Finding Joy in Joyce:
A Readers Guide to Ulysses

John P. Anderson

Universal Publishers/uPUBLISH.com
USA • 2000

Finding Joy in Joyce: A Readers Guide to Ulysses

ISBN: 1-58112-762-6

Universal Publishers/uPUBLISH.com
USA • 2000

www.uPUBLISH.com/books/anderson2.htm

TABLE OF CONTENTS

SOURCES

To Prof. Louis Leiter, whose inspiration survived 35 years in the desert.

To Linda, Egan and Cameron, who gave me the strength.

To Leo, for encouragement.

ACKNOWLEDGMENTS

Excerpt (part of Figure 1) reprinted by permission of Princeton University Press.

Photograph (figure 2) reprinted by permission of Self-Realization Fellowship Church.

THE MASTER SPEAKS:

"[copulation is not the death of the soul because] there you are dealing with a mystery which can become anything and transform everything. Love-making can end in love, it often does, and so its possibilities can be limitless."[James Joyce as reported by Arthur Powers]

INTRODUCTION

Welcome to the most important novel of the 20th century. Published in 1922, Joyce's *Ulysses* still speaks forcefully to the subject of the human condition through art whose appeal transcends time and national boundaries.

The principal issue in this novel is creating individual meaning in modern life. This continues to be the principal issue for human kind as the 21st century opens. Stephen Dedalus, a principal character in this novel representative of the young Joyce, has the modern disease of the spirit, narcissism.

Joyce's medicine for the diseased spirit is a custom blend of self-realized individuality combined with a detached respect for the human unity. This blend combines Jesus and Buddha, not as they have been marketed by institutional religions but as they lived their lives as humans. In Joyce's blend, the respect for the unity does not limit human possibilities. Indeed, it is designed to maximize them. Joyce's Way to the eternal is for each individual to maximize his or her own human possibilities within recognition of the unity. Founded on his own personal experience of the human condition, Joyce's existential medicine can provide spiritual health in the 21st century.

The sublime joy in Joyce is the art by which the levels of existential meaning are brought forth. Many consider Joyce's art as seminal for modern literature. He enlarged the possibilities of prose with revolutionary techniques and methods of coherence. And his methods carry meaning. In Joyce's architecture, the material is cyclical and the part implies the whole. These patterns bear the imprint of Joyce's views of historical and ultimate reality: history is cyclical, and the human condition (the part) implies the nature of the powers that be, the gods (the whole). Joyce's art is, in my opinion, one of the wonders of Western civilization. My purpose is to make its power and beauty accessible to you.

But readers beware; reading Joyce can fundamentally alter your entire outlook on life. This is what Joseph Campbell, pre-eminent mythographer and life long Joyce reader (may he rest in peace), said

5

about reading Joyce:

> But when you are reading Joyce, what you get is radiance. You become harmonized, and that is what it's about. It is not teaching you a lesson. It is feeding you, giving you spiritual balance and spiritual harmony.[1]

If you want some of that some spiritual balance and harmony, that soul food, read on.

Magnitude of Subject and Power of Order

Joyce's novel confronts subject matter of immense magnitude—the nature and meaning of the human condition through the experiences of three principal characters in Dublin during the circuit of just one spin of the earth, about 20 hours. The subject is the human condition, not the gay or black or Irish or female condition, but the basic human condition. This confrontation takes place in the lives of three intense characters: Stephen Dedalus, a most narcissistic young artist; Leopold Bloom, a most compassionate adult; and Molly Bloom, Leopold's wife, a most passionate woman. Youth and adult, male and female. Joyce's focus through these three characters on the full tapestry of human consciousness, not just an expurgated version, insured for this novel both its titillating initial reception and mature continuing appeal.

Joyce's order has immense power. Each of 18 separate episodes of this novel is dressed in its own separate style. That style is designed from the pattern of its individual unifying subject theme. The novel has an independent beginning (Part I—3 episodes). The beginning leads to a middle that looks back and forward (Part II—12 episodes). It ends with closure (Part III—3 episodes). The plot portrays each of the three main characters at the center of a succession of fluid moments of the here and now surrounded by a maternal past. The names of persons, places and streets that carry important symbolic associations are largely drawn from actual Dublin. Through this satisfying structure, calamity moves to better fortune in a self-reflective format—the author writes about his earlier soul voyage that made him the author of this book.

This Guide and How to Use It

This guide is, as far as I know, unique in its attempt to give the reader a rendition of the deep meaning of each part of the novel. Much of my interpretation is totally new. Not being an academic gives me liberties.

I suggest that after reading this Introduction, you read *Ulysses* episode by episode using this guide as follows. First read the episode of *Ulysses* through and don't worry about understanding it. Just read it through. Then read the related chapter of this guide. And finally reread the episode, this time deeply. That's right, it's not going to be easy, even with this guide. Joyce is worth the effort. Your investment will be returned several fold.

Because the individual episodes generally stand alone, you can have a satisfactory overall experience even if you have to lay the book aside from time to time. The *Ulysses* line references in this guide are to the Vintage Books 1986 corrected edition available in paper. Having that edition is not necessary, however.[2]

The episodes of this novel are related to parts of that grand old aristocrat, *The Odyssey of Homer*. The descriptions in this guide of the related chapters[3] of Homer are sufficiently detailed so that reading that masterpiece as well should not be necessary. Homer's hero is Odysseus, which in Latin is Ulysses. Joyce chose his title to direct the reader to Homer's epic.

Since they have now been cited formally several times, let's just call *Ulysses* Ulysses or the novel and *The Odyssey of Homer* The Odyssey.

Meaning

This novel is an "open work," which even as to fundamentals is susceptible to various supportable interpretations. The ending is notoriously ambiguous in its implications for the Bloom future. Joyce wanted it that way. His work, which is a paean to individuality, is what it is to you. You can customize your own projection of the future of the Blooms. It is designed to work that way, as an individual truth. The costs of relativism are accepted.

The action begins on Thursday, June 16, 1904, the day Joyce had his first "date" with Nora Barnacle, the woman to be his partner in exile and eventually his wife for life. She reportedly "took him in hand" on that first date. This novel is dedicated to the change in his life and soul that their relationship initiated. The search for meaning in this novel must start there. Based on my interpretation of the novel, Joyce found himself, his fundamental creative self, through his sexual love for Nora.

Joyce's Other Works and Interpretation of Ulysses

Joyce first wrote poems. One collection he named *Chamber Music*. In the time period covered by the novel, the artist character Stephen is still in the poetry stage. Joyce is not remembered for his poetry, and Joyce's critical view from maturity about his first efforts is important in understanding the presentation of Stephen in this novel.

At various times Joyce wrote articles on intellectual subjects now collected as *The Critical Writings* (CW). Some of the positions staked out in those articles return in the attitudes assumed in writing this novel.

Dubliners is a group of short pieces portraying spiritual corruption in Dublin and drawing for symbolic imagery on the Catholic Mass. That same subject and imagery appear in every other book he wrote. Next came *Stephen Hero* (SH), which Joyce eventually rewrote in tightened form as *A Portrait of the Artist as a Young Man* (AP). Note the title is A Portrait not The Portrait, emphasizing possibilities rather than the one reading.

Joyce's first sustained masterwork, AP is concerned with the development of character and consciousness of one Stephen Dedalus and is largely if not wholly autobiographical. Since the same Stephen is in this novel, AP and SH provide important interpretive material for Ulysses. In AP, Stephen thinks the restrictions on his self-realization possibilities derive from Irish culture and the Catholic Church. In this novel, which continues the story of Stephen's maturation, he comes to realize the real enemy is closer to home.

In preparation for writing this novel, Joyce made notes on an episode by episode basis. The notes contain facts or ideas in highly summary form. These are referred to as Joyce's Notes and are obviously important in terms of the artist's intent.

Joyce wrote Ulysses from 1914 to 1921. During the early part of this same period, Joyce wrote an unsuccessful play *Exiles*. Its subject is the necessity, as part of love, to allow one's mate to be unfaithful. Love, like the creation of art, must derive from the freedom to choose, not possession. This theme provides important material for the plot of this novel, which hinges on Bloom's reaction to his wife's adultery. Joyce's explanatory notes to *Exiles* are particularly helpful in this regard.

Joyce's last work, ***Finnegans Wake***, is written largely in the language of dreams and without significant reference to external space/time reality. The achievements of the Wake include its own language and magnificent internal correspondences. The closing episodes of this novel register a gravitation pull in that direction.

Organization

This novel is organized into three parts. Part I features Stephen, part II Leopold Bloom, often referred as just Bloom, and part III Bloom together with Stephen and Bloom together with Molly.

The individual episodes are the jewels of this novel. Joyce's highest art blesses their internal organization. My explanations, organized episode by episode, are relatively longer for the early episodes since they set out tools for the entire novel. The Endnotes following each section of this guide provide details.

The "traditional schemata" provided for each episode refer to descriptions given by Joyce to Stuart Gilbert and to Carlo Linati as to his basic structuring techniques for each episode. These schemata, often tongue in cheek, give limited clues as to the meaning of the episode and serve to relate one episode to another through common structuring devices. The items in the schemata include for each episode a Greek name to indicate the parallel chapter of The Odyssey and a particular art, color, symbol, narrative technique and human organ.

Conceptual Structure of Episode

Each episode is based on a single concept, usually derived from Joyce's interpretation of the parallel chapter of The Odyssey. The unifying concept is most accessible in the opening and closing portions of each episode. Sometimes the unifying concept is encoded in the episode's first letter considered as a pictograph. In order to indicate thematic importance, all editions published while Joyce was alive magnified to full-page size the first letter of each part and capitalized the

9

first line of each episode.

Joyce loved to generalize, and his unifying concept for an episode is usually a highly generalized version of the point of the related Odyssey chapter. For example, Homer's Sirens sing to invite Odysseus and crew to stop at their island and retell old war stories. Joyce, in his Sirens episode, generalizes from the specifics of retelling old war stories to the concept of the sterility of living in the past as a special case of repetition without redemption.

Having established a single unifying concept for an episode, Joyce then collected into that episode as many of his own personal experiences and as many mythical, philosophical, religious or other cultural references as he could relate to the unifying concept, consistent with his notions of good taste. All of these references participate in the unifying concept. Extending in multiple dimensions and directions, Joyce's octopus-like sense of generalization is broad and powerful. The Jocotopus swings far and wide.

In some cases, Joyce incorporates references by including in the episode just some of the facts or names or incidents out of a myth. These partials I refer to as the "Connector Facts." They are designed to bring the entire myth or cultural reference into the episode.

The result of Joyce's procedure, building the episode from materials related to one concept, is that the entire episode resonates with the basic meaning and produces a kind of reverberation. Like a hologram, each part of the episode implies the unifying concept of the entire episode. In Joyce's artistic architecture, the part implies the whole. And this process is not accidental; this architecture carries the imprint of Joyce's view of ultimate reality—that the microcosm of humanity reflects the macrocosm of the gods. Life and art, fundamentally connected.

Art of the Episode

The episode is the format through which the author's aesthetic theory, presented in SH and AP, is implemented. This theory is fundamental to understanding the art of this novel. Here is the heart of the theory from those earlier works. Stephen gives Joyce's aesthetic theory using Latin terms (*integritas, consonantia and quidditas*)

10

borrowed from the theology of one of Joyce's gurus, the Catholic theologian-philosopher Thomas Aquinas:

> The first phase of apprehension is a bounding line drawn about the object to be apprehended. An esthetic image is presented to us either in space or in time. What is audible is presented in time, what is visible is presented in space. But temporal or spatial, the esthetic image is first luminously apprehended as self-bounded and self-contained upon the immeasurable background of space or time which is not it. You apprehended it as one thing. You see it as one whole. You apprehend its wholeness. That is *integritas*.
>
> . . .
>
> Then, said Stephen, you pass from point to point, led by its formal lines; you apprehend it as balanced part against part within its limits; you feel the rhythm of its structure. In other words, the synthesis of immediate perception is followed by the analysis of apprehension. Having first felt that it is one thing you feel now that it is a thing. You apprehend it as complex, multiple, divisible, separable, made up of its parts, the result of its parts and their sum, harmonious. That is *consonantia*.
>
> . . .
>
> You see that it is that thing which it is and no other thing. The radiance of which he speaks is the scholastic *quidditas*, the whatness of a thing. This supreme quality is felt by the artist when the esthetic image is first conceived in his imagination. The mind in that mysterious instant Shelley likened beautifully to a fading coal. The instant wherein that supreme quality of beauty, the clear radiance of the esthetic image, is apprehended luminously by the mind which has been arrested by its wholeness and fascinated by its harmony is the luminous silent stasis of esthetic pleasure, a

11

spiritual state very like to that cardiac condition which
the Italian physiologist Luigi Galvani, using a phrase
almost as beautiful as Shelley's, called the
enchantment of the heart.[4]

. . .

. . . This is the moment which I call epiphany. First we
recognize that the object is one integral thing, then we
recognize that it is an organized composite structure, a
thing in fact: finally, when the relation of the parts is
exquisite, when the parts are adjusted to the special
point, we recognize that it is that thing which it is. Its
soul, its whatness, leaps to us from the vestment of its
appearance. The soul of the commonest object, the
structure of which is so adjusted, seems to us radiant.
The object achieves its epiphany.[5] [first three
paragraphs from AP and the last from SH]

Now this is fairly serious stuff. You don't have to plumb its depths right
now, but you may want to revisit these principles of analysis as you go
along episode by episode. Note the source of Joyce's aesthetics principles
in theology. Acquinas used these terms in connection with a description
in the Trinity of the Second Person, the Son. Acquinas used the terms
"blaze of being" and "certain splendor" to describe *quidditas* or
epiphany. Joyce will use these same ideas in describing the creation of
art. Joyce's connection of art to theology is not accidental.

Measure each episode according to these principles. Joyce
designed his episodes to be apprehended as art objects in and of
themselves, not as images of space-time or emotional reality. Consider
each episode as the bounded object you apprehend. The parts to be
related to each other and to the whole include the subject, narrative style,
symbolic subtext, texture and atmosphere produced by the narrator or
narrators and the degree of realism used in the presentation. The radiance
or epiphany of the overall effect is successful only if the reader manages
a deep penetration of the meaning. The epiphany is usually the unifying
concept for the episode.

Proper Art

In terms of Joyce's objectives, his theory of proper and improper art is instructive:

> The tragic emotion [result of proper art], in fact, is a face looking two ways, towards terror and towards pity, both of which are phases of it. You see I use the word arrest. I mean that the tragic emotion is static. . . .The feelings excited by improper art are kinetic, desire or loathing. Desire urges us to possess, to go to something; loathing urges us to abandon, to go from something. The arts which excite them, pornographical or didactic, are therefore improper arts. The esthetic emotion (I used the general term) is therefore static. The mind is [by proper art] arrested and raised above desire and loathing.[6] [material added]

Note the emphasis on aesthetic arrest, which raises the mind "above desire and loathing." Consider preliminarily the common aspects shared by aesthetic arrest and general Buddha-like detachment, in whose gentle arms the ego-induced emotions of aggression and desire are arrested.

The emphasis on proper (static) and improper (kinetic) is in relation to art—what is proper to or the property of art. For example, advertising, which just happens to be Bloom's business, would by necessity be kinetic or pornographic under this definition since it is designed to create desire for the advertised product.

Since pity and terror are proper effects of art but their near relatives desire and loathing are not, the definitions of pity and terror are key:

> Pity is the feeling which arrests the mind in the presence of whatsoever is grave and constant in human sufferings and unites it with the human sufferer. Terror is the feeling which arrests the mind in the presence of whatsoever is grave and constant in human sufferings and unites it with the secret cause.[7]

The phrase "grave and constant" means what is "irremediable" or inherent in the human condition; and the "secret cause" refers to inevitable death of humans, the ground of all that is grave and constant in human sufferings.[8] These grave and constant aspects of the human condition are the mortar in Joyce's art. This is the material with which he intends to connect with the reader. This is the principal Joyce subject matter, the eternal aspects of the human condition which transcend time, culture and locale.

These academic concepts are critical to understanding the subtleties of this novel because they indicate what Joyce is trying to accomplish. Notice that pity and terror, the static emotions produced by tragedy, inherently involve a connection or unification with other humans—**uniting** with the human sufferer or **uniting** with the secret cause. As a consequence, an assumption of some sort of human unity is built into the very foundation of Joyce's theory of literary art.

This human unity is the common ground where the artist Stephen and the compassionate Bloom meet. This is also the common ground where Joyce meets his reader. The human condition, the natural human condition, is Joyce's subject, not the latest whims or hot subjects. That is why his art lives on and on through time and crosses language boundaries.

And these basic concepts of proper art translate into important lessons as to the proper method of literary composition. They suggest how to do it to get the right result. Here are the lessons as to proper composition method issued by Stephen for Joyce in AP:

> Even in literature, the highest and most spiritual art, the forms are often confused. The lyrical form is in fact the simplest verbal vesture of an instant of emotion. . . . He who utters it is more conscious of the instant of emotion than of himself as feeling emotion. The simplest epical form is seen emerging out of lyrical literature when the artist prolongs and broods upon himself as the centre of an epical event and this form progresses till the centre of emotional gravity is equidistant from the artist himself and from others. The narrative is no longer purely personal. The personality of the artist passes into the narration itself, flowing

14

round and round the persons and the action like a vital sea. . . .The dramatic form is reached when the vitality which has flowed and eddied round each person fills every person with such vital force that he or she assumes a proper and intangible esthetic life. The personality of the artist, at first a cry or a cadence or a mood and then a fluid and lambent narrative, finally refines itself out of existence, impersonalises itself, so to speak. The esthetic image in the dramatic form is life purified in and reprojected from the human imagination. The mystery of esthetic like that of material creation is accomplished. The artist, like the God of the creation, remains within or behind or beyond or above his handiwork, invisible, refined out of existence, indifferent, paring his fingernails.[9]

In other words, the detached, restrained dramatic form is best. In that mode, the characters have independent existence on their own terms. The author does not possess them in order to make a personal statement for or against something; the actions of the characters are born of their own nature. The author frees his characters from the author's own subjectivism and in an impersonal process creates more possibilities. Is this beginning to sound like unconditional love? Following this line of association, the detached charity or compassion of the Buddha and Jesus would be the counterpart of the dramatic mode in art.

In the dramatic mode, the object of the writing is presented only in relation to itself. Explanatory lead-ins and background information are intentionally omitted. The author shows but doesn't show and tell. Nothing is spelled out, and the reader must participate to supply the missing pieces. Objects, characters and thoughts are presented objectively, just as they appear in real life. Characters are only in the immediate present. They may remember the past or project into the future but they do so from the present. These characteristics make the material hard to come by, but ultimately satisfying.

By contrast, the romantic lyrical mode is guided by the artist's self-indulgence and is an immature pursuit of beauty and truth. In that mode, the end product is slave to the author's emotional subjectivism and agenda. For this reason, the end product does not have access to the unlimited possibilities that flourish only in artistic independence. In this novel, the intentional use of improper tools by Joyce is a signal to look for limitations in the characters or their behavior in that episode. The style used by Joyce serves as a metaphor for a particular mentality.

The most basic human passions propel the plot of this novel. Indeed, the summary reads much like a daily soap opera—artist Stephen struggles for freedom and human connections, compassionate Bloom is cuckolded and hot-blooded Molly has her first sex in many years. The curve of this plot of passions is shaped by Joyce's theory of proper art. During the course of this novel, the characters change in the direction of the human psychological equivalents of the dramatic literary mode that produces arrest. Life and art, art and life.

Proper Art and the Reader

So much for the artist. But what's in it for you the reader? What is this about your soul being transformed?

The detached artist produces art that can arrest the reader. This arrest is a kind of fascination that "stops the clock." The reader must be receptive and open to possibilities in order to have this kind of experience. In this fascinated state, the reader leaves his or her normal ego state, which is characterized by a sense of separation, isolation and emptiness and which is standard equipment for many materially successful persons. In fascinated arrest, this ego state collapses, at least for a moment.

Leaving the ego state, the arrested reader enters a new realm in which detachment and a special sense of individuality and unity prevail. That's right—individuality and unity. In the right dimensions, they are mutually supportive, not opposites. The sense of individuality is intense, nurtured by the companion sense of unity. This is a soul altering experience for many, an experience of greater depth of existence. Don't be put off by the fact that several previous attempts to reach this same ground have been rather tawdry. And it is no coincidence that the effect of Joyce's art is a prescription for Joyce's existential medicine for life.

Because of the power of the art, the reader unites with the

human sufferer or the secret cause, and the reader's soul is changed in proportion to the strength of the detachment.[10] Here's Joseph Campbell talking about Joyce's notions of dramatic art and aesthetic arrest in Buddhist terms (the Buddha was known as the one "thus come"):

> . . . And whenever anything is experienced that way, simply in and for and as itself, without reference to any concepts, relevancies, or practical relationships, such a moment of sheer aesthetic arrest throws the viewer back for an instant upon his own existence without meaning; for he too simply is—"thus come"—a vehicle of consciousness, like a spark flung out from a fire.[11]

Read Joyce and you can feel the Buddha. And by the way, the Buddha can reach the suburbs. He is not put off by nice yards and big houses.

Art and the Gods

One of Stephen's main concerns in this novel is the relationship of the individual, particularly the artist, to the forces of the macrocosm, to the gods.[12] The artist has, Joyce believed, a particular interest in this issue because the artist must reach the eternal domain of the gods in order to produce the highest art. That which is grave and constant in the human condition necessarily involves, in this view, the issue of the relation of the cosmic forces operative in our universe to our brief individual human passage in and out of energy consciousness. Act One in this drama is the subject of the legend of the Fall in the Garden of Eden, the last time the Big Guy and the little guys were together. That legend, bathed in Joycean interpretations, is an important construct in this novel.

In the case of Joyce as reflected in Stephen, the two institutional religious controllers of this relationship of the macrocosm with the individual microcosm were (1) from his upbringing, the Roman Catholic Church and (2) from his readings in the then popular Theosophical movement and the powerful writings of Hegel and Schopenhaeur, the transcendental Hindu/Buddhist traditions. The Catholic Church controller offered a brokered, indirect and guilt oriented relationship with a distant god, definitely a second-hand, second-best experience. The Hindu/Buddhist traditions promised the divine spark in everyone but emphasized passivity and caste in the face of inevitable suffering in life.

17

As traditionally depicted by his institutional representatives, Christ is hanging on the cross and the Buddha is in passive position, lying down.

Both of these traditions protected the faithful from suffering but at the cost of restricted possibilities. The Catholics offer protection from suffering at the cost of guilt. Joyce rejected this trade-off because guilt corrodes and reduces the spirit whereas suffering increases human possibilities. The Hindu/Buddhist tradition offered a way to avoid suffering but at the cost of passivity and caste. Joyce rejected passivity because, as he might have put the point, the Buddha lying down all the time misses most of life.

Joyce cherry-picked from both of these sources in developing a customized spiritual approach to life that made sense to him and which is expressed in this novel through Stephen and Bloom. In his quest for maximum self-realization, Stephen gravitates away from the institutional religious controllers and back to the genuine original articles, Jesus and Buddha as they lead their lives, Jesus and Buddha as humans. They are viewed as radical apostles of profound personal experience and personal illumination, proponents of growth of soul or self-realization. In addition, since Joyce found kindred concepts in Tantric Yoga, images from that tradition are used throughout the novel.

Joyce practices metaphysics in this novel and equates the divine with potential. The essence of "being" and of god is more possibilities, not just in the human realm but in nature and evolution. That which promotes more human possibilities is sacred and that which restricts human possibilities is profane. More possibilities in art and more possibilities in life. For Joyce, god is in the possibilities.

In the first episodes, Stephen struggles against the forces of restriction that limit possibilities. In the last episode, we are given a glimpse of the sacred realm of possibilities through the fluid thoughts of Molly as earthmother. With this ending, the liberating Flow of the Mothers replaces the restrictive Law of the Fathers.

Joyce's ultimate philosophy is based on the human, the natural human not the hair shirt ascetic human. If the image of god is reflected in humans, it must be reflected in what is most natural to humans. What is most natural is most god-like. And for Joyce the most natural human

18

functions are the sexual instinct and the creative imagination. In his life, these functions came bearing the most energy. When liberated from self-indulgence, these functions serve as portals to expanded perception, to Joyce's gods. In their mature form, their core is impersonal, reflective of the distant Father recumbent in the void.

The Soul, The Mass and The Trinity

Elements of Ulysses are framed on the Catholic concepts of the Mass and the relation of the Father and Son in the Trinity. Joyce approaches these concepts as attempts to understand the relation of man's soul to possibilities and to the gods, not as dry speculation on the nature of the godhead. Joyce approaches the gods as the sum of all forces in the universe but, unlike the trend of current theories, treats the creation of mankind as an important event. By the way, I use the terms god and gods with and without capitalization as interchangeable terms.

The Mass is necessary, in the view of the Catholic Church, because the only possible portal for the connection of humans to god is a humiliating sense of sin, separation from and loss of god, and the corresponding constant need for renewal. The Mass, the Catholic instrument of change, is used throughout this novel as a structuring device to frame the changes in Stephen.[13] But Joyce uses the Catholic Mass in a way to point out its failure as a passport to the universal powers. Joyce's human mass is used to elevate the real and liberating connections that he believed humans share with the universal powers, the creative imagination and the sexual instinct.

The Trinity is the Catholic Church's version of the relationship of god to humans. The Father created the universe and sent His likeness the Son into the world of time and space in the Incarnation, and together they send the Holy Spirit into human hearts. Joyce, following the lead of St. Augustine, brings the Trinity into the human soul. Indeed, Joyce will find in the different theories of the Trinity analogies for Stephen's youthful self-indulgence and more mature self-realization.

Vico Patterns

The cyclical theories of history of Giambattista Vico, an 18th Century Italian philosopher, provide important patterns for this novel. Vico viewed as inevitable four stages of history: (1) mythical age of the gods or theocratic (2) heroic or aristocratic (3) human or secular and (4) chaotic to be followed by a recorso, a return to the first stage. Each Vico stage has a language, character, jurisprudence and method of reasoning in tune with a basic mind set.[14] In this system, language and history are parts of the same whole. In this system, you will sense the fundamentals that historical reality is cyclical and the part implies the whole.

The parts of this novel are sequenced by reference to the Vico cycle. In Part I, the first episode reflects attempts by the theocratic forces to control Stephen's soul, the second episode presents a similar attempt by mock heroes and commercial aristocracy, and the third episode is ruled by the thoughts of Stephen, his own secular productions. Part II is built on the chaotic stage and a recorso in the movements of Bloom, the wandering Jew. He starts at home, leaves and returns. The Vico cycle repeats in an artistic dimension in the last three episodes of Part III, as the three step sequence governs the basic mindset of the narrator.

Bible Connections

The Bible, like The Odyssey, is an important structuring device for Ulysses. Like the Bible, this novel is written largely in the literary language of myth and metaphor,[15] is an open work with several meanings,[16] and presents existential wisdom with an emphasis on human concerns.[17] One central myth of the Bible is deliverance, from the Exodus of the Old Testament (OT) to the redemption promised by Christ's crucifixion in the New Testament (NT).[18] Likewise, in the novel both Stephen and Bloom are delivered to an increased freedom and an enlarged view of the possible dimensions of life. In addition, the progression of styles in this novel tracks the movement in the Bible from the more realistic, more historically "world" oriented OT to the more spiritual "word" oriented NT.[19] This novel, like the Bible, moves from the objective to the self-referential.

Joyce uses several biblical characters in this novel, particularly the Jewish prophet Elijah. He figures prominently, both on the surface and in the coil springs of the plot. As the master of transitions, Elijah charts courses in a novel about redemptive changes.

In attempting to create a modern sacred text, Joyce co-opted the primary technique used by the NT authors and editors to bind the NT to the OT.[20] This technique is known as typology (types that share traits in common). The NT was apparently constructed so that events in the NT would be viewed as "fulfilling" the events in the OT, as Christ came to "fulfill" the Jewish Law. The typological method of interpretation of scripture was developed by early Church fathers, such as Chrysostomos who shows up in Stephen's very first thought in the novel.

In this system, as interpreted by Eric Auerbach:

> Figural interpretation establishes a connection between two events or persons in such a way that the first signifies not only itself but also the second, while the second involves or fulfills the first. The two poles of a figure (the two events) are separated in time, but both, being real events or persons, are within temporality. They are both contained in the flowing stream which is historical life, and only the comprehension . . . of their interdependence is a spiritual act . . . .
>
> This type of interpretation obviously introduces an entirely new and alien element into the antique conception of history . . . . a connection is established between two events which are linked neither temporally nor causally—a connection which it is impossible to establish by reason in the horizontal dimension. . . . It can be established only if both occurrences are vertically linked to Divine Providence, which alone is able to devise such a plan of history and supply the key to its understanding. The horizontal, that is the temporal and causal, connection of occurrences is dissolved; the here and now is no longer a mere link in an earthly chain of events, it is simultaneously something which has always been, and which will be fulfilled in the future; and strictly, in the eyes of God, it is something eternal; . . . .[21]

Joyce uses the typological technique throughout this novel. Joyce believed that in order to have maximum power, his art must both rest in the concrete here and now and reach by symbolism to the eternal beyond. In this emphasis, it shares fundamentals with typology. But in his use of this technique, Joyce replaces the Church fathers' vertical dimension of divine reality with his own version of the structure of divine reality. In his view, the vertical dimension of ultimate reality is self-realization because self-realization is the only human path to divine proximity. Moreover, Joyce uses the typological technique in a degrading sort of way in order to undermine the Church's "Law of the Fathers," the sense of the Law as an external source of control and personal justification.[22]

This novel is also full of other concepts that share fundamental traits with Biblical typology. In reincarnation, a favorite Joyce subject, a previous soul is reborn in a new body. The experience in the new body, influenced by karma, gives new meaning to the results of the prior life. Through Joyce's abundant use of Dante and Shakespeare, their works are given new meaning in Dublin and "fulfilled" in the intensification of modern consciousness. Art in general fulfills prior experience on which the artist based the art. The soul, as expounded by Stephen, reads backward as an expression of prior experience and forward as the potential for the future. These similar concepts, like typology, do not operate on the basis of cause and effect or logic.

In the end, for Joyce the associations and connections resulting from the typological and similar processes become values in themselves. Compassion and connections. His revelations in the human realm become open-ended. As Iris Murdoch has one of her characters say, "The good feel being as a total dense mesh of tiny interconnections." Interestingly, this approach foreshadows the current model of the quantum connectedness of the entire universe.

Stephen, Bloom and Molly as Joyce

Stephen and Bloom started out in Joyce's mind as parts of himself— young and older, idealistic and practical, artistic and scientific, and centrifugal and centripetal. Then Joyce gave them artistic life in the dramatic mode and independent action in the story line. While they function as independent characters, they remain connected through the text by common experiences, dreams and thoughts. Ultimately, they connect through Molly, who represents a magnified version of Joyce's experience with Nora.

In symbolic association, Stephen generally represents a version of Jesus and Bloom a version of Moses. Together they share a version of the Buddha and Dante, both of whom were exiled, highly individualized and giving (Dante means the "giver"). Molly represents the feminine principle in all its manifestations: temptress, mate and earthmother. These symbolic associations are not fixed and bend and merge throughout the novel.

Notice that all three main characters have had fractured family experiences. Bloom lost his father to suicide, Stephen his mother to cancer and Molly her mother to desertion. They all have what has become a very modern problem, as individual liberty has fed selfishness. Joyce's family life was fractured by his selfish father's spendthrift habits, drunkenness and lack of support for the individual development of his many children. During Joyce's youth, their family fell from the garden of respectability and inherited financial independence to the hardship of poverty. Joyce's mother died of cancer (on August 13, 1903) when Joyce was 21, basically worn out from child bearing and family stress. As the novel opens, Stephen is still, ten months and three days later on June 16, 1904, in mourning over her death and feeling guilty as a result of refusing her deathbed call for submission to her Catholic faith.

Attitude

This Book is full of playfulness and humor, some of it quite juvenile. And as for the basic purpose of it all, comedy and joy are the summit of art:

> For desire urges us from rest that we may possess something, but joy holds us in rest so long as we possess something. . . . All art which excites in us the feeling of joy is so far comic and according as this feeling of joy is excited by whatever is substantial or accidental in human fortunes the art is to be judged more or less excellent: and even tragic art may be said to participate in the nature of comic art so far as the possession of a work of tragic art (a tragedy) excites in us the feelings of joy.[23]

23

Joy produced by arrest—that's the right stuff.
Read on and find the Joy in Joyce.

****

ENDNOTES

1. Campbell, J. *Mythic Worlds, Modern Words* (New York: Harper Collins, 1933) p. 272.
2. For help with unfamiliar places and names, Gifford, D. *Ulysses Annotated* (Berkeley: University of California Press, 1988) is excellent, but it is not needed for a basic understanding of the novel.
3. The divisions of Homer are actually called Books, but I use the term chapter to avoid confusion.
4. *A Portrait of the Artist as a Young Man* (New York: Viking Press, 1956) pp. 212-213. This work is hereinafter referred to as AP.
5. *Stephen Hero* (New York: New Directions, 1944) p. 213. Thomas Aquinas used these three Latin terms to describe the Second Person in the Trinity; Joyce, for reasons which will become clear, found that source most appropriate for a description of apprehending art. Watch for the images of the Son and artist to be joined.
6. AP, p. 205.
7. AP, p. 204.
8. Joyce, J. *The Critical Writings* edit. by E. Mason and R. Ellmann (Ithaca: Cornell University Press, 1959) p. 144. This work is hereinafter referred to as CW.
9. AP, pp. 214-215.
10. Frye, N. *Words with Power Being a Second Study of The Bible and Literature* (San Diego, Harcourt Brace Jovanovich, 1990) p. 71. This work is hereinafter referred to as Frye II.
11. *Myths to Live By* (New York: Penguin Books, 1972) p. 137.
12. In the interests of even-handedness, I will not capitalize references to deities unless required by the context.
13. For all the detailed information concerning the Mass, see Lang, F. *Ulysses and the Irish God* (Lewisburg: Bucknell University Press,

24

1993).

14. Klein, M. *A Shout in the Street* (New Directions) pp. 327-345.
15. Frye II, p. 99.
16. Frye, N. *The Great Code The Bible and Literature* (San Diego, Harcourt Brace Javanovich, 1990) p. 65. This Book is hereinafter referred to as Frye I.
17. Frye I, p. 67.
18. Frye I, p. 50.
19. Restuccia, F. *Joyce and the Law of the Father* (New Haven: Yale University Press, 1989) p. 53.
20. For the material in this and next paragraph, see Restuccia p. 20 et. seq.
21. Auerbach, E. *Mimesis The Representation of Reality in Western Literature* (Princeton: Princeton University Press, 1953) p. 73.
22. Restuccia, p. 20 et. seq.
23. Paris Notebook as quoted in Kenner, H. *Dublin's Joyce* (Bloomington: Indiana University Press, 1956) p. 156.

Part I – Summary

Part I introduces Stephen Dedalus, a young and self-absorbed artist with a fragmented soul and primed for a change. This is the same Stephen from AP and generally representative of the young Joyce. This initial focus on Stephen and his narcissism prepares for a marked contrast with our unlikely but compassionate and integrated hero, Leopold Bloom, who is generally representative of the older Joyce. The zone between the younger and the more mature Joyce, the zone of change, is the terrain of this novel.

The three episodes of Part I are related to the first chapters of The Odyssey that focus on Telemachus, the young son of Odysseus. The narrative in Joyce's first three episodes proceeds chronologically through the morning. Part II will revert to the same hours covered by Part I. By these most direct methods, Joyce lays the subject of youth and the heavy hand of time in the opening of the novel.

As these three episodes proceed chronologically, the focus moves inward. Stephen is first in his temporary residential quarters with companions, then in his teaching job with students and his boss, and finally alone in his own thoughts on the beach. The progression of episodes pays heed to Vico's cycles, the sequence of chakras from Tantric Yoga and Joyce's theory of literary forms.

These initial episodes present the external adversaries of Stephen's self-realization: Church and state claiming cultural control, his family claiming loyalty and normal employment claiming deference. Guardians of the Law of the Fathers, these mutually reinforcing adversaries use as their main weapon the blessing of respectability. These adversaries, when successful, produce a kind of societal conformity, not unity, which restricts possibilities in individual development. Against these adversaries, Stephen has been in the opposition mode for several years. This opposition has preserved his independence but at the cost of a sense of separation and a fragmented soul.

Since Joyce founded his spiritual, metaphysical and artistic systems on independence, this opening theme comes as no surprise.[1]

****

ENDNOTES

1. Gorman, H. *James Joyce* (New York: Rinehart & Company, Inc., 1939) p. 110.

Episode 1 (Telemachus)

Basic Themes

Betrayal of potential.

Ulysses opens with Stephen's struggle to control his own self-realization. His adversaries are the religious and secular authorities in his culture. Youthful Stephen seeks freedom from the restrictive Law of the

Fathers in order to control his own destiny. In our time and thanks in part to Joyce, this is now a familiar theme.

Stephen is living at close quarters in a highly unusual stone tower with the young bachelors Buck Mulligan and Haines (no first name). These emotionally unfulfilled bachelors attempt to pull Stephen in the direction of their own values, to control him. Through this effort, Buck and Haines serve as reflections of Stephen's cultural adversaries. In Stephen's field of reference, they are the Roman Catholic Church and the United Kingdom, then (1904) the ruling institutions in Ireland. These adversaries seek to betray Stephen by expropriating his potential for their own ends.

Joyce presents these expropriating institutions as the latest incarnations of a long and distinguished ancestor line of institutional forces of control over the individual, particularly the gifted individual. These forces produce a kind of unity that restricts rather than increases human possibilities. The justification offered is that humans are limited in potential anyway, a kind of self-fulfilling prophecy. Thus the novel opens showing the wrong kind of unity.

Buck and Haines embody these cultural forces as the hitman from the future in the movie *Terminator II* incorporated multiple beings. The hitman's seemingly human form concealed his real and lethal identities, which emerged out of and then merged back into that human form. During the progress of this episode, the lethal forces reflected by Buck and Haines emerge out of and then merge back into their normal human identities.

In the very first sentence of the novel, Buck is presented in the skins of the ancient Greek snake god that avenges kindred blood, an ancestor of the Roman Catholic Church. When no one is looking, the snake is out of the cage:

> Stately, plump Buck Mulligan came from the stairhead, bearing a bowl of lather on which a mirror and a razor lay crossed. A yellow dressing gown, ungirdled, was sustained gently behind him on the mild morning air. He held the bowl aloft and intoned: -
> *Introbio ad altare Dei.*

27

The initial letter of this novel, S on "Stately," looks just like the upright giant snake god from ancient Greek tablets (see figure 1). In all editions published while Joyce was alive, this single letter S takes up the entire first page. This Greek snake god is a bearded snake. Buck comes up to shave in the interests of respectability. As a god requiring placation, this giant serpent produced fear and superstition, and thus limited possibilities for self-realization. And given Buck's "ungirdled," yellow dressing gown, the gold snake is shedding its slightly faded yellow skin, signifying a rebirth of the dark forces. This menacing snake figure then proceeds to conduct a mock Catholic mass. This connection identifies the guilt-based Catholic Eucharist as the modern manifestation of this ancient, lethal force, a hitman from the past.

Stephen's potential betrayal by these modern hitmen is amplified by references to the restriction of individual realization by the interests of control in the theologies and mythologies of many other ages and cultures. These interests betray the individual by expropriating potential personal realization in the interests of the institution. For example, the Catholic Church takes potential by restricting activity and fostering guilt, all in the interests of control. The universal scope of this message, true across time and cultures, magnifies the importance of Stephen's personal struggle.[1]

The other meaning of betrayal, to give oneself away, is also in play in this episode. Indeed, to allow the institutional betrayal of one's potential is to give oneself away. For example, guilt gives one's potential to the church. Stephen brands such institutional appropriators as "usurpers," those who would wrongly appropriate for their own interests Stephen's realization.

Stephen senses these lethal identities and the risk they pose to his soul. At this point, he is more vulnerable to these risks than the Stephen described at the end of AP because of guilt engendered by his mother's recent death (some ten months ago).[2] His guilt has produced an identity crisis because his narcissistic identity is shaky. His identity crisis has lead to a life of debauchery. This life limits his possibilities and results in disrespect of his own realization. He has exercised his freedom in favor of self-indulgence of the lowest order, and this condition makes him more vulnerable to his adversaries.

This all important first episode also establishes the problem that Stephen deals with in the novel: in his successful defense against these institutional adversaries of the soul, he has become   narcissistic, withdrawn, and self-protecting.[3] His condition will be familiar to most modern readers. He is now his own enemy in self-realization in art and life.

Having learned how to avoid spiritual submission, he is now unable to connect with other humans to create a meaningful emotional life. In this condition, he has no insight into the grave and constant, the foundation necessary for the highest art. This shell was necessary to protect the young Stephen from the adversaries of his independence. He eventually realizes that this shell limits his art, and on this day, the day Joyce had his first date with Nora, he gains sufficient courage to take it all off.

Structure of Episode

This first episode of Ulysses is based on Chapters i and ii of The Odyssey and Scenes i and ii of Act I of *Hamlet*.[4] The ancient Greece of Odysseus is suitable framing material for this Irish tale and Stephen Dedalus bears a Greek name because, Joyce believed, many of the earliest settlers in Ireland were Phoenicians like Odysseus.[5] The Hamlet reference rests on the common theme of soul struggle.

Dublin—Tower

The entire novel takes place in and around Dublin on one day and one long night, June 16 and 17, 1904. The first episode starts in the morning in the Irish spring, suggesting promise.[6]

The first episode takes place in and near a tower named by Buck as the Omphalos (navel), which is located on the beach in Sandymount near Dublin. The tower in the novel is based on an actual "Martello" tower that existed at that location in 1904 (and still exists as a tourist attraction). As in Joyce's life, Stephen has been living in the tower after his return from Paris to attend his mother's last illness and funeral.[7] The actual tower, built as one of several, has walls eight feet thick and narrow slits for windows that grudgingly admit little light. A spiral staircase built

29

in the wall connects the main room to the top, which originally housed canon in gunrests.[8] These features are carefully duplicated in the novel. This cold, dark tower houses three bachelors eating, eliminating and sleeping.

The navel is, according to the ancients, where the soul resides.[9] Any round tower also serves as a figure of the lingam, a symbol of the male sex organ, in the yoni, a symbol of the female sex organ. Accordingly, the primal individual energies—soul and sex—are represented by the tower.[10] Here these primal individual energies are under the control of the Catholic Church, as its representative Buck takes possession of the key to the tower from Stephen. The tower is initially locked from the inside, suggesting imposed control and a hard inner orientation separated from others. The fact that the key is found in the lock on the inside suggests that an important solution can be found within. The key would be made of copper in order to avoid sparks, which could set off munitions originally stored inside.[11] Sparks within, the mystical approach to god, is denied by the Catholic Church.

These towers were originally built to by the British to protect British control of Ireland from French invasion in favor of Irish independence. Since Stephen has just returned from a run to freedom to Bohemian Paris, we can anticipate that those in the tower will oppose his introduction into Ireland of the forces of freedom.

The hard, enclosing and defensive Omphalos tower is in sharp contrast to that famous Hindu navel, the navel of Vishnu. From his cosmic navel, the lotus flower of the world unfolds and blooms. These lotus and bloom images from Hindu mythology will grace our soft and compassionate hero Leopold Bloom. In the hard tower, Stephen is focused on himself and is extremely cold and hostile in his relations with others.

Action in Ulysses

The action starts abruptly without prelude, background or explanation. Joyce doesn't set the scene or introduce the characters. This is one aspect of the dramatic method.

Early on a spring morning, Buck emerges from the spiral staircase onto the top of the tower. He is wearing only a yellow robe open

30

in front and is carrying shaving gear. Otherwise, he is naked. He calls Stephen to come up from below in the tower. Notice that Buck's first interaction with Stephen is a church-like instruction, raise yourself up. Then for an unexplained purpose, Buck looks sideways and up and whistles once slowly. The answer from an unknown source is two "strong shrill" whistles. Then Buck thanks the other whistler and calls for the "old chap" to shut off the current, presumably instructing Haines below in the tower to turn off the light on the top of the tower. Stephen, having been called up by Buck, stops at the top of the spiral staircase.

The first visual presentation of Stephen is just of his head. He is standing on the stairs with his head above the level of the roof of the tower, part in and part out of the body of the tower. His elbows are resting on the roof. Buck can only see his head. With Stephen in this half-exposed position, Buck uses his shaving bowl as a mock chalice and pretends to conduct a mass before Stephen, apparently in an effort to mock Stephen's seriousness. Stephen is wearing mourning clothes (black) because of his mother's death. He has been mourning for some time.

Stephen responds to Buck's mock mass with just one thought, "Chrysostomos." At Buck's urging, Stephen obligingly moves up the rest of the stairs to a round "gunrest" on the top of the tower and sits down. Notice the second church-like instruction, rest your gun, a gun with sexual overtones.

Buck shaves while talking to Stephen. Stephen does not shave. Buck mentions Stephen's ancient Greek family name Dedalus and Hellenism. They talk about Haines, and Stephen complains about his violent tendencies, which have surfaced in nightmares. Stephen asks how long Haines will be staying in the tower. Buck doesn't answer. Buck instead talks about the sea as the "mighty mother" and repeatedly charges Stephen, only partly in jest, with the murder of his own mother. Stephen is charged with matricide because he refused his cancer-ridden mother's deathbed request to kneel and pray to her god.

Buck offers Stephen more hand me down (second hand) clothes and, showing his emphasis on appearances, compliments Stephen's when well dressed. Stephen shows no interest in appearances.

Buck reports to Stephen that on the previous evening, Buck heard that Stephen has "g.p.i.," general paralysis of the insane, a mental condition resulting from the last stage of neuro-syphilis. Buck says he heard this at a pub named "The Ship" from one who worked at an asylum ("Dottyville"). Stephen's reaction, if any, to this ominous report is not given.

Buck has Stephen look at himself in the shaving mirror, which prompts a discussion about Irish art. Stephen characterizes Irish art as the "cracked looking glass of a servant." Buck takes Stephen's arm, and Stephen thinks about Cranly, a friend of his, doing the same. Human contact feels odd to Stephen. Finally, Stephen tells Buck that Haines can stay in the tower since he is only a problem at night. To wipe his razor, Buck borrows Stephen's noserag. Buck jokes about snot green as the new art color for Irish poets. Buck sings blasphemous songs about Jesus and Mary Ann.

Buck asks Stephen why he is cold and distant ("Why don't you trust me more . . . Then what is it . . . Cough it up. I'm quite frank with you. What have you against me now?"). This set of questions is apparently prompted by Stephen's terse responses to Buck's garrulous conversation. Note Buck's use of "cough it up," no doubt an intentional reminder of Stephen's mother's violent coughing in her death throes. This aspect of his mother's death throes is registered in Stephen's memory in a bedside bowel, a bowl that she used to contain her expectoration of bile.

As an explanation of his cold and distant attitude, Stephen reminds Buck of a comment Buck made earlier ("It's only Dedalus whose mother is beastly dead"). Stephen thinks this comment belittled his value as an individual human. Having seen people "pop off" and cut up every day in the hospital where he is a medical student, Buck scoffs at Stephen's claimed value for the human aspect of each individual. Buck claims the harm in his statement belittling Stephen is nothing compared to the harm in Stephen's refusal of his mother's deathbed request to kneel and pray. Note that Buck is doing his best to make Stephen feel guilty and belittle his value as an individual human. He would belittle and reduce Stephen—be little. The Church would shrink its subjects. His lost

32

potential would be sacrificed on the altar of respectable society and religious control.

Called down by Haines, Buck goes down the stairs inside the tower to prepare breakfast. As he leaves Stephen on top, Buck continues his assault on Stephen's brooding with the line "And no more turn aside and brood." This line is part of a poem by the Irish Yeats about "love's bitter mystery" and one Fergus ruling "the brazen cars." Stephen stays up top by himself, muses about the sea and reviews a repeating dream he is having. This dream, apparently fueled by guilt, involves terrifying visits by his mother from the grave. He begs her memory to leave him alone and let him live. Stephen repeats in Latin the layman's prayer for the dying: "Liliata rutilantium te confessorum. . . ." [May the glittering throng of confessors, bright as lilies, gather about you. May the glorious choir of virgins receive you (translation by Gifford)]. In this thought sequence, Stephen recalls the song about the boy "that can enjoy invisibility." This song is about the youth of Christ, during which period he is reputed in non-canonical sources to have appropriated his divine power for playful ends, such as making himself and animals temporarily invisible. Eventually the disappearing act will be performed by the author in the dramatic mode.

Buck calls Stephen down for breakfast, another instruction, with reference to "coming" and Jesus. Buck comes back up the ladder momentarily to suggest confidentially a money raising idea to Stephen: since Haines thinks clever Stephen's definition of Irish art, Stephen should touch Haines for a quid. Art for commercial gain. Stephen does not carry out this suggestion that betrays Buck's commercially oriented values. Learning that Stephen is to receive his salary that morning, Buck excitedly mentions "four omnipotent sovereigns," and with this royal reference enthusiastically sings a song about drinking on coronation day, the traditional phrase for the day of the second coming. Note when Stephen receives his salary in the second episode that Buck has overestimated the amount. Stephen retrieves the shaving bowl Buck has carelessly left on the tower's parapet and characterizes his actions as those of a "server of a servant," Stephen's view of the faithful in the Catholic Church.

Haines has been below in the tower the entire time. Back down in the tower with Buck and Haines, Stephen makes the tea. Buck's cooking makes too much smoke. Haines opens the door to the tower to let the smoke out but only after Stephen locates the key in the iron lock on the inside of the door. Buck thought Stephen had the key, and Haines couldn't find it even though it was quite visible in the lock. After order is restored, Buck jokes about the trinity as he divides up three eggs. All three eat breakfast and talk. An old woman arrives in the nick of time to deliver milk for the tea. Stephen uses bitter lemon instead of rich milk in his. Buck jokes about making tea (read spirit) and water (read urine) but not in the same pot (read the human can not contain the divine). Buck mentions the Mabinogion and the Upanishads in jokes about the tea and water pots. Buck pays the old woman for most but not all of the past milk bill. Haines shows off his command of the original Irish language for the milk woman; she is humbled by her ignorance of her own native tongue. Stephen notes that she pays respect to Buck and Haines but not to him.

After breakfast, Buck carefully dresses in front of the mirror and talks about "dressing the character." Buck throws Stephen's Parisian "Latin quarter" hat (black with wide brim) to him. Prior to leaving, Buck whets Haines's appetite for Stephen's theory of Hamlet. Stephen sardonically asks if he will be paid for this rendition, apparently in an effort to mock Buck's values. All three climb down the ladder (outside) to leave the tower. Buck advertises that Stephen paradoxically ". . . proves by algebra that Hamlet's grandson is Shakespeare's grandfather and he himself is the ghost of his own father." Haines talks to Stephen about Stephen's theory of Hamlet and religious faith. Haines, the collector, brings up well-known theories about Hamlet, including the theological concept of atonement of father and son.

Shortly they reach the forty-foot swimming hole, and Buck rushes toward it pretending to fly. Buck takes off his clothes for a bath in the hole, which was in 1904 and is still part of Dublin Bay. Taking off his trousers, Buck proclaims superman status by reference to the rib of Adam and Nietzsche, the philosopher patron of aristocratic power. Two other swimmers are already in the hole. Neither is identified and only one is known to Buck. The known swimmer asks Buck if he coming in. Buck responds, quoting from Wilde, "Yes, Make room in the bed." The known swimmer asks about Buck's brother. Buck says he is "down" in Westmeath with the Bannons. The known swimmer mentions that Bannon has found a girlfriend, a "photogirl." Later we learn this is Bloom's daughter Milly, who is working in a photo shop. Notice that photography is a form of reproduction. Buck jokes about the photogirl with the quip "brief exposure."

The unknown swimmer in the hole is older, has his hair in an old-style tonsure, and seems to frighten Buck. Haines says he will swim later after he digests his breakfast. While Buck is bathing, Stephen and Haines see two boats in the harbor, a steam-powered mailboat making for Bullock Harbor and a sailboat coming up from the south. Haines tells Stephen this sailboat will come in on the tide "about one," a typical Joycean pun combining time (one o'clock) and identity (one). Later the sailboat is identified as the *Rosevean* and as carrying bricks in the belly of her hold. Stephen encounters her in the third episode.

As Stephen expects, Buck asks Stephen for the key to the tower. He also asks for two pence for a pint of beer. Stephen reluctantly complies with this expropriation by Buck of key and coin. Buck asks Stephen to meet him and Haines at 12:30 ("half twelve") at a pub named "The Ship," expecting Stephen to play the host with his salary ("kip") that is due that morning. Stephen seems tacitly to agree to these expropriations.

Upon departing, Stephen repeats in Latin part of the Catholic layman's prayer for the dying. This time he leaves out (see full text above) the parts about confessors and about being received by the virgins. Upon seeing a priest's gray nimbus (halo—head garment) in a discreet dressing area (probably used by the older swimmer), he predicts he shall neither return to the tower that night nor be able to go home. This nimbus and Stephen's iconoclastic hat are the first of many head garments to signify spirit. Haines has a soft grey hat, respectable grey, Stephen a Latin quarter hat, an emblem of exile and independence, and Buck a Panama, the icon of imperialistic control of others.

Walking on an "upwardcurving path," a symbol of the spiritual quest, Stephen hears and sees Buck swimming out in the Bay. He

35

compares Buck to a "seal." The closing phrases of the episode are instructive in tone and subject:

> A voice, sweettoned and sustained, called to him [Stephen] from the sea [image combines mother and church]. Turning the curve he [Stephen] waved his hand. It [Buck's voice now depersonalized as "it"] called again. A sleek brown head, a seal's far out on the water, round.
>
> Usurper. [Stephen's thought] [parentheticals mine]

This image is of the call of the normal life, a life pursued for the respect of others. The tone is seductive. The image of Buck bathing in the water signifies the submersion of the individual in the imposed conformity of the sea of respectable society. First the image of Buck becomes an impersonal "it," then just a head and finally just a shape, round, the shape which produces the least resistance. This sequence of images is a picture of the loss to imposed conformity of individuality.

This comparison makes a connection to the third episode, which features seals. Moreover, this initial connection also starts a process of association that is fundamental to this novel. The seal of Solomon, signified by two interlocked triangles, is the symbol in esoteric Buddhist conceptions of the relatedness of all things to the powers that be.[12]

Action in The Odyssey

The related chapters of The Odyssey (i and ii)[13] open with some of the Olympian gods in council discussing the free will of man, which they state is greater than humans imagine. Athena, daughter of Zeus, and Pallas plead to Zeus for the release of the human Odysseus from captivity. Odysseus is being held captive because he incurred the wrath of the "earth shaker" god Poseidon by blinding one of Poseidon's many progeny, the one-eyed giant Cyclops. As Poseidon's punishment, Odysseus has been held captive for many years after the Trojan war. His prison is on an island, called the navel of the sea, and his warden is the young female nymph Calypso. An unusual warden, Calypso has regular sexual relations with her prisoner. With this captivity, Odysseus's victorious home coming after the Trojan war has been delayed and betrayed by Poseidon.

The gods also discuss, as a potential version of Odysseus's future fate, the homecoming betrayal of Agamemnon, another Greek warrior king. After returning home from Troy, he was killed by his wife and her lover Agisthos. His murder was eventually revenged by Agamemnon's son Orestes, the Greek Hamlet.

Poseidon being absent from the council (these gods apparently have to be present to have any influence), Athena easily persuades daddy Zeus to let her help her favorite Odysseus and his young son Telemachus. Then, motion picture-like, the action cuts to Odysseus's mansion in Ithaca, two small islands west of Greece in the Ionian Sea. There Odysseus's wife, Penelope, and their young son, Telemachus, are living in the family mansion. Telemachus means "decisive battle"[14].

Odysseus has for several years been missing in action in the Trojan war. His son was born shortly before his departure for the war. While Odysseus has been gone, Telemachus has grown to a young man in a single parent household, without the benefit of a male role model. Given the male vacuum, many lords from the neighborhood have come to Odysseus's mansion to plead for the "hand" of Penelope. They are referred to as the "wooers."

The wooers wait impatiently for Penelope to choose one of them as mate. In the meantime, the numerous members of this expectant male group are staying in Odysseus's mansion and eating Penelope and Telemachus (as the heirs of Odysseus) out of house and home, rapidly consuming their flock and stored up wine and grain. They order the servants about and consort with some of the female slaves as if they own the place. Young Telemachus stands helplessly by as the wooers mock him and dishonor his home and his heritage. In response to the wooers' demands, Penelope declares the waiting time for her hand will end when she completes a big weaving; she works on the weaving during the day but, in order to delay the process, secretly undoes it at night.

Athena, in disguise and conspicuously carrying a spear, arrives at Odysseus's mansion. Athena takes Telemachus aside to tell him she has seen Odysseus and that he will be coming home soon. Athena asks if

37

he is the son of Odysseus, and Telemachus makes the provocative comment that no one really knows his own father, only his mother. Athena encourages Telemachus to be bold with his mother and the wooers. With this encouragement, Telemachus commands his surprised mother to stay in her room and demands a meeting of the city assembly in order to argue his case against the wooers. At this city meeting, the wooers defensively blame Penelope for giving them hope by promising to give her hand when the weaving is done. Mentor, whom Odysseus left in command at the mansion, tries to support Telemachus. Initially Telemachus seems to gain some momentum in the argument before the assembly but ultimately fails to bring the matter to a head. Two eagles appear and fight above the assembly, which is taken by some as an omen.

Back at Odysseus's mansion after the assembly, one of the leading wooers, Antinoös, tries to befriend and convince Telemachus to accept the inevitable and to go along to get along. Telemachus responds by threatening him and the rest of the wooers. The wooers laugh at his threat. In the face of mounting personal danger, Telemachus escapes in a ship arranged by Athena in order to learn more about his father's fate. In Chapter iv, the wooers wake up to the dangerous implications of Telemachus's departure and lay a naval ambush for his return.

Parallels to The Odyssey

The basic parallels with The Odyssey that give reinforced meaning to the Telemachus episode of this novel are as follows:

Stephen is the counterpart of Telemachus. In spite of multiple references to Stephen's deceased mother, there is no reference in this first episode to Stephen's father. This lack of paternal presence for Stephen reflects Odysseus's absence from home and Telemachus's comment about not knowing his father. Stephen is searching for his spiritual father, the knowledge and experience that will allow him to take control of his own life and maximize his self-realization. Achieving this state is traditionally referred to as the second birth through the father. Since Athena was born directly from the forehead of Zeus, she symbolizes the process of the second birth in the mind. Since Joyce believed that the important human issues have not changed over time, Stephen can be viewed as a reincarnation of Telemachus. Stephen's struggle for realization is the "decisive battle," the meaning of Telemachus' name.

Stephen's drive for self-realization relates to the discussion of the Olympian gods about human free will—humans have more than they think. Buck and Haines in the tower are the wooers at Ithaca. The wooers try to convince Telemachus and Stephen to take the easy path blessed by society, to go along in order to get along. The wooers would consume Telemachus's and Stephen's independence by expropriating the father function. They are would-be false fathers.

The old milk woman symbolizes Ireland[15] and is one counterpart to Athena in disguise.[16] Stephen says this third master, Ireland , wants him for "odd jobs" but nothing important. Living in Ireland does not suit Stephen's artistic mission in life and would result in menial employment. Attracted to the simple soul of the milk woman, Stephen (as Joyce) will feature Ireland in his art in an attempt to redeem her "Celtic inheritance" from the Roman Catholic and British usurpers. Without redemption, she gives respect only to Haines and Buck.

Traditional Schemata

The traditional schemata given by Joyce for this episode are art—theology, colors—white and gold, symbol—heir, and technique—narrative (young). That is to say, the art of the episode is based on theology, the colors emphasized are white and gold, the symbol for the subtext of meaning is heir, and the technique of the narrator's presentation is a chronological narrative given by a young person. Note no organ, usually included in the schemata, is involved. Stephen the cold-hearted brain is present. He is only head at this juncture, a point made by his first visual presentation.

The correspondences given by Joyce are Telemachus—Hamlet and Stephen, Antinoos—Mulligan, and Mentor—the milkwoman. Both the milkwoman, representing Ireland, and Mentor, Odysseus's second in command, have lost command of their own mansions. Linati lists as symbols Hamlet, Ireland and Stephen and for persons Penelope as the Muse. As the Muse, Penelope weaves and unweaves the symbolic sub-text of this episode.

The traditional schemata, however, give only a faint hint of the delicacies this episode has to offer.

39

First Letter, First Word and Opening

The first letter of the episode and Part I is **S**, which announces Stephen's preoccupation with Stephen. Part II will open with an **M** for Bloom's preoccupation with his wife Molly, and Part III with **P** for Stephen's and Molly's preoccupation with Poldy, Bloom's nickname.[17] The first word "Stately" announces Buck's concern for appearances. The novel starts and ends with the letter s, but the ending s is part of Molly's yes to fundamentals rather than Buck's concern for stately appearances. Note the first and last words of the novel begin and end with s and y and y and s respectively. What goes around comes around.

The opening of the first episode, with a perverted Mass and Stephen ascending in the tower, conditions the reader from the very outset to interpret the entire novel as a form of extended initiation rite and transition for Stephen. Stephen's first words are "How long is Haines going to stay in this tower?" In other words, how long are the forces represented by Haines going to be instrumental in Stephen's soul? Fortunately, the answer is not too long.

Themes

This episode introduces several themes basic to the novel. They include the personal values of Buck and Haines, typology, the ritual of the Mass, Hellenism, art, Hamlet, church and state as enemies and usurpers of realization, the Trinity and the soul. In addition, the episode touches lightly on the subject of syphilis, a condition for which Joyce probably received treatment in March of 1904, the year in which this novel is set.[18]

Buck and Haines

Buck, an Irish medical student focused on the body, mocks Stephen's serious emphasis on the world of the spirit. Buck's main values are respectability and the favorable opinions of others, not self-realization and integrity. Haines, a well-heeled Britisher collecting "native" Irish material, is freeloading in the tower while Stephen pays the rent from his meager teacher's salary. Haines's propensities to violence, which trouble the peace-loving Stephen, have surfaced in Haines's dreams.[19] Haines is staying in the tower at the invitation of Buck and eventually displaces Stephen in the tower. Buck's motivation in this regard is suggested by his statement at the end of the episode quoting Oscar Wilde, "Make room in bed"[20].

Typology—Chrysostomos

Stephen's first thought and his only reaction to Buck's mock mass show and his gold tipped teeth is the thought "Chrysostomos." He was one of the early fathers of the Greek Church (the Greek Orthodox Catholic Church) and known as "Golden Mouth."

This early church father (d. 407) was famous for the typological interpretation of scriptures. In that interpretation, Old Testament events are real historical events and prefigure later real historical events in the New Testament. These "horizontal" events in time are connected by a common "vertical" reference to divine reality. Chrysostomos also down—played the role of the Holy Spirit, believing that individual gifts of the spirit were no longer operative after the Church was established. No more individual charismata. Instead, the restrictive Law of the Church Fathers.

The first typological combination in this novel is the one slow whistle by Buck and an answer from an unknown source of two strong and shrill whistles. While giving his one whistle, Buck looks sideways and then up, a reference to the horizontal and vertical connections of events in typology. The first single whistle suggests the events in the Old Testament, those energized by the presence through the vertical dimension of the "Old Chap," the Father and the first Person in the Trinity. The shrill two whistle reply suggests the events in the New Testament, those energized by the dual presence of the Father and the shrill, sermonizing Son, the second Person in the Trinity.

In the view of Chrysostomos, the Son proceeds in the world in relationship to the Father in order to fulfill the events in the Old Testament, the counterpart of the Law of the Fathers. The role of Christ in the world was to confirm the Law of the Hebrew Fathers, not to strike out on his own. In Buck's world of the spirit, the functions of father and son are separate and the son must respect the father's rules, that is fulfill the rules laid down by church and state in order to gain the respect of others. As we shall see, for Stephen father and son must be the same and he will respect only his own rules.

41

Both the legacy of Chrysostomos and the attitude of Buck belittle the independence and importance of the individual human spirit. By contrast, Stephen believes in individual charismatic and a divine reality of uniting with god through self-realization. The inevitable inheritance from both Buck's quest for respect from others and Chrysostomos's theology is a group of camp followers with small human spirits enjoying less possibilities. So, Stephen's first thought in the novel is a negative reaction to the Law of the Fathers.

The Ritual of the Mass

Buck intones the first words of the Mass spoken by the Priest: *"Introibo ad altare Dei,"* or "I will go in unto the altar of God." The next line in the Mass is to be spoken by the younger server (acolyte). The next line, pointedly omitted in Ulysses, is "unto God who giveth joy to my youth." Young Stephen does not give this answer. He refuses to be the server. And Stephen refuses to serve in a deeper sense, the sense declared by Lucifer and known in Catholicism as the sin of pride, the opposite of supplication. Like Lucifer, Stephen dares to be great, even at the cost of eternal damnation.

Buck continues his mock mass with "Back to barracks," arbitrarily calling Christ to his military duty in the Eucharist. He continues in a "preacher's tone" with "For this, O dearly beloved, is the genuine christine: body and soul and blood and ouns [wounds]. Slow music please. Shut your eyes, gents. One moment. A little trouble about those white corpuscles. Silence, all."

In the ritual of the Catholic Mass, the bread and wine are transubstantiated or changed by a transfer of energy into the substance and accidents of Christ, the divine substances that end up in the accidents of the bread and wine. The substance of the bread and wine as such has gone. Buck's mock attempt at transubstantiation falls short because Christ's white corpuscles have not been received in the transporter room. In the body, white corpuscles fight disease. In spiritual terms, a lack of white corpuscles corresponds to an individual's lack of ability on his or her own to fight spiritual corruption, a lack which the daily Mass assumes. Buck's joke champions institution over individual.

42

The breakfast of eggs, bacon, bread and tea is presented as a mock Eucharist. The three eggs in the skillet for the trinity carry the episode's colors yellow and white. The etymology of the word "mass" combines sacrifice with blazing or flaring up of the smoke, which carries the food spirit to the gods.[21] But Buck's smoke from cooking the breakfast gets trapped in the hard tower and doesn't make it up to the gods, until the door is opened from the inside.

The consumption of the body of Christ in the Eucharist, with its basic connection in The Odyssey to plundering by the wooers, is spread like heavy hors d'oeuvres throughout this episode.[22] As one example, during the breakfast Buck "lunged towards his messmates in turn a thick slice of bread impaled on his knife." Read mass for mess; the mass is a real mess, everyone eating Christ. The knife in the bread would signify the spear in Jesse's side during the Passion.[23] The references to the mass support the usurper/betrayal theme since the foundation for the mass is the Last Supper from which Jesse's betrayal was predicted by him and initiated by Judas. In Stephen's view, the inheritance as heir from church and state is betrayal of the spirit, restriction and expropriation of individual possibilities.

The mock mass conducted by Buck opens the novel and is prominent in this episode (first 29 lines) because it is used as the principal symbol for the changes to take place in Stephen. Since the novel takes place on Thursday and Friday, it is useful to know that the Friday Mass is the Mass of the Presanctified, the only Mass during which the host is not consecrated. The remaining and already consecrated host from Holy Thursday is used in the Friday Mass, leftovers or a "second hand" host.[24] The Host is removed from the altar during the Thursday Mass, and the light indicating the presence of the Host in the Tabernacle is put out. Other important items are removed. This is referred to as stripping the altar. In order to provide a Connector Fact to the Thursday Mass, Buck says "Mulligan is stripped of his garments." Removing the Host and turning out the light are reflected in Buck's direction to Haines on Thursday morning to turn off the "current," and thus the light on top of the tower. The removal of the consecrated Host from the Thursday

Mass signifies the spiritual condition of Stephen's depraved life and his current companions.

Good Friday was not so good because Jesus was crucified on Friday. He arose on Sunday; in between is Holy Saturday, the day characterized by waiting in uncertainty about how grief from the crucifixion is to be overcome. Jesus is in hell on Holy Saturday.[25]

The Mass breaks down into two parts, the first part being the Mass for the Cathecumens known as the Mass for the Learners, those not yet baptized. The second part is the Mass for the Faithful, in which only the baptized were allowed to partake in early Christianity. The Mass for the Faithful begins with the Offertory, includes Communion and ends the service.[26] Initially, Stephen is identified with the Cathecumens portion and Bloom the Faithful, but eventually they both partake of a combined secular mass.[27]

The Catholic cult of the Sacred Heart is also important throughout the novel. This is the particularly guilt oriented and *quid pro quo* based cult of Catholicism that was popular with Irish women in 1904. This cult is based on visions of one Margaret Mary Alacoque on June 16 (our same day) in 1675. Margaret Mary reported visions of the Savior with his heart exposed outside his body and pleading for "reparations" for his unappreciated sacrifice.[28] This cult promises final absolution conditioned on the believer attending every Friday Mass for 9 months (another gestation period as well). Stephen's mother followed this cult, and Stephen believes that Irishwomen serve as accomplices of the Catholic Church. The exposed heart motif and its icon the crimson halter appear frequently throughout the novel. The Sacred Heart emphasizes the guilt aspect of the Eucharistic ceremony and can be analyzed as a projection of the feelings of most Irish women that they are not properly appreciated either. Buck, who wears a primrose waistcoat, calls the cult visionary "Margaret Mary Anycock."

The name Malachi associates Buck with the Old Testament Book by the Minor Prophet Malachi, the last in the Christian arrangement of the Old Testament. Malachi means "my messenger,"[29] and the Catholic Church interprets this last chance Old Testament Book to prefigure the Mass. The message of the Book of Malachi is faith and

44

conventional obedience and is delivered to a doubting community.[30] Significantly, the last line of the Book of Malachi refers to reconciliation between fathers and sons through god. Reconciliation of father and son is an important concept in the trinity and in this novel.

Hellenism

In the ancient Greek tradition, a man or woman is important only for a heroic aspect of his or her personality. In the heroic tradition, the hero "goes it" alone and achieves heroic status by reason of his or her deeds acting alone. This tradition and its mutant progeny of Nietzschean supermen and modern narcissists are associated in this novel with youth and the lyrical mode of art, that mode in which the possibilities of art are held hostage to the artist.

The ancient Greek heroic tradition is in sharp contrast with the Jewish tradition, which is represented by the older Leopold Bloom. In the Jewish tradition, every human who leads a life of justice and righteousness in connection with his fellow humans is considered sacred. In the Jewish tradition, divinity can be found in anyone, whether of heroic or humble deeds.[31] This tradition is associated with the mature dramatic mode of art.

Irish Art

Typical Irish art is paraded in this episode: poems, bawdy songs, legends, riddles, Yeats's esoteric poetry and Wilde's wit. Stephen criticizes Irish art as lacking in independence and serving the wrong masters, "a server of a servant." This criticism initiates the issue of independence in the artistic realm in an episode about Stephen's struggle for freedom in the spiritual realm. Life and art.

Hamlet

The characters in the first episode quote from and discuss the meaning of *Hamlet*. Like the Prince of Denmark, Stephen is struggling to "do his own thing," to identify himself by his own values and to ward off those who would dictate his identity.[32]

In scenes i and ii of Act I, Prince Hamlet is first seen in mourning for the death of his father and at odds with the new King, Prince Hamlet's uncle, and the Queen, his mother, together the betrayers of Prince Hamlet's father (also named Hamlet, King Hamlet). The usurpers, the new royal couple, encourage young Prince Hamlet to stop mourning and to get along with the new regime. Likewise, Stephen is first seen in mourning for the death of his mother in the tower equivalent of Elsinore and at odds with Buck Mulligan. Like the uncle king, Buck scoffs at Stephen's prolonged mourning and tries to betray Stephen's legitimate spiritual inheritance, as his Uncle did to Prince Hamlet's right to the throne.[33] To his uncle's question "How is it that the clouds still hang on you?", Prince Hamlet replies "not so, my lord, I am too much in the sun"[34]. These same themes, sun god principles and the heirship pun (sun-son), are larded into Joyce's Telemachus episode.[35]

The father-son issue in **Hamlet** is the foundation of the plot in this novel as it relates to Stephen. The issue is maturation: what is the process by which the son acquires "manhood"? By manhood, I mean self-respect and secure identity. Note that the issue in **Hamlet** can be explored in terms of the concept of the Trinity: Will the heretofore intellectual Prince Hamlet become like his warrior father King Hamlet? In the Trinity, the object is for the Son to proceed in the likeness of the Father.

The human soul reflects the Second Person in the Trinity. The ghost of King Hamlet hounds Prince Hamlet to behave like the warrior King would have. This is Prince Hamlet's affliction. Prince Hamlet struggles to build his own consciousness and values.[36] The blood father functioning properly can help the son achieve the proper heirship. So can a spiritual father. However, Stephen's blood father is of no help in this department and all would-be spiritual fathers have thus far threatened his independence. So Stephen believes at this point that this most valuable acquisition can only be made by him acting alone.

Church and State: Usurpers and Betrayal

Buck Mulligan represents the demands of the Roman Catholic Church in pursuing Stephen's faith and obedience. Both Buck and the Church seek to expropriate Stephen's spiritual and material assets for their own purposes. The mysterious British guest, Haines (no first name), represents the UK state or culture and would instruct Stephen how to live his life. These are the Priest and King that Joyce boasted of banishing from his "marriage" to Nora (for many years no license or ceremony) and attempted to banish from his life.[37] Now Priest and King are bed mates cooperating in the expropriation of potential.

Stephen has not decided to try to change or rid Ireland of these forces but only to banish them as effective forces in his own life. These adversaries of his independence and values are branded at the very end of the episode as "usurpers"; they would take his most precious asset, his realization potential. In order to avoid them, Stephen decides to leave the tower, even though he has nowhere to go.

In reacting as a reader to the immoderate attention given to Catholic doctrine and influence in this novel, keep in mind that Stephen is pledged to an uncompromising life of the spirit and was, throughout his impressionable youth, subjected to the magnificent, intellectually consistent doctrines of the rigorous Jesuits of the Roman Catholic Church. With this orientation and great respect for recurring images of human spirituality, Stephen can not just brush Catholicism aside, as materialists now do without a second thought. He must confront it and deal with it. And he does so with an attitude, an attitude born of respect for its power and scorn for its purposes.

Buck asks to have the "current" turned off, presumably for a light on top of the tower. These efforts signify the Church's preoccupation with the hereafter, as opposed to the "current" here and now. They also suggests the absurdity of the Church's position that even a corrupt priest (signified by Buck and the "Old Chap," the nickname for Satan) can turn the Holy Spirit, the current of the Trinity, off and on at will in the sacraments. Note that in the last episodes, Molly turns the current and a light on in her house at a critical moment in the novel. She turns on what Buck turns off.

Buck's repeated questions as to whether Stephen is "coming" signify the Church's obsession with sex to the exclusion of many other values. The Church's unstated preference for masturbation over copulation for pleasure hides in the undertow of this episode. These sexual strictures are connected to the destruction of Ireland through the betrayal by the Church of Charles Parnell. He was the Irish independence patriot whose political career was destroyed by the influence of the Church because of an adulterous affair with Kitty O'Shea.[38] At the same time, the questions as to whether Stephen is "coming" inevitably connect to the "second coming" of Christ and the Buddha as the "one thus come." In this case, the questions would be an institutional inquiry whether Stephen is trying to reach the divine all by himself. Together these "coming" references connect the human sexual instinct and the divine, a major Joycean theme.

Roman Catholic theology would betray Stephen's quest for self-realization through its insistence that his soul carries the virus of original sin, not the divine spark. Buck has Stephen look at himself in a **cracked** mirror. Stephen needs, according to this doctrine, constant atonement with a distant God that can be provided only by the Church acting as a bridge or broker. These concepts, like the ancient Greek snake god requiring placation, operate on the principles of fear and guilt. Fearful Catholics are to believe and beget, submit not soar. In essence, the Church and Buck try to belittle Stephen's spirit and take his realization potential.[39] That is heirship in the Catholic Church, the inheritance of fear and guilt that restricts human possibilities.

The clothes that Stephen wears, "hand me downs" from Buck, symbolize the second-hand spiritual experience provided by the Roman Catholic Church, the Church acting as broker with a distant God. Buck's mirror "to flash the good news abroad" refers to the good news of the gospels, the word of god in Roman Catholic theology.[40] Gospel was originally spelled "godspell," [41] and in this novel, the reversed spelling of god as dog (a palindrome) plays a major symbolic role.

The reference to the old style tonsure (hair style) of the priest in the 40 foot swimming hole reflects the initial independence of the Irish clergy from Rome's dictates. In the eyes of Rome, the Irish missionaries erred as the shape of the tonsure.[42] Representing the interests of the centralized control function of the Church, Buck instinctively doesn't like this independent priest.

While alone, Buck first blesses the tower, the countryside and the mountains. The tower represents fertility and the countryside nature. The invisible gods of ancient Ireland, the Tuatha de Danaan, were believed to dwell in the mountains. So Buck first appears as a snake, and while he is alone blesses first the concept of fertility, the original primitive mythology, then the concept of a nature god and finally the ancient Irish gods. The Druid priests of the ancient Celts practiced human sacrifice, and their modern successors are still sacrificing potential.[43] When Stephen emerges, Buck abruptly shifts from his pagan ceremony and gurgles in traditional Catholic mode before Stephen mocking him as Christ. All of this suggests more of a pagan influence on Christianity than the Roman Catholic Church would want to acknowledge.

The Trinity

The Catholic Trinity of Father, Son and Holy Ghost is a fundamental doctrine of the Catholic faith. The doctrine of the trinity is a reading of the relationship of the eternal powers to all of humanity: The Father as the creator of the universe, the Son in the Incarnation as Christ on earth and the Holy Ghost in the sacraments and the hearts of humans as love. The doctrine of the Trinity is also a reading in love relations—the Holy Ghost or Spirit issues when the relation of Father and Son is proper.

Buck, Stephen and Haines make a trinity of sorts, with Buck as the would-be father influence, Stephen as the developing son and Haines as the spirit. The opening scene pays homage to the Catholic view that the Son comes from the Father in a type of "procession," not in a birth but a coming forth. Buck, as the would-be first mover father, comes up first and then calls Stephen to "Come up," a procession up and out into the world. The symbolic role that Haines plays, as the presence of the state and culture in the world, is in the same dimension as the Holy Ghost, the presence of God in the world. Haines is also associated with the Holy Ghost by his dream of the panther, Panthera being the name of the alleged Roman illegitimate father of Jesus.

A trinity of Buck, Stephen and Haines suggests that something fundamental is amiss. Under Catholic doctrine, a distortion in the Father/Son relationship results in an absence of the Holy Spirit, the giver of love and life. If Haines is the spirit immanent in the world, then that spirit was sent by Satan, not by a loving god. The presence of the spirit of the devil, the "old chap," rather than love informs us that the Father/Son relationship is distorted in Stephen's case.

49

The references to Chrysostomos and the Greek Orthodox Church also prepare us for Stephen's association of Buck with Photius, a patriarch at Constantinople in the 9th century whose views on the procession of the Holy Ghost were accepted by the Greek Church but not by Rome.[44] Stephen associates Buck ("pseudo Malachi") with Photius and other mockers; in this case, mockers refer to those who belittle the importance of the individual human spirit. The Photius reference takes us into the father and son issue in the trinity.

Stephen gives the trinity a totally new reading, a human and existential reading: the father aspect is the control function in human realization; the son aspect is the youthful energy for personal self-realization; and the spirit is the soul that results. The soul is the potential for the future. When the father/son relationship is distorted, the soul is limited compared to its potential. For Stephen, the father and the son must be the same person. He refuses to develop along lines dictated by others. He must be his own spiritual father. Moreover, he feels the divine spark within himself in the energy of his own genius; for this reason, he refuses to believe that he as the son is not of the same substance as the father. These dual requirements, same person same substance, lead the youthful Stephen to adopt the Sabellian view, the view that the father and the son are the same person and of the same substance. This view is heretical in the Catholic Church.

By contrast, Buck leads his life on the basis of standards set by others in order to gain their respect. The image of the trinity which corresponds to Buck's view of life is a father that is separate from the son. Photius fills that bill. Photius started with the assumption that the Son could not be his own Father, reading the Father-Son relationship in terms of birth rather than procession in general. From that starting point, he came to the conclusion that therefore the Holy Ghost did not proceed from both the Father and the Son, but just from the Father. Otherwise, the Holy Ghost who impregnated the Virgin Mary with the Son would be the father or grandfather of himself. This view of the Trinity appears in Buck's reference to Stephen's theory of Hamlet as the ghost of his own father.

Stephen classifies Photius, Buck and all others who require a separate father or separate source of authority in order to make them feel good about themselves as mockers of the human spirit. Stephen is to be his own father in terms of independence and his effort to assimilate to the divine. His soul, his spirit, is to proceed from his own personal realization directed by himself. He will control his own spirit rather than allowing Church and State to direct and take it.

By contrast to the Sabellian view, the orthodox version of the Trinity stipulates three difference Persons in one Divine Substance. The Son is not just a mode of the Father but proceeds separately from the Father in a procession. If the Son is in the perfect likeness of the Father, if their relationship is in pure love, then the Holy Spirit of love in the world issues from both. Note that this view involves love and relationships, which have not yet been part of Stephen's experience. Stephen at this point is projecting his own youthful image on the Trinity. His youthful experience has led him to the Sabellian view.

Also included in the episode as mock baptisms are a morning swim for Buck [45] and a reference to a drowned man on the nearby beach.[46] In Catholic theory, the baptism is the sacramental sign for experiencing the death (immersion) and resurrection of Christ (reemergence) into the eternal values. In this Dublin baptism, however, the swimming hole contains an old swimmer who symbolizes Poseidon. Since Poseidon is the master of time and space, this process is depicted as leaving one right where one started—a human creature in time and space. Buck is cleansed by the swim only in the dimension of social respectability.

Several times in the episode Stephen remembers the Catholic prayer for the dying that can be administered by the layman in the absence of a priest. Stephen is going to save himself.

Soul: Aristotle and the Kundalini

Since Stephen's soul is the battleground in Part I, Aristotle's key words "soul" and "form" (the soul is the "form of forms") permeate the first three episodes.

In defining the soul in *De Anima*, Aristotle reviews earlier theories, including those that the soul is sperm and the soul is blood.

Hints of sperm and blood, instruments of continuity, are smeared all over this episode. Rejecting earlier views, Aristotle offers the personal view that the soul represents the potential future action of each living being and the world soul represents all living potential. This potential is what Stephen and Joyce mean by soul.

The faculties of the soul are described by Aristotle as moving upward in a hierarchy from the lowest of nourishment and reproduction, to sense perception and desire, to imagination, and then to the highest of intellect. Within intellect, knowledge of universals is the ultimate achievement. Aristotle also speculates on one of the basic themes of this novel—whether any continuity exists through time and souls, his mentor Plato having believed in reincarnation of souls.[47]

A parallel pattern is presented by the chakra centers in Kundalini Yoga practice, a symbolic system in Tantric Yoga that Joyce uses throughout the novel. The chakra centers are imaged at various points in the body, and each location corresponds loosely to a certain type of psychological orientation. The image of the kundalini is as a narrow white snake that can move up and down in certain tracks in the body. The objective in this system is to move the kundalini from the lowest point located between the anus and the genitals (first chakra) to the highest at the crown of the head (seventh chakra) and thereby achieve the related, advanced psychological orientation. Each point or chakra has certain symbolic correspondences in elements, organs, sensations, colors, animals, numbers and in a certain representation of the lingam (male sexual principle) and yoni (female sexual principle). At the bottom, the snake is wrapped three and one-half times around the lingam. The energy of the lower chakras supports the higher chakras (in Jung speak, sublimation). Later in the novel, explicit reference is made to breathing exercises used in this practice. Chakra is Sanskrit for wheel, and the wheel of life signifies the constant round of rebirth produced by a failure of spiritual achievement.

This episode presents Buck and Haines in the lowest portions of the Aristotle model of the soul and in the bottom chakras, the lowest points of spiritual development with limited nourishment and reproduction interests and without the ability to generate their own ideas, being mere collectors.[48] Buck suggests the snake wrapped around the phallic lingam, controlling the tower as the Church would control Stephen's sexual energy. In the first chakra, a shell surrounds the kundalini and lingam, a role played in this episode by the tower. Buck moves from the first chakra associated with the element of earth (which he blesses), the color yellow (his robe and the egg yoke) and the organ feet (Stephen is wearing Buck's cast off shoes) to the second chakra associated with the genitals (showing while he is in his robe), the element water (Buck shaves and bathes), the color white (white shaving soap), the sensation taste (Buck's line "you can almost taste it") and the organ hand ("hand" over the key).

The goal of Kundalini Yoga is union with the Supreme Self by rousing the cosmic power, the kundalini present in every individual, to rise through the chakras to higher states of individual illumination. Failing to reach the higher chakras and to recognize the universal presence of the divine results in a sense of separation, known as "maya." The fourth chakra, that of the heart, is particularly important since it is the first spiritually oriented chakra. It is associated with Bloom, our compassionate hero. Moreover, the symbol of the fourth chakra is two interlocked triangles, the same symbol used to depict the seal of Solomon, which signifies the connection of god to events on this earth. This correspondence through triangles builds a bridge from the human heart to Joyce's view of the interconnectedness of the entire universe.

Syphilis

The subject of syphilis is broached in this episode in an entirely off-hand manner. This dark subject is deeply hidden in the folds of his novel. Consider that Joyce was probably treated for this disease in the year 1904, the year this novel is set, and struggled for most of his life with the guilt of the possibility that he infected his wife and their second child. The later stages of this disease may explain Joyce's recurring eye, stomach and gait problems as an adult.[49] In this novel, this highly sensitive subject is deflected into the guilt and masochism in Bloom's soul.

Ladder

The movements up and down the spiral staircase in the tower condition the reader for the use in this novel of the image of Jacob's ladder. In the desert, Jacob had a dream of a two-way staircase to heaven.

Ovals

During the time Stephen and Buck are on the top of the tower, the oval or circular shape is emphasized.[50] The tower's round top, the round gunrest, the round shaving bowl, and the movements of Buck and Stephen have this shape. They present circles within circles. As an enclosure or limitation, the circular shape is associated with limitations on the possibilities of the human spirit. Later in the novel the same image signifies the limitations associated with ego lock and Dublin spiritual paralysis (for example at the pub named the "Oval").

Eventually, the circle reappears, much in the manner of Biblical typology, in the orbit of comets. Fully transformed, the circle finally appears in the image of infinity or the eternal, an 8 (two interlocked circles) on its side, and in the image of the godhead borrowed from Dante, three intersecting and mutually reflecting circles. In the last episodes, Joyce uses Dante's image of interconnected ovals to symbolize the union of humans as producing an union with god.

Plato's Dialogues

Euthyphryo, an early dialogue by Plato, bears striking resemblance to parts of this episode. This dialogue features Socrates and the definition of holy (for Stephen, self-realization not supplication). Socrates is at the King's Porch (Stephen is on the top of the tower with Buck) to answer a charge of impiety (Buck's and Stephen's mother's complaint about Stephen). Socrates compares himself to Daedalus, another wordsmith, and claims him as an "ancestor." This form of heirship relates Socrates directly to Stephen, who bears the last name Dedalus. The dialogue portrays Socrates as a humble and wise man of historic integrity, a fitting reference for Stephen's and Joyce's view of themselves. This reference also carries the betrayal theme as Socrates was condemned to death by the council in his own city.

Independence Theme

Stephen's quest for independence is dramatized through the action.[51] Stephen is the only character who has independent thoughts. By contrast, Buck sings songs and recites poems written by others. Stephen has the brilliant insights; Buck and Haines seek to collect them. Only Stephen's thoughts are given in the text while Buck and Haines only move and talk.

Stephen is associated in the text with independent spirits, such the intellectually rigorous Jesuits, certain heretics of the Roman Catholic Church, mysticism and then trendy esoteric paganism. He is also directly associated with Jesus and Buddha whose lives, Joyce believed, manifested fundamental independence and integrity.

Buck and Haines as characters are weighted down by heavy symbolism, while Stephen remains light and clear in his own person. Indeed, Buck as a character becomes flat and wooden as he repeatedly asks for Stephen's faith. Haines plays the straight man in the episode; he obligingly brings up Hamlet, the trinity and freedom of spirit. Buck plays the jester. Stephen is serious.

The basic independence theme is reinforced by a father-son or heir theme. In the family, the son is initially controlled by the parents and then seeks his own way. Stephen must challenge his father and, in general, the Law of the Fathers, the repository of the cultural heritage and order.

Stephen's Mother

Stephen's mother threatened Stephen's independence by asking him to kneel and pray to her god at her death bed and thereby at least momentarily renounce his rejection of her religion.[52] This he refused to do because of the perceived threat to his soul. Now, however, he feels guilty about his refusal, and this guilt fuels his continuing dreams of her return from the grave. Stephen remembers his mother in connection with apples (Eve's betrayal) and lice (original sin which according to Catholic dogma he inherited from her). She appears three times in this episode. Just before Stephen begins to think about her, the cloud covers the sun.

In order to escape mother guilt, Stephen must untie once and forever the apron strings of control—faithfulness, loyalty and devotion. In Freudian analysis, a prolonged mother attachment produces narcissism and potentially homosexuality; in mythology, the mother attachment produces impotence or even self-castration or suicide. Echoes of these blind alleys reverberate in this episode. Stephen believes that guilt and loyalty controls result in self-abuse of a very important nature—in limited realization.

In view of Stephen's mother image problem, it is interesting to note the findings of Dr. Edmund Bergler in *The Writers and Psychoanalysis* that most of his writer patients suffered from the conflict of a masochist at war with the pre-Oedipal mother image.

Mythology

This episode is laced with mythological, religious and philosophical references.[53]   These reflect the struggle between the individual spirit and authority. Joyce borrows them for his personal myth based on the principle of analogy.[54]

Buck as the Bearded, Golden Snake

The ancient Greek snake god is described in the early pages of Jane Harrison's *Prolegomena to the Study of Greek Religion* (first published in 1903), a book I feel certain Joyce read and used.[55] The image of the ancient Greek snake god is unusual, an upright and bearded snake. Buck comes up to shave. Buck's yellow, ungirdled robe suggests a gold skin being shed. The result of the ancient Greek snake worship was fearful superstition.[56] Gilbert Murray describes the snake while commenting on the ancient Greek Zeus Meilichios rites called Diasia:

> The Diasia was said to be the chief festival of
> Zeus, the central figure of the Olympians, though our
> authorities generally add an epithet to him, and call
> him Zeus Meilichios, Zeus of Placation. A god with an
> 'epithet' is always suspicious, like a human being with
> an 'alias'. Miss Harrison's examination (Prolegomena,
> pp. 28 ff.) shows that in the rites Zeus has no place at
> all. Meilichios from the beginning has a fairly secure
> one. On some of the reliefs Meilichios appears not as a

god, but as an enormous bearded snake, a well-known representation of underworld powers or dead ancestors. Sometimes the great snake is alone; sometimes he rises gigantic above the small human worshippers approaching him. And then, in certain reliefs, his old barbaric presence vanishes, and we have instead a benevolent and human father of gods and men, trying, as Miss Harrison somewhere expresses it, to look as if he has been there all the time.[57]

Like Zeus and the Roman Catholic Church, Buck has put on an educated and sophisticated Zeus-like veneer, among other things by shaving off his beard. However, his lethal primitive identity remains—the power of fear created by spiritual ancestors.

The primitive placation ritual bears a striking resemblance to the Catholic Eucharist and the concept of man's guilt for Christ's death—he died for us. The theories of the Eucharist convict mankind as guilty of the murder of Jesus, our spiritual ancestor, and sentence all to the continuous need to placate the transcendent god.[58] Joyce views this kind of spirituality as on the same plane with the ancient Greek snake god that demanded constant placation. An expanded version of this same kind of fear is also present in the souls of persons who are "other directed," who live to placate the opinions of others.

Stephen As His Own Jesus and Buddha

Stephen seeks his maximum potential, guided as to values by his own personal ecstasy. Stephen treats this approach to life as justified by the precedents of Jesus and Buddha. Stephen views their lives as models to be emulated, not as a source of guilt. Jesse's purification on the cross, separation of His divine element from his human nature, is treated as the prototype for the spiritual awakening in each person.[59] This approach requires suffering, which, unlike guilt, expands the possibilities of life.

As Jung would say years later:

[Compared to the Tao which grows out of the individual] the *imitatio Christi* (imitating Christ) has this disadvantage: in the long run we worship as a divine example a man who embodied the

57

deepest meaning of life, and then, out of sheer imitation, we forget to make real our own deepest meaning—self-realization. . . .The imitation of Christ might well be understood in a deeper sense. It could be taken as the duty to realize one's deepest conviction with the same courage and the same self-sacrifice shown by Jesus. . . .Then we would have attained, in a European way, the psychological state corresponding to Eastern enlightenment.[60]

Jesus was the "first coming" and the Buddha, who also preached self-realization, was known as the "one thus come." Stephen is associated with both in this first episode.

Jesus and Buddha. The dream team!

Stephen As Daedalus

With the direct reference in the text to the Greek derivation of Stephen's name, the myth of Daedalus, the "cunning artificer" and Greek patron of the arts, comes into play. In AP, Stephen adopted Daedalus as his life patron. Daedalus expanded possibilities by creating arts then unknown.

According to Greek myth, Daedalus was in Crete on the lam from the murder in Athens of Talus, his nephew and apprentice. In Crete, King Minos and Queen Pasiphae, apparently using his criminal status to control him, kept Daedalus busy building things for them. Despite all of Daedalus's good works, the King attempted to betray Daedalus by imprisoning him and his son Icarus in the labyrinth they had built at the order of the King. Daedalus got into trouble with the King because of following orders from Queen Pasiphaë. When the King was away, Daedalus built a wooden cow at her order because she had developed the hots for a white bull that had been given by Poseidon to King Minos. The King was supposed to sacrifice the white bull to the gods, but instead the King kept it as a pet. The Queen used the wooden cow built by Daedalus, with the Queen hidden in the "belly," to approach the white bull for rutting. The result of this bizarre pasture union of Queen and bull was the minotaur, half-man half-bull, that had to be kept hidden in the maze. Pasiphae's birth pains are not discussed.

Not so hidden in the maze of this myth are the lessons for Stephen. Following orders, the rules of established religion and society, and succumbing to guilt will build walls that ultimately imprison your soul; and the use of a divine gift such as artistic talent for the wrong purposes produces a beast.

Daedalus and his son Icarus escaped from the labyrinth on wings they fashioned from wax, using arts then unknown to mankind. Daedalus made it from Crete to the Greek mainland (Stephen's flight to the Continent). But his son Icarus flew too close to the sun and his wing wax melting fell from the sky into the sea. Likewise, Stephen is attempting to escape from his own oppressors and soar to his maximum potential, away from his provincial background and culture. The Icarus risk of youth is to burn out by soaring too high, too fast and too young.

Stephen As the Martyr Stephen

Our protagonist bears the same first name as the first reported martyr of the Christian Church (the first after Jesus). The earlier Stephen had the temerity to declare the temple order no longer necessary because of the coming of Jesus. For this impertinence, the earlier Stephen was indicted before the Supreme Court of the Temple, the same people who railroaded Jesus in the middle of the night, and was stoned to death. A man called Saul (later known after his conversion as St. Paul) made the stoning official (legal). Martyr Stephen is an early example of the sacrifice of human potential on the altar of institutional authority.

Stephen as Narcissus (Buck and Haines as Echo)

The myth of Narcissus is woven through the first three episodes and a statue of Narcissus plays an important role in the last two episodes of the book.

As told by Ovid, Narcissus was famous for his physical beauty but was filled with a "hard pride." Echo, a nymph (a goddess mind you), fell in love with him. But she had a mental impairment; she could not initiate speech but only speak the last few words she had just heard from others, thus her name Echo. One day Narcissus met Echo. He was out in the woods with others but (significantly) had lost sight of his friends. He called out "Is anyone here?" Echo answered "Here." Narcissus responded: "Let's meet here" (that is you come to me). Echo of course answered "meet here" (which could be confusing but Narcissus is so keyed on himself that he knows here means where he is). Echo, the nymph goddess and presumably attractive, approached Narcissus in the woods, but he backed away saying, "I would die before I would give my power to you." Narcissus apparently believed that striking up a relationship with Echo would involve **giving** her something and that he would lose that something in the process. He was afraid of emotion. Faithful Echo echoed "I would give my power to you." Rejected and frustrated by Narcissus, Echo lost her body and became a mere voice.

Then Narcissus approached a water pool remarkable for its stillness and smoothness, never having been disturbed by either human or animal. As Narcissus bent down to drink, he saw his own image in the water and had an intense psychological experience. Narcissus marveled at the watery image of the neck, which he described as ivory. True to form, Narcissus wanted to possess this image, which at some level at least he didn't know was his own. To possess the image, Narcissus reached into the water, but to no avail. The narrator Ovid intervenes to preach: "What you are looking for is nowhere. Turn your head away and what you love will be lost."

So at least Narcissus was attracted to something other than himself—at least an image of himself (Joyce and his literary works). He found this image in water, his birthright from his father a river god. He even talked to the trees seeking consolation. He became more moist and flexible.

In his new depth, Narcissus entertained thoughts of death. Having undergone some kind of an initiation, he took on a red glow, the image of fire and for Joyce aesthetic arrest, and burned with love for the image in the pool. Transformed and arrested psychologically by this experience of love, he lay down on the grass by the pool and quietly disappeared into the underworld. He became the pool. Later, his companions looked for his body but instead found only the narcissus flower, which has a yellow center and white outer petals.

Joyce uses this myth with a multiple focus. Like Narcissus before his transformation, Stephen is cold, hard and afraid to connect. Like the classic narcissist, he experiences inner emptiness, fear of dependence and poor relations with other men and women. Under pressure, the narcissist with a shallow identity has an identity crisis—thus the popularity of the couch and the bottle in our times. Narcissus began his transformation by looking at an image of himself in a remarkably smooth and clear pool; the image is of Narcissus as others see him. Buck has Stephen look in a cracked mirror, and Stephen remarks that he is seeing himself as others see him. Water symbolism is important throughout the novel; it reflects both the light above and reveals the murk below.

Buck and Haines play the role of Echo. Buck repeats and Haines collects Stephen's sayings. Buck and Haines fade as full characters as this episode progresses much as Echo lost her body and became a "mere" voice. Stephen, who has an initiation in our story, looks into the ocean in the third episode and wonders if he would have the courage to brave the waters and save a drowning man. That man turns out to be himself. He saves himself from narcissism by finding his spiritual father within himself, ushering the father principle into his life and gaining the power of compassion.

Horn of a Bull, Hoof of a Horse, Smile of a Saxon

The end of the episode provides a partial clue to some of the mythological references in the episode with the following: "Horn of a bull, hoof of a horse, smile of a saxon," apparently a thought by Stephen.[61] The phrase was traditionally used as a warning.[62] As discussed below, I believe this phrase refers to Dionysus, Poseidon and Mercury/the legendary Irish clown King.

Horn of a Bull—Stephen as Dionysus/Orpheus

In Dionysian iconography, the horned bull was the usual representation of Dionysus/Orpheus.[63] Stephen plays the part of Dionysus seeking personal fulfillment and Buck the treacherous Titans who betrayed him. Frazer in *The Golden Bough* tells us that:

> Like other gods of vegetation Dionysus was
> believed to have died a violent death, but to have been
> brought to life again; and his sufferings, death, and
> resurrection were enacted in his sacred rites. His tragic
> story is thus told by the poet Nonnus. Zeus in the form

of a serpent visited Persephone, and she bore him Zagreus, that is, Dionysus, a horned infant. Scarcely was he born, when the babe mounted the throne of his father Zeus and mimicked the great god by brandishing the lightning in his tiny hand. But he did not occupy the throne long; for the treacherous Titans, their faces whitened with chalk, attacked him with knives while he was looking at himself in a mirror. For a time he evaded their assaults by turning himself into various shapes, assuming the likeness successively of Zeus and Cronus, of a young man, of a lion, a horse, and a serpent. Finally, in the form of a bull, he was cut to pieces by the murderous knives of his enemies.[64] [They also eat the pieces].

The white chalk on the faces, the mirror and knives[65] of the Titans are reflected in Buck's shaving lather, mirror and razor. The mirror was used as a toy to distract Dionysus into capture. Buck has Stephen look in the mirror in an effort to belittle him and capture his smaller spirit to the respectability of the shaven and of the institutional faith. As Dionysus is the god of wine and ecstasy and the life blood of nature, Stephen seeks his own fulfillment. The lightning in Dionysus's youthful hand would be Stephen's youthful writing. The early emphasis in this episode on Buck's teeth and the Eucharist reflects the eating of the remains of Dionysus by the Titans.

Stephen is strongly associated with Orpheus, who taught that man himself could become god. [66] However, this Orphic sanctity is achieved by union with, not by submission to the gods. Orpheus is believed to have been human flesh and blood—a seer, prophet and teacher—and was considered the spirit of music, order and peace.[67] Orpheus's music calmed the beast through its restrained style, as Joyce's art produces stasis.

Jane Harrison in the *Prolegomena* notes the forms of lyrical, epic and dramatic Greek poetry in the same terms as presented in Joyce's aesthetic theory outlined in the Introduction. Perhaps her book was the inspiration for Joyce's theory. She makes the point that the impulse toward the third person dramatic form and away from the lyrical first person form was fueled by the inspiration that the worshipper/author could become a god.[68]

Hoof of a Horse—Poseidon

Since the real power behind the captivity of Odysseus was Poseidon, it is not surprising to find chemical traces of Poseidon in Buck and Haines. Poseidon, also known as Hades-Pluto the lord of the abyss, was closely associated with horses.[69] Buck is described very early as "equine" in length. Poseidon was also the ruler of the seas. Likewise, the British were known as the rulers of the sea. Violent Poseidon sired savage offspring,[70] as the Roman Catholic Church gave birth to the inquisition practices and the UK to frequent war. The elderly male swimmer in the forty-foot hole is described in terms similar to Poseidon, and Buck is deferential and slightly afraid of this old swimmer in his natural element.

Smile of a Saxon—Mercury and Irish Legend

Buck's mocking and clownish ways are rooted in Celtic mythology. The father figure of the gods of ancient Ireland, the Tuatha De Danann, was a kind of a clown. He was noted for the milk-stew drinking contest he held with the king of his enemy.[71] These aspects are reflected in Buck's merry ways and his love of the milk brought by the milk woman. As such, Buck plays in a long line of tricksters, an epitome of all the inferior traits in humans.[72] Among the ancients, the trickster was signified by Mercury with whom Buck is directly identified in the episode. In psychological terms, the trickster corresponds to the earliest and least developed period of life, when mere physical appetites dominate behavior.[73]

Hinduism and Buddhism

In the Hindu-Brahman religion, an institutional religion of India, the unity of all life is recognized and detachment is promoted as the spiritual freedom that allows for maximum realization of the self. By contrast to the Catholics, the realization process is approached by the Hindu on the assumption that a divine spark more or less realized is contained in each one of us, and this understanding sponsors the unity of all living beings.[74] No beings can be treated as trash or objects in this

63

system. In the institutional version of this religion, conservative ritual and repetitive sacrifice are emphasized. This same religion enforced the static caste system. In Dublin, rows of cast steel for the trams suggest spiritual paralysis.

Ancient texts codifying the doctrine of unity include the various Upanishads, mentioned in this episode. They emphasized individual self-realization of the unity, rather than conservative institutional ritual. The word Upanishad denotes sitting down together,[75] which in a later episode Stephen and Bloom do for a long time as part of their process of liberation.

Buck's joke about making tea (spirit) and making water (urine), but not in the same pot, refers to the Catholic Church's view that humans can not carry the divine within. Buck asks Stephen whether the tea and water pot are spoken of in the Mabinogion or the Upanishads. The point is that Buck doesn't know which of these totally different sources would supply the answer. The Mabinogion is a collection of Welsh tales about strife mostly based on heroic legends. The spiritual teachings in the ancient Indian Upanishads support Stephen's view that tea (stimulant of the divine) and water (urine of the human) can be made in the same pot, that he can reach the divine in himself by self-realization.

The Buddha, known at birth as Prince Gautama, inspired a movement away from conservative institutional Hinduism and toward personal illumination based on the right type of detachment. Because of the prophecy that Prince Gautama would either be a famous king or a famous monk, his father (a local king) hoping for the king alternative maintained the future enlightened one in a false world protected from all the miseries of life, a false type of detachment. At this point Stephen is also in a false kind of detachment, narcissism. Proper detachment proves to be the cotter pin for many of the fundamental concepts in the book.

Sea Mother

The references in the text to the sea, the great sea mother and Stephen's mother dream call up images of the original figure of all mythology and worship—the goddess Earth. Joseph Campbell tells us that:

In the earliest period of her cult (perhaps c. 7500-3500 BC in the Levant) such a mother-goddess may have been thought of only as a local patroness of fertility, as many anthropologists suppose. However, in the temples even of the first of the higher civilizations (Sumer, c. 3500-2350 BC), the Great goddess of highest concern was certainly much more than that. **She was already, as she is now in the Orient, a metaphysical symbol: the arch personification of the power of Space, Time, and Matter, within whose bounds all beings arise and die: the substance of their bodies, configurator of their lives and thoughts, and receiver of their dead.** And everything having form or name—including God personified as good or evil, merciful or wrathful—was her child, within her womb. [76] [emphasis added]

In the next to last episode, Molly is identified as the Earth Mother and Bloom as the manchild in the womb of the Earth Mother. Through Molly's thoughts, the fundamental process of life is depicted as promotion of the species with less regard for the individual human. Molly, whose formal name is Marion, is foreshadowed in this episode in Buck's song about the lusty Mary Ann who doesn't give a damn.

In the "Oriental" mother goddess world view, god is immanent in all things and life is an endless round of birth and rebirth. All opposites are illusions. This view of ultimate reality does not work at this point for youthful Stephen because it would dull his quest for self-realization. The potential dulling power of this view of "oneness" can be felt in the following passage, which is right in the middle of that part of the episode dealing with Stephen's mother:

Wood shadows floated silently by through the morning peace from the stairhead seaward where he gazed. Inshore and farther out the mirror of the water whitened, spurned by lightshod hurrying feet. . . . The twining stresses, two by two. A hand plucking the

harpstrings, merging their twining chords. Wavewhite
wedded words shimmering on the dim tide.

The twining stresses would be the rhythm of life and death and
other seeming opposites, such as male and female and good and evil.
They are merged by the hand of the Great Mother.[77] The unification of
opposites and the Earth Mother return to greater glory in the liberating
Flow of the Mothers in the closing of this novel after Stephen has
experienced Bloom.

Sun Gods

At this point, the separated Stephen feels more in tune with the
heroic sun gods, who appear in Yeats's poem of Fergus ruling the brazen
cars. This poem is quoted by Buck and was sung by Stephen to his
mother on her deathbed. These sun gods are associated with the male-
oriented patriarchal myths, such as Yahweh, Zeus and Mithra, and the
assumption of separation of opposites. Again Joseph Campbell:

`The patriarchal point of view is distinguished
from the earlier archaic (sea mother) view by its setting
apart of all parts of opposites—male and female, life
and death, true and false, good and evil—as though
they were absolutes in themselves and not merely
aspects of the larger entity of life. This we may liken to
a solar, as opposed to lunar, mythic view, since
darkness flees from the sun as its opposite, but in the
moon dark and light interact in the one sphere.[78]

This separated point of view, Stephen is about to discover, is the
rebar in the Law of the Fathers, his primary enemy.

The anxiety expressed in the Fergus poem about who rules the
brazen cars brings in the myth of Phaeton from Ovid's *Metamorphoses*.
Phaeton was the youth who was allowed to drive the family car, his
father's sun chariot, for just one day—with disastrous results.[79] This
refers to the danger of youthful Stephen of being in the driver's seat of
his own life without the insurance of family, religion or country.

Alchemy

With frequent references to gold and silver and the direct
allusion to Mercury, alchemy is included in the symbolism. The colors

white and gold, the colors of this episode, represent god in the symbology of the Roman Catholic Church. These same colors were sought by alchemists in heating base metal. The ranks of alchemists included some spiritualists attempting to achieve soul transformation but more chemists attempting to achieve material wealth through transformation of base metal into gold and silver. The effort at transformation puts them in the company of the Church with the Eucharist and the collection plate.

The alchemical stone was the lapis philosophorum or green stone. It was used in attempts to achieve transformations. This power shows up humbly as the green stone on Haines's silver cigarette case. With cigarettes, the transformation is the menial task of turning tobacco into nicotine laced smoke, a parodied reference to the spiritual goals of alchemy.

Irish Legend—Fergus, King Conor and Honey

The textual reference to Fergus is an invitation into the world of Irish legend, where betrayal and treachery reigned supreme.

The Yeats poem Fragment quoted by Buck is:

And no more turn aside and brood

Upon Love's bitter mystery

For Fergus rules the brazen cars

Fergus was a faint hearted and easy going poet warrior who voluntarily gave up his throne short term to Conor.[80] Fergus was not possessive even of the throne. But King Conor (MacNessa) usurped the throne long term and ruled as the King of Ulster supported by the Red Branch Knights. The connection of Buck to the usurper Conor is made by Buck's "primrose waistcoat." Since rose is the symbol of Ireland, this reference reflects general Irish heritage as well as "prim" Buck's inordinate concern with dress and appearance. If Fergus rules the brazen cars (and the spirits of humankind), then love without possession would rule human hearts. On the other hand, love governed by possession is love's bitter dimension.

Usurper King Conor betrayed the three sons of Usnach, who accompanied the beautiful Deirdre in her escape from King Conor's lecherous interest. Pursuing Deirdre from his usurping position of authority, King Conor treacherously sent Fergus, his knight trusted by all, to tell Deirdre and the three sons that they were fully pardoned and asked to return to Ulster with Fergus as a safeguard. In response to this bidding, Deirdre had a dream:

> Three birds came to me in my sleep last night. Out of Emain Macha they came, and in their bills were three sips of honey. The three sips of honey they left with us, but they took with them three sips of our blood.

> The three brothers asked Deirdre to explain her dream, and she told them that the three sips of honey were the false messages of peace and pardon that Conor had given to Fergus for them. And the three sips of blood were the three Sons of Usnach who would be betrayed by Conor.[81]

Her prediction of treachery comes true as Fergus the safeguard is side tracked by King Conor's prior arrangement that he be invited to a banquet, which he apparently can't refuse. Fergus sent his son as a substitute to protect the sons of Usnach and Deirdre, but the son wasn't up to the job.

This legend, which is humorous rendition of the Christ story, is reflected in this episode by the following Connector Facts: honey on the breakfast bread, which itself is a symbol for the Eucharist, and the several references to three pints of blood and three pints of ale. This connection places the Eucharist in the role of a false pardon, and as an instrument of betrayal of Stephen's self-realization.

Meaning of References

What do all these mythological, theological and philosophical references mean? Why does Joyce use them? First, they force the imprint of the past and the collective memory experience on the present. Their insistence to be a player in the present precludes a pedestrian "I here now" limited view of reality. In Jungian terms, they fund the collective unconscious. Second, these references elevate the meaning of this novel above the limited one-time one-person aspect associated with merely personal experience. They elevate Stephen onto the world stage

68

as an example for all who would follow his attempt to soar and transcend.

Joyce brings archetypes out of their dark corners and myth and god down to the streets of Dublin. This episode begins in Joseph Campbell's phrase to present life in Dublin "recooked in the brew of mythological themes"[82]. The nesting of many of these mythological references in the ordinary details of then current Dublin indicates the view that extraordinary force fields infuse the ordinary. Biblical typology is one rendering of this infusion of depth. Like the shaman, Joyce presents a vision of "something far more deeply interfused" inhabiting both the round earth and one's own interior, which gives to the world a sacred character; an interaction of depth . . . ."[83] These extraordinary force fields are the masks of the gods. They have been visited by shamans, mystics and artists. And now Joyce will give you a peek.

Love

"Love's bitter mystery" in the poem by Yeats about Fergus brings up the tricky issue of love. Joyce is reluctant to deal with this issue head on, particularly in view of the many varied emotions that are grouped under that same word. The Christian concept of love is as close as Christianity gets to the unity in Hinduism; god is love and when you love without possession you participate in god. God loves humankind without possession since god gave them free will.

Echoes of Shaw, Milton and Dante

In revealing two of the usurpers, Stephen tells Haines that he is the servant of two masters,[84] an Englishman and an Italian. Stephen identifies them as the Imperial British state and the Roman Catholic Apostolic Church.[85] The Englishman and the Italian have, however, additional references in this novel.

George Bernard Shaw's 1904 play *Man and Superman* (superman is mentioned in the text) centers around the struggle of the artist against the mother goddess. Does that ring a bell? The artist equates respectability with cowardice and expresses the view that the life force acting through philosophers (the supermen) will improve the direction and soul of mankind. The Devil says, in this play, that the false

69

view of him is due to an Englishman and an Italian. In the Devil's case, it is Milton and Dante.

This second English and Italian pair plays a significant role throughout this novel. Their initial influences are felt in this episode. Through Milton's *Paradise Lost*, Stephen's drive for independence is tied to the theme of man's disobedience in the Garden of Eden. Stephen's current spiritual condition contains echoes of the opening of Dante's *The Divine Comedy*, in which the author/protagonist has "lost the way"; lost after the death of his mother, Stephen is spending his time and money, even borrowed funds, on drink and whores.

With these references and Mr. Respectability in charge of the key to the tower, moral corruption covers the first episode as it draws to a close. It feels like the world of Kali Yuga, the phase the world is passing through now according to Hindu belief, during which "property confers rank, wealth becomes the only source of virtue . . . falsehood the source of success in life, sex the only means of enjoyment, and when other trappings are confused with inner religion"[86].

Structure, Art and Aesthetics

The main theme of both the Telemachus episode and the first two books of The Odyssey is betrayal. Note the parallel to the betrayal of Bloom by his wife Molly, the hinge of the plot of this novel.

The episode is presented in super-realism, both as to actions and Stephen's thoughts. Most of the narrator's voice is in the objective third person, with occasional "lapses" into Stephen's interior monologue. Compared to the increased use of Stephen's interior monologue in the second and third episodes, this objective emphasis reflects the importance of external forces in Stephen's life at this particular moment. The language is sharp and clear, father image type language with fixed meaning. Like Penelope's weaving, the symbolism in this episode is tightly woven and relatively invisible in the beginning but is at least partially unraveled at the end.

The third person narrator, while generally objective, has many tones. Sometimes the narrator's voice takes on the color of the subject character in focus at the moment, while at other times the voice reflects the author's views of the character. This is the literary counterpart of the effect on the soul of seeking the respect of others.

A prime example of the voice being influenced by the subject character in focus is the first sentence that introduces Buck: "Stately, plump Buck Mulligan came from the stairhead, bearing a bowl of lather on which a mirror and razor lay crossed." Now read that line again. Joyce probably worked hours and hours on it. Notice "cross." Notice "came." Feel how dull the language and syntax are; the effect is flat, stale and dead. The sentence just lies there; it has no energy, no soul. It sort of trails off at the end. Think of the many other ways the language could be organized and the effect this particular combination produces. It focuses first on Buck's outward characteristics, proud and fat, not his inner nature. It indirectly tells us Buck's soul is dead.

Later in the episode, the language concerning Buck becomes trite: "he said frankly"; and "He shaved warily over his chin." For the great master, the use of these pulp novel techniques is designed to convey meaning: as an individual, Buck is trite. Even Stephen, when he is showing fear and small soul, comes in for a mockingly trite description: "Stephen said with energy and growing fear"; and "He shook his constraint from him nervously." These techniques are the Joyce jewels, the pearls of indirection.

When the conversation turns to the mighty sea mother, in whose realm sharp opposites disappear, the third person voice softens and fades: "his fair oakpale hair stirring slightly"; "woodshadows floated silently by through the morning peace from the stairhead seaward where he gazed . . . ." The alliterated Ss lower the blood pressure of these sentences. For the mother dream, the sentences are soft and fuzzy and the rhythm languid, as concepts are run together: "In a dream, silently, she had come to him, her wasted body within its loose grave clothes giving off an odor of wax and rosewood, her breath, bent over him with mute secret words, a faint odor of wilted ashes." The feeling tone of that sentence is motherhood herself, softly bending over her child. Rosewood is included in this image because rosewood trees decay in their heart before maturity.

Sometimes the feel of the language reflects the event described: for example, "fumes of fried grease floated, turning". Reading this aloud

71

emphasizes the change from the past tense "floated" to the gerund "turning," which gives a syntactical feel similar to a slow smoke float and a faster smoke turning. When Haines is near, "the key scraped round harshly twice. . .," an illiterate use of round and an awkward combination of harshly and twice, as befits the lower order of the brain of (in the Irish view) the Englishman. When the representative of the Catholic Church is at the breakfast mass, the language becomes formalized, stiff and ritualistic: "He [Buck] lunged toward his messmates in turn a thick slice of bread, impaled on his knife." Change impaled to stuck and feel the loss of potency and ritual. When Buck sings the bawdy song about Mary Ann, the language is eight-grain brawny and vital: "he growled in a hoarsened rasping voice as he hewed again vigorously at the loaf."

The simple milk woman is described without frills, simply and with dignity: "she said" and "the old woman asked." In the narrator's description of some of Stephen's thoughts, the language is pretentious: "the proud potent titles clanged over Stephen's memory the triumph of their brazen bells . . . the same growth and change of rite and dogma like his own rare thoughts. . ." For Poseidon's entrance at the swimming hole, the language is a model of Grecian clarity and lightness and intentionally rhymed for a cohesive effect: "An elderly man shot up near the spew of rock a blowing red face. He scrambled up by the stones, water glistening on his pate and on its garland of grey hair, water **rilling** over his chest and paunch and **spilling** jets out of his black sagging loincloth" [emphasis added].

Some paragraphs are a confusing mixture of Stephen's interior monologue and the narrator's voice. For example, consider this sequence: "He watched her put into measure and thence into the jug rich, white milk, not hers. Old shrunken paps. She poured again a measureful and a tilly." In this group, "not hers. Old shrunken paps" are Stephen's thoughts, the rest is the voice of the narrator. The use of the rural word "tilly," an extra measure not paid for, reflects the presence of the rustic Irish milk woman. An extra measure not paid for also conditions the reader for Stephen's view of a sentimentalist: he who enjoys without paying in suffering.

The presentation is highly neutral in terms of everyday reality, including small details. The surface is highly polished and the thematic integration of the episode is intense, as you would expect when control is the object of the institutional adversaries. Lying shallow beneath the surface of the action is a fastidiously interwoven net of allegories.[87] The high art of this episode resides in the thematic integration and the ultra-stable relationship between the realistic surface of the text and the underlying allegorical references. All this is accomplished while the episode introduces major themes of the novel.

The sexual allusions in this episode are exclusively male—sperm and ejaculation, white foam like Buck's shaving soap. As is appropriate in the case of a young man in the presence of the Church and the cultural mores of the time, this theme is basically underground in the first episode. As befits Church and state, much of the conversation is didactic—one person instructing another.

This episode introduces a key Joycean technique, reverse iconography or simonizing (simony is the Church's term for improper use of Church sacraments or doctrine). Trained by the Jesuits, Joyce was immersed in the medieval view that everything was created for a purpose, and a specific purpose at that—a sacrament to the one supreme and totally good god. In this view, all natural sciences point beyond "themselves" to religion; and the universe is a vast sacerdotal system for man's salvation. Man's meaning is as a child of god who needs to accept without question the value transfers of the father. The religious icons and symbols served to take one "out of oneself" to humility and to point beyond to the after-life assimilation with god.

Joyce reverses this orientation and points many of the same images back into human life. This redirection of the search lights gives that human life, with an emphasis on what is natural to humanity, more meaning or vitality. In this process, religious icons are converted into archetypes or human life models or stimulants. This reversal of orientation from out to in produces startling combinations of the old with the new.

The art of this episode in Joycean terminology is mostly in the dramatic form, the third person objective. In most of the writing, the force of the aesthetic image surrounds all of the characters and appears to come from an outside source, not from Stephen. The author is distant. Even if you view Stephen as a stand in for Joyce, this form is nonetheless in the dramatic because Stephen is a younger version the older author is writing about.

The relationship between the parts and the whole of this episode is consistent and mutually supportive. For example, the realistic surface presentation is the aesthetic counterpart of control. The mythological themes fold into the heir or inheritance symbol.

Under Joyce's definition of proper art, the episode is static. In my view, it does not create a desire for or a loathing of any of the characters. Buck could invite loathing as a potent enemy of Stephen's efforts, but in this role he is so wooden that loathing doesn't arise. The allegories are designed to establish the tragic-terror combination that arrests the mind in the presence of what is grave and constant in human suffering (oppression by authority) and unites the mind with the secret cause (the inevitability of death). The comic is a harsh mocking variety, not joyful. This is fitting because the episode portrays the land of the dead under the Law of the Fathers.

However, a certain aspect of the magic is limited for me and, I suspect, for many readers. Being accustomed to our current US culture of the cult of the individual, I can't feel the force of the betrayal by church and state depicted in the novel. In our culture with little church and state, the prime enemy of the soul is the job; Stephen confronts the job dragon in the very next episode.

The real strength of this episode is unity and integration. If you read this episode as one piece and can hold it in mental solution all at one time, you shall behold a brilliant architecture of themes intensely integrated. Because the metaphors and images have dual and often triple meanings and are intensely interrelated, they cast multiple beams of meaning and interlock with other images. In this respect, the integration reflects exoterically the medieval Catholic framework of typologically inspired order, which "provides an unlimited chain of relations between creatures and events," and esoterically the interlocked triangles in the seal of Solomon. The next two episodes display more flexibility, as Stephen's determination to live freely gains in strength.

This episode about struggle for control ends on an ambiguous note, with Stephen declaring his own independence but giving up the key to Buck. This gives the tone of the episode a note of uncertainty. Stephen sees a boat making for Bullock harbor, which prepares us for the second episode Nestor,[88] and the allusion to Buck as a seal in the harbor prepares us for the third episode Proteus.[89]

****

ENDNOTES

1. See generally Campbell, J. *The Masks of God Creative Mythology* (New York: Arkana, 1968).
2. Schwartz, D. *Reading Joyce's Ulysses* (New York: MacMillan Press, 1987) p. 73.
3. See Gorman, p. 111 for the same experience of Joyce. Joyce also covered himself in a reckless Bohemian life with medical students in a desire to forget himself.
4. With remarkable parallelism, the second episode of Ulysses (Nestor) will be based on Chapter iii of The Odyssey and scene iii of Act I of *Hamlet* and the third episode of Ulysses (Proteus) on Chapter iv of The Odyssey and scene iv of Act I of *Hamlet*.
5. CW, p. 156.
6. Schwartz, p. 61.
7. Joyce actually lived in this very tower after his return from Paris because of his mother's last illness. This residence was his headquarters for a life of drink and whoring with Oliver St. John Gogarty, the model for Buck. Joyce and Gogarty were close buddies during this period, but Joyce has retroactively projected into this period his attitudes resulting from their later estrangement.
8. Colum, p. 61.
9. See Blavatsky, H.P. *Isis Unveiled* (Pasadena: Theosophical University Press, 1976) vol. I, p. xxxix; Gilbert, S. *James Joyce's Ulysses* (New York: Vintage Books, 1970) p. 51. We learn this

tower was built by Billy Pitt, for pit of the stomach.

10. We may also see the tower as the body that imprisons Stephen's soul. This partial set of birth tools, the male sex drive together with the navel as the tie for the umbilical cord, also introduces the theme of continuity of souls through space and time, one of the main themes of Ulysses.

11. This fact is not given directly in the text but may be inferred from the description of the lock as iron and the large size of the key. The actual tower had such a copper key. Colum, p. 60.

12. Gilbert, p. 45.

13. *The Odyssey of Homer*. Translated by Butcher and Lang (which in my version doesn't have line numbers).

14. Graves, R. *The Greek Myths* (London: Penguin, 1955) p. 779.

15. Serving her conqueror the U.K. and her gay betrayer the Roman Catholic Church.

16. The milk maid can't understand Haines's Gaelic, and Athena states she has come "unto men of strange speech." The milk maid receives payment for her milk, and Athena suggests a fair exchange of gifts.

17. Gifford, p. 12.

18. Ferris, Kathleen *James Joyce and the Burden of Disease* (Lexington: The University Press of Kentucky, 1995).

19. The model for Haines eventually committed suicide. Colum, Mary and Padraic *Our Friend James Joyce* (Garden City: Doubleday & Company, 1958) p. 65.

20. Schwartz, p. 76.

21. Jung, C. *Psyche and Symbol* (Princeton: Princeton University Press, 1991) p. 160. The fact that the blasphemous Buck conducts a mock mass reminds us that the Roman Catholic Church decided in response to the Donatists that a corrupt priest could administer an effective Eucharist, the power believed to reside in the consubstantial bread and wine not the unclean hands of the priest. The fact that Buck gives the milk maid short measure, does not pay her bill in full, suggests the Church is a taker.

22. For a few examples: Buck Mulligan has a razor , the sign of the

76

slaughterer and the priest as butcher (Gifford, p. 13), and as a medical student he watches surgery; "Introibo ad altare Dei" is the first line of the Mass; Stephen looks well when he is "dressed"; Buck calls Stephen to breakfast for "Jesus' sake"; the Eucharist is suggested by the joke about the candle melting; and references to the sacred pint do the same. The reference to Chrysostomos, among other things, brings in an historical Jew hater. The reference for Odysseus (Leopold Bloom) will turn out to be a Jew. Hugh Kenner notes that with dismemberment themes, Joyce strews the parts all around the episode. Kenner, Dublin's Joyce, p. 16.

23. I try to use Christ to refer to divine character and Jesus to human.

24. Lang, F. *Ulysses and the Irish God* (Lewisburg: Bucknell University Press, 1993) pp. 57, 98, 126, 132.

25. *The Oxford Dictionary of World Religions* edit. J. Bowker (Oxford: Oxford University Press, 1997).

26. Lang, p. 105.

27. Lang, p. 106.

28. Lang, p. 231.

29. Buck is also associated with Mercury, another messenger, who is the guide to the dead.

30. Stephen is the prime example of that doubting community. The Book of Malachi discusses problems such as the impurity of sacrificial offerings and that some priests "parade their sins on their cloaks." The same problems are certainly present in this episode as well. The Book predicts that in the end Elias "shall reconcile heart of father to son, heart of son to father; else the whole of earth should be forfeit to my vengeance." Buck is a false father for Stephen and no reconciliation is possible. The Book of Malachi concludes with the advice "to respect your own life . . .", advice which Stephen has taken to heart.

31. Schwartz, p. 41.

32. This concept is neatly introduced in the opening lines of *Hamlet* when the guard coming on duty asks "Who's there?", instead of waiting for the guard already on duty to ask for the password. That already on duty guard responds: "Nay, answer me. Stand and

unfold yourself." In Telemachus, Buck is first seen in a dressing gown that is ungirdled. See the discussion in the third episode concerning the nature of being and unfolding.

33. Buck and Haines are directly linked by textual reference to Hamlet's uncle and mother. After Haines's obliging introduction of the Hamlet subject, Stephen sees his own image in mourning clothes between the other two (Buck and Haines) dressed in party attire, reminding us of the party Hamlet's uncle and mother enjoyed while Hamlet was in mourning. Hamlet's uncle Claudius is the usurper, as are Buck and Haines and the wooers in The Odyssey. All are, however, only temporarily successful.

34. The sun connects back through patriarchal myths to the Law of the Fathers.

35. If the son is not his own father, he can be disinherited.

36. Harold Bloom reads **Hamlet** as the rise in consciousness and civilization generally.

37. Joyce, S. **My Brother's Keeper** (New York: The Viking Press, 1969) pp. 154-5 referring to Blake's couplet that "King and Priest must be tied in a tether before two virgins can meet together." Also see CW at p. 172 for poor Ireland in the "double yoke" of the Church and England.

38. Gifford, p. 12.

39. He tries to make Stephen feel guilty for refusing his mother's request to kneel at her death bed, leads him around in the tower, calls him "poor dogs body" which reverses to "god's body," tells him he has "general paralysis of the insane," or has contracted syphilis from his sexual activity, tells him he is a "dreadful bard," uses Stephen's noserag to clean his razor (as the Church will use artists to enhance its image), generates in Stephen doubt and lack of self-resolution, creates "fear in the lancet of [its] art," claims that Stephen should trust him, tells Stephen his death means nothing, tells Stephen he is an "impossible person," tells Stephen to stop brooding, prepares to take Stephen's money, seeks the key and control of the tower-Omphalos, damns Stephen for his independent Paris fads, criticizes Stephen for not washing, and eventually takes

his key and money.

40. The mirror was also capable in Irish lore of carrying away a living soul if in the presence of the dead. Costello, P. *James Joyce Years of Growth* (New York: Pantheon, 1992) p. 212. So Buck the dead soul tries to get Stephen to look in the mirror.

41. Lang, p. 151.

42. Russell, B. *A History of Western Philosophy* (New York: Simon and Schuster, 1972) p. 394.

43. The description of Buck's hair as "grained and hued like pale oak" probably refers to tree spirits, an early form of Celtic spirit worship. The Celts worshipped various trees, including the oak, and the priests who served the Celtic god were called druids —which means "knowing the oak tree." Bile (connected in the text to Stephen's mother's illness, the color snot green and the divine essence in each person) means sacred tree in the Celtic religion. The druids committed great numbers of verses to heart, and Buck quotes much verse in this episode. They worshipped the sun, and Buck quotes Yeats's poem about the brazen cars. Mercury, with whom Buck is identified as Malachi the messenger, was the principal god of the Celts.

44. Lang, p. 115.

45. Buck is described as like a bird when he approaches the swimming hole. Perhaps this associates him with the fighting eagles in Book II of The Odyssey. As "Mercury" like, he would take human sacrifices in terms of the lost potential of believers.

46. This can also refer to Icarus, Daedalus's son who flew too high while escaping and fell into the sea. This poses the danger of Stephen's independent course. This also connects to the mother-sea image, the mother who can kill your independence ["scrotumtightening" to reduce machismo]. It can also be Odysseus. Telemachus describes the wooers as eating ". . . up the substance of a man whose white bones lie out in the rain and fester somewhere on the mainland. . . ."

47. This theme is lightly announced in this episode and treated more seriously later.

48. Like the lordly wooers in The Odyssey, Buck is presented in sexual overtones as follows: his first name Buck (which Buck himself uses in its sexual connotation "Redheads buck like goats"); in his first entrance in the episode, Buck "came from the stairhead" of the tower and "mounted the round gunrest"; he has "lather" in the shaving bowl; he "thrusts"; he "lunged"; and he "plunged." Like the lordly wooers, Buck is presented with substance consumption overtones by eating breakfast, making plans for drinking, seeking Stephen's ideas, taking the key, and living at least in part off Stephen's salary. His name Mulligan is slang for a stew originally made by tramps consisting of "odds and ends" thrown in by the many, a reference to his intellectual collection practices. See Mr. Deasy in the next episode as a collector of gold and aphorisms.

49. Ferris.

50. Lang, p. 120.

51. The quest for independence by Stephen is presented by multiple references in the text: he is "cold" or independently distant; his first name Stephen—the first recorded Christian martyr; his last name Dedalus who in Greek mythology (Daedalus) put on artificial wings to escape Crete by soaring (the name Dedalus compared to Daedalus sounds more like dead); in the Church-Christ relationship, the real Jesus was too hot for the Church (Buck to Haines during the mock mass--"turn off the current"); he follows Buck only halfway; his nickname Kinch the knifeblade suggests intellectual rigor and as pointed out a difficult path to follow; Stephen refused to kneel as requested by his mother on her deathbed; he wears without concern for the opinion of others frayed mourning clothes and refuses to wear respectable grey; his name is Stephen or steel pen or "cold steel pen," suggesting the hard lance of his art (this image is related to Hamlet's ghost who appeared in "complete steel"—Stephen's art drives him on to revenge against those who would hold him back); he thinks about trendy new paganism as opposed to Catholicism; he frees his arm from Buck's; he is personally offended by Buck's remark that "it's

only Dedalus whose mother is beastly dead . . ."; he cries out to his mother's memory "No mother. Let me be and let me live."; he feels he has a choice (free will) at least for the menial act of whether to bring down the shaving bowl ; he has the key to the tower or knows where it is (in the door); he enjoys Paris fads (tea with lemon); he makes the decision how much milk to buy; he refuses to wash; Stephen conceives the original thoughts which Buck and Haines seek and collect; Stephen has already made a freedom run to Paris; he wears a Latin quarter hat; he refuses to wash and by implication to shave; he is the only one making a salary and paying the rent (Buck is a student apparently receiving money and instructions from his aunt, and Haines is apparently a free loader); he describes himself as a "horrible example of free thought"; he associates himself with heresies and change in dogma; he declares he can't sleep in the tower with Buck and Haines anymore or go home; and he eventually (as we learn later) spurns Buck's command to meet at the pub "The Ship."

52. See also AP, p. 239 where his mother tries unsuccessfully to convince Stephen to do his "Easter duty."

53. In this respect it reminds us of the Book of John, the "logos" Gospel, which is built on a similar basis. The logos will become manifest in the third episode.

54. Kimball, J. *Odyssey of the Psyche* (Carbondale: Southern Illinois University Press, 1997) p. 9 characterizes Joyce's as "a stunning sense of analogy.".

55. (Cambridge: University Press, 1922) pp. 18 and 20.

56. Harrison, p. 5.

57. Murray, G. *Five Stages of Greek Religion* (New York: Columbia University Press, 1925) pp. 28-29.

58. The primitive placation rite also suggests another reason why Hamlet plays such an important role in this episode; Hamlet had to deal with the ghost of his father, who demands the blood of revenge. We can also see in this light Stephen's mother dreams as a ghost Stephen needs to placate. The ancient Greeks poured milk and honey into trenches to placate these ghosts. We find milk and

honey at the Eucharist breakfast in this episode. Honey was also used to embalm the dead. The ghosts that needed to be placated were often depicted as winged creatures, known as Keres or Erinyes (Erin or Ireland – yes). They represented bringers of evil, corruptness in man, and old age and carried off souls and ate the flesh of the dead. Like these spirits, Buck is identified as winglike when he bathes. He is the very spirit his ritual is designed to placate. This aspect reinforces the allusion in the episode to Buck as Satan—with our memory of medieval goat devils (Buck himself says "Redheads buck like goats," which reduces to buck like goats). Buck is first seen shaving. Shaving is connected to Kouros, or the power of annual rebirth. In Buck, however, rebirth is limited to whiskers which he cuts off and thus denies. Later we see him beating down the leaders of young plants, the envoys of rebirth. Buck, the barbaric power of death and denial in action.

59. Jung, Psyche and Symbol , p. 65.
60. Jung, Psyche and Symbol, pp. 382-383.
61. Vreeswijk, H. *Notes on Joyce's Ulysses Part I* (Amsterdam: Van Gennep, 1970) p. 59.
62. Colum, p. 63.
63. Frazer, J. *The Golden Bough* (New York: MacMillan, 1963) Vol. 1, p. 451-453. The references to the memory of cutting off trousers at school and "Don't play the giddy ox with me" may refer to horned bull jumping ritual in Crete.
64. Frazer, pp. 450-51.
65. Dionysus was killed by the Titans using a labrys, a double edged axe and an instrument of sacramental castration. This ties together the sexual controls, the Great Mother and realization themes.
66. As summarized by J. E. Harrison:

> The religion of Orpheus is religious in the sense that it is the worship of the real mysteries of life, of potencies (oaluoves) rather than personal gods (Oeoi); it is the worship of life itself in its supreme mysteries of ecstasy and love. Reason is great, but it is not everything. There are in the world things, not of

82

reason, but both below and above it, causes of emotion which we cannot express, which we tend to worship, which we feel perhaps to be the precious things in life. These things are God or forms of God, not fabulous immortal men, but 'Things which Are,' things utterly non-human and non-moral which bring man bliss or tear his life to shreds without a break in their own serenity.

In this quote you can sense worship of human possibilities, Joyce's god.

Details of the Orphic religion find noticeable places in this episode. Orpheus, like Stephen, was an exile returned. Orpheus is slain by Zeus because he reveals the ultimate mysteries to man, as Stephen would with his art. As a child, Orpheus was nearly killed by a snake as the young Stephen's soul was nearly killed by the Catholic religion represented by the snake-like Buck. Orpheus was torn to pieces by the female Maenads (echoes of the Eucharist). In the ritual of this religion, Dionysus/Orpheus is ritually eaten by devotees who actually tear apart with their teeth live bull flesh (more echoes of the Eucharist). The head of the original Orpheus (minus the torso) was saved and became an oracle. (This is another reason why no organ other than the brain is used for this and the second and third episodes.) Orpheus, like Stephen, was aloof and remote, a self sufficing artist. He was even considered by the Catholic Church fathers to be the prototype for Christ. In this Orphic religion, the duty is to god or the divine potential in yourself, not to your neighbor, a creed Stephen and Joyce lived out in their lives. This Orphic religion promulgated the expansion, liberation and enthusiasm that Stephen eventually achieves in the teeth of Buck's check, negation and restriction. Buck will pay for Sandy cove milk (sacrifice for placation) but not for booze (Dionysus).

67. Harrison, p. 464.
68. Harrison, p. 568.
69. *Poseidon*, Encyclopedia Britannica, 1983 ed., Micropaedia, Vol. VIII, p. 148.

83

70. Poseidon, p. 149.

71. Campbell, Joseph *The Masks of God Occidental Mythology* (New York: Arkana, 1991) pp. 301-302. While this and other books cited were published recently, the authors use source materials that were available prior to 1917. I don't have Joyce's library card.

72. Jung, C. *On the Psychology of the Trickster Figure* in Radin, R. *The Trickster* (New York: Philosophical Library, 1956) pp. 197-99.

73. Henderson, J. *Ancient Myths and Modern Man* in Jung, C. *Man and His Symbols* (New York: Doubleday & Company, Inc., 1964) p. 112.

74. Coomaraswamy, A. *Dance of Shiva* (New York: Noonday Press, 1957) p. 4 ff.

75. Hinnells, A. *Esoteric Buddhism* (Boston: Houghton, Mifflin & Co., 1883) p. 21.

76. Campbell, Occidental Mythology, p. 7.

77. The references in this episode to green bile and green snot are a parody of the vital godlike essence supposedly in all of us under this "Oriental" theory. Buck wonders what Stephen "has up his nose against [Buck]?" The vital essence is linked to art in Buck's lame joke that snotgreen is the new art color for Irish poets. Buck, with his mind always on the Eucharist, thinks about eating it: "You can almost taste it, can't you." In the third episode, the vital essence emerges as art, and Stephen, reflecting on whether anyone will ever read his work, will leave his own personal dried snot, a "booger," on the rock for someone to read.

78. Campbell, Occidental Mythology, pp. 26-27.

79. Ovid *Metamorphoses* (London: Penguin, 1955) p. 51.

80. O'Faolain, E. *Irish Sagas and Folk Tales* (Oxford: Oxford University Press, 1954) pp. 43-44.

81. O'Faolain, p. 93.

82. Campbell, J. *The Novels of James Joyce* audiotape, Big Sur Tapes (Tiburon, Ca).

83. Campbell, J. *Primitive Mythology* (New York: Arkana, 1991) p. 252.

84

84. The name of play by Carlo Goldoni, an 18th century Italian playwright who introduced realistic comedy, perhaps an apt description of Joyce's method. Thank you Cameron.

85. Remember also that Ireland was given by the Roman Catholic Church first to England (Pope Adrian IV to Edward II) and second to an Italian (Gregory XIII to a "bastard of the papal court"). See CW, p. 170.

86. Zimmer, Myths, p. 15.

87. Allegorical writing in this episode seems appropriate since much of Greek mythology proceeded by allegory. Murray, p. 199. [This book was originally published in 1910; the first episode was finished in 1917.] Canto I of The Divine Comedy opens with allegory.

88. Sacrifice of bulls at Nestor's palace.

89. Proteus has a herd of seals for mates.

Episode 2 (Nestor)

Basic Themes

The education dragon and the job dragon serve the Law of the Fathers. Homoeroticism and strife among the students foster separation among humans and competitiveness and war in the world soul. Deference demanded by employers produces weak willed victims.

At the end of the first episode, Stephen left the tower to go to his teaching job on payday. In the second (known as Nestor), he is teaching in a boys school headed by Mr. Deasy.[1] At the boys school, a memorization and repetition learning process conditions their impressionable minds. They perform for external approval, the report card system. The proud, arch-materialist Mr. Deasy prepares the souls of his young student charges as a herd of neophyte materialists on the path described by Joyce in SH as "remunerative respectability"[2] and to the "commercial prison".[3]

The psychological foundation for this commercial approach to life is to teach the students to seek personal satisfaction only in the favorable opinions of others, Buck Mulligan's approach to life. The culture at the school is competitive and strife oriented combined with a homoerotic atmosphere. Creative imagination and the heterosexual instincts, Joyce's portals to the eternal, are discouraged. As headmaster, Mr. Deasy masters their heads. The education dragon guards the values of society. Control.

Working for Mr. Deasy for three months has stunted Stephen's effort at promoting his own spiritual values and maximum self-realization. Interested in control, Mr. Deasy subjects Stephen to intellectual harassment—unless you defer and agree with me, you lose your job. The job dragon weakens its victims.

This school experience is the breeding ground for materialism, greed and pride, and these traits in turn result in a continuation of strife and misery in the world, the state of the soul of the world throughout history. This condition continues without any improvement to "reincarnate" from age to age in endless cycles because of the lack of proper education. The corrupt souls of the students continue the corruption of the world soul.

History is the backdrop for this episode. As the study of what happened in time and space, history foregrounds these two "nets" in which most souls are prisoners.[4] History restricts because it limits the possibilities of the future. In an attempt to find a way past these nets, Stephen tries to energize the students to use their creative imagination, but the students are already caught fast. Stephen feels an urgent personal need to break away from this paternity ward for the forces of greed and pride. At the end of the episode, Stephen makes a Buddha-like escape.

School

The school where Stephen teaches is not Catholic but is private, so it is probably Protestant, those Irish which favor English occupation. Mr. Deasy is an Orangeman, a Protestant. The time is before 10:00 a.m. In this school setting, Stephen learns an important lesson in life.

86

Action in Ulysses

The action again begins abruptly, in the middle of Stephen's class in Greek history. The limited learning process is rote memorization. This particular history lesson consists of questions and answers in ancient Greek history about the battle of Asculum and the famous remark by Pyrrhus, "Another victory like that and we are done for." The 17th episode returns to the more general issue of the limitations inherent in the process of questions and answers.

During the session, Stephen loses his focus to his own imagination. With limited governance, the attention of the class quickly slips away through word association from Pyrrhus to pier to Kingstown Pier (the local lovers' lane). Stimulated by this subject, Stephen remembers by their names his heterosexual partners. He tries unsuccessfully to energize the students to imagine a pier as a disappointed bridge, which suggests peer group pressure against individual extension through realization.

Stephen abruptly shifts the class from history to poetry recitation and has one student attempt to recite a poem from memory. The reciting student surreptitiously keeps the book open in front of him; when he has trouble remembering, Stephen, aware of this game, suggests he turn the page. The poem is by Milton about Lycidas not being dead "sunk though he be beneath the watery floor." This poem attempts to confront the meaning in god's universe of the seemingly senseless death of a young religious person. His death was by drowning, and the poem suggests Christ, who walked on water, saves him. The important point is that while the text is memorized and recited, the meaning of the poem, the product of the creative imagination, is not discussed. As the novel continues, water is the symbol of human unity.

Throughout the school lessons, Stephen thinks about various theories of history and about the students as visions of the future. At the end of the class, Stephen tells a riddle in an effort to kindle the creative imaginations of the students. But no student even tries to give an answer, because they haven't memorized it. The riddle Stephen asks is "The cock crew/the sky was blue/the bells in heaven were striking eleven/ tis time for this poor soul to go to heaven," a famous Irish riddle. Stephen nervously gives his extemporized answer—a fox burying his grandmother under a holly bush. While momentarily held by the puzzle of the riddle and Stephen's answer, the students gleefully adjourn class to go outside to play hockey. There they make noise and argue.

After class Stephen tutors a slow boy named Sargent in math sums. Stephen tries to help him understand, but Sargent can only memorize. Stephen compares him to a snail and contemplates the power of a mother's love that could have nurtured this limited boy. Sargent is presented as the characteristic product of this system.

After Mr. Deasy restores order in the hockey game, Stephen receives his monthly salary of 3 pounds and 12 shillings (Buck thought 4 pounds) in Mr. Deasy's office. The office walls hold several pictures of racehorses, icons of commercial competitiveness. Mr. Deasy didactically counsels Stephen in a fatherly way to save his money. Stephen can't stand Mr. Deasy and wants to escape. Mr. Deasy asks Stephen to carry to Stephen's newspaper editor friends Mr. Deasy's letter to the editor about a means of curing Irish cattle of hoof and mouth disease. Anxious to leave, Stephen agrees.

In their conversation, Mr. Deasy gratuitously berates the Jews. Stephen counters effectively using argument by definition. They have a discussion about god and history at the end of which they disagree. Mr. Deasy is frustrated that Stephen does not defer to him in argument. Mr. Deasy preaches the traditional Christian position that history is linear and moves toward the manifestation of god. In a Beckett-like response, Stephen refers to god as a "shout in the street." This startling remark is based on the view that the world soul continues to be violent, has not improved as Mr. Deasy suggests. It views history as cyclical, described by Stephen as a "nightmare" from which he is trying to awake.

Stung by Stephen's lack of deference in the discussion, Mr. Deasy predicts Stephen won't be at the school very long and wasn't born to be a teacher. Stephen archly replies, "A learner perhaps." In an ironic gesture, Stephen bows to Mr. Deasy's back and leaves. Mr.

Deasy runs out to catch him and tell an anti-Semitic joke. Upon leaving, Stephen would think, in the current vernacular, "I'm history."

Action in The Odyssey

In the related chapter iii of The Odyssey, Telemachus with Athena still by his side has arrived from Ithaca at the Greek mainland to seek out Nestor for news about Odysseus. Athena has assured Telemachus that Nestor will provide history not lies. Telemachus arrives, after a short overland journey, at Nestor's "citadel" to find Nestor's people providing methodical sacrifice of black bulls to Poseidon.[5]

Nestor is an elderly man of considerable means. He lives in a "splendid dwelling" with a "towering doorway," "polished stones" and a large "echoing portico." Nestor is proud and obsessed with wealth; he goes out of his way to comment proudly on his golden goblet (gold cup) and his possession of an "abundance of fine rugs and blankets." He reveals without hesitation that at Troy he "cruised after plunder." Nestor is famous as a tamer of horses.

Having been a fellow warrior with Odysseus at Troy, Nestor brags to Telemachus that Nestor and Odysseus always agreed on battle strategy. On being asked by Telemachus about the fate of Odysseus, Nestor does not come to the point immediately. Instead, he tells from only his own personal point of view the Trojan war experience and the return home. Nestor over-states and is focused on his own importance in a constant effort for the approval of others. Nestor brags about the correctness of his judgment about when to sail back from Troy. In not answering Telemachus's question immediately and especially in bragging about his return strategy, Nestor shows insensitivity to the grief of Telemachus.

After emphasizing his own exploits, Nestor finally informs Telemachus that Nestor has only hearsay information about most of the others but doesn't even have hearsay information about what happened to Odysseus. Telemachus tells Nestor about the suitors. Nestor advises that since Athena showed love for Odysseus during the Trojan war, Athena should now help Telemachus, who surely must have divinity in his blood (not very helpful advice, we note). Telemachus asks why the son Orestes didn't protect his father Agamemnon upon the father's return from Troy. Nestor relates that the winds caused by Zeus delayed Orestes in his return home to his family. (We would have guessed Poseidon, rather than Zeus, would make such winds over the ocean, but Nestor sacrifices to Poseidon). Drawing the wrong moral from Agamemnon's experience and projecting his own values, Nestor advises Telemachus to stay at home and guard his possessions.

Nestor flatters Athena, and her surprising response is to take on the characteristics of Nestor; she leaves in order to collect a debt and flies off in the form of a "vulture." Recognizing Athena from her transformation into a vulture (this is a format he can appreciate), Nestor sacrifices a cow after its horns have been gilded with gold (Nestor's highest form of sacrifice, his own gold). Nestor finally points Telemachus to Menelaus at Sparta for further information. In short, Telemachus comes a long way for very little information.

Nestor has an anal retentive psychological profile—obsession with wealth accumulation, self importance, ultra-organization (each of 9 settlements with 500 bulls in each providing 9 bulls for sacrifice), fastidiousness in sacrifice, tendency to preach to others, punctiliousness, "righteous" character, insensitivity and his tendency to bitch and moan.[6] One of his many sons, Pisistratus, is still a bachelor and sleeps by Telemachus in the hallway.

Parallels to The Odyssey

The references in this episode to the Nestor chapter of The Odyssey include the following:

Stephen continues as the reference for Telemachus. Stephen is also, as the apparently fatherless son fighting his foes, the reference for Orestes trying to come home in the teeth of the winds while his father is being murdered. Potential realization in Stephen is reflected by Nestor's reference to potential divinity in Telemachus's blood. Stephen's earlier trip to Paris and his study there as part of his self and artistic realization serve as a parallel to Telemachus's escape/voyage to find news of his father.

Mr. Deasy is the reference for Nestor. Both dote on gold and are interested in cattle and horses. Both share the psychological profile

90

of anal-retentive. Both are fond of giving advice. Both the school and Nestor's citadel have imposing gates. The students being sacrificed to the commercial life are the reference for the bulls being sacrificed to Poseidon, the master of time and space but not the eternal.

The traditional study of history is the reference for Nestor's only hearsay information about the fate of the other Greek warriors and the lack of information about Telemachus' father. Most history is only hearsay and, according to Joyce, leaves out the important matters. The normal Irish educational process is the reference for Telemachus coming a long way for very little useful information. Stephen wants to limit his time with Mr. Deasy so that his character doesn't rub off on Stephen, as Nestor's apparently rubbed off on Athena. The powerful effect of the desire for approval from others is reflected in Athena's conversion into a vulture after being flattered by Nestor.

Traditional Schemata

The traditional schemata given by Joyce for this episode are art—history, color—brown, symbol—horse, and technique—personal catechism (question and answer). Again no body organ is mentioned, but the buttocks and anus get much attention. Brown for scatological. The correspondences are Nestor—Deasy, Pisistratus—Sargent and Helen—Mrs. O'Shea (Parnell's mistress).

First Letter

The first letter **Y** in the first word "You" looks like a pictograph of word association, an intersection of two words. It also looks like conforming to the opinions of others (two become one).

Soul of the World

The episode presents the view that history repeats and that little improvement has occurred in the soul of the world throughout recorded history—from 279 BC and Pyrrhus a Greek war general to the present and men like Mr. Deasy. He is the materialistic, proud, ultra-competitive, misogynistic and anti-Semitic headmaster currently in Stephen's hair, particularly on payday. World history has proved, in Bryon's phrase, to be the "devil's scripture," and the Holy Ghost as the love of God in the world has been conspicuously absent. This episode describes Stephen's third payday after which, like Christ's three days in

91

the tomb, Stephen arises from this dead world.

The philosophy of this episode echoes the position taken by Joyce in his 1903 review of a book on Buddhism:

> Our civilization, bequeathed to us by fierce adventurers, eaters of meat and hunters, is so full of hurry and combat, so busy about many things which perhaps are of no importance, that it cannot but see something feeble in a civilization which smiles as it refuses to make the battlefield the test of excellence. There is a Burmese saying— "The thoughts of his heart, these are the wealth of a man."[7]

The risk to higher self-realization resulting from this type of competitive civilization is demonstrated in matured form by the diseased soul of Mr. Deasy. The same virus is being implanted in the younger student versions, particularly the failing student Sargent. As his military name would suggest, Sargent follows orders and stays after class to do "sums" by rote as directed by the schoolmaster, training for the future practice of counting money.

The concept of the world soul that reflects the souls of all individual humans is an aspect of Joyce's megacept that the part implies the whole, which is signified by the seal of Solomon. Giordano Bruno, a 16th century Italian philosopher-mystic regarded by Joyce as the father of modern philosophy,[8] espoused a similar holographic view of the world soul:

> Everything we take in the universe has in itself that which is entire everywhere; and so it comprehends in its mode the whole world soul. . . .That soul is entire in any part whatever of the universe. Therefore, as act is one and constitutes a single being, wherever it is, we are not to believe there is in this world a plurality of substance of that which is truly being.[9]

Sargent's failure as a student is shown as the result of the memorization and repetition educational system. This is education in the service of the state.[10] Like Echo from the myth of Narcissus who

92

can only repeat what is said to her, the students can only repeat what they have memorized.

Mr. Deasy's anal-retentive psychological profile is linked to the homoerotic theme by word play as well as psychological theory. The students relieve their sex drive through the only means available—masturbation and predatory or less frequently voluntary homosexual practices.[11] These practices are cast by Joyce as futile, inward looking and strife producing in league with selfishness and greed. Repeated references to the game "hockey" characterize the effect of the Deasy academy of learning—hocking the key to the soul.

The connection of homoeroticism and strife is made through word association in the text of the student history lesson concerning Greek warfare. The students' early tendency to strife is shown through their general clamor, their overriding interest in playing competitive games (hockey) and their natural tendency to arguments on the hockey field (sports are described as "hardy brutality" and "mimic warfare" in SH). The competitive tendencies of the students set the stage for strife in life. Hockey sticks become lances become bombs. Stephen, though, only pokes with a book.

In this school, the ABC's prepare the ground for the "Waste Land." As Joseph Campbell says:

> the Waste Land . . . is any world in which . . .
> force and not love, indoctrination, not education,
> authority, experience, prevail in the ordering of lives . .
> . .

Stephen's reaction to this waste land is a desperate desire to "awaken from the nightmare of history" and free himself from the job dragon, the practical requirements of earning a salary that force him to subject himself and superficially defer to men like Mr. Deasy.

Sex/Strife Theme

The connection of homoeroticism and strife is made through the following multiple instances of word association in the student history/poetry lesson:

Cochrane for cock rain and cock reign and masculine rule.

93

Tarentum for tear into them, sodomy without lubricant, and direct assault.

Asculum for ass and famous battle.

Another victory like that and we are done for for ejaculation and battle.

Blowing by Mr. Deasy for fellatio and anger.

Armstrong for masturbation and strength of soldier.

Comyn for coming or ejaculation and attack.

Other homoerotic allusions include the following

Talbot for tall but.

Jerks of verse for ejaculation.

Turn over Talbot for preparation for sodomy.

Talbot . . . bending forward for preparation for sodomy.

A hard one for erect penis.

The cock crew for effect of sex drive as pride.

Get your stick and go out to the others for preparation for homosexual acts.

By multiple and obvious repetitions of these gross puns, Joyce sticks to the reader this association of homoeroticism and strife. For Joyce, sexual interest is perverted unless it results in emotional as well as physical connections.

The failing student Sargent is described in similar terms: the references to his "copybook," his tool for copying or procreation, is open; and his head is associated with the head of a penis, "His tangled hair (read pubic) and scraggy neck (read penis) gave witness of unreadiness. . ." On his copied "sums," Stephen notices a blind loop and a blot. His first name is Cyril for surreal.

The tie between materialism and warfare is demonstrated in many ways. For example, in the following early part of the school scene:

> A bag of figrolls lay snugly in Armstrong's satchel. He curled them between his palms at whiles and swallowed them softly. Crumbs adhered to the tissues of his lips. A sweetened boy's breath. Welloff

people, proud that their eldest son was in the navy.

Vico Road, Dalkey.

Note the association between well-off, pride, and the navy. Dalkey gives us "key" again (the key to the soul from the first episode) and plays either as doll key or donkey, in either event a compromised soul key. Vico gives us cycles, repetition of violence and misery. Joyce uses Vico as a street name because Vico means "little street," a meaning in tune with the implications of the cyclical theory of history—each event is little in importance because everything has happened before and will happen again.

Riddle

The riddle Stephen gives is "The cock crew/the sky was blue/the bells in heaven were striking eleven/ tis time for this poor soul to go to heaven," a favorite Irish riddle. This can be read as the sexual interest of an eleven year old, the probable age of the students. Stephen's customized answer to the riddle is the fox who buries his **grandmother** under the holly **bush**.

Since the traditional answer to the riddle is a fox burying his **mother** under a holly **tree**,[12] the changes should be the clue to Stephen's intended meaning. The change from tree to bush and burying something in a bush suggest the heterosexual act. Stephen is excited and stands up while giving the answer. In other works, Joyce referred to the Roman Catholic Church as the "Grandmother Church,"[13] since it gave birth to his mother's values. Fox was the false name used by Parnell in his adulterous affair with Mrs. O'Shea.[14] The fox/Socrates association represents the power of independence.

Given these clues, one possible interpretation of Stephen's answer to the riddle is to bury or rid oneself of the restraint on realization resulting from genetics, parental environment, childhood and the Church (represented by the grandmother) by means of intercourse with the opposite sex (represented by the holly bush).

Rewards and Controls

The episode begins with a directive from Stephen to a student: "You. Cochrane. . . ." This protocol puts the student in the responding rather than the creating mode. No exercise of the creative imagination in this school. Proper behavior is rewarded from without, by the teacher's praise, rather than inward through personal satisfaction. To a correct answer, Stephen praises but then quickly asks for more, "Very good. Well?"

This system imprints on the blank slate of the students the system of direction and reward from outside, the instruments of control. These students are being trained to do what they are told as part of a transmission of cultural values from one generation to the next. This is reincarnation in the world soul of the Law of the Fathers. The students are taught not to seek their own version of satisfaction. This restricts possibilities and creates the psychological system common to society of doing things to seek the approval of others, rather than for personal satisfaction.

This misdirection in the training of the students translates on the national stage into the jester of Ireland before its Master England:

A jester at the court of his master, indulged
and disesteemed, winning a clement master's praise.
Why had they chosen all that part? Not wholly for the
smooth caress. For them too history was a tale like any
other too often heard, their land a pawnshop.

By the jester image, the Buck chord from the first episode sounds. The smooth caress anticipates the dog image in later episodes.

In mythological terms, Stephen is standing head to toe with two big dragons—the job and the transmission of cultural values through education. The fathers in most societies have traditionally controlled these dragons. Stephen must slay or by-pass these dragons in order to achieve maximum growth possibilities.

Mr. Deasy

The dragon schoolmaster falls well short of his self image as an intellectual. He takes a martial pleasure in winning arguments, rather than joy in mutually beneficial discussions. He describes his discussion with Stephen as "breaking a lance." This phrase recalls the name of the only English born Pope, Nicholas Breakspear. He blessed the English conquest of Ireland.

96

Deasy likes to dictate his views. In the letter to the editor, he states there can be "no two opinions" about the subject. When Stephen disagrees with Mr. Deasy's view that history manifests the will of god (the orthodox Christian typological view of linear history), Mr. Deasy becomes frustrated and beats a cowardly retreat. He claims that he is happier for his views than Stephen is for his and issues the cowardly threat that because Stephen does not defer in their discussions, Stephen will lose his job. This is another humorous reference to the quotation "another victory like that (victory in argument) and we are done for (job lost)." Stephen does bow upon entering and leaving, apparently what Mr. Deasy expects. Even the horses in the pictures on the wall are shown in "homage" with "meek heads."

Mr. Deasy's propensities are portrayed in the details: his job is to restore order among the students even though he does not understand the problem, namely Comyn (coming) and Halliday (holiday) being on the same team; he yells but doesn't listen; he steps "fussily"; his head is "illdyed"; he treats folding money with unusual care, even has one taped together; he puts his billfold away immediately (his billfold is described in terms which suggest a condom); he has a "strong room" for gold; he has shells (former currency and dead souls) in mortar display; he advises Stephen to save his money; and he is proud he has "paid his way."

Deasy's association with Judas, the treasurer for the group of Jesus and his Apostles, is made by references to Deasy's collection of silver spoons bearing figures of the Apostles (12 silver spoons) and to his paying Stephen "three twelve" (three for the Trinity and 12 for the Apostles). Judas and Deasy would rather have 12 pieces of silver than Jesus and the Apostles. Deasy is also associated with Poseidon through the wind images, "blowing" as he typed and prompt "ventilation" of the question. The fallible Mr. Deasy makes several mistakes in his discussion of Irish history and hoof and mouth disease.[15]

The masturbatory/homoerotic references to Mr. Deasy are numerous: his very name suggests DC of AC-DC, or direct current for sex with the same sex; he turns about in his hand the coin dispensing box from which he shoots a coin; he quotes Shakespeare "Put but money in thy purse," which in this context is an injunction against copulation; Stephen responds "Iago," the name of a Shakespearean character but also a pun on I go (go is the Indo European root for god[16]); while typing Deasy "prodded the stiff buttons of the keyboard," another masturbation image; and even his letter to the editor sounds the homoerotic themes, "may I trespass on your valuable space" and the "hospitality of your columns."

Mr. Deasy believes that the difficulties he has experienced in advancing his views as to the cattle trade are caused by others, particularly Jews, as opposed to his own lack of talent. He halts in the light (of reason), and he blames Jews and women (Leopold and Molly, our two other main characters) for the problems of the world reflected in history.

Putting Mr. Deasy in deeper historical light the most that can be said for him and his commercial warriors is that they are faint echoes of the warriors in the *Iliad*. The aristocratic warrior world of Achilles was the world of brutal vitality, guarded by the code of honor and shame. This was the pre-ethical world of the sword and the moody self-preoccupation and rage of Achilles. This was a savage world but without hypocrisy where you were not good or bad but ". . . strong or weak, beautiful or ugly, conquering or vanquished, favored by the gods or used"[17] . This robust nobility is but a faint echo in Mr. Deasy and his future merchant warriors.

Protestantism

The quarrels of the students about who is on what hockey team reflects the tendency to division within the Protestant ranks that resulted in hundreds of denominations. The symbolic imagery in terms of allegories and metaphors is weak in this episode, compared to the first, reflecting the poverty of symbols in most of the Protestant denominations. The lack of coherence and logic and even correctness as to fact in Dr. Deasy's argument reflects Joyce's view of Protestant doctrine; when asked about becoming a Protestant, Stephen replies in AP, "I said that I had lost the faith, but not that I had lost self respect. What kind of liberation would that be to forsake an absurdity which is logical and coherent and to embrace one which is illogical and incoherent?"[18].

The use in this episode of word association, as opposed to Catholic visual imagery and allegory, parallels the Protestant emphasis on the word. The typical Protestant practice of lining the walls with pictures of family ancestors suggests Mr. Deasy's ancestors are horses, or symbols of Poseidon. Dr. Deasy's proud claim that he paid his own way reflects the lack of a mass or Eucharist in most Protestant churches and the Protestant emphasis on the priesthood of all believers.

Theories of History

The Nestor episode encodes several theories of history:

1) In Saint Augustine's *The City of God*, history is described as metaphorically reflecting two cities: the Heavenly City whose constituents love God, which results in love among mankind; and the Earthly City whose less fortunate constituents love themselves, which results in strife and hate. The first resident of the metaphorical Earthly City was Cain, whose name means possession, the instinct of the materialist. According to the Bible, Cain actually founded the first town.

Saint Augustine numbers among the primary blessings of mankind his seed and the power to procreate in order to "Increase, and multiply and replenish the earth," sees God as involved in the creative energy producing human generations, sees beauty in the erect carriage of mankind and recounts the progress made by mankind. Elsewhere Saint Augustine flatly rejects cyclical versions of history and soul reincarnation and instead postulates the movement in history toward the manifestation of God, when the divine direct current will rule the world.

This episode begins with: "You, Cochran, what city sent for him?" The student answer is Tarentum or "tear into them." The answer in Augustinian terms is Cain's Earthly City of strife and hate and desire for possession. Saint Augustine's procreation theme shows up in Stephen's memory: "woven on the Church's looms . . . my father gave me seeds to sow." The students' homoerotic, like any selfish, sexual activity is in the futile realm of self-love in the garden of earthly delights. The upright beauty of humans is mocked by the appearance of the stooped Sargent and his sloping math figures, not even his copied sums are upright. A prisoner of the Earthly City because of his exclusive interest in material realization, Mr. Deasy is the ironic voice for Saint Augustine's theory of linear progress in history toward the heavenly city as the manifestation of God.

2) The nature of history is explored in Stephen's first thought during the history lesson:

> Fabled by the daughters of memory. And yet it was in some way if not as memory fabled it. A phrase, then, of impatience, thud of Blake's wings of excess. I hear the ruin of all space shattered glass and toppling masonry, and time one livid final flame. What's left us then?

These expressive phrases are graftings from Hesiod and Blake root stock—history is fabled by memory and the history of violence is the product of impatience and desire for excess. Stephen wonders what the end will be if strife from impatience and desire for excess have characterized the beginning and the middle: "What's left us then?" The end of time is depicted in "time one livid final flame." These questions hunt the larger game of the meaning of time and space.

In this and related connections, remember that immortality is a concept related to time, time extended indefinitely, whereas the eternal in human concerns relates not to time but to the inherent, timeless aspects of humans beings and the cosmos that do not rise and fall with birth and death. These eternal aspects are the rebar in Joyce's aesthetic masonry.

The little bricks of history are explored in little phrases such as "after," " go on," " went on again," and "remembered." The mansions are explored in the consideration of the theoretical historical possibilities that could have but didn't take place. Like restraints on realization, history shuts down possibilities. Proper art can transcend and is not bound by history. Through the creative imagination, art produces events that could have but did not take place. Art can expand the possibilities.

3) Recurrent cyclical theories of history (such as those of Vico and Plato) make limited appearances by repetition throughout the episode. Their signatures, as characterized by Saint Augustine as "worlds without end," pop up repeatedly throughout the episode. The episode views the Greek wars and the students' delight in strife as part of the same cyclical continuum. This continuum is part of Joyce's justification for his use of The Odyssey, old myths and other tools from the past in shaping his Dublin world.

Vico is the name of a street used in this episode. As indicated in the Introduction, the cyclical theories of history of Giambattista Vico, an 18th Century Italian philosopher, provide important routing in this novel.[19] The attitude of this episode—that the student brand of homoeroticism, anal retentive behavior and ambition lead to world strife and misery—is the kind of mega-analysis inspired by Vico.

4) Aristotle's theory of history as the potential becoming actual is replayed in Stephen's own thoughts. The Aristotelian concepts of "form" and the soul as the "form of forms" are used repeatedly in the episode.

5) Mr. Deasy gives a version of modern Irish political history. Ireland, mythically founded by the daughters of Cain, has historically been a hot bed of tyranny and violence. The betrayal theme continues in the history of Irish-British state relations and Irish Catholic-Protestant relations. Mr. Deasy is an Orangeman, a Protestant, who is happy with British rule over Ireland (this ended in 1921 except for Ulster).

Independence Theme

Stephen's quest for freedom is reflected in the names of the horses in the pictures on the wall in Mr. Deasy's office: "Repulse" (deny authority), "Shotover" (shot over to Paris), "Ceylon" (so long) and "Prix de Paris" (freedom prize of Paris). These names refer to Stephen's prior rebellion and freedom run to Paris. He remembers one horse "Fair Rebel." The condition of the horses also reflects Stephen's condition; he is eager for freedom but held hostage in the stable. These horses, despite their rebellious names, run competitively for others under tight controls for material rewards.   Personal history through

101

ancestors and the experience of youth are also included in the template of historical restraints on the possibilities of realization. Stephen calls childhood "tyrants, willing to be dethroned." He can escape his inheritance and his past.

Buddha

The part of the Buddha story reflected in Stephen's experience in this episode is Prince Gautama's experience of the four signs and his subsequent escape from home. The young prince has been imprisoned in a false material world created by his father in which the Prince experiences no unhappiness or want. One day when the forests were carpeted with tender grass (Mr. Deasy is first seen stepping over wisps of grass[20]), the young Prince goes out for a picnic in the "city groves—beloved of women." The King carefully prepares the way to avoid any experience that could unsettle his son's mind, but the "gods" plant an old man, a sick man and a dead man for the Prince to see. From his charioteer, the Prince learns for the first time that these are the inevitable condition of every man (this Prince has really been sheltered). In the Buddhist system, these are the signs of the inevitable sorrows of all life. Shortly thereafter, the Prince sees the fourth sign, the fact that plowing the field for food cultivation kills insects (life eats life). Contemplating the meaning of the fourth sign, the Prince sees a beggar who says he lives now only for the highest good and then suddenly disappears into the sky (this must be some form of sky blasting).

The Prince begs his father to allow him to leave home and adopt the way of life of an ascetic monk, like the one he saw disappear into the sky. His father refuses. With the help of the gods, the Prince defies his father and escapes the castle on his horse. [21] This is another reason why the horses in the pictures in Mr. Deasy's study have names associated with independence.

As the Buddha escaped on his horse from his father's castle, he let out a "lion's roar"[22]. As Stephen escapes from Mr. Deasy's dark study and gains in strength in the light, he passes the lion statutes. Joseph Campbell aptly catches the lion spirit in the Buddha myth:

The lion roar, the sound of the solar spirit, the principle of the pure light of the mind, unafraid of its own force, had broken forth in the night of stars. And as the sun, rising, sending forth its rays, scatters both the terrors and the raptures of the night: as the lion's roar, sending its warning out across the teeming animal plain, scatters the marvelously beautiful gazelles in fear: so that lion roar of the one who had thus come gave warning of a lion pounce of light to come. Along the way of the one who had thus broken forth from the palace of nets of gold and gossamer set to catch and trammel lion hearts, heavenly beings strewed light . . . [23]

The images of solar light and leaves of the Buddha's tree of enlightenment inform the last line of the episode, which wonderfully can refer either to Mr. Deasy or Stephen or both: "On his wise shoulders through the checkerwork of leaves the sun flung spangles, dancing coins." In the light filtered through the leaves of the tree of enlightenment, Mr. Deasy's coins begin to dance, materialism turns to art.

Mara

This episode shows the school ruled by proxies for Mara, the Lord of Illusion or Desire and Aggression, who challenged the Buddha after his enlightenment. Mara rules over the world of maya or illusion for any individual trapped in the ego nets of desire and aggression. The Buddha had passed through these nets by dissolving the concept "I" and the correlative concept "you," so he was not vulnerable to Mara's challenge.[24] By contrast, the episode starts with Stephen as an "I" calling "you" to Cochrane and continues with the emphasis on separates in Mr. Deasy's office. These scenes are securely within the world of maya. Desire and aggression are the fuel for the sex/strife theme.

Mara paraded before Buddha, in an attempt to distract him, Mara's "three attractive sons . . . Mental-Confusion, Gaiety and Pride, and his voluptuous daughters, Lust, Delight and Pining"[25]. While the

103

Buddha did not yield, these temptations have found distracted converts among the school students. Mara then called for soldiers and monsters, which also had no effect on the Buddha but which are ingrained in the clamor and strife and future of the students.

Poseidon and Medussa in the Wallet

This school is in the land of the horse, the province of time and space ruled over by Poseidon, Mr. Deasy's Olympic counterpart. Poseidon's chief festival was the Isthmia, the scene of famous athletic contests. This historical background presides over the hockey game, as the students are trained as warriors, not poets.

Poseidon was the father/lover of Medussa, who ends up in Mr. Deasy's hip pocket. One look at Medussa would turn the observer into stone. Perseus cut off her head and carried it back in his wallet.[26] Mr. Deasy has in his billfold a torn bill which has been taped together, the Medusa redux. As one look at Medusa would turn the observer into stone, a material orientation (the billfold) turns the soul into stone.

Parallels to Hamlet

The Hamlet theme continues with Mr. Deasy as Polonius. In scene iii of Act I, Ophelia is instructed by both Polonius (her father) and Laertes (her brother) to stay away from Hamlet since Hamlet's attentions as a prince could only be transitory. Polonius's motive in giving this bad advice to his daughter, to belittle herself and not follow her heart, was to curry favor with the King, thus betraying his daughter. Likewise Mr. Deasy betrays his soul and his children charges to greed.

Use of Aristotle's View of the Soul and the Kundalini

The depressing condition of the soul of the world and the individual students and headmaster is framed in Aristotelian terms as being stuck at the level of desire in the soul hierarchy. This is just above nutrition and reproduction, the level reached by the usurper wooers in the first episode.

From the Kundalini Yoga point of view, these students are being trained for life in the third chakra centered near the navel and associated with worldly power and control. In this chakra, fire is the element (war), red the color (blood), sight the sensation (Sargent is nearly blind) and anus the organ (anal retentive). In this mode,

> . . .the energy turns to violence and its aim is to consume, to master, to turn the world into oneself and one's own. . .and even sex becomes an occasion, not of erotic experience, but of achievement, conquest, self-reassurance, and frequently, also, revenge.[27]

The animal, which represents this chakra, is the ram, which finds its meaning in the allusions in this episode to predatory sodomy, an unfortunate tradition at British sponsored all boys' schools.

Plato's Dialogues

In the dialogue *Apology*,[28] Socrates speaks before the Athenian assembly to answer criminal charges of impiety and corruption of the youth of Athens. Despite the dangers of a possible death sentence, Socrates refuses to cow-tow to the assembly and instead criticizes them for pursing only material ends, rather than the virtuous life.

In his presentation, Socrates is arrogant and uses "big talk"[29]. The speech itself uses the techniques of rhetoric, but its aim is not rhetorical. It is full of irony, which at the time was conventionally considered a defect of character and was associated with foxes. Socrates was thought to have this defect.[30] Socrates preached the truth rather than trying to get off easy. He jeered the judges.

The parallels to the Nestor episode are significant. Stephen again appears as Socrates to battle conventional wisdom and pursuit of materialism (impiety). Stephen is teaching and trying to liberate the minds of his students (the charge of corrupting youth). He refuses to defer to Mr. Deasy in argument and in fact irritates him (Socrates before the assembly). Stephen uses Socrates's rhetorical devices, argument by definition and irony, in his argument with Mr. Deasy. The fox shows up in the answer to the riddle.

Psychoanalytical Theory

The aggression drives proceed from the id forces in the unconscious, which were represented in the first episode by Haines.[31] In this episode, this role is played by Mr. Deasy. He and Haines are connected by Stephen's description of both of them as the sea's ruler.

Structure, Art and Aesthetics

The action of this episode is almost exclusively conversation between Stephen and the young male students and between Stephen and the headmaster Mr. Deasy. As suggested by the imposing gates at Nestor's citadel and the school, these conversations produce no emotionally fruitful connections. Stephen's thoughts protrude into the text more in this episode than the first. While Mr. Deasy frustrates him, Stephen is much more independent and stable in his own person in the school situation than he was in the first episode in the tower.

The art of the episode consists of the successful intertwining through word association of the themes. The reader is alerted to look for the word association technique by its conscious use in the conversation between Stephen and the students. The interwoven themes play like counterpoint in music.

Compare, if you will, the implications of the use of word association as the main tool in this episode compared with allegory in the first episode. Allegory pulls the meaning out of the concrete and into the realm of abstract ideas, as the Church would pull the attention of the faithful away from this life to the abstract beyond death. On the other hand, word association involves a connection, an intersection of two words, in the here and now. However, their separate meanings are more important than the connection. By contrast, in a pun the connection is more important than the two separate meanings. Likewise, the human characters in this episode associate but remain unconnected.

Sexual symbolism is much more on the surface compared to the first episode, as would be expected in the world of the school and away from the Church in the first episode. The reality lens is set at surreal caricature (student Sargent's first name is Cyril). The vision is overripe and maya inspired, not a neutral picture of the world. Unlike the first episode, small details as to reality outside the theme are missing. The relationship of part to the whole is extremely hot and intense. The two themes, skewed sex and strife, dominate all action and all description.

The art of this episode in Joycean terms is the quasi-epical. Compared to the first episode, the voice is more in the first person or interior monologue and less in the third person objective, signaling Stephen's increasing independence and "descent" into himself. The emotional gravity of the episode proceeds from Stephen's mind. The artistic image flows between and around Stephen on the one hand and the students and Mr. Deasy on the other. This time Stephen feels more like the author. **Quasi**-epical because Stephen does not fully represent Joyce the author. Quasi-**epical** because the artistic image doesn't vitalize the students or Mr. Deasy, only Stephen's thoughts. The students and Mr. Deasy are servants of the artistic image, as is appropriate for the message. The art "descends" from the first episode in the dramatic, to the second episode in the quasi-epical and then to the third episode in the quasi-lyrical.

The third person narrator, like the orchestra in opera, continues to provide mood information, but is subdued compared to the first episode. Hear the warm sounds (even using Middle English) of recently satisfied oral pleasure: "He curled them (figrolls) between his palms at whiles and swallowed them softly. Crumbs adhered to the tissue of his lips. A sweetened boy's breath." When the boys laugh, the words are abrupt: "All laughed. Mirthless high malicious laughter." When the narrator wants to describe a student as simple, the adjective is used as an adverb: "What sir? Talbot asked **simply,** bending forward." Sargent the slow student "came forward **slowly.**" Words describing the run of symbols across the page dance and turn in their own rhythm: "Give hands, traverse, bow homage to partner." Even the symbols bow homage to others, rather than standing independently by themselves.

This episode continues in the tragic with oppression by commercial authority. The comedy is not joyful, only parody. Whether you are "arrested by its wholeness and fascinated by [the] harmony" of this episode depends on your own individual chemistry. For my own taste, the episode is brilliant exactly because it is overdone. The reality lens supports the message. This episode is not a period piece; its dramatic weight can be felt at anytime, anyplace.

This caustic episode closes with Stephen shaking free of Mr. Deasy past the lion statues but only after Mr. Deasy's last second joke about why Ireland never discriminated against the Jews: "because she never let them in. . . . A coughball of laughter leaped from his throat dragging after it a rattling chain of phlegm." This presents the last link in the episode between strife and hate with homoeroticism (**she** never let them **in**).[32] The phlegm-sperm shoots out from Mr. DC's mouth with the joke. We leave him with his mouth open, the symbol of desire and the expression of one of the two cherubims guarding against the return of humans to the Garden of Eden.

****

ENDNOTES

1. Joyce taught at a private Protestant preparatory school in Dalkey, the Clifton House School, after returning from Paris. Costello, p. 222.
2. SH, p. 49.
3. SH, p. 30.
4. AP, p. 206.
5. The very god who has caused the captivity of Odysseus.
6. Freud, S. *Dictionary of Psychoanalysis*, p.11 " . . . orderliness, parsimoniousness and obstinacy . . . persons possessing these characteristics proceed from the dissipation of their anal-eroticism." *APA DSM–III-R Diagnostic Manual of Mental Disorders, 3rd Edition*, revised at p. 354: "Preoccupation with rules, efficiency, trivial details, procedures and form interferes with the ability to take a broad view of things . . . . People with this disorder are stingy with their emotions and material

possessions . . . time urgency, hostility-aggressiveness, and exaggerated competitiveness."

7. CW, p. 94. Joyce characterized England as a materialistic civilization (p. 173) compared to the idealistic Ireland.

8. CW, p. 133.

9. Bruno, G. *Cause, Principle and Unity* trans. J. Lindsay (New York: International Publishers, 1962) p. 139.

10. See in general the article in CW, p. 109.

11. Other writers have been explicit about the homosexuality at Clongowes, Joyce's grade school. Joyce always associated the British "public" school system with homosexuality. Costello, p. 76. Joyce took the position in the article *Oscar Wilde: the Poet of Salome* collected in CW, p. 204, that Wilde's sexual preferences were the "logical and inescapable product of the Anglo-Saxon college and university system, with its secrecy and restrictions."

12. Gifford, p. 33.

13. See the poem *The Holy Office* in CW, p. 151.

14. Costello, p. 97.

15. Vreeswijk, pp. 79-88.

16. Dannielou, A. *Shiva and Dionysus*, trans. K. Hurry (London: East - West Publications, 1982) p. 49.

17. Dunbey, D. "Does Homer Have Legs" **The New Yorker**, September 6, 1993, p. 52.

18. AP, p. 277.

19. Klein at pp. 327-345 takes the position that Vico's four stage cyclical theory of history can be read continuously in a line by line analysis of this episode.

20. His gaitered feet probably pulls us into word play on Romeo, which means one given over to lovemaking or desire and also means a type of gaiter.

21. Summarized from the description in Campbell, Oriental Mythology, pp. 259-265.

22. Ibid, p. 265.

23. Ibid, p. 265.

24. Ibid, p. 274.

25. Campbell, Oriental Mythology, p. 265.

26. Campbell, Occidental Mythology, p. 152.

27. Campbell, Joseph *The Mythic Image* (Princeton: Princeton University Press, 1974) p. 350.

28. Apparently the second dialogue.

29. *The Dialogues of Plato*, trans. by R. E. Allen. (New Haven: Yale University Press, 1984) vol. 1, p. 70.

30. Ibid, p. 66.

31. Haines supplies the current, may mean hate, raved all night about a black panther, is associated with guns, is a lunatic, is in the dark below in the phallic tower, is "stinking," his father was associated with aborigines, doesn't ' know who Stephen (the ego) is, apparently lit the fire in the hearth, is described in impersonal terms on the first entrance as "seated," speaks right after "serpent's prey," speaks in languages not understood, is described as a spot that can't be cleaned with conscience, is associated with the "hold fast" of the hammock, is a Jew hater, and remains below in the tower while Buck and Stephen talk. Haines for the tea gives everyone two lumps, for the id and two testicles.

32. Both spittle and sperm have been thought to be substance of life and soul.

Episode 3 (Proteus)

Basic Themes

Alone and separated, Stephen's turbulent imagination produces poetry in the lyrical mode. His agitated soul and separated condition distort his views of reality.

Stephen is alone on Sandymount Beach. He has separated himself from Buck and Haines and has just burned his bridges to Mr. Deasy and his teaching job. He has left behind his religious upbringing, family home, temporary lodging in the tower for which he paid the rent, job and companions. He is totally homeless, literally and figuratively. He wanders aimlessly on the beach where the constant

110

change of fleeting reality is most visibly registered. In this milieu, Stephen's imagination registers an agitated jitter.

At this point, Stephen believes that he can realize the meaning of his existence and the metaphysical foundation of his art solely through uncompromising independence.[1] With this independence, Stephen creates his own life values and a world determined by his art that no father can disinherit.[2] However, these gains are achieved at the cost of separation.

He declares his independence with the manifesto "*As I am. As I am. All or not at all.*" It is no coincidence that the repeated phrase *As I am* sounds like the Sanskrit words *sa ham sa ham* (which mimic the sound of inhalation and exhalation). This phrase and its counterpart *ham sa*, which means gander, are used in Yoga meditation. They reveal the "secret" that the human individual, even though bounded by maya, may rise like the gander and soar to unlimited consciousness.[3] In this episode, a dog chases on the beach the shadow of a flying gander. The dog's pointedly limited consciousness reminds Stephen of dependent slave-like humans who restrict their potential by living for rewards from others.

In this exiled state, Stephen pays the price of his independence. He is thrown into his own turbulent and agitated being. In this condition, he exercises his freedom to create poetry. Stephen's condition suggests that the poetry, which is not disclosed at this point, is composed in the romantic temper using the lyrical method, the literary counterpart of ego fixation.[4] Later we learn that the poetry is romantic indeed and features a vampire. Reflecting the limited possibilities of art produced in this mode, the poetry nearly plagiarizes an old Irish love song.

Stephen tries to read the language of nature through sight and hearing and to relate his own sense of self to time and space. He describes the sensations of sight and hearing as the "ineluctable modality of the visible and audible," that is the inevitable way humans view reality second hand, not directly into the essence. The result is the "Limits of the diaphane," the limits of the translucence of meaning. He tries to see beyond the veil to the holy of holies, the ultimate reality in

111

nature, but in his current condition is not able to do so. He believes that darkness, the "adiaphane," is behind the veil.

He muses about the separating effect these modalities of sensation produce, in sight objects side by side and in sound one after another. Stephen also experiences the separating effects of the subject-object duality (separate "I" subject views separate object). This musing is framed through the German terms (*Nebeneinander* and *Nacheinander*) used by Schopenhauer, whose philosophy emphasized the unity. Stephen, though, is not ready for the unity. At this point, he seems to reach the common sense conclusion with Aristotle that his self is real and separate, the world out there is real and separate from himself and opposites are never unified. Joyce has Stephen close his eyes and pretend to be blind because at this point he is blind to the ultimate reality as perceived by the matured Joyce.

In contrast to Stephen's conclusions, the episode hints that the separating assumptions Stephen is making condition and limit his existence as a human and as an artist. This point of view is inspired by the doctrines of Kant. These restricting limitations are similar to the limitations of the lyrical romantic mode in literature, the mode of Stephen's current efforts. In that mode, the artist is not tuned to the grave and constant and remains separated from his readers. They are also similar to the limitations of the second hand religious experience with the separate divine provided by the Catholic Church.

The main point of the episode is that all these modes (in sensation, art and religion) are flawed in the pursuit of the eternal. They all share the same split weld in the foundation, the separation of the individual from others and the divine ground of being. In later episodes and after his life enhancing experiences, the dividing line for Stephen between the self and the outer world blurs and memory and imagination through art transcend time and space to reach the eternal.[5]

In my favorite interpretation, Stephen's thoughts in this episode are spawned as the more generalized version of the specific subject most on his mind, his upcoming date that afternoon with Nora and hopeful thoughts about what her soft hands will be doing. The potential relationship with Nora prompts Stephen's thoughts about

112

relationships in general, between two existences and between subjects and objects. The artistic counterpart of relationships is rhythm, the relationship in art of part to part and part to whole and whole to part. Stephen combines these subjects as he considers artistic rhythm in connection with poetry lines about a mare on Sandymount Beach, the site of his first date with Nora.

Stephen's sexual interest in Nora and females in general serves as midwife to artistic creation. Stephen flashes spontaneously on a line of poetry in the midst of thoughts about women as sexual creatures. *Eros* serves as midwife to art, but without compassion the art is limited, limited as to possibilities by the author's subjectivity and romantic temper. The contents of the poem (about a vampire mouth to mouth) and Stephen's fearful musing about trying to save a man drowning in the ocean off "maiden rock" convey misgivings about an emotional attachment with Nora. So in his current mode of ego, Stephen is both drawn to her and fearful of a relationship, desire and loathing. These are the two faces of kinetic art and the inevitable byproduct of the lyrical method and the romantic temper.

In Buddhist terms, the subject-object duality rests on ego fixation, as opposed to a world *detached* immersion in the eternal. Like the ever-changing beach environment, his ego-driven soul remains turbulent and not detached. Stephen is free at this point to produce art that is independent of church, state and their inevitable didacticism, but his art is still hostage to his own self-indulgent emotionalism. Through his poem, that kind of emotionalism is now symbolically associated with the image of the vampire, whose victims once bitten were willing and described as the "undead."

As the episode proceeds in images of creation and change, allusions to the Buddha's enlightenment promise subsequent improvement in Stephen. This promise is issued by striking allusions to those events in the life of the Buddha that immediately preceded his enlightenment. The Buddha's milk bowl that miraculously floated upstream appears here in the form of the *Rosevean*, the three masted schooner. She is floating upstream in the Liffey River of life on the tide from the eternal ocean. This is a message "about one" from the calm eternal to the busy and messy temporal.[6]

Joyce named this episode for Proteus, the sea creature in The Odyssey who gave correct information about the fate of Odysseus. But Proteus provided this information only after Proteus was captured, struggled to escape, changed physical forms, and was held in a firm grasp. Joyce uses this heavy image as a symbol of Stephen's current immoderate and turbulent imagination (Proteus changing forms). It forecasts his ability to reach truth and beauty when his imagination is firmly held by classical restraint (firm grasp). The abuses of Stephen's current romantic mode involve distortions resulting from immoderate enthusiasm. These abuses in literary art appear most clearly in this episode in the descriptions of the movements of a dog on the beach. These descriptions are made by unnatural, unconvincing and constantly changing references to several other types of animals, much as Proteus first changed into other animals. So the dog with limited consciousness serves as the vehicle of the limited romantic mode, and god (reversed spelling of dog) serves as the vehicle for the eternal, which only classical restraint can reach.

Stephen explores his turbulent soul in the edifying context of metaphysics as this episode stages two magnificent themes: (1) the meaning of the human experience, or metaphysics breeds detachment and existentialism and (2) the spectacle of creation, or sperm becomes art. In both themes, logos plays a vital role. Logos, the word, the very stuff of the episode. This exploration for deeper meaning is made in the cave of the secret cause, the implications of death for the meaning of Stephen's human experience. And concerning that meaning, a disguised appearance is made by Anubis from the Egyptian *Book of the Dead*. Anubis served as the gatherer of souls for the final judgment (before Osiris). Anubis is representative of the view, shared by the Catholic Church, that life is a one-way ticket to be punched in the final judgment of the quick and the dead. Stephen rejects the submission necessary for a life sacrificed in preparation for the final judgment. In the individual pursuit of the eternal, he accepts the costs of relativism and the lack of objectivity. Stephen anticipates what post-modernism thinks it discovered.

Beach

Stephen is at the beach between 11:00 a.m. and 12:30 p.m. Because the episodes are contiguous but not continuous, we have to guess that he went to the beach directly from the school.

The beach is the borderline transition zone where ocean and land meet. Water, the mighty mother, in whom life was first created and which *in utero* nurtures the unborn human child. Land, where higher life first crawled and where the great human creation show now takes place. The beach, where life and death are on show as "seaspawn and seawrack." Dublin Bay, where the River Liffey carrying the sewage life of Dublin dies by enfoldment into the ocean. The river, which recycles to the ocean the water that has evaporated from the ocean, fallen as rain and collected in the river. Cycles.

Stephen is under the sun at noon. The sun provides light for the visible, indirectly provides air for the audible and provides energy for creation and growth. However, on the beach, lacking soil, nothing much grows, even in the sun. Only in nearby Cock Lake are there any plants. Stephen, under the sun, nonetheless begins to grow (in the famous phrase of W. Pater) in the "soil of his own individuality"[7].

Action in Ulysses

Stephen is hanging out on the beach pending his scheduled meeting at 12:30 p.m. with Buck and Haines at the pub "The Ship." He walks in a triangular pattern on the beach. The first leg is on the edge of the beach. The second leg is toward the Bay and ends on the rocks on the south retaining wall of the Liffey River. The wall retains the river as it flows through the beach into the ocean. At the end of the episode, he returns on the third leg via the sea wall to the point on the beach where he started. Stephen's return to the staring point suggests his development is stalled because in the romantic mode he always returns to himself.

He thinks about visual and auditory perception using Schopenhauer's terms, about Aristotle the bald millionaire, and about theories of subject and object duality and time and space. For details,

115

see the line by line analysis at this endnote.[8] He watches two midwives come down to the beach from the Dublin slums. They are described quite obviously by reference to seals. One is a widow. Seeing them he contemplates causation through the dimension of creation: Eve as the original mother of all human creation, the continuity of human life and death, and various theories of the creation of the world. He imagines calling the gods in Edenville using the omphalos as a telephone. The wind is blowing, the tide is coming in and the waves are up.

He thinks about going to live at his Aunt Sara's since he has already left home and is leaving the tower. He imagines how his "consubstantial" father would complain about this residential choice. Stephen imagines a visit to his Uncle Richie's house (same as Aunt Sarah's) where at first they don't recognize him. In the imagined visit, Stephen's cousin Walter fawns before his father Richie (unlike Stephen before his father), and the Uncle teases Stephen about his high pretensions as to the value of his future literary output and his lust for girls. Enthusiasm for sexual intercourse is coded into the names of his youthful epiphanies (youthful eros and youthful art). Apparently the creative and sexual instincts visited Stephen early in life.

Back in the here and now, Stephen spots various items on the beach. He remembers in the there and then good times with friends, books, clever sacrilegious poems, his prior plans to be a missionary, Paris, Kevin Egan the Irish revolutionary living in Paris, food and spurned lovers. In connection with Kevin Egan, Stephen remembers that one of the Invincibles, the "head centre," escaped from jail disguised as a bride.

Proteus appears in Stephen's thoughts in his Irish mythical counterpart Mananaan MacLir. As the tide is coming in, Stephen's feet sink in the wet sand. This reminds him of being trapped in the tower and the loss of the key to Buck. Stephen predicts he will not sleep in the tower that night.

Stephen sees a dead dog and thinks about the dead prose of earlier writers. He watches a live dog chase the shadow on the sand made by a flying bird. The dog eagerly fawns to his master, a man gathering cockles on the beach with a woman. Stephen reviews historical events that took place on the beach, from the first conquerors to the whales that washed up and were butchered by the locals. He believes the conquerors' lusts are in his blood and that he himself is a "changeling."

As the dog barks, Stephen experiences fear and in this condition thinks about Buck, political and court pretenders and saving a drowning man. He tries without success to recall the details of his dream involving a Turkish man and a watermelon. He contemplates the pleasure of sex in general by reference to Thomas Aquinas's terms for this popular pastime ("morose delectation"). The cocklepickers pass without speaking to him and, at least in Stephen's mind, notice his "Hamlet" hat (Parisian Latin Quarter hat). Stephen thinks about the naked philosophers Alexander the Great (the epitome of the heroic and separate individual) and his entourage reportedly encountered on a hot rock in India; these philosophers would have espoused the unity and detachment.

Stephen shapes an O with his mouth and lips and thinks about womb and tomb (the obvious hallmarks of the human unity), his own shadow, erotic kissing, and about a woman fondling him (his date with Nora is scheduled in just a few hours). In this erotic mental framework, a poetry image spontaneously erupts in his mind: "He comes, pale vampire, through storm his eyes, his bat sails bloodying the sea, mouth to her mouth's kiss." He wants to memorialize this image ("Put a pin in that chap, will you?"), so he writes it down on a piece of paper he tears off of Mr. Deasy's letter to the editor. Stephen usually uses library slips for this purpose. He considers changing the last image to "Mouth to her kiss" but rejects the change on the ground there must be two mouths for a connection. Then Stephen's mouth "mouthed fleshless lips of air: mouth to her moomb. Oomb, allwombing tomb." He goes on to mimic the sound of the "roar of cataractic planets," which are involved in the theories of esoteric Buddhism.

He contemplates his short shadow falling on the rocks and wonders why it doesn't reach endlessly to the stars. This is a metaphor for the reach of his art. He is prone on the rocks of the wall holding the Liffey River and wonders if he is alone and whether anyone will read

117

the poetry he is writing. He thinks about his feet, borrowed clothes, homosexuality, and about drowning. In nearby Cock Lake, a lake in the beach, he watches the wind-made waves and then urinates. He imagines a drowned man washing up on the beach. He wonders if he could go into the ocean to save a drowning man. He can't find his handkerchief (Buck had it) and leaves dried mucous on the rocks.

While walking back to the beach on the retaining wall, he turns to the rear, west, to see a three masted ship moving silently upstream in the Liffey River. This is the *Rosevean* coming "about one," as predicted by Haines in the first episode.

Action in The Odyssey

Telemachus was last seen leaving Nestor's citadel on the Greek mainland. In Chapter iv, Telemachus and Nestor's son arrive at Menelaus's mansion in Sparta after an unrealistically fast trip (bent reality). When they arrive, Menelaus is celebrating a double wedding feast, the wedding of his son by a slave woman to a girl of Spartan royalty and of his daughter to the son of Achilles. Menelaus is living with the famous Helen, whose betrayal of her husband Menelaus started the war with Troy in the first place. She is now barren.

One of Menelaus's guards stops Telemachus and Nestor's son outside and then goes inside to ask Menelaus whether to bring the strangers in, since the wedding feast is in progress. Menelaus replies yes of course and is deeply vexed at his guard for insulting the strangers by keeping them outside. The guard returns to welcome the Telemachus party and quarter their horses. They admire the mansion. They are bathed and served food as Menelaus plays the perfect host. Menelaus seems to leave the wedding feast in favor of talking to the strangers.

In a whispered aside to Nestor's son, Telemachus admires Menelaus's mansion and compares it to Zeus's. Menelaus overhears this remark and replies that his are no rival since Zeus's mansions are immortal. Without any further prompting, Menelaus launches into a description of his own personal suffering and wanderings on the way back home from Troy with the plunder that decorates his mansion. Unlike Nestor, Menelaus wishes for an alternative reality—that he had

118

less in plunder and that the men of Troy were still alive. He mentions Odysseus and says his child and wife must be grieving. At this point Telemachus, who has not yet been identified, begins to cry.

At this critical moment in the conversation, Helen makes a royal entrance and starts weaving wool on a gold and silver loom (imagine that!). She asks pointed questions and correctly identifies Telemachus as the son of Odysseus. Menelaus quickly agrees based on a likeness of feet and hands. Telemachus is too choked to speak for himself, so Nestor's son confirms Telemachus's identity and his grief. Note that considerable conversation takes place even before Nestor and Helen know to whom they are speaking. This must be the Spartan way.

Menelaus claims Odysseus was a great friend. Then they all weep, all that is except Helen. While the rest are distracted, Helen drugs their wine with sleep medicine she obtained in Egypt. Before they fall asleep, Helen recounts her own war story: that inside Troy she encountered Odysseus who had entered disguised as a beggar; that she recognized him but decided not to give him away; and that at this point she had realized her mistake in coming to Troy in the first place. In a pointed response, Menelaus recounts that later when the Trojan horse was brought inside Troy, Helen served the Trojans by mimicking the voices of the wives of those Greeks she thought might be inside, in an unsuccessful attempt to betray them. This response contradicts Helen's prior claim of which side she was on at the earlier point. After this exchange, they all fall asleep from Helen's drug. Once again Telemachus and Nestor's bachelor son cozy up together on the porch.

In the morning Menelaus comes out with his sword conspicuously strapped on and asks Telemachus what he wants. Menelaus is ready to get down to business. Telemachus asks for news of Odysseus and tells Menelaus about the wooers back at Ithaca. Menelaus is angered by the Ithaca news and predicts that eventually the wooers will die like deer fawns in the lion's den. Menelaus finally tells Telemachus what Menelaus learned in Egypt from the "Old Man of the Sea," Proteus, who has the powers of prophecy. Menelaus describes being held up at Pharos, an island in the mouth of the Nile, in his attempted voyage back home because of the lack of favorable winds.

Just as his provisions were running out, he was befriended by Eidothea, the daughter of Proteus. In order to play a trick on her father (notice the rebellion theme), she tells him how to escape—by catching Proteus when he comes at noon onto the beach to join the sleeping seals. They must hide among the sleeping seals disguised in sealskins. She advises that Proteus must be caught and held firmly, that during confinement he (it) will change shapes, return to his normal shape, and then correctly answer their questions. Eidothea even gives them ambrosia to counteract the bad smell of the sealskins in which they are to be disguised.

According to plan, Menelaus and two of his men lay disguised on the beach and the seals come. Proteus comes punctually at 1:00 p.m. and lays down among the seals. Menelaus and company promptly catch him. Using "the subtlety of his arts," Proteus changes forms in this order: into a lion, serpent, leopard, bear, water, tree and finally back to his original form. Then Proteus asks what they want. Menelaus asks how to get off the island. Proteus advises to return to Egypt, sacrifice more to the gods and then sail home. Menelaus also asks about the fate of the other Achians (Greeks). Proteus tells them about Asias who was lost on the rocks because of his hubris, about the homecoming tragedy of Agamemnon, and finally about Odysseus. Proteus discloses that Odysseus is still alive and is detained on an island by the nymph Calypso.

Thus Telemachus finally learns through Menelaus about his father from Proteus among the seals. Telemachus wants to leave at once and gives the horses as presents and Menelaus returns a silver mixing bowl.

The text abruptly shifts to the wooers back at the mansion. They are amusing themselves by throwing spears. What else would sex charged wooers be doing? They learn of Telemachus's return voyage and plan his assassination. Penelope finds out about their plot but doesn't do anything except fret and grieve. A goddess assuming the form of her sister visits to tell her not to worry.

Parallels to The Odyssey

Chapter iv of The Odyssey and the third episode of this Book are tied together as follows:

Stephen's creative imagination and art are the reference for the power of Proteus though "the subtlety of his art" to assume different forms and to speak the truth. Stephen is referred to as the "changeling." Proteus was considered the primary essence of nature, so Stephen thinks about what the signs in nature mean. Proteus is also related to the ship *Rosevean* because both arrive at 1:00 p.m.

Since Proteus must be restrained firmly in order to speak the truth, Stephen's imagination will have to firm up in order to speak the truth. At this point, his imagination creates an artificial reality informed by his ego, his own alternative reality. Since Menelaus came to Proteus by way of a female, Stephen will come to proper art through the female side.

The midwives, coming down to the shore "flabbily" with their "splayed feet," are the references for the seals; experience with the female will midwife artistic creation in Stephen, as the seals helped Menelaus catch Proteus.

The dangers of the romantic mode in literature are presented by Helen, first seen weaving on an incredible loom of silver and gold. Her specialties are betrayal, lies and drugs, and her womb is barren.

The delay by Uncle Richie's family in recognizing Stephen in the imagined visit is the reference for the delay in recognizing Telemachus & Company as proper guests. Stephen's thoughts about his feet and borrowed shoes (borrowed identity) reflect identification of Telemachus by his hands and feet. The multiple musings by Stephen about perfume suggest the ambrosia used by Menelaus and his men to ward off the dead seal skin stench.

Traditional Schemata

The traditional schemata given by Joyce for this episode are organ—none, art—philology, color—green, symbol—tide, and technique—monologue (male). The correspondences are: Proteus as primary matter of nature; Menelaus as Kevin Egan in Paris (both wishing for alternative realities); and Megapenthus (son by slave of Menelaus) as the cocklepicker (both share the slave mentality).

First Letter and First Word

The episode stars with the letter **I** in "Ineluctable." This announces the focus of Stephen on himself ("I") and the emphasis on the eye or visible ("Ineluctable modality of the visible. . . . "). The etymology of ineluctable is "not to struggle out of," which shares fundamentals in mythology with Proteus and, as we shall see, in metaphysics with the definition of being.

Mental Images

Stephen's mental images are kinetic; they flicker and shift in undisciplined association, producing a Proteus-like turbulent world of fragmentary thoughts. This turbulence is the result of his freedom, the lack of structure in his life and his youth. His memory microwaves hot emotional reactions to his experiences; he still lacks the cooler and firmer objectivity of maturity. In Joyce's terms, Stephen displays the romantic temper in his imagination, the hot house of his art.

The unsettled nature of Stephen's soul is reflected through images given in yoga training. Joseph Campbell instructs:

> The analogy is given of the surface of a pond blown by a wind. The images reflected on such a surface are broken, fragmentary, and continually flickering. But if the wind should cease and the surface become still—nirvana: "beyond or without (*nir-*) the wind (*vana*)"—we should behold, not broken images, but the perfectly formed reflection of the whole sky, the trees along the shore, the quiet depths of the pond itself, its lovely sandy bottom, and the fish. We should then see that all the broken images, formerly only fleetingly perceived, were actually but fragments of these true and steady forms, now clearly and steadily beheld. And we should have at our command thereafter both the possibility of stilling the pond, to enjoy the fundamental form and that of letting the winds blow and waters ripple, for the enjoyment of the

122

play (*lila*) of the transformations. One is no longer afraid when this comes and that goes; not even when the form that seems to be oneself disappears. For the One that is all, forever remains: transcendent—beyond all; yet also immanent—within all.[9]

Stephen's mind pond is not still: "airs romped around him, nipping and eager airs"; "they are coming, waves"; "the new air greeted him, harping in wild nerves, wind of wild air of seeds of brightness"; and "their lusts my waves." His kinetic soul, driven by youth, is still trapped in ego formation. He searches for the divine or ultimate meaning in nature but Kant find it, only ripples on the pond, changing form and deceiving masks.

Here in the vortex of mental masturbation, Stephen takes an adolescent step in art while lying down (for a more stable center) on the retaining wall of the Liffey River. He spontaneously spits out a little bit of art in the midst of energizing mental images of women in "moondrawn" menstrual cycles. By this, Joyce associates a menstruating and thus barren woman with romantic art. The relation of the female to creativity sponsors Stephen's recollection of the escape of the jailed Irish freedom fighter disguised as a bride: "How the head centre got away, authentic version. Got up as a young bride, man, veil, orangeblossoms, drove out the road to Malahide. Did, faith. Of lost leaders, the betrayed, wild escapes. Disguise, clutched at, gone, not here." The head centre, the leader of a cell in the secret independence movement isolated for security reasons, symbolizes Stephen's current ego condition. He is isolated in order to protect himself. The leader manages to escape from jail, and Stephen will escape from the limits of his condition, when associated with the female, the bride.

Unable to make contact directly with the inner meaning of nature, Stephen nonetheless spits out a poem that he hopes will mirror nature. Stephen barely finds room to write his poetry on a strip of paper torn off of Mr. Deasy's letter to the editor, commercial writing leaving precious little room for creative work. Like all young writers, he wonders whether anyone will read his work. As a proxy for his poetry with limited power to connect, he leaves on the rocks for all to see a "booger," dried mucous. And in the words of the "logos" gospel of John, the word was made flesh.

Proteus

Proteus appears in the episode under the guise of the ". . . steeds of Mananaan," his legendary Irish counterpart Mananaan McLir. He is in the foam and in the waves, "white manned seahorses." Both Proteus and Mananaan could change form but retained an underlying unity of reality. Proteus was a subject of Poseidon, our Field Marshall for time and space, and was regarded as a symbol of the primary or original matter from which the world was made.[10] The legendary Mananaan is said to have founded the Manx nation on the Island of Man, an island off Ireland.

The nature of reality Stephen experiences on the beach is patterned after the famous Conclusion by W. Pater in *The History of the Renaissance* (1873). Paraphrasing Pater: reality consists of forces and elements that fade away almost immediately—wind, waves, life and death; only to us in our flawed experiential mode do these events have any tangibility or apparent presence; and on reflection, they dissolve and the world appears to be incoherent and unstable. In this episode, many objects change or mutate in the hot house of Stephen's mental association. Even Joyce's language changes. And don't forget the most famous change artist of all time. Christ changed from god to man-god Jesus Christ and then back to god.

Stephen's Impending Change

The Alibi

Joyce puns on "arrest" by the authorities. Stephen muses about carrying a punched ticket as an alibi for murder and identifies the murderer as the "other me." The alibi would prove him not guilty and thus arrest his arrest, which gives us the very pun that is at the heart of this episode. His ego condition—his narcissism and his very personal alibi—prevents his art from producing arrest.

The Earth Moves and the Buddha Bowl Floats Upstream

Striking allusions to the legend of the Buddha promise change in Stephen in the way of arrest and detachment. They relate to events that took place immediately before the Buddha's enlightenment, the knowledge that life is suffering and detachment cures suffering.

In the milk bowl story, Buddha had been fasting as a means of seeking enlightenment. However, the fast was not working so the Buddha decided he needed more strength in order to gain enlightenment. So the daughter of a cow herder took the milk of a thousand cows, fed it to a hundred, their milk was fed to ten, their milk to one and its supercharged milk was fed to the Buddha. He drank and was refreshed. He threw the empty bowl in the river and said, "If this bowl goes **upstream**, I shall become a Buddha." Low and behold, it floated **upstream**, silently. That night the Buddha realized illumination.[11]

At the end of this episode, a much larger vehicle moves upstream: "He turned his face over a shoulder, rere regardant. Moving through the air high spars of a threemaster, her sails brailed up on the crosstrees, homing, **upstream**, silently moving, a silent ship." Since the three masted schooner is silent and thus not under motor, it is moving upstream against the current of the Liffey River of life. With three masts in the forms of crosses, it is a memorable image representing the struggle, sacrifice and compassion of Christ moving against the current of life on the incoming 1:00 p.m. tide from the eternal ocean. This image shows the force of suffering and compassion that can transcend the time aspect of the river of life.

This image of the ship is a foretaste of events to come, and suffering Bloom is right around the corner. Like the Buddha, Stephen is now prepared to reach enlightenment since he has suffered through uncompromised independence. When he does, we know that the proper medicine is detachment.

Like the Buddha's fasting, Stephen's life to date has made him spiritually thin, a threadbare ascetic. This morning Stephen preferred bitter lemon to rich milk in his tea; later with Bloom he will take rich cream in his cocoa. The shift from the lesser milk bowl in the

125

Buddha story to greater three masted schooner here suggests the lesser and greater ferryboats in Buddhist theory. The "lesser" ferryboat for achieving enlightenment is the withdrawal to an ascetic monkish life. By contrast, Stephen sees the much larger ferryboat, the three masted schooner, which represents the greater vehicle in the Mahayana Buddhist tradition. In this tradition, one does not withdraw from but participates in life with the point of view that all things including oneself are Buddha things. Illumination is referred to as reaching the far shore; Stephen is still on the near bank in Ireland, not in France.

In looking at the three masted schooner, Stephen receives an advance look at the event that will change him forever. But he doesn't know it yet. He has already had the benefit of several time warps in the first three episodes, seeing things that figure prominently later on.

The Wild Gander

The wild gander (in Sanskrit *Hamsa*) is a yoga symbol of the two-fold nature of each human being. The wild gander can swim on the surface of the ocean or walk on land but is not bound to either. When it wishes, it can arise to fly and soar. With these capacities, it symbolizes the divine essence that abides in each individual and can arise when the individual is detached from desire and loathing as to the events of individual lives.

At this point, I turn you over to Heinrich Zimmer, Joseph Campbell's guru:

> The melody of inhaling and exhaling, which the Indian yogi hears when he controls through exercises (*pranayama*) the rhythm of his breath, is regarded as a manifestation of the "inner gander." The inhalation is said to make the sound *ham* and the exhalation *sa*. [By uttering] *ham-sa*, the inner presence reveals itself to the yogi-initiate.... The song of the inner gander has a final secret to disclose. "*Ham-sa*, *ham*-sa" it sings, but at the same time, "*sa-ham*, *sa'ham*." *Sa* means "this" and ham means "I"; the lesson is, "This am I." I, the human individual, of limited consciousness, steeped in delusion, spellbound

126

by Maya, actually and fundamentally am This, or He, namely, the Atman, the Self, the Highest Being, of unlimited consciousness and existence. I am not to be identified with the perishable individual, who accepts as utterly real and fatal the processes and happenings of the psyche and the body. "I am He who is free and divine." That is the lesson sung to man by every movement of inhalation and exhalation, asserting the divine nature of Him in whom breath abides.[12]

The declaration of independence by Stephen comes as: "As I am, As I am. All or not at all." Keeping in mind the image of the inner gander, you can hear *sa ham* in the phrase *As I am*. This is Stephen's own declaration of independence. He can arise and soar to unlimited consciousness and existence.

Metaphysics Breeds the Detached Mode and Existentialism

With Aristotle and Schopenhauer on stage and Presocratic Greek philosophers in the pit, Stephen explores his favorite subject, himself, in an edifying fashion through the issues of metaphysics—the nature of time, space and being. Stephen experiences color, shapes and sounds, and looks for Proteus, the ultimate meaning within nature: "If you can put your five fingers through it it is a gate, if not a door." The gate would be a portal for understanding, a door a barrier. A gate would be a soft barrier between the self and other reality, the door a hard barrier.

As explained by Martin Heidegger in **Introduction to Metaphysics**, the original Greek meaning of *physis* from metaphysics was "self-blossoming emergence (e.g. the blossoming of a rose), opening up, unfolding, that which manifested itself in such unfolding and perseveres and endures in it"[13]. By this the early Greek philosophers understood an erect standing there and enduring, something that comes up and "becomes intrinsically stable [and] encounters, freely and spontaneously, the necessity of its [inherent] limit. . . its end. . . in the sense of fulfillment. . . . the supreme term that Aristotle used for being, *entelecheia*-the holding-itself-in the-ending (limit)"[14]. Remember the etymology of our first word ineluctable, not

127

to struggle out of, the same concept as *physis*. So that we don't miss the point about Stephen's being, he sits or lies down for much of the episode. No erect being here. He still has tremor and is not finished; he is not united or gathered in himself. He doesn't have the classical temper that is P.C. in Joyce's aesthetic theory.

Many of the concepts and images used in this episode are from the writings of Pre-Socratic and classical period Greek philosophers:

Aristotle. The episode starts with references to Aristotle and in a clear Aristotelian organizational style (first sight, then sound, then memory). Aristotle is on stage in this episode because Aristotle believed that the phenomenal world as experienced by humans is the "true guise of reality"[15]. In his view, there is only one world—the world of actual things as we see them. At this point, Stephen is sympathetic to Aristotle's view. From this starting point, however, he sees only a jumbled world of unconnected signs.

Pythagoras taught that all is change and that human souls reincarnate in plants, animals and humans. Pythagoreans laid great emphasis on the "perfect" triangle called the tetraktys.[16] This is the shape of Stephen's walking pattern. The episode echoes the "logos" doctrine of Pythagoras that numbers are the deep reality. To the Pythagoreans, the number 10 was the perfect number as the sum of first four numbers 1, 2, 3 and 4 (the ratios involved in the consonant musical intervals and the sum of the four parts of the Mandala). In his current, imperfect state, Stephen counts 5. . .6, right after the magic first four. Pythagoreans believed numbers translated to points and to lines and shapes and thus to reality. Thus Stephen first sees the moving dog as a point. The treatment of the dog in the text echoes the Pythagorean beliefs in the transmigration of souls from humans to humans and humans to animals and the kinship of all creatures. [17]

Parmenides postulated that the changing forms and motions in nature are but the appearance of a single, eternal reality that he called "Being." All is one. Change is not the reality because there is no fixed reality that exists and then changes. The reality is change itself, a **pre-existing** process. With this concept, time disappears as an important

128

function. The change is always there as the pre-existing reality. Currently this concept is referred to as "process." The reality is process; and in human life that process is built into the DNA and is inevitable. In Parmenides's view, being comes out of concealment, emerging and appearing, becoming manifest. Consider the similarities of this approach with Biblical typology.

In framing this episode, Joyce drew heavily from Parmenides's poem *On Nature*. [18] Parmenides's theory resurfaces when we reach Stephen's view of the soul—that because of prior experience the future for a particular individual is in a sense predestined.

Heraclitus. The feeling of constant motion in the wind and waves and in Stephen's thoughts reflects Heraclitus's basic theory of constant flux resulting from the struggle and tension of opposites in a fundamental unity. [19] This emphasis on opposites is embedded in the use of many pairs of opposites in this episode. [20] According to Heraclitus, a man's character is his fate, the ultimate concept in responsibility. Heraclitus was nicknamed the riddler because of the obscurity of his writings. Remember Stephen's riddle in the second episode.

God Becomes. The chain of mutation "**God becomes man becomes fish becomes barnacle goose becomes feather bed mountain**" parodies the Pre-Socratic Greek philosophers' typical theories as to evolution of primal matter, the Proteus of nature. In these theories, the purported fundamental elements of creation changed into each other in an upward or downward path (e.g. water becomes earth becomes air becomes fire).

In Stephen's system, **God becomes man** is Christ Jesus, as man eats the Eucharist. **Man becomes fish,** as man eats fish, was part of the view of Anaximander as well as the sign for Christians.[21] Fish implies fin, and Nora was working at Finn's Hotel when Joyce met her. **Fish becomes barnacle goose,** as goose eats fish, is the secular lift off Nora gave Joyce. Goose is the wild gander, and Barnacle is Nora's maiden name. **Barnacle goose becomes featherbed mountain** refers to the use of goose feathers in featherbeds and in the weighing by Anubis of souls of the dead in a scale against a feather. Summarizing this sequence, the "descent" is from God to Christ/Joyce, to Christianity/Nora, to his soul, and to death. Notice that Stephen's sequence is not that of elements but of the spirit. Notice also that each link in the chain involves some kind of death. God kills man, man eats fish, geese eat fish, and geese are killed for feathers.

Three Paths. In the discourse of the ancient Greek metaphysicians, the concept of the ultimate being of reality is explored through the connections and tensions between three pairs of concepts: being and becoming, being and appearance and being and thought. These three subject pairs are mirrored in the Stephen's thoughts on the three paths forming the triangle that he walks during this episode: (a) First path (lines 1-158), most of the musing in this section involves subjects related to being and becoming;[22] (b) Second path (lines 159-269), most of the musing in this section involves being and appearance;[23] and (c) Third path 270-end, most of the musing in this section involves being and the mind and resulting realization.[24]

Metaphysics Breeds Detachment. The theories of metaphysics are related to the theory of literary creation (Joyce's main interest) through the resulting implications of metaphysics for human detachment. Those metaphysical theories alluded to in this episode—which hold ultimate reality to be a process, a change and a series of events of becoming—support detachment and lack of ego. In these views, humans are constantly changing so how can there really be any significant "I" for the ego. The ultimate reality is not a continuing person that changes but a succession of moments of consciousness in a changing process.[25] Further, it would be pure nonsense to cling with attachment to a series of events that are forever becoming and cannot be grasped.[26] This, I believe, is the real lesson to be learned from Proteus, the change artist with the message. Here Stephen is still trapped in ego and thus still emphasizes his "I" and resulting solipsism (separation of viewer and object). But in this episode, this "I" is shown to have a fundamental weakness; it can't see deep reality. This retina is blind because it is not detached.

Stephen struggles to find an inner meaning by reading the signs of nature, but without a firm grasp on himself, he only finds the ineluctable experience of change. In this mode, he will produce romantic art. If he would only listen deeply to the change going on around him, he would realize the true nature of things at whose center detachment is the junction for art, metaphysics and spiritual freedom. Moreover and perhaps unexpectedly, detachment is the proper path to unity.

Existentialism.

Alone now with himself and without the benefit of the ultimate meaning of his being, Stephen finds the world hostile and inhospitable. And in this world he does act—he composes poetry. Lacking a grand theory that would provide vouchers for life, he is responsible to himself based on his own experience. His painful loneliness and alienation are the necessary corollaries of his egohood, separation, and consciousness of his own existence. Stephen gains courage thinking of Kevin Egan, the Irish revolutionary he visited in Paris. Like Jesus, Kevin Egan is willing to risk all for his objective. And Stephen admires him for that dedication, even though he doesn't share the same affinity for forcing political change with dynamite.

The threat to Stephen of being stuck in the world of dependence and potential failure in his existential soul struggle are symbolized by the danger of sinking in the sand and mud, which threat is presented immediately together with "the cold domed room of the tower waits . . . silent tower, entombing them blind bodies"[27]. As he decides not to return to the tower, "He lifted his feet up from the suck and turned back by the boulders. Take all, keep all. My soul walks with me, form of forms." Sinking in and being trapped in the sink holes would result in drowning: "The flood is following me. I can watch it flow past from here."

This existential theme follows organically out of the notion of Stephen as his own Jesus, discussed in connection with the first episode. In this view, Jesus is a model of the struggle we must all experience, not a proxy to protect us from the necessity of the struggle. No pain no gain. Stephen identifies directly with Christ's struggle on the cross: "Come. I thirst. Clouding over." Even with Lucifer's struggle: "All bright he falls, proud lightning of the intellect.

131

Lucifer. . . ." Lucifer, to Stephen the youthful romantic Christ, who said that the mind is its own time and space.[28]

Stephen wonders if he would have the courage to face another threat to his independence: to save a drowning man, to enter the sea and to risk drowning. This is a question about a sea change in attitude. Below the surface of this question is the issue whether Stephen can connect with anyone at all, for example Nora. More generally, the issue is whether Stephen has the potential to immerse in the mighty mother of unity, dwell in the divine spirit, penetrate behind the veil and connect with that divine unity.

This way of framing the question, whether to save another, is based on Schopenhauer's notion that the unthinking emergency reaction to save another person even at grave personal risk is based on the instinctive recognition of the fundamental unity. The fear of drowning is the fear of death of the separate ego, which in turn makes us timid.

Slaves—the Dog and Cocklepickers

A couple picking cockles passes by on the beach with their dog. Dwelling as he is on the issue of independence, Stephen projects the dog as a symbol of humans whose souls are enslaved by promises of future rewards and projects the male cocklepicker as Anubis, the Egyptian judge of the hearts of the dead. In these projections, Stephen is torturing reality, typical of the lack of limits in the lyrical romantic mode.

The dog's movements are described by overblown references to several other animals. Compared to the changes by Proteus, the list of changes in the description of the dog is missing only the lion, sudden like the present. The dog fawns before his master hoping for strokes of praise. His master kicks the dog unmercifully and yet the dog still fawns. Stephen calls the creature "the dog of my enemy" in relation to the fawning desire for approval from others, an attitude destructive of independence. When Stephen fears the dog, he thinks about fear in general, fear of hell and then "A primrose doublet, fortune's knave, smiled on my fear." Given the primrose doublet, this

132

reference is to Buck as representative of the Catholic Church, pleased that fear has been created for soul control.

The fawning dog is a symbol of the faithful in all religions that promise a final judgment of all souls. The male cocklepicker wears a brick muffler on an unshaven neck and views Stephen with a surreptitious side eye. Stephen characterizes the cocklepickers as "the red Egyptians." Since cockles are muscles (sea creatures) with two heart shaped chambers, they strongly suggest the heart or soul. Given the Egyptian reference, the male suggests the Egyptian god Anubis, the god with the jackal head and thus an unshaven neck and a dog style "side eye," as opposed to a human head with more forward eyes. Anubis in the ancient *Book of the Dead* guides the deceased in the underworld and produces his or her heart/soul for judgment.[29] The heart/soul was judged for purity by weighing it against a feather. If found heavy, the heart/soul of the unfortunate "unjustified" was eaten by a giant dog named AMAM.[30] On the beach, the representative of Anubis side eyes Stephen's Hamlet hat, which would be an unsettling reminder of rebellious genius, Anubis representing the established state religion interested in control. Note the dog's name Tatters, reflecting his uncoordinated behavior, in the context of the purpose of Egyptian religion to bring "maat" or order in life. [31]

The dog sniffs the carcass of a dead dog washed up on the beach. For this transgression, he is punished by the cocklepicker. Notice the analogy with sin. The dog is just doing something that is natural for a dog. Stephen speculates the sniffing dog is "Looking for something lost in past life," suggesting reincarnation. With the cocklepickers in the role of Anubis, their desire to punish is understandable. The reincarnation view would release the pressure to be under the control of institutional religious authorities in this **one** life. There would be many other lives in which to do better, and one could conceivably slack off in this one. With this reference, the cyclical changes in nature. . . waves, tides, shells. . . begin to merge with the cycle of reincarnation.

The view that life is a one-way ticket with opportunities to be grabbed or missed with critical one time results produces a life of fear, a lack of soul courage and a watered down guilt ridden soul that does not strive for the most. You never get a report card and don't know for sure where you stand. It produces souls who, like the dog in this episode, fawn before their cruel master. The potential god in each person is reduced to a dog.

The Two Partners

The ancient Egyptian references also take us into the "Secret of the Two Partners." In this mythology, Horus/Osiris and Seth were nominal enemies. Horus/Osiris was represented by the falcon and corresponds to our would be flyer Stephen Dedalus. Seth was represented by the bull, which as we shall see in the next episode refers to our hero Leopold Bloom. Behind the scenes this Egyptian pair agreed to a peace in which the Pharaoh ruled in "maat".[32]

In the eternal reality beyond, this pair of opposites merges to unity, the morphic field in which all forces play.[33] In our representative Dublin force field, Stephen meets Leopold Bloom, and something very important happens to both of them. Something like a minor merger of the two seemingly opposite partners. But let's not get too far ahead of our story, just enough to note this rock old mythical presentation of the same theme at the Temple level on the Nile.

References to Creation

This episode contains repeated references and allusions to creation and various theories of creation.[34] Stephen is trying to create his own character and destiny by striking out on his own. Man plays his part in creation by reproducing. Artists create art as a refinement of the cognitive process, which is itself a process of procreation of mental images, concepts and forms.

Perhaps the most elaborate creation symbol involves the rocks upon which Stephen rests and creates. These rocks suggest the myth of post-flood recreation of the human race from Ovid's *Metamorphosis*. The basic theme of that venerable work is " . . . to tell of bodies which have been transformed into shapes of a different kind." How appropriate for the Proteus episode. In this myth, Saturn was displeased with the human race and sent a flood. Deucalion and Pyrrha, left after the flood as the only humans, visited the oracle Themis whose temple had been fouled by dirty water and foul moss (see the description of Cock Lake, the Dublin counterpart of the temple to restore life). Themis issued the oracle "Depart from my temple, veil your heads, loosen the girdles of your garments and throw behind you the bones of your great mother." The enterprising human pair figured out that the bones referred to the rocks of the mother earth. After veiling their heads and loosening their tunics, they threw rocks over their shoulders. The stones changed into humans. Other animals were produced by the earth warmed by the sun.[35] To help us get this point, Joyce describes the boulders in the river wall as skulls.

Logos—the Link in Creation

Logos is the pattern or morphology of creation. In the sphere of human thought, logos is the word. With philology as the art of this episode, the word gets a big play. The writer's words are akin to the physical signs Stephen sees on the beach. Stephen plays with words. The episode plays with words. Words are the **logos** of the episode.

Listen to Martin Heidegger about the logos and the struggle:

To the opinionated life is only life; death is death and only death. But life's being is also death. Everything that enters into life also beings to die, to go toward its death, and death is at the same time life. Heraclitus says in Fragment 8: "Opposites move back and forth, the one to the other; from out of themselves they gather themselves." The conflict of the opposites is a gathering, rooted in togetherness, it is logos. The being of the essents is the supreme radiance, i.e. the greatest beauty, that which is most permanent in itself. What the Greeks meant by "beauty" was restraint. The gathering of the supreme antagonism is polemos, struggle in the senses of setting apart . . . .[36]

In this view, which is quite similar to Joyce's concept of the epiphany, creating art is participating in the struggle and power of being. When properly done, this process unfolds in epiphanies of being within the limits of classical restraint.

135

At the present time, Stephen is not gathered existentially. His mode is flawed. When he is rooted in togetherness and gathered in classical restraint, he will produce beauty in art by reference to the common unity of being. But not until then.

Sperm Becomes Art

Stephen's poetry is produced as part of a broad discourse about creation. The episode drum beats womb tomb time and sex. In this context, the power of sperm or sexual potency becomes art. Eve's pregnant belly is "taut vellum," writing paper for the artist. Many artists report a connection between libido and artistic production.

Art shares fundamental continuity properties with human reproductive processes: to the next generation sperm passes life and art passes illumination, both forms of reincarnation. Stephen's experience is on display in this episode through the museum of his memory and is the sperm for the birth of his art.

Narcissus

Like Narcissus in the forest who had lost his friends, Stephen is alone on the beach having rejected everyone in his life. Like Narcissus who found a pool, Stephen is near the ocean and Cock Lake. Like Narcissus who saw an image of himself in the still pool, Stephen feels an image of himself in the changeling Mananaan, feels the lusts of other beach invaders in his own blood and senses his own turbulence in the winds and waves. Narcissus disappeared into the pool, and Stephen urinates into Cock Lake. As his urine yellow and white foams in the water of Cock Lake, Stephen notes the following: "It flows purling, widely flowing, floating foampool, flower unfurling." His urine trace in Cock Lake mimics the yellow and white narcissus flower in the pool after Narcissus slipped underground.

Stephen wonders about the drowned man. As he imagines the drowned body on the beach, Stephen thinks, "I want his [the drowned man's] life still to be his, mine to be mine. A drowning man. . . . Five fathoms out there. Full fathom five thy father lies. . . ." Here is the counterpart of the image in the pool that Narcissus wanted to possess, the man drowned in the unity. Stephen wants to remain separate. He projects his father as the drowned man.

The Big Word

In thinking about creation as the first father of causation, Stephen thinks about his own creation and that God has willed his being. He wonders if this divine will is "the divine substance wherein Father and Son are consubstantial?" Putting the question another way: Is the divine will the substance that both the gods and humans share? If so, humans would possess divine will, presumably in their free will, the engine of possibilities. This question is more than a theoretical question for Stephen. Acting on the Jesus model, he is searching for maximum realization, which may include his share of the divine.

The relation of Father to Son or the powers that be to humans is the subject of Stephen's famous big word "contransmagnificandjewbangtantiality." This big word is made up of con . . . tantiality or consubstantiality (Church's view, Father and Son of same substance), trans . . . tantiality or transubstantiality (heretical view of Arius, not same substance, Father controls Son[37]), magnific (magnficat, the Virgin's song of thanksgiving for her mother role in the logos) and the phrase "and jew bang." The references to consubstantiality and transubstantiality debate the nature of Stephen's maximum artistic potential (as the counterpart of the Son), god-man reaching the eternal or mere man stuck in time and space. Can every son be divine? Can any? The phrase "jew bang" describes the Jewish Virgin Mary being impregnated by the Holy Ghost through the ear (in the same sense as a "gang bang" is a rape). "Bang" being a sound suggests the ear. By contrast, in Yeats's poem *Leda and the Swan*, Zeus's conjugal visit to Leda is treated as actual carnal intercourse.

This phrase "Jew bang" also anticipates, in that wonderful Joycean sort of way, the experience that gives Stephen the bang he needs to go over the hump into the divine in literature—meeting the Jewish Bloom. The related event of the date with Nora is very much on show in Stephen's thoughts: "Touch me. Soft eyes. Soft soft soft hand. I am lonely here. O, touch me soon, now. What is that word known to all men: I am quiet here alone. Sad too. Touch, touch me."

137

Toothless Kinch

The toothless kinch that appears in Stephen's imagination no doubt refers to Thomas Hardy's poem:

"Know, Time is toothless,

seen all through;

The Present, that men but see,

Is phasmal: since in a sane purview

All things are shaped to be Eternally."

Toothless Kinch equates toothless time with peaceful Stephen. When no longer agitated and eventually peaceful, Stephen will worship the eternal in the here and now.

Parallels to Hamlet

Since Stephen's soul is the focus of this episode, this episode is heavily wired into *Hamlet*. Giving us a clue, Stephen describes his own hat as "my Hamlet hat."

Like this episode, scene iv of Act I of *Hamlet* starts with references to the time and natural conditions in which human souls are locked. The temperature, the time (12 midnight vs. 12 noon in Proteus) and hearing (bells being struck) are mentioned. Hamlet meets the ghost that will talk only to him and only privately, a limited modality of reality that suggests the romantic mode in art. Hamlet is described as one who "waxes desperate with imagination." Stephen's agitated imagination and by extension his art are his ghost. Hamlet says "I'll follow them" and "my fate cries out." Stephen accepts his fate. Stephen's art becomes his own father, his ghost, driving him on.

At 12:30 p.m. Buck and Haines are waiting for Stephen at the pub "The Ship." Hamlet's uncle and mother are having a party complete with drums and trumpets while Hamlet goes to the ghost on the fortress walls. In scene v of Act I, Hamlet finds out about his father's fate through the ghost. In Chapter iv of The Odyssey, Telemachus finds out about his father's fate from Proteus through Menelaus. But Stephen is still left hanging. The next episode starts with Leopold Bloom, our Dublin Odysseus.

138

Several direct or nearly direct quotes or correspondences tie Hamlet to this episode. See this footnote for details.[38] In terms of Hamlet puns, Stephen is the son of the sun, the heir of the nipping air, and the father of his own spiritual birth.

Use of Aristotle's Theory of Soul

In this episode, we take another step up Aristotle's hierarchy of the soul to perception and imagination, away from the ring of desire in Nestor. Most of this episode is made up of Stephen's perception and creative imagery. The Kundalini imagery is missing; the next chakra is the heart. Bloom is just around the corner warming up.

Plato's Dialogues

The reference for this episode is the dialogue *Parmenides* and others in which the subject of metaphysics is discussed.

Structure, Art and Aesthetics

The very writing of this episode changes like Proteus. The voice, tense, mood and even type of language shift abruptly. As just one of many examples, consider the following description of the dog on the beach: "He rooted in the sand, dabbling, delving and stopped to listen to the air, scraped up the sand again with a fury of his claws, soon ceasing. . . ." Notice the shifts from the past tense to current gerunds to past tense to current gerunds: rooted, to dabbling and delving, to stopped and scraped, to ceasing.

The voice is mostly Stephen's interior monologue. The narrator's voice is limited in quantity and scope, is often neutral in tone and its subject matter is mostly confined to the environment, the waves and the wind. The limited scope of the narrator's role, compared to the first and second episodes, reflects the movement of Stephen through the first three episodes toward greater individual independence. Stephen has reduced the importance of the independent environment (Buck, Haines and Deasy) by his own soul stretch. In fact, Stephen "himself" is the only order, the only logos in this episode. The language used in the construction of this episode is, compared to the first, more fluid and capable of multiple meanings or a shift in meaning.

Most of the meaning of the episode is below the surface, the analog of what Stephen looks for but can't find. The surface of this

139

episode is rough and rag tag, reflecting the turbulent soul of Stephen, unlike the smooth polished surface of the first episode in which control is king. One example of the rag tag surface is the following:

> He had come nearer the edge of the sea and
> wet sand slapped his boots. The new air greeted him,
> harping in wild nerves, wind of wild air of seeds of
> brightness. Here, I am not walking out to the Kish
> lightship, am I? He stood suddenly, his feet beginning
> to sink slowly in the quaking soil. Turn back.

The first sentence in this paragraph is the neutral narrator's voice in the third person. It contains in miniature our prime elements of time and space—the visible "near the edge" and the audible "slapped." The second sentence is again in the third person but this time not so objective. Its nervous language and syntax reflect the jitter in Stephen's nervous soul. The alliterated **W**s whirl. The third sentence is pure Stephen interior monologue. The question creates a fragmented rhythm. The fourth sentence is again a mixture of the narrator as influenced by Stephen—"stood suddenly" and the "quaking" soil. The last is pure Stephen monologue.

The many instances in which Stephen's mental state affects the narrator does not just show Stephen "rubbing off" on the environment. It underlines an important message about the cost of the subjective author whose emotional reactions rub off on and limit the possibilities of his artistic productions. It also demonstrates that his current version of individuality must be paid in the coin of relativity. With individual relativity and no one fundamental truth in nature or in life, all may act differently, pursue different goals and will read signs differently producing emotional, spiritual and intellectual relativity. The many voices of Babylon.

The narrator's voice ends the episode with a beautifully smooth but somehow threatening sound for the arrival of *Rosevean*, the three masted schooner carrying bricks in her belly. This ending sequence itself is a picture of Proteus, the secret of nature:

> He turned his face over a shoulder, rere
> regardant. Moving through the air high spars of a

threemaster, her sails brailed up on the crosstrees,
homing, upstream, silently moving, a silent ship.

The word "brailed" refers to drawing in a sail or a net (to
which subject this episode is closely attuned) and speaks to us from the
ancient caves of Middle English and Ancient Celtic. The intensity of
this description, patterned in the ineluctable visual and audible, is
enhanced by the use of the present tense gerunds (moving. . . homing. .
. moving). They suggest that within a moving and changing pattern of
nature there is a continuous presence homing toward an ineluctable
end, a presence that is always there if we would only look.

****
ENDNOTES

1.   See Gorman, p. 100 for Joyce's identical philosophy.
2.   Cixuos, H. *The Exile of James Joyce*, trans. by S. Purcell (New
     York: David Lewis, 1972) p. 4.
3.   Zimmer, H. *Myths and Symbols in Indian Art and Civilization*
     (Princeton: Bollingen, 1946) p. 49-50.
4.   "The romantic temper . . . is an insecure, unsatisfied, impatient
     temper which sees no fit abode here for its ideals and chooses
     therefore to behold them under insensible figures . . . it comes to
     disregard certain limitations." CW, p. 78. In other words, the
     expression of the artist's emotion can not be held within the reality
     of nature.
5.   Ellmann, R. *The Consciousness of Joyce* (Toronto: Oxford Univ.
     Press, 1977) p. 66.
6.   In fact, Joyce apparently took the first steps toward detachment
     when, ironically enough, he started writing prose material about
     his own life. He could gain "a certain detachment from what
     happened to him, for he could reconsider and re-order it for the
     purposes of the book." Ellmann, R. *James Joyce* (Oxford: Oxford
     University Press, 1982) p. 149.
7.   Pater, W. *The Renaissance* (London: MacMillan, 1873) p. 219.
8.   The first three paragraphs are worth exploring in detail. They are

among the most satisfying in all of the book.

Lines 1--9: Stephen first thinks about space and time. Space under the " Ineluctable modality of the visible." Ineluctable means inevitable. Modality means the way of being, not being or the essence itself. The visible brings us information about space, second hand. And sight is the principal sense in Aristotle. Imagination, the locus of this episode, derived its Greek name from light. "At least that if no more." Stephen accepts the limited version that enhances the role of the rational structure. "Signatures of all things I am here to read." Stephen is looking for the divine essence or message or logos in matter (Proteus). All he has, though, are the signs (these concepts are related to theories of knowledge). Snot green is included (the divine essence from the first episode). He can't see through to the essence. Note the skillful transition to "reading" nature, which opens the subject of art and nature. He is at the limits of the diaphane, where vision ends. Stephen concludes by thinking about Aristotle and notes Aristotle's common sense acceptance of matter in space through a slip in the rigor of Aristotle's logic. Stephen happily returns to an acceptance of matter as it is, not as signs of the divine. Stephen then shuts his eyes "to see." This would be to allow his inner eye to "see" the ultimate realities.

Lines 10--20: Stephen then closes his eyes and thinks about the nature of time—*Nacheinander* (Schopenhauer's term). In this realm, reality is separated because presented one after another. By contrast the visual *Nebeneinander* is presented all at once but side by side. The art reference to the visual all at once is painting; the art reference to time is literature or music. Stephen breaks time down into small segments and thinks about the corresponding small units of space, space/time. You will remember Zeno's paradox of the tortoise and hare, showing that this is a false view of reality—it can't be understood by reductionism. Stephen wants to open his inner eye but is afraid that would give him the Hamlet problem: it would be too much; he would fall over a cliff through time. He pretends he is blind, since he is blind to the divine

142

essence. Like Hamlet's sword of steel and words, he has his ashplant. He jokes that his feet are in Buck's "hand" me down boots and trousers. He hears the sounds made by his walking, shells crushing. Shells are leftovers, as our sensory perceptions are indirect, second hand experiences. They are "wild sea money." He then remembers Mr. Deasy from the second episode, because of his collection of dead sea shells. We then get the poem "Won't you come to sandymount. Madeline the mare?" which probably brings in Epona, the Celtic mare goddess, as well as a continuing reference to anti-heterosexual behavior from the Nestor episode. Mr. Deasy would "decline the mare." We must also remember that being locked in time, space and matter is to be under the control of Poseidon, who still has our hero Odysseus locked up with Calypso. Los Demiourgos introduces Blake's position (in The Book of Los) in art and nature of the impossibility of being a poet in a father world. The los is sol or sun backwards, the sun providing the means for the visible. Waves are present as a metaphor of what the flow of reality looks like from a more distant and slower perspective.

Lines 23 –24: Stephen then thinks about rhythm, in the realm of time. Rhythm is, however, also the relationship of part to whole and part to part. Keep in mind that what we are experiencing here is art exploring the relationship of art and reality. Stephen's art, writing, cannot explain all at once like the visual but must of necessity proceed one at a time while you are reading it. However, when you have finished reading it and can perceive it as a whole for what it is, then you can see it all at once. Isn't that just splendid? He continues "Rhythm begins, you see. I hear." This is pure joking on the meaning of "see." "I hear" also suggests "I here" - I hear therefore I am. This is all play in the fields of the lord—knowledge and phenomenology and the relationship between consciousness and reality. Who would decline the mare? He opens his eyes and the world is still there (is there a noise if no one is there to hear?). This is concluded with "see now. There all the time without you: and ever shall be, world with end." This is a tribute to reality as its own end *a la* Parmenides. By using a religious phrase (in whose theory the corporeal world will end), Stephen gives his view an ironic twist.

We then abruptly switch to seeing the midwives (29). Notice the straight forward language that registers Stephen's perception. They are immediately identified with the seals through their splayed feet (and spayed souls). Stephen shifts to the mighty mother of all creation (31-32) whom we recognize from the first episode as the symbol of fertility and the power of "Space Time and Matter within whose bounds all beings arise and die." Here you relate art as creation to creation of life from nothing (a hot bed of controversy in the Catholic doctrine surrounded this phrase). Art is creation from imagination of the divine essence. Life is creation from sperm. Stephen considers the continuity of all souls through time and space through sperm and the naval cord.

9. Campbell, J. *Masks of the Gods Oriental Mythology* (New York: Penguin, 1962), pp. 27-28.

10. *Proteus*, Encyclopedia Britannica, 1983 ed., Micropaedia, vol. VIII, p. 251.

11. Campbell, J. *The Campbell Companion* (New York: Harper Collins, 1991) p. 211.

12. Zimmer, Myths, pp. 49 - 50.

13. Heidegger, M. *An Introduction to Metaphysics* (New Haven: Yale University Press, 1959) p. 14.

14. Heidegger, p. 60.

15. Beets, M.G.J. *The Coherence of Reality* (Holland: Eburon, 1986) p. 159.

16. *Pythagoreans*, Encyclopedia Britannica, 1983 Ed., Macropaedia, Vol. 15, p. 322.

17. Guthrie, W.K.C. *A History of Greek Philosophy* (Cambridge: Cambridge University Press, 1965), vol. I, p. 200.

18. See Diels, Fragmente der Vorsokratiker (available in German in 1897) translation by Kathleen Freeman in *Ancilla to the Pre-Socratic Philosophers* (Oxford: Basil Blackwell, 1948) pp. 41-50. Detailed comparison of Fragments and episode available on request (pat@greencafe.com).

19. Guthrie, History, p. 435.

20. Limit - unlimited (U3.4); odd - even (U3.9, 16, 136); one - many (U3.123) Occam's theory about the many hosts; right - left (U3.159, 270); male - female (many references); rest - motion (many references); straight - curved (Stephen walks straight, the dog moves in a curve U3.339, 356); light - dark (Stephen in sun, Buck in dark tower U3.275); good - evil (U3.385); and square - oblong (handkerchief normally square, taken up would be oblong - U3.498).

21. Freeman, p. 62.

22. The subjects include perception, birth, creation, Adam and Eve, Stephen's youth, the coming age of the Holy Ghost, the change in the eucharist, sex, reading and learning. At the end of this segment we have sewage breath, a sacrifice, ashes, thirst, broken hoops, graffiti and crucifixion (these are decay events, the result of becoming).

23. In this path, Stephen is walking toward the Pigeonhouse, originally a safe house for sailors and fishermen forced to take refuge from the stress of the weather. Likewise, appearances would be a place of refuge in the soul struggle. In this section the appearances include: the Holy Ghost as the pigeon, pregnant Mary in the eyes of Joseph, Patrice posing as an atheistic socialist, dressing the character, alibis, proudly walking, pretentious plans to be a missionary, "pretending to speak broken English. . . ," appearances that Stephen killed his mother, keeping the appearance of decency in Buck's family, marching in "proud rhythm," rocks appear as skulls, light appears as gold, incense in Paris, changing faces with acid, Paris men dressed up for conquest, sauces to hide bad meat, eucharist, appearance of father in son, appearance of Queen Victoria to journalist, appearance in bath, disguise for escape of Irish revolutionary, false love, hiding in Paris, false reputation as gay Paree and dress for the young.

24. The subjects include not returning to the tower, avoiding the waters (the flood), interpreting tide as language, realizing the threat of the dog and related risks, cataloging the history of invaders on

145

beach, recognizing his blood legacy of lust, recognizing pretenders as enemies, saving a drowning man, considering reincarnation, thinking about the cocklepickers, analyzing his dream the night before, considering Aquinas on sex, the sun and womb to tomb, writing a poem, casting his shadow to the stars, wondering whether anyone will ever read his work, day dreaming about women and women fondling him, and musing about Pan's hour, his shoes, homosexuality, speech of the waves, the drowned man, toothless kinch and the three masted schooner.

25. Coomaraswamy, A. *Buddha and the Gospel of Buddhism* (New York, G.P. Putnam's Sons, 1916) p. 944.

26. Coomaraswamy, Buddha, pp. 95, 98.

27. The phrase "them bodies" is from Yeats, W.*Rosa Alchemical in Mythologies* (New York: Collier, 1959) p. 289, which like this episode features J. Abbas, J. Swift, Pico della Mirandola and alchemy. In the Rosa Alchemical, the line is: "that the gods may make them bodies out of the substance of our hearts." This is a cry by a supernatural being while the author is undergoing an initiation dance in order to enter the Order of the Alchemical Rose. (Buck would entomb the bodies and the hearts making them blind to the true love of God.) In this series that includes The Tables of the Law and The Adoration of the Magi, we learn that the order of the Holy Ghost which is supposed to supplant the Church will be revealed by colour, music, softness and a sweet odour (p. 300). These we do not find on the beach where Stephen is; instead we find the opposite: the bright sun (the alchemical flame) rather than colors, waves and wind rather than music, sharp shells and sticky sand and mud rather than softness and sewage breath (seal skin stench) rather than sweet odour.

28. Ellmann, The Consciousness of Joyce, p. 66.

29. Budge, E. *The Gods of the Egyptians* (New York: Dover Publications, 1969) Vol. ii, pp. 261 and 262.

30. Budge, Vol. ii, p. 262.

31. *Egyptian Religion*, Encyclopedia Britannica, 1983 ed., Macropaedia, vol. 6, p. 503.

146

32. Campbell, Oriental Mythology, p. 81.
33. Zimmer, Myths, p. 46.
34. [All references to U3] 12 noon with the sun above—Hindu fire god of creation; time, space and human beings (1-20)—the residue of creation; vision and hearing (1-20)—the human's connection with the creation: vision all at once (Nebeneinander) like painting and hearing one after another (Nacheinander) like writing and music; Los—Blake's spoofing poem about creation, the Book of Urizin (Urizin representing the power of wisdom, part of the original unity, is separated out and builds a womb roof to protect himself from the celestial fire; he has difficulties because he is separate; Los representing the power of love brings order and invents time and brings Urizin under control); rhythm (23)—aspect of time and relationship of part to part in creation; "There all the time without you: and ever shall be world without end" (27-28)—concept that matter exists independently of observer, ironically described with the Catholic ritual phrase for the Kingdom of God and parallels Greek theories of the primal stuff; midwifes (32)—help with birth (as experience helps with birth of art); ocean as mighty mother (32); late Pat MacCabe (34)—death (the ineluctable companion of life); creation from nothing (35)—Hebrew theory of creation; continuity through naval cords (36-39)—continuity of human creation; Adam Kadmon and Heva (41)—first humans created by Hebrew god who created the human race; womb of sin (44)— original sin created in garden by Adam and Eve and passed to human race through the genetic bottleneck; creation of Stephen "made not begotten" (45)—Christ is the only begotten not made son in Catholic theology; lex eterna stays about Him (48)—Catholic theory of eternal God, outside time; sperm as common divine substance between God and Christ (49); Arius' clotted hinderparts (54)—homosexuality (see episode 2) hinders creation (Arius believed in the humanity of Christ and that he was subject to time and space, was born at a point in time and was like humans separated off from the Father; this view also hinders the mystical union with Christ described by St. Paul); Steeds of

147

Manaan (56)—the necromancer who combines Nebeneinander (all at once) sex and death which are normally spread out in time; Nacheinander---a Necromancer must have to press hard, particularly if rigor mortis has set in, so the next line (58) is about remembering the letter for the "press"; Stephen's father (62) referred to as "consubstantial," the theological phrase for the host turning into the blood and body as Stephen's father's sperm turned into Stephen; boys up in the hay loft (66)--Olympians(?); The cornet player (67)—Gabriel(?); Jesus wept (68) before raising Lazarus; Richie creates legal documents (80); Wilde's Requiescat (83)—poem about death of sister; malt (86)—creates whisky; little bedpal lump of love (88)—sex and sperm and incest; houses of decay (105), stagnant bay (107), fading prophecies (108)—theories of creation and decay of matter; creation of host simultaneous (all at once) in Catholic masses (120)—Occam's solution and general theory that beings should not be multiplied unnecessarily for explanation purposes (which is very Proteus like); hypostasis (124)—union of god and man in Christ in Catholic theology, the essence; creation through pray (130); sell your soul (132) for sex—create different reality a la Faust; women "invented" for sex (135); reading (136)—creating knowledge; writing books (139); Mahamanvantara (144)—Hindu theory of soul of universe from which all things emanate and return, flex and reflex; reading work similar to transmigration of soul of author (146); sewage, porter bottle, broken hoops, graffiti and human shells (148-157)—residue of life to death; Pigeonhouse (160)—Virgin Mary, virgin birth and creation of Jesus by pigeon; Kevin Egan (164)—who has become a different kind of bird (wild goose) by his revolutionary activities, he creates bombs; inventing theories about life of Jesus (166); dressing or creating the character (174); creating alibi (179); creating proud walk (184); creating plan to be missionary (192); mother died (199); Stephen creates mental images of Paris (209); cosmetics creating odor (213);   creating sauces (220); journalist creates phrase (232); creating disguises (244); teaching songs (258); forgetting (263)—decay; flood (282)—life to death;

drowned dog (286)—life to death; live dog (294)--grows visually from "a point"; legacy of blood lust (306)—creating character; pretenders creating images and generating praise (312-317); "waters: better death: lost" (330)—life to death; lost in a past life (333)—transmigration of souls; vulturing the dead (363)—death to life; dream (364)—creating images; "bride bed, child bed, bed of death, ghost candied" (306)—the creation process one after another; Oomb, all wombing tomb (402)—birth to death; creating shadows (414); emblems "hatched" on its field (417); "green heaving serpent plants, milk oozing fruits" (443)—life; from the Cock Lake the water flowed full (453)—birth; baby fish minnows come from the drowned man's trouser fly (477)—as man came from fish now fish

comes from man, life to death to life—the famous chain follows immediately (God becomes man becomes fish. . .); "dead breaths I living breathe, tread dead dust" (479)—life to death to life.

35. Ovid, Metamorphosis, pp. 39-40.
36. Heidegger, pp. 131-132.
37. In the debate as to the relationship of the Father and the Son, Arius, included in Stephen's thoughts, was branded as a heretic because of his view that Jesus did not partake of the same divine substance of the Father but instead was a perfect human, but a human nonetheless. To Arius, Jesus was at most a secondary deity or Logos subject to and subordinate to the Father.
38. For details, see the following:

Hamlet	Proteus
A nipping and an eager air (I.iv.2)	Nipping and eager airs (U3.55)

149

(ghost) tempt you toward the flood . . . or . . . the cliff that beetles o'er its base into the sea (I.iv.69) sable silvered (I.iii.240)	The flood is following me (U3.282) . . . I pace the path above the rocks, in sable silvered, hearing Elsinore's tempting flood (U3.280)
Hamlet's father says "Adieu, adieu. Remember me" (I.v.110). Note the lyrical mode!	Stephen writes a poem - "scribbled words" (U3.337) and wonders if anyone will read his work (U3.414)
Vicious mole of nature (I.iv.24) (Hamlet calls the ghost) old mole (I.v. 161)	mole of boulders (U3.279) edge of mole (U3.356)
sun breed maggots in a dead dog (II.ii.180)	dead dog (U3.286)
cockle hat and staff and his sandal shoon (IV.v.25) At his heels a stone (IV.v.32)	cockle hat and staff and hismy sandal shoon (U3.487) Stephen resting prone on boulders (U3.437)

Grapple them unto thy soul with hoops of steel (I.iii.63)	broken hoops on shore (U3.154)
Hamlet talks to Ophelia "with his head over his shoulder turned" (II.i.97)	"Stephen turned his face over a shoulder, rere regardant." (U3.503)
Queen says Hamlet has cleft my heart in twain (III.iv.160)	That gives you a cockle. We have cocklepickers (U3.342).
To try conclusions (III.iv.199)	To try conclusions (U3.50)

Further conceptual ties include:

•The ghost is in full steel and Stephen is nicknamed "steel pen" in the first episode.

•The "rose clad" morning chases off the ghost and Buck's primrose waistcoat in the first episode.

•Hamlet's speech about the uses of the world being "weary, stale, flat" (I.ii.133) and "unwholesome sandflats" (U.3.150) and tidal flats along Sandymount Strand.

•Hamlet's real father is like a sun god (I.ii.140) as 12 noon ushers in Stephen's inner freedom and art.

•The falcon call (I.v. 116) after Hamlet has seen the ghost suggests Stephen's menacing raptor like view of the world as opposed to the submissive dove (prey of the falcon) of the Holy Ghost—which should rule the world according to J. Abbas mentioned in the episode. The symbol of John, whose Book of John begins with a reference to the logos, was the eagle.

•Hamlet describes a cloud as like a whale (III.ii.351) and Stephen remembers whales on Sandymount beach (which the starving Dublin natives ate). (Unlike the fish, which in Christian iconography represented invulnerability to death and manna for the multitude, the whale blubber provided only temporary Proteus-like relief.)

•"The limed soul struggling to be free" (III.iii.68) prepares us for Stephen's feet sinking and sticking in the sand. Notes to Hamlet explain that lime is a sticky substance such as birdlime used for catching birds—see above for the falcon.

•The reference in Hamlet to the baker's daughter who was turned into an owl when she gave short measure to Christ in the baker's shop (IV.v.41) is echoed by the Proteus metamorphosis theme in general and the giving of short soul measure by not striving. And remember Buck who gave short measure to the milk maid by not paying the bill in full.

•The many changes in Hamlet's plans—go back to Wittenberg to school, stay in Denmark, go to England and return from England and his famous indecision—recall Proteus's changes.

•Hamlet changes his own destiny by forging a new commission to England over the King's signature (V.ii.33) as Stephen begins to change his own destiny by writing a poem which forges his emotions or view of nature.

The cockle hat and staff appear in Ophelia's "mad poem" (IV.v.25) in which she wonders how to identify true love (her love for Hamlet having been betrayed by her father's ambition). The cocklehat suggests the cocklepickers in this episode. They are gathering cockles and symbolize the Egyptian version of the final judgment. The cockle hat is, according to the Hamlet notes, the symbol of a pilgrim to the shrine of St. James of Compostela in Spain (martyr recorded in the New Testament). Apropos of the themes in this episode about the meaning of time and being, this same James, son of Zebedee, is the apostle whose question about the end of time sparked Christ's eschatological discourse in Mark 13.

Part II—Summary

This episode starts what is marked off as Section II. This formal division prepares for a shift from Stephen to Mr. Leopold Bloom and for a shift of the clock back to about the same time as the first episode with Stephen in the tower. Modeled on a similar shift in The Odyssey, this narrative tactic breaks the stranglehold of time on the narrative, as the message from the eternal enters our story in the unlikely person of Mr. Bloom.

Forced out of his own home by visit to Molly of Blazes Boylan, Bloom wanders around Dublin all morning, afternoon and evening. With Bloom in the legendary role of the wandering Jew, Part II captures the restless spirit of that part of The Odyssey known as the wanderings of Odysseus and Vico's chaotic stage, characterized by individualism and sterility. Bloom wanders from the butcher's to the bath, the cemetery, the newspaper office, a pub for a light lunch, the library, the bookmart, another pub for another lunch, yet another pub for an argument, the beach for fireworks, the maternity hospital, and finally to the whore house. He wanders midst the plagues of individualism and sterility.

The initial presentation of Bloom sets up an elaborate set of conjunctions and contrasts with Stephen. Betrayal is the conjunction, Stephen's artistic spirit by his family, church and state and Bloom's love and charity by the impending unfaithfulness of his wife Molly and community anti-Semitism. Betrayal exiles both from home; Stephen is displaced from the tower by Buck, and Bloom is displaced from his own home by Blazes. In the way of contrast, Stephen has a hard, cold inner orientation like the tower, Bloom a soft, compassionate nature like the lotus. Stephen strives as a heroic artist driven by images of mythical figures; Bloom is content to live a quiet and just life based on experience and memories.

Stephen is at this point independent of all emotional relationships; he is totally separate. Bloom is at the other end of the spectrum, slave to his wife Molly in a marriage in which he is wittingly cuckolded. Thus indentured, Bloom is a caricature of the risk in emotional relationships that Stephen fears—the risk of the loss to love of

153

his hard won intellectual freedom and integrity. Despite his emotional indenture, Bloom manifests an independent force field of compassion and empathy resulting from loss of ego.

As Part II opens, the main forces in Bloom's current emotional life are the sense of separation and loss in his marriage and his racial identity. Bloom and Molly have not had normal sexual relations since the death approximately 11 years ago of their 11 days-old son Rudy. Bloom has made do with substitutes. Bloom's name change from Virag to Bloom, his uncircumcised penis, and adoption of both the Protestant and Catholic faiths reflect Bloom's lack of integrity to his racial identity. His Hebrew is limited and his knowledge of Judaism weak. Masochism and guilt plague Bloom's soul because of his lack of integrity to his role as husband and his attempted assimilation that anti-Semitic Dublin society rejects.

Bloom helps Stephen through an identity crisis produced by his shallow subjective orientation. As a result of experiencing Bloom's empathy, Stephen begins a fundamental change across the whole of his soul. Helping Stephen helps Bloom to purge his soul and live his identity.

In the last episode of Part II, Joyce extends the Jewish assimilation issue to the psychological problem every human faces—the attempted assimilation of disturbing individual experiences into the collective unconscious. Part III extends the issue even further to the assimilation of every separate human individual into the collective human race.

Bloom's Jewishness is Joyce's passport for the themes of unity, continuity and the epiphanic moment as an extended moment filled with meaning, all traditional Jewish concepts.[1]

The liberating experiences of Stephen and Bloom take place in the context of the spiritual relation of father and son. Their experiences are accompanied by symbolic references to purification procedures in the Catholic Mass and Jewish ritual. Parallel references are made to the factors that influence the strength of art.

The wanderings in Part II prepare for the homecoming in life and art in Part III.

ENDNOTES

1. Nadel, I. *Joyce and the Jews* (Iowa City: University of Iowa Press, 1989) pp. 35,41,158.

Episode 4 (Calypso)

Basic Themes

Buddha and Moses Bloom has a delayed release.

This episode introduces Leopold Bloom and highlights his Buddhist-like spirit, his compassionate nature and lack of ego. He has managed a general state of compassion despite having suffered anti-Semitic discrimination. He is even compassionate with his wife despite her pending infidelity, which is (in current jargon) in his face. Bloom's immunity, which enables him to be compassionate despite what he endures, is a remarkable degree of detachment concerning his personal situation, which results from loss of ego. By contrast to those of competitive males, his soul is passive and feminine.

Bloom unifies body and soul ("kidneys were in his mind"). By contrast, Stephen's body and soul are implacable separates at this point. For Stephen's three episodes, no body organs were included in the symbolic template. Bloom starts out eating them. And given his integration of body and soul, Bloom accepts the influence of one or more organs of his body. In many ways, the presentation of Bloom anticipates Jung's view that all the organs of the body, not just those related to sex, produce energies that affect the soul, some being subject to conscious control and some not. As recommended by the good doctor Jung and his successors, Bloom is in touch with these energies and they are integrated into his psyche. Bloom, like the Jews in general, celebrates the body, the human.

It is no accident that the integrated Bloom is introduced in the fourth episode, as four symbolizes completeness and the most famous Buddha (Prince Gautama 563 BCE-483 BCE) was the fourth earthly manifestation of the Buddha spirit. Bloom is presented as a Bodhisattva (pronounced Bode he **sott** va), an elevated status in the Buddhist tradition. This status is achieved by negating the ego but remaining in the world to help others. The Bodhisattva delays his total release from the world, nirvana, in order to help others. His heart still makes room for compassion or mutual concern for others. In this respect he still suffers, but he no longer generally suffers because of his own unsatisfied personal desires, just for others. His reaction to Molly's infidelity will be the proof of the pudding on that score. By contrast, the narcissist Stephen is indifferent to others and concerned for himself. Bloom's delayed release is reflected in the intentional delay in the release of his bowels. Buddha Bloom has a delayed release.

Bloom is slave to his wife Molly. The episode opens with Bloom preparing her breakfast to order. We understand that this happens every morning. He picks up her dirty clothes. As he picks up her bra, he becomes her Brahman. The dull feeling tone allusions to institutional Hindu ritual register his indentured marital status. This slave relationship is a caricature of the risk the narcissistic Stephen senses in any emotional relationship.

Despite his marital indenture, Bloom is more free in important respects than the unattached Stephen. Bloom, our modern Moses, is free from ego; this personal Exodus has given him the gift of compassion and shared suffering and a home in the unity; and that home has given him a stable identity, which Stephen lacks at this point. To emphasize his association with Moses, Bloom's movements in and out of Molly's bedroom track Moses's movements in and out of Egypt. Moses Bloom has a delayed release from his Pharaoh.

The first paragraphs describing Bloom's preferences for inner organs are composed with classical restraint in the dramatic mode. This style of writing announces Bloom's spiritual condition. In this typically Joycean way, the point is made that this particular spiritual condition is necessary to produce this kind of art. This restrained style is used to indicate what Bloom likes. Personal preference is the usual fare for the lyrical romantic mode: I like this; I like that. Contrast this patient presentation of Bloom with the presentation of Stephen and his lyrical poetry. The dramatic method requires a delayed release of experience.

The last episode closed on the image of the brick-laden, three masted schooner coming upstream on the Liffey River. It carried the combined images of the Buddha's detached enlightenment and the suffering of the Jews (they were forced to make bricks in Egypt). The first image of this episode repeats those themes with Bloom as the detached, Semitic sufferer. Bloom is a Dublin representative of Mahayana Buddhism, the greater ferry boat for whose passengers love and knowledge are the path to release. Stephen is currently a representative of the ascetic, monkish Hinayana branch, the lesser ferry boat for whose rowers knowledge alone is the hard path to release. How they will come together is the secret of the two partners.

As with the Eucharist breakfast in the first episode, this time related episode starts with another breakfast, another ritual offering. This offering is prepared by Bloom for his wife Molly, an offering or sacrifice of ego to Molly, the great vessel of life and sex. Molly is in bed for all of this episode and is presented in reflections of the image of the Hindu goddess Maha Kali. She is the dark one who represents time, undifferentiated energy and undifferentiated consciousness. Molly is representative in Buddhist terms of craving and thirst in life. Her bed is presented in the Hebrew context as the Ark of the Covenant, this time the covenant of sex. Both covenants are suspended at this time.

Home

This episode takes place from about 8:00 a.m. to 9:00 a.m. in and near Bloom's home at 7 Eccles Street in the northeastern portion of Dublin. The scenes are set in the kitchen downstairs, the hallway near the upstairs bedroom, the way to and in the nearby butcher shop, the return home, the bedroom, the kitchen, the bedroom and then the kitchen again. Bloom moves around a lot. The clock strikes 9 bells at the end of the episode.

Action in Ulysses

The episode opens with a third person narrator's remarkably calm and extended statement about Bloom's preference for kidneys and other inner organs. Bloom is first seen down in the kitchen making

157

breakfast for Molly, whose very definite requirements he is careful to heed. The air in the kitchen is "gelid" (cold) and he feels "peckish"; by contrast, outside is "gentle morning everywhere."

The kitchen stove is heated by coals which are "reddening." He takes a water kettle off the "hob," a platform in the fireplace, and puts it directly on the coals in the stove. He anticipates his morning tea. The cat comes in, and Bloom thinks about her, talks to her and feeds her. For himself, he decides against ham and eggs because of the drought conditions in Ireland and decides instead in favor of a pork kidney at Dlugacz's, the local butcher shop. Bloom goes upstairs quietly to ask his wife, who is still asleep, if she wants anything special for breakfast. She rolls over in bed and says "Mn," which he interprets as no. He hears the loose quilts on the bed jingle and thinks about getting them "settled." He recalls the acquisition of the bed as an auction purchase by Molly's father. Her father rose in army rank from non-commissioned to officer status; such a person is known as a ranker. In his personal finances, her father made a "corner" in an unspecified kind of stamp, a monopoly seller's position designed to eliminate competition in price.

Bloom has odd personal habits. He carries a potato around in his pocket. He wears second-hand hats and coats. He goes out without locking the door because he is basically the trusting sort. Besides, he has left the key in his other pants, which signifies Bloom's condition generally (he is not "wearing the pants" in the family). Note that both Stephen and Bloom are keyless. Walking in the sun and wearing black clothes for Dignam's funeral (Stephen is also wearing black), he tries unsuccessfully to remember the word for the effect of black clothes on heat (conducts). He is more in tune with giving heat. He thinks about daily bread, daydreams about following the sun and imagines a scene that seems to be set in ancient Egypt.

He thinks about his business, canvassing ads for the *Freeman* newspaper as an independent contractor. He muses with pleasure over a thought someone else had concerning the meaning of the homerule logo for the *Freeman* newspaper (read a man is free only if he rules himself). He passes a pub and goes out of his way to be pleasant to the owner Larry O'Rourke. O'Rourke, in turn, is curt. Accustomed to this anti-

Semitic treatment, Bloom is not phased. He continues on and thinks about the pub business in Dublin.

Bloom arrives at the butchers just in time to get the last kidney. He has to wait in line behind a girl, a housemaid in his neighborhood. Her rear end awakens his sexual interest (it doesn't take much). Especially attracted to the female rear, Bloom takes joy in ass (joyass—Joyce).[1] While waiting, he reads two ads in old newspapers used in the shop as wrapping paper. Both are about business opportunities in Palestine, the home of the Jews. One is a cattle farm near Lake Tiberias organized by Moses Montefiore. The second is for Agendath Netaim (Hebrew for "Plantations Association"), a German company that for investors plants melons in the Holy Land. As the novel progresses, melons are associated with the female spheres, the human holy land. Bloom hurries out to follow the girl's rear end, but loses track of her. On the way home, he thinks about importing citrus and cattle, Sodom and Gomorra and the Dead Sea.

Upon returning home, he finds the mail has been delivered while he was out. From the bedroom, Molly calls "Poldy" (his nickname) to find whom the letters are for; she is expecting one but couldn't be bothered to get out of bed and come down herself. She apparently wants Bloom to notice a special letter. And her special letter has arrived—from Blazes Boylan setting up an appointment for that very afternoon. The delivery also contains from their daughter Milly a card for Molly and a letter for Bloom.

Bloom delivers the mail (but not the male) to the bedroom. Molly is still in bed. She is rough and impatient with him because she is hungry and thirsty. He dutifully returns to the kitchen to finish her breakfast preparations, which bear the stamp of exacting ritual. The water in the kettle has boiled, and he pours it into the teapot and puts butter and the just purchased kidney in a frying pan on the coals now vacated by the kettle (note his efficiency). He gives the wrapping paper, which contains the promises of the Promised Land, to the cat to lick. Then he skims Milly's letter and reminisces about Milly when she was five years old (she is now 15). After making sure all is in order, he carries up to Molly

159

the breakfast tray holding toast (4 pieces), butter, sugar, spoon, cream and the teapot.

Despite his first class service, Molly complains Bloom took too long. He "calmly" watches her ample breasts under the nightgown. She has opened the special letter from Blazes and partially hidden it behind her pillow. Molly reports that Milly's card tells of receiving the birthday package. Bloom asks about the special letter, and Molly tells him about her scheduled meeting with Blazes that afternoon to practice for the upcoming musical tour. The special letter is addressed to Mrs. Marion Bloom rather than Mrs. Leopold Bloom, which is a slight to Bloom's position as husband. He masochistically repeats this slight in his mind several times during the day. The name issue brings up the possession theme. Is she an independent Marion or Leopold's wife? She asks about the time of the funeral for Dignam, showing an interest in how long he will be out of the house. He understands.

Bloom picks up Molly's bra and other clothes; she is as messy as a teenager. Her mouth full of toast, she asks him to find her current book by pointing. He finds it under the bed near the orange chamberpot, which is behind the valance (curtain). Joyce intends that the reader associate this domestic image with the ultimate sacred room in the Jewish Temple, the holy of holies, which was covered by a veil. It plays that role in the last episode.

She asks Bloom for the pronunciation and meaning of the word "metempsychosis," a key concept in Hinduism/Buddhism. She has encountered this word in her popular "romantic" novel. She pronounces the word as "Met him pike hoses." She asks the question using the phrase "Who's he when he's at home?" This is the relevant question for Bloom in his marriage. Bloom explains metempsychosis as reincarnation and in the process looks at the picture of a nymph above her bed. Molly doesn't understand the explanation but doesn't persist in her effort to understand. She shifts the conversation to her current book, *Ruby: The Pride of the Ring*. She asks Bloom if Ruby was in love with "the first fellow all the time." Bloom, not having read the book, doesn't know. As this novel progresses, look back on this question as a foreshadowing of the relationship between Molly and Bloom. Molly asks Bloom to get her another book, this time by Paul de Kock, with whose name she says she is in tune. The absence in the Blooms' marriage of full sexual intercourse for approximately 11 years gives this remark a sadistic edge. Joyce indicates in his Notes to *Exiles* that Paul de Kock's novels begin a shift in sympathy toward the cuckolded husband in cuckold based novels.

Bloom randomly opens *Ruby* to an illustration showing an Italian man with a whip in hand standing over Ruby on the floor, S and M. Bloom is reminded, by the word "Ring," of cruelty to animals in the circus, a foreshadowing of events in the later Circe episode and signifying separation as did the oval in the first episode. Bloom thinks "Bone them young so they metamspychosis." This curious word, a mutation of metempsychosis, seems to read "me tames psychosis (spirit)."

Bloom tries again to explain metempsychosis. Molly still doesn't understand but does smell the kidney burning downstairs, which Bloom has forgotten. He stumbles ineptly in his rush downstairs, but manages to save most of the kidney, giving the burnt part to the cat. He eats breakfast slowly savoring each mouthful. Molly calls the cat upstairs with "Come come pussy. Come." The feline predators lounge together.

He reads the letter from his daughter Milly and muses about the correlation of her 15th birthday with the 15th day of the month. Milly is living independently in another city and working in a photography shop, another form of reproduction. Bloom accepts her sexual initiation as inevitable and part of the natural order of things.

After breakfast, his bowels begin to move, and he visits the outdoor "jakes," which they share with neighbors. While intentionally delaying the release of his bowels, he thinks about flowers and fertilizer and reads a prize-winning article in an old newspaper. The title of the article is "Matcham's Masterstroke." He enjoys the pleasure of the delayed release and thinks about writing himself (in association with Molly of course). This connects the bowel release and writing. He wipes himself with the newspaper containing the article, and leaves the jakes as the bells of a nearby church strike 9 "Heighho" sounds for 9:00 a.m.

Bloom hears the overtone, a third above the original tone. The original tone is produced by the clapper striking the bell, and the

161

overtone is produced by the continuing vibration of the bell itself. The episode ends with Bloom's own vibration, thinking compassionately about "Poor Dignam," who died recently and is to be buried that day.

Action in The Odyssey

Chapter v of The Odyssey presents Odysseus for the first time. The reliable Athena describes him as kind, righteous minded and gentle as a father. Now, however, he is suffering, chained to the "halls" of the Nymph Calypso on an isolated island. She is a goddess with significant powers, including the power to bestow on humans a certain kind of immortality. She eats the food of the gods, which requires no bowel movements, and apparently has regular sexual relations with Odysseus. He is suffering because even though Calypso bestows her favors on him, he still misses those aspects of life that are natural to and the essence of the human condition—his family, his ships and his companions. Zeus sends Hermes to this island, named "Omphalos" (also the name of the tower), to instruct Calypso to release Odysseus and to point him toward Phoenicia, which apparently is on the way home to Ithaca.

Hermes on his "lovely golden sandals" carries out his charter to Calypso, described as the "nymph of the braided tresses." Upon arriving, Hermes finds Calypso singing in her cave with a big fire going in her hearth. But Odysseus is sitting apart on the seashore and crying. Crying! Our big hero is first seen crying. As they used to say, mark that. Boys don't cry. Note that Calypso doesn't seem to care that Odysseus is crying. He cries, she sings. Calypso prepares for Hermes a welcoming meal of ambrosia and nectar, the comforting food of the gods.

Hermes informs Calypso that he has a message from Zeus. He adds, on a personal note, that he would never have come to her isolated island on his own initiative because of the lack of cities, and thus sacrifices to him, on the way. Hermes seems to be self rather than other oriented. He deliverers Zeus's instruction to release Odysseus. Upset by these instructions, Calypso whines and complains that the other gods are just jealous of her relationship with Odysseus. During her tirade, we learn that Athena was responsible for the death of many of Odysseus's companions and that Calypso saved Odysseus from the waters. Now our brave soldier pouts and cries on the shore during the day and studs for

Calypso at night. Calypso eventually relents and informs Hermes she will heed Zeus's command.

Calypso informs Odysseus that he may leave and offers to help him make a raft. Odysseus is astonished, but he quickly gains his wits and refuses to leave without her oath of support for his departure. She so swears, affectionately calling him a rascal, and prepares for him one last meal and one last night. She once again offers him immortal life without suffering, if he will only stay with her. She predicts much suffering if he leaves. Odysseus diplomatically refuses her offer and says he will take the risk.

The next morning Odysseus starts to make a big raft using auger bored holes for fittings. Skilled in this sort of thing, he finishes after a few days. Calypso gives him wine, food, clothes and steering instructions for the journey, including corn for his wallet (a leather bag). He sails toward Phoenicia for 17 days without incident, right on schedule as prescribed by Zeus. However, Poseidon, on the way back from Ethiopia, recognizes his old enemy and creates a storm at sea that threatens the hero and upsets Zeus's plan. In the storm, the raft's mast and rudder break. Ino (think about that name for a second), the daughter of Cadmus, rises from the sea to have "compassion" for him and give him a magic veil for protection. She was formerly a mortal, but is now a marine goddess, another ranker.

After two days in the water and a prayer of supplication to Poseidon, Odysseus finally manages to swim ashore on an unknown island at a tidal river outlet. His flesh is bloated, and he removes and throws away the protective veil he received from the goddess Ino. After worrying about the "female dew and evil frost of the night," he falls asleep in a protected arbor in the woods near the river.

Parallels to The Odyssey

The references in this episode to this charming chapter are legion:

Bloom is our reference for Odysseus. This is surprising at first, because Odysseus is a great warrior and Bloom is but a henpecked husband and at best a man of modest commercial achievement. Our hero Bloom is first seen in the gelid light and air, frosty for the "female dew

163

and evil frost of the night," preparing breakfast, a wifely role in 1904 Dublin. In general, Bloom demonstrates the compassion then traditionally reserved for the female sex. This indicates that Bloom has already learned the feminine side wisdom that Odysseus learns on his journey. Most significantly, both Odysseus and Bloom value the essence of humanity, what is natural to the human condition. Both experience a delayed release.

Molly is our reference for the nymph Calypso. Bloom is chained to Molly's "halls." A cheap picture of a sea nymph hangs above her bed. Both Molly and Calypso feature braided tresses. The nymph sings; Molly is a famous singer. The dark kitchen where Bloom prepares breakfast is the counterpart of Calypso's cave. While even the goddess Calypso prepares meals for Odysseus, Molly makes Bloom prepare breakfast in bed for her. True to the reference, however, Molly eventually changes and prepares breakfast for Bloom at the end of the novel. Calypso means "she who conceals things,"[2] as Molly partially conceals from Bloom the letter from and her scheduled infidelity with Blazes.

Calypso's island is out of the way time wise, from the old realm of Kronos (pre-Zeus). Her immortal world stands in the dead zone between life and eternity. For seven years, Odysseus has seen only Calypso and big birds of prey, violets and alders, cypresses and black poplars, all emblems of the dead.[3] Calypso's kind of immortality is death to the human spirit. Calypso apparently never leaves her small island, restricting her possibilities. Odysseus protects his humanity by avoiding the elimination-free food of the gods, which would make him immortal. Likewise, Bloom enjoys the release of his bowels and takes delight in his very humanity. Odysseus's delayed release from the island is the analogue for Bloom's delayed bowel release and his spiritual condition of delayed release. Note that Odysseus's relationship with the goddess is based on sex.

The movement of sunlight in the street during Bloom's trip to the butchers reflects the image of Hermes on his golden sandals. The kettle assumes the role of Odysseus on the beach and the breakfast tray his raft (more on this later). Calypso placed corn in Odysseus's wallet as Bloom has a potato (Irish corn) in his pocket.

Bloom's lack of ego is the reference for Ino ("I" no), who in compassion helps Odysseus. Negation of the "I" or ego principle helps Odysseus. He is saved by his prayer of supplication to Poseidon. We learn later in The Odyssey that Odysseus's name in a play on words means "no man." The lack of ego also protects Bloom from suffering. His detachment is Bloom's protective veil. The name Ino also prepares us for the word Ikey, which is used in this episode and means smart.

Odysseus is known as the man of many turns ("polytropos"). Notice that Bloom starts a day that has many turns. Bloom thinks about whether it would be possible to cross Dublin without passing a pub—which would require just the right number of turns. He says to Molly, "I'm going round the corner."

The many references in this and other episodes to Bloom's hat reflect a charming story in *The Illiad*. When the Greek draft board (Agamemnon, Menelaus, and Palamedes) drafted Odysseus for the Trojan War, he tried to preserve his peaceful status by feigning madness in the fields, plowing with salt. As part of this attempted ruse, he wore the pointed hat of an initiate in the Cabirian society, a mystery religion. Likewise, Bloom's hat serves in this episode as the material manifestation of spiritual principles.

Note that Calypso represents one kind of exile and immortality. Living on her own island, she is normally alone and separated from the rest of the gods. While other gods seem to like to be together and discuss matters, she is happy to live apart from her own kind without contact. She is not overjoyed to see Hermes after what must have been a long absence of her divine kin. In this separated state, she sings away in her cave near her fire midst the signs of death. She feeds on and even begs for a one-sided relationship with a human, a relationship totally lacking in mutuality. This same dead spiritual state also currently affects our main characters Stephen and Molly. At this point, they are both on separated islands of their own making, bound in ego-based exile. They both need the kind of connection that can be provided by the compassionate Bloom. He will give them a dose of the fundamental ground of being among humans in its male/female and male/male versions.

165

Traditional Schemata

The traditional schemata given by Joyce for this episode are organ—kidney, art—economics, color—orange, symbol—nymph, and technique—narrative (mature). The correspondences list Calypso as the nymph in the picture over the bed, the recall (in the sense of Hermes recalling Odysseus) as the flyer advertising return to the Holy Land, and Ithaca as Zion. Linati also lists as persons Callidike, a queen Odysseus marries in one version of the sequel to The Odyssey, and as additional symbols vagina, exile, family and Israel in bondage.

First Letter

Our hero is introduced with an **M** in the first word "Mr." This **M** stands first of all for Molly, his obsession for the day. Her first word is "Mn." The formal Mr. also introduces the restraint and impersonal aspects of the dramatic literary style. As detailed below, the M also outlines Moses's movements in and out of Egypt and Bloom's in and out of Molly's bedroom.

The fourth through the seventh episodes featuring Bloom are introduced with the letters MBMB, indicating Bloom's obsession with Molly as his wife. The nature of any obsession is to limit the possibilities of action. The time related first and fourth episodes are introduced by S and M, for the sadistic and masochistic forces that limit Bloom's character at this point .

Bloom

Leopold Bloom, in sharp contract to Stephen, has "bloomed." His soul is open, and he is caring and compassionate. He shares the sufferings of others. He manifests the marks of charity— detachment, tranquillity and humility.[4] Aside from his problems with his wife and his racial heritage, Bloom is centered and sure of his identity. Indeed, as an advertising man, he helps others establish their identity. Bloom uses the word "Ikey," which means Jew or Jewish or alternatively smart or alert. Remember hockey and Dalkey from the second episode. Bloom has the key within—the "I" key. Bloom's name unfolds to Om Blo. Om (or AUM) is the sacred sound that depicts the divine energy in the universe, and Blo for blow or breath is the pnema or the spirit.

Leopold Bloom. Leopold for the People's Prince. Nickname "Poldy" for a flower soft and unfolded, the lotus image of the ego negated and being in self-blossoming emergence.

Bloom knows what he likes, particularly kidneys. This organ separates water and waste from the blood, leaving only the purified blood as the desired substance. Purification is also the result sought by much of Jewish ritual, by the Eucharist, and by the proper literary method. As a general theme of Part II, purification and the delayed release of blood are announced by this initial emphasis on kidneys.

Bloom is anchored in the here and now of this world. He is in tune with his nature. He is frugal and objective, scientific in outlook, patient, attentive, conscientious, objectively self-critical and modest. Indeed, he is the model of an adept in Buddhism and Jung's model man. He is careful but not proud of his dress (black today for the funeral). He shows a sensual vitality. He enjoys the simple sensual pleasures—eating, eliminating, and being warm.

Bloom is first seen near the "reddening" coals of the fire. This early sentence stands all alone as a one-sentence paragraph, indicating thematic importance. Joyce's favorite image of aesthetic arrest was from Shelly in his **Defence of Poetry**—the mind becomes a ". . . fading coal, which some invisible influence, like an inconstant wind, awakens to transitory brightness . . . ." By the image of the reddening coals, Joyce signifies Bloom's compassion and that Bloom's spiritual character has developed the potential for aesthetic arrest.

Bloom cares for the cat in a kindly manner; he even thinks how the world must appear to her. Always considering the other person's point of view, even a cat's. He cares for his wife even though she criticizes him and orders him around. His lack of ego even allows him to hear his own voice.

Bloom's clothes indicate his basic character. He has no problem wearing second-hand clothes that bear the nametag of some one else. He buys them in the tram lost and found department. By contrast, second-hand clothes disturb Stephen. Homerule is what Bloom has in himself but lacks at home with Molly. Bloom muses on the identification implied by the homerule logo of the *Freeman* Newspapers: "homerule sun rising . . .

167

behind the Bank of Ireland." The scene of Joyce's date with Nora, from which his homerule started to rise, is located directly behind the Bank of Ireland when viewed from 7 Eccles Street.

Hindu Breakfast Ritual and Bloom as Bodhisattva

Bloom uses the kitchen fire to prepare for the thirsty and hungry Molly her daily breakfast, the counterpart of the continuous Hindu sacrifice of Soma to the god Agni. In institutional Hinduism, the Brahman priests conduct an endless ritual of sacrifice according to exacting rules and standards. The favorite items for Hindu sacrifice are kidneys and butter, Bloom's choice for his own breakfast. Bloom's preparation and delivery of Molly's breakfast (as her Brahman) are vested with exacting ritual. This procedure, like that of the Catholic Church, offers salvation at the cost of sacrifice. Like Calypso, these institutions, in Joyce's view, offer immortality at the cost of human death.

The Upanishads, mentioned in the first episode, reflected an effort to reduce the importance of institutional ritual sacrifice and to emphasize instead the priesthood of all believers, individuals changing their own mental outlook. The Buddha, operating within this Hindu tradition, moved even further towards individual enlightenment, just as Christ moved away from institutional Judaism. The main effort in both Hinduism and Buddhism is to negate the sense of ego in order to gain freedom from desires that produce suffering and reincarnation. But unlike institutional Hinduism, the Buddhist way is individual with each person. Here is the last reported speech of the Buddha to his followers: "Therefore . . . be ye lamps unto yourselves. Be ye a refuge to yourselves. Betake yourselves to no external refuge. . . . Look not for refuge to anyone besides yourselves. . . ."

The opening of this episode is structured with reference to Hindu/Buddhist doctrines in order to emphasize Bloom's nature as a Bodhisattva, an advanced soul who with gifts of charity and shared suffering helps others in this world get off the wheel of karma and into nirvana.[5] This spiritual enhancement comes from elimination of desire and ego. As Joseph Campbell put it: ". . . through selflessness one is released from self, and with release from self there is release from desire

168

and fear. . . . what the Bodhisattva is doing is participating in the nature of things. He is benevolence without purpose [without personal advantage]."[6]

In much of Buddhist art, the Buddha himself is not physically present because he has reached nirvana and lost his "I" status. Likewise, Bloom, who is only partially released, is missing from public view part of the time, while he is in the jakes enjoying his delayed release.

In the Hindu/Buddhist tradition, the object is to concentrate on your own Atman, you as a piece or manifestation of the divine energy. With this focus, you relate to others as pieces or manifestations of the same divine energy. In this way, love for another is love of unity in the divine energy, which is also your own Atman or Self. In other words, love of another is at the same time love of your own essential self (does that sound familiar?).

When the Buddha appeared on his throne post-enlightenment, the world burst into flowers. Our Dublin Buddha sits on a wooden throne above the aroma of his very own internal productions. However, he sees outside only a sparse flower show: "a lean file of spearmint growing by the wall." The flowers are lean because of spears (warfare) and mint (materialism). Bloom thinks of having more flowers in "bloom": "Make a summerhouse here. Scarlet runners. Virginia creepers. . . ." Runners and creepers bring to mind Kundalini or serpent power. He goes on to ruminate about organic fertilizers, since fertilization is never far from his mind.

By contrast to Bloom, the cat and Molly personify desire or selfishness, which was generally referred to in the Hindu/Buddhist traditions as "thirst." The cat is thirsty for milk and is described by reference to her rough tongue, tendency to seek attention, vindictiveness, cruelty, unreasonable fear and greed. Molly's rough tongue abuses Bloom unreasonably since she is parched and thirsty for her tea. Molly, the vessel of desire, is so hungry she doubles the toast in her mouth so she can get it all in right away. Reincarnation is symbolized as the "road of smoke," which is produced by the burned kidney right after Bloom defines metempsychosis and reincarnation for Molly. Molly only smells smoke (read endless rebirth), but Bloom returns to be near the fire, the symbol for the proper road to release.

You are What You Eat and Buddha Bodies

The first paragraph, detailing Bloom's love of eating inner organs, is a comic rendition of the Hindu/Buddhist doctrine "Thou art that." This doctrine paraphrases the notion of the fundamental unity of all creation and the creator. In this case, the doctrine is comically reduced to you are what you eat. Our ancestor warriors believed that they would assume the strengths of the enemies they had defeated by eating their testicles or their hearts. Bloom eats the inner organs of tamed animals.

He "ate with relish the inner organs of beasts and fowls." Here we are told that Bloom follows the practices of a very reformed (free) Jew and has a healthy orientation towards innards. He likes soft, moist organs, particularly kidneys with the tang of urine. Contrast Stephen with his hard inner orientation. Notice Bloom's simple pleasure in food. By contrast, Stephen intellectualizes food as the Eucharist. Bloom eats all day long, Stephen only breakfast. Kidneys are the sacrificial organ of choice both for the Hindus and the Hebrews.

The doctrine of three bodies of Buddha is encoded in the second paragraph describing the outdoors, the kitchen indoors, and the breakfast preparation. This doctrine is a presentation by visual metaphors of metaphysical concepts. The introductory phrase "Kidneys were in his mind. . ." paves the way for this allusion from intangible (mind) to tangible (kidneys). The doctrine describes the three manifestations of the divine ground of being by reference to three Buddha bodies: the first is the Primordial Buddha body, the manifestation of the primordial ground of being, described as the "Clear Light of the Void"; the second is the personal body, the manifestation in religion—what was then institutional Hinduism; and the third is the material Buddha body, the manifestation of the Transcendent in the human Prince Gautama.

The first body, the Clear Light of the Void, is signified by "Out of doors gentle summer morning everywhere," where manifold possibilities reign in freedom and softness. The second body, religion, is coded in the slavish preparation by Bloom of breakfast for Molly in the cold kitchen, separated from the gentle and warm summer morning. This

170

description indicts ritual servitude and sacrifice pursued by earthly institutional representatives of the second manifestation. Through sacrifice, they limit possibilities. Our earth Buddha, the third manifestation in our very human Bloom, is warming up in the kitchen as the counterpart of the human manifestation of the divine.

Hymn to Food

Bloom is introduced with a hymn to inner organs. One of the early Brahmanical searches to unify the microcosm with the macrocosm, part with the whole, identified food as the divine building material of the universe. Combining as it does matter and force, food was viewed as the life sap. Creatures fed on each other, but the divine sap lived on undiminished. The eaten were "reincarnated" in the eaters. This doctrine, celebrated in the ancient classic *Hymn to Food*, was highly life affirmative and led to rules of life characterized by dialectics of the body rather than logic, the reason of nature not the human mind. Bloom is introduced with a personalized menu from this Hymn.

Hebrew/Jewish Legacy

Bloom is also presented in the context of the Hebrew/Jewish legacy, particularly the Exodus from Egypt, the famous political detachment or delayed release from the forces of the Pharaoh. Since Bloom is slave to his wife, Joyce has him daydream about being in Egypt.

Bloom is associated with several personalities from the Hebrew tradition. Following the tradition of the renowned dream interpreter Joseph, Bloom has several daydreams and speculates on their meaning. The Connector Facts to the Joseph story are Bloom's being down below in the kitchen and having a second-hand coat. Before being sold to passing traders, Joseph was thrown into a pit by his brothers. They stole his coat and tore it up to support their story to their father that beasts had killed Joseph.

Bloom is most identified with Moses and the freedom of the Exodus. The name Moses is used in the episode in Moses Montefiore, a modern Moses. The biblical Moses's essential characteristics were his humility and his affinity with the father figure Yahweh. With egoless compassion, Bloom will bring Stephen out of his subjective bondage and into the father principle.

In the call by Jahweh of Moses recounted in the Book of Exodus, Moses experiences the bush burning with the fire that does not consume and through which Yahweh speaks. Yahweh's first words are "Moshe! Moshe!" Moses responds: "Here I am." Then Yahweh says, "Don't come any closer" (Ex. 3:14).

Our Dublin Moses uses a more detached response in his first speech. Upon seeing the cat that is seeking attention and food, Bloom responds not "Here I am" but "O, there you are. . . ." So Bloom refers not to himself but to other, signifying his detachment. Completing the connections, the Buddhist name for ego is "Aham," which literally means "here I am."

Despite Yahweh's injunction not to come closer, the compassionate Bloom spends the rest of the episode trying to come closer to everyone he meets: the cat, Larry O'Rourke, the girl from next door and to Molly. Molly's connection to the burning bush is the product of her sexual longings, which after 11 years are quite natural.

This interpretation of Bloom's opening remarks in the context of Moses and the burning bush casts the cat, the symbol of selfishness, as Yahweh! This must be the tribal god that was only interested in the Jews. The cat puts up with Bloom's affection only before getting the milk and then leaves immediately (continuous sacrifice to Yahweh required). The cat, initially related to Yahweh by the all-important first speaking lines, is also tied to the black panther in Haines's dream in the first episode by the cat's description as "the lithe black form." The cat as the panther tamed would reflect the impotence of Yahweh while the Jews were in bondage in Egypt. Bloom muses about clipping the cat's whiskers, as Yahweh's horns were clipped during the bondage. Here our Dublin Moses is in bondage to his own Pharaoh, his wife Molly. These references, considered in combination, view Jahweh the Old Testament god as a projection of aspects of the human mind, in this case a projection of the jealous and violent forces of the human unconscious onto a jealous and violent deity.[7]

According to the Jewish Legends (only some of which are in the Bible), Moses's political prominence peaked during his first stay in Egypt after he had led a military victory over invading Ethiopians. The record of this victory contains the first recorded use of an air force. Moses used birds to eat the serpents that otherwise infested and thereby blocked the land route he wanted to use. With this route cleared ecologically by birds, Moses and the Egyptians gained the element of surprise and drove the Ethiopians out of Egypt and back to their own fortress. There the standoff was ended by the Ethiopian Princess who agreed to marry Moses if he would lift the siege. Moses agreed.[8] We hear nothing of this wife afterward. The Dublin representative of the Holy Ghost (the spiritual air force), Bloom counts sausages in the butcher shop, sausages that have the same form as dead serpents. He has married Molly, a dark Spaniard, after a courting siege.

After Moses's military victory, the Pharaoh became jealous and concerned about Moses's political power and betrayed Moses to his political enemies at court. Moses was driven out of Egypt. Likewise, Bloom's Pharaoh Molly selfishly betrays Bloom during the day and drives him out of the house.

Out of Egypt and in Midian, Moses helped three young girls obtain water at a well by driving off shepherds who were blocking their access. Apparently water was scarce. He was rewarded by Raquel (AKA Jethro), the father of these girls, with the hand of one of them. For his new father-in-law, Moses tended cattle. Here Bloom daydreams about cattle, and the parallel Dublin drought is reflected in Bloom's thoughtful decision not to have ham and eggs for breakfast.

While tending Jethro's cattle at a remote and traditionally sacred location, Moses encountered the burning bush and heard Yahweh exhort him to return to Egypt to free his people. So Moses returned to Egypt with his brother Aaron as his mouthpiece, Moses being insecure as a stand up speaker. They carried as signs of their authority a magic staff and the knowledge of the sacred name of Yahweh—an archaic verb form of the verb "to be" that means something like I AM THAT I AM or I WILL BE THAT I WILL BE. Note that the name Yahweh is fundamentally connected with being and independence.

Moses first used the magic staff with the Pharaoh, in an effort to free the Hebrews, by turning the staff into snakes. The Pharaoh's house magicians matched this trick, but Moses's snakes ate the Egyptian snakes. This victory is echoed in the sausages Bloom sees:

> He halted before Dlugacz's window, staring at the hanks of sausages, polonies, black and white. Fifteen multiplied by. The figures whitened in his mind, unsolved: displeased, he let them fade. The shiny links, packed with forcemeat, fed his gaze and he breathed in tranquilly the lukewarm breath of cooked spicy pigs' blood.

The white sausage would presumably be the Hebrew's snakes and the dark sausage the Egyptians. The "forcemeat" would be the result of one snake eating another.

The captive Jews in Egypt were forced to make bricks for the Pharaoh's building projects. They worked in the "brickfields." The three masted schooner *Rosevean* is carrying bricks in her hold. In the last of the plagues caused by Moses to force the Pharaoh to give the Jews their delayed release from brickfield slavery, the avenging angel killed the first born of the Egyptians in the "Passover." Here Bloom daydreams an Egyptian scene in which a mother nervously hides her children from him. Bloom's previous argument with his daughter Milly about her bracelet recalls Yahweh's order, recounted in Ex 33:6, for the Jews to remove all their ornaments (ego oriented) during the exodus.

Moses and Yahweh spoke of the promised land, which didn't pan out right away. Moses got to see it from a mountaintop but not enter, a voyeur of sorts. Here Bloom reads ads for business schemes in Palestine that involve restoring the land. As an ad man himself, he knows enough to suspect these come-ons, but nonetheless blesses them as a good idea. These represent a return to Zion by restoring the land to production. In biblical typological interpretation, the restoration of the Promised Land of Israel is treated as a type (the first of two related events) for the Kingdom of God. Here it is used as a symbol of potential renewal of Bloom.

Through very subtle allusions, the restored promised land is identified as the consummated marital and family life. The first ad for cattle raising near Tiberias, the city founded by Herod Antipas, suggests spiritual and emotional slavery. The second ad for raising oranges, citrons (a type of watermelon) and olives near Jaffa suggests the consummated marriage as the promised land. The ad claims "Your name [is] entered for life as owner in the book of the **union**." The promoter's address is Bleibtreustrasse 34, Berlin 15. Molly's age is 34 and Milly's 15. Bleibtreustrasse means "stay true street." Citrons, signifying Molly's female spheres, are juicy indeed but grow on a plant with thorns. Melons are popular dream subjects for both Stephen and Bloom. In keeping with this symbolism, Bloom sees the current reality of the Promised Land, and the current state of his marriage, as the Dead Sea. This is where the Jews actually ended up, and Bloom calls it "the gray sunken cunt of the world."

On their journey in the wilderness, the Jews ran out of food, and Yahweh provided "manna from heaven," a bread like substance that came each day with the morning dew. The Jews were commanded to eat it and not save it for the next day, seemingly an anti-accumulation or "trust me every day" suggestion. True to the commandment, Bloom thinks about hot daily bread, but Molly likes day old (which is harder).

Moses starts in Palestine, comes to Egypt, leaves, returns and leaves. Our hero is likewise first in the kitchen and away from Molly's bedroom on his errand, then in the bedroom with the letters, then out to the kitchen, then back in the bedroom with her tray and finally back to the kitchen from which he leaves the house. He is in and out with reference to her bedroom, the bedroom of Bloom's captivity, in the same pattern as Moses was in and out with reference to Egypt. This common pattern, when drawn horizontally with time running from left to right and with Egypt (or the bedroom) as the top points and Palestine (or freedom from Molly) as the bottom points, looks an "M," the first letter of the episode.

The famous Ark of the Covenant shows up here as Molly's bed. Her bed has "loose brass quoits" on the posts that jingle when she turns over. Quoits are rings used in a game the object of which is to get a pole through the ring (suggestive?). Poles inserted through gold rings carried the Ark. The top of the Ark was decorated with pictures of cherubims; above Molly's bed is a photograph of a nymph. Bloom cut the photograph out of a magazine *PhotoBits*. Bloom would like to get the bed "settled," as he wishes Molly would settle sexually. This leaves sex as the covenant in Molly's world. The covenant of life is sex. The ark is Molly and her vagina. Her sexual and maternal instincts fuel the species, but not necessarily the individual. The only covenant with the vessel of life is sex, the "gift" or curse from the Garden of Eden, sex and death.

Hebrew or Hapiru originally described their practice of hiring themselves out for pay. Our Bloom is a free lancer, an independent contractor in the ad business. As the Jews wear talismans of their heritage, Bloom carries a potato (Irish) around his pocket. As Moses's people broke their first stone tablets, Bloom uses the prize essay to wipe himself, the essay that begins and ends "morally." It was titled "Matcham's Masterpiece," and Matcham translates to Yahweh of the burning bush: Matcham or Match I am.

Moses, an Egyptian name, means "He Who Pulls Out."[9] Likewise, Bloom has pulled out in regard to his role as sexual lover to his wife. He now ejaculates on her buttocks, his Sodom.

Wandering Jew

Bloom, who wanders all over Dublin while shut out of his own house, is representative of the legend of the wandering Jew. In this legend, Jesus paused while carrying the cross on the way to Golgotha. He leaned for a moment against the house of a Jew. The Jew came out and ordered Jesus to keep moving. Jesus moved on, but in the process condemned the Jew to wander the earth forever. As Part II unfolds, we discover that Bloom's marital problem, which causes him to wander around town all day, is based on guilt.

Kundalini

Bloom starts in the bottom of the third chakra. In the arena of mastery and control, he is slave to Molly but generally in control of himself. Molly is in the converse position, in control of Bloom but generally not of herself. The symbols of the third chakra are reflected in the organs around the navel that Bloom eats, fire that he uses for sacrifice, the color red for the "reddening coals," the sense of sight that he uses keenly throughout the episode, and the anal cavity that hosts his delayed bowel movement.

He warms up to the fourth chakra of the heart, in Sanskrit *Anahata* (notice hat). Its symbols are the heart, air, smoky, touch, penis and the sound of Om made without objects striking each other. These represent experiences Bloom has in this episode, the energies of the third chakra properly sublimated feeding the fourth chakra. He goes out into the gentle summer morning air, uses the fire to produce reddening coals, makes smoke and would like to be in touch particularly with his penis.

Bloom warmed by the fire is at the fourth chakra, the level of the heart represented by a luminous, 12 petalled red lotus, here in the form of the reddening coals. In the auditory realm, the fourth chakra is represented by the sound of Om "not hit"[10]. The sound not hit, that is not made by two objects struck against each other, appears as the third overtone that Bloom hears as the church bells ring. An overtone is made by the bell itself due to its own continuing internal vibration, not by being struck. The overtone is a delayed release from the bell. Bloom's own continuing internal vibration is his detached compassion signified by his delayed release. In the presence of this auditory metaphor of non-violence, Bloom feels compassion for the deceased Dignam. He unites in pity with the family sufferers and with the memory of Dignam in the secret cause, the artistic subjects that reflect the attitude of the fourth chakra.

A Bodhisattva remains in the fourth chakra, having rejected the complete release of the ultimate seventh chakra. That last chakra is centered on the crown of the head and is represented by the flames of illumination. The internal band of Bloom's hat, which sits on the crown of his head, carries the manufacturer's logo "Plasto's High Grade Ha" (the t is missing). The emphasis on Bloom's hat also relates to the Sanskrit words *arahat* and *mahatma*, which mean release from desire. In this episode, Bloom forgets his hat because of his concern about his wife.

When the kundalini is roused, she is felt as heat. Each of the chakras "blooms" as the kundalini passes through. In order to start her up, she must be centered in the correct channel and removed from the

177

two side channels (Ida and Pingala of male and female), each of which separately pursued is a dead end.[11] This centering in the correct channel requires the combination of male and female attributes that Bloom represents. In relation to the gods, the human soul is always passive and feminine.[12] When the kundalini falls back down in lowered realization, she is felt as chill. Here she falls back in Bloom as he worries about Molly: "Cold oils slid along his veins, chilling his blood"; and "A soft qualm, regret, flowed down his backbone, increasing."

Molly

Bloom as Brahman serves Molly as Maha Kali, the Hindu Time Goddess and the destructive manifestation of the divine energy. Bloom is yoked to her, the original meaning of Yoga. She is asleep in the dark. Her shape is covered by her nightclothes. Feel the image as she wakes up for breakfast:

> She set the brasses jingling as she readied
> herself briskly, an elbow on the pillow. He looked
> calmly down on her bulk and between her large soft
> bubs, sloping within her nightdress like a shegoat's
> udder. The warmth of her couched body rose on the
> air, mingling with the fragrance of the tea she poured.

Bloom picks up her bra and thus becomes her Brahman. The bra, designed to create illusion and desire.

As Maha Kali maintained burning grounds for her victims, Molly instructs Bloom to scald the teapot. She requires his submission to her rhythmic order of breakfast just so and not too late. Like Maha Kali, she must have her own way, is dark (Molly is part Spanish) and is large.

Molly is first seen asleep, in the unconscious world where the instincts rule. She doesn't want to wake up. Her several grammatical mistakes and her pornographic reading preferences reveal her basic connections. Her first word is "Mn" in a "soft grunt." This sound contains from the mystic word AUM the M sound; it signifies the undifferentiated consciousness (A for waking, U for dreaming and M for undifferentiated consciousness).

Molly indirectly tells Bloom to stay out of the house by asking him at what time the funeral is scheduled. She makes Bloom get the mail even though she has heard it arrive. She expects a letter from Blazes and wants Bloom to see it. She rubs his nose in it. He asks about the letter, and she tells him Blazes is coming that afternoon at 4:00 p.m. to organize their upcoming concert tour. Boylan is bringing the "programme"—no doubt. Even the song chosen for their practice is a story of seduction, *La ci darem* from **Don Giovanni** . She hides the letter and then in a "you know that I know that you know," she tells him to stay out of the house. Bloom plays this game on the blinds; Bloom asks if she wants the blinds open.

Selfishness

Selfishness is the opposite of compassion. Compassion is related to self-generated warmth and selfishness to coldness. "Gelid light and air were in the kitchen but out of doors gentle summer morning everywhere." This is our first description of the atmosphere or surroundings. Gelid is an unusual word that attracts your attention, and it means cold or frosty. So we have cold on the inside in the kitchen (where servitude reigns) and warm on the outside (where freedom reigns). This makes Bloom feel "peckish," a word meaning hungry and irritable no doubt chosen for its association with henpecked. He is hungry and wants to be warm on the inside. The kidney breakfast fuels his soul. The next line is "The coals were reddening."

The next objects of attention are the kettle and the teapot. They, too, are warmed up. The kettle is taken off the "hob." "It sat there, dull and squat, its spout stuck out." The hob is a shelf in the fireplace for keeping the kettle warm. Another meaning of hob is a rustic or a lout. Is this our Odysseus crying on the beach? Could be this our hero before he warms up because Calypso lets him go? Odysseus is first seen on the rocks on the beach, a shelf of the land, as the kettle is on the shelf on the fireplace. Both are sitting. The kettle is described by a peculiar reference to the spout, which in this seam of associations seems vaguely phallic. Odysseus is squat because he has short legs and a long trunk. He is pouting on the beach.

Then comes the cat, the model of selfishness. Cats are only affectionate when they want something. And this pussycat wants milk and blood on her rough tongue. After she gets what she wants, she

179

deserts Bloom and joins Molly in the bed. Molly calls her with "come, come, pussy. Come." You don't have to be a sexual pervert to realize the lust-oriented connotations of that line. The cat's green eyes recall the green jewel on Haines's cigarette case.

Bloom muses about cats going after mice. He unconsciously compares himself to a mouse that does not squeal; he doesn't complain even though he is Molly's plaything. Similarly, he laughs at the cat's fear of chickens, as Bloom is henpecked. His attitude suggests masochism, a frequent subject in Bloom's magazine *PhotoBits*. He thinks about the cat's face whiskers as feelers in the dark, the darkness of ego exile.

Selfishness operates through possession. Consider this sentence that is framed by the references to his father-in-law's monopolistic corner in stamps:

> "His hand took his hat from the peg over his initialed
> heavy overcoat and his lost property office secondhand
> waterproof. ."

Four "hises," the indicia of possession and the sound of snakes. Bloom thinks "stamps: sticky back pictures." Here sticky is for possession, which has entered Bloom's mind because of his memory of his father-in-law's corner in stamps, an economic achievement in possession. Molly has inherited this trait, the desire for possession. The association of possession and ego continues in the next reference to his hat's manufacturer, "Plasto's." Bloom laughs at this name because the apostrophe suggests possession and plast means combining. These are the opposites: possession proceeds from separateness and combining from unity.

Stephen and Bloom

Through connections between this and the first three episodes, the secret of the Two Partners begins to develop between Stephen and Bloom. The details in this episode repeat numerous subjects contained in the first three episodes (schoolboys, pier, black cat, lips, kiss, dog, hat and bell ringing). These common details begin to build a web between Stephen and Bloom.

The nature of this web has received several possible explanations. Joseph Campbell is of the view that many of these common details serve as premonitions, which if we were only sufficiently sensitive are there for us to read. He also suggests the events are tied together by a process that Jung called synchronicity. This concept is a mysterious relationship of events producing a common course but not in the nature of cause and effect. Jung finds this relationship in the *I Ching*. Other suggestions include the theory of parallax—different events as seen from different angles by two separate viewers.

My preferred interpretation of the developing connections between Stephen and Bloom involves the traditional concepts of unity and relativity, but with a modern twist. Under this concept, each human is like a separate ship floating in the sea of unity of being. The view from each ship is relative, like parallax. The nature of the unity of being is not strong like a solid but weak like a fluid and partial, producing both separateness and connections and thus endless possibilities. The unity is also reflected in the common land marks encountered. These common land marks are registered in the connections between the worlds of Bloom and Stephen. In current theoretical terms, this type of influence is called morphic resonance and operates at a distance like a force field (in the theories of Rupert Sheldrake in *Presence of the Past*).

Hermes

Hermes is the messenger in The Odyssey who carries Zeus's release instructions to Calypso. He carries out the compassion/selfishness theme because of his remark to Calypso that he wouldn't have bothered to come to her area without an order from Zeus, since there were no sacrifices to him on the way.

In addition to his role as the messenger of the gods, Hermes was also representative of consciousness and wisdom, with a tinge of shrewdness and larceny (which returns in the Jewish expression "Ikey"). Hermes's image appears in the streets at the same time as Bloom: "Quick warm sunlight came running from **Berkeley** Road, swiftly, in slim sandals. . . ." By this association, Joyce connects Hermes in his wisdom role with the philosophical doctrines of George Berkeley, the Bishop of Cloyne, whose radical theory of perception was summarized as "To be is to be perceived."

181

Like Bloom, Hermes was associated with cattle and dreams. His sacred number was four. This is the fourth episode. In later episodes, Bloom appears as Hermes in his role as guide to the eternal. In this episode, Hermes's role as the spirit of commerce neuters the language describing Bloom's commercial transaction with the butcher:

> His hand accepted the most tender gland and slid it into
> a sidepocket. Then it fetched up three coins from his
> trousers' pocket and laid them on the rubber prickles.
> They lay, were read quickly and quickly slide, disc by
> disc, into the till.

The persons involved in this commercial transaction are reduced to the absolute minimum. Bloom becomes his hand. The rest of the transaction is described in terms of the coins; the butcher is not mentioned.

Milly and Molly

Milly is Molly's and Bloom's 15-year-old daughter who is working and living away from home. She has met a student named O'Bannon where she is working. Buck's brother, we learned in the Telemachus episode, is down with the O'Bannon's. She is probably near sexual initiation since her physical circumstances are certainly free. Note how liberal Bloom and Molly have been with her at such an early age. Later Molly tries to read a sinister purpose into Bloom's cooperation in this regard. Note that Milly sends her message about the new boyfriend in a letter to Bloom; this hides the news from Molly. Too involved with her own plans, Molly doesn't ask about the letter to Bloom from Milly.

I can't resist the comparison in names: Milly to Molly, change an "i" to an "o." This symbolizes the comparison of virgin to a maternally tested vagina, as well as a more egoistic personal approach of the young ("I").

Purification

Our hero Bloom starts off his day with a sacrifice and then is off on his wandering voyage. Later the narrator will refer, in terms of Jewish ritual, to the preparation of breakfast as the "burnt offering" and to the "intestinal congestion and premeditative defecation" as the "holy of holies."

In Jewish ritual, the regular burnt offering, as opposed to the holocaust, involved burning only part of the animal in sacrifice to god. The rest was retained by the party making the sacrifice for personal consumption. Bloom himself is the burnt offering in this novel. He offers sacrifice through compassion. To make this identification, Bloom eats kidney, the part normally sacrificed, after it has been burned partially while Bloom is taking care of Molly. The holy of holies was the ultimate room in the Temple in Jerusalem (destroyed by the Romans 70 CE) where the ark held the Torah, the most sacred items to the Jews. The Bloom bedroom at this point holds only pornography. Bloom's most sacred items are his humanity and compassion, signified by his delayed release – his premeditative defecation.

In the Mass, Bloom's sacrifices to Molly correspond to the Offertory, when the bread is brought into relation to Christ and marked for the sacrifice. In art, the corresponding reference would be the sacrifice of patience through a delayed and cooled release of experience inherent in the dramatic method. Purification is underway.

Structure, Art and Aesthetics

The references in Part I to Hamlet, Aristotle and Plato's dialogues are not continued. This episode is based on a series of movements away from and back to Bloom's house, action in the physical world rather than the conceptual nightmare of Stephen.

The language for our hero Bloom is light and clear. When the narrator's voice takes on its own identity, it is scholarly, supportive of the picture of Bloom. The episode alternates between a very restrained and controlled third person narrator's voice and Bloom's own thoughts. Molly's thoughts are not presented. Neither are the cat's, the butcher's, the girl next door's or Larry O'Rourke's, the only other characters who appear in this episode.

The symbolism in this episode commingles with Bloom's character in a more integral way than the earlier metaphors did with Buck, Haines and Stephen. The Hindu/Buddhist and Hebrew legacies are presented as a fundamental part of his character. The episode gives off the impression of organic wholeness.

****

ENDNOTES

1. I first saw this correspondence in Brivic, S. *The Veil of Signs* (Evanston: University of Illinois Press, 1991).
2. Graves, Greek Myths, p. 730.
3. Graves, Greek Myths, p. 370.
4. Huxley, A. *The Perennial Philosophy* (New York: Harper & Row, 1944) p. 92.
5. Basham, pp. 274-275.
6. Campbell, Myths to live By, p. 155.
7. Several pre-Jungian psychologists in the 19th century identified the unconscious with god. Noon, W. *Joyce and Acquinas* (New Haven: Yale University Press, 1957) p. 135.
8. Legends, Vol. III.
9. Cahill, T. *The Gifts of the Jews* (New York: Doubleday, 1998) p. 103.
10. Campbell, J. *Early Hindu and Buddhist Myths* audiotape, Big Sur Tapes (1993).
11. Avalon, A. *The Serpent Power* (New York: Dover Publications, 1953) pp. 229-230.
12. Campbell, Oriental Mythology, p. 165.

Episode 5 (Lotus-eaters)

Basic Themes

Bloom loses touch with himself.

Wounded by expected spousal betrayal, Bloom seeks the comfort of his secret life. In his secret life, Bloom pretends to be a writer. Under the alias Henry Flower, he has advertised seeking typing help for a "literary gentleman," and an apparently normal initial response from Martha Clifford has developed into an intoxicating pen pal relationship. Bloom substitutes giving mail to Martha for giving male to Molly. Since

184

Molly received mail from Blazes, Bloom goes to the post office to see if he has mail from Martha. He does! Bloom has mail!

Bloom's seductive secret life is presented as one of the lotus forces that compromise integrity to identity. For Odysseus and his crew, eating the local lotus fruit meant losing their initiative and desire to go home. Momentarily under the lotus influence, Bloom loses touch with his essential identity. For Bloom in particular, this includes loss of his Judaism in the interests of assimilation in Irish society. For all Dubliners, the lotus forces include stimulants, intoxicants, masturbation, ambition, advertisements and most of all the Catholic Eucharist. Now add TV and drugs. Like the corresponding pornographic mode in literature, these seductions produce only limited, temporary satisfaction while the true way requires suffering but produces long-term satisfaction.

Bloom temporarily falls from grace in order to emphasize what grace is—living your life without compromise, with sincerity, on the basis of your own identity and realization and, if necessary, in the teeth of suffering. The lotus forces compromise this effort through addiction to temporary comfort and avoidance of suffering. Bloom's fall from grace is traced in myth through lotus fruit to the apple in the Fall in the Garden of Eden, the crime in the park. The effect of the Fall in the Garden appears in the submission called for by the Eucharist and the Sacred Heart cult, forces on show in this episode. The Fall is reproduced in Bob Doran's annual bender, an all day drunk, and even produces totally vertical poetry, one word per line, the ultimate fall in words.

The personal force necessary to resist the seduction of temporary comforts is personal control or will power, the domain of the fifth chakra. In this episode, Bloom's will power waxes and wanes against the lotus forces. His status in this struggle is indicated by the location of the Henry Flower identity card, in his waist coat pocket when losing and in his hat band when winning.

In the initial part of the episode, the identity card is in his lower waist coat pocket, and Bloom's orientation is that of the lower inner and sexual organ chakras, the body counterparts of temporary comforts. This episode is the time counterpart of the Nestor episode, in which the same forces of the second and third chakras are in full play in the school. In this state, Bloom treats rudely an acquaintance who is being perfectly civil. To his credit, Bloom's display of these lower energies is definitely low voltage.

The Hindu image of Dancing Shiva flits through the episode. Shiva's gracefully raised left leg symbolizes release from the temporary passions. Shiva is the god resident in the fifth chakra and, true to himself, all of his gestures are born solely of his own nature. Shiva appears in the image of a dignified woman Bloom sees across the street, and Shiva's form is traced in abstract outline in the seemingly indirect and wandering movements of Bloom on his way to the post office. Under the influence of the lotus forces, Bloom fails to sense in the dignified woman the aspects of self-control. Drawing the wrong lesson from this experience, he concentrates on getting a sexually arousing, temporary glimpse of the dignified woman's leg as it is raised to mount a carriage.

The first commandment of personal integrity is to "know thyself." Since "know" is used biblically to mean sexual relations as well as understanding, lotus-mode Bloom thinks about masturbating in his bath, sex with himself or the wrong form of knowing himself. But he doesn't. In both senses Bloom loses touch with himself.

Eastern Dublin

During this episode, Bloom walks in the easternmost portion of Dublin. The shape of the city looks like the head of a penis.[1] The area where Bloom walks would be the opening of the penis. The penis is the organ for this episode, and the symbol of Shiva. Many of its uses qualify for the temporary comfort lotus-eater category. This portion of the City holds many of the purveyors of lotus leaves: the Salvation Army, the Church, the undertakers and the tea company. The time is between 10:00 and 11:00 a.m.

Action in Ulysses.

Hoping he has mail (read male) from Martha, Bloom walks indirectly to the Westland Row Post Office. He uses this post office, which is distant from his house, so he won't be recognized. A letter from Martha would be particularly sweet for his bruised male ego, given Molly's letter from Blazes, and is a low grade Old Testament "eye for an eye." To pick up his secret mail, he uses a printed identity card under the

186

alias Henry Flower. He normally hides this card in his hat band. He is pretending to be someone he isn't.

While walking toward the Post Office, Bloom's thoughts are driven by whatever he sees along the way: a boy picking through garbage cans with a cigarette in his mouth; a young girl eyeing the boy; Bethel, the Hebrew name used by the Salvation Army; the undertakers, for the last address; and the Tea Company. Bloom strolls along and sings dance type songs, a Connector Fact for Shiva's dance.

Twice he takes off his hat to cool his head and brush his hair. If Joyce has something happen twice, it contains a message. Bloom thinks about the logo in his hat: "high grade ha." The "t" has been worn off the manufacturer's logo inscribed on the internal hat band—"Plasto's High Grade Ha(t)." In the lotus mood, Bloom is in for a low go. He moves the identity card from the hat band to his waist pocket, near the inner organs. He thinks about living in a hot climate and the resulting lethargy. The Oriental lotus-eater imagery is fairly direct:

. . . (tea) made of the finest Ceylon [so long] brands.
The far east. Lovely spot It must be: the garden of the
world, big lazy leaves to float about on . . . lobbing
about in the sun in *dolce far niente*, not doing a hand's
turn all day.[parenthesis added]

The Orient beckons with idleness, comfort and fatalism. He thinks about floating without effort in the salt laden Dead Sea and, under the lotus influence, tries without success to remember the scientific formula for volume/weight displacement. He tries to walk like the neighbor girl he saw at the butcher's shop (in the 4th episode) and saunters with a careless air, the lotus walk.

After approaching the post office in an indirect manner and making sure no one is present to recognize him, he asks for any letters using his Henry Flower identity card. The card avoids the need to give his false name out loud, which might be overheard. While waiting, he sees a military recruiting poster and contemplates military discipline as a type of hypnotism. He does receive a letter from Martha, which he is hot to read. He rips open the envelope, but his satisfaction is interrupted by the arrival of M'Coy, who happens by in front of the post office.

Bloom and M'Coy pass the time talking about Dignam's funeral. M'Coy's wife is also a professional singer, and he brings up the subject of upcoming singing prospects for his wife outside Dublin. Bloom believes that M'Coy plans to use this subject as a stalking horse to try to borrow a valise from him and then not return it, as M'Coy has allegedly done with others. Rudely, Bloom fails to pay attention to what M'Coy says in this conversation. Instead, Bloom is distracted by the sight of a dignified and elegant woman across the street. She is waiting to board a horse drawn carriage in front of the Grovesnor Hotel. A passing tram blocks his anticipated view of her uncovered leg as she rises to the carriage. Frustrated, Bloom muses about being blocked out of paradise. In this distracted state, Bloom blunders in the M'Coy conversation, appearing not to know about the death of Dignam. Forgetting about death is one of the main purposes of temporary comforts. Bloom even reads the newspaper during the conversation; he reads the ad for Plumtree's Potted Meat. This ad announces plums, trees and potted meats, important subjects for the rest of the novel.

Bloom feels that M'Coy is trying to pull Molly down to the same level as M'Coy's wife's lesser talents. So Bloom, with a touch of misguided one-upmanship, tells him about Molly's upcoming multiple city engagement. M'Coy naturally asks who is organizing the affair ("getting it up"). The answer to this question is Blazes, an embarrassment to Bloom, so he doesn't answer the question. He responds vaguely about a committee and "Part shares and part profit" (read sharing Molly). M'Coy believes Bloom is hiding information that M'Coy could use to advance his own wife's prospects. As he leaves, M'Coy asks Bloom to put down M'Coy's name as attending the funeral. Bloom agrees to participate in this subterfuge. Bloom muses, uncharacteristically for him, in a critical vein about the poor quality of M'Coy's wife's singing talents, compared to Molly's. Bloom even wonders if M'Coy has been "pimping" him.

While moving to a safe location to read Martha's letter, Bloom looks at ads, thinks about actors, and thinks about the play *Leah* scheduled for performance that evening. From this play, he remembers the scene in which blind Abraham unmasks the anti-Semitic Nathan as a

Jew. The identification is made by the sound of his voice and, more traditionally from the Jacob/Esau Bible story, by feeling his face. Bloom's father often referred to this scene, which presents the biblical archetype of lack of integrity to oneself. Bloom's father did not score well in this department either; he left the Jewish faith for better commercial prospects and changed his name from Virag to Bloom. He eventually committed suicide and died in Bloom's arms. Bloom himself, removed from his Jewish roots, has been baptized in both the Protestant and Catholic faiths, Bloom the spiritual wanderer.

As he goes around the corner to find a safe place to read the letter, Bloom sees gelded horses eating from nosebags. He thinks about the limited life of the gelded horses and the results of castration as "one solution." He passes a cabman's shelter where temporarily idle carriage taxis wait for business. He muses about the carriages and drivers having no will of their own, moving around as they do at the commercial call of others. He sings from *Don Giovanni*, Mozart's opera about seduction, a particularly popular form of the lotus. He notices the marks of a hopscotch pattern and a child playing alone at marbles. He puts the letter inside the newspaper he is carrying so he can read the letter while pretending to read the newspaper, a traditional ruse for reading pornography. Under an arch that carries the tram tracks above, he reads the letter hidden within the newspaper. The arch carries symbolism of prostitution, the fall to the base in personal sexual relations.

This letter is part of a regular correspondence with Martha Clifford that started as the result of an ad placed by Bloom for secretarial help for a "literary gentleman." We don't know if Martha Clifford is her real name. The initially business correspondence has become quite personal. However, they have never met, even though Martha has apparently made the suggestion that they meet some Sunday after church service. But Bloom appears reluctant to consummate. Her letter uses incorrect English, uses "world" when she means "word" and mentions a special word, which we can only guess at. The world/word confusion suggests the logos theme. Logos refers to both the pattern in the world created by god and the structure of human consciousness that allows understanding of that world through words. Logos is a kind of two way

189

ladder, world/word or structure/understanding. In the Jewish Kabalistic tradition, the world reflects the Hebrew word of the Torah.

Martha's letter also contains heavy overtones of S and M. The letter has a yellow flower pinned to it. With this allusion to Narcissus, Bloom thinks about flowers and then reconstructs the letter in his mind using flower words. He guesses Martha is near menstruation. Trams pass overhead on the fixed rails.

Her letter gives him "weak joy," and he thinks in macho male terms about meeting Martha for S and M flavored adultery. In his mind, adultery is associated with cigars and the narcotic effect. He throws away the pin (control) that held the flower to the letter. The pin reminds him of songs about "keeping it up" and about roses with thorns.

Thinking of the name Martha, he recalls a painting that depicts the Bible story (Luke 10: 38-42) about Martha (sister of Lazarus). In the story, Martha was preparing food and, in a "distracted" state, complained to Jesus about her sister Mary. She was just sitting and listening to Jesus and not helping Martha. Jesus defended the idle Mary in a lecture to Martha about having the right attitude and Mary being absorbed in highest calling. The moral of the story is that Martha was "distracted" by menial duties from the prime spiritual occupation. Likewise, Martha is a distraction for Bloom, compared to his role as husband to Mary/Marion (Molly's full name).

In the lotus mood, Bloom gives the Martha/Mary painting the wrong interpretation. He thinks about the domestic comfort depicted in the picture and the pleasures of being a couch potato, "No more wandering about." He also confuses this Mary with Mary Magdalene the prostitute, no doubt because of his Marion's plans for the afternoon. Reference to this Bible story prepares us to look for others.

Bloom tears up the envelope and thinks covetously about the wealth of the owners of Guinness. He associates the noise made by trams above the arch with drums of liquor spilling in his head, liquor which deadens the spirit. Notice that in this state Bloom is violating the Commandments against coveting.

As he goes into the nearby Catholic Church named All Hallows (you get that one), he puts the Henry Flower identity card back in his hat band, signaling his return to enlightenment. Rev. Conmee (read con me), the priest here, will next be preaching on the African Mission. This causes Bloom to think about conversions in general, taking the unsaved away from their natural religions (as a result, they lose touch with themselves). He compares the indolent Buddha reclining on his side to Ecce Homo, "Behold the Man," the vision of Christ with the thorn crown and carrying the cross. In this comparison, the Buddha comes across as a fatalistic couch potato and Jesus as will power and suffering. The about to be converted heathen are compared in Bloom's mind to a cat lapping up milk.

Many of the All Hallows congregation appear to be part of a group and are wearing crimson halters, the sign of the Sacred Heart cult. They are observing June 16, the anniversary of the day of the big vision by Margaret Mary Alacoque (see 1st episode). In Bloom's analysis, the Church and this cult of solidarity are merely sources of comfort, like the other lotus factors.

Bloom contemplates the cannibal character of the Eucharist ceremony and, like an ad, its narcotic and enslaving effect. Through guilt, the faithful lose touch with themselves. He thinks about meeting Martha after Mass to do it on the sly. Contemplating the commission of a sinful act right after communion, he recalls that attending communion every morning had no beneficial effect on the famous Irish Invincible. Despite his regular attendance at Mass, he was involved in the Phoenix Park murder of an Irish leader and British representative and then turned state's evidence on his co-conspirators (another crime in the park with fall out for others). Bloom confuses the conspirator's name with that of a priest (both betrayers).

In church, he thinks about Molly singing older sacred music, composed with discipline and grace by Rossini, Mozart and Palestrina. He thinks specifically of the **Seven Last Words of Christ**, music based on the last seven utterances of Christ. The first of the seven was "Father, forgive them, for they know not what they do." This suggests surrender by "them" to the temporary "passions." The reference contrasts the suffering of Christ in His Passion with the common everyday passion for lotus leaves and comfort. The last of the seven utterances is "Father, into

191

thy hands I commend my spirit." Compare this acceptance with Molly's last seven words that end this Book: "yes I said yes I will Yes."[2]

As Bloom gets up from kneeling in the church, he notices that his trousers are unbuttoned (lack of control) and muses with male machismo that women like themselves neat but their men untidy. Leaving the building, he associates the low tide of holy water in the basin with nearby trams. The trams with fixed-end destinations signify the conventional life of comfort. He proceeds to the chemist (drug store) to get some face wax (read false appearance) for Molly. He remembers that he has forgotten the formula and that the chemist should have it in his records (read control). He thinks about the aging effects of drugs after mental excitement. He contemplates old-fashioned recipes for cures and then a bath at the nearby Turkish bath. He anticipates masturbating in the bath and buys some soap.

Leaving the chemist, Bloom bumps into Bantam Lyons. He wants to read in Bloom's copy of the newspaper about the Ascot Gold Cup horse race, which is being held that same day. Bloom unwittingly uses the name of one of the horses in the race, Throwaway, which Lyons treats as a veiled tip. This misunderstanding causes Bloom much trouble later in the day. As Lyons leaves, Bloom puts the soap into the newspaper and thinks about the stupidity of betting. He moves toward the bath house, which looks like a mosque (the comfort of Islam). He sees a poster ad for a college bicycle race and mentally redesigns the poster as a wheel with "sports" on the spokes and "college" on the hub. He greets Mr. Hornblower, the porter at the gate of Trinity College,[3] who sometimes lets Bloom walk in the college grounds. But not this time—no vision of the Trinity while under the spell of the lotus. He makes small talk with Hornblower and then, apparently because of the college, Bloom thinks about cricket and the time Captain Culler with a mighty hit broke the window in the Kildare Club. The name of the club reappears in this novel in the context of the general subject of the fear of death (kill dare).

Thinking about his up-coming bath, Bloom visualizes a scene in the bath looking down at his own body and remembers the words from the mass, "This is my body." He imagines his body soaped with the lemon soap he just bought, floating in the water (as in the Dead Sea), his navel in flower terms, and in the tangled curls of his pubic bush his penis as the "limp father of thousands, a languid floating flower." This image of anticipated masturbation and ejaculation of thousands of sperms into the water is what Bloom foresees, and is not presented as what happens. The actual bath itself is not presented. We learn later that he does take a bath but doesn't masturbate.

Action in The Odyssey

Joyce now goes out of order compared to The Odyssey. He uses part of Chapter ix. This one is short enough to quote in full (from the Butcher and Lang edition):

> Thence for nine whole days was I borne by ruinous winds over the teeming deep, but on the tenth day we set foot on the land of the lotus-eaters, who eat a flowery food. So we stepped ashore and drew water, and straightway my company took their midday meal by the swift ships. Now when we had tasted meat and drink I sent forth certain of my company to go and make search what manner of men they were who here live upon the earth by bread, and I chose out two of my fellows, and sent a third with them as herald. Then straightway they went and mixed with the men of the lotus-eaters, and so it was that the lotus-eaters desired not death for our fellows, but gave them of the lotus to taste. Now whosoever of them did eat the honey-sweet fruit of the lotus, had no more wish to bring tidings nor to come back, but there he chose to abide with the lotus-eating men, ever feeding on the lotus and forgetful of his homeward way. Therefore I led them back to the ships weeping, and sore against their will, and dragged them beneath the benches, and bound them in the hollow barques. But I commanded the rest of my well-loved company to make speed and go on board the swift ships, lest haply any should eat of the lotus and be forgetful of returning. Right soon they

embarked, and sat upon the benches, and sitting orderly
they smote the gray sea water with their oars.

Parallels to The Odyssey

The parallels are fairly obvious this time:

Bloom's pseudonym Flower and his pretend life are the counterpart of the "flowery" lotus fruit eaten by the natives. Both prevent making it home. The fruit is an appropriate symbol for this purpose because it is temporary by nature and designed for reproduction (contains the seed), reminding us of the temporary human life of sex and death. The many substances and modes of behavior in modern Dublin life that produce temporary comfort but prevent the homecoming to true realization reproduce the narcotic effect of the lotus.

As the herald, Bloom unwittingly predicts the winner of the Gold Cup horserace, Throwaway, which in this case signifies throwing away your own potential. Will power or Shiva is the reference for Odysseus who drags his men back to the ship and binds them to the benches. All Hallows Church is the reference for the "hallow barques," where the lotus initiates were dragged and fastened to the oars. The Church benches receive the knees of those bound to the Cult of the Sacred Heart.

Traditional Schemata

The traditional schemata given by Joyce for this episode are organ—genitals, art—botany and chemistry, color—none, symbol—Eucharist, and technique—narcissism. Narcissism is the psychological counterpart of the lotus-eater. Linati also lists as symbols "Host, Penis in Bath, Foam Flower, Drugs, Castration, Oats." Linati lists Eurylochus, a crew member of Odysseus's ship who in a later chapter leads the crew to eat the sacred Oxen of the Sun to satisfy their temporary hunger. Linati also lists Polites, killed during the fall of Troy. Soldier Polites must refer to Captain Culler and the Kildare Club (the Army). Note that Bloom's temporary fall from grace into narcissism is into the basic condition of Stephen.

First Letter

The first letter of the episode is **B** in the first word "By," which has an obvious connection to Bloom. But there must be more to it than

194

that. The letter B looks like a half section of the numeral eight (8). The numeral eight is an upright version of the sign for infinity or eternity, a symbol used prominently in later episodes. Compared to the symbol for infinity or eternity, the half section letter B signifies that Bloom in this episode is not all that he can be. The first word "By" also suggests missing something.

First Line

That all important first line:

> By lorries along sir John Rogerson's
> quay Mr. Bloom walked soberly, past
> Windmill lane, Leask's the linseed
> crusher, the postal telegraph office.

Note that the author has bent this sentence out of shape in order to start with By and B. The initial adverb clause "By lorries along . . . quay" is out of place; it should, in parallel construction, be at the end of the sentence with the other adverb clauses "soberly, past . . ." Used as an initial adverb clause, it should end with a comma, for sense control. The series of remaining adverb clauses at the end of the sentence should be separated by "and" just after "crusher." The end of this opening sentence feels crowded and without proper shape. This is a grammatical example of the lotus effect, which can artificially shape sentences as well as human priorities.

Major themes are hidden in this first sentence. Lorries are horse drawn carriages without sides. These are lined up to carry things away, as the lotus does to the spirit. Without side panels, they can't control much of a load. They have wheels signifying the chakras and the wheel of reincarnation for the lotus-eaters. Perhaps lorries also suggest the lorelei, the Rhine River siren who bewitched fishermen. Sir John Rogerson was a famous barrister whose verbal eloquence announces the importance of the voice in this episode.[4] Windmill lane would suggest pipe dreams, in the lotus-eater family. Linseed oil, from the linseed crusher, was a popular home remedy for burns. Here Bloom fends off the heat of higher realization. The crusher indicates the effect of lotus forces on the spirit.

After the first line, the description goes on and on in terms of where Bloom is and what he sees. For example, he sees the sailor's

195

home, where Odysseus's men would end up if they continued to eat lotus fruit.

Word Play

Bloom muses about the frowning face of Bethel, a Salvation Army Hall.[5] Bethel in Hebrew means House of God. It was the name of the town north of Jerusalem where the Ark was kept. The House of God is frowning because Bloom has renounced his Hebrew heritage and Molly's ark. Bloom thinks about the name: "Bethel. El, yes: house of: Aleph, Beth." Bloom unfolds the name Bethel to El Beth. El means house, Beth means god. Here is your authority for unfolding the name Bloom to Om Blo. Later Bloom muses: "Table: able. Bed: ed." Using the same procedure on Flower, we get lower, which is where Bloom is in this episode. Note that Bloom uses a form of word association that emphasizes the common letters.

Shiva

Shiva peeks through the details of this episode as the symbol of self-control and integrity to self. Shiva is traditionally portrayed as Dancing Shiva with four arms and the left foot lifted. One of the two left arms is crossed over—see Figure 2. Manifesting immaculate self-control, Shiva's head remains still during his dance. His dance is to his own drummer, all movements borne of his own nature and making. The purpose of this image is to promote release from illusion and resulting freedom, symbolized by raising his left foot off the ground.[6] His bottom foot rests on "concealment planted in forgetfulness." He carries deerskin in the two lower hands, a drum in his upper right and a tongue of flame in his upper left. His symbol is the lingam, which is held in hand during worship. Shiva has wild hair, the power of life energy.[7] His Greek counterpart Dionysus was excluded from the Olympian community, an outsider.[8] He dances below an arch composed of lace and tongues of flame. His weapon is the bow. Shiva combines many of the contradictory qualities found in nature: ascetic and sensual, destroyer and restorer, herdsman of souls and avenger, and female and male.[9] As such, he represents choices among opposites to be made by humans according to their will.

The icons of Shiva are present in the image of a dignified woman Bloom sees across the road. The Connector Facts are numerous. She is in front of the Grosvenor Hotel, a name which signifies governor or control. She is composed. She wears deerskin gloves, as deerskin is carried by Shiva in two of his hands, and Bloom obligingly associates to a drum head, which Shiva also carries. She lifts her leg to mount the carriage, as Shiva lifts his leg signifying release. Bloom thinks of caste, which in the Hindu social order limits realization. Her stocking is white, the color for Shiva and of the second and fifth chakras. Bloom thinks "Two strings to her bow," Shiva's weapon. She travels in a carriage called an outsider, as Shiva/Dionysus remained outside the community of Olympus. Bloom tries to walk like a woman, as Shiva combined both male and female. As her carriage leaves, Bloom sees ". . . her rich gloved hand on the steel grip. Flicker, flicker: the laceflare of her hat in the sun: flicker. flick." Steel grip for control. Flicker for an image that changes with the dance. Laceflare of hat for the laced arch of fire over Shiva's head. Bloom's sexually aroused reaction to this image is, in terms of Joyce's aesthetics, a pornographic one. Shiva is designed to produce arrest and realization, not sexual heat.

Will power or control of oneself is the realm of the fifth chakra, where purification is achieved by redirecting the sexual energy of the second chakra. Bloom is purified physically by his bath and spiritually by control of his desire to masturbate. The body location of the fifth chakra is in the throat—for the voice that gets a big play in this episode. The related element of the fifth chakra is ether or air through which the voice is carried.

The clue to the influence of the chakras in this episode is found near the end of the episode in an otherwise totally out of place focus on the bicycle race ad. Bloom reconstructs this ad in his mind as a wheel, since chakra means wheel. The wheel also signifies the wheel of reincarnation for the lotus-eaters in life who do not reach the higher chakras. He thinks of the spokes as sport, the enlightened and detached attitude toward the dance of this life.

With the Flower identity card in his waist coat pocket near the inner organs of the third chakra, Bloom denies Shiva and the heat of the higher chakras (sixth in the forehead and seventh on top of head). Twice he takes off his hat to cool his head and smooth down his oiled hair. Bloom's vision of Shiva is occluded by the passing tram cars, which move without will of their own according to someone else's schedule.

Shape of Path

The part of Bloom's trip described in this episode doesn't begin at home but rather at a point that is most of the way to the post office. This starting point suggests that we look at the pattern he traces, since we know that Joyce has crafted it very carefully. It looks like this:

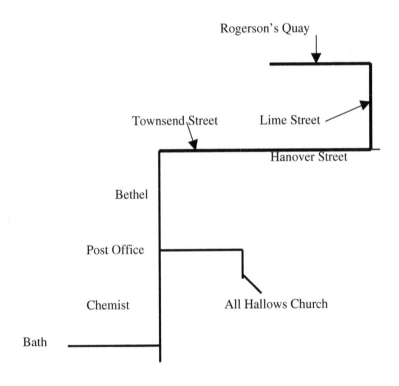

Please compare this abstract outline, which is roughly to scale, with Figure 2. This outline traces, I submit, the figure of an abstract

Dancing Shiva. The first segment is named for a barrister, suggesting the voice, the air and the drum, and Shiva's upper right hand. The third segment is on Hanover, suggesting the left arm and "hand over." As befits Bloom's condition in this episode, the dancer's leg is reversed. The right not the left leg is raised just at the point, at All Hallows Church, where Bloom reads the letter in pursuit of a temporary comfort release from the suffering of his marriage. He brushes his hot forehead with his right hand, while Shiva holds the tongue of flame in his left. He forgets the formula for his wife's face wax prescription at the counterpart location of concealment planted in forgetfulness. The lingam in hand shows in Bloom's vision of his own body in the bath and in the following Bloom thoughts: "Who has the organ here [in the Church]"; the priest "holding the thing [water dish] in his hands". The arch of lacefire shows up several times in the episode; Bloom reads the letter right under the arch.

The Arch of Lace and Fire

Shiva dances inside and immune from the arch of lace and fire, which suggests desire in the world. Through self-control, Shiva is immune from these desires. In our sordid world of temporary comforts, lace and fire frame the prostitute. She dresses pretty and inspires flame. Bloom culminates his profane and artificial withdrawal from genuine life by reading Martha's letter under the arch, which is emphasized in the text. In a book maintained in Joyce's permanent library (Beverland's *Law Concerning Draped Virginity*),

> . . . Joyce would have learned that the word "fornicate"
> derives from the latin 'fornex' or arch under which the
> Roman prostitutes used to ply their trade. . . . In
> Finnegans Wake a prostitute is described as an "arch
> girl". . . .[10]

Through the name Merchant's Arch, the profanity of the prostitute indicts commercialism in general. The arch carries those trams running on schedules dictated by others, the symbols of a life without will power prostituted to commercial interests.

Jewish Legend—The Stone Tablets and Bloom's Letter

The Jews were moving around in the desert, having left Egypt and the brickfields in a hurried Exodus. During this arduous desert journey, they were sorely tempted to return to the "flesh-pots" of Egypt for the temporary comforts of food and warmth, even if return meant slavery.

When they stopped, Moses pitched his special tent outside the regular camp. This special tent was known as the Tent of the Meeting. When Moses went out there, everyone stood by his own tent. The pillar of the cloud, representing the power of Yahweh, would show up at the entrance to the special tent. When the people saw the pillar of the cloud, they would bow. Joshua, son of Nun, always stayed in the special tent. The pillar of the cloud, apparently a cyclone type of affair, moved to show the Jews which way to go. At night, the pillar of fire did the same. For some 40 years, they faithfully followed the pillars and wandered around in the desert.

After arduous desert travel, the Jews reached the sacred mountain where earlier Moses had first encountered the burning bush and this time believed he would encounter Yahweh again. The Jews purified themselves to get ready (purification for the fifth chakra). The trumpets sounded, and Moses went up alone on the fire-belching mountain. There he received the stone tablets containing the Ten Commandments and the Covenant. Compliance with the Ten Commandments requires will power and control. The Covenant contained details about building the Tabernacle and the Ark and the future of the Jews. After many days on the mountain, Moses came back down with the tablets, only to find that his group, impatient for his return, had constructed a golden bull idol in an attempt to please Yahweh (pornographic sculpture). Having read the very first commandment prohibiting idols, Moses was incensed and threw the stone tablets to the ground. They broke and the chiseled writing on the broken tablets disappeared. Moses organized an internal massacre, caused the golden bull to be melted down and mixed with water, and forced the surviving turncoats to drink the gold-laden water. Later he goes up again for a second set, which according to some was different.

200

The Connector Facts are unusual items in this episode. Young Joshua at the special tent outside the camp is reflected in the solitary child playing marbles outside the church. The pillar of the cloud appears as the piled balks (did Yahweh balk?). The hopscotch court with its forgotten stone, which when thrown in the right way gives the player a turn, is a game in which the player can not tread on the lines or pass beyond the appointed square. Yahweh in Exodus 19:21 says, "Go down and warn the people not to pass beyond the bounds. . .(and not to come up too high where they can see Yahweh)." A round hopscotch court (it can be square or round) would look like the cross section of a mountain. The trumpets appear in the name of the Trinity gate guard, Hornblower. The throwing of the stone tablets is echoed in the horse named Throwaway, which like Yahweh was a dark horse. Bloom wonders if the extra object in the envelope (the flower) is a photo or a badge, which would be prohibited idol images. The letter is addressed to the covenant or relationship between Martha and Bloom. She says she thinks about him all the time, as Yahweh must have done with the Jews since he had only one people to look after. Bloom reads the letter under the railway arch where there would be smoke and noise, like the belching mountain.

The envelope that Bloom tears apart signifies the stone tablets containing the Ten Commandments, which were broken by Moses. Like the envelope, the Ten Commandments are only the laws, the outward manifestations holding the internal message that informs all the rules, which is love. The reference in this episode to M'Coy borrowing but not returning the valise, particularly the fancy one Bloom thinks about, refers to the Ark of the Covenant. The ark was used to carry the stone tablets and later was lost in a battle with the Philistines, the traditional enemy of the Jews.

Bloom's Condition

Bloom's condition in this episode is determined largely by the digestion of his breakfast. This diversion of internal energies pulls him down to the second and third chakras, especially during the early part of the episode. In the secret correspondence, he pretends to be someone he isn't, a writer. He muses about using sadistic love techniques on Martha and engaging her in love scrimmages. This is not our compassionate, centered Bloom accepting of himself and his condition.

The loss of Jewish heritage is the reason Bethel frowns on him and the reason behind his thoughts about *Leah*, a play being put on that evening. He recalls the scene from the play in which Jewish Nathan, hiding his identity by acting as an anti-Semite, is unmasked by Abraham who recognizes Nathan as Jewish by his voice (what else in this episode). Then Bloom thinks:

Nathan's voice! His son's voice! I hear the voice of
Nathan who left his father to die of grief and misery in
my [Bloom's] arms, who left the house of his father
and left the God of his father. [parenthesis mine]

Bloom's thought merges the Nathan story with Bloom's personal story by equating Nathan's father with Bloom's father. Bloom recalls his own father dying in his arms, his father who left the Jewish heritage for the Church of Ireland and presumably better commercial prospects, the loss of the spiritual father principle. Then the author sticks in "Every word is so deep, Leopold." This must be the lotus affected author because the author in the dramatic mode would not show up in the text. Note that Bloom is haunted by memories of his father while Stephen is haunted by memories of his mother.

Leah

The play *Leah* contains a warning that Bloom overlooks, just as Jacob missed his warning and ended up initially with the wrong wife in the tent.

In the Bible story, Leah was originally promised to Esau and Rachel to Jacob. Jacob worked faithfully for seven years for Rachel's father Laban in order to earn his beloved Rachel as wife (will power and patience). But after Esau turned out so poorly and married outside the faith, Laban wanted to get rid of his older daughter Leah first. He also wanted to keep Jacob around longer since he was good for their luck (lots of rain). Laban knew that Jacob, loving Rachel as he did, would work another seven years to earn Rachel as his second wife. So Jacob unwittingly got the older Leah in the tent on the first wedding night (the candles were put out).[11]

Likewise, Bloom misses the point about which female is the right one (Molly/Mary or Martha). His mistake is to divert his energies away from his role as a husband.

Comfort and Control

The list of temporary comforts includes the following: nicotine, alcohol, popular music, tea, loafing, fatalism, floating in the Dead Sea, the caste system, Catholic solidarity, confession, Eucharist, Holy Water, drugs, masturbation, wagering, watching cricket and a bath.

Bloom's loss of control is suggested by the following: his inability to remember the weight/volume law; inability to read the letter when he wants to; lack of attention to the conversation with M'Coy; loss of control in the conversation with M'Coy by bringing up a subject that embarrasses him; his unbuttoned waistcoat; and his forgetfulness concerning the face wax formula. The same subject runs through the images about safety pins being used to keep skirts up and the cabmen who move without a will of their own.

Loss of identity appears in references to soldiers in uniform, actors, male impersonators, renunciation of heritage, conversion of Gladstone, conversion of natives and Chinese, Pilate who was swayed by the crowd after finding no fault with Jesus, chanting and eunuchs.

The Mass and Purification

The Mass devoted to the Sacred Heart cult, which Bloom observes in the church, brings forward the image of Jesus with the exposed heart, Jesus seeking to take reparations from the guilty. By contrast, Bloom's heart is exposed in his compassion and charity; he only gives and doesn't take. The Mass parallel proceeds with the Lavabo, the washing of hands that follows the Offertory.

Bloom's bath is designated in a later episode in terms of Jewish ritual as the Rite of John. This is Joyce's name, by reference to John the Baptist, for the micvah, the Jewish ritual bath designed to purify defiled persons. Bloom's exercise of self-restraint in the bath purifies him of the defilement of yielding to other temporary comforts.

John the Baptist repeatedly spoke of the one "who would come after me." Given Bloom's masturbation later in the day and Stephen's date with Nora later in the day, the reference to purification takes on an aspect of sperm buildup reduction.

These references begin to turn the Mass parallel toward the earthly.[12] Joyce consecrates the earthly Bloom through his thought "This is my body," the line used by Jesus in the Last Supper. Joyce co-opts the ritual of the Eucharist for Bloom's very human body.

Avoiding pornography (as defined by Joyce) through self-control is the artistic analogy in the purification process. Without self-control, the author tries to create desire or loathing or a lesson for the reader.

Parallels with Nestor

This episode takes place at about the same time as the Nestor episode, between 10 and 11 a.m. Both episodes show enemies of the human spirit in league with sexual energies. Stephen showed some flashes of realization before his students as Bloom shows some realization in his evaluations of church ritual. Bloom's overreaction to M'Coy's friendly overtures—"Wonder is he pimping after me?"—projects in homosexual terms. The student soldiers following the charted commercial path are the counterparts of the lotus-eaters. Hockey in Nestor appears here as cricket which breaks windows.

The type of word association technique used in the Nestor episode emphasized separate meanings more than connections. By contrast, Bloom's word technique is the comparison of one word with another that contains most of the same letters, a word association technique that suggests common substance.

Structure, Art and Aesthetics

This episode is structured much the same as the last one. A calm, third party classical style narrator's voice is mixed with Bloom's thoughts. Compared to the last episode, the narrator's voice seems slightly more pedestrian. This shift is reinforced by the many, relatively less interesting references to places and names of places. The overall mood suggests surrender. We learn more about Bloom by his thoughts and his actions. We still don't have a physical description of Bloom, only his actions and thoughts, echoes of his soul.

The art of the episode is only as strong as the Hebrew-Hindu combination. For my taste, the references to Shiva are too light to be dramatically effective. The Shiva-Moses concepts are intellectually satisfying because of their common parallels, but for some reason this one doesn't play for me. Further, Bloom's motivation in entering the church, "the call of the sacred stones," is not convincing.

As to the aesthetics of the episode, I feel the force of the tragedy of the human condition, what is grave and constant and unites the reader with the human sufferer. Joyce's concept of pornographic is deftly drawn into the episode as the literary counterpart of eating lotus fruit.

While we don't find this out until a later episode, Bloom does gain control and thus is purified by the bath. Even though he anticipated the pleasure, he doesn't masturbate in the bath. Thus purified into the realm of Shiva, in the next episode Bloom sits shiva as the Jewish death rite, in order to guard Dignam's soul.

****

ENDNOTES

1.   Gifford, p. 83.
2.   Blamirez, H. *New Bloomsday Book: A Guide Through Ulysses* (New York: Routledge, 19960 p. 32.
3.   Gifford, p. 99.
4.   Gifford, p. 84.
5.   Gifford, p. 84.
6.   Zimmer, Myths and Symbols, pp. 152 et. seq.
7.   Ibid, p. 157.
8.   Ibid, p. 186.
9.   **Shiva**, Encyclopedia Britannica, 1983 Ed., Micropaedia, Vol. IX, p. 245.
10. Brown, R. *James Joyce and sexuality* (Cambridge: Cambridge University Press, 1985) p. 121.
11. Legends, Vol. 1, p. 360.
12. Lang, p. 138.

Episode 6 (Hades)

Basic Themes

The dead bury the dead. Inhumanity in inhumation. Death teaches life.

What speaks to us across the certainty of own death? You "gotta have heart" and "little things mean a lot." While our blood still flows, we must live vitally and pursue the really important things, loving kindness and "warm fullblooded life." As we are one in death, we should be one in life. Death, the secret cause, the cause of all that is grave and constant in the human condition.

In The Odyssey, ghosts of the dead in Hades are able to relate to Odysseus only after receiving fresh blood. Without blood, the ghost of Odysseus's mother can't relate even to her own son. The shades crave human blood, having learned the lesson of life. In this episode, the mourners at Dignam's funeral other than Bloom lack the heart and warm blood of compassion that derives from the knowledge we are all in one boat. Like the deceased Dignam, they have suffered "breakdown of the heart" and died to the spirit (pun intended).

On the way to and at the burial, the inhumation, other mourners treat Bloom inhumanely. The lack of compassion also fuels grudge keeping and critical remarks about the nature of the service. As Jesus said, the dead bury the dead. Bloom continues valiantly to reflect the human unity, as he reacts only with kindness and thinks about everyone being in the same boat.[1]

The lessons to be learned about death are part of the terror aspect of tragedy—that which arrests the mind before what is grave and constant in human suffering and unites the human sufferers in the "secret cause." That secret cause is the knowledge of certain death. That knowledge causes suffering that can only be overcome with loss of ego and detachment into the unity. Even though face to face with certain death in the cemetery, these Dubliners have not learned the secret to be learned from death. They remain in ego-fixed suffering.

To cover or conceal is the etymological derivation of Hades, as

206

the dead are buried or covered. This episode about a funeral features hats and "covering," putting them on. The non-family mourners in the Dignam funeral wallow in a kind of empty vanity, which results in fear of death and conceals the human unity. Empty vanity is the subject of the Book of Ecclesiastics, which characterizes this attitude as a metaphorical mist (in Hebrew *hebel*).[2] Mist and light rain fall on the funeral procession. The parallel in the Mass is the Secret, which is concealed from the congregation.[3]

Dublin is controlled by the dead. Statutes of the dead preside at important intersections. Old times and customs rule the conversations. Grudges are kept for years. The loss of living identity is manifested most directly in the anonymous character MacIntosh, who is identified only by his coat. He is named after the inventor of the water proof coat. It sheds water, the symbol of unity. MacIntosh is associated throughout the novel with the Anti-Christ.

Bloom contrasts the ritual of the Catholic burial with the rules for sitting Shiva, the Jewish rite for protecting the soul of the dead. The episode touches on different funeral and burial practices and theories of the after-life in several cultures, including the symbology of the Tibetan Book of the Dead (correct name—Natural Liberation Through Understanding in the In Between or "Bardo"). According to the Bardo, immediately after death the deceased experiences a descent through the chakras toward rebirth as human or animal. In this descent, the "in between" or "Bardo" is from death to rebirth. In this descent, the deceased starts at the highest chakra and if he or she can hang on to the fourth or higher chakra, rebirth as a human or animal is avoided. Dignam apparently can't hang on high enough. A donkey brays at the moment of his burial.

The Hebrew trail in the desert centers on the death of Aaron. He had to die (naked on the mountain) because his brother Moses failed to have sufficient faith that Yahweh would lead the Jews into the promised land of Canaan. Aaron's death was a fratricide by lack of faith. The Connector Facts in the episode include the Childs fratricide murder case. Hindu symbolism provides the elephant and the rat, the symbols of Ganesha who is the son of Shiva and Lord of Obstacles. Ganesha breaks a path through obstacles for the devotee. He is protection against disaster in the jungle of the world, protection even for those who have been his enemies.[4] He is compassion, the lesson from the certainty of death.

As the funeral proceeds, father and son pairs are featured to emphasize that death to the flesh is defeated only by the procreation of children. The pairs include Ganesha and Shiva, Bloom and his father, Stephen and Simon, Rudy and Bloom, Triton and Poseidon and the wet son of Dodd. Christ as the son of god and son of man returns in two jokes. Stephen's natural father Simon and his future spiritual father Bloom sit in the same funeral coach. Stephen walks by the carriage. Significantly, Bloom sees him but Simon doesn't.

References to Hume and Berkeley Street return to the issues raised in the time related Proteus episode, subject-object duality and the resulting inability to see the unity, again symbolized by water.

Funeral Procession and Cemetery

The time is 11:00 a.m., the time when Stephen walks to the beach where he was in the 3rd episode. Bloom sees him walking in that direction. The funeral procession starts at the Dignam residence at No. 9 Newbridge Avenue in Sandymount. Newbridge because new children bridge the death of their father into the future and Sandymount for the mountain in the desert where Aaron had to die. The service is held at the Prospect Cemetery located north of Dublin. The name Prospect suggests the main theme of the episode—given the certainty of a final visit to the cemetery, what is the prospect for life?

Action in Ulysses

Fresh from his bath, Bloom attends the funeral for Dignam (Latin for worthy). The first section dwells in detail on how four persons enter their horse drawn "creaking carriage." Martin Cunningham is "first" (ego and importance) and "poked" (aggressive) his fancy "silk hatted head" in the carriage. He has his hat on; he is "covered." With this emphasis, Joyce associates respectability and death. Then Mr. Power. We later learn that Power is part of a paramilitary force to support British rule and interests, the political police. Then Cunningham, already in, shows his interest in control by telling Simon Dedalus, Stephen's father, that he should "come on" in third, ahead of Bloom. Simon seems

208

reluctant to enter but "covers" (puts on his hat) and enters. Bloom shows his politeness by deferring, "After you." After only three are in, Cunningham asks if "all are here now," when obviously the seemingly inconsequential Bloom isn't in yet. Cuningham's disregard of Bloom is blatant.

Once safely in the last seat, Bloom secures himself prudently through the arm strap; he is apparently the only one who uses it. He immediately notices the effect of the funeral procession on persons in the street and muses about the effect of death on the living. This is the main theme, the effect of the certainty of death on your soul or philosophy. Seeing a woman peeping at the procession through her window, Bloom muses on the woman's role as mother in bringing males into the world and as surviving spouse in ushering them out.

The procession doesn't start right away so "All waited" appears twice, all waiting for death, the inevitable human condition. The start of the procession is registered in terms of the wheels of the carriages ahead starting first, as we watch others die first. They leave the home of the deceased at number nine Newbridge and move out on Tritonville Road, Triton being the son of Poseidon. The effect of the carriage ride is registered in the position of the occupants' knees and their "trunks" (think elephant). Some of them can't tell which way they are going, suggesting limited vision. The procession goes through Irishtown, including Ringsend (the bell rings no more for Dignam). Simon applauds the route through Irishtown as old custom. Simon appears trapped in the past. He repeats phrases, he dwells on memories, and he loves the old Irish customs.

The carriage travels part of the way on the tram tracks, a symbol of fixed destiny. The language of death is in the details: custom has not "died out"; friend of yours "gone by"; and son and heir. Bloom has his newspaper, the daily record of time and space and obituaries, and its movements are detailed throughout the episode.

Just as Bloom sees Stephen walking by, the carriage leaves the tramtracks and moves on to Watery Road (read the unity). The other carriage occupants talk about everything else except the deceased and the lessons of death. Simon delivers a diatribe against Mulligan as a bad influence (*fidus Achates*) on Stephen. In the diatribe, Simon uses the same phrases that Stephen imagined his father using. From this, we know that Simon is predictable; he repeats pat phrases. Showing ignorance as to the basics about his son, Simon assumes from Stephen's location that Stephen is staying at the Gouldings. Simon goes on and on about what he is going to do about Mulligan, but we understand that he is just hot air (where else but in Hades). Bloom characterizes him as a "noisy selfwilled man," the opposite of the enlightened who can escape the suffering of death.

Bloom thinks about what life would have been like if his son Rudy had grown up rather than dying shortly after birth: "Me in his eyes. . . . From me." He remembers Molly, just before the conception of Rudy, heating up watching two dogs go at it. She was wearing a cream gown with a rip that was never stitched. He thinks of Molly and Milly in water/unity terms: "Same thing watered down."

The funeral procession passes several pits, four rivers, and gasworks, all appropriate to the Hades image. The dominant colors are gray and brown and black, the colors of death. The occupants recognize they are behind schedule (read in realization). They discuss having a better yoke, which would make the ride (read of life) more pleasant. They discover crumbs on the seat of the carriage, suggesting the last occupants enjoyed a picnic. Bloom wishes his socks had been darned better, since they are now on view. Cunningham twirls his beard repeatedly. Their carriage stops at the Grand Canal, which goes to the west coast of Ireland through locks.

It starts to rain. Bloom notices that the rain drops are separate (no water of unity here), as if the rain were strained through a "colander." This is a straining device the holes in which are usually in the shape of the Star of David. Seeing the home for stray dogs, Bloom remembers his father's dying wish for Bloom to take care of their dog Athos. Bloom continues to be haunted by images of his father, as Stephen is of his mother.

The procession starts again with references to wheels, trunks and Cunningham twirling his beard. The carriage occupants continue to talk about extraneous subjects, including last night's pub revelry by Tom

Kernan and Paddy Leonard, "who took (Tom) off to his face" (mimicked him). The words "trenchant" and "retrospective arrangement" (read reincarnation) are mentioned in this connection. In this mode, the unity is reduced to similarity feigned in the interests of sarcasm. Bloom at least looks at the obituaries in the newspaper. Their trite sentimental messages prompt the following chilling symbol of the brevity of life: "Inked characters fast fading on the frayed breaking paper." The short human life span and the transient newspaper. He remembers a four line ditty about meeting the deceased on high (read Aaron).

Bloom remembers Martha's letter, which is in his waist coat pocket. He sees the yard near Meade's, where he first read her letter, and sees two horses eating at the cabman's shelter, the "hazard." Bloom describes the feeding horses as being as "full as a tick" (a blood image). He notices the number of horses (two) because there were three when he went by earlier. He sees the tram "pointsman," who points the tram cars. Bloom considers improving the tram operation by changing the placement of the wheel (read chakra), the device that the pointsman uses to change the vehicles from one track to another (read rebirth).

Bloom begins to think extraneous thoughts (just like everyone else), about the play *Leah* and Blaze's pending visit. Then he thinks "Plasto's" for possession. At that moment, the carriage passes Blazes Boylan, who is walking on the sidewalk. The other three carriage occupants go out of their way to greet him, Cunningham with a salute. Blazes does not remove his hat to show respect for the dead. He remains covered. Reacting to the proximity of Blazes, Bloom looks at his fingernails and wonders what women see in Blazes. Since the possession instinct is weak in Bloom, his nails are paired. Note the contrast with the talons of Simon, the claws of the vampire and the related possessive mode. Just to rub it in, Power and the others ask Bloom about the concert tour that they all know will involve Molly with Blazes. They sadistically ask him if he is going along. Bloom misses the point, and the text focuses on what he does with his hands, which clasped together make the Buddhist sign of respect to the divine in each person.

As they pass the statute of the Irish hero Farrell, their knees are thrown together and "united," at least in their Irish faith. Immediately

211

thereafter they see O'Callaghan selling bootlaces four for a penny. Formerly a solicitor, he suffered professional death by losing his license ("struck off the rolls"). He says "oot," which is "too" reversed. "Too" would suggest the unity. Formerly, he was chief solicitor for Waterford, a name that suggests fording the water and thus avoiding the water/unity. His office was on Hume Street, for the subject-object separation. His dilapidated silk hat (cover) is mentioned. He is covered. Notice that no one helps him. No unity among the living.

Bloom thinks about Molly being out of bed and doing her hair and the arrival of their cleaning lady, Mrs. Fleming. He remembers Cunningham's background and his mistress, who used to work in a bar. Since they are reputed not to engage in full carnal relations, he brings her "rumpsteak" (read anal intercourse). The carriage occupants see by Elvery's Elephant House (which according to Gifford sells waterproof gear) Mr. J. Reuben Dodd, a Jewish money lender who is bent over with curvature of the spine. Simon, who no doubt owes him money, curses him by the devil.

In a highly naive social move in an effort to be one of the boys, Bloom decides to tell an anecdote about Reuben and his son. As Bloom tells it, Reuben's son had got a girl in trouble. Reuben was escorting his son to a boat headed to the Isle of Man, an island just off Ireland, so as to avoid his responsibilities. However the son, described as the "young chiseller," bolted and jumped into the River Liffey. A boatman fished the son half dead out of the river, and the father rewarded the boatman with a florin. Bloom tells the story in such a way that Simon initially confuses father and son in terms of who fell in the river (joking on theories of the Trinity and the nature of the godhead that arrived in time and space). The others rudely butt in on Bloom's story and appropriate it for themselves. They laugh at Simon's response that the father's reward of a florin (two shillings) was one and eight too much. This would, in Simon's estimation, leave the son worth four pence. After the laughter, proper Cunningham suggests that they should at least look serious. As they pass Nelson's pillar, a peddler shouts "Eight plums a penny." These plums figure prominently in the next episode.

The carriage occupants talk about excess drink as the cause of

Dignam's death and in general the dangers of drink. Simon expresses sympathy with the problems of drinkers, being one himself. Bloom expresses the view that since Dignam died suddenly, he had the best death. The other three are shocked by this perfectly rational statement. Rebuffed by their reaction, Bloom retreats to his thoughts about the part of town they are passing through, being dead in terms of business potential. A coffin of a child passes them. The white colors indicate the child was illegitimate.

Power talks about the evils of suicide, not knowing that Bloom's father took his own life. Cunningham tries to divert the conversation out of consideration to Bloom. Bloom compares Cunningham's face to that of Shakespeare's (remember this comparison when we do the 15th episode). Bloom mentally notes the lack of humanity in the Catholic burial custom of marking a dead child as illegitimate, more inhumanity in inhumation. Bloom thinks about the continuous effect on Cunningham of his alcoholic wife in terms of the mythical Sisyphus rolling the stone up the hill over and over again. Bloom remembers drunk Mrs. Cunningham singing the song "I am the jewel of Asia." Bloom thinks about the inquest for his father's death; "Boots," who appears in a later episode, gave evidence. Bloom remembers the red labeled bottle by the side of his father's bed, from which he took the overdose. The red labeled bottle image returns as a beer bottle in the 14th episode. The others talk about the German auto race, competition not unity.

In Berkeley Street, they hear the street organ play "Has anybody seen Kelly," a title which combines the subject-object duality with human separation. They pass Bloom's street Eccles. *Ecclesia* in Greek and *Ecclesiastes* in Hebrew mean the gathering in of those summoned, as all humans are to death. The funeral procession has to stop for a "divided drove" of cattle (even the cattle are separated) and sheep "bleating their fear" on the way for sale in England, another gathering in of those summoned to death. Remembering that the next day is slaughter day, Bloom suggests in the interest of avoiding traffic congestion that the City Corporation run a tramline line from a point in the City to the quays, where the sheep and cattle leave on boats to be slaughtered. To complete the connection of animals to humans, Joyce has Bloom also suggest a similar tramline to the cemetery for humans. Simon characteristically thinks about a drinking car on such a train. He offers to buy the first round after the service. Always in the past, Simon remembers another procession marred by the fall of the coffin out of the hearse onto the street. Bloom imagines Dignam falling out and asking "What's up now?", a reference to the resurrection. Bloom, the scientific one, wonders if a corpse would bleed.

As they pass, Power points out the traditional post-funeral watering hole Dunphy's. On the canal, they all watch the passage of a boat named *Bugabu* (Celtic for devil). Bloom thinks about a surprise visit to daughter Milly by walking or cycling the canals, "To heaven by water" (the unity again). Later he decides a surprise visit could be dangerous. On Finglas Road, they pass the stonecutter's yard, see ghost-like white statues and immediately thereafter a bum on the corner. No compassion for him either.

They pass the Childs house and talk about the fratricide murder case in which the accused Childs brother was successfully defended by the lawyer Seymour Bushe (read see more bush, for Moses). As their carriage reaches the walls of Prospect cemetery, they see more ghost-like forms inside: "Dark poplars, rare white forms. Forms more frequent, white shapes thronged amid the trees, white forms and fragments streaming by mutely, sustaining vain gestures on the air." Vain for the life of the ego. Vanity is the subject of the Book of Ecclesiastes, the gathering in of the vain to dust.

At the cemetery, they dismount in the same order (of rank) as they got in. No one helps any one else. Bloom uses the moment to shift the soap (he bought in the last episode) to his inner handkerchief pocket. He thinks about funerals in general and observes in hurried departure a distraught and hard looking woman with a child looking for guidance, the only mourners for the illegitimate child. No one else seems to notice or care. During the short service, Bloom thinks about the priest and the Catholic burial ritual. Father Coffey presides, and the service is short and perfunctory. Attending the funeral are twelve known persons and a 13th in the MacIntosh coat whom no one can identify. Stephen is not at the funeral. Bloom's mind wanders to the subject of bad gas produced by the

214

dead. As they leave, Simon Dedalus vainly feels sorry for himself as he passes his wife's grave.

After the service, Bloom talks with Tom Kernan who, even though right in the midst of this solemn occasion, makes critical remarks about the Catholic service compared to the Protestant version. In this conversation, Tom obligingly repeats Christ's direction for the spirit: "I am the resurrection and the life." In context, this direction is about spiritual resurrection during your life, the main theme of this episode. This direction for the spirit was a rejoinder by Jesus to Martha, the sister of Lazarus, about her lack of faith in connection with Jesse's late arrival to aid the mortally sick Lazarus, Martha's brother. Since Jesus arrived late, after Lazarus's death, Jesus had to raise him from the dead, rather than cure his illness. Jesse's rejoinder puns on resurrection and directs it into this life.

The emphasis on the life of the living is also the subject of the following statement attributed to Jesus in Mark 12:26-27 about the focus of God: He [the God of Abraham, Isaac and Jacob] is not the God the dead, but the God of the living. . . ." To emphasize this point, Joyce has the cemetery caretaker John O'Connell tell the joke about two drunks in the cemetery. Upon finding the grave of their friend and looking up at the statue of Jesus over the grave, they agree that the statue doesn't look a bit like their friend. This joke comments on the spiritual state of most of those at the funeral.

Seeing Bloom, John Henry Menton has him identified and by name remembers the grudge he bears Bloom from a bowling game many years ago. Bloom bested Menton in this game in front of Molly. Even in the midst of this solemn occasion, Menton does not curb his years-old grudge developed in the context of a mating competition.

Bloom contemplates life and death ("In the midst of death we are in life"), most poignantly in terms of speculation about the cemetery caretaker meeting women at the cemetery. Bloom thinks about what it must be like under ground with all the bugs. He also thinks about all humans being "in the same boat" and what would happen if suddenly each living person were turned into someone else, a form of advance reincarnation.

215

Taking names for attendance for the newspaper, Hynes asks Bloom for his first name and the name of the man in the MacIntosh. Bloom doesn't know MacIntosh and asks that M'Coy be recorded as in attendance. Hynes informs Bloom that M'Coy used to work for the newspaper *Freeman,* but due to an embezzlement lost that job and now works in the morgue. This signifies the loss of freedom to materialism and fear of death.

The funeral party returns by Parnell's grave. Due to the opposition of the Catholic Church, the plinth base for a commemorative statute is empty. Seeing many expensive grave stones, Bloom thinks the money would be better spent on the living. Bloom notices a tame bird on a branch and remembers a painting, whose artist Bloom misremembers as Apollo. The painting was so realistic that real birds tried to eat the painted grapes but ignored the painted child, just as the Dubliners in the pubs ignore their families. Immediately after the tame bird memory, Bloom notices in the cemetery a Sacred Heart of Jesus statue, Jesus with his heart outside in order to tame the faithful. Bloom also considers possible improvements in the information conveyed on headstones and has the idea that the dying make phonograph recordings of their voice.

Bloom observes an obese, gray rat moving pebbles (obstacles) and crawling under a crypt. He thinks about what the rat is doing to the buried bodies and the various means of taking care of dead bodies used in other cultures. Bloom is happy to leave the cemetery, feeling that each time he is there he is closer to death. Given the dead souls of the other mourners, this is certainly true and not just in the realm of time. Bloom thinks about his ghost haunting others after his death.

Not aware of the grudge, Bloom stops to tell John Henry Menton that he has a crease in his hat: "Your hat is a little crushed." Again, the hat plays the role as a manifestation of the spirit. Menton, feeling the grudge, can not bring himself to thank Bloom. Cunningham intervenes to remove the crease. Then Menton begrudgingly gives thanks to Cunningham, but not to Bloom. Bloom feels the hate, which he doesn't understand, and is "chapfallen."

The episode ends with Bloom reacting to Menton's hate and naively thinking that old "oyster eyes" (signifying Menton as an oyster shell opened up or uncovered) will eventually regret the way he has treated Bloom. Continuing the Hades pun, Bloom thinks he will be getting the "pull over him that way" (more covering and concealment). Then Bloom, apparently reconstructing the event in his imagination to include thanks to him from Menton, thinks "Thank you. How grand we are this morning!" This imaginative reconstruction would involve Menton learning the lesson of death and expressing it through "we" in this statement.

Action in The Odyssey

In Chapter xi, Odysseus recounts for the Phoenicians and their King Alcinous his trip to the land of Oceanus at the limits of the world. Oceanus was the river that ringed the world (flat) beyond which lay only the land of Cimmerii, the land of dreams and the dead. Odysseus took this trip because Circe had instructed him to go to Hades to receive a prophecy from Tiresias. Hades is the land of the dead. The Greek push-off on the voyage for Hades is described in great detail, several of the men being reluctant to leave or to go. During the journey, they are guided by an anonymous helmsman and by the wind. As the sun sinks, they reach the land of the Cimmerians, constantly in mist and cloud where never the sun does shine.

Immediately upon arriving, Odysseus orders a sacrifice of sheep they brought with them. The sacrificial blood from the sheep is poured into a trench, first with mead, then with sweet wine, then with water and finally with white meal. Immediately a horde of ghosts appears around the trench crying for blood. The dead have finally learned to appreciate blood and all that it stands for. The dead have learned the lesson of death. Odysseus has to guard the blood with his sword, so passionate are the ghosts for it. Apparently a bloodless ghost can be hurt by a sword.

Odysseus then meets ghosts of persons from his life experience. The first is his kinsman Elpenor, who was left dead but unburied; he asks not for blood but to be buried. Honor before compassion. Odysseus agrees. Then Odysseus receives his mother; she died in Ithaca of a broken heart because her son was gone so long. Without blood, she doesn't even recognize him. No blood for her either, at least not yet since he must make sure there is enough blood for Tiresias. Finally Tiresias

217

arrives and immediately asks for blood. Odysseus consents, Tiresias drinks and then gives Odysseus the following prophecy: Odysseus will have more trouble from Poseidon; he must stay away from the flocks of Helios; he will return to his own house full of wooers; and Odysseus will avenge the wooers. After that success, Odysseus will go by oar to the land of men who do not know the sea and do not eat meat with salt. There he will experience in old age a gentle death from the sea. Note that the prophesied end game for Odysseus is full of paradox.

Having received his prophecy, Odysseus then gives blood to his mother. She drinks and then recognizes him. They catch up on the news, and he learns that she died for loss of his "loving kindness" and that his father has fallen on hard times, is basically homeless and is reduced to sleeping outside. Odysseus tries to embrace her but can't. A bloodless shade can be hurt with a sword, but a blood-filled shade can not be embraced. So much for logic in Hades.

Other famous women ghosts arrive, and Odysseus forces them to drink blood one by one so he can hear their stories one by one. They tell of being mated by Poseidon, Zeus or some other god, including one who bore the tallest men on the earth. In their youth, these tall ones even threatened the immortals but were defeated before reaching the full height of maturity.

Odysseus offers to stop the long story but King Alcinous urges him on. Odysseus continues to tell of meeting the following ghosts: of Agamemnon, who had met death at the hands of those closest to him and who advised Odysseus to be cautious upon returning to his wife; of Achilles, who said he would rather be lowly and alive rather than famous and dead; of Ajax, who still bore a grudge over a contest Odysseus had won for which he was awarded the arms of Achilles; of Orion, who was with the beasts he had slain; of Tityos, who was eaten by vultures because he had angered the gods; of Tantalus, who was in constant thirst near the receding water and the fruit blowing away; of Sisyphus, who pushed the stone uphill over and over again; and of Hercules, who created clamor and fear. Notice that every shade Odysseus meets has no peace in his or her soul and continues to suffer. Fearing the risk of a longer stay and being crowded by thousands of shades, Odysseus successfully exits the Land of the Dead.

Parallels to The Odyssey

The parallels in this case are more detailed than usual and provide important background relief for the main themes of the episode.

The reference for the blood the ghosts must drink before they can relate to Odysseus is the blood of loving kindness, the sap that binds the human unity. The other Dubliners act like the shades without blood, not relating to each other at all. The shades' desire for blood is reflected in Bloom's musing about whether a corpse could bleed.

The reference for the ride in their ship by Odysseus and his crew to Oceanus, the limits of the world, is the ride in the carriage to the cemetery. When Bloom leaves the cemetery, he says, "Back to the world again." The River Oceanus and other rivers in Hades sponsor the references to four rivers in Dublin. The sky clouds over at the funeral, as the sun never shows on the land of the Cimmerians. The reluctance of Simon to enter the funeral carriage captures the reluctance of Odysseus's crew to leave for Hades. The unknown driver of the funeral carriage is the nameless helmsman of Odysseus's barque. The sacrifice of blood with mead comes back as Meade's timberyard, and the sacrifice with white meal shows up as the picnic remains on the seat of the carriage. The bums begging on the streets of Dublin are the reference for the homeless condition of Odysseus's father as disclosed by Tiresias. Elpeanor's first priority to be buried prompts the references to the burial practices in many societies.

Mr. Power, who has to bend his height to enter the carriage, is the reference for the tall sons who threatened the gods but were cut down before they completed their realization. John Henry Menton bearing the grudge against Bloom plays Ajax or Aias (means brotherhood and sounds like I ass); his creased hat and grudge keeping reflect Ajax's continuing madness in reaction to not receiving the arms of Achilles instead of Odysseus. Orion with his slain beasts appear as the cattle and sheep going to slaughter, the poor souls who live and die without realization. Bloom's memory of the Parsi practice of leaving the dead on poles for the vultures to eat is echoed in Tityos being eaten by vultures. Bloom's decision not to surprise Molly at home reflects the warning by

Agamemnon to Odysseus to be careful when he arrives at home.

Odysseus was able to obtain the prophecy of his future fate from Tiresias in Hades, as the knowledge of the certainty of death gives humans the understanding central to life. Even Jesse's main ad man and love advocate St. Paul gets mentioned. Before Kernan quotes Jesus ("I am the resurrection and the light"), Bloom has been depressed by the occasion. After this point in the episode, Bloom gathers himself and leaves the cemetery on a high note.

Traditional Schemata

The traditional schemata given by Joyce for this episode are organ—heart, art—religion (religion as an art?), colors—white and black, symbol—caretaker (take care for others) and technique—incubism. White and black are the colors of ghosts and the dead. In this case, incubism suggests the ghosts but more importantly the nature of the brooding that Bloom does about the dead. Most of his thoughts emerge from an association process born of brooding on death. Dignam with the red face of an alcoholic stands for Elpenor, whose name according to Berard means blazing face; neither is buried yet. Father Coffey officiating at the funeral plays Cerberus, the many headed dog who keeps the dead in the underworld. The cemetery caretaker John O'Connell plays Hades the ruler of the underworld.[5]

Linati also lists Eriphyle (another wife who betrayed her husband), Orion the hunter, Odysseus's father Laertes, Prometheus with the bad liver like Paddy Dignam's, Proserpine the Roman queen of Hades (the hard unwed mother at the cemetery), Telemachus for Stephen and Antinoos for Buck Mulligan.

The Secret Cause and the Colander

The secret cause is the fundamental epiphany in Joyce's aesthetic system. The secret cause is part of the definition of terror, "the feeling which arrests the mind in the presence of whatsoever is grave and constant in human sufferings and unites it with the secret cause." The secret cause, which Joyce does not specify, is given as the ground of all that is grave and constant or irremediable in the human condition. I believe the secret cause is the inevitability of death of humans. That is to say, all instances of pity, in which the mind is arrested before that which

220

is grave and constant in human sufferings and unites the reader with the human sufferer, are based on the fundamental human condition of mortality. This is the fundamental ground in Joyce's aesthetic system, and this episode focuses on it. Compare this with the separate attitude of Stephen in the time related 3rd episode.

Given this focus, the episode presents the odd trope of rain falling in separate drops as if strained through a colander, a bowl which allows liquid to flow out holes in the pattern of the Star of David. Water is the symbol of unity, but in this case is falling in separate drops because of the vanity of those involved. The straining device suggests an emphasis on what is left in the strainer after the separate drops are gone. What residue is left when separating vanity is strained out? The residue is the secret cause, the certainty of death that is the source of potential unity. The water of unity passes through in the pattern of the Star of David, the interlocking triangles signifying the unity of macro and microcosm.

The Secret in the Mass and the Sacred Heart

The parallel in the Mass for the Faithful is the Secret. The Secret is a petition to God that is recited by the priest inaudibly during the Mass and thus kept secret from the congregation. The petition recited on June 16, 1904 was a petition to the charity of God to accept the Mass as "an acceptable gift and in atonement for our sins"[6]. The Latin phrases, translated below, scattered throughout this episode make up a petition of sorts:

> In the name of the Father.
> Enter not into judgment with thy servant, O Lord.
> And lead us not into temptation.
> May the angels lead you into paradise.

These petitions ask unrealistically for protection from suffering and death and for a direct transit to Heaven by the lead of angels, rather than by the normal route death. These petitions do not ask for what is really needed, the living strength necessary to come to terms with suffering and death. By contrast, the secret disclosed by the Secret Cause is that only dissolution of ego and detachment bring relief, not the Mass or prayers for deliverance from death.

The secret disclosed by the statue of Jesus as the Sacred Heart is that a Jesus who asks for reparations for his sufferings has lost his own heart. His heart is outside and still dependent on human reparations; this Jesus seeks more blood of sacrifice because he has not been fully appreciated for his sacrifice. No wonder this cult was popular in 1904 with Irish women. This is a sadistic Jesus trying to produce guilt in his masochistic faithful. In this condition, his heart has been exposed because he "burst sideways," the description used by Simon to describe the corpulence of the cemetery keeper. Guilt and fear to tame the congregation, signified by the tamed bird on the poplar tree. Joyce at his best.

First Letter and First Word

The first letter **M** of the first word Martin repeats from the first of the Bloom episodes (M also opened the fourth). In this case, I believe the reference is to M of AUM, the deep sleep beyond dreaming where the mystical union into universal consciousness reportedly takes place. Here that condition is in death. Opening with the name Martin Cunningham emphasizes separate existence. Martin is also the name of a bird in the swallow family.

Sitting Shiva

Much of Bloom's attitude about the Catholic funeral process is in tune with Jewish rituals for burial and for post-funeral grief. The Jewish rituals are designed, like the Bardo, to help protect the soul of the dead as well as the grieving relatives. The right attitude in this process is to de-emphasize the individual ego.

The philosophy of the Jewish death ritual is that all are the same in death.[7] Looking on the face of the dead is not permitted. Bloom remembers that he was not allowed to look on his dead father's face. During the service, the surviving spouse cuts "Keriah," tears her garment and wears it for seven days, never to be repaired. This sponsors the reference to Molly's ripped gown, which she was wearing just before Rudy was conceived and which has never been repaired.

The reading in the Shiva ritual is from Psalm 49, "The futility of riches." It contains the following lines: "But man could never redeem himself or pay his ransom to God: it costs so much to redeem his life, it is beyond him; how then could he live on for ever and never see the Pit." This is the main message of the episode, recognizing the implications of the pit of death. Continuing in the Psalm: "Their tombs are their eternal home, their lasting residence. . . ." This returns in "The Irishman's house is his coffin." More Psalm: "Man in his prosperity forfeits intelligence: he is one with the cattle doomed to slaughter." Dubliners—like the cattle doomed to slaughter they encounter on the road.

The casket should, according to Jewish ritual, be brought in feet first to prevent the deceased from looking back. Bloom thinks: "Which end is his head?" Grass is thrown over the right shoulder in the Jewish ritual, and here one gravedigger plucks a long tuft of grass from the "haft," a word meaning both the handle of the shovel and a new residence.

Back at the home of the deceased, 12 ritually purified Jews should sit Shiva. Twelve Dubliners plus Macintosh, the death in life, attend this funeral. Those sitting Shiva sit for three days without wearing shoes, leaving, working, shaving or having fun. They are not to call attention to themselves by dress or actions. Here Bloom has just been purified in the bath and worries about his socks being properly darned and about the "soles" of his feet. Unlike the other Dubliners, he is properly respectful of the dead, thinks about what death means and does not try to impress the others. The others pursue their separate ego identification by trying to impress each other.

The Shiva rituals carry out the message of the Book of Ecclesiastics, that all of life's material rewards and personal pride and achievements are empty vanity. The Hebrew word used for vanity is *hebel*, which suggests mist or vapor.[8] Rain falls on Eccles Street and the vain mourners.

Ganesha

Death is defeated in the realm of the flesh only by having children. For this reason, the father-son theme is presented repeatedly.

An appearance is made by Ganesha, the son of Shiva. Shiva presided over the last episode. Ganesha is traditionally presented visually as an elephant-headed man whose vehicle is the rat. The elephant can overcome any large obstacles, and the rat can get in the smallest places.

223

The elephant characteristic shows up in the descriptions of the "trunks" swaying in the funeral coach. This unusual word is used repeatedly. The word elephant is also mentioned as part of the name of a store. The rat shows up *in persona* in the cemetery doing its thing.

The sacred utterance associated with Ganesha is "Thou art That," the formula that declares the connection between the absolute (that) and the relative in existence (thou), the basic unity of the whole and part. "That," representing the limitless, transcendent principle or Father, and "Thou," representing the relative presence in the Universe or the Son, are welded together by the third term "art," or existence.[9] This weld also suggests that art as in literature provides a connection from the relative individual to the absolute human condition, the part to the whole. Thou art that or the Father art the Son through art, Stephen's formula for personal and artistic realization. For the rest of us, this realization of the human unity removes obstacles to realization. In this episode about heart, we contemplate along the same lines HEART as HE ART, or third person dramatic art.

In his traditional pose, one of Ganesha's four hands holds a noose and a hook, which appear in the carriage armsling that only the cautious Bloom uses. Ganesha's trunk is bent to indicate that he goes around obstacles[10] as Bloom bobs and weaves in the conversation in an effort to avoid acrimony, despite the obvious anti-Semitism being directed at him.

Tibetan Book of the Dead—Bardo or Do Bar

This ancient classic contains a description of the soul journey shortly after death in "bardo"; the bardo is the period "in between" death and rebirth in reincarnation. The procedures in the Book of the Dead are designed to de-emphasize the ego during life in the interest of avoiding adverse reincarnation after death during the bardo process. Immediately after death, the soul passes downward through the chakras starting from the top one, the seventh. If the soul has been sufficiently advanced during life, it holds on to the fourth (heart) or higher chakra, thus reducing the fall to less than five chakras. If not, it will fall five or more chakras to the third or lower and certain reincarnation as a human or animal or object. This concept returns in Bloom's musing about Jesus raising Lazarus:

224

"Come forth, Lazarus! And he came fifth and lost the job. Get up! Last day!"

In the all important fourth chakra of the heart, the reigning Buddha is Amitabha, whose shakti or consort is the "Woman in White." This reference gives us Molly in the cream gown. Amitabha's virtue is compassion, and the correlative obscuring vision of the deceased is attachment. If the deceased's mind has been attached to the things of this world, then the deceased experiences the world of the hungry ghosts, inconsolable spirits with insatiable stomachs.[11] Your Dubliners.

The state of bardo or in between for our Dubliners is a failure of spiritual rebirth between birth and death. Their twist on bardo is let's do bar, where the in-between state is intoxication.

The Ghosts

The ghosts from Homer's Hades appear in the cemetery statues being prepared in the Stonecutter's yard: "Crowded on the spit of land silent shapes appeared, white, sorrowful, holding out calm hands, knelt in grief, pointing." But make no mistake, the real ghosts here are the other occupants of the funeral carriage. While condemning suicide ("But the worst of all . . . is the man who takes his own life"), they have already committed suicide of the living spirit. As one of them says, "The crown had no evidence. . ." Given the association of the crown of the head in the chakra system with ultimate realization (seventh chakra), this is tantamount to saying there is no evidence of realization at the crown. The Dubliners dead to life are counterparts of the tame bird perched on the poplar branch; this bird, the symbol of soul flight for Stephen, doesn't rise to the occasion.

The Dubliners pray to memories and to the complex molecule. As Simon offers to buy the first round of drinks after the funeral, Cunningham says, "Praises be to God!" For them, drinks in the pub are the blood of life. After many years, their faces turn permanently red in superficial vitality.

Tramline

The tramline emerges in this episode as a symbol for a life without willpower, a life run on a pre-established route according to schedules dictated by others. People of this sort are reliable and often

225

used by others.

Reuben Dodd and Son

The story about the money lender and his son is a obvious parallel to the Jesus story. The son of the money lender is referred to as the "chiseler." Jesse's occupation was probably that of a stonemason as well as a carpenter. The story suggests that God should have left Jesus on earth, as Reuben's son should have stayed with the pregnant girl. The concept of Jesus staying on the earth promotes Jesus as a living example, not as a bridge.

Sisyphus

The overt Sisyphus reference to Cunningham and his alcoholic wife suggests the unending nature of ego suffering, but also invites a deeper analysis of that legend. Sisyphus is most famous for his rock pushing exploits; lesser known is his paternity of a famous son whom he sired because of a chain of events that started with the theft of his cattle by Autolycus. After Sisyphus's herd shrunk and Autolycus's swelled, Sisyphus had his cattle branded with the monogram SS. After the next theft, Sisyphus confronted the thief and in the process seduced his daughter. The result of their union was our hero Odysseus.

Tantalus

Tantalus ("tantalizing") is best known for his punishment, eternally thirsty while in the midst of water and fruit that receded whenever he reached for them. This is a powerful image of the frustration inevitably involved in seeking identification just through the individual ego. Tantalus is less famous for one of his recipes for father-son stew. Having called a banquet and invited the gods, Tantalus put the body of his son Pelop in the stew; and the gods claimed they were aghast. [12] Think stew when you read this: "A dwarf's face, mauve and wrinkled like little Rudy's was."

This legend, I believe, is the underlying reference for the relationship between Simon and Stephen, which surfaces when Bloom spots Stephen walking near the procession. This episode contains the background energy echo of Simon's attempt, witting or otherwise, to curtail Stephen's realization, or put him in the common stew like everyone else. Simon repeatedly talks about the past. As pointed out by

226

Helene Cixous, Simon tries to deny his son by living in the past of the good old days, killing time and associating life with memory and thereby refusing his son the right to live as himself realized in the present[13] Compare Bloom's attitude toward a son—make him independent and even teach him German, so he could read Hegel and Schopenhauer about the unity.

MacIntosh

Continuing the influence of the derivation of Hades from covering or concealment, the unknown 13th mourner is described by reference to his cover—a macintosh rain coat. The association with the number 13 suggests the Devil. His presence makes everyone at the funeral capable of being described as the 13th person.

The famous rainproof material invented by Charles MacIntosh was composed of two layers of material joined by rubber that had been dissolved in naphtha. Mr. MacIntosh developed this fabric in the process of searching for commercial uses for the waste products of gas works, which are mentioned in the episode.[14] Since water is the symbol of the unity and the eternal, the association with the Devil makes sense, particularly here in the context of death. Also consider the construction of the raincoat as a symbol for vain humans such as these Dubliners—devil gas inside two layers of skin.

After the funeral, MacIntosh disappears quickly, and his identity is confused by the reporter Hynes. Watch for this character to be reported anonymously in the newspaper account of the funeral and to reappear mysteriously in the last drinking scene in the Oxen of the Sun (14th) episode and in the brothel scene in the Circe (15th) episode. Like the Anti-Christ in Rev. 17:8, "the beast that once was, and is not, and yet is," this creature appears and disappears repeatedly in this novel.

Connections with Proteus

In the time related Proteus (3rd) episode, the only constant was change, endless becoming. The endless becoming in the human sphere is through procreation, here emphasized in the father-son theme. "Cockles of his heart" are mentioned here, one of the basic structures of the Proteus episode. The gate, here to the transcendent, reappears. As do the navelcord and the dog. Separated Stephen matches the vain Dubliners.

227

Purification

In a later summary, the funeral in this episode is referred to in terms of Jewish ritual as the "Rite of Samuel." There is no rite of Samuel that I can find. But apropos of this episode, the prophet Samuel (I Samuel 28) was raised from the dead by King Saul through the offices of a necromancer, "the witch of En-Dor." The King went to these efforts because the King could not get in touch with Jahweh and the battle with the Philistines was going badly. Moreover, David was a threat to Saul's throne. The witch raised the ghost of Samuel from the dead, and the King bowed down in homage. The King explained the situation and asked Samuel to help him with Yahweh. Samuel told the King that Yahweh had already told him all he needed to know about his future and added that he and his sons would die the next day in battle with the Philistines. Despite knowledge of certain death the next day, the King doesn't change his attitude. The next day the Jews lose to the Philistines and the King falls on his own sword.

Like the witch, the Dubliners are necromancers; they stay in touch with the dead and bow in homage to dead heroes at the expense of the living spirit. Like the King, the Dubliners don't learn the lesson from the knowledge of certain death, the Secret Cause. The ultimate prophecy is death.

Structure, Art and Aesthetics

This episode continues the actions and thoughts of Bloom in the dramatic style. The thoughts of the other characters are not reported. The composition style remains the same, an objective third party voice blended in with Bloom's stream of consciousness. Like Stephen in the time related 3rd episode, more of Bloom's thoughts are reported compared to the last two episodes.

The subject is death and its relationship to life—the very essence of Joyce's concept of terror, that which arrests the mind before the grave and constant in human suffering and unites the reader with the secret cause. The knowledge of death teaches Bloom compassion and the others fear. Fear that reduces their spirit to ego and their life to booze and covers their soul. Fear buries their spirit. This is the major issue of modern life "in spades," how to come to terms with death in the post-

Christian world.

I feel the poignancy of Bloom's position, the vulnerability of compassion against hate. In this respect, the episode is highly successful for my money. The pace of Bloom's thoughts is governed by the nature of brooding. This episode drags near the end in order to portray Bloom's increasing desire to get out of the cemetery.

My principal objection to this episode is the kitchen sink. Joyce has thrown into this episode a multitude of aspects of death, burial practices and the conceptualized reality after death. I can't coordinate them all in mental solution in a way so that they all add to the dramatic effectiveness of the episode. Aside from their loose association under common subject matter, they don't for me effectively reinforce the main message of the episode. The *integritas* or mark off function has not been sufficiently narrow for my money.

****
ENDNOTES

1. *James Joyce's Ulysses Critical Essays* edit. C. Hart and D. Hayman (Berkeley: University of California Press, 1974) p. 110.
2. Frye I, p. 123.
3. Lang, p. 140.
4. Zimmer, Myths and Symbols, pp.183-4.
5. Gifford, p. 104.
6. Lang, p. 141.
7. All of the following information comes from Syme, D. *The Jewish Home* (New York: UAHC Press, 1974) pp. 106 -115.
8. Frye II, p. 127.
9. Ibid, p. 294.
10. Ibid, p. 296.
11. Campbell, The Mythic Image, p. 403.
12. Ibid, p. 387.
13. Cixous, p. 44.
14. *MacIntosh, Charles* Encyclopedia Britannica, 1983 edition, Micropaedia, Vol. VI, p. 449.

Episode 7 (Aeolus)

Basic Themes

"Cruel Karma blocks Promised Land."

Hereditary and cultural karma threaten Stephen's independence as he flirts with the profession of journalism. Spiritual governance is the main theme, free will versus karma and the Law of the Fathers. Stephen's exercise of independence is associated with a short circuit of Dublin's tram system.

The alcoholic editor of the *Freeman* invites Stephen to join the pressgang. The editor praises him as a chip off the old block of his father, the karma of hereditary inheritance. The editor compliments Stephen's abilities and invites him to "write something for me" with a "bite in it." Reacting to this praise, ego inflation momentarily blushes Stephen's cheeks. Fortunately for his future, Stephen quickly realizes the deflation potential of this job and that its bite would drain him vampire-like of the artistic independence on which he has staked his realization.

Stephen realizes that writing even part-time for the newspaper about the transient and superficial topics of the day with a view to increasing newspaper circulation would compromise and corrupt him as an artist. The "purple prose" of the newspaper style is on display in the unusual headlines and writing devices used in this episode. A successful newspaper must reflect the opinions of the times, or cultural karma.

After explicit references to Moses and the Promised Land, Stephen gives his response to the press job offer in the form of an extemporized "vision." This vision he gives two titles: in florid newspaper style, "The Pisgah Sight of Palestine," referring to the fact that Moses gets to see the Promised Land from Mt. Pisgah but not enter; and in restrained style, "The Parable of the Plums." In Stephen's vision, two Dublin virgins ascend the pillar bearing the statue of Lord Nelson, the English naval hero described as the "one-armed adulterer." From the top of the pillar, they spit plum pits onto the barren ground below. The message of the parable is that Stephen believes that this press job even on a part time basis would result in lack of fulfillment in his artistic realization because of the necessity of writing for the wrong reasons,

230

through corruption of his soul effectively bar Stephen from the promised land of art, and thereby waste his seed. As with even one prayer for his mother, the corruption of this job would pollute the spirit.

Focused on the promised land of art, Stephen refuses to make the same mistake Moses made, inheriting the cultural attitudes of the old generation. That cultural karma cost Moses entrance into the Promised Land. Only the new Jewish generation born in the desert and not in Egypt was allowed to enter. Stephen breaks away from hereditary and cultural karma and levels the "Law of the Fathers"[1]. He is the leader of the new generation of artists who can enter into the artistic promised land. His exercise of freedom brings to a full stop the Dublin trams that signify fixed destiny. The story of the Jews continues with allusions to the pillar of the cloud, a whirlwind powered by Jahweh that led the Jews in the desert. Since the Jews wandered for 40 years, the pillar proved an unreliable guide to freedom. The editor of the newspaper plays Balaam on his ass to Bloom's Moses.

In the related chapter x of The Odyssey, Odysseus sails almost all the way home with help from King Aeolus. The King had tied up all the bad winds in a wallet (leather sack), but members of Odysseus's crew greedy for treasure open the wallet, while Odysseus is asleep, only to release the bad winds. The bad winds force their ship all the way back to the King's island. These winds are associated with dead ancestors and thus with hereditary karma. This lack of progress and frustration of fulfillment is the fate Stephen would experience if he were to inherit the role of the chip off the old block.

This episode is full of images of wind, inflation and deflation, movement out and back and out and in. These images toss this episode to and fro and generate an over-all mood of transience commensurate with the typical concerns of the newspaper. In the middle of this low pressure zone, Bloom is at work in the "gentle art of advertisement." He uses understanding, tact and quiet diplomacy in an unsuccessful effort to place into the newspaper an ad for the House of Keyes with a crossed keys logo. The editor frustrates fulfillment of Bloom's business prospects.

The episode is chock full of rhetorical devices and is broken into unnaturally short or unnaturally long sections, newspaper article length being governed by space considerations rather than content. The section titles are composed in the overcooked newspaper headline style.[2] These devices are used for their own sake and do not integrate into the text. The use of headlines makes the narrative flow choppy. These effects, no doubt deliberate, emphasize the results of writing for a purpose other than beauty, in this case to ease comprehension and to promote newspaper circulation. These effects help make the contrast between the impatient purple prose of the newspaper about transient and superficial topics of the day and the proper art of Stephen's restrained parable about the grave and constant in human affairs.

With an emphasis on Old Testament events and newspaper printing, "Typology becomes typography"[3]. Both reflect restrictions on Stephen's realization, typology by holding the present hostage to the past and typography by merely copying others. The use of Biblical events in tawdry newspaper headlines deflates the patristic solemnity of biblical typology. One headline is "From the Fathers." For these solemn Fathers, Moses was the type (first event) for Christ's anti-type (second event) and Christ fulfilled Moses through their divine vertical connection. But the Fathers focused on the Exodus, not on Moses's failure to make it to the Promised Land.

Stephen's refusal to yield to karma franchises a stylistic break in this episode away from traditional realistic presentation.

Newspaper Offices

This episode begins with a description of Dublin activities near the offices of the **Freeman** newspapers and continues mostly inside their offices. Two newspapers are published from his location, the *Weekly Freeman and National Press* and the *Freeman's Journal and National Press*. Crawford is editor of the Weekly and Brayden of the Journal.

Nelson's Pillar, where the episode opens and ends, is adjacent to the newspaper offices. Two blocks away is the River Liffey, one block away the pub "The Ship," where Mulligan and Haines are scheduled to meet Stephen, and three blocks away Dillon's auction room. This is in the eastern most portion of Dublin.

The episode starts about 12:00 noon and progresses for some time. Later in the episode, Stephen arrives at the newspaper offices from the beach where he was walking at noon in the Proteus (3rd) episode. Both Stephen and Bloom are involved.

Action in Ulysses

This episode starts with animated descriptions of several processes that, like the winds, involve repetitious movements back and forth or in and out.

The first process, under the purple prose headline "In the Heart of the Hibernian Metropolis," is the municipal electric tram system. Hibernian is Latin for Ireland, and metropolis means both chief city and bishop of the city. Accordingly, the episode opens with the occupation of the heart of the city by the Law of the Fathers and fixed destiny.

Nelson's pillar is the central control and changing point for the tram system; there in-bound cars are shunted, a process of transfer, onto new tracks for the next run out-bound. The cars come in, change tracks and go out again. The various names in the text (Black Rock, Kingstown and Dalkey . . .) are the terminal point destinations for each line, the last stop where they are bound to go. Double and single deck tramcars are mentioned. Nelson's pillar, a copy of one in England, celebrates an English naval hero and symbolizes English control of Ireland through power. The admirable Admiral lost one arm in action and famously engaged in adultery in foreign ports, thus the "one armed adulterer."

The second process, described under the "The Wearer of the Crown" headline, is the Royal mail service, which receives letters and then sends them out. The third process, curiously described under the "Gentlemen of the Press" headline, is the loading of beer into barrels that are being shipped out on floats and no doubt returned empty.

Then under the headline "William Brayden . . ." the episode cuts abruptly, like a wind shift, to inside the newspaper plant. Bloom and Red Murray, a copy editor, have located in an old newspaper an ad previously used by Alexander Keyes. Mr. Keyes, Bloom's client, now wants to renew the ad using a new logo, crossed keys. (Remember the importance of key in earlier episodes — the key for the tower, Dalkey, hockey, Ikey.) Bloom and Red discuss in advertising jargon the preparation of a new ad to advertise the commercial identity of the House of Keyes, a store that sells liquor or spirits.

233

Bloom is working. He is an ad canvasser, a go-between. He goes between the commercial establishment who wants an ad and the paper that sells advertising space. The word canvasser plays back to canvas, sails and ships.[4] He makes connections in order to sell space-time in the newspaper to advertise commercial identity.

Just about then it hit me. House of Spirits. Souls and metempsychoses. The *Freeman* newspaper, free will. These perfectly normal little scenes near or at the newspaper offices are symbols for the process of creating new human souls; in this process, karma and reincarnation are at odds with free will. This follows from the last episode dealing with Bardo and death. The municipal tram system delivering current to the tramcar on an outbound route, the Royal mail service receiving and sending out letters and the beer enterprise of loading spirits (read souls) into empty barrels (read bodies) and shipping them down the Liffey River of life are symbols of governance in the process of creating new human bodies, minds and spirits.

The tram system always stops at the same locations.[5] These stops are selected on the basis of where customers have wanted to go in the past. Destination karma. Delivery by royal mail service suggests the powers that be. The reuse of the same beer barrels suggest the repetitious role of karma and heredity that restrict human freedom and possibilities. Just to emphasize the repetition, Joyce does it in the text in a pattern of out and then back (ABC—CBA):

> Grossbooted draymen rolled barrels dullthudding out
> of Prince's stores and bumped them up on the brewery
> float. On the brewery float bumped dullthudding
> barrels rolled by grossbooted draymen out of Prince's
> stores.

Our Mr. Bloom, the master of go-between or compassion, tries to bring to this process spiritual illumination symbolized by the crossed keys in the ad for the House of Keyes. To emphasize this point, Joyce lets us know that the same symbol is used to designate the House of Parliament for the Isle of Man (read governance of man). The copy editor talks about throwing in a "par," a paragraph that is an ad but designed to look like a news item, or in reincarnation just another average person with a lack of integrity. Bloom and the editor cut and paste; in karma and heredity the results of the last life are cut and pasted into the new life. Bloom will "rub it in" (into the new life) as they make the new ad. Bloom thinks about the unity of creation: "We."

As the action continues, other governing influences in the "life" of the newspaper make their appearance. In order to signal the association of newspaper governance with spiritual governance, the editor Brayden (bray as in donkey) is compared superficially to Christ, for the soul the "way in" and the "way out." The dullthudding barrels of spirits are repeated right in the middle of the description of the editor. His Grace the Archbishop, a chief exponent of the Law of the Fathers, has phoned twice in an effort to influence coverage in the paper.

Bloom smiles meekly as he walks through the newspaper plant, which is described in ways to suggest the human body. He goes through the counterflap (a one-way valve) down the warm dark stairs and passage (a blood vessel) to the sounds of the printing press (the beating heart). Joyce emphasizes the words "circulation" and "organ," which are common to the body and the newspaper. Under the "With Unfeigned Regret . . ." headline, machines are directly compared to the human body.

Under the headline "How a Great Daily Organ is Turned Out," Bloom thinks about Nannetti, the business manager of the newspaper, and Hynes delivers his write up of the funeral for the next edition. Bloom considers subjects that sell newspapers: jokes, pictures, and human interest stories such as the double wedding of sisters. Bloom surveys the material normally contained in the paper and, since the Weekly is just that (in more ways than one), about old "news" in papers that come out only weekly. A mule is mentioned (for Balaam's ass). The phrase "an organ turned out" suggests the image of the Sacred Heart of Jesus (heart exposed). Seeing Hynes about to be paid for covering the funeral, Bloom tries to remind him gently of the debt Hynes owes Bloom. Bloom is so gentle Hynes doesn't feel any pressure to repay.

Under the ". . . Canvasser at Work" and "House of Key(e)s" (Keyes the name and keys the symbol) headlines, Bloom talks to Nannetti, the business manager for the newspaper, about the ad for the House of Keyes. Nannetti is bald and blunt. Successful as a local politician, a city councilor, he is about to run for mayor of Dublin (more governance). Nannetti scratches like a monkey when considering the crossed keys ad. This reference to our primitive ancestors suggests the inherited governance of mankind leaves us with an itch, a suggestion confirmed by the last lines of the episode. Bloom considers asking Nannetti the proper pronunciation of the Italian word *voglio*, but decides not to do so out of sensitivity to Nannetti's possible reaction to mention of his nationality. Compare this sensitivity with the anti-Semitism experienced by Bloom.

Bloom explains the ad with the crossed keys. Nannetti agrees to run the new ad in exchange for an advertising commitment of three months. A "limp" galleypage (read baby) is brought in for examination by Nannetti. Under the ". . . Occasional Contributor" headline, a man named Monks is mentioned. He is the "Dayfather" (read the ego function), who is serious and conservative.

Under the ". . . Feast of the Passover" headline, Bloom watches the typesetters laying type backwards and is reminded of Old Testament events and of his father reading to him in Hebrew (read back to front). This suggests Biblical typology and its emphasis on connecting back to earlier events, the historical counterpart of karma. In typology, events in the present are measured against earlier events and serve principally to fulfill the earlier events. Present events are not evaluated on their own terms. This kind of control of the present by the past is similar to karma.

Bloom remembers the Exodus, perhaps with a Freudian slip: " . . . out of the land of Egypt and into the house of bondage . . . ." Formal Judaism with its many detailed rules for life would be a house of bondage. He recalls, from Passover Seder chants, the references to the 12 tribes and the long list of killers in the chain (the angel kills the butcher, the butcher the ox etc.), or in summary life eats life. In the original version that Bloom incorrectly remembers (memory as mental karma), the lowest item on the food chain is a baby lamb, a kid signifying Israel.[6] This reference links the newsboys, the kids, with Israel. Note that technically Bloom is not Jewish since his mother wasn't. In Dublin, however, either parental line is apparently enough for discrimination.

Bloom remembers Keyes's telephone number as 2844. Under the ". . . Soap" headline, Bloom leaves the printing room and notices match made graffiti on the walls and a greasy smell. He moves the soap he purchased in the 5th episode from his breast pocket to his hip pocket. He imagines going home and surprising the lovers.

Under the "Erin . . ." headline, Bloom walks into the room where Ned Lambert, Professor MacHugh and Simon Dedalus are talking about Dan Dawson's speech, which was reprinted in the morning newspaper. No one greets Bloom, even though all other arrivals receive friendly greetings. Bloom is connected to Hamlet's ghost through MacHugh's remark "The ghost walks . . ." This follows immediately after "He (Bloom) entered softly." MacHugh is, though, speaking of salaries being paid in the inner office.[7] He sees the payments being made by looking through the window to the inner office.

Kindly as ever, Bloom mentally makes excuses for Lambert not working (because of the funeral). Now Bloom and Stephen's father are in the same room. But not for long. The Dawson speech, entitled "Our Lovely Land" and about Ireland's beauty, is being read aloud. Like the newspaper, the speech is composed in overblown or inflated purple prose. Simon Dedalus tries to show off with Greek references: "And Xenophon looked on Marathon . . . and Marathon looked on the sea." By contrast, Bloom charitably thinks about Ned Lambert's family.

Under the "Short But To The Point" headline and in reference to "Our Lovely Land," Bloom asks Whose Land? This question sounds the promised land and anti-Semitism themes and, in a deeper sense, whether Joyce will be able to redeem Ireland from the influences of Catholicism and England (certainly not as a newspaper writer).

O'Molloy comes into the room hitting Bloom in the back with the doorknob. Under the "Sad" headline, Bloom thinks about O'Molloy's loss to booze of a promising legal career (alcohol karma). Dawson's speech, still being read, goes on to references about "serried mountain peaks," which begin to connect the speech with the Moses story.

The deflating potential for Stephen of the pressgang job is paraded in the form of underachieving Gabriel Conroy (from *The Dead* in **Dubliners**). Likewise, the Professor is forced by commercial

237

considerations to teach Latin, which he despises, instead of his beloved Greek. More frustrated fulfillment. Bloom thinks of the pressgang's pursuit of the transient in wind related terms—"wind of a new opening" and "blowing hot and cold in the same breath."

Under the "Wetherup" headline, the editor Myles Crawford first appears. He is described in bird terms ("scarlet beaked face, crested by a comb of feathering hair") and by reference to his harsh voice. Simon Dedalus and Lambert prepare to leave for a pub named the "Oval" and invite editor Myles (but not Bloom) to join them. The editor smiles (vampire like) at Bloom and, under the "Memorable Battles" headline, recalls notable Irish military victories in the US War for Independence (note that the Irish military was on the side of the British oppressor). The editor appears to be slightly off kilter ("jiggs") due to alcoholism. Under the "Harp" headline, the editor oddly cleans his teeth with dental floss in front of the group. Bloom leaves to make a call to Keyes about the ad. He now correctly remembers the number as 2044, not 2844.

Under the "Spot The Winner" headline, Lenehan comes into the room with the pink (read new born) sports edition and makes reference to the Ascot (British) Gold Cup horse race. The newsboys, who are waiting impatiently for the sports edition, push into the room. In the process, the tissues of the sports edition are blown on the floor, and Lenehan picks them up with his "paw." At the urging of the editor, Professor MacHugh throws one newsboy out of the room.

By phone Bloom finds out that Mr. Keyes is at the nearby auction room, so he leaves to find him there to communicate the *Freeman's* offer of three months. On the way back from using the phone in the inner office (under the "A Collision" headline), Bloom opens the door into Lenehan. The newsboys (read the Jewish tribes) are heard outside singing a military song. Under the "Exit Bloom" headline, Bloom explains to the editor he is going out to catch Keyes. The editor tells him "Begone! . . . The world is before you." Under the "A Street Cortege" headline, the newsboys follow Bloom like a "kite's tail" (kike's tail or the Jewish multitude following Moses). Seeing this procession out the window, Lenehan imitates Bloom's unusual walk: "Taking off [mimicking] his flat spaugs [clumsy feet] and walk."

238

The editor gets ready to leave and, like Balaam on his famous ass, he walks "jerkily" and can't find the keys (of illumination). Under the "Calumet . . ." and "Grandeur . . ." headlines, the group continues to shoot the breeze and deride British culture by reference to its ancestor Roman culture, which featured the water closet as its throne and Pilate as its prophet. This is a direct reference to cultural karma. Myles says to O'Molloy that the Irish are the "fat in the fire" and "haven't got the chance of a snowball in hell."

Stephen comes into the room with Burke to deliver Deasy's letter to the editor. The editor greets Stephen warmly, praises him, and calls his father his "governor." Lenehan tries for the first time to tell his opera riddle. Stephen is prompted to remember the poetry he wrote in the Proteus (3rd) episode about the "pale vampire, Mouth to my mouth." The poem is in the lyric mode, and this association relates praise from others with the bite of the vampire. Praise drains personal independence as the romantic lyrical mode drains the characters of independent life.

Under the "Lost Causes" headline, the Professor bemoans the lack of spirituality in the practical British culture. Under the "Limerick" headline, Lenehan describes the Professor by reference to his clouded vision and his ebony glasses.

The editor tells Stephen that Mr. Deasy's letter will be included in the newspaper. Lenehan finally gets his riddle off—what opera is like a railway line? The answer is Rose of Castile and rows of cast steel. The fixed rows of cast steel, such as those in the Dublin tram system, suggest restraints on freedom such as caste, karma and heredity. The joke is not well received. The professor accuses Stephen of looking like a revolutionary because of his loose tie; Stephen prophetically says "they" are only thinking about it.

Under the "You Can . . ." headline, the editor tries to recruit Stephen for the pressgang and asks him to write something with "bite in it" (read the vampire). The editor attempts to recruit Stephen by recounting a famous moment in Irish journalism—when Gallaher, a *Freeman* reporter, telephoned a report to a New York newspaper describing the escape route used by the Invincibles. They had murdered in Phoenix Park two top political leaders deemed traitors to Irish

239

independence. Another crime in the park, which like the Fall in the Garden, left its own karma. The route was described by Gallagher by reference to an ad in a former edition of the Irish newspaper, which was on hand in New York (no fax then). This alerts us to watch for other escape routes out of Dublin paralysis. Mention is made of the local presence of two of the Invincibles, Fitzharris and Gumley. They reappear in the later Eumaeus (16th) episode. Contrary to the editor's intent, Stephen sees how thin it is when it's as good as it gets.

The inbreeding of the press corps is mentioned under the "Clever, Very" headline. Stephen begins to think about his poem and how he can make it more general in interest, removing it from the lyrical toward the grave and constant. Under the "Rhymes and Reasons" headline, he thinks about mouth and south in his poem and rhymes in general. In the lines given in the text in Italian, Stephen contemplates Dante's use in *The Divine Comedy* of quiet rhymes to build an image of temporary arrest from the winds of Hell and his use of the image of three approaching women wearing various colors. Stephen compares the hell winds with the bluster in the newspaper office and contrasts the colorful women with the drab men of the press before him: the pressmen are "penitent, leadenfooted, underdarkneath the night: mouth south: tomb womb." By these images, Stephen registers the drab down side of the press job compared to the arresting yet colorful effort of the poet. Under the "Sufficient . . ." headline, O'Molloy says the newspaper is good enough for the day (art is for the eternal).

The "Links. . ." headline moves closer to the Moses story with references to Seymour (read see more) or Kendal (read kindle) Bushe and the Childs fratricide murder case. Bushe's inability to get on the bench (become a judge) because of an affair is mentioned (Moses married a Midianite woman not a Jew). More frustrated fulfillment. Stephen remembers the line from *Hamlet*, "And in the porches of mine ear did pour," as the ghost told Hamlet about being poisoned through the ear, which frustrated King Hamlet's fulfillment of his reign. Stephen wonders how the ghost found out he had been murdered (not in the newspaper).

Lenehan lights cigarettes for others so he can bum one. The author intrudes with a comment that the lighting of the match for the cigarettes determined the "entire aftercourse of both our lives." This explicit comment about karma is delivered in typical newspaper hyperbole.

Moses is brought up directly under the "A Polished Period" headline. Under the "A Man of High Morale" headline, O'Molloy tells of the reported late night visit by Stephen to A.E. (George Russell the famous Irish poet) to talk about planes of consciousness. This subject suggests a psychological orientation to ascending Pisgah mountain. Stephen resists the urge to ask what A.E. thought of him, as Stephen has resisted praise and staked his soul on independence.

The next several headlines feature the recitation of an earlier speech made by Taylor in favor of the Irish language by analogy to the Jews maintaining their independence in Egypt. This is one of Joyce's favorite passages. Moses's failure to enter the Promised Land and his mysterious demise on Mt. Pisgah are mentioned. Using corporate board room type talk, Stephen suggests adjourning to a pub, and the editor calls him a chip off the old block (what the editor would like to make him). Sure enough, the editor can't find the keys (Stephen, Bloom and the editor are all keyless).

Under the "Let Us Hope" headline (read hope that Stephen will be an artist), Stephen begins his vision as the newsboys race by with the sports special in hand. As Stephen begins the parable with the Professor, Bloom runs up to the editor to report that Mr. Keyes will commit to two months not three. Note that the three months requirement was stipulated by Nannetti, and, so far as we know, the editor doesn't know about it. The editor responds, for the first of three times, to "kiss my arse . . . from the stable." The editor strides on "jerkily," as if riding on an ass. O'Molloy tries unsuccessfully to borrow money from the editor. No compassion in the editor; compare Bloom who has loaned Hynes three shillings and only gently reminds him of the debt.

Stephen's parable is spread out under several headlines because of interruptions (by Bloom). It showcases two Dublin vestal virgins. Stephen has chosen for this purpose the two midwives he just saw on the beach, that is from his own experience. The vestals raid their "letterbox moneybox" for funds for provisions and an outing to Nelson's Pillar, where the trams start. They buy brawn, panloaf and 24 plums, plums at the Pillar having been prefigured in the last episode. They are superstitious, users of Lourdes water and double X. The 50 and 53 year olds huff and puff up the inside stairs of the pillar to the top of the pillar. The statue of Nelson rests on the top of the pillar. Looking out at the City, they fear the pillar will fall, search for and argue about the location of various churches, and look up at Nelson the one-armed adulterer. Their necks stiff and hot, they pull up their dresses, sit down, eat the plums and spit the plum pits over the railing down on to the ground far below. The style of the presentation by Stephen is a model of calm objective prose. But the accompanying headlines become increasingly pretentious and self-conscious.

Stephen finishes telling the parable right under Nelson's Pillar. This parable contains a heavy echo of frustration of fulfillment—virgins in the tower throwing away their seed. The virgins look out at the City and its manifold possibilities, but given their limited life choices, this view of manifold possibilities only makes them nervous. They look for churches for reassurance in their life choices built on limitations. They see from the tower the Promised Land of the manifold possibilities of the City but don't wish to enter.

The Professor thinks the title of Stephen's vision should be (delivered in his despised Latin) "God has made this peace for us." Stephen rejects the Professor's proposal since it suggests passive acceptance of limitations, which at least gives peace. Stephen instead gives the vision two titles: A Pisgah Sight of Palestine or the Parable of the Plums. Both of Stephen's titles suggest lack of fulfillment or frustration with limitations. Note the contrast in these two titles: the first is in the impatient, inflated newspaper headline style, and the second is in a restrained style, like proper literature or even a parable by Christ. The first focuses on what happened, the second on the meaning.

This vision is Stephen's negative reply to the editor's invitation to join the pressgang. Right after this reply is delivered, all the trams on the Dublin United Railway come to a halt "becalmed in short circuit." The karma and reincarnation of family and culture has been short circuited, at least momentarily, by Stephen's exercise of free will.

Professor MacHugh understands the relation of the parable to Moses and masturbation (seed on the ground) and even seems to understand the parable as a negative response to the pressgang offer. The Professor compares Stephen to Antisthenes, the Greek Cynic who counseled restraint in pleasure in external goods and emphasis on internal goods of the soul, even at the cost of pain and suffering.[8] The editor, on the other hand, understands only the masturbation part and, in the last words of the episode, opines that the same "tickled the old ones too . . ." Tickles and itches, the favorite subjects of the newspaper, sufficient for the day. Tickles and itches which restrict action to scratches. Reference to the old ones, for biblical typology and restrictive repetition in karma.

Stephen continues with the group to the pub Mooney's, where Stephen will host drinks for the group, deteriorating specimens of "All the talents. . . Law, the classics. . .   The Turf. . . Literature, the press. . . ." Note that Simon had tried unsuccessfully to get this group to go with him to the "Oval" pub and Buck and Haines are waiting for Stephen at "The Ship."

Action in The Odyssey

In Chapter x, Odysseus is on a floating island where Aeolus, the master keeper of the winds, is King. Aeolus received this position from his patron Kronos, the older generation of pre-Zeus Greek gods. His unusual island has sheer rock walls and ramparts of bronze. The King has 12 children and showing a strong local emphasis (as does the news), the six brothers are married to the six sisters. Odysseus and crew are hosted royally for a month. Noises of imprisoned winds are prominent features of the island.[9]

As requested, Odysseus receives help in returning home in the form of an escort and an ox hide wallet (bag), in which King Aeolus magically contained the bad winds. With these boons, Odysseus and his companions sail nine days and get close enough to their Ithaca home to see the beacon fires. At that point, Odysseus falls asleep (come on!). Members of his curious, jealous and greedy crew open the wallet seeking treasure, only to release the bad winds. Later sources specify that the bad winds are the spirits of the dead.[10] The bad winds drive their ship all the way back to Aeolus. Back on the same island, they explain to King

243

Aeolus what happened. The King refuses to help them a second time, being of the view that they must be cursed by the gods.

Parallels to The Odyssey

The bad Aeolian winds from the spirits of the dead are the winds of karma blowing about Stephen, the influence of his paternity and his culture. The lack of progress in Ireland through generations reflects Odysseus's blown return to the starting place and to the now hostile island King (UK). The noises of the printing press, capturing the news to print, suggest the imprisoned wind noises at Aelous's island.

The movement of the pressgang from job to job is the reference for the floating island. The old-boy network in press jobs is the reference for the incestuous royal brothers and sisters, whose off-spring would have access to a limited gene pool. Coverage of a double wedding of sisters with the grooms laughing is included in Bloom's musings about the type of article that sells newspapers.

Stephen senses his proper role as an artist as Odysseus's ship came close to home. The failure to reach home is reflected in Bloom's failure to place the ad and Stephen's failure to improve the "mouth south" poem by generalizing its interest. Many in the episode have failed to arrive at their Promised Land: Simon, with nothing to do and nowhere to go, who moves to the pub; Professor MacHugh, a would-be scholar, sometime teacher and full time show off, who spends his day at the newspaper offices; O'Molloy, the promising young lawyer, who was brought down by booze; and the lawyer Bushe, who never made it to the bench because of an affair.

First Letter, First Word and Telephone Numbers

In this context, the letter **B** of the first word "Before" (disregarding the headline for this purpose) looks like two sails full of wind extending from a mast. The first letter B is the same opening letter as in the Lotus-eaters (5th) episode. As there, I submit the point is the contrast of the letter B with the figure 8, which stands for infinity or eternity and/or for the joinder of two personalities in the unity, two complete closed circles. The letter B as a vertically severed 8 would stand for the limited realization potential associated with the press job; both Bloom and Stephen would be working for the paper so the circles are joined, but Stephen would not be realized as B is a severed half of the 8.

The first word "Before" has two meanings. One is in the present in the dimension of space, meaning in front of as in "Before Nelson's Pillar." The second is a reference to the past in the dimension of time, which clues in hereditary and cultural karma, history and biblical typology.

Bloom first thinks the telephone number for the House of Keyes (illumination) is 2844, but remembers it correctly as 2044 when he dials. This substitutes 0 for 8, 0 for the closed circle of personality and 8 for eternity excluded by separate personality. Our best examples of this type, Simon Dedalus and Ned Lambert, leave to go to the "Oval" (O) pub. The rest go to Mooney's, where like the moon they can wax and then wane. Given the structure of the episode with the first half for Bloom and the second half for Stephen and their failure to meet, I read their continued separateness in the substitution of the 0 for the 8 in the telephone number.

Traditional Schemata

The traditional schemata given by Joyce for this episode are art—rhetoric, organ—lungs, color—red, symbol—editor, and technique—enthymemic (in logic a syllogism in which one of the premises is based only on probability instead of being true for all cases, more rhetorical than logical). Correspondences are incest—journalism, Aeolus—Crawford, and the floating island—the press. The Linati scheme states that the meaning of the episode is "the mockery of victory," that is a Phyrric battle victory—one more victory like that and we are done for. These include a victory won by mere rhetoric rather than art, the job done for the pay and the day, and in general the life of survival. These are all Phyrric victories in which the spiritual war is lost. The editor, who controls the paper, suggests the control function of karma.

The many types of rhetorical device used in this episode range from abbreviation to zeugma. These devices, typical for the newspaper, show Joyce as a virtuoso in his craft and are used deliberately for their own sake, a deliberate show off in writing in order to make a point. The conversations among the pressgang and the hangerons are similar. They are trying to impress each other. Joyce interpreters report that the three types of oratory as classified by Aristotle are used in this episode—expository in the Dawson speech, forensic in the Bushe speech and deliberative in Taylor's speech.[11] The main point, to my mind, is that all these classifications are based on achieving the desired response in the three different kinds of audience. In other words, the text is custom tailored in order to achieve a certain positive reaction of a specific audience, rather than one truth founded in the grave and constant for all. Likewise, the newspaper panders to ease of comprehension and the expected interests of the readers in controversy. This is all pornographic in Joyce's aesthetic theory. In the realm of personal development, the counterpart is living your life for the praise or the coin of others, poison to independence.

The functioning of the lungs is one example of the repetitious in and out process whose generalized implications are explored in this episode. Appropriate to the general message, the lungs provide only transient relief.

The color red is for blood, which vampire praise would drain and which must be continuously replenished by oxygen from the lungs. Red appears in the red mail vans, the name Red Murray and the editor's scarlet face. In the alcoholic, red rises to the surface of the face registering only superficial vitality and underlying degeneration. In the same "vein," Stephen blushes twice while being wooed for the pressgang. The cosmetically rougy cheeks of Mario the tenor liken superficially unto Jesus. All of them — the newspaper, the blush to praise, the cosmetics, and the alcoholic "buzz" — are transient and superficial.

The editor Crawford is like Aeolus because they both give and take. Aeolus first helps and then drives Odysseus off. Crawford would give Stephen a job but take his independence. The use of enthyme, a syllogism with a premise suppressed because probable rather than certain, is seen in the arguments of the characters in this episode. According to Aristotle according to Stuart Gilbert, the orator often must

246

use enthymemic reasoning to support the argumentation designed to support a desired conviction in the audience.

Newspaper

One concept that permeates this episode is the difference between the newspaper of the day and literature of the ages. The newspaper contains items of passing interest, matters that are transient and superficial. It is written in purple prose. It is "sufficient for the day," as opposed to what is grave and constant. The news items are selected and written with a view towards increased circulation. This limits the possibilities. The newspaper is similar to the lyric mode in which Stephen's poem was written, and even similar to enthymemic reasoning; all three proceed from premises that limit the force of the result. Stimulated by rejecting the press job, Stephen quotes his lyrical poem and tries to think how he can make it more general in interest.

Newspaper production is described repeatedly in terms of the human condition. The printing press is the heart, the lungs the pressgang and the editors and business manager the governance. The smell of grease is for the stomach. Bloom tries to bring illumination to this process in terms of the crossed keys. The interests of the readers, to which the newspaper caters, poison the process.

As Odysseus finds out, it matters who your companions are in your effort to get home. Here are the companions that Stephen would have on the pressgang. They stand around the empty fireplace without fire in their souls, shoot the breeze and then at noon go to the pub.

Moses Story

Several explicit references to Moses and his failure to enter the Promised Land suggest a detailed review of that part of the story. Moses was frustrated in his fulfillment because he was not allowed to reach the Promised Land. According to some sources, he was denied because he was the last of the old Egyptian-born generation. Jahweh detested them, and all of that generation except Moses had died in the 40 years of desert wanderings. Consequently, long-lived Moses had to stop short on the east side of the Jordan where some tribes had already settled in the "cities of refuge"[12]. The newspaper, you noticed, is in the eastern most portion of Dublin.

247

The new generation of Jews, born in the desert, made it to the Promised Land, but they did not have the pillar of the cloud or fire. These forces disappeared when Moses died. The pillar of cloud by day and the pillar of fire by night had guided, covered and protected the first generation in their desert wanderings.[13] When the cloud disappeared, the new generation could see the sun, moon and stars for the first time. Stephen goes to Mooney's Pub rather then the Oval, which is the shape of the pillar.

The pillar of the cloud, a whirlwind generated by Jahweh, led the Jews in the desert. Since their quest took same 40 years, the pillar of the cloud can be seen as an unreliable guide to freedom and promise. Like the winds of Aeolus of the old generation of gods, the pillar of the cloud could not take Moses of the old generation to the promised Jewish homeland. His ancestry held him back.

The pillar of the cloud and fire reappears in this episode as Nelson's Pillar, which represents the cloud and fire of UK control of Ireland, which has blinded the old Irish generations. Stephen is not blinded by this political issue or others of only transient interest, fit for the newspapers but not for art. From Nelson's pillar, the Dublin trams of fixed destiny start. Earlier trams went to Blackrock, Kingstown, Dalkey and Clonskea. They reflect the Jewish experience in Egypt: Blackrock for making bricks, Kingstown for the Pharaoh's place, Dalkey for compromised soul and Clonskea for cloning bricks. The next trams are going to Rathgar and Terenure. These names recount the story of the Jews in the desert through their ancestor-like etymologies: Rathgar for rage at being stuck in the desert; and Terenure for tere, which means to be made round and smooth as by blowing sand. After that are ("Come on . . .") Sandymount Green for the oasis of Canaan in the desert and Palmerston for Palmer, which means pilgrims from the holy land carrying palms.

The vestals in Stephen's parable who climb Nelson's pillar and look for churches, the other cloud on Ireland, become "stiffnecked" because of the other reason given for Moses's punishment denying him entrance into the Promised Land. In an argument over from which desert rocks water would flow, each group of wandering Jews argued for their own rock where they were already lined up to be first. Moses became enraged with Yahweh's chosen people and called them "stiffnecked." Yahweh did not like his people being badmouthed, even by Moses and even if true.

The denial by the Moabs of access across their land by the Jews on their way to Canaan is echoed in the several instances in the episode where one person blocks the door being opened. The Jews faced early losses in the conquest of the Promised Land as a result of not trusting Yahweh and instead resorting to spies. They brought back false reports describing the enemy as giants. The spies falsified their reports because they thought they would lose their leadership positions once they entered the Promised Land (job denies art). One of the spies' name means empty handed.[14] This tale returns in the scene in which one newsboy sneaks into the office in an unsuccessful attempt to get the sports edition first. When caught, he blames the big boy (the giant). Carrying the Aeolian incest theme, the Moabs were the descendants of Moab, the son of Lot who impregnated his daughters after their mother was turned to a pillar of salt.[15] Incest karma is particularly bad. The allusion to the newsboys following Bloom like a kite's tail and the mocking of Bloom's unusual gait recall the Amelikites. They attacked the Jewish stragglers who were at the rear of the Jewish migration because lame or injured.

Nannetti plays Korah, a political competitor of Moses among the Jews. Korah means bald or blunt,[16] and Nannetti is both. Korah tried to unseat Moses, and Nannetti is an ambitious politician. At this point he is a City Councilor running for Lord Mayor. He demands of Bloom, our Moses, that the House of Keyes (illumination or in this context Yahweh) provide a three month commitment, or a guarantee of good times for the Jews for awhile.

The shoeblacks near the mail trucks could signify the Moabs; the Jews painted the Moab faces black after defeating them in battle. They were painted black to mark them as unclean and to mock their god Chemosh, usually depicted by the Moabs as a black stone in the form of a woman.[17] The Professor's glasses, which he uses to read despised Latin, have "ebony" rims.

The editor Crawford is described at his first entrance in raptor terms, by reference to beak and head feathers. Characteristic of a raptor nearing new prey, the editor's first words are "What is it?" Ironically, this is the literal meaning of the word manna. These raptor references suggest Balak, the King of the Moabs. King Balak's forces squared off militarily against the Jews, who had camped near Balak's Kingdom. Balak did not know that the Jews had been instructed by Yahweh to leave the Moabs alone. The editor is described in raptor terms because Balak used a metal bird for prophecy. It would divulge occult secrets when placed by the window and properly worshipped (the editor is first seen through the window to the inner office and demands job dependency). The bird's tongue would move if pricked by a golden needle, writing for pay.[18]

Balak, in an effort to repulse the Jews, consulted the Prophet Balaam, whose name means "Devourer of Nations"[19]. The editor conspicuously picks his teeth with dental floss. Balaam was rebuked by his own ass because Balaam couldn't see the angel of mercy of the Lord blocking the road. Simon Dedalus prepares us for this allusion with his quip—give you "heartburn on your arse." Heartburn because of lack of mercy and arse for ass. The editor repeatedly tells Bloom, our local angel of mercy, to tell his client that he can kiss my ass. Yahweh counted Balaam's blessings as curses, and Stephen treats in the same vein the editor's blessing of Stephen as a chip off the old block.[20] Balaam had earlier advised the Egyptian Pharaoh to force the Jews to make bricks, our leitmotif of suffering.[21] Yahweh withdrew the gift of prophecy from Balaam, and the editor is now resigned to reporting events that have already happened.[22]

One of Moses's last acts was to set down the law (preserved in Deuteronomy), which shows up in Bloom's thoughts about *lex talionis*. Moses unsuccessfully begged (using mostly enthymemic arguments) to be allowed to enter the Promised Land, if only for a short while. This in and out request was denied by Yahweh, who took Moses's soul by kissing him on the mouth.[23] Likewise, the editor's kiss of praise and continuation by Stephen in the mode that produced the romantic vampire poem "mouth to mouth" would take his soul by denying his promise of true literature, short of the Promised Land.

While the Moses/Irish language speech is being repeated, Stephen has the following chain of thoughts: "Nile. Child, man, effigy. By the Nilebank the babemaries kneel, cradle of bulrushes: a man supple in combat: stonehorned, stonebearded, heart of stone." Stephen reaches the essence of Moses in the hard hearted justice (flexible only in combat) for which he was famous, cold stone horns not rays of illumination coming from his head. By implication, this attitude is short of the promised land where love and compassion emerge naturally from recognition of the human unity.

Biblical Typology

The many Old Testament events referred to in this episode and the blatant headline "From the Fathers" bring typology (see Introduction) into the foreground. The seriousness of the Church Fathers in this effort at analysis of ultimate reality is burlesqued by the appearance of these events in tawdry newspaper headlines. Stephen, like Jesus, follows Moses, not in the traditional relationship of the first event (type) to the second event (anti-type), but in the way of avoiding Moses's mistakes that meant denial of entrance into the Promised Land. With the newspaper type clamoring in the background, Stephen rejects the value transfers of the older generation and maintains freedom in reacting to his experience, all in his new generational effort to gain the Promised Land of highest art.

With this subversion of typology and the associated Law of the Fathers, Joyce moves away from realistic presentation, which has prevailed in the episodes up to this point. As Stephen continues to grow in strength, the episode style becomes more and more inventive. Notice that the style is the most radical in those episodes of Part II which feature Stephen together with Bloom.

Crossed Keys

The symbology of the crossed key logo that Bloom takes pains to create and include in the ad is explained in *Isis Unveiled*, whose author Blavatsky is explicitly mentioned in this episode. The crossed keys symbolized exoterically the illumination residing in understanding of the mystic formula AUM, which signifies creation, conservation and transformation. Esoterically it symbolized the even more secret word kept under lock and key by the chief priest, the Brahm-atma.[24] He bore on his tiara two crossed keys supported by two kneeling Brahmans. That secret is not revealed here and is withheld until the last episode.

Rhymes, Dante and Inferno V

The connection between Bloom and Stephen and the corresponding connections in literary theory are the subjects of the following thoughts of Stephen under the "Rhymes and Reason" headline:

Rhymes: two men dressed the same, looking the same,

two by two . . . He saw them three by three,

approaching girls, in green, in rose, in russet, entwining

. . . in mauve, in purple . . . gold of oriflamme . . . .

Given the comparison of rhymes to two men dressed the same and given that Bloom and Stephen are both dressed in mourning clothes, their relationship is pointed into literary theory. Then Stephen remembers the quiet rhymes used by Dante in *Inferno* V to signify arresting the winds in hell (the Italian in the text).[25]

Inferno V is appropriate background material for this episode because in that section Dante deals with destiny and the heart wrenching story of Francesca and Paolo. Judge Minos, resident magistrate in the second circle of Hell, warns Dante to be careful how he approaches the area: "Look how thou enter here; beware in whom thou places thy trust; let not the entrance broad deceive thee to thy harm." The memory of this warning rises to Stephen's consciousness (literary karma) while the members of the pressgang are in front of him (Joyce memorized long passages from Dante). The Judge describes those in charge of destiny as those in whom "will and power are one." Compare the tram system in which there is no will only power. Will power and independence from hereditary and cultural karma are different names for the same liberating condition of freedom.

The rhymes in Italian convey in their quieting tones the arrest of the winds in Hell so Dante can hear from Francesca her story of love doom. She and Paolo were swept away in love adulterous to the desires of the Duke of Ravenna, who had them killed. Upon reflection from hell, she attributes her troubles to reading the stories of Lancelot. Bad karma from reading choices. Still in hell, Francesca is not very far along in self-analysis or a sense of responsibility. Her reason numbing passion translates to the bluster of the newspaper, and arrest from the winds of hell translates to the dramatic method. Dante's rhymes quiet Stephen's soul sufficiently to allow him to sense the problems inherent in the press job.

The colors Stephen chooses for the three approaching girls are meaningful. Perso, a kind of murky purple, is the color of the air in this region of Dante's Hell. Purple is for purple prose of the newspaper. The other colors are good news when used as rhymes by Dante: green as an emerald for Dante's edifying love for Beatrice; rose or russet for one of the three colors of stone steps at Purgatory's gate; and gold of oriflamme for the image of the peace in the soul of Virgin Mary.[26] All the good news colors are associated with arrest. The good news colors are brought by three approaching girls, as Stephen's artistic imagination anticipates the effect on him of heterosexual love.

Hindu Themes

In Hindu doctrine, the one and only reality that inhabits every human soul, the "we" that is addressed by Bloom's compassion, is known as the "Lord of Breaths"[27]. Controlled breaths would be the result of arrest while raging winds would be the result of passion and the subjective mode.

With the emphasis on the name of the newspaper (Freeman) and free will, consider the basic Hindu proposition that human kind is free and has free will only when enlightened as to the human unity. Free will inheres in the general sense of being, but not in the sense of individual personality or being a certain person.[28] One must be born again into a sense of the unity in order to gain this real freedom. Herein lies a path for Stephen's independence that is consistent with emotional involvement.

Kundalini and Purification

The fifth chakra makes its presence felt in the episode in the larynx for breath and plum for color. The fifth chakra involves turning inward the sexual forces of the second chakra that were pointed outward.

In and out, like the breath and the winds. Perhaps pointing the sexual forces inward is spoofed in the incest theme—all in the family.

The goal of the fifth chakra is purification, which Stephen pursues by rejecting the press job. The lotus symbol for this chakra has 16 petals, one for each of the vowels in Sanskrit. The complete vowel inclusion in the symbol franchises Joyce's complete survey of rhetorical devices. This region of the psyche is known as the Gate to the Great Liberation.[29] Stephen is at the gate, but he must still pass its many guardians. The central symbol is a white disc, for the full moon. Stephen invites to the pub named Mooney's specimens of all the arts. Independence of the artist is the counterpart of purification.

In a later episode, the House of Keyes ad is referred to in terms of Jewish ritual as Urim and Thummin. These refer to stones, prophetic dies, thrown by Jewish leaders who believed the resulting patterns would reflect divine guidance (I Sam. 14:41). The counterparts in this episode are the plum pits thrown from the tower by the virgins in Stephen's vision. Urim and Thummin "graduated" later to the system of colored stones on the breast plate of the High Priest. Divine guidance was sought by detection of which colors shined the brightest.[30] Here Stephen senses a message from the eternal in the colors used by Dante, Joyce's high priest of the imagination. Since all the letters of the Hebrew alphabet were contained on the breastplate stones, all possible messages could be received. In the last episode, the House of Keyes ad will reveal Joyce's version of divine guidance.

Structure, Art and Aesthetics

This episode consists of a short prologue, then two halves, the first with Bloom and the second with Stephen, and then an epilogue in which they both share the action. They come close but only when Stephen is off to the pub Mooney's. Both strive, Bloom on the ad arrangements and Stephen on vitalizing his poem with generalized interest. Both are frustrated in these efforts.

Only Bloom's and Stephen's thoughts are shown; the other characters are presented in the third person: Lenehan said, Simon Dedalus said, Crawford said, etc. This is the first episode featuring the thoughts of both of our two main male characters.

The use of rhetorical devices and the pattern of in and o
rhythm extend in a *tour de force* in several dimensions. The use of these
patterns is masterly. That they call attention to themselves is deliberate.
You can object that fewer would also do the job, but the master Joyce is
as exhaustive as normal life is exhausting. The heavy hand on the
Freeman of biological and cultural karma gives this episode its dose of
grave and constant.

****

ENDNOTES

1. Restuccia generally.
2. Gilbert at p. 179 fn. detects a change in the titles as the episode progresses from the dignified Victorian to the vulgar modern.
3. Restuccia, p. 20.
4. Burgess, A. *Re Joyce* (New York: WW Norton, 1965) p. 119.
5. The call of tram stops by the hoarse United Railway timekeeper suggests the similar call by Charon of stops in Hades (in *The Frogs* by Aristophanes): "Who's for the Lethe's plain? the Donkey -- shearings. Who's for Cerberia? Taenarum? or the Ravens?"
6. Gifford, p. 132.
7. Gifford, p. 133.
8. *Antithenes* Encyclopedia Britannica, 1983 ed., Micropaedia, Vol. I, p. 427.
9. Gilbert, p. 183.
10. Graves, Greek Myths, p. 730, par. 10.
11. Gilbert, p. 188.
12. Legends, vol. III, p. 416.
13. Legends, vol. III, p. 330.
14. Ibid, p. 264.
15. Ibid, p. 352.
16. Ibid, p. 287.
17. Ibid, p. 352.
18. Ibid, p. 353.

24. Blavatsky, Vol. II, p. 31. See Gilbert at p. 192.

25. Reynolds, M. *Joyce and Dante* (Princeton: Princeton University Press, 1981) p. 87.

26. Ibid, p. 87-88.

27. Coomaraswamy, A. *Selected Papers*, Vol. 2 (Princeton: Princeton University Press: Bollingen Series LXXXIX, 1977) p. 71.

28. Ibid, p. 91.

29. Campbell, The Mythic Image p. 368.

30. Legends, Vol. III, p. 172.

Episode 8 (Lestrygonians)

Basic Themes

Instincts rule.

As Bloom gets hungry, food and sex possess his thoughts. Until he eats, his instinct-driven personal ego cannibalizes Bloom's compassion. Both food and sex are "sticky," a word used repeatedly in this episode, and thereby associated with the stick, the archetypal tool of competition and aggression. These instincts are linked to the Fall in the Garden of Eden through the first word of the episode, "Pineapple." Pining after the apple in the Garden led to the big time out, expulsion from the effortless and eternal life in the Garden and creation of the need to compete for food and sex.

In the related Chapter x of The Odyssey, the Lestrygonians cannibalize most of Odysseus's unsuspecting men lured initially into danger by the King's winsome daughter. Odysseus's men are tenderized by rocks thrown down on them from the twin headlands of the Lestrygonian harbor. The twin headlands made difficult the Greek naval escape out the harbor mouth, as the twin instincts hunger and sex trap many souls. These twin instincts combine in Bloom's memory of his first sex with Molly; for preliminaries, she passed a partially masticated seed cake from her mouth to his. Mouth to mouth from Stephen's vampire poem. The mouth is the scouting party for both sex and hunger.

Cannibalism is the ultimate form of possession; and possession commands the wrong kind of love and the wrong kind of art. Carnal cannibalism begets spiritual cannibalism. Religious institutions suck their faithful dry through sacrifice of realization. Survival instincts produce large families whose members in turn cannibalize each other spiritually. Men totally consumed by the instincts show in this episode as "sandwichmen," those carrying advertising signs on their backs and chests. The devouring process also promotes this episode's use of colons (puns with the end of the digestive tract), rather than commas and semi-colons.

Spiritual cannibalism from the Hebrew tradition takes the center altar. The passive Bloom/Jacob ducks into the library (home of the nerds) to avoid the aggressive hunter Blazes/Esau. Blazes is preparing, as the representative of the instincts, to claim the "birthright" by possession of Molly's loins. The prophet Elijah haunts the episode in the guise of several minor characters as Bloom's prophetic thoughts create time warps.

The devouring process unfolds in this episode as the implicate order of life.[1] "Eat or be eaten. Kill! Kill!" The episode is consumed by the depressing Vedic worldview that the process of eating, the devouring process transforming life into life, is the ultimate reality. The process of eating, not the eater or the eatee, is the important thing. In the continuous Vedic sacrifice designed to replicate this process, the offering (Soma) is consumed through fire (Agni). In this episode, fire appears as sun, stomach, hunger and lust and the offering as moon, food, the victim and sperm. The demands of the devouring process and of the big daddies metempsychosis and karma boil spiritual freedom in the cannibal pot of grim necessity.

The twin headlands, which impeded the Greek escape from the Lestrygonians' harbor, are echoed in the image of the two-headed octopus that Bloom overhears George Russell use in conversation with his female friend Twigg. Joyce refers to the octopus because it moves by ejecting fluid in spurts, like the peristaltic movement of the digestive canal, and because it uses instinct-like black ink to hide and blind its prey, as the spurt-like instincts blind the human spirit.

Sublimation of the instincts in the interest of detachment and soul progress, at least post-lunch, is suggested by Bloom's affiliation with the Freemasons, who started as foundation (read instincts) builders and now spread light.

In terms of literary theory, the instincts are linked to the lower order lyrical subjective mode. The vegetarian diet, good for the dreamy poet, seems to be associated with sentimentalism as defined by Joyce—writing not out of your own experiences. The cannibal would include the plagiarist, who would eat another writer's substance, and the pitiless, who would not be in sympathy with the human grave and constant.[2]

Scene

Bloom is in eastern Dublin between 1:00 and 2:00 p.m. Having left the editor and Stephen without successfully placing the ad, he walks across the Liffey River on O'Connell Bridge, past the Bank of Ireland and Trinity College to Duke Street. He is on his way to the library to find the crossed keys ad in an old newspaper. He is cannibalizing an old ad. (Will he cut it out of the library's copy of the newspaper?) He helps a young blind man cross Dawson to Molesworth Street that opens to Kildare Street, the location of the National Library and Museum. Just Bloom, not Stephen, is involved.

Action in Ulysses

The action starts with food and sex. Bloom looks into the window of Graham Lemon's, an ice cream and candy store. The first words of the episode are his thoughts about food in the form of three flavors—"Pineapple rock, lemon platt and butter scotch." Pineapple, pining for the apple, brings in the Fall in the Garden. Then sex as Bloom notices the "sugarsticky" (the first of many uses of "sticky") girl scooping melon shaped creams (read female flesh) for a Christian brother, a layman temporarily under the vow of chastity. This image gives off an echo of Eve tempting Adam. Bloom thinks "Some school treat," as the Christian brother is probably connected with a school. In addition, the school reference registers the use by religious institutions of the legend of the Fall to teach obedience.

Bloom associates from food to bad for the tummies, an allusion to pregnancy that is the ultimate in physical possession and sacrifice by the mother. From there he associates to medicine with the royal seal and to god as King vampire sucking a red candy white. This initiates a heavy blood sacrifice theme, as food for the gods and the associated priesthood. In the Catholic Church (at least at this point in history), the sacrifice to god is of human potential.

Bloom is handed a religious tract (a "throwaway," same as the name of the horse) by a young representative of the YMCA. It contains the phrase "blood of the lamb." In reading the word "blood," Bloom momentarily thinks the bloo will continue as Bloom, placing Bloom as the sacrifice. This ego-oriented hypersensitivity to his name suggests that with hunger, Bloom's normally egoless and compassionate identity is shaky and is threatened with possession from below.

The tract advertises a sermon by Dr. Dowie, billed as the restorer of the Church in Zion, that Elijah is coming. Note in terms of our major themes that the good Doctor's name phonetically is "do we," or do the unity. Bloom thinks about the constant sacrifices that the gods want: "blood victim. Birth, hymen, martyr, war, foundation of a building, sacrifice, kidney burntoffering, druids' altars." Elijah is to precede the redeemer, who will take possession of space-time. Bloom thinks skeptically about religious scams as a "Paying game," polygamists, evangelists and night glowing crucifixes that contain phosphorus extracted from fish.

Walking along, Bloom sees Stephen's sister outside the auction hall where the Dedalus family furniture is being sold to pay creditors (the Dedalus family is cannibalizing their furniture). Bloom thinks about the harm to both parents and children of large families encouraged by the Catholic Church, while priests, without families, eat well. He feels compassion for Stephen's sister. He sees the Guinness barge taking barrels of spirits out for export (the sea air sours it) and thinks about dead rats in the porter vats and Reuben's son in the river.

He notices gulls on the river and admires their greed and cunning and survival skills; they refuse to chase fake food, the crumpled religious tract he throws in the water. Always charitable, Bloom buys from a female seller of apples (Eve again) two banbury cakes, breaks them into small pieces (mass like) and throws them into the river. These goodies the gulls do chase and devour. Bloom apparently fashions his own verse about them: "The hungry famished gull /flaps o'er the waters dull" (hunger instincts—spirits dull). Then Bloom associates to the ghost in *Hamlet*, a spirit consumed by revenge who seeks to devour only his brother but not the Queen. He thinks of the banbury cake as manna. He wonders why some but not all animals take on the taste of their food or environment (some remain independent of the life eats life process): "Eat pig like pig."

He contemplates an ad for Kino's Trousers, "Kino's ll/-Trousers," on a sign resting on a boat rocking at anchor in the Liffey River. This boat and ad for commercial identity are rocking because of the flow of the Liffey River. It carries to the sea the instinct-driven sewage of Dublin. Instincts threaten identity. Feel the gentle rock in the language: " . . . rowboat rock at anchor on the treacly swells lazily its plastered board." He thinks about life as a stream like the river, as his thoughts are possessed by cliches. Since the boat ad is not paying rent for the river, he thinks about another non-paying ad, for the venereal specialist that appeared in the "greenhouses" or public restrooms. These ads were placed on the restrooms because the venereal condition is manifested as a burning sensation during urination. Then Bloom is momentarily obsessed with worry about unspecified matters, which I believe would be Blazes giving Molly a dose of venereal disease. Bloom forces his thoughts to move on, and he associates from Timeball to Sir Ball the astronomer, to parallax (one time and space aspect of personal relativism), and to metempsychosis. He uses the expression "O Rocks" several times, a reference to the rocks thrown by the Lestrygonians. He thinks about Molly's clever phrase "base barreltone," base for the instincts.

Bloom watches the "sandwichmen" carrying shoulder signs (one board in front and one in back and thus the sandwich with the men as the meat). The signs advertise Bloom's prior employer Wisdom Hely's. Each letter of the name is on a sign. The Y and thus the 'S are lagging behind because the bearers are eating. The remaining signs read "Wisdom Hel," or the wisdom of hell, which is to curb your instincts. Bloom thinks about concepts for ads he proposed to this former employer. These included girls writing while riding in a horse drawn cart in order to advertise writing supplies, the well known use of sexual attraction to sell products, and the name Kansell for an inkeraser, punning on cancel the ink and can sell the product. He disparages the Plumtree's Potted Meat ad, which "no home should be without." He remembers in the Hely job the difficulty of collecting the bill at the Mt. Carmel convent.

Bloom passes close to the apostrophe S from the sign (read possession) and is consumed by memories: a party at Glencree attended by several men later designated by Bloom as Molly's suitors; the fire at Arnott's ("are not"—the fire of the instincts destroys the egoless detachment); and Molly's elephantgray dress with the frog pattern. He masochistically remembers several of his social *faux pases* that particularly distressed Molly. Masochism is taking possession of Bloom. He is eating himself.

Bloom recalls happy times with Milly as a baby. He tries to remember the name of the "priestylooking chap." He tries Pendennis. We later learn it is Penrose and *a la* Freud, the memory loss is associated with priest and rose, icons of Buck in the 1st episode. Bloom thinks of heredity for the first of several times (the past cannibalizes the future possibilities). He remembers nostalgically the night Prof. Goodwin (the good one or Adam) was talking with Molly and the wind blew her fur boa (a scarf signifying the serpent in the Garden) in his face and nearly smothered him. Bloom also remembers warm Molly in bed.

Bloom runs into his old flame, now married as Mrs. Breen. Their conversation is constrained within the limits of their current situations; they chat about Molly and Milly and her husband and family. Bloom is courteous, and she appears to be a passive type. While talking to his old flame, Bloom feels the tickle of hunger at the bottom of his esophagus in response to food smells coming from nearby Harrison's (read the hairy son—Esau). A nearby Arab boy barefoot (read no sole or soul) takes in the same smells. Hungry Bloom, attracted to his old flame, doesn't help the boy, even though earlier Bloom fed the gulls. Mrs. Breen offers the influence of the new moon as the explanation for her husband's recent odd experiences—his dream of the ace of spades walking up the stairs and his receipt of an anonymous postcard the next day containing just the word U.P. Mr. Breen is now obsessed with the notion of suing for libel, whom he doesn't know, and consults unsuccessfully with various lawyers for this purpose.

Because of the postcard, Bloom changes the subject to Mrs. Beaufoy, which is another Freudian slip, Beaufoy being the name of the author of the *Tidbit* newspaper prize. Mrs. Breen corrects his reference to Mrs. Purefoy, whom Mrs. Breen has just visited in the "lying in" hospital in her third day of birth labor. Bloom utters in pity "Dth! Dth!" Notice that with Bloom's slip in names (Beaufoy and Purefoy), creative writing and birth labor have been placed side by side. This association comes into full bloom in the Oxen (14th) episode.

As Farrell comes rocking by, Bloom pulls Mrs. Breen out of the way and comments on Farrell's odd and apparently obsessive habit of always walking outside lampposts (habits cannibalize possibilities). Farrell's dustcoat and umbrella are mentioned repeatedly. Mrs. Breen sees her husband with two large law books in hand and leaves saying she must go after him. Bloom notices Mr. Breen's odd dress and in Hebrew calls him eccentric: "Meshugah. Off his chump." Breen is described as "Blown in from the bay. Like old times" and suggestive of an Old Testament figure. Bloom thinks, "Going the two days." Bloom speculates that one of the local boys has sent the postcard as a practical joke. Bloom follows the three of them, watching Farrell's rocking walk outside the posts and contemplating Mr. Breen's unusual clothes.

Bloom walks by the offices of the *Irish Times* newspaper and remembers the ad he placed in that paper: "Wanted, smart lady typist to aid gentleman in literary work." This ad brought him 44 replies (double 4's for separates) and the now hot correspondence with Martha, his secret life that now possesses his ego. Counting conquests like Don Giovanni, Bloom thinks there may be other answers to the ad "lying there" in the newspaper office. He remembers one reply from Lizzie Twig that mentioned George Russell as a former employer. Bloom goes on to think generally about ads in this and the related paper *Irish Field* and its owner Carlisle. This paper apparently covers equestrian activities of the upper classes. The Irish fields in turn remind him of the masculine women ("Weightcarrying huntresses") involved in horse riding in the fox hunt at Rathoath (you get that one). From there he associates to memories of the dignified woman in front of the Grovesnor Hotel and the Spanish American woman who without embarrassment sold him used black underclothes. After this obsession with masculine women in control, he associates to another famous Bloom *faux pas* –putting mayonnaise on plums thinking it was custard (remember plums from the parable). More masochism.

He thinks about Mr. Purefoy's regular eating and conceiving habits and his well connected relative. Having decided to lunch at Burton's since it is on the way to the library, he thinks about Mrs. Purefoy lying in waiting to give birth, again utters "Dth, dth, dth," thinks of the child trying to "butt its way out blindly," and about being pregnant himself (talk about being in touch with the feminine side). Charitable as always, Bloom contemplates an effort to reduce the pain of childbirth and a national scheme to provide all children with a sum of money at birth that is automatically saved for them (avoiding the spending instinct).

As Bloom watches a flock of pigeons, he remembers his youthful chums playing the game monkey and his kid nickname mackerel. With the earlier reference to fish extracted phosphorus on crucifixes, this nickname paints Bloom as a walking luminous crucifix. He watches the squad of constables marching out to their posts post-lunch (food going to parts of the body[3]) and another squad returning to eat: "Prepare to receive cavalry. Prepare to receive soup." He walks under the statue of Tommy Moore, an Irish poet famous for sentimental and mild patriotism, located over a public urinal "Where the waters meet"[4]. Bloom charitably thinks there should be public urinals for women.

Bloom remembers the time he nearly got into trouble with the police at the pro-Boer student demonstration and a similar experience another time when he celebrated graduation with some medical students ("swept along with those medicals"). Since we are in a prophecy episode, you know a similar experience awaits Bloom and Stephen. Bloom recalls the resulting connection with student Dixon who, subsequently and recently as Dr. Dixon, dressed Bloom's bee sting on his belly (the bee, a social creature, stings the source of Bloom's instincts). Contemplating the small world, Bloom uses the phrase from Ezekial "Wheels within wheels." This phrase also signifies sublimation and the energy interconnections of the chakras (means wheels)—one feeds six and two feeds five and three feeds four. He thinks about the instinctive enthusiasm of youth for causes, their survival after graduation by selling out and going on to work for the British and the greatest of all turncoats the one Invincible who ratted on the rest of them. He can't remember the turncoat's first name. He thinks about political subjects: the danger of talking sedition with anyone because of the many plainclothes police spies; the security based isolated cell organization of the Sin Fein (pronounced shin fain and means ourselves alone—for human separation in general); and the charisma of certain politicians. The line "There are great times coming, Mary" is the typical line used by cautious revolutionary students with their girls and is also appropriate for the annunciation of the pending birth of Christ to Mary, who was possessed by the Holy Ghost.

As the sun goes behind a cloud shadowing the front of Trinity, the Protestant college symbolic of English colonization of Ireland, Bloom ties together several thoughts:

> Trams passed one another, ingoing, outgoing, clanging.
> Useless words. Things go on same, day after day:
> squads of police marching out, back: trams in, out . . . .
> Dignam carted off. Mina Purefoy swollen belly on a
> bed groaning to have a child tugged out of her. One
> born every second somewhere . . . .

Do you feel the dullness? This is the kind of pessimistic thinking the instincts produce, no gumption to accomplish anything:

No-one is anything. This is the very worst
hour of the day. Vitality. Dull, gloomy: hate this hour.
Feel as if I had been eaten and spewed.

Bloom, like the plums in the parable, is down to the pit, the base instincts.

The sun returns as Parnell's brother walks by just after Bloom had been thinking about Parnell. Then George Russell goes by on a bicycle with a young woman, and Bloom overhears Russell say to her: ". . . Of the twoheaded octopus, one of whose heads is the head upon which the ends of the world have forgotten to come while the other speaks with a Scotch accent. The tentacles . . ." This occult gibberish—plagiarized in part without acknowledgment from Walter Pater's essay on the Mona Lisa—expresses Joyce's views about such occult groups and the practice of writing from other than your own experience. Bloom contemplates this coincidence as his second time warp since he had just been thinking about Russell. Bloom speculates on the meaning of Russell's famous initials A.E. Bloom broods about vegetarians and scorns dreamy symbolism. He assesses vegetarianism as good for the poet.

Bloom crosses Nassau street and looks at field glasses in the window at Yeates and Son (Yeats the Irish mystical poet and his successors). They are of German manufacture (influence of Goethe on Yeats, as artists cannibalize earlier works) so Bloom thinks about economic competition. He extends his finger to blot out the image of the sun and thinks about sun glasses. He imagines visiting Prof. Joly to ask about parallax, which Bloom doesn't understand; Bloom in the unity has trouble understanding personal relativity.

He thinks about the new moon, which is blacked out by the earth's shadow—like the spirit blacked out by the instincts. He remembers masochistically an event a fortnight back when Molly was walking with Blazes setting up their tryst. He tries to force the thought away. This recollection excites him, and he tries to calm himself with the conclusion that her adultery was inevitable, an event possessed by destiny. He passes Adam court (you know what that means) and sees Bob Doran on his annual bender (here Joyce cannibalizes a character from **Dubliners**). Bloom thinks about earlier times with Molly and

265

wonders if he is the same person. Bloom's version of events (truth cannibalized by rationalization) is that Molly never liked sexual intercourse after Rudy died (11 years ago). Bloom is denying responsibility.

He thinks about Molly leaving pins lying around and considers the possibility of buying her a pin cushion for her birthday, September 8th (same as the Virgin Mary). He feels a scrape on his arm from a pin injury. He walks by shops selling silks, thinks of women, beautiful things, fruits, Israel, and wealth and is mentally possessed:

> A warm human plumpness settled down on
> his brain. His brain yielded. Perfume of embraces all
> him assailed. With hungered flesh obscurely, he mutely
> craved to adore.

Joyce claimed that he worked on this passage for an entire day in order to include a hint of The Odyssey's seduction theme. That hint comes with perfume, embraces and craving.

Contemplating food and sex, Bloom enters Burton's, but he is immediately revolted by what he sees—men eating like savages among noise, clamor and heavy odors. The serving girl gathers plates that are "sticky" (there's that word again). The exclusively male customers sit on high stools and at tables. Rocks are mentioned. Bloom responds to the scene: "Eat or be eaten. Kill! Kill!" After that outburst, Bloom more characteristically thinks of a communal kitchen to feed everyone regardless of station. Even then, he thinks, they would quarrel and fight.

Bloom retreats out of busy Burton's and goes near by to Davy Byrne's, a "moral pub," morals versus the instincts. Unlike popular Burton's, this moral pub is nearly empty. He exchanges greetings with a regular Nosey Flynn, whose name suggests that morals are enforced by a nosey community. Nosey is in his regular nook. Running over the luncheon prospects in view, Bloom thinks hungrily about what to eat, sardines or ham, and even remembers a limerick involving cannibals. He muses about Plumtree's potted meat in connection with cannibals. Connections between food and religion are surveyed. He thoughtfully orders a glass of burgundy and a modest cheese sandwich. No killing is involved in this lunch as the cheese is still alive.

Flynn sadistically asks Bloom about Molly's singing tour and who is getting it up. Bloom tries to avoid the question, but Flynn already knows the answer and indicates he has been talking to Blazes. Bloom has an attack at the mention of this name. After the attack, Bloom is uncharacteristically rude and doesn't say much, even though Flynn tries to make pleasant conversation. Flynn seems to be drunk; his first question is "Doing any singing those (sic) times?" Bloom critically notices Flynn's big mouth and dripping mucous (remember the vital essence). Flynn advises that Blazes is promoting boxing (aggression) and recently won a bet on a civilian versus a soldier bout by helping the civilian stay off booze by sucking duck eggs. Flynn states out of the blue that Blazes is a "hairy chap" (hairy also means clever). While Flynn and the bar keeper talk about the Gold Cup horse race, Bloom quietly savors his sandwich and his wine. Contrast the savage eaters in Burton's pub.

Flynn and Byrne discuss the horses, moral Byrne being against betting. Not deterred by Byrne's lack of interest, Flynn continues to talk about betting the Gold Cup race and his recent unrealized chance to bet 7 to 1 on St. Amant, named after a 17th Century French poet of the pleasures of the table and tavern.

After his lunch, Bloom's thoughts become more lucid and controlled. He finds beauty in the curve of the bar and surveys with his normal, detached speculation the food on the shelves. He thinks about what people eat. In this passage, he reviews in the following terms what he saw in Graham Lemons: "Tempting fruit. Ice cones. Cream. Instinct." Tempting fruit helps associate pineapple with pining after the apple in the Garden of Eden and the instincts with the Fall. He thinks about being a waiter (always helpful) and rich food and female patrons (looking down their blouse). Stuck flies buzz on the pane, signifying sticky and stuck. He remembers his first time with Molly and her passing seedcake between their very active mouths. Her lips were "Soft warm sticky gumjelly lips." This memory, compared with his current situation, ends in depression: "Me. And me now. Stuck, the flies buzzed."

He thinks about beauty, even fashions a theory of beauty, and about the gods eating and drinking their electricity-like food without the need to eliminate. The gods have no limiting instincts. He decides to look in the museum to see if the statues of the gods have a messial groove, the line dividing the symmetrical human form down the middle, for an anal opening. Notice the identification of the art, the statue, with the real thing, the gods. Feeling the instinctive urge to eliminate, Bloom gets up to use the bar urinal to complete the trinity of the base instincts—food, sex and elimination. The sensation of the pulsating need to urinate and its mind numbing effect are reflected in the rhythm of the language and the elementary words used: "Dribbling a quiet message from his bladder came to go to do not do there to do."

While he is gone to the urinal, the bar keeper and Flynn talk about Bloom and inform us that Bloom's reputation is as a good, measured man who is a member of the Freemason's order, the mutual help society ("Light, life and love. By God"). They note that Bloom only has a drink after looking at his watch, and is never drunk. Flynn opines he must have extra income from somewhere, notes that he helps others in trouble and assigns as Bloom's only fault the refusal ever to commit in writing. Byrne, but not Flynn, has noticed that Bloom is in mourning clothes.

Paddy Leonard, Bantam Lyons and Tom Rochford come into the bar while Bloom is in the urinal. Tom has on a claret waistcoat. They order, only Paddy takes alcohol and chides the other two for not being real men. Tom takes medicine in water for a stomach ailment. They talk about the horse race. Lyons says Bloom gave him a tip.

Bloom comes out of the urinal and leaves the bar, raising three fingers in some kind of greeting. He thinks about following an object in the alimentary canal and then outside the pub watches a dog eat its own throw up. Consider the dog as god and the vomit as creation and then reconsumption as human sacrifice. Bloom contemplates Tom Rochford's invention, which is explained in a later episode. He continues to work on remembering the lines from **Don Giovanni**, particularly the last supper scene when the Don, the addicted seducer, goes to dinner. The Don is sucked into Hell, merging the symbols of love and death.[5]

While counting up his expected income and considering a gift of a silk petticoat for Molly, Bloom notices a parked dyeworks (read death in the works) van. He passes a bookstore and remembers Protestants

268

using food to bribe starving Catholics to convert. At this point, Bloom sees a blind "stripling," a slender young man. Stripling is a textile based term, which in that trade means a narrow strip of a garment. Bloom decides to help him. The blind boy is uncertain about where he is, and Bloom informs him. The blind boy points his cane toward the dyework's van. Bloom tells him about the van and helps him across and to find Molesworth and South Frederick street, his destination. Bloom makes casual conversation, the rain kept off, but the boy doesn't answer. Bloom holds his hand and notices food stains on his coat.

After they separate, Bloom thinks about being blind, the resulting heightening of the other senses, and what it must be like to be blind and with a girl. Thinking that the boy has the face of a priest, he finally remembers the name Penrose. Bloom refers to blind men as dark men. He decides to send Martha two shillings. He compares his own hair to straw and feels the fat on his belly. He thinks about karma and metempsychosis, which cannibalize free will. He sees lawyers and judges going into the Freemason's hall for a fancy lunch.

Just as Bloom comes to Kildare street, he runs into Blazes: "Straw hat in sunlight. Tan shoes. Turnedup trousers. It is. It is." Straw signifies Cain, which means possession. Tan is for the hunter Esau. Turned up trousers is for Esau who turned up late in the Jacob/Esau story. Bloom's heart takes off, and he instinctively ducks into the museum, short of his objective the library. He pretends to be busy in his pockets and pulls out the Israel flyer he got in the butcher shop in the Calypso episode. By looking at the flyer, he pretends to be reading about the building in the flyer, but his thoughts are troubled: "Sir Thomas Deane was the Greek architecture [sic]." He looks for his soap and after a few seconds feels "Safe." Safe from Blazes, safe from the instincts, and safely out of the Lestrygonian harbor.

Action in The Odyssey

In Chapter x, immediately following their depressing return to Aeolus, downhearted Odysseus and his crew row their boats for six days. They come to the stronghold of the Lestrygonians, a protected bay surrounded by two high headland cliffs. The other Greek boats, motivated by habit to convenience, enter inside the bay past the cliffs, but

269

Odysseus cautiously anchors his boat outside near the opening. The sense of time and space is distorted in Lestrygonian land because night and day overlap.

Seeing no sign of men or oxen, only smoke, Odysseus orders out a scouting party of three. The scouting party meets a comely lass who convinces them with her winning female ways (seduction theme) to come to her house the castle to meet the King. At the castle, the unsuspecting Greeks first meet the Queen, who is big and ugly, but they don't sense any danger. The King, a giant, comes out and promptly grabs one of the Greeks and eats him. The instincts rule here. Note in passing that while the King and Queen are big and ugly, the daughter is comely enough for sexual attraction.

The other two Greeks escape from the castle, but the King sounds the alarm and the rest of the Lestrygonians take to the high headlands. From there, they crush the boats in the harbor below by throwing rocks down on them. They kill, spear like fish and then eat every Greek from all the boats other than that of the cautious Odysseus. His crew is able, cutting the anchor ropes, to get out fast and safely because his boat is not in the harbor. Odysseus and his only remaining crew quickly leave the "beetling" cliffs behind. This phrase "the cliff beetling" was apparently plagiarized by Shakespeare for *Hamlet*.

Parallels to The Odyssey

The instincts that surface in this episode to possess Bloom are the direct descendants through karma and metempsychosis of the cannibal Lestrygonians. The first sign of the Lestrygonian habitation is smoke, from the fire of the instincts that cannibalize the higher aspirations. The two headlands at the harbor mouth are references for the hunger and sex instincts that impede the escape toward realization. Night and day metaphorically overlap because the dark instincts are out and in control in the Dublin dayfather, not just in nighttime dreams.

The messy eating scene in Burton's and the spiritual cannibalism in the episode are the references for the eating of Odysseus's men by the Lestrygonians. The high harbor cliffs are echoed in the high stools in Burton's. The seductive effect of the thoughts of food, women and lace on Bloom's mental process is the reference for the seduction of

270

the search party by the King's daughter, seduction in the interest of food for her father. The rocks used to crush the Greek boats reappear often in the episode in the expression "O rocks."

First Letter and First Word

The first letter **P** of "Pineapple" is the curtailed top half of the **B** that began the last episode (when both Stephen and Bloom were present). Here we have just Bloom, not both Bloom and Stephen as in the two-part **B**. As in the Aeolus episode, a powerful factor limiting realization is operative, here the instincts, and thus the continuing comparison of the first letter **P** to the sign **8** for infinity or eternity.

P also serves as one letter of the word up or U.P., the mystery word in the telegram to Breen. The letter **U** looks like a symbol for the female; **U** starts the next episode where it symbolizes a whirlpool—very sticky. **P** looks like a club. Together they combine the passive female instincts with the aggressive male instincts, but separated by periods (menstrual). **U** and **P**, Ulysses and Penelope. They also look like a bowl and spoon for eating. Sex and food.

The first word Pineapple suggests pining for the apple in the Garden of Eden and the apple tree itself. After being banished from the Garden, Adam and Eve had to compete for their own food as a means of fending off an early death, and Eve like Mrs. Purefoy had to endure painful child birth in order to continue the species.

Traditional Schemata

The traditional schemata given by Joyce for this episode are organ—esophagus, art—architecture, color—none, symbol—constables, and technique—peristaltic. The correspondences are Antiphates (Lestrygonian cannibal King)—hunger, the decoy (King's daughter)—food, and Lestrygonians—teeth. The Linati adds the sense of the episode is "dejection."

Bloom feels hunger at the bottom of his esophagus. Architecture plays a minor role, probably because the arts are weak in the presence of the instincts. The constable is the symbol because the constable, like the super-ego, is in effective control only if the body is fed; the constables march out to duty post-lunch. The peristaltic movement is a succession of waves of involuntary contraction in the walls of the intestine that force

271

the food onward toward further digestion. You can feel this kind of periodic pulsing movement in the dynamics of Bloom's thoughts. They rest on one subject for awhile and then are propelled "ahead" to a different subject. This kind of movement is also similar to the birth contractions in Mrs. Purefoy and the movements of the octopus. The involuntary aspect of the peristaltic movement is felt in the powers of the blind instincts.

The correspondences are self-explanatory at this point. The sense "dejection" is a Joycean joke, since it means both low in spirit and excrement, aptly signifying two results of the instincts.

Unconscious

The free will of humans is threatened by forces from the unconscious (in Freud's term "unknowable") part of the mind. Forces like the instincts, heredity and repressed energies and experiences are stored "there." Of these forces, the conscious mind is unsuspecting, like the Greeks in the harbor. These forces "seep through" in dreams and in waking life in memory problems and slips of the tongue like the ones displayed in this episode. These forces also energize concepts such as karma, metempychosis, masochism and other restrictions on free will. If operative, original sin would also be stored "there" with its sibling forces in the unconscious. Religious institutions feed off the sacrifice made necessary by original sin.

Cannibals, Instincts and Ice Cream

Why do cannibals eat other humans? Instinct. And by the way, early inhabitants of Ireland, the Picts, were reputed to be cannibals.[6]

This episode starts off with Bloom looking in the window of an ice cream and candy store. Because he is hungry, his thoughts are cannibalized by the flavors: "Pineapple rock, lemon platt, butter scotch." Each of these three flavors is a miniature reproduction of the cannibal feast. The first word of each flavor is something alive, the last word something associated with aggression. Pineapple alive and rock. Lemon alive and Platt is a stick. Butter alive and scotch derives from the root that means to injure or obstruct for a period of time. The stick suggests the upright serpent. The instincts arose because of expulsion from the stasis of paradise in the Garden of Eden.

272

Cannibals carnal and spiritual fill this episode. Starting with the blood of the lamb as a cannibal sacrifice to the gods, Bloom thinks momentarily the word blood might be Bloom. Fake evangelists and luminous crucifixes scam money, and church doctrine sponsored large families eat each other's potential. Bloom eats his own confidence by masochistic memories of his *faux pases*. Practical jokes are played on Mr. Breen. Unborns are eating their mothers; the earth is eating the dead; economic competitors dog eat dog for market share; and ghosts yearn for blood.

The instincts cast their long black shadows in the many references to corruption, darkness and blindness. Venereal disease, which Bloom worries Blazes might give to Molly, causes blindness. Our spirit symbol, the export of stout, grows sour in the sea air, and rats die in its parental vats. The barrel of Bass for base spirit. Sewage swills in the Liffey on which the hungry gulls hunt, hungry greedy cunning gulls rather than soaring ganders. Bloom's eyes are troubled. Bloom's ad suggestion is for an inkeraser or instinct eraser. Fire at Arnott's is the fire of instinct destroying loss of ego (are not). The frogs on Molly's dress were the ancient Egyptian symbol for fertility. Milly coming of age is a "house on fire." Sex "Pleasure or pain is it?" The Ace of Spades stands for death. The blind baby instinctively struggles to emerge. Tom peeping through the keyhole is struck blind. The octopus ejects black ink. Bloom thinks about black glasses and sun spots. Like the limerick Bloom remembers about cannibals, the instincts "grew bigger and bigger and bigger." Buried cities. The blind stripling, a textile based word, feels the presence of the dyeworks van (spiritual death venue), "something blacker than the dark." Blind men are called dark men. "Want to try in the dark to see."

Bloom's expression "Dth, dth, dth" is death with ea removed, associating death and pity, the sources of arrest in Joyce's aesthetics. These removed letters will return in the initials of George Russell, A.E. short for aeon, and also are the letters left out of Yahweh, the esoteric unutterable name, when coded exoterically as YHWH.

In the maelstrom of the instincts, identity signified by the boat supporting the commercial advertisement for Kino's Trousers rocks in

273

the Liffey River carrying the instinctual sewage of the City out to the Ocean. Identity is associated with a commercial aspect because our identity is what traffics with others. The price for Kino's trousers is advertised as "11/—," which look like pictograms for Rudy's death at 11 days (upright slash then prone dash), when marital stability was lost for Bloom. Bloom's compassionate identity is shaky until he eats. Much of his hungry thought appears to issue from the Freudian preconscious.[7]

With the heavy emphasis on instincts and death, I am tempted to conclude that Joyce had heard of or foreshadowed Freud's theory in **Beyond the Pleasure Principle** (1920): that a basic human instinct is to return to the original stasis condition, in our case to inanimate dust. Freud refers to this instinct as the death wish, the ultimate self-cannibalizing instinct.

Elijah, Jacob and the Angel of Death

Elijah, conspicuously announced at the beginning of the episode, lived as an iconoclastic, itinerant prophet in the Old Testament time of King Ahab and his Queen Jezebel. Elijah wore a garment of hair, used uncouth language and generally exhibited the outward signs of social rebellion. After wrestling with the angel of death, Elijah was taken into heaven by "translation," that is without being subjected to death. In heaven he performs as the "Psycho-pomp"; he stands at cross roads to guide the pious to their appointed places (much like Hermes). He often reappears in the world in various guises, a form of spiritual rumination, to help deserving souls and savants. Elijah's most important reappearance will be to precede by three days the arrival of the Messiah, in the second coming for Christians and the first for Jews. During those three days, Elijah is to resolve all legal disputes—good luck![8] As indicated in the Introduction, Elijah is the master of transitions.

King Ahab was big on sacred poles. His wife Jezebel had allowed the worship of Baal and ordered the rebuilding of Jericho, both forbidden by Jewish wisdom. In Jericho's foundation walls two sons of Hiel of Bethel were buried—so Bloom includes foundation walls in his list of sacrifices. Baal demanded the sacrifice of the first born. Bloom has already experienced the sacrifice of his first born. The sacrifice of the first born for Stephen would be of his most important "calling."

274

The Ahab kingdom was suffering a drought. Elijah claimed that as a representative of Yahweh, he was in control of the rain. He challenged the priests of Baal to a shoot-out on Mt. Carmel to decide once and for all whether Yahweh or Baal was the true God of Nature. Bulls were to be sacrificed, and the competing gods were to display their powers by igniting an altar. The Baal priests were unsuccessful, even though they were 450 strong and tried to cheat; one was hidden under the altar but died there. No fire appeared. While they were praying to Baal all morning long, Elijah tormented the Baal priests with remarks such as Baal must be absent relieving himself. No show from Baal.

Then Elijah prepared a simple altar for Yahweh. It burst into flames upon his first imprecation. The crowd, seeing the power of Yahweh, killed all 450 Baal priests; coming in second was not good. Shortly thereafter Elijah summoned the drought relieving rain. It arrived in a cloud off the Mediterranean.

Retreating to the mountains still in fear of Queen Jezebel, Elijah experienced a theophany—Yahweh appeared to Elijah as he hid in the crevice of a rock. Elijah experienced a big wind, earthquake and fire. But Yahweh was not in any of these instinct-like violent natural events. "And after the fire came the sound of a delicate silence." This was Yahweh, like simple compassion.

Apropos of Elijah's repeated returns in various guises, the legend of Elijah lives on in this episode in several characters. First, in the irascible and oddly dressed Mr. Breen, who is described as "blown in from the bay" (like the rain cloud), has had a dream of the Ace of Spades (the angel of death) and has received a mysterious post card inscribed with the one word U.P. (Elijah's direct translation to heaven without death). He struggles in the courts against all comers, as Elijah is to end all legal disputes. Bloom calls him a Meshuggah, or eccentric, and thinks two more days (for a total of three). The barefoot Arab boy echoes Elijah's appearance as a destitute Arab to test the charity of others.[9] Note that before lunch Bloom doesn't help the Arab boy since Bloom is under the rule of the hunger and sex instincts. After lunch, Bloom does help the blind stripling across the street to his desired destination, Bloom in the role of Elijah as the Psycho-pomp.

The Baal/Jahweh contest on Mt. Carmel sponsors Connector Fact references to the Feast of Our Lady of Mount Carmel and the candy caramel. Baal's fire failure is reflected lovingly in the recollection by Bloom of the big fire at Arnott's (Baal are not). The theme of the sacred poles appears in the lampposts outside of which the lurching Farrell always walks (superstition). His repeatedly mentioned dustcoat and umbrella recall the drought. Control over the rain appears in Bloom's measured drinking habits and resulting control over his spirit and urination.

The near sacrifice of Isaac by his father Abraham and the competition for the birthright between Isaac's two sons Jacob and Esau are among the most memorable stories in the Bible. Saved by angels from sacrifice by his father, Isaac was blinded by the tears of the angels. Of Isaac's two sons, the younger Jacob was the studious and pious one and the elder Esau the materialist and the hunter. In the famous story concerning the first blessing or birthright (right to be priest and double inheritance), Jacob, urged on by his mother, disguised himself as the older and hairy Esau by covering himself with animal skins and Esau's garments. With this ruse, he received the first blessing from the blind Isaac. Just as Jacob left the tent with the fraudulently obtained first blessing, Esau finally returned late ("turns up") from his hunting expedition expecting to receive the very same first blessing. Esau had been out hunting Isaac's favorite game, but came back late because each time Esau caught an animal and tied it down to come back for it later, it got away. Esau visited his father to obtain the blessing and discovered the ruse used by Jacob. Livid Esau threatened to kill Jacob, who hid and then fled to Haran. Much later after establishing his family and wealth, Jacob returned to Canaan and at the Jordan fought with the angel of death. In this fight, he was slightly injured. Esau remained the sworn enemy of Jacob for many years, always pursuing him as the aggressor. Esau, true to his hairy condition, turned out to be a rapist and interested only in the hunt.

Bloom has already experienced the sacrifice of his first and only son Rudy, who lived for only 11 days, so Bloom has already played the part of Abraham "in spades." Here Bloom plays Jacob to Blazes's Esau.

Bloom is the passive and spiritual male who avoids contact with Blazes before Blazes goes to Molly as the aggressive male hunter representing the instincts claiming the "birthright." Blazes/Esau can't tie down his prey permanently; as a bachelor he has only temporary sexual relations. Nosey Flynn pulls Bloom's chain by asking the question everyone is asking, who is getting up (there's that word again) the tour featuring Molly, and telling Bloom that Blazes is very hairy. Blazes is wearing hunter's brown. The blind, passive Isaac is reflected in the young blind man Bloom helps across the street. The blind man wants South Frederick Street, and the very next street is Kildare, for the near sacrifice of Isaac by Abraham. The blind man is concerned about the dyeworks van, which is parked in the intersection he wants to cross; this puns on dying and also relates to the near sacrifice of Isaac. Blind Isaac mistook warm water for wine,[10] and Bloom muses about the need for two senses in identifying food and drink. Bloom rubs the minor scrap on his arm, from Jacob's fight with the angel of death.

The other famous Old Testament aggressive/passive male pair is Cain and Able. Cain is mentioned explicitly in this episode, and Bloom, feeling his relative lack of hair on his body (compared to Blazes), compares his own to straw. Since Cain means possession or straw, this Connector Fact refers to this second famous pair. Bloom is temporarily possessed by the instincts that constantly possess Blazes. An aggressive/passive female pair also shows in this episode in the comparison between the passive Mrs. Breen, to whom Bloom is attracted as like to like, and aggressive horseriding women, who frighten Bloom. Joyce made the aggressive/passive male and female pairs a regular part of the archetypal structure of *Finnegan's Wake*. The Old Testament dating of this aspect of human experience suggests that these drives proceed from the archetypal instincts.

Melchisedek

In a later episode, the light lunch of Bloom in this episode is referred to in terms of Jewish ritual as the rite of Melchisedek. Also identified as Shem, this Old Testament character first surfaces as one of Noah's son whose job on the ark was to feed the animals, as Bloom feeds the gulls. The deluge was sent to punish mankind for his instinct-driven

277

sins. The priestly garments of Shem-Melchisedek were passed down to Esau and stolen by Jacob.

As the priest King of Jerusalem, Shem-Melchisedek blessed Abraham after a military victory in which Lot was rescued from the bad guys (Genesis 14:18). Abraham gave 10% of the spoils to the priest. After that, King Melchisedek offered the rest of the spoils of victory to Abraham. He refused except for the food his men had eaten and the shares for the men who came with him. Abraham refused to partake personally of the spoils. Likewise, Bloom has a "light lunch," he does not partake of the spoils of cannibalism, carnal or spiritual.

Later on in the New Testament (Hebrews 7:3), the claim is made that Jesus was superior as a priest to the Levites, the hereditary priests of the Jews, because his priesthood derived from the earlier priesthood of Shem-Melchisedek. A faint allusion to bread and wine in the Old Testament in connection with Melchisedek is used to justify the Eucharist in the New Testament. These are surprising and unconvincing uses of Biblical typology and appear to be merely cannibal plagiarisms of the authority of the Old Testament.

The Cannibal Mass

The parallel to the Mass of the Faithful (for Bloom) continues with the reference to the blood of the lamb. This phrase, repeated in this episode, is used frequently in the *Agnus Dei* portion of the Mass.[11] It is based on John 1:29: "Behold, the Lamb of God, who takes away the sin of the world!" This portion of the Mass stresses the theme of sacrifice and echoes the Old Testament legends about Isaac, the sacrifice of the first born and the substitution of animals as proxies.

The Mass involves two-way cannibalism. First, the Mass involves eating the dead Jesus to reflect his sacrifice for sinners. Second, the guilt produced by the Mass eats the soul potential of the celebrants, the very souls God created "in his own likeness." God with a guilt complex who demands human sacrifice. Bloom compares the Mass he saw in All Hallows to the "sandwichmen." More and more Bloom is being identified with the bread or body in the Mass, as Bloom serves as Joyce's transsubstantial heir.[12] Bloom's is the body of the living compassionate. Later Stephen will show as the wine.

278

In Byrne's moral pub, "The curate served." In Dublin, curate means either bartender or a clergyman.[13] The Gold Cup horserace, for the gold cup used in the Mass to hold the wafer, is mentioned again. Who will win? Sceptre for control by church and state, Zinfandel for mystic spirit or Throwaway for detachment.

Structure, Art and Aesthetics

The episode consists mostly of Bloom's thoughts—which until he eats are increasingly under the influence of the primal instincts. His thought patterns shift in a peristaltic type movement dwelling on one subject and then jumping to another. The flow is jerky. A few guides from the objective narrator provide clues to what is happening.

The art of the episode is realized in the impact of the instinctive forces on the very construction of the episode and the thoughts of Bloom. Even colons (puns with the end of the digestive tract) are used as temporary stopping points, rather than commas. As Prof. Tindall said: "Sentences, responding to stomach and bowel, lose shape, go soft and mushy"[14] . This must have been particularly difficult and to my mind is brilliantly realized. The Hebrew background lays in the episode much in the manner of hazy archetypes, which appear on the surface occasionally. Despite the dire subject matter, the tone is light. For an energizing exercise, compare this episode with Conrad's *Heart of Darkness.*

****

ENDNOTES

1. See generally Bohm, D. *Wholeness and the Implicate Order* (New York: Ark Publications, 1980).
2. Ellmann, The Consciousness of Joyce.
3. Burgess, p. 122.
4. Gifford, p.167.
5. Blamirez, p. 73.
6. Graves, R. *The White Goddess* (New York: Farrar, Strauss and Giroux, 1948) p. 51.
7. Critical Essays, p. 135.
8. Legends, Vol. IV, pp. 195 et. seq. for all of this material.
9. Ibid, p. 208.

10. Ibid, p. 329.
11. Lang.
12. Lang, p. 152.
13. Ibid, p. 152.
14. Tindall, W. *A Reader's Guide to James Joyce* (Syracuse: Syracuse University Press, 1995) p. 169.

Episode 9 (Scylla and Charybdis)

Basic Themes

Immanence and transcendence: sentimentalism and projection.

Like the Catholic God of creation who is contained in creation but arises above it, the human creative artist must be in but above his material. The material of the artist must be of his or her own personal experience (the artist immanent in the work) but the treatment impersonal (transcendent). Here the artists, Shakespeare as analyzed by Stephen and the narrator/author of this episode, fail the impersonal test. They are hot for revenge and project their attitude into the material.

This middle of the book episode, which Joyce thought ended the first of two parts, deals with the issue recently set forth in the following letter from older writer V.S. Naipaul to younger writer Paul Theroux:

> But above all this is the work of a man who has come to a resolution about a particular experience (we have discussed this before). A poor word, but Mailer, say, doesn't have it. His work is a writer's self-display, a display of writing, a display of the self. Here you have gone beyond that to the true artist's detachment (which is not unconcern, far from it) . . . . though I fear that by dealing in subtleties and getting rid of the ego-display you are ruining your chances in the US market.[1]

This episode is based on actual experiences in Joyce's life. Stephen is involved in a library discussion with Dublin literary heavies drawn from "real life." He sucks up particularly to Geo Russell, then a famous Irish bard, and serves up the best he has to offer, his theory of the relationship of art to life in Shakespeare. Nonetheless, he is unsuccessful and humiliated in his desire to be invited to that evening's intellectual entertainment and to be included in a collection of verse by young Irish poets being organized by Russell. In response, Stephen commits to revenge, "remember this," a restriction on future possibilities.

The question presented by this episode is whether Joyce had adequately detached from or had resolved his reaction to those experiences before writing this episode. I think not. Joyce takes his revenge in this episode on those real life Dublin literati who claimed sophistication but failed to recognize Ireland's answer to Shakespeare even though he was in the same room. They humiliated the future Irish Shakespeare for poets now lost to memory's favor. I think Joyce expects the reader to consider the Dublin heavies totally out of it because they didn't respect his talents. In short, I think in Joyce's theory this episode is pornographic.

Stephen's theory is that Shakespeare wrote *Hamlet* because Shakespeare himself was humiliated by his wife's unfaithfulness with his own brothers. Thus the play passes the immanence test; it is based on Shakespeare's own personal experiences. Stephen thinks Shakespeare was in the hot revenge mode in writing *Hamlet*, as indicated by the excess violence in the play, and that the famous play is pornographic in its desire to expose his unfaithful wife. For this reason the play fails the transcendence test; the treatment is not impersonal. In Stephen's theory, Shakespeare's inability to resolve his reaction to the marital betrayal is reflected in Hamlet's inability to resolve his reaction to the unsettling information about the murder of his father and in his corresponding inability to act decisively. Likewise, Stephen is presented in this episode as self-conscious and insecure, lacking his own father.

Stephen's theory is that the play *Hamlet* acts as a revenge piece because it informs the character Hamlet, as a proxy for his real then dead son named Hamnet, and more importantly the world, about the betrayal. Note preliminarily that the play as a revenge piece didn't work well because no one except Joyce got it. Joyce's works better. The effect on the author of a hot reaction to experience is expressed in the concept of the effect of the "unquiet father" (author) on the "unliving son" (his work). Shakespeare's son Hamnet is dead; he died at 11 years. Bloom's son Rudy is dead; he died at 11 days and would be 11 years had he lived. Stephen's son, his own artistic realization, will remain unliving until he cools off.

The theme of the relationship of art to life and life to art can been seen feeding on the surface of this episode. The relationship of art to life is part of the more general Joycean megacept that the part implies the whole. Shakespeare's life is in his art. Art implies life. Shakespeare's and Joyce's characters imply all of humanity. This is especially true of Bloom, the Jews being known as the people of the body. And the human, fashioned in the image of god, implies the eternal.

Joyce's megacept that the part implies the whole funds an episode whose progress is based on the Socratic dialogue, a dialectic process (proposition, opposition, and synthesis). That process itself implies the megacept since each synthesis (whole) carries seeds of all resolved antecedents (parts). Hegel, the famous proponent of the dialectic process, viewed this process as the only valid truth seeking process since in his view all reality must be seen as part of a whole.[2] Likewise, Socrates thought that individual aspects of virtue, such as courage, could be understood only in terms of an understanding of all virtue.

As Stephen lectures about Shakespeare, he is at the same time indirectly speaking about himself and every artist: "A great poet on a great brother poet." Stephen reviews the inclusion of the intimate details of Shakespeare's personal life in his plays and sonnets. Similarly, the drama of this episode presents the personal experience in Joyce's life that lead to the writing of this very episode. In Stephen's theory, Shakespeare lost his self-confidence because the older Anne, his wife to be, seduced him and got pregnant. Here Stephen, the younger Joyce, is sucking up to the older Geo Russell and is full of himself and insecure.

Stephen reacts to various theories of the relationship of life to art and part to whole at the highest plane of generalization, his view that the Father and Son must be the same person in the Trinity because self-realization is the only path to true fatherhood of oneself. Stephen quotes with approval

282

> Sabellius, the African, subtlest heresiarch of all the
> beast of the field, held that the Father was Himself His
> Own Son.

Stephen brands as mockers of the human spirit the orthodox Roman Catholic doctrine of the Trinity, which assumes at the base that Father and Son cannot be the same person, and all those who live for the approval of others. The counterpart in art is to serve external authority in the production or interpretation of art. The author's intent to produce desire or loathing in the reader (i.e. pornography) would be such an external authority. Art must serve itself.

The connection to the Trinity is legitimate in Stephen's view because in the production or the reception of art, the most poignant reflection is obtained of the human soul, that vessel made in the likeness of the powers that be. Human part implies the eternal whole. In Trinity theory, this is expressed as the logos, the Son as the Word:

> Formless spiritual. Father, Word and Holy
> Breath. Allfather, the heavenly man. Hiesos Kristos,
> magician of the beautiful, the Logos suffers in us at
> every moment.   This verily is that. I am the fire upon
> the altar. I am the sacrificial butter.

The Father is the Son, as This is that or Thou art that. The son is the immanence, the father the transcendence. Fatherhood in this sense can not be the blood father because:

> Fatherhood, in the sense of conscious begetting, is
> unknown to man . . . [It is] founded, like the world, macro and
> microcosm, upon the void. Upon incertitude, upon unlikelihood.
> ****
>
> [The son] is a new male: his growth is his father's
> decline, his youth his father's envy, his friend his
> father's enemy.

In the Sabellian view of the Trinity, there is no separate father. The son is fatherless. When Shakespeare wrote **Hamlet**, his father had already died. As far as Stephen is concerned, his father Simon might as well be dead as far as spiritual paternity is concerned. Shakespeare is a Sabellian because he is in all his works.

Understanding this point is necessary to see this episode in clear focus. The Father is the Son is the Holy Ghost is the soul in all of us. We suffer in our soul like the Son suffered. The suffering artist is the word, the "magician of the beautiful." These concepts give us the paternity side of art. The maternity side is coming up later.

Through references to Shakespeare's *The Tempest*, this issue is extended to perspective as authority in life. Prospero in his first line recommends Buddhism to his beloved daughter, "be collected." In the play, illusion gives way to reality. Prospero, the Anti-Faust, throws off his magic mantle of art and buries his staff to leave the magic island and return home to collected humanity. Stephen, in this episode, is definitely not collected. He is still in illusion. Bad art equals illusion. Being collected is the classical temper.

This episode explores the necessity of detachment in life (the classical temper) for dramatic resolution in art. Later episodes explore the necessity of compassion for the empathy inherent in the grave and constant. And going beyond artists, does this need for radiators of the soul tell us anything useful about spiritual development and freedom in general? Does the case of the artist teach us something about spiritual life for all of us, not just for artists? Are we more free in an important way in general if we are cooler, more detached, more Buddhist, more like Bloom? Are we more open to new experience? Can we grow more? Can we gain a deeper experience from art?

The Triple Cheeseburger

This episode reminds me of a triple cheeseburger. Stacked together are three meaty layers: Shakespeare's personal betrayal and revenge writing of *Hamlet* as expounded in Stephen's theory; Stephen's betrayal of his own independence by his insecurity and desire for revenge; and Joyce's revenge writing of this episode. The juice of these themes mingle as you turn the episode over in your mind. The cheese that binds the taste is revenge and revenge requited, from the basic image of the father ghost in *Hamlet*. The bun which holds the meat, cheese and juice together is the relationship of the artist's life to his art and his art to his life. Despite some scholarly contention to the contrary, I don't think

284

this very thick cheeseburger is cold. I don't think Joyce is pretending to be in the revenge mode.

Action in Ulysses

Before the action reported in this episode, Stephen has had several drinks with the pressgang but no lunch. As a result, he is wired and supersensitive. Following drinks with the pressmen, Stephen sent a telegram to Buck and Haines at the nearby pub, a real extravagance perhaps to avoid them. He then proceeded to the library, apparently for the purpose of finding Geo Russell to ask him to place Mr. Deasy's letter in *The Irish Homestead*, a paper devoted to agricultural affairs[3] of which Russell is an editor.

In any event, it appears that Stephen is using Deasy's letter as a pretext for his real purpose, which is self-promotion. He tries to impress Russell to the end that Russell will include Stephen's verse in the upcoming book of promising young Irish poets. Stephen and Geo Russell have discussed Deasy's letter in the conversation before the episode begins. Also, someone has already specifically mentioned Freud (the "Viennese school"), the first English edition of Freud's *The Interpretation of Dreams* having been published in 1913. The Hamlet subject is already on the table when the scene opens. The episode presents part of what happened, and from the part presented the reader must deduce the whole conversation. Accordingly, the very structure of the episode shares the concept that the part implies the whole.

The action starts in a dark office in the National Library, probably that of the assistant librarian, apparently a normal venue for intellectual conversation.[4] Only one poor light is on in this dark office, suggesting that both truth and light may be absent in this den of theory. The Quaker head librarian Lyster, the assistant librarian and well known literary critic William McGee (literary name John Eglinton) and the famous bard Geo Russell (literary name AE) are with Stephen as the scene opens in this dark office. Stephen is wired from his beers and is extremely self-conscious, prime breeding grounds for the hot, subjective mode. Russell is sitting near the one lamp in the office.

Lyster curiously steps forward and back, hesitates and then leaves almost immediately. Eglinton needles Stephen about his previous pretension to rewrite *Paradise Lost* as The Sorrows of Satan. This signifies the loss of the paradise of the classical temper to youthful pride in the context of Stephen's theory that Satan represents the youth of Christ. Stephen thinks about being held hostage to his prior follies, and then about Ireland being held hostage to England. Eglinton bemoans the lack of an Irish Shakespeare.

The opening subjects carry the art and life theme. Stephen's previous boast that he would dictate The Sorrows of Satan to "six brave medicals," presumably non-poets, reflects blind Milton's dictation of *Paradise Lost* to his non-poet daughters.[5] The "Jolly Old Medical" poem Stephen recites refers to a doctor drawing urine from a female with a catheter, but only after visiting the tickle and patting zones. These extra-circular interests would be improper for a doctor, as a hot temper would be for the artist. A similar theme governs the lines of Milton that Stephen remembers about the leader (orchestral) Satan weeping during his presentation to his army of fallen angels. The Italian from Dante (*"Ed egli avea del cul fatto trombetta"*) translates "And of his arse he made a trumpet." Art and life in the basics.

Russell scorns as a domestic reading of art Stephen's theory that Shakespeare's plays grew out of and reflect his life. Russell gives an opposing theory of literature associated at least in Russell's mind with Plato. Its aim is to approach just the plays, not the biography of the author, to find the formless essences, the eternal truths. Stephen disagrees forcefully in his mind, but in the conversation is superpolite to Russell. Stephen is greatly affected by his presence. Stephen even reacts hopefully to a report that Russell had been talking about him; Stephen in his self-consciousness is clutching at straws. Since Russell is a Theosophist, Stephen thinks through the father-son duality in terms of the basic Theosophist doctrine. Magee gets angry because Stephen champions Aristotle over Plato (talk about lack of detachment). Stephen uses the argumentation tactics of Aristotle in the discussion.

Mr. Best, also an assistant librarian, enters the office. He is beautiful and a bachelor. Best carries a notebook, suggesting he spends his life collecting the thoughts of others. He has to his credit an English translation of a book about Celtic mythology, originally by the French

286

author Jubainville, and has just helped the other collector Haines look for some similar materials. Best talks about Mallarme's view of *Hamlet*, reading the "book of himself," and a French version of *Hamlet* he saw advertised with the pun—piece **of** Shakespeare. Best quotes these ideas of others but doesn't express any ideas of his own.

Stephen starts his unique theory of Shakespeare with an emphasis on the identity of the ghost. Joyce apparently issued the same literary bull to Gogarty (the model for Buck), Best and Magee in the National Library.[6] Stephen identifies the author Shakespeare with the ghost of King Hamlet, instead of the usual identification of the author with the son Hamlet. Stephen opens the way for this interpretation with the suggestion that ghosts can be in several dimensions—ghosts by death, by mere physical absence and even by a change in manners. Stephen indirectly relates Shakespeare and himself to the ghost by physical absence, Shakespeare in London absent from Stratford and his wife and Stephen in Paris absent from Dublin. Bloom is a ghost by manners, since no one greets him.

In order to involve his audience (the objective of pornography), Stephen paints a picture of Shakespeare starting his typical day in London. This picture reminds us of some of Bloom's activities earlier in the day. Stephen describes the theater, the mascot bear named Sackerson (read sack the son), the audience, the start of the play and the ghost's entrance. He suggests that through the ghost, the acting part that Shakespeare actually played, the playwright Shakespeare is speaking to his own real son. Shakespeare's real son named Hamnet died at 11 years. Shakespeare's purpose, according to Stephen, is to seek revenge by disclosing to his son's memory and to the world at large that Shakespeare himself, just like the ghost, was betrayed by his wife with his brothers.

Russell bluntly rejects Stephen's domestic interpretation of the play since it involves the raw material of the artist's life, not the Platonic formless essences. In response, Stephen thinks about a line from a Russell play involving the Irish sea god Mananaan MacLir, surely a formless essence not in Russell's experience. Stephen also thinks about the pound he owes Russell, a subject not mentioned in the actual conversation. Stephen thinks momentarily that he shouldn't owe the debt

287

since his molecules (his Platonic essence) have changed and he isn't the same person. But then returning to Aristotle's notion that his identity is not the changing material but the internal built-in form that directs the change, he ineluctably concludes he still owes the debt. This thought sequence plays with the issue of which human part implies the whole. Stephen plays with the vowels to state this continuing debt obligation - AEIOU (AE I owe you). This emphasis on vowels suggests that we be particularly alert to the use of vowels in generating meaning, such as the letter U that begins the episode.

Stephen defends his Shakespeare theory against challenges from Eglinton and Best. Russell gets up to leave right in the middle of Stephen's presentation, indicating profound indifference. Given Russell's pending departure, the discussion centers on George Moore's soiree scheduled for that evening. Eglinton invites Russell and talks of inviting even Mulligan and Haines right in front of Stephen. Stephen has not been invited. Best also mentions the upcoming collection of young Irish poets that Russell is organizing. Stephen has not been included in this either. An irritated Stephen thinks, "See this. Remember."

Feeling left out, Stephen compares himself to MacLir's loneliest daughter Cordoglio. He also makes a connection to Cordelia, the faithful and left out daughter in Shakespeare's *King Lear* who would not flatter her father to make him want to give her a fair inheritance (that is use pornography). She remained detached. Summoning his will power, Stephen asks with his "best French polish" for Russell to place Deasy's letter in the newspaper run by Mr. Norman. Russell is non-committal.

In response to more discussion about other writers invited to the Moore soiree that evening, Stephen imagines being asked (as if his imagination could force reality—art to life), is still not asked and then in his humiliation has to sit down. Lyster returns and shows interest in Stephen's theory. Russell leaves. Immediately Stephen feels more relaxed. Demonstrating his increased feeling of confidence and independence, he thinks in Aristotelian terms and refers to the books in the library as having "an itch of death . in them . . . urge me to wreak their will." This is the pornographic theory of art, that is art designed to produce kinesis rather than stasis.

Eglinton picks up the Shakespeare theme again, and Best reflects that *Hamlet* feels very personal. This view supports Stephen's theory. Stephen thinks in terms of ancient Irish legends and associates to Robin Hood, the medieval successor to many of the heroes in Irish legend. We could say that art robs from the rich in experience, the writer, and gives to the poor, the reader. Stephen continues with a general speech about the effect of the "unquiet father" on the experience of the son/artist: as long as the father is unquiet, the art of the son will be too subjective. He continues to develop his theory that the plays depict the raw material of Shakespeare's personal life. The part, his art, reflects his life, the whole. He notes that Shakespeare keeps coming back to the betrayal theme even after *Hamlet*, like licking an old and unhealed wound.

Buck comes in, having received a telegram from Stephen at the pub "The Ship" where they (with Haines) had agreed to meet. The telegram contains the following definition of a sentimentalist: "he who would enjoy without incurring the immense debtorship for a thing done." On the surface, this definition suggests Stephen enjoyed the Pub party without paying for it either in cash or by attending.

Buck guesses the subject of the library conversation, having heard Stephen's Shakespeare theory before. Stephen thinks of Photius, pseudo Mallachi, and Johann Most as mockers of the spirit, and in his mind runs through the father-son relationship on the assumption that father god is his own son, the one person one substance Sabellian heresy.

Ever the comic, Mulligan compares Shakespeare to Synge. Note that this comparison bears out Stephen's theory that Shakespeare has been burned ("singed") emotionally. Singed also means to burn the feathers of a bird, leaving only the meat. Best, the collector without his own ideas, brings up Wilde's theory of Shakespeare and Shakespeare's purported homosexual lover Willie Hughes. Buck finally brings up Stephen's telegram, which he reads. Buck describes their wait in the pub in mock Syngese and jokes that Synge, signifying Buck heated by his impatient wait, is looking to murder Stephen. With Buck present, the intellectual conversation breaks up.

Just then, Bloom comes ghost-like into the adjacent part of the library looking for an old edition of the Kilkenny newspaper, to find the crossed keys logo. He presents his regular identity card, which is brought in to Lyster. Lyster leaves and, after hesitating, helps Bloom personally, even though assistants are available. Their initial conversation can be overheard in the office. Reviewing Bloom's name on his card, Buck makes anti-Semitic remarks and relates that he just saw Bloom in the museum looking at Aphrodite's messial groove. We remember that Bloom was going to find out if the gods had an anus. At Eglinton's urging, Stephen continues his theory. Shakespeare's last will and testament provision to his wife of his "second best bed" is discussed. The conversation runs on puns from Will, to last will and testament, to will power.

When pressed, Stephen says he doesn't believe his own theory and agrees the author Shakespeare is in all his characters, including the youth to mature man in Prince Hamlet and from Prospero to Othello to Iago.

Inspired by Stephen's theory that Shakespeare was his own father and Stephen's hermaphroditic vision of heaven (man is his own wife), Buck composes the outline of a pornographic play featuring masturbation, entitled "Everyman His Own Wife" or "A Honeymoon in the Hand." Because of its light tone, the poem promotes masturbation, more pornography. Buck feels that he can't discuss these subjects in front of the bachelors Best and Lyster, so he makes Stephen leave with him. As they leave the library into the full light of Kildare Street, Buck reads his outline to Stephen. Then, in a significant moment, Bloom passes in between Stephen and Mulligan; the lesson of Bloom will separate Stephen from the Buck type of egoism and its literary counterpart the lyrical mode.

Ever the two-faced devotee of respectability, Mulligan greets Bloom with surface courtesy. Stephen thinks about the "seas between" them and escaping from Mulligan, but apparently doesn't do that right away. Mulligan warns Stephen that Bloom has a lustful eye on Stephen, Mulligan who sees lust in compassion. And Mulligan's all too ready detection of homosexual interest of Bloom for Stephen suggests a projection of his own soul and the reason Buck wants Stephen out of the tower while Haines is there.

Stephen recollects having been in the same spot on the library porch previously. At that time, he looked at birds in flight for signs of prophecy and thought about his dream that involved flying, a street of harlots, and "in" the melons. He associates Bloom with the dream and sees smoke arising from two housetop chimneys across the way (smoke in June?). The episode ends with Stephen's recollection of lines from Shakespeare's late play *Cymbeline.*

Action in The Odyssey

In Chapter xii, Circe warns Odysseus about the water routes away from her island. All involve the Sirens. Beyond that, there is a choice of dangers—one way involves the Wandering Rocks and the second the passage between Scylla and Charybdis. We get both of them.

The Scylla and Charybdis way itself features a choice. On one side is a cave inhabited by Scylla, a fearsome monster with six necks and three rows of teeth in each of her six heads. She hides in wait in her cave and bends down into the narrow passageway for prey. Her voice is like that of a new born whelp. Across the narrow way is the other choice Charybdis (pronounced Ka **rib** dis), the black water whirlpool that three times a day spouts and sucks. Just above the whirlpool is a fig tree bearing rock cliff. Circe recommends passing near Scylla, even if it means losing some of the crew because Charybdis risks all. Odysseus asks about taking revenge on Scylla, and Circe chides his martial temperament, explaining that Scylla is an immortal plague to which there is no defense. Circe recommends calling on Cratais, the mother of Scylla, for assistance.

Odysseus chooses Scylla and Charybdis over the Wandering Rocks and Scylla over Charybdis, but he doesn't tell the crew about Scylla. Against the advice of Circe, Odysseus puts on his war gear in preparation for Scylla. And he hasn't called on Cratais. As their ship is caught in the current in the narrow passageway, Odysseus directs the ship away from the whirlpool. As the crew is distracted by the whirlpool, Scylla picks up six crew men in her as many jaws.

Coming back later and alone, Odysseus passes through on the Charybdis side. The remains of his ship are sucked down into the whirlpool, but he clings to the fig tree in the rock above until the remains of his ship come back up and he is saved. With less baggage, the Charybdis side is preferable.

Parallels to The Odyssey

Stephen alternatively sucks up or spouts off in this episode, much like the whirlpool. He is still caught in the youthful subjective swirl. The revenge writing is sponsored by Odysseus's foolish martial desire for revenge on Scylla. The whirlpool effect is manifested in some of the language. The inevitability of suffering involves the frequent necessity in life of a choice between two evils: Scylla and Charybdis, the devil and the deep blue sea, or a rock and a hard place.

Aristotle is the rock of objective, secular truth from experience, and the dagger definitions of Aristotle used by Stephen are the reference for the teeth of Scylla. The mysticism and ethereal forms of Plato as given in the literary theory of Geo Russell are the reference for Charybdis the whirlpool. Scylla represents youth: her new born whelp, the inevitability of the condition and the mother influence all signal youth.

In the table of associations, we have the following:

Scylla	Aristotle	Dogma	Specifics	Youth
Charybdis	Plato	Mysticism	Generalizations	Experience

Art and Life and Fathers

The issue of the relationship of life to art and art to life plays out in this episode on both the production side in artists and the reception side in consumers. The character of soul conditions the message generated or the message received. "A book is a mirror. When a monkey looks in, no apostle can look out."[6]

The first connection of life to art is made on the reception side in the case of the bachelor and Quaker librarian Lyster. His view of *Hamlet* is conditioned by, indeed equated with, his own soul. Through his movements and reactions, he is presented as hesitating, quaking and uncertain. In interpreting *Hamlet*, he only quotes others on Shakespeare but never proposes an original thought. His interpretative view, taken from Goethe, is a picture of himself: "A hesitating soul taking arms against a sea of troubles, torn by conflicting doubts, as one sees in real life." Lyster is the quaking one seen in "real life."

With the remark that Palice was alive before he died, Stephen sneers at Lyster's shallow view as a rendition of the obvious. Further, the Quaker Lyster is throughout the episode walking not according to his own will but under the influence of other forces. In Quaker lingo, walking is a general symbol for behavior. Their leader George Fox, combined in Stephen's thoughts as Christ/Fox, contrasted the "strait walkers" with the "disorderly" walkers (unseemly behavior).[7] Lyster is an uncertain walker directed by others. The limited soul like Lyster's is not capable of resolving growth experiences, so it seeks shelter from them; he seeks comfort not growth ("Lyster . . . to comfort them"), less not more possibilities. The hesitating soul becomes the beautiful ineffectual dreamer pursuing matters not of this life. In short, Lyster's soul conditions, indeed limits, his view of *Hamlet* and all art. His limited soul produces a limited reading of *Hamlet*.

The conversation continues with Eglinton chiding Stephen for his youthful boast to rewrite *Paradise Lost* as The Sorrows of Satan. This is life and art on the artist side of the equation. Stephen's youthful soul conditions the art he expects to produce and his theory of the Son as Satan, Stephen's view of Satan as the youthful Christ.

Russell oracles his position that art must seek Plato's universal realm of forms. In Stephen's view, this divorces art from life. This removes the artist to the realm of the occult and limits the readers to the adepts, such as those in Russell's Theosophy movement. Ordinary people (OP) need not apply. Here is art as the distant father reached only by a few through the artist as broker/priest, a view the reader will note is similar to the basic doctrine of the Catholic Church. In Stephen's view, this art suffers because it has no connection with the here and now and the human grave and constant. As Stephen says, Plato not Aristotle would have banished him from the state (*Republic* — art must serve the state). Stephen's view that Plato's ideas about the afterlife were as shallow as Hamlet's reflects his scorn for the idea that a personalized or ego based soul continues in the afterlife.

In a lovely moment, Best informs us that Haines, the voyeur of things Irish, has just left to buy a book of lovesongs recommended by the bachelor Best. As to this type of lovesong, both Best and Haines are sentimentalists as defined in Stephen's telegram. They have not experienced personally the kind of love in the lovesongs. They are not "immanent" in the lovesongs. So any enjoyment of the lovesongs would be sentimental. Stephen earlier plagiarized one of these lovesongs in creating his vampire mouth south poem. He too, so far, is a sentimentalist as to this kind of love.

Mallarme's phrase that *Hamlet* is "reading the book of himself" is exactly what artist and reader alike are doing in connection with the arts. Art is experienced through the reader's own soul, which in proportion to the depth of the soul either restricts the import of the art or allows it full sway. Monkey in, monkey out. Apostle in, apostle out.

In nearly identical life and art, Stephen predicts, in this episode, writing this episode in the future: "So in the future, the sister of the past, I may see myself as I sit here now but by reflection from that which then I shall be."

In Stephen's theory, Shakespeare is presented as still licking the same old wound in the plays after *Hamlet*, as he continued to write about emotional banishment in general. Note that Joyce also appears to be licking the old wound of humiliation and seeking revenge by the very writing of this episode. In Stephen's view, Shakespeare kicked the revenge habit only with love for his granddaughter and the reconciliation is found in *The Tempest*. In this theory, I believe Joyce shows Stephen projecting his own personal condition onto his reading of Shakespeare. Shakespeare the writer is resolved even if Stephen isn't.

The issue of the relation of Father to Son in the Trinity is woven in and around the issue of the relationship of art to life. When Buck comes into the library office, Stephen thinks "Brood of mockers: Photius, pseudo Malachi, Johann Most." Photius (9th century patriarch of Constantinople) believed that the Holy Spirit must proceed only from the Father, not from both the Father and Son, because otherwise the Son would be his own Father. This view, in Stephen's opinion, mocks the human spirit because it insists on a external father. Stephen runs the

Father/Son equivalency concept through the Apostles' Creed: "He who Himself begot middler the Holy Ghost and Himself sent Himself, Agenbuyer, between Himself and others . . .. " In this rendition, Joyce is building on the prose of Johann Most (a 19th century anarchist).[8] The Apostles' Creed was the battleground for the official version of the relationship of Father and Son. Those who demand a separate father are equated by Stephen with mockers and even "Eve. Naked wheatbellied sin. A snake coils her, fang in's kiss." Eve, you remember, listened to the serpent.

In reaction to Stephen's concept of self-sufficiency of the soul and in heaven, Buck projects his own interests onto these concepts and creates a play based on masturbation. Like the others, his limited soul limits his creations. Stephen is not amused. One of the titles is "Everyman His Own Wife," which at this point describes Stephen's narcissistic attitude. He is his own wife and would be his own father.

Plato and Aristotle

You will remember from Philosophy 101 the conflicting views of metaphysical reality proposed by Plato and Aristotle. Plato proposed separate, eternal forms by which physical reality was influenced to become a horse or other object. Aristotle believed that the form of an object resided in the built-in pattern contained in the object itself, very similar to the modern view that DNA contains the instructions for an object's form.

These views of reality resonate with other major topics Joyce has treated: the divine is inevitably separate from or potentially part of each human; personal realization is based on the approval of others or on individual self-sufficient development; and highest art reaches for the eternal truths or is an integral part of the experience of the artist. Aristotle's view of the soul is in tune with Stephen's current views on these other major topics.

The Artist's Soul

In presenting his Shakespeare theory and in his related thoughts, Stephen proceeds from the assumption that the following three conditions are necessary for highest art:

295

1. The artist must create from the raw materials of his own life experiences and their record in his soul. Any artist who creates not from his own experience is a sentimentalist.

2. The artist must sufficiently resolve or detach his imagination from these life experiences before creating from them. Otherwise, the inevitable suffering or other emotional reaction to the experiences can disturb the detachment or equilibrium of the imagination necessary for the highest art. The creative imagination must be able to give the artistic creations their own life so they can speak to eternal human truths applicable to and realizable by all. This requires a composed or centered sense of self-confidence and security; it is no accident that these are the very aspects of identity and the Aristotelian definition of being.

3. The artist must be free of the objective to create pornographic art, that which is designed to attract or repel or teach or project an attitude. The only acceptable objective for proper art is aesthetic arrest.

All three principles are aspects of the relationship of an artist's life to his art. Principles 2 and 3 are about freedom, freedom from the artist's own subjective dislocations and from external or internal objectives that would limit the freedom of the artist to choose. This is the freedom that gives art its eternal aspect; it must proceed from the potential of all possibilities.

In the case of the artist, he must become sufficiently secure to the point that he (as son) can experience life and suffer without damaging the father imagination or the "quiet father"; the son serves as a sort of heat shield. Persons who experience too much too early are overwhelmed. They are represented by Lyster's view of the hesitating Hamlet and the name of the playwright Synge or singed—perhaps a reference to the riots caused by his plays. The singed ones protect themselves from suffering by comfort shelters such as bachelorhood. This in turn limits their soul and thus their art possibilities, both as artist and consumer ("of arts a bachelor").

Brunetto and False Fathers

When Stephen experiences resistance to his theory of *Hamlet* in the "bane of [their] miscreant eyes glinting stern under wrinkled brows," he thinks of a "basilisk" and thanks Brunetto for this word, since he apparently found it in a treatise by Brunetto. The basilisk was the king of the serpents, which with just one look could poison a man.[9] The glaring audience reminds him of this serpent (a hyper-extended metaphor, we note). Its ancestor in the Garden of Eden convinced Eve to follow his advice, poison in her ear, not the voice of her own soul.

This reference goes deeper than Stephen's overt credit gives it. Brunetto, a teacher of Dante, is principally famous as a character in Dante's *Inferno* XV. He serves his sentence in the dry hot desert of the third compartment of the seventh ring. It is so hot there that the condemned wanderers can not stop even for one second (no arrest here). This area was reserved for sodomites and is populated by teachers such as Brunetto, who was a teacher of Dante. This sounds like a false father. This area of Hell serves as a general comment on this episode; this area housed those who did violence against god, against nature and against art.

Traditional Schemata

The traditional schemata given by Joyce for this episode are organ—brain, art—literature, color—none, symbol—Stratford and London, and technique—dialectic. Correspondences are as follows: Scylla's rock—Aristotle, dogma and Stratford; the whirlpool—Plato, mysticism and London; and Odysseus—Socrates, Jesus and Shakespeare.

The time 2 p.m. is associated with Mars, the god of war. So here we have in the library an argument, a dialectic in which some get angry, some learn. The dialectic first encountered in Lyster's hesitating to and fro movements sponsors a number of instances of synthesis: the compromise resolution of the Shakespeare discussion; the multiple and contending voices in Stephen's mind; and the general course of the episode. Literature and the brain are, of course, right up Stephen's alley. Apparently not in favor of the siesta, Joyce felt that early afternoon was the highest point of mental activity.[10] Shakespeare left Stratford and his wife for London and then returned to Stratford in retirement. Socrates is the symbol for personal integrity, and here we encounter a Socratic dialogue. Jesus, who passed between the experiences of the divine and human, continues in the ever present father-son motive.

Stephen's Behavior

Stephen sucks up while the heavy weight George Russell is present. Stephen is highly self-conscious, conscious of his audience ("Two left") and self-conscious about his smile. He even smiles Cranly's smile, somebody else's smile. He is self-conscious about his method of presentation. As Erik H. Erikson has reminded us, you can't be your self if you are self-conscious.[11]

Stephen thinks with energy about Russell talking to someone about him. He speaks to him "superpolitely." He is quite willing to present to Russell his theory of Shakespeare, something he wouldn't do for Haines at the tower. He begs their hearing with his glance. He is sensitive to the debt he owes. He looks at their faces anxiously when Russell's young Irish poets collection is mentioned. Not invited, he hotly commits to revenge: "See this. Remember." As Russell is leaving, Stephen gears up, even though "Nookshotten" (pushed into a corner), to speak with his best French polish about Mr. Deasy's letter to the editor.

After Russell leaves, Stephen suddenly relaxes: "Rest suddenly possessed the discreet vaulted cell, rest of warm and brooding air." Note the allusion to the cell of Prospero from Shakespeare's *The Tempest*. After that, he is stronger. He can withstand "the bane of miscreant eyes glinting stern . . . . " He laughs and his inner thoughts return to his customary erudite subjects. He is bold and more secure. This change is a miniature version of what must happen to any artist in order to produce the classical temper.

Father, Son and the Lapwing

The main images in Stephen's speech and thoughts are the spiritual father-son duo and the flying trio of Dedaelus-Icarus-Lapwing. These images carry the theme of the relationship of art to life or the artist's life to his work. How does the intense imagination, the fading not burning coal, transubstantiate human experience into works of art?

Daedalus-Icarus-Lapwing serve as an ornithological artistic trinity with the lapwing displacing the Holy Ghost. Stephen repeatedly thinks of himself as a lapwing. The lapwing was renown for its cunning deceit of injury in protection of its nest and accordingly was used as a symbol by the Celtic Bards under the pressure of Christian censure to signal their esoteric intentions.[12] Like the deceit of the lapwing, this episode serves to hide Joyce in Stephen, Stephen in Shakespeare and Shakespeare in the play *Hamlet*.[13] The lapwing is so named because in slow flying one can see its wings move. Compared to Daedalus and Icarus, the lapwing-like Stephen in this episode doesn't soar because he is self-injured by his hot subjective temper.

Shakespeare was, in Stephen's theory, still shaking his spear about the betrayal issue and creating an even darker passion even into his last plays until *The Tempest*, in which he was at least partially reconciled, due to the love for his new granddaughter:

> He goes back, wary of the creation he has piled up to hide him from himself [the father artist from the suffering son], an old dog licking an old sore. But, because loss is his gain [he as a genius can use it in his art], he passes on towards eternity in undiminished personality, untaught by the wisdom he has written or by the laws he has revealed. His beaver is up. He is a ghost . . . . [parenthetical expressions are mine]

Thereafter he returned home.

With a detached or spiritually balanced father, the quiet father or classical temper, the son is sent to suffer and experience the heat of life to gather more material for art.[14] The detached father watches his son undergoing the experiences of life. This dualistic approach leads to two contending voices[15] within Stephen, which appear several times:

> Do you know what you are talking about? Love, yes . . . .
>
> * * *
>
> What the hell are you driving at? I know. Shut up.
> Blast you. I have reasons.

This duality is also presented in the pictograph "I, I and I. I." The first dual I with a comma in between shows the father and son as a work in progress and the dual I with a period in between shows the father at rest, the quiet father.

Stephen has two monologues (one interior and one a part of his lecture) about fathers and sons. In the first (line 61 "Formless spiritual"), Stephen's thoughts are pressed into the theories of the Theosophists, since he is talking to Geo Russell, the famous local Theosophist from whose court Stephen is exiled. In this formula:

Logos who suffers in us at every moment. This verily
is that [remember thou are that]. I am the fire upon the
altar. I am the sacrificial butter . . . The Christ with the
bridesister . . . repentant sophia, departed to the plane
of buddhi . . . Ordinary person must work off bad
karma first. [parentheticals are mine]

The "plane of buddhi," where the self is felt clearly and intensely but also as one with others, is the equivalent of the restrained and balanced classical temper in tune with the grave and constant in the unity of humanity.

In the second (line 828 "A father . . . battling against hopelessness, is a necessary evil"), the blood father hates the son because the son ". . is a new male: his growth is his father's decline, his youth his father's envy, his friend his father's enemy." This sums up Simon's view of Stephen. The succession of the spiritual father is not to be found in the blind rut of the blood father but more like the apostolic succession in the Catholic Church—the transfer of authority from Jesus to Peter and down through the Popes. Stephen believes he must receive the succession of the spiritual father in the church of his own experience.

Bachelors

Stephen saves his most ruthless exhibition of the limitations in the field of emotional life for the bachelor librarians. They are "of arts a bachelor" since a bachelor in life. They perform as adolescents in Stephen's play, worrying about their names like young boys. Their expected masturbation, the ultimate subjectivism, is the subject of Mulligan's mock Shakespeare play. Shakespeare's possible and Oscar Wilde's declared homosexuality are included as limited experiences. In this equation (in Ireland in 1904), homosexuality equals a limited

300

emotional experience and masturbation is subjective art. Mr. Best is blond and handsome and the second best bed. Stephen isn't very far along either, having only reached the whore's bed, paid for with the pound he borrowed from AE—the pound of flesh. Never forget that this book is dedicated to the day Joyce took Nora out on their first date and she reputedly "took him in hand."

Grandfathers

Buck indicated in the first episode that in Stephen's theory of Shakespeare, "He proves by algebra that Hamlet's grandson is Shakespeare's grandfather and that he himself [Shakespeare] is the ghost of his own father." In deciphering this riddle, it is helpful to know that Dante has Virgil say in *The Divine Comedy* that art is the grandchild of the gods (gods—artist—art). Using this kind of formula, experience could also be the grandfather of art (experience—artist—art).

Hamlet's grandson: King Hamlet's grandson is the soul of Prince Hamlet (King Hamlet—Prince Hamlet—Prince Hamlet's soul). Shakespeare's grandfather: The soul of Prince Hamlet is Shakespeare's grandfather because it represents Shakespeare's experience (experience—father imagination—Shakespeare as author). Ghost of his own father: Shakespeare created and thus was the creative father of the ghost of King Hamlet. This makes Shakespeare King Hamlet's father and Prince Hamlet's grandfather (Shakespeare—King Hamlet—Prince Hamlet). Shakespeare was also the father of his own soul, his own son so to speak, and thus the creative ghost of his own father.

Soul

In Stephen's system inspired by Aristotle, sensation is primary in human knowledge and the artist's self image or soul acquires experience through sensation. Aristotle describes the acquisition of experience as incorporating in the soul the "form" of the experience. Note that in this analysis, the term soul is used in a different sense than in current usage; it means something like one's total consciousness, including memory. The soul, which is a "form," collects the "forms" of experience and thus becomes the "form of forms."

The soul changes with new experiences. Moreover, the soul at any one time regulates the potential to experience new possibilities. The maximum soul would have the potential to experience all new possibilities. A limited bachelor soul would not. The range of possibilities the soul encounters depends on the internal and external degree of freedom enjoyed by the soul. In this sense, the soul viewed at any one time conditions the scope of future experience. That future experience in turn conditions the soul. This process gives total mental development a degree of inevitability. The final result of this process Aristotle calls "entelechy" or "form." The "form," the destined whole, is the essence of being.[16] Stephen thinks, "In the end is my beginning." The goal of change is being. This is the point of the following thoughts of Stephen:

> But I, entelechy, form of forms, am I by memory because under all experience, material and moral.
>
> ***
>
> His own image to a man with that queer thing genius is the standard of all experience, material and moral.
>
> ***
>
> He found in the world without as actual what was in his world within as possible . . .. If Socrates leave his house today he will find the sage seated on his doorstep. If Judas go forth tonight it is to Judas his steps will tend. We walk through ourselves . . . but always meeting ourselves.

Aristotle analogized the soul to the hand; the hand is the tool of tools, as the soul is the form of forms. Stephen considers his "Shrunken uncertain hand." The soul doesn't, in Stephen's view, come from the blood father but is developed by god and the person's own experiences. As the soul develops with experience, it is measured by the epiphanies it has acquired. Then the artist creates out of the inventory of his soul. As he acquires self understanding of his own soul, he reacts to new experiences not in kinetic terms colored by his subjective desire or repulsion. These kinetic reactions limit future possibilities. Instead, he reacts with more understanding, patience and deliberateness: "free his mind from his mind's bondage." This freedom in turn maximizes the possibilities. This condition is the classical temper in art.[17]

Dialectical Resolution of Classical and Romantic

The compromise in the dialectical discussion between the classical (Stephen—Aristotle) and romantic (Russell—Plato) approaches invites an exploration of the common base that binds them and avoids the dangers of each of the separate approaches.

The classical approach, linked here with Scylla, was defined by Joyce in an earlier essay as "a method which bends upon these present things [read here and now] and so works upon them and fashions them that the quick intelligence may go beyond them to their meaning, which is still unuttered [read the epiphany]." (CW, 74). The romantic approach, linked here with Charybdis, is criticized in the following: "So long as this place in nature [read here and now] is given us, it is right that art should do no violence to that gift, though it may go far beyond the stars and the waters [exaggeration] in the service of what it loves." (CW, 74). The gift of nature is the fruit of the senses lodged in experience and memory, the soul; that gift can be destroyed by an exclusive pursuit of the subjective experiences of inner being. Both approaches seek something "higher," and the danger in the classical approach is to get bogged down in pure materialism (the rock) while the corresponding danger in romanticism is incoherence (the whirlpool).

The Joyce synthesis approach achieves a "higher" objective and avoids both dangers. His synthesis of the dialectic is to show both the truth of the visible world (from Scylla) and the truth of the being of humans (from Charybdis). This is accomplished by art which manifests the eternal truths of humanity in normal human circumstances.[20] In this approach, there is no higher objective than the "grave and constant" of the human condition built into Joyce's aesthetic theory. Since Shakespeare on the page and Bloom in the flesh are most in touch with this aspect of the human experience, they represent the way.

Celtic Mythology

Ancient Celtic lore sponsors several references in this episode. First, Mr. Best in "real life" actually translated a book by Jubainville titled *The Irish Mythological Cycle*. In the novel, Best shows his own book to Haines. This episode's Celtic sauce includes references to druids, Aengus of the birds (an artistic bird-headed figure looking for an ideal

303

mate), Lir (tied to King Lear), mother Dana (of the Irish gods Tuatha De Dannan), an ollav, Irish Bards, old Irish myths, the mulberry tree sacred to Dana and augury by birds.

The ancient Irish bards connect many threads. They produced the legend of Llew Llaw Gyftes, which prefigures Red Robin Hood[19] and perhaps even Hamlet. Llew couldn't get a name, or horses or fighting gear (his identity) without the approval of a woman. The episode contains several direct ties from Celtic legend to Shakespeare. We have Lir and Lear and Prospero the druid and the soothsayer in Cymbeline, which ends the episode.

The druids serve as a general symbol for the perspective of the classical temper. Their goddess Dana points to the creative mother principle of possibilities. The main creed of the druids was that man develops by experience in different states of being,[20] which sounds very much like Aristotle. Their idea of god is said to have sprung from thunder and the barking of a dog,[21] two subjects that are prominent in this novel. Bloom looks for the crossed key logo in the Kilkenny newspaper; the Kilkenny Transactions are a famous set of metamorphosis by the Druid Laban.[22]

Sentimentalist

Stephen sent a telegram to Buck at the pub "The Ship," since Stephen did not show up there for their agreed meeting. This was an extravagance since Stephen was only a short distance away. This suggests Stephen wanted to avoid them. How Buck finds Stephen in the library is not revealed.

The text of the telegram, apparently taken from Meredith, is "The sentimentalist is he who would enjoy without incurring the immense debtorship for a thing done." This line was included in a sequence of poems by Meredith entitled "Modern Love."

In Buck's case, he is a sentimentalist under this definition because he enjoys serious subjects without ever having made a serious attempt to come to terms with them. He only mocks. An author who would write from imaged not actual experience would fall in the same category. As would a voyeur. Christ as a scapegoat rather than an example would be included. Include those who write books about other

304

books (like this one) or who like Mr. Best only translate a book. Stretching a bit, the Platonic view of art as a reach for objective eternal forms existing independently and not through the key hole of actual experience of the here and now would also be sentimental. And finally, Stephen's use of Meredith's quotation without an acknowledgment of source makes him a sentimentalist, and the telegram itself is an example of the definition contained in it. Stephen in a sense has enjoyed the scheduled meeting at the pub without having paid for the drinks.

Parallel in the Mass

In reaction to Mulligan's entrance, Stephen applies the Sabellian heresy to the Apostle's Creed. Compared to the Nicene Creed, the version now cited in the Mass, the older Apostles' Creed is consistent with both the orthodox and heretical versions of the relationship of the Father and Son.[23] That flexibility is presumably the reason for its inclusion in this episode.

Right after the tortured Apostles' Creed, Stephen makes reference to the following: "He lifts his hands. Veils fall. O, flowers! Bells with bells with bells acquiring." This is the ritual that follows the Blessing of the Baptismal Font on Holy Saturday.[24] This ritual precedes the baptism of the Catechumens on Saturday. Stephen, the Catechuman, is to be baptized in his own self-realization.

First Letter, First Word and Opening

The first letter is **U** in the first word "Urbane." First of all, the letter **U** looks like a whirlpool, Charybdis. This would reflect subjective mysticism, the swirl into oneself. This must be overcome to achieve the classical temper, the quiet father. Breaking down urbane into "ur" and "bane," the etymology of "Ur" is primitive and "bane" is murder especially by poison, suggestive of King Hamlet's murder and indicative of Joyce's view of the subjective as primitive art. The combined word "urbane" suggests refined sensibility, which is also close to the concept of the stable imagination. In this reading, this one word would contain both of these opposed forces treated in this episode.

In the imagery of the Symbolist poets that Joyce studied (Mallarme is mentioned), the letter U stands for green,[25] which in turn colors Stephen's jealousy. R. Graves advises that the letter U was

305

rigorously excluded by druids from certain important cryptographic sequences of letters to numerals since the letter U represents the Goddess of death in life.[26] How appropriate for the classical temper drowning in the whirlpool.

The episode opens with the Quaker librarian Thomas Lyster. He is described as urbane, his speech is designed to comfort and he is purring. When he enters, he hesitates by coming forward and then stepping back. He speaks tentatively: "we have, have we not . . . " He says he will go directly, but then hesitates. Lyster's movements, backward and forward, are the apparent movements of an object caught in a whirlpool—while going around and around it appears to be coming forward and then going away. His movements are described in the trope of the dance—the "sinkapace" (used by Shakespeare after the French *qinque pace*) and "curanto." The names of these dances, containing sink and current, stay in the whirlpool image.

The dance is the Dionysian counterpart in personal entertainment of the whirlpool. The shape of the whirlpool, the oval, and the reference to the cat (purring) pull the whirlpool image into the service of selfhood, the tyrannical master of the subjective lyrical mode. Like selfhood and the lyrical mode, the whirlpool never goes anywhere; it just continues to dwell on itself and possess those items it can. Mysticism is the ultimate extension of selfhood, where license is given to disregard the truth of everyday life in the direct pursuit of personal eternal beauty.

The Tempest in the Library and the Last Mole

Two of Shakespeare's last plays, *The Tempest* and *Cymbeline*, portray the direction of change in the artist as he matures.

The totally detached artist would be like Prospero in *The Tempest*. He is in command on a mysterious island through the magic of his art spirits. He was previously betrayed as the Duke of Milan by a group led by his brother. The very usurpers who originally betrayed him are most conveniently forced ashore on Prospero's island by a storm (the tempest) raised by Prospero's magic. Even though their very survival on the island is in doubt, all the addicted usurpers continue to scheme and plot against each other, creating their own personal tempest. All, that is, except the good son Ferdinand, who does not wish to usurp his father's position as King. Prospero marries his daughter, "his future," to the good son Ferdinand. With his enemies in his power and vulnerable to his revenge, Prospero, the anti-Faust,[27] adopts compassion and drops his powers by planting his staff in the ground. The bad guys repent in the face of this compassion (this part was hard to swallow).

In terms of symbology, the tempest is the emotional reaction of Stephen in the library. Joyce is Prospero controlling events and finding atonement through self restraint. Notice that Prospero brings about the reconciliation through the agency of the tempest.

The episode ends with an image from *Cymbeline* and the peace of the druid priests. The wager plot in this play about the chastity of the heroine is featured in Stephen's earlier line about the influence of Ophelia on Hamlet: "That mole is the last to go." By this reference, Stephen means that sexual attraction is one of the last powers or experiences to resolved by the classical temper. In *Cymbeline*, one of the parties to the wager, the Italian, hid in the heroine's bedroom in a trunk, and as she undressed saw a mole on an intimate part of her body ("A mole cinque-spotted"). The Italian used this knowledge of the intimate mole in a false attempt to prove that he himself had been the cause of her loss of chastity. This deception was unmasked in a happy lovers' ending. The other part of the plot featured the reunion and reconciliation of long lost royal sons to their father the king as a result of noble fighting. In this reunion, the sons are united with their spiritual as well as consubstantial father.

Cymbeline, a very odd play, has some parallels with the episode. In the play, the heroine is presented in "aesthetic dignity" amid a throng of absurd characters.[28] Perhaps this suits Joyce's view of himself among the Dublin literati. The play reflects authorial self parody,[30] as Joyce is parodying his hot earlier self as Stephen. The plot synthesis through family reconciliation is reflected reductively in Stephen becoming his own father. Shakespeare's sickness of spirit in this play[30] is echoed in Stephen's hot emotional mood.

The druid peace registers the peace of the soul attained by the power of the classical temper. These peaceful powers are "hierophantic"—they reveal the sacred through the epiphany drawn from

307

the here and now of real life. The penultimate closing lines of the episode feature the "frail . . . two plumes of smoke ascended, pluming, and in a flaw of softness were blown." The soft merger of the two plumes reflects the synthesis of the two approaches, classical and romantic. In this synthesis, soul and experience interact. The soul resolves experience and grows. The broadened soul seeks broader experience. Two plumes of smoke ascending, pluming—interacting.

The chimney smoke makes Stephen think: "Cease to strive. Peace of the druid priests of Cymbeline: hierophantic: from wide earth an altar." And then the episode ends with the lines from *Cymbeline*, to which Stephen's mind has been drawn by the twin plumes of smoke:

Laud we the gods

And let our crooked smokes climb to their nostrils

From our bless'd altars.

Notice the balanced physical composition of this material. The top line on the right is balanced by the bottom line on the left, making a picture of the classical temper. This druid priest, this artist with the classical temper, can use the base of the wide earth, signifying the natural world of the here and now, as an the altar and achieve the hierophantic—that is read the sacred mysteries. Both growth of realization through resolved experiences and a stable imagination are necessary to read the mysteries. By this growth, not by the sacrifice of limitation, we laud the gods by growing closer to them.

The Library as the Temple

The visit to the museum and library is described in a later episode in terms of Jewish ritual as the visit to a "holy place." The holy portion of the Jewish Temple in Jerusalem could be visited only by the priests. The holy of holies within the holy portion was the "book room"; it contained the Torah given to Moses by Jahweh and the Ark.

Likewise, the sites in this episode are the holy place, not because they contain books, but because they are the sites for the discussion of Joyce's holy of holies—the relationship of art to life.

Structure, Art and Aesthetic

This episode is hard to read but one of the best. Featuring a growth path for Stephen, the style is highly inventive. It contains, in my view, arresting living truths about the human condition that will be felt by each generation. The metaphysics will fall away, but the heart will remain.

The form of the episode is like the dialectical process, back and forth. Lyster steps forward and then back; Stephen theorizes and then retracts; the choice of Scylla or Charybdis. Resolving the various theories of art and about Shakespeare gives the episode the aspect of the transcending of opposites. That in turn suggests the unity.

The narrator is much the same as in the first three episodes, dominated by Stephen's point of view. Note, however, that the narrator, unlike Stephen, refers to Russell and Magee by their literary pseudonyms.[31]

Literature as the art of the episode conditions how the scene is delivered to the reader and the sharing of depth among the characters. For example, Best and Lyster are relatively flat characters. In the literature mode of art, they can usefully serve more powerful and in depth characters and the episode's symbology; this inequity in depth of characters would not work in drama. Joyce should have learned this lesson from writing the unsuccessful play *Exiles*.

The episode contains examples of poetry, blank verse and even a play. In the play, some characters are self-conscious and therefor lyrical (those making a big issue about their names) while Stephen is restrained and dramatic. Much of the episode is made from pieces of the plays of Shakespeare and the poetry of Milton, Blake and Dante. There are several references to actual studies of Shakespeare.

Stephen's thoughts at certain points take on the nature of a whirlpool—the sentences get progressive shorter and "circle" around the same subject. His thoughts about the meeting of the Theosophical Society have this construction—"Yogibogeybox in Dawson's chambers. . ." starting at line 279. This material even includes "whirled, whirling. ." He is thinking about the Theosophist's mystical doctrines in thought patterns that resemble a whirlpool. The same is true of Stephen's thoughts about Shakespeare's second-best bed being left to his wife, starting at line 701:

"Leftherhis
Secondbest
Leftherhis
Bestabed
Secabest
Leftabed
Woa!"

This even looks like a whirlpool in which the words get mixed up as objects would in the water. This is appropriate to the subject matter because the will provision reflects, in Stephen's theory, continuing anger that has not been resolved—Will's last will and testament carrying out his pornographic will to humiliate his wife.

****

ENDNOTES

1. Letter dated May 16, 1969 reprinted in the July 3, 1995 issue of *The New Yorker*.
2. Russell, B. *A History of Western Philosophy* (New York: Simon & Schuster, 1945) p. 743.
3. Critical Essays, p. 148.
4. Gifford, p. 193.
5. Ellmann, James Joyce, pp. 118.
6. Georg Christoph quoted by Robertson Davies in *A Voice From the Attic*.
7. Critical Essays, p. 160.
8. Lang, p. 152.
9. Gifford, p. 218.
10. Budgen, F. *James Joyce and the Making of Ulysses* (Bloomington: Indiana University Press, 1960) p. 107.
11. Erickson, E. *Childhood and Society* (New York: W.W. Norton & Company, 1950).
12. Graves, White Goddess, p. 53.
13. Cixuos, p. 566.

14. Goldberg, S. L. *The Classical Temper* (New York: Barnes & Noble, 1961).

15. Cixous refers to this as the artist and his double. See Cixous at p. 564.

16. Greene, M. *A Portrait of Aristotle* (Univ. of Chicago Press, 1963), pp. 63, 211-212, 229, 230.

17. Goldberg, pp. 66-99 and particularly p. 76.

18. Critical Essays, p. 157.

19. Graves, White Goddess, pp. 304 and 318.

20. Bonwick, p. 63.

21. Bonwick, p. 76.

22. Bonwick, p. 53.

23. Lang, p. 155.

24. Lang, p.149.

25. Herring, P. *Joyce's Uncertainty Principle* (Princeton: Princeton Univ. Press, 1987) p. 149.

26. Graves, White Goddess, p. 296.

27. Bloom, H. *Shakespeare: The Invention of the Human* (New York: Riverhead Books, 1998) p. 663.

28. Bloom, p. 618.

29. Bloom, p. 622.

30. Bloom, p. 638.

31. Critical Essays, p. 162.

Episode 10 (Wandering Rocks)

Basic Themes

Hell on earth administered by church and state. Priest and king crush human possibilities.

In The Odyssey, Circe cites to Odysseus the perils of the wandering rocks. Coming together in a pincher movement, the wandering rocks had crushed the ships that tried to sail through them. Only one, the *Argo* captained by Jason with an all-hero crew, had managed to pass through the mobile crushers.

In this episode constructed of 19 small episettes, the

wandering/crushing rocks are church and state featured on the move in the first and last episettes. Father Conmee stands for the church and is on a mission, motivated by political considerations, to place one of the Dignam children in an orphanage. The Viceregal Calvacade stands for the state and is on a mission, motivated by control considerations, to benefit a local hospital.

Trapped between them in the rest of the episettes are the crushed souls of the ordinary people of Dublin. This trap is Hell on earth: coffin sellers, police informants, one-legged sailors begging hand outs, poor children begging for food from their drunkard father, adulterers, pornographers, gamblers, family abusers, soldiers, disasters, bribes, lawyers, drunks, lechers, tyrants, boxers, the blind and cursers. You name it, these episettes have got it.

This earthly Hell is presented with Connector Facts from *The Divine Comedy* and *Paradise Lost*. Through the middle of this Profane Comedy in Dublin, the crumpled handout announcing Elijah's imminent return sails unnoticed down the Liffey River to the ocean. Elijah is the symbol of freedom and is to precede the redeemer; and the redeemer is the most famous victim of the crushing rocks, the Jewish Temple leaders and the Roman Pilate. Jason and Jesus made it through the rocks and so can you—that is if you are willing to pay the hero price. Bloom, like Odysseus, goes another way altogether.

In this earthly Hell, time is the ruler. Again and again the occupants reset their watches or ask for the time. Time rules the organization of events in the episettes; each contains contemporaneous events, even at the cost of including one more "intrusions" of contemporaneous events that are removed in space and meaning from the rest of the material in the episette. These arbitrary intrusions come (like the rocks) crashing in without explanation or apology, emphasizing the rule of time in the Hell on this earth. Time is the condition initiated as a result of the expulsion from the Garden of Eden; time is the measure of human degeneration; time is the format of human internal consciousness; and time is the substratum of subjectivity. On this earth, time is arrested only momentarily by echoes from the original Garden condition in the eternal.

The promise of transcendence issued by the synthesis of the dialectic process featured in the last episode is rescinded in this one. The opposites, church and state, come together in a crushing pincer movement.

Parallels To *The Divine Comedy* and *Paradise Lost*

In Dante's *The Divine Comedy*, Virgil guides Dante through the circles of Hell. At the bottom they see Lucifer, the ruler of Hell. Hell is shaped like a cone of space in the earth. Lucifer is at the point at the bottom of the cone; there the possibilities are totally limited to Lucifer. Huge physically, Lucifer is covered up to his waist in ice and makes chilling winds with his bat-like wings. He has a total of six eyes in his three heads. The three heads stand for impotence, ignorance and hate. He is eating Judas, Brutus and Casius. He sports heavy hair all over his body.

In the region of Hell near Lucifer, the spirits of dead humans (the shades) ". . . were wholly covered, and showed through like a straw in glass. Some are lying down; some are upright . ." With no possibilities other than Lucifer, there is no movement. The shades are frozen, signifying a total lack of free will. Dante describes the experience of being near Lucifer as being neither alive nor dead. In order to reflect stylistically the effect of Lucifer, Dante's otherwise highly structured verse is grossly distorted in this section. Those intentional gross distortions in Dante's poetic syntax sponsor the intrusion distortions in this episode.

Hay and straw and related materials cut from Dante's images of shades are used as Connector Facts in this episode. Straw and the Dubliners are neither dead or alive, the condition generated by proximity to Lucifer. By contrast, Lenehan guesses that Bloom is reading the book entitled "Bloom is on the Rye," when the plant material is alive. As all who enter Hell abandon hope, Stephen's music teacher and guide, Artifoni, describes life as a beast but recommends hope. With hope, Virgil and Dante climb out of Hell by climbing over Lucifer's buttocks, his "swelling . . . haunches."

In this episode, Blazes prepares to go to Molly's house for seduction and betrayal of her marriage covenant. The very name Blazes suggests the fires of Hell. We already know that like Lucifer, Blazes is very hairy. Consider Blazes's testicles as the wandering rocks.

In Milton's *Paradise Lost*, Satan sees the universe of reality as a ball with a hole on top suspended from the floor of heaven by a gold chain. The Connector Facts for this image are Father Conmee's gold pocket watch on a fob chain and the watch chain in the lapidary shop. Milton's Satan was, and the characters in this episode are, obsessed with time. After the fall of Adam, Milton's God distorted the world and stars. In this episode, distortion and confusion are rampant. The earthly flame, Milton's image of the degenerated version of the celestial fire, is projected through the limited fire potential of the hay, straw, twigs and peat repeatedly mentioned in this episode. After Satan had permanently opened the gates to Hell, his agents Sin and Death built an "arch" bridge from earth to Hell. Bloom spends this episode looking for a new porno book for Molly under the Merchants' arch, the arch carrying the symbol of prostitution or commercial sex. Like the piano tuner in this episode, Milton was blind.

If these and other indirect references to Hell weren't enough, specific mention is made of Hell in the 15th, visions of Hell in the 16th and Purgatory in the 18th episette.

Jason, Action in The Odyssey and Parallels

The Connector Facts in this episode from the hero voyage of Jason through the wandering rocks are numerous. They indicate the trials and tribulations that are necessary for a hero's soul journey past the rocks of church and state. The hero must avoid the influence of the priest and king in order to reach the maximum possibilities in life and realization. The Odyssey doesn't tell the story of Jason, but other sources[1] relate the following concerning his famous voyage. The wandering rocks guard the narrow end of a body of water, the Bosporus at the northern end of the Sea of Marmara. Like Lucifer at the bottom of his cone, there the possibilities in terms of navigation are few.

Jason's voyage was made because Pelias, a son of Poseidon (tied to church and state in earlier episodes), usurped the throne of Iolcus from Aeson. Here church and state have usurped the Dublin throne. Because of an oracle that a son of Aeson would overthrow Pelias, the usurper Pelias killed all of Aeson's children except one, Jason, who escaped into exile. Our hero Stephen has just returned from exile. Jason means healer, which is what Stephen hopes to do for his country's soul. An oracle specifies that a one-footed man will undo Pelias. Jason returns home to Iolcus wearing just one sandal, a fighting mode for the mud. An one-legged sailor begs in this episode, and Jason's final fate as an outcast justifies the allusion.

Upon confronting Pelias, Jason forthrightly demands the throne as his rightful inheritance. Crafty Pelias agrees to give the throne back if Jason is able to bring home to Iolcus from Colchis (at the eastern end of the Black Sea) the golden fleece and the soul of Phrixus. Phrixus had left Iolcus in order to avoid being the subject of royal sacrifice (royal draft dodging) and died in distant Colchis in disgrace because without burial. Pelias predicts the return of the fleece and Phrixus's soul will cure the draught and plague in Iolcus. Likewise, Stephen has left Dublin to avoid soul death, and the draught and plague remain behind in Dublin. The return of Stephen's soul is this novel. The golden fleece is the fleece of Dublin souls by church and state. The voyage of Jason and his crew also seemed to have had political and economic overtones. Up to this point, the Troy-lead league of cities had kept the Greeks out of the Black Sea, the source of grain imports for Greece, particularly Athens.

Jason's destination is known as the land of the mighty, and only heroes are recruited for the job. Their ship is huge, and its imposing main beam is of wood from Zeus's oak. Only heroes can seek soul freedom in Dublin. The select crewmembers are known as the Argonauts. The name itself makes the point about the multitude of ordinary people—are go naut, are for the plural multitude go not past the rocks.

The heroes' first stop is Lemnos, where the women have murdered all the Lemnian men. The now sex starved Lemnian women send food to and bestow womanly gifts on the Argonauts, who stay in Lemnos distracted from their mission. Eventually Hercules recalls them to duty. This stop has ominous overtones as a requirement for the hero quest. In the Sea of Marmara (past the Dardanelles), the Argonauts land at Archton where six-handed giants have to be beaten off. The Argonauts dedicate their anchor stone to the marriage of King Cyzicus, a ruler in this area.

At Bebryos, King Amycus challenges their best to a boxing match. The Greek Polydeuces (many twos) wins killing the King. The boxing match causes a battle rather than a catharsis of aggression. Boxing matches are featured in this episode as a reflection of the tortured and aggressive desires of the Dubliners.

Next the heroes land at Salmydessus, where the blind Phineus rules. Blinded by the gods for accurate prophecy, he is plagued by harpies. In this episode, a blind man (later identified as a piano tuner) gives a prophetic assessment of the Dubliners as "bitch's bastards," or Eve's legacy. In the Argonaut legend, the blind King warns the Argonauts about the Symplegades or terrifying rocks that guard the entrance to the Bosphorus. Armed with this information, the Argonauts send a bird, a symbol of the spirit, ahead of the ship as they approach the rocks. The rocks close on the bird nipping its tail feathers. As the rocks recoil open, Jason's ship rows through quickly, losing only its tail ornament as the rocks shut again. Timing is everything. After that, the rocks remained open to the heroic passage.

Notice that the spirit of the soaring bird precedes the heroes through the rocks and that the bird's guidance tail feathers are temporarily injured in the process. In this episode, Elijah precedes the redeemer. The Elijah tract floating down the Liffey is crumpled like the bird's injured tail. And the church has co-opted the bird. Father "Swan" is in charge of the orphanage to which Father Conmee is making a visit. Like the swan that can't fly, Father Swan is presiding over an orphanage more interested in control than self-realization. Children without parents ruled by the church. Birds that don't fly. No more charismata from the Holy Ghost. Don't fight city hall.

On an island in the Black Sea, Apollo appears briefly to the Argonauts in a huge human form with bond hair in ringlets and carrying a silver bow. The earth shakes and the Argonauts are afraid to look directly at Apollo; the narrator tells us that Apollo glides above the water. Apollo appears in this episode as the dancing instructor who glides along dressed like a peacock.

Near their destination Colchis (at the far end of the Black Sea), which is famous for its gold, defending birds drop brazen plumes (metal feathers) that injure the Argonauts. The female temptations in the Ormond Hotel bar in the 15th episette have alluring hair of "Bronze by gold." Aphrodite convinces Eros to help Argonaut Jason by giving Medea, the daughter of the King holding the golden fleece, the passion arrow for Jason. For this purpose, Aphrodite bribes Eros with a golden ball with blue rings. When thrown, this special sphere leaves a comet's trail. In the 9th episette, Bloom discusses the stars and comets while Lenehan is ejaculating (comet's trail) while feeling up Molly's magic orbs with blue veins. The passion given to Medea by Eros is kept going by a live wryneck (a kind of bird) spread on a firewheel, the wryneck being known for its ability to twist its neck into contortions. This episode contains multiple references to a poster of Marie Kendall (fire), the famous pantomime.

The King of Colchis agrees to let the fleece go if Jason performs more heroic tasks (constant testing of the hero). Jason does so with help from Medea's magic potions. One of the tasks involves sowing a field with serpent's teeth, which hatch as soldiers. Soldiers enforcing British rule in Ireland are in evidence in the 6th episette. Even after Jason performs all the assigned tasks, the King renounces the deal and refuses to let the fleece go (heroes face treachery). Using Medea's sleep potion, Jason manages to steal the fleece from the guardian dragon. Jason, his accomplice lover Medea, her brother and the other Greek heroes leave, and the King's men give chase by ship.

On their chased return to Greece, Medea slows down their pursuers by murdering her own brother, cutting him into little pieces and dropping them in the water. The pursuers slow down to pick up the royal pieces. Kernan in the 12th episette remembers Robert Emmet, the Irish patriot who was drawn and quartered. Everything must be risked in the hero journey, even family. Stephen refuses to help his sister in the 13th episette.

Medea eventually kills the bad King Pelias using the cauldron of regeneration. The Dedalus daughters featured in the 4th episette have two pots, one to wash clothes for others and one for charity soup, regeneration through compassion. After he achieves everything he wants with her loyal help, Jason deserts Medea. For this treachery and insincerity, the gods punish him. The hero must be careful about means and ends. Deserted by the gods, Jason roams homeless from city to city and eventually returns to the scene of his former glory, the Argo, only to die by way of a beam falling from the ship.

Action in Ulysses.

1st **Episette**. The first episette features Father Conmee (con me). He is moving around—one of the wandering rocks. The sanctified Church built on Peter should be a solid rock, but as reflected through Father Conmee, it is off its moorings and wandering. It moves around seeking respect and denying charity.

Time and disorientation, from Milton's conception of the fall from paradise, lurk in the very first sentence:

"The superior, the very reverend John Conmee S.J. reset his smooth watch in his interior pocket as he came down the presbytery steps."

When reading "reset his smooth watch" before reading "in his interior pocket," the meaning of reset is ambiguous; it could mean resetting the time on the watch or resetting the watch back in his pocket. This is typical disorientation for these episettes, a literary portrait of the distortion in time and space caused, according to Milton, by the fall of man. By this opening, Joyce deftly ties disorientation with time. Orientation is to the eternal.

Then consider the watch, a pocket watch held by a fob or chain, in the context of Milton's image of Satan coming into reality (where time rules) through the hole in the top of the universe, a reality that is suspended from the floor of heaven by a golden chain. This is a typical Joycean symbol—reality is ruled by time. Conmee's watch is smooth because he pulls it out often. Now, however, he is behind in his vespers, his holy duties.

Father Conmee comes into Gardiner Street from the presbytery steps, from that part of the Church reserved for the clergy. And Conmee is safely reserved from the real problems of the world. He likes it cheerful and smooth, smooth like the back of his pocket watch. Superior, he is addicted to respect. Reverend, he would revere the end in the after-life. This life is not his concern; his lifetime pursuit is the past, and he has written a book with the title *Old Times in the Barony*.

Conmee is on a seemingly charitable mission, to place one of the Dignam children in the Artane (read are tame) orphanage. But he is doing so for the wrong reason—the political or business reason of mutual favors with Cunningham. Here are the thoughts of the superior, the very reverend:

> What was that boy's name again? Dignam. Yes. *Vere dignam et iustum est.* Brother Swan was the person to see. Mr. Cunningham's letter. Yes. Oblige him, if possible. Good Practical catholic: useful at mission time.

Conmee puns on the name Dignam. Conmee's transition from Dignam as a recently deceased father and husband to one word in church ritual (in Latin) is too easy. Father Conmee's mind dwells on propriety, not compassion. In Latin, *dignam* means "fitting" in the phrase from the Mass "it is indeed fitting and right." The phrase continues in the Mass to give thanks to the Lord. Given the hell conditions in Dublin, thanks is not the most natural reaction. Brother Swan runs the orphanage so Conmee is to "see" him. Mr. Cunningham has asked by letter for help in placing one of the Dignam children in the orphanage. Conmee is doing so for practical and political reasons, not out of compassion. And you have to ask why only one Dignam child?

Conmee thinks about the problems of life, but without involvement. Detached without compassion, he is like the shades near Lucifer, neither alive nor dead. Ever mindful of social standing, he speaks respectfully to the notables, down to the school boys but not at all to the one-legged sailor beggar, the Dublin version of the golden fleece who is most needful of charity.

The beggar extends his hat to Conmee to ask for alms, but Conmee refuses since he has only one coin, one silver crown (5 shillings), which Conmee thinks would be too much. Notice Conmee didn't prepare for the beggars by bringing some small coins. His "silver crown" protects him against charity.

Father Conmee considers soldiers and sailors who, like the beggar, have lost limbs in war and then been reduced to poverty. He concludes uncharitably that if they had served their god as well as their state, they would have no problems. More insulation from the need to extend charity. Neither church nor state helps the limbless veterans.

Conmee meets Mrs. Sheehy, wife of Sheehy M.P. (read he she empty). He doffs his "silk hat" to her. He tells her he will soon be taking the "waters" at Buxton, a fashionable resort for curing physical ills. Note the emphasis on prestige and the secular. Conmee feels secure about his social smile because he cleaned his teeth with arecanut paste (made from palms)—arecanut for Argonaut.

She inquires when Father Vaughn is scheduled to return to preach, not when Conmee will be preaching. Vaughn is a Welsh father who preaches fervently in brogue. Conmee's fire has gone out, and the congregation wants entertainment. Conmee remembers a line of Father Vaughn's about Pilate, in whose time the crushing rocks of church and state closed on Jesus.

At Mountjoy Square, Conmee meets three schoolboys from Belvedere. The three schoolboys are depersonalized in Conmee's thoughts; he thinks of them as six eyes, not three individual souls. The six eyes of the boys suggest Lucifer's six eyes. Conmee does remember a letter to be mailed to father provincial, his Rome representative or his Pilate. To mail this letter, he uses one of the schoolboys, so the lazy and important Father doesn't have to cross the street. Conmee warns the boy not to be swallowed by the mouth of the red mailbox, reminding us of Lucifer's mouth.

Conmee likes the trams, the symbol of predestination, since the end of the journey is known and struggle is not necessary. Conmee passes the basics of life in the here and now—the grocery store, the tobacco shop, the ever-busy pub and the mortuary—without a major thought. They are all open but the "free church" is closed. He enjoys the salutes of respect he receives. Conmee views as idyllic the barge he sees below in the canal ferrying peat, which is burned to heat poor homes. The bargeman has a dirty straw hat and is looking up.

320

On his mission, Father Conmee thinks about the aged and virtuous but bad tempered females in St. Joseph's Church, reminiscent of the women of Lemnos. Conmee wallows in nostalgic daydreams of being back in the fields of Conglowes (where he was rector when Joyce attended Conglowes Wood College) and of his relative of yore, Don John Conmee.

The repeated emphasis on palmoil, greasing the palm, the crucifixion through the palms and the bloodless sacrifice begins in the first episette. These references suggest the betrayal of Jesus and of the Dubliners by church and state.

Conmee boards the tram at Newcomen bridge. This event is repeated in the text to emphasize the stranglehold of time. He pays for his ticket this time. Conmee is more interested in good cheer than dealing with the ills of the world in this life: ". . . he disliked to traverse on foot the dingy way past Mud Island . . . . The solemnity of the occupants of the [tram] car seemed to Father Conmee excessive for a journey [life] so short and cheap . . . . " [parenthetical expressions added]. His concern as a waste of souls for all the unbaptised yellow, black and brown souls is priceless (his next sermon is on the foreign missions of the Church). He reads his Nones or prayers for the noon hour; the word Nones originally referred to the hour Christ died, the ninth hour. He is behind in his daily prayers.

He gets off the tram at Howth road and walks on Malahide Road, which is quiet. He thinks about the book he wrote, *Old Times in the Barony*, and about the saucy first countess of Belvedere whose house is nearby. Word has it that she was adulterous with her husband's brother. She was "not startled when an otter plunged."

Just as Conmee reads in the Palms under the Hebrew letter *res* the verse "Blessed are the undefiled (*Beate immaculati)*," Conmee meets a young man (later we learn Lynch) and woman coming out of the fields, the fields of privacy. Lynch raises his hat in respectful salute. The woman is not abashed. She rubs Conmee's nose in what they have been doing: "the young woman abruptly bent and with slow care detached from her light skirt a clinging twig" [emphasis added]. Feel the twig as the tree of knowledge of good and evil and the unabashed girl as Eve, the goddess and the power of sex and death before whom Conmee is impotent. Sex is further suggested by Mountjoy Square and children newly born by Newcomen bridge. Conmee continues on in the Palms under the Hebrew letter *sin* and begs off the struggle in this life with the thought that God's ways are not our ways. The point of all this is that Conmee misses the connection of what he is reading to what he sees before him. His reading is perfunctory.

Sometimes what Conmee says is reported, sometimes not. He is concerned with appearances and social station, but he is confused in the presence of Mrs. M'Guinness, since she is a pawnbroker but nonetheless has a queenly carriage. We gather that sometimes Conmee does not buy a tram ticket: ". . . he reflected that the ticket inspector usually made his visit when one had carelessly thrown away the ticket."

Malahide (bad hide) Road suggests bad skin and must reflect the absence of God from the world. Yahweh would never show himself, even to the prophets.

Conmee's episette ends with his reading from Psalms 119 under the letter Sin : "*—Principes persecuti sunt me gratis: et a verbis tuis form idavit cor meum.*" Translation: Unjustifiably though princes [the state] hound me, your [God's] word is what fills me with dread." It goes on: "I rejoice in your promise . . . Universal peace for those who love your Law, no stumbling blocks for them . . . you know how I keep to your paths." In context, Conmee seems to place blame for the hell on this earth exclusively on the state (princes) since God creates universal peace.

2nd. The second episette features the mortuary and the coffin lid held vertically, a Connector Fact for the shades in Dante's Hades frozen at various angles by the near presence of Lucifer. Kelleher chews hay and spits out hay juice. In an intrusion, Conmee gets on the tram. Kelleher, a police spy, receives a report from a constable about the activities of an unidentified "particular party."

3rd. The one-legged sailor passes Katey and Boody Dedalus, Stephen's sisters, and begs by singing "For England home and beauty." In an intrusion, O'Molloy is trying to find Lambert in order to borrow money. Molly throws a coin out the window to the beggar. It lands on the path. The urchins, poor as they are, honestly and charitably retrieve

Molly's coin for the beggar. Molly's "generous white arm" puts out her welcome sign for Blazes— "Unfurnished Apartment." Now what apartment is that? What part is meant? The sign means Bloom is out and the coast is clear.

4th. The Dedalus daughters are taking in laundry, and the only thing between them and starvation is charity soup from the nuns. The laundry and soup pots reflect the cauldron of regeneration used by Medea. Here the question is put whether Stephen's books were "put in." At first this seems, as part of the general disorientation, to mean in the pot (of regeneration), but later is clarified as in the bankruptcy sale of the Dedalus possessions being held that day. Stephen's books for the cauldron of regeneration. In intrusions, Conmee walks through Conglowes fields in his daydreams, the bankruptcy sale bell rings, and the Elijah throwaway passes the Customhouse old dock, moving on beyond civil custom.

5th. Blazes buys his seduction present for Molly (fruit, port and a jar of something) at Thorton's (for thorn), and the package goes by tram to Molly. The gift precedes him. Blazes lies (the recipient is invalid) in order to convince the store to deliver for free.

Notice the suggestive language: The clerk "bedded" the bottle with "rustling fibre." The ripe peaches are "shamefaced." Blazes is the model of self-confidence and pomposity; he flirts with the clerk and looks down her blouse at every opportunity. He is especially sensitive to smells. Remember that he is hairy like Lucifer. The HELYS sign goes by. Blazes checks his watch, mindful of his 4 o'clock with Molly. In an intrusion, Bloom looks for books for Molly under the Merchants' arch. Blazes takes a carnation without paying for it and puts it in his mouth. Think about carnation (etymology—flesh) as the opposite of incarnation. At the end, he makes a call on the store phone. As indicated below, this may be a call for Miss Dunne at the office or a long distance call to London to find out which horse won the Ascot Gold Cup Race.

6th. Stephen and Artifoni, the music teacher, are speaking in Italian. They have been having a philosophical conversation that causes Artifoni to miss his tram, which signifies predestination or the blind life. This is a typical Joycean method of making a point. Yes it's subtle, but its right there up front. Artifoni, Virgil to Stephen's Dante, says that when he was young he too thought life was a "beast." Stephen has apparently used the word beast in their conversation. Artifoni, the music teacher, advises Stephen that he is sacrificing his singing career to his writing career. Stephen responds the sacrifice is bloodless. Artifoni advises him to have hope. The gate above Dante's Hell read "Leave every hope, ye who enter." They connect through the eyes. A soldiers' band unloads off a tram. No straw in this episette.

The episette mentions English tourists ("palefaces") who are in the area in order to see Trinity College (the Protestant controlled college) and the Bank of Ireland, which face each other across College Green. These two institutions provide another visual presentation of church and state. The tourists have "stunted forms." Pigeons sit on the Bank of Ireland.

Artifoni's "sturdy" trousers (his own philosophy of hope) are mentioned repeatedly. Osiris, the Egyptian Lord of rebirth, means sturdy.[2] We remember Stephen's second hand pair and the use of trousers generally to connote identity—who wears the pants? Trying to leave, Artifoni can't get the attention of the tram conductor because Artifoni is hidden among the disembarking band musicians who are "smuggling implements of music through Trinity Gates." This suggests that hope and art assist in the passage through the wandering rocks. Note that Stephen is not with Buck even though they left together in the last episode. Importantly, there is no intrusion in this episode, perhaps because it features hope.

7th. Miss Dunne works for Boylan in an ad agency, the same business that Bloom is in. They use gaudy notepaper. Even though on the job, she is reading a book, *Woman in White*, which involves general disorientation—madness, murder and confused identities.[3] Miss Dunne wonders if "he" is in love with Marion (Molly's name), puts the book far back in her "drawer" and thinks she will get another book by an author named Haye (read hay and straw). When she types a letter, the date June 16, 1904 is used. In two intrusions, the number 6 (symbol for the beast from the Book of Revelations) shows on Rochford's invention (see the 9th episette) and the HELYS sign turns around.

Miss Dunne looks at a large poster of Marie Kendall, apparently in the office, which is associated symbolically with the fire of *eros*. Miss Dunne is anxious to get off early to go to a dance, that power of sex again. Boylan gives her instructions by phone, perhaps from the store where he buys the seduction package, which assume that he personally will not be available for the rest of the afternoon. She tells him that Lenehan, associated with *Sports* (a weekly racing form), is looking for him about Rochford's invention and will meet him at the Ormond at 4:00 p.m.

Blazes gives her some figures. She is to call these figures in to an unidentified contact but only after 5:00 p.m. It relates to "only two for Belfast and Liverpool." She repeats what Blazes says as "Twentyseven and six," and the second time she repeats it as "one, seven, six." This is probably a reference to an amount of money, 27 shillings 6 pence (27s 6d) being equal to one pound (20s) 7 shillings 6 pence. My guess is that Blazes is placing bets through factors in Belfast and Liverpool on the Gold Cup Race. If so, it is being placed after the race is over, suggesting a fraudulent betting scheme. The losing betting tickets left by Blazes at Bloom's house in a later episode (the 17th) bear the numbers 8 87 and 88 6. Since Blazes bet for both himself and Molly, I think Blazes bet on different horses and after the fact assigned to her the losing and kept for himself the winning tickets, perhaps fraudulently obtained. The race was run at 3:00 p.m., but the official results have not yet been announced in Ireland. This delay and the fact that Blazes' phone call from Thorton's had to be made at a certain time suggests he is betting on the race already knowing, by the phone call, which horse won.

8th. Ned Lambert is in the basement chamber under Saint Mary's abbey, formerly (in order of time going forward) the oldest religious center in Dublin,[4] a Jewish synagogue and the spot from which silken Thomas declared his rebellion against Henry VIII. Now it is the storeroom for a seed merchant for whom Lambert works. Lambert is serving as tour guide and showing the historic spot to Rev. Love, who has a "refined accent." Lambert and Love are the two pink faces in the flare of the "tiny torch." Hard-up O'Molloy seeks out Lambert for a loan, even in this remote location. When asked to identify himself, O'Molloy replies Ringabella and Crosshaven. These Cork references apparently identify Jack O'Molloy. Love's light dies after O'Molloy comes in; the vesta, a short wooden match, goes out leaving them in "gloom." The Rev. Love is writing a book about the Fitzgerald family, apparently Irish hero types (Jason and his all pro crew). Next time he wants to take a photograph through one of the old windows, which would present the religious view, and asks Lambert for permission. Lambert can arrange it.

The basement occupied by the Rev. Love suggests Purgatory in Dante's conception, out of Hell and into Purgatory. The first description of Purgatory in *The Divine Comedy* is a "natural dungeon which had a bad floor, and lack of light." The light of love can just barely be seen in Purgatory. Rev. Love is from St. Michael's, as archangel Michael was the main adversary of Satan. The seed bags stored in the basement suggest the irrepressible march of humanity. Carob (locust beans) and palmnut oil (palm again) are being shipped out, probably for cattle feed (the masses). Lambert has caught a cold, resulting from "a Hell of a lot of draught"—from the ice lake of Lucifer. He exclaims "Mother of Moses." You Bible scholars remember that Moses's mother Jochebed was a Hebrew midwife who refused the Pharaoh's order to kill all male Hebrew children. She eventually mothered Moses, who saved from the waters lead Israel to freedom from the Hell of captivity. The normal appeal by a Catholic in this sort of situation would be to the Virgin Mary, but her name may not be uttered in Hell (*Inferno* Canto II 85 fn. 2). So the mother of Moses, not of Jesus, is used. Lambert sneezes, the moment when the soul is exposed to the devil.

The intrusions are Parnell playing chess (16th episette) and the girl coming from the field with a twig on her skirt (1st episette). Irish heroes of yore who tried to burn the archbishop are discussed. They could run the rocks.

9th. The main subject is Rochford's invention, a device that records by the number on the last disc standing what vaudeville act is currently on. This is information for a prospective customer while the act is in progress. The latest disc, inserted from inside the tent where the show is taking place, knocks over the previous one and registers for the prospective customer outside which act is on. The disc numbers correspond to the act numbers in the handbill, which a customer would have. The device is called Turn Now On, turn being an act in vaudeville. This is a chilling symbol of the process of life, a vaudeville act in which death and the new born knock over the dying old. The number 6 comes up here from the 666 beast in the Book of Revelations, which has already emerged in Stephen's discussion with Artifoni—a beast of a life. The number six is also included in most of the betting numbers.

The intrusions feature the following: lawyers of the past (lawyers were some of Dante's most notable residents of Hell), current lawyers and an elderly lady with false teeth and a big skirt; Dignam's son coming out of the butcher shop; Molly replacing the Unfurnished Apartment sign; and the start of the Viceregal calvacade.

Rochford wants to talk to Blazes and asks Lenehan to find him. Two puns are used—good turn and turn now on (charity in life) and Boylan and boiling (Boylan's behavior is the path to Hell). Mention is made of Rochford's heroics in saving a man from a gas filled manhole, another indirect reference to heroes and Hell. Betting on the Ascot Gold Cup horserace is going on (even though the actual race is already over). Lyons was going to bet on Throwaway, a long shot, based on his inadvertent tip from Bloom, but Lenehan talks him out of it. Lenehan and McCoy see Bloom looking at books under the Merchant's arch. The Elijah handbill thrown away by Bloom is floating down the Liffey, a spiritual long shot indeed.

Lenehan tells McCoy about a late evening cab ride with Molly and Bloom after the Glencree dinner. During the ride Lenehan felt up Molly's boobs while pretending to settle her "boa," a fur neck piece. This reminds us of the ball with blue veins used to bribe Eros. Lenehan apparently ejaculated in this process: "I was, so to speak, in the milky way." During the same ride, Molly mocked the stature of Bloom's manhood by comparing his penis to a pinprick. McCoy initially smiles at this story but then becomes grave. Lenehan, perplexed, says in contrition that Bloom is cultured and has a "touch of the artist."

10th. The middle episette features Bloom doing a good turn for Molly, renting her a new soft pornographic novel titled the *The Sweets of Sin*. He does this good turn for her even though he knows she is preparing to cuckold him. The names of other authors—Masoch of *Tales of the Ghetto* and Lovebirch of *Fair Tyrants*—add spice to his shopping experience. Bloom thinks that he has already "had" Masoch, for whom masochism was named. Bloom is in the self-imposed ghetto of masochism. Disorientation appears with a book by Aristotle, which turns out to be another mildly pornographic book and not by the real Aristotle. In an intrusion, Professor of dancing Maginni, the fallen Dublin Apollo, with "grave deportment and gay apparel" is observed on O'Connell Bridge.

Bloom samples passages from the *The Sweets of Sin,* fallen Dublin literature, about an adulterous liaison between Rauol and an unfaithful wife. This scene, redolent of the classic trappings of Masoch's novels, haunts Bloom for the rest of the day. In the spirit of masochism, Bloom becomes passive and warm in the presence of these images. A second intrusion features the elderly female again, this time leaving the court buildings having heard a case in lunacy and a case in maritime (crazy seas or wandering rocks). Perhaps she is Persephone, the mistress of Milton's Hell, tending to her interests. The title *The Sweets of Sin* suggests the trap of the church, to brand as sin that which is sweet to humans.

The bookseller Bloom deals with suggests Dante's Charon, one of the many boatmen in Hell. His jaws were "fleecy" and his eyes were round wheels of flame. The bookseller's ruined mouth smells of onions and his eyes blaze with old rheum. That these porno books encourage greater sin is confirmed by the presence in Dante's Hell of the illicit lovers Francesca and Paolo, who had read books about Lancelot and Guenever.

Up to this point, Bloom has been described by reference to a "darkbacked figure under Merchant's arch." Perhaps this is the counterpart of Lucifer's "haunch" on which Dante and Virgil escape from Lucifer's realm. Bloom's compassion and Rev. Love, they are the escape. Why is Bloom darkbacked? Because Dante moved out of dark Hell into the light in Purgatory in front of him. The arch of Merchant's arch combines commercialism and sex because of the association of arch with prostitutes in ancient Rome. Here the arch is associated with commercial pornography, prostitution's cousin. In the later Circe (15th) episode, Stephen will very nearly compromise his values in favor of commercial survival in the presence of prostitutes.

11th. Simon Dedalus psychologically abuses his daughter Dilly. She is begging for funds to buy food to keep the Dedalus children alive. He is, as usual, in the pubs and has spent borrowed money on a shave by a barber for the funeral and for booze. He expects her to understand that these social matters are more important than healthy food for his children. Simon sees no human unity even in his family; this attitude is Stephen's spiritual inheritance. Milly's burden is reflected in her bent back, which Simon mocks as a matter of social appearance. He in effect bribes her by giving her a penny for herself (the palm), so she will stop asking for more money for the family. When she still pesters him for more, he curses her and threatens to send all of his children to the nuns.

In an intrusion, the bells ring for the bankruptcy sale of the Dedalus possessions. The bell ringer at the auction house vainly looks at himself in the mirror of a fancy mirrored cabinet, formerly a Dedalus possession. The mirror has chalk on it for identification, suggesting the treacherous titans from the 1st episode. The bidding for the cabinet goes 4 pounds and 9 shillings, 4 the number for material order and 9 for sadness and pain. Nine years at Troy, nine years of wandering for Odysseus and the ninth hour (3:00 p.m.) when Christ died. Simon threatens to leave his children where Jesus left the Jews, without hope (the ticket to Hell). Another bell (for the last lap) rings for an intrusion about the bicycle race (the "halfmile wheelman"). In other intrusions, Kernan has just received an important business order and the Viceregal calvacade passes out of Parkgate (echoes of the rocks).

12th.　　Kernan, a commercial salesman, struts and wags, celebrating with pub gin his recent important business order. He passes "Shackleton's offices," signifying the shackled state of his soul. He recalls the conversation with the buyer about the explosion in America aboard the ship *General Slocum*. Playing to the expected opinions of the buyer, he attributed the dangerous condition of the ship to graft to the safety inspectors. Ireland's failure to qualify as the land of the free is mentioned.

Kernan vainly preens his dress like a peacock. To him, social character and dress are all. He thinks the buyer admired his fancy coat. In an intrusion, Simon Dedalus and Father Cowley meet on the sidewalk.

The Elijah skiff sails by the quay that provided the initial scene of the Lotuseaters (5th) episode; the hero must foreswear the easy aspects. Notice the grammatical construction of each Elijah appearance is different. This one is distorted, perhaps because of hell, the lotus effect or Kernan's pathetic vanity:

> North wall and sir John Rogerson's quay, with hulls and anchorchains, sailing westward, sailed by a skiff, a crumpled throwaway, rocked on the ferrywash, Elijah is coming.

Kernan remembers the place where the Irish patriot Emmet was drawn and quartered, Emmet who tried to enlist Napoleon's help for Irish independence. Kernan, interested only in commerce, thinks of social unrest as "bad times." He goes by the Guinness visitors' room and the Dublin Distillers, symbols for the corrupted spirit. There he sees our symbol for the individual spirit, a mode of conveyance. This time it isn't a tram but a horse drawn wagon. It is not secured, signifying a free soul. Reflecting the common view between the rocks, Kernan thinks this freedom is dangerous.

Kernan thinks about gambling and dueling gentlemen, his self-image. He just misses the Viceregal calvacade and is disappointed, since social standing and dress are his values.

13th. Stephen looks in the windows of Old Russell's lapidary (gem cutters) shop. The first thing Dante sees in Purgatory is the "sweet color of oriental sapphire," in that case the sun, and in Milton the Heavenly Gate is covered with "orient gems."

Stephen sees through a dust webbed window (read maya) a "timedulled" chain (clock chain) being "proved," the symbol from Milton of time ruled reality. Stephen considers jewels and other valuables sought for wealth and conspicuous consumption in serpent terms: "dull coils of bronze and silver, lozenges of cinnabar, on rubies, leprous and winedark stones." Time's dust covers everything. Stephen thinks of the jewels being born in the earth where the fallen angels threw the "stars of their brows." Pigs now root them out.

His thoughts pass to an image of "she (who) dances in a foul gloom where gum burns with garlic." This is the Lordess of this episode, Mali Kali or the devouring goddess of time. She dances in a foul gloom as the image of the dark side of energy.

Hearing the sound of the Dublin municipal dynamo powerhouse, Stephen associates from the jewels in front of him to the "The Island of the Jewels." In this yantra, an aid to meditation in yoga, the creative goddess of energy is shown on an island in the sea of universal consciousness. This island is known as the "Point of Power," the drop that spreads and becomes changed into the limited consciousness of each individual. Stephen thinks: "throb always without you and the throb always within." This is the Hindu concept of the divine energy, present everywhere and within everyone. The goal is to harmonize the two energies. This energy is what Stephen worships as genius in his own soul. He strives to harmonize his genius with the eternal powers. And seeing the Hell created by Mali Kali, he feels caught "Between two roaring worlds where they swirl," the energy without uncoordinated with the energy within.

He either imagines talking to or does talk to the store clerk about whether the clock whose chain was being proved keeps good time. Only the clerk's response is given. Stephen refers to Monday, the first day of creation when presumably time was created. Then Stephen walks down the street where he sees an old print showing boxers. He thinks of boxers as heroes, from the legend of the Argonauts. Keep in mind in this connection that the anniversary of the death of the Martyr Stephen (by stoning) is Boxing Day.

Stephen stops at a book cart containing books for sale, and wonders if he will find his pawned school prizes. In an intrusion, Father Conmee walks through the hamlet of Donnycarney still saying his vespers. The 8th and 9th Books of Moses referred to are part of the missing "magic" books of Moses, the first five being the Torah or the first five books of the Old Testament and the hypothesized remaining four being about magic. In this context, Stephen thinks about the seal of

331

King David, also known as the Seal of Solomon, the interlocked triangles signifying the interaction of the human and the gods.

In one of the saddest scenes of the book, Stephen denies financial and moral support to his sister Dilly. She has just bought a French language primer (with the penny from her father), so she can escape to Paris like Stephen did. Stephen has money in his pocket that he is spending for drink, just like his father. And just like his father, Stephen feels that helping her would pull him down too; this thought is framed in the symbol of drowning. He feels guilty, so he thinks "agenbite of inwit." Bite for the vampire that stops heroes. At least Stephen feels the pain: "Misery."

14th. Rueben Dodd, the money lender, is trying to collect from Father Cowley, who needs just a little more time (known as grace). With the debt overdue, Rueben has called out the Sheriff's deputies, who have surrounded the Father's house. Cowley has barricaded the house to deny entrance and seizure of his personal property. Ben Dollard, a lawyer, helps Cowley. His legal solution is that the landlord has a prior rent claim ahead of the Rueben the unsecured lender. Dollard has apparently arranged this with the landlord. The landlord is Rev. Love, from the 8th episette, who is senior in claim to the Jewish god. Dollard mentions Barabbas, the thief set free instead of Jesus, to help us get the point. Dollard returns from convincing the subsheriff to recall the deputies.

Even in this situation where Dollard is helping a mutual friend, Simon Dedalus ever concerned with appearances can't help criticizing Dollard's clothes. Simon passively follows the others, having nothing to do. In the intrusions, Farrell is walking his beat outside the posts on Kildare Street and Rev. Love is leaving St. Mary's abbey.

15th. Cunningham, Power and John Nolan are trying to collect donations to help the Dignam family. They try Jimmy Henry, the assistant Town Clerk, and Fanning, the subsheriff. Henry escapes by complaining of his corns. Fanning says he didn't know the deceased. Contrast these responses with Bloom's willing and generous donation. We learn of bedlam in the recent City Council meeting over the issue of the official status of the Irish language; the Marshall Parnell should have

332

been there, but he was playing chess at the time. While the council debates the official language, children are starving.

With his act of charity, Cunningham is described as passing out the Castleyard gate, and we read past the rocks. Politicians come and go speaking of each other. The calvacade goes by carrying the lordlieutenant governor and general governor of Ireland, representative of state, the other wandering rock. In the intrusions, Misses Douce and Kennedy (stars of the next episode) look out the window of the Ormond Hotel Bar and Blazes talks to Bob Doran. Doran is on his annual bender and headed to the red light district. Doran was the marriage victim in *The Boarding House* story from **Dubliners** and probably has to do this once a year to remain sane. His is a loveless marriage of incompatibility, the subject of a tract by Milton. More Hell on earth.

16th. Buck sponges off Haines in the tearoom of DBC (Dublin Baking Company). Buck tries to entertain Haines and position himself as the ticket to Stephen. They agree that Stephen has been unbalanced by something. Buck thinks the fear of Hell; Haines thinks this is odd since Irish myth contains no concept of Hell. Haines's reaction is the product of his limited tunnel vision—Stephen's condition must relate to what Haines is studying. Haines is absolutely trivial and officious. Buck does accurately predict that Stephen will not be a successful poet. In intrusions, the sailor begs on Nelson street and the floating Elijah handbill makes it to the mouth of the Liffey just as Buck discusses Stephen's prediction of successful artistic creation in 10 years. The floating handbill passes the schooner *Rosevean* from Bridgwater (bridge the unity). Stephen saw her in the Proteus (3rd) episode. She is loaded with bricks, bricks for suffering that our hero must endure.

17th. Artifoni, Farrell and the young blind man are walking on the same street in the same direction. Farrell continues to avoid street lamps and turns around near the house of the parents of Oscar Wilde, the ultimate subjectivist and the subject of Hell on earth. Continuing back the other way, Farrell sees Elijah's name on a handbill at Metropolitan Hall and responds in Latin, "Having been forced, I was willing." This would be a reference to Jesse's experience in having been chosen as the son of man and the foxhole Christian belief in the face of Hell. Farrell's obsessive walking patterns present an example of habit closing down possibilities.

Farrell continues on without caution and his dustcoat brushes the tapping stick of the young blind man, whom Bloom helped across the street in an earlier episode. The blind man curses and accuses Farrell of being blinder. The curse is "you bitch's bastard." Since this phrase is redundant, I think we are pointed to Eve's progeny, the hell resulting from original sin. The blindness here is the occlusion that prevents the beatific vision. Occlusion means closing, which is what the Wandering Rocks do. They close down the potential of most people.

18th. Patrick Dignam is walking home with the just purchased porksteaks for the wake for his deceased father. This is how the family spends the charity money, playing to the expectations of others. He is "dawdling" since the wake at home bores him. He remembers his father beating him for smoking. He distracts himself with thoughts about boxing matches, including the soldier/civilian bout in which Blazes was involved.

In this mood, he sees Pat Doran on his annual bender and on his way to the red-light district. Doran is talking momentarily to the smiling Boylan, who is about to start off for his adulterous visit to Molly with the carnation still in his mouth. By this association, Joyce equates the moral level of their activities.

Patrick plans to exploit his father's death for another day off from school. In his vanity, he hopes others will notice his mourning clothes and that his picture will appear in the newspaper. Not finding a tram on his street, young Dignam finally thinks about his father's last words and death and begins to come to terms with it. His thought language matches our expectation. Purgatory is mentioned.

19th. The other wandering rock, the state represented by the viceregal calvacade, passes all the characters in this episode and some of the others in the novel (even including the brown MacIntosh eating dry bread, day old manna forbidden by Yahweh). The state's representatives do not, however, pass Stephen or Bloom. Stephen will pass the rocks, and Bloom has gone the other way. Since we are in Hell, the cavalcade leaves from the **vice** regal lodge. The reaction of each observer to the calvacade is in character. Note the mock serious newspaper type language.

The episode ends in a rushing sentence as Artifoni's "sturdy" trousers go through the closing door, signifying passing quickly through the Wandering Rocks. Many of the characters in this episode are depressed because squeezed by poverty or problems. Here the philosopher of hope is sporting trousers, the symbol of identity, which are sturdy, like the main beam of Jason's ship fashioned from Zeus's oak. He passes through the Wandering Rocks.

First Letter

The first letter is capital **T** in the first word "The." I think this "stands" for the cross in its relation to the sins of the world, which we see in full force in this episode. The traditional cross would be a lower case t. In the hands of the Church, however, the cross has been capitalized, formalized and decapitated. Like Father Conmee, the capitalized cross no longer really suffers for the world.

Scene

The scenes of this episode are located on the streets of Dublin between 3 and 4:00 p.m.

Traditional Schemata

The schemata given by Joyce for this episode are as follows:

The organ is blood in the sense that everyone is moving around in this episode, but not in the sense of nourishing. Most of what happens in this episode is denial of a human connection; the only connection, like that between the frozen shades around Lucifer, is the sharing of time and space. Artifoni's attempt to cheer Stephen with hope is the one exception.

The art is mechanics, which is in the foreground in Rochford's machine and in the background in the mechanical nature of most lives, a form of predestination symbolized by the trams. Like a mechanical device, the episodes interlock by way of the intrusions.

The symbol is citizens or groups of citizens through which Hell on earth is seen. Like the wandering rocks, these groups also squeeze their own members between loyalty and violence, such as the treatment by Simon of his daughters. The technique is the Labyrinth, which sponsors the detailed movements of the characters in this episode.

The Bosphorus is the Liffey, where the Argonaut heroes and the Elijah handbill go. As the Bosphorus joined Asia and Europe, the Asiatic shore is represented by the detached Father Conmee and the European shore by the active Viceroy. The Linati lists the sense of the episode as a "hostile environment," a tongue and cheek description of Hell.

General Slocum

The textual reference to the disaster involving the *General Slocum* and its lack of life boats extends the Hell on earth and crushing rocks images. The *General Slocum* was a passenger ship that burned in the East River in New York. She was caught in the Hell Gate rocks and couldn't turn to shore and safety, which was only a short distance away. The victims were mostly women and children.[5] The Dubliners are caught in Hell on earth like these ill-fated passengers, in a dangerous and hostile environment without lifeboats.

Parallel in the Mass

Conmee jump starts the allusion to the Preface portion of the Mass with the inappropriate pun on Dignam: "Dignum, yes. Vere dignum et iustum est" (It is indeed fitting and right). He puns his way into the Preface, the central act of the Mass, keeping pace with this episode's position as central in the Book.

The Father is behind in his reading for the day from the breviary because of his social engagement with Lady Maxwell. His prayers emphasize the passive, deliver me and make me undefiled. He doesn't like Mud Island. His readings are from Ps. 119 that begins with different letters of the Hebrew alphabet. He reads the verses associated with the Hebrew letters *Res* and *Sin*, signifying the tools of State (res—things decided) and Church (sin and fear of Hell). His readings frame the return of the carnal pair from the fields of privacy.[6]

Stephen assists in secularizing the Mass with his own personal and modified version of the Sanctus in the 13th episette: "—*Se el yilo nebrakada femininum! Amor me solo! Sankus! Amen.*" This Tower of Babylon mixture of several languages probably translates as "My little heaven of blessed femininity, love only me. Holy! Amen"[7].

These modifications point the meaning of the Mass literally to the flesh and move the Eucharist as a symbol closer to Joyce's view of sexual intercourse as one of the real connections humans share with the gods.

Purification

With Sanctus in the Mass, the reference in a later episode for this episode in terms of Jewish ritual describes Bloom's book hunt as the Simchath Torah, the Joy of Torah. This ritual marks the beginning of the cycle of reading of the Torah, which derives from the root for instruction or teaching. Like the reading of the Torah, the book hunt for pornographic materials never ends. The cycle of desire continues.

The equivalent in art is didacticism, the usual fare for art sponsored by the church or state, which crushes the possibilities of art.

Art, Aesthetics and Structure

Like the labyrinth of time and space as we experience it, and according to Milton as God fashioned it after the big fall, the text is deliberately full of traps, misdirections and ambiguities. The narrator's view point shifts suddenly and apparently without reason, and only parts of conversations are heard. Correlations and connections are especially dangerous. The same names appear for different persons; the same places appear under different names and errors are made.[8] The crashing intrusions, reminding us of the rocks, also contribute to the general confusion.

The characters stand in a different sort of foreground in this episode. The only word I can think of is vulnerable. Every episette begins with a person right out front, stark and on point. As the *Entr'acte* between but not significantly connected plot-wise to the two halves of the book, this episode is cold and separate, like Lucifer's Hell.

In order for the net of symbols to work, the reader must be willing to accept that Hell on earth is the product of church and state. This was a given to Joyce but like the betrayal theme in the first episode, I don't feel the jaws of the rocks at work. We only see the result and are expected to make the connection. I don't and that reduces the power of the episode for me. We still have Hell on earth in the United States with very little church and state.

337

****
ENDNOTES

1. All of this material is from Graves, Greek Myths, pp. 577-621.
2. Plutarch *Moralia* trans. F. Babbitt (Cambridge, Harvard University Press, 1936), Vol. V, p. 91.
3. Gifford, p. 267.
4. Gifford, p. 268.
5. Gifford, p. 186-187.
6. Lang, p. 159-160.
7. Gifford, p. 277.
8. Critical Essays.

Episode 11 (Sirens)

Basic Themes

Repetition without redemption.

Sirens were island-bound female singers who bewitched passing sailors with their irresistible "sirens song." The bewitched sailors jumped ship and swam ashore. But on the sirens' island with their ship long gone, the sailors quickly turned to rotting flesh and bone. The sirens' come-on song was custom tailored for each passing crew, and in Odysseus's case was an invitation to rehash the memories of the Trojan war. Accepting that invitation would mean living on memories, the voice of the past, which is death to the redeeming possibilities of the present and future.

In the Ormond Hotel Bar, siren barmaids serve booze and smiles, at least to paying customers. Siren Simon Dedalus, Stephen's father, provides music to drink by. Siren Simon is singing for free drinks under an arrangement with the bar. His singing draws other customers into the bar. They drink and sing the same old mournful songs. And these repeat customers pay dearly, in the coin of their own degeneration.

Joyce builds this episode on a highly generalized, philosophical version of the sirens theme, Schopenhauer's pessimistic concept of repetition without redemption. The German philosopher Schopenhauer (1788-1860) held that music is a direct copy of the Will to life. This Will force has, in his theory, produced all being and our world. The Will force is characterized by a blind, endless and repetitive striving that inevitably produces a life of repeated suffering, repetition without redemption. In an endless chain, life moves from one wish to satisfaction to another wish waiting to be satisfied: song and drink, song and drink. This is the root source of pessimism in this episode.

Joyce casts the sirens as a metaphor for this pessimistic reality. The sailors could only see the attractive top half of the sirens. Hidden below were the legs and talons of birds of prey. Their hidden lower half indicated the real intentions of the sirens and accounts for the bones and rotting flesh in the meadow. Likewise, the sexy barmaids are dressed well above but poorly below the waist, that portion hidden by the bar. The reality below the surface is pessimistic.

Repetition supplies the design for the episode: an overture presenting summaries of the themes repeated in the "body"; a body constructed according to the rules for a fugue, which involves repetition of voices; repetition of words or sounds within nearly every theme; and heavy repetition in this episode of incidents from previous episodes. Repetition also characterizes many subjects of the episode: the life force producing repetition of the human species through sex; song lyrics and musical techniques involving repetition and contrast; daily repetitive consumption of alcohol; mirrors repeating visual reality; song reflecting life; song as self expression; and the repetitive cycles of time. Repetition is audibilized in the sounds made by the blind man's tapping stick, tap tap tap. Freud readers will hear the footsteps of *Beyond the Pleasure Principle.*

The lack of redemption in the repetition is featured in the general pessimism of the Irish, the sorrowful songs, the corruption of alcoholism, several puns without literary redemption, and continuous suffering, including masochism. The bar patrons, like the mariners who jump ship for the Sirens' island, subject themselves to a series of restrictions on human potential that deplete their redemptive resources. They are doing the same old things—drinking, dwelling on the past and singing the same mournful songs. By drinking and worshipping the past, they borrow against their future. By worshipping the past, they divert energy away from the present and future and neglect current relationships. Their basic problems seem trivial and without alcohol manageable, particularly in comparison with the deaf waiter and the blind piano tuner, both of whom deal with their severe handicaps.

The music in the bar is most sorrowful, full of suffering. The sorrow is, however, self-indulgent rather than empathetic. The drinkers feel sorrow for themselves, not empathy for the sufferers in the song. Moreover, this self-indulgent, sorrowful musical experience doesn't produce any cathartic resolution, only more drinking. Drink, song, sorrow and more drink, song and sorrow. Repetition without redemption.

By contrast, our man Bloom, in the Ormond dining room for a substantial late afternoon dinner, is redeemed through the exercise of restraint, even at the moment of his greatest suffering. Even though he hears Blazes leave for his 4:00 p.m. appointment with Molly, Bloom doesn't try to stop him, doesn't drink and doesn't resort to whores. In this episode, Bloom seems in Harold Bloom's phrasing ". . . (though) scarcely middleaged, . two thousand years older than anyone else in Dublin"[1].

Bloom's behavior serves as an overture to the path to redemption. The last theme in the overture is simply "Begin," for begin anew; this is the only theme announced in the overture section that is not repeated in the body of the work, which ends with "Done." This beginning, Bloom's mission of hope, leads this episode into the last half of the novel, the regenerative and redemptive New Testament portion. Through typological repetition of themes from the first half of this Book, the New Testament regenerates itself out of the Old. Repetition with redemption with Bloom.

The style of this episode is a new beginning, a total change from the first part of the novel (Aelous headlines excepted). The episode is made of an overture of theme summaries and a body fleshing out the themes summarized in the overture. As such, it is a double mirror reflecting itself. The overture refers to the body and the body refers to the overture. The episode's stylistic truth is internal, not as a representation of external time and space reality. In the last part of the novel, literary integrity is no longer measured in terms of submissive fidelity to objective external events or standards, which signify the Law of the Fathers and the Old Testament Jewish Law. In the last part, literary integrity is measured in terms of internal stylistic integrity, a text reflective of and reacting to text. This is the style chosen by Joyce to signify the Law of Self Realization and Christ's New Testament internal message of the spirit. With this shift in style, punishment by the ruling fathers yields to a softer relationship made of puns and connections.[2] With this new stylistic integrity, time and space are transcended. Bloom, our ad for this internal integrity, separates himself from the degenerating crowd.

Faithful to the sirens, this episode is the song of songs. The narrative text is put together in ways that reflect musical lyrics and melodic progression. Repeats are frequent, and announced phrases are followed by repetition of their constituent pieces. Music is made and heard and reacted to throughout. Music, experienced in the time domain, is time made audible, time the substratum of hell on earth and subjectivism explored in the last episode. The bar is the common denominator of the Ormond and music. The bar in the Ormond Hotel separates the customers from the sirens and their supply of alcohol and hides their lower torso, and the bar in the musical score separates the flow of the music into time intervals, one after another. In the bar, the patrons are killing time but none the less watching the clock.

Bloom and music both reflect the power of restraint. In order to be pleasing, music must be composed according to certain patterns that limit the selection of notes to be used. For example, in tonal music the selection is generally limited to those notes contained in a key. Bloom's restraint, which marks him off from the degenerating crowd, is symbolized by a cats cradle that he makes with a catgut thong (used to make stringed musical instruments) binding his own hands (which would raise the glass). Restrained, he avoids the temptation to stop Blazes, which would in effect possess Molly and, in any event, only provide temporary possessive relief. He leaves the bar before anyone else and without drinking. On the way out, Bloom creates flatulence, his own Chamber Music.

The contrast between the eye and ear provides meaning for this episode. The sirens are attuned to the eye and Bloom to the ear. The distinctions of eye and ear derive from the concepts of St. Paul that faith comes through the ear, "the evidence of things that are not seen" (Heb. 11:1).[3] The power of the eye is for "things seen," the rational pursuit of matters in the everyday world. The power of the ear is for "things not seen," matters of faith accepted by resignation. In Joyce's terms, eye is for the flesh and ear is for the spiritual. Weak in matters audible, one siren barmaid listens to a sea shell and misinterprets the source of the apparent sound as the ocean, as opposed to the reality of the sound of blood in her ear. Likewise, the bar patrons feel sorrow listening to the sad songs, but in reality they feel sorry only for themselves, not empathy for the subjects of the songs or others.

Translating the music experience into literary theory, the sirens' song deals with the grave and constant but is pornographic because it produces kinesis. Popular song is cast in the same category. The pornographic limits the power of the art of popular song because the possibilities are limited by the program to produce attraction or repulsion. The pornographic is, in Siren terms, artistic corruption and death.

Action in The Odyssey

Circe warns Odysseus about the sirens. Only two in number, they sit in an island meadow full of human bones and rotting skin corrupt in death (these warning signs are apparently not visible from the passing ship). Circe advises Odysseus to put wax in the ears of his men and, if he likes, to arrange for himself to be tied to the mast with cords so he can hear the sirens. Odysseus tells his men about the sirens and adds, unexpectedly, that they sit in a field of flowers, all that can be seen from the ship. The lower half of the sirens and the rotting flesh cannot be seen.

Odysseus also tells the crew that Circe recommended that Odysseus listen to the sirens but tied to the mast (this is not quite true, desire distorting truth). As their ship arrives near the sirens' island, a calm ensues, the crew rows and Odysseus puts wax plugs in their ears. They leave his ears open but bind him securely to the mast head. The crew can see but not hear. Odysseus can see and hear but not move.

The two sirens see the approaching ship and sing the following in their "high thrilling song":

Hither, come hither, renowned Odysseus, great glory of the Achaians, here stay thy barque, that thou mayest listen to the voice of us twain. For none hath ever driven by this way in his black ship, till he had heard from our lips the voice sweet as the honeycomb, and hath had joy thereof and gone on his way the wiser. For lo, we know all things, all the travail that in wide Troyland the Argives and Trojans bare by the gods' designs, yea, and we know all that shall hereafter be upon the fruitful earth.

Because of their precautions, Odysseus's ship does not stop and no one jumps ship, even though Odysseus tries to convince his men to release him. Unsuccessful, the sirens are said to commit suicide. Earlier the sirens had tried to charm the Argonauts, but were unsuccessful with them as well. Orpheus, the classically restrained musician in the Argonaut crew, did them one better in the music department. Only Butes jumped ship and tried to swim ashore, but Aphrodite rescued him.

The sirens are traditionally described as servants of the death goddess or daughters of hell.[4] The word Sirens means those who bind with a cord or those who wither.[5] The etymology of "sirens" is not Greek but Hebraic and Arabic. The meaning of the root in Hebraic slides in the zone between singers of enchantment and singers who shackle and in Arabic moves all the way from rope or chord (as in strings for stringed instrument) to sexual impotency.[6]

Action in Ulysses

It is particularly important, in order to understand the action, to pay attention to the smallest details in this episode. As in Sherlock Holmes stories, important clues include what doesn't happen, as well as what does.

The scene opens in the Ormond (means our world) Hotel bar with the siren barmaids, Lydia Douce and Mina Kennedy. They are "Bronze by gold," a description of their hair color that repeats danger omens from the last episode. The brilliance of the scene is to open with the psychology of the idle sirens. What do they do while waiting for the next ship? They talk about men and former conquests, addicted to their repetitive tease.

With no one in the bar, Douce rushes to the window to see through the "crossblinds" the viceregal calvacade going by (it started to move in the last episode). Douce believes (unrealistically) that one male participant in the royal calvacade is looking at her. She presses her face on the glass "making a halo of hurried breath" and announces to Kennedy, "He's killed looking back." There it is, all in one line framed in the domain of the eye—sex, death and memories (looking back), principal manifestations of repetition without redemption. The possibilities of the present and future are killed by dwelling on the past (". . . killed looking back."). Sounding the note of pessimism, the sirens bemoan their own personal situation in comparison to men ("it's them has the fine times. . . ."). Kennedy sounds this note while twinning her hair behind her ear.

Bloom walks by nearby antique and old plate shops, signifying repetition (reuse) with potential redemption. He is carrying the book entitled the sweets of sin (lower case in the text). Back in the bar, the tea delivery boy, described only as "boots" (remember Butes), comes in the bar. Focused in the visual, the sirens don't hear him right away. He sets the tea tray down with a bang in order to get their attention. He teases Douce about looking for her boyfriend out the window. An expert teaser herself, Douce threatens his insolence with a word to Mrs. de Massey (read Mass say), apparently his employer, about his "impertinent insolence." This makes Boots stutter as he tries to say impertinent,

344

"Imperthnthn thnthnthn." The barmaids put the teas down behind the bar, ". . . safe from eyes, low." Behind the bar is where the lower halves of the sirens are hidden. The barmaids have teas waiting to tease, a pun without literary redemption.

The sirens deal with Douce's sunburn contracted on a recent trip to the shore (Blazes's song about those lovely seaside girls). They laugh about seeing (the eye) an old fogie in Boyd's, where Douce went to buy sunburn lotion, and about a night in the Antient Concert Rooms when he apparently gave them the eye. The phrase "your other eye" sets them off laughing uncontrollably; later Molly refers to the opening in as the eye of the penis. The barmaids give the impression of losing control easily, exaggerating their appeal to males and living only for the interest of males; like drinking, sexual teasing doesn't satisfy long term and must be repeated over and over.

The action cuts back to Bloom who passes Aaron Fignater's and, as usual, thinks Figather (gather for together). He considers statues of virgins (note the contrast with the sirens). He walks by the Ormond ("By went his eyes.") The sirens see him. They continue to laugh, now about Bloom's eyes and greasy nose, old "greaseabloom." They laugh uncontrollably about the prospect of being married to him. Bloom can't hear them and continues to walk, apparently without aim, around the area of the bar. He goes by Cantwell's offices (read can't do well signifying pessimism) and Ceppi's frame makers shop (read limits). He thinks depressingly about time moving toward 4:00 p.m. and Raoul, the sadistic protagonist of the book he is carrying and the counterpart of Blazes.

Simon Dedalus idly strolls into the Ormond bar. No other customers are in the bar at this point. He enters picking chips off one of his "rocky" fingernails, his paternal talons connecting him in spirit to the sirens' lower half. In friendly tones he welcomes Miss Douce back from her trip to the seashore, and she responds making references to herself. Note that she does not reciprocate; locked in a personal shell and without respect for him, she doesn't ask after Simon's well being. The sirens give song but not succor. Simon practices casual sex talk with her about luring unsuspecting males. Smoothly she works into the drink order:

And what did the doctor order today?

Well now, he mused, whatever you say yourself. I
think I'll trouble you for some fresh water and a half
glass of whisky.

She fills it with the "grace of alacrity," an odd use of the word grace. One
of the translations of sirens in French is chanteuse de grace, graceful
singers. Simon says he wished he could visit the "Mourne mountains" for
the air, but concludes pessimistically, "But a long threatening comes at
last. . . ."

No mention is made of Simon paying for this drink, unlike with
other customers and even the waiter whose drink payments are
specifically noted. Since Simon almost immediately goes into the concert
room in the back to sing and the barmaids don't listen to him, I think that
Simon is getting free drinks to sing. Later he says he has no money.

Simon asks if Lidwell has been in (he hasn't). Simon takes out
his smoking pipe (a favorite personal item for Schopenhauer). As Simon
puts tobacco in the pipe, the ambitious narrator affected by Simon tells
us: "He fingered shreds of hair, her maidenhair, her mermaid's, into the
bowl. Chips. Shreds. Musing. Mute." In the presence of the satin clad
sirens, Simon's thoughts mutate tobacco strands into maidenhair.

In the presence of Simon, Douce begins to sing a song starting
with the line "O, Idolores, queen of the eastern seas!" Little of this song
is reported, but for your information the first stanza refers to a tryst in a
garden and the second to an island in the western sea where the lovers
will linger and "the past but seem an idle vision . . . . Happy songs we
were singing, Songs of a bygone day." The past. With Idolores, a
combination of idol and dolores (sorrow), the stage is set for a group
which worships the past and suffering.

Lenehan the leach comes in, looks for Blazes, and looks for
someone else to buy him a drink. In time related intrusions like those in
the Wandering Rocks episode, Bloom crosses the Essex Bridge and
thinks about buying writing paper and the jingle of Blazes's car is heard.
Lenehan tries to talk to Kennedy. She snubs him, by continuing to read
the newspaper, since at this point he isn't a paying customer. He tries to

get a free drink from her by telling the story about the fox who asked the stork to put his bill in the fox's mouth in order to pull out a bone, which was supposedly stuck in the fox's throat. But she won't even look at him (the eye). Later when Blazes buys him a drink, she does listen to Lenehan.

Having failed with the bar maid, Lenehan tries to get a free drink by buttering up Simon, but chooses the wrong subject—a greeting from his famous son. We know this is artificial since Stephen has no use for his father. Lenehan doesn't sense Simon's coolness to this subject and continues on to tell Simon about Stephen's intellectual exploits earlier that day with the newspaper group. Simon goes numb at this news ("I see") since Simon had unsuccessfully invited the editor to join him at a different pub. Simon is pleased only by his own exploits, not by those of his son. Simon is trapped in ego and the past when he was more important and was treated with respect. He does not sense life as continuity. Depressed, Simon starts to withdraw to the piano, which he notices has been moved recently (he knows where it usually is) from the bar to the concert room ("I see you have moved the piano"). Douce tells him the blind piano tuner was in earlier and played exquisitely, "the real classical." The piano tuner who prefers classical music can hear but not see.

Pat the deaf waiter comes in and orders a lager with his lunch. He can see but not hear. He has to pay for the lager. It is served "without alacrity." Simon goes to the piano, which is described as a coffin. He opens the lid and tries the keys.

The action cuts to Bloom in Wisdom Hely's, where he used to work and perhaps still gets a bargain. He is buying three sheets of writing paper and an envelope to write a letter to Martha, having received one from her that day. He thinks about her letter and the "language of flow," sees a poster ad featuring a mermaid smoking a cigarette and, right after thinking about Raoul, sees Blazes in his taxi car on "supple rubbers." Bloom ranks this Raoul-Blazes coincidence as his third foreshadowing experience of the day. He decides to follow Blazes, and in his haste almost forgets to pay for the writing supplies. The young female clerk is nice, but Bloom knows why.

Back in the concert room adjacent to the bar, Simon strikes to a "dying call" the tuning fork left behind by the blind piano tuner. Accompanying himself on the piano, Simon sings "Goodbye, Sweetheart, Goodbye," a song by a lover who tries but can't leave his loved one.[7] Those sirens are sticky, like tar babies. His singing is given in italics. The first line is "The bright stars fade . . .," in line with the corruption theme. Lenehan and the barmaids ignore Simon's singing, as if they had heard it often. She continues to read the paper, and he tries another joke on her, his Rose of Castile pun. Rows of caste steel for caste repetition without redemption.

Blazes enters the bar, and Lenehan calls him the "conquering hero" (a line from Handel's *Judas Maccabaeus*[8]) in a successful effort to get a drink—a bitters, again signifying suffering. The barmaids smile at Blazes. Blazes asks if the results of the Gold Cup race are in (they aren't) and orders a slow (read time) gin fizz, which requires the barmaid to reach up to a high shelf to get the ingredients. She reaches them on the high shelf, "But easily she seized her prey and led it low in triumph." The sirens in the meadow. The "Clock clacked."

Bloom, the conquered hero who has been following Blazes, walks by the front of the bar. He is saved by Richie Goulding, Simon's brother in law, who invites Bloom to join him for dinner in the separate dining room of the Ormond Hotel. Richie and Bloom enter by a separate door into the dining room. Bloom checks the time and can't understand why Boylan would late for his engagement with Molly.

At this point, the barmaids, Lenehan and Blazes are in the bar, Bloom and Richie are in the next room, and Simon is alone in the concert room still singing "Goodbye Sweetheart Goodbye." Bolstered by his association with Blazes, Lenehan asks Douce to do the garter snap on her thigh—known as Sonnez la Cloche (the bell rings)—by saying "Let's hear the time." This phrase associates sex, music and time. Interested in Blazes, she agrees and smacks her thigh with her garter, raising her skirt in the process. Douce flirts with Blazes, who is momentarily seized with lust. "Boylan, eyed, eyed." His eyes are "spellbound." Lust through the eyes. While Blazes can't take his eyes off her, Douce moves down the bar, just as music does. But Blazes decides on going to Molly. Just as

348

Blazes is leaving, Lenehan finally remembers the message he is to deliver to Blazes from Rochford; we don't hear the message that is given as Blazes walks out to his car (horse drawn), which has been waiting all this time. Bloom hears Blazes leave, he knows to go to Molly's bed, and even in the depth of his depression orders only cider.

As Blazes leaves, he greets Ben Dollard who is walking by with Father Cowley. From the last episode, we know Dollard has been helping the Father with his debt to the money lender. Dollard is an expert at debts, which like boozing involve borrowing against the future for the benefit of the present. Even though at poverty's edge, these two unfortunates are lured into the bar by the sound of Simon's singing and playing. Simon comes out of the concert room into the bar; apparently he has been crying—he rubs an eyelid. Simon says to Dollard he has only been "vamping." They go back into the concert room, and Dollard sits down at the piano and suggests that Simon sing the old favorite "Love and War." Simon says "God be with old times."

Douce wonders why Blazes left so soon, particularly after she had gone so far as to raise her skirt for him. She lowers "the dropblind with a sliding cord" as he leaves. The bar, like a gambling salon in Las Vegas, should not allow light in and should create its own artificial atmosphere.

We learn from Bloom's musings that Dollard was formerly in the ship supply business, ruined his life on Number One Bass ale (number one for ego), and now lives in an institutional home for indigents. Cowley is also in financial trouble, as we learned in the last episode. Simon is in deep financial trouble, now reduced to tears of self-pity in his fallen condition.

These three failures in the present, Simon, Dollard and Father Cowley, reminisce about the more attractive past. They recall the time when Goodwin, the pianist to accompany Dollard's singing, was too drunk to play. Also, Dollard didn't have the right formal wear ("wedding garment"). With pathetic post-mortem vanity, Cowley recalls that he saved the situation by coming up with the idea to borrow formal wear for Dollard from the Blooms. The trousers borrowed generously without charge, even though the Blooms were in tight circumstances at the time, were for Dollard too tight, especially in the crotch. The tight fit caused considerable exposure in outline and merriment. On the subject of the Blooms, Father Cowley recalls that was the time Molly was playing the piano and singing for money in a coffee house and suspected of prostitution (remember Bloom is in the next room). Simon makes a joke along the same lines about all the fine clothes she has taken off. They continue to discuss Molly's background in the same vein, as daughter of the regiment and Irish from Gibraltar. The barmaids are bored because Molly is now the center of attention.

Bloom and Richie eat their dinners (Bloom has liver), and we learn by omission that Bloom can't hear the conversation in the bar. Bloom continues to think about Molly and his depressing experience that morning in her bedroom: "Mrs. Marion. Met him pike hoses. Smell of burn. Of Paul de Kock. Nice name he." These reflections continue the theme of possession by memories, metempsychosis being the ultimate in that domain. Repetition of memories without redemption. In a time related intrusion, Boylan on his way to Molly's unfurnished apartment registers his impatience with a "flick of the whip," hints of more masochism to come. These strains are woven together in the text with the conversation of Bloom and Richie and the action in the concert room.

Dollard begins to sing "When love absorbs my ardent soul" from "Love and War," a tenor/bass duet. But Dollard, a bass, begins to sing the wrong part, the higher tenor part. This he sings too loudly. Crowley reminds him that his is the war or warrior part, the lower bass part. Dollard says he was thinking about Rev. Love in singing the higher love part. They joke about his "organ" being big. Only a few lines are heard, but in this song both the lover and the soldier absorbed in their ardent soul "think not of the morrow" and cure their pains with rosy wine.[9]

Without any warning or lead in, two more patrons are in the bar. They are described as gentlemen and order tankards. Soon they are referred to just as tankards, bodies holding alcohol, and no longer as gentlemen. They make trivial conversation with Kennedy and ask where the viceregal calvacade is going. She doesn't know (to a charity hospital) and tries unsuccessfully to look it up in the paper. The sirens are not research scholars.

Bloom is eating liver and bacon and mashed potatoes (for repetition without redemption try he "mashed mashed potatoes"). He remembers independently the same incident when Dollard borrowed trousers from the Blooms—"tight as a drum." In musical terms, his recollection is a repetition of the theme in a different voice. The solicitor Lidwell (read drum) comes in, and Miss Douce is most charming to him. She solicits the solicitor.

Dollard convinces Simon to sing, but "shy, listless" Simon refuses to sing "Love and War"; Simon would have to sing the love part. Dollard alternatively suggests that Simon sing the aria "M'appari" from the opera *Martha*, and even sings a few words in Italian to urge him on. Simon doesn't openly disagree but instead sings "A Last Farewell," which is described in prose as about a farewell, a girl, a veil, a headland and wind. Apparently Simon's repertoire has dwindled. Finally, Simon agrees to sing "M'appari" and starts to play the piano part but falters (perhaps this is why he initially sang "Farewell" instead). Dollard wants him to change to the original key (one flat for pessimism). This Simon can't do anymore (because of drink), so Dollard takes the piano and starts to play. In intrusions, Boylan on the way to Molly's goes by Graham Lemon's pineapple rock (the ice cream store symbol for the Fall in the Garden) and Elvery's (which sells waterproofs, for separate identity resulting from the Fall).

Bloom hears the piano again and, showing his astuteness in musical matters, correctly guesses from the sound alone (ear) that Dollard is playing. Bloom characterizes Dollard's skill with the piano as a "mutual understanding," a unity in music making. Bloom thinks about his first time with Molly on Ben Howth headlands above Dublin Bay under the rhododendrons. He concludes: "We are their harps. I. He. Old. Young." By this Bloom says that his wife has played him and Blazes like a harp and, in a different dimension, that the failure of his relationship with Molly has separated his personal identity (I Old) from what he was earlier (He Young).

Richie remembers in grandiose terms hearing the aria "Tutto e Sciolto—All is Lost Now" [10] from the opera *Sonnambula* sung by the famous tenor Joe Maas (read all is lost in the Mass). Bloom believes Richie is mostly making this up, does not respond appropriately to Richie's claims and thinks critically about Richie's lack of frugality. Bloom can be temporarily excused for being less than kind now that he knows the adultery is certain. He is trying hard not to associate "All is Lost Now" with his personal situation. Bloom thinks about an English drinking song, "Down Among the Dead Men," which Bloom characterizes as "appropriate." Bloom remembers from *Sonnambula* the scene where the innocent woman sleeps walks into bedroom danger, an example of moving blindly into harm's way. His thoughts ineluctably return to Molly and "all is lost now." Bloom sees himself in the bar mirror as the "Face of all is lost."

Simon begins to sing an air from *Martha* (sung by Lionell in the opera). This Richie and Bloom want to hear better so they have the waiter open the door between the dining room and the concert hall. Bloom starts his internal joke about the "waiter, waited waiting to hear." He repeats this joke in his mind many times; it is another pun without literary redemption. Sailors no doubt waited on the sirens' island; the singing probably stopped and they felt trapped. In the opera, royal ladies on a lark hire out as servant girls to a peasant and become trapped.

The aria touches Bloom: "Braintipped, cheek touched with flame, they listened feeling that flow endearing flow over skin limbs human heart soul spine . . . . Love that is singing . . . ." While Simon sings, Bloom alternates between a passive mental state dominated by the music and an objective analysis of music. Bloom begins to play with the cat gut band that bound the expensive stationary he bought for the letter to Martha. He winds the cat gut around his fingers in a cats cradle pattern. He associates to the song "Those Lovely Seaside Girls," a song to be sung by Molly on the upcoming tour with Blazes. Bloom thinks about how Simon ruined his own life and wore out his wife with children, perhaps to give himself an excuse why he hasn't sired more with Molly.

Bloom focuses on the coincidence that he is about to write to Martha and an aria from an opera by the same name is being sung. Further under the influence of music, he remembers meeting Molly the first time, their playing a game of musical chairs and her singing "Waiting." He believes they were fated to get together. At the end of Simon's singing with the concluding line "Come to me," the narrator says "Siopold! Consumed." Everyone claps. The text repeats several events that have already happened in the episode: "Blazes Boylan's smart tan shoes creaked on the barfloor, said before . . . ."

Dollard tells Simon abstaining from alcohol (seven days in jail) would improve his voice. Tom Kernan struts in for more gin; he just had several during the last episode. Richie recalls for Bloom the night Simon sang "Twas Rank and Fame," with emphasis on the line "love lives not." The pedigree of the Dedalus family is given. Now the family must pawn furniture and books so Simon can booze while his children eat charity soup.

Bloom releases the cats cradle. Then he transforms the string into a musical instrument. He stretches the cat gut as a single string and plucks it making a sound. He stretches the string tighter and plucks a higher pitched sound. Bloom muses about the fact that Simon doesn't even talk to his brother-in-law Richie (Richie's sister, Simon's former wife, is now deceased) and that Richie admires him all the same. Bloom thinks: "Thou lost one. All songs on that theme . . . . Cruel it seems. Let people get fond of each other: lure them on. Then tear asunder. Death . . . Her wavyavyeavyheavyeavyevyevyhair un comb:'d." This long phrase features repetition in general and sea-like repetition of waves and Eve's seaweed-like hair in particular: wavy (wayyav) yeavy heavy eav (eve) yevyevy hair. This version of repetition suggests original sin from the Garden of Eden repeated in subsequent sin. More repetition without redemption. Thinking of Plumtree's potted meat and the missing ingredients in his marriage, Bloom stretches the string tighter until it breaks.

Bloom asks the waiter for writing materials and begins to write his most personal letter to his siren Martha right in front of Richie. He partially covers the letter in progress with a newspaper. He is sending her a money order for 2 shillings and 6 pence, an expensive gift that would prostitute their relationship. As the novel progresses, try to determine if he ever mails this letter.

Bloom thinks about the scientific and psychological aspects of music— "musemathematics . . . Time makes the tune." Simon attributes his soft Cork voice to Italian seamen whose singing he heard as a boy. Blaze's progress on the way to Molly at the Bloom home is documented; he is now in a hired hackney car—so his own will not be parked in front of Molly's house.

Richie asks if Bloom is answering an ad; Bloom says yes, a town traveler. In the postscript to the letter, Bloom asks masochistically "How will you pun? You punish me?" (Joyce punishes reality with puns in this episode.) The music affects what Bloom writes to Martha. Despite his best efforts, Bloom keeps repeating the thought of Blazes arriving at Molly's.

Douce has Lidwell listen to the sea shell she brought back from her vacation. Seaweed hair over the ear, from the image of Eve, is mentioned; this associates the sirens with Eve's seduction come-on "come eat the apple." Bloom scientifically analyzes the sound apparently coming from the shell as actually an echo or repetition of the sound made by blood in the ear of the listener. We note that this is similar to the effect of sad popular music. Bloom then extends the connection from blood back to islands and Sirens with the thought, "Well, it's [blood is] a sea. Corpuscle islands." Dollard continues to play and his thoughts mix his financial problems and time in music: "The landlord has the prior. A little time . . . One: one, one, one, one, one: two, one, three, four."

Bloom thinks about music in nature: "Sea, wind, leaves, thunder, waters, cows lowing . . . . There's music everywhere." He also considers the gruesome reality of the situation in the **Don Giovanni** seduction scene, when the Overlord Don tries to seduce the serf Zerlina on her wedding day. This seduction attempt takes place in the context of the former legal right of the overlord to possession of all his female serfs. The distraught bridegroom (Bloom's counterpart) and the horrified peasants watch, "Green starving faces eating dockleaves," while the dancers think "Look: look, look, look, look, look: you look at us." Repetition and vanity in possession.

Mozart's classically composed opera provides contrast with popular song. In this opera, the Don, the serial seducer, is invited to dinner by the ghost of the father (the Don killed him) of one of his female conquests. The Don thinks he will celebrate fearlessly his sexual conquest. Refusing to repent, the Don is sucked into hell. The Don's destruction is itself a dramatic picture of arrest in a moment of attraction to ego celebration.

Bloom considers the joyful transcendence of music across time and makes a pun on Chamber Music (try heart, sex, farts and also the name of an earlier collection of poems by Joyce). Bloom imagines "Paul de Kock with a loud proud knocker with a cock carracarracarra coc. Cockcock." Repetition and phallus.

Dollard begins to sing "The Croppy Boy," a sad song about the treachery of a false priest, actually a British police captain disguised in priestly robes as Father Green. The false father Green captures a confessing Irish lad asking for blessing to join the resistance—Father let me go. This is a version of Bloom's psychological problem. Bloom thinks about the soul limiting effects of the Mass and death. At the depth of his depression, Bloom thinks about paternity and whether it is too late for him. Despite everything, he remains somewhat hopeful, still feeling the will to life.

Getting up to go, Bloom charitably leaves with Richie his portion of the bill plus a little extra, since Bloom knows Richie has money worries. Richie unsuccessfully urges him to stay. Bloom leaves through the bar, but the barmaids don't see him leaving, caught up as they are watching Dollard sing. The text commingles Bloom's thoughts, the song being sung and the tap of the approaching blind piano tuner. Since Bloom is suffering from what he could have stopped, Bloom thinks about Christian martyrs as voluntary sufferers. The barmaid Lydia Douce, lost in the song, has her hand on the white, smooth beerpull (read penis). The narrator calls Bloom the "Scaring eavesdropping boots croppy bootsboy Bloom in the Ormond hallway." He hears the applause for the last song. Simon blows his nose, ". . . trumping compassion from

355

foghorn nose . . . " Overweight Dollard speaks of his weight as the "fat of death," an allusion to the rotting skin on the sirens' isle. Eating as repetition without redemption.

The tap of the sounding stick of the blind piano turner, returning to retrieve his tuning fork, is heard as he gets closer to the Ormond. Tap grows to tap tap grows to tap tap tap etc. The crowd, which increased during the music, moves from the concert room to the bar for a drink. The text doesn't say who pays. Someone tells Simon and company that Bloom has been in the bar. Somewhat abashed by their earlier slanderous remarks about Molly, they mutter nice things about Bloom.

Leaving the bar, Bloom runs into a whore whom he had known earlier. He avoids her this time by looking in the window display of the antique shop. She has on a black straw sailor hat, straw from hell in the last episode and sailor for the sirens. In Bloom's thoughts warped by the presence of the prostitute, wind instruments suggest blow jobs. This association of prostitute and siren is the harshest condemnation of the barmaids and Simon; they are no better than whores because they lead men to ruin and disease.

Bloom remembers the final speech of the Irish patriot Robert Emmet just before he was executed by quartering—a rapid form of degeneration. His last words were that he would have his epitaph written when Ireland took her place among the nations of the earth. Only then could people understand his motivation. This speech sandwiches identity and independence, the very attributes the sirens and repetition of the past take away. During this sequence, the blind piano tuner passes the Ormond, goes by the store east of the Ormond (Daly's) and then mysteriously reappears in the now empty concert room and finally the door to the bar. By omission we gather that no one helps him and that he is still looking for the tuning fork. My guess is that bankrupt Simon took it. The text uses its last literary device without redemption, which continues the emphasis on the limitation of the visual, "Hee hee hee hee. He did not see."

Outside the bar, Bloom farts, making his own internal music. Ever thoughtful of others, he releases his opus only when he is clear and the sound is covered by that of the passing tram. Bloom believes his internal music must have been caused by the burgundy (read spirits) he drank at lunch. The music of the spirit is realized in the body.[11] The episode ends as his fart ends, "Done." This the last note of the episode sounds in its double meaning the principal theme—dwell on the past (done) and you are finished (done).

Parallels to the Odyssey

Like Odysseus tied to the mast listening to the sirens, Bloom voluntarily subjects himself to suffering by following but not stopping Blazes. The deaf waiter corresponds to the crew which could see but not hear. They both serve, the waiter serves Bloom and the crew serves Odysseus. Bloom corresponds to Odysseus who could see and hear but does not seek the sirens because of prior restraint.

The sirens' amazing claim to know the future of anyone who came to the sirens' island is more easily understood as a self-fulfilling prophecy. Their visitors never leave their island. Their future is limited and easy to predict. Likewise, singing mournful songs is a self-fulfilling prophecy; the singers become sad and then drink some more. The barmaids know the future of their regular customers, because they only leave stiff.

The opening is an example of Joyce's masterful technique of creating parallels to The Odyssey. Here are the first item in the overture and first sentence of the corresponding body:

Bronze by gold heard the hoofirons,
steelyringing.

*****

Bronze by gold, miss Douce's head by miss
Kennedy's head, over the crossblind of the Ormond bar
heard the viceregal hoofs go by, ringing steel.

The bar maid/sirens are immediately associated with the usurping state from the previous Wandering Rocks episode. The "steelringing" from the overture suggests the tuning fork; siren also means a noisemaking device producing a certain pitch. A state of imprisonment is suggested by the reference to "hoofirons"; boatless travel from the sirens' island would be impossible and the bar is a prison of memories.

357

Note the parallels between the picture of (i) the sirens sitting in the meadow on the island with only their heads visible to the passing ships and (ii) the picture of the head of the barmaid above the "crossblind" and their torsos above the bar. In all cases, the lower bodies are hidden. What danger lurks in the bodies of the sirens such that they sit rather than stand (which would be more natural) when a ship comes by? Myth presented them with the upper torsos of attractive human females but with the lower torsos of birds of prey which would attack the sailor jumping ship just as soon as he reached the island. The sirens were also depicted as bird ghosts that stole the living.[12] Likewise, the Dubliners in the bar are blind to the suffering in store for them; they are "crossblind," blind to the suffering. In addition, the word torso means partially completed, in tune with the meaning of this episode.

Arthur Power reported that Joyce "[pointed] out that the barmaids, with careful hair-do, make-up, and smart blouses, looked well only to the waist, and that below the waist they wore old stained skirts, broken and comfortable shoes, and mended stockings."[13] Like the sirens, their attractive upper torso is a come-on for the treachery of the lower torso. The treachery of the commonly dressed lower torso of the barmaids is the common obsession with sex, the come-on to corruption in the bar. The sex instinct gives repetition without redemption except in new life.

The episode ends with another reference to upper and lower torso. In this case, the upper is the spirit of Bloom's heart or soul (represented by the burgundy wine) and the lower is the instrument for his fart. Bloom's fart, caused he thinks by the burgundy wine, is chamber music of the unified body and soul. His chamber music is presented together with phrases from Emmet's proclamation of emancipation. Unification of body and soul are necessary for freedom.

The names of the two sirens in The Odyssey mean "white body" and "shrill"[14]. Miss Douce is sunburned and Miss Kennedy is shrill. They are behind the "reef" of a bar counter and stand on upturned crates, signifying both bones and staves for notes. In the bar, an island in the city, the barmaids promote the sale and consumption of booze through sexual teasing and pleasant conversation, available only to paying customers. Simon, himself a Siren, sings in the bar for free booze, and his singing brings in other customers. In this bar/island refuge of temporary pleasures, our Dublin mariners raise their cups and rehash memories, share gossip and hear the same old mournful songs. These limited experiences produce "feelings of loss, self-pity, depression and petty vindictiveness that interfere with passionate relationships with others . . . ."[15] These social forcefields are the modern sirens' spell and attract the Dubliners to further drink. But pleasure turns by repetition to corruption. Like the sailors who jump ship for the sirens' island, the Dubliners rot from booze.

Butes was a mariner on the Argo who was tempted by the sirens, jumped ship and swam toward them but was saved by Aphrodite. Butes appears here as the messenger boy, referred to only by his boots, who brings the teas to the teasers. He teases the sirens and is no longer enchanted by them. When he is attacked, he begins to stutter, perhaps a reflection of Butes's near-miss experience with the sirens.

The corrupting effects of the sirens' bar have reached an advanced stage in Simon Dedalus. The booze has ruined his singing voice, not to mention the health and security of his family. In his role as siren of old songs and guardian of the past, he is totally displaced as to his identity by the news that his son, the future, had earlier in the day intellectually charmed Dubliners deemed important by Simon. Simon's personal degeneration is coded with images from the Hindu god Shiva/Rudra, the centrifugal energy of disintegration and annihilation.

Shiva-Rudra

Images from the Hindu pantheon explain much otherwise difficult detail in the episode.[16] The basic players are Shiva (AKA S'iva) and Rudra, representing different aspects of the forces of disintegration and annihilation. Shiva represents the peaceful and Rudra the violent. These are forces that have been given names, not individual gods who have powers.

The odd discussion between the barmaids about Bloom and the "other eye" reflects the three eyes of Shiva, the third eye being the inner eye of fire. The three eyes allow Shiva to see past, present and future, while the activities in the bar are designed specifically to dwell selectively on the past and most importantly avoid thoughts of the future. Bloom as Shiva explains Bloom's musings about the drum, since the hour glass shaped drum, which keeps time in music, is a common symbol of Shiva. Shiva is also blue throated as Bloom's name in the narrator's voice goes from Bloowho to bluehued.

Shiva's color is white and Rudra's red so one barmaid, the white one, gets a red sunburn, by itself and symbolically disintegration brought on by behavior. Rudra is sweet scented so the sirens wear perfume. Rudra's form is water so the bar maids lips are wet, one jokes about getting all wet (in the pants) from laughing and the several references to Eau du Nile. Rudra is the Lord of Songs and the Lord of Tears, as sorrowful songs proliferate in this episode and Simon rubs his eyelid. Rudra means the removal of pain, which alcohol accomplishes on a temporary basis. By contrast, Bloom voluntarily takes on pain by not stopping Blazes. The bar mates drink to drive away the effects of time and death, but Shiva alone can drink the deadly poison necessary to free the world from the effect of death.

The force complimentary to the Shiva/Rudra complex is Vishnu, the cohesive or centripetal force represented by Bloom. Bloom understands the effect in the human ear of the sea shell since it is typically carried in one of the four hands of Vishnu and is the image of the cohesive or centripetal tendency. The conch, the symbol of the origin of existence and born of water, allows one to hear oneself, the goal of Yoga and the Hindu religion.

In this same belief pattern, controlled sexual energy allows man to conquer the celestial worlds of the spirit. Control and restraint—our man Bloom. And compare, if you will, the addicted flow of booze into the pub patrons with the "grace of eternal life pouring into the world." Grace was represented by the rose in medieval Christian symbolism.[17] Here the rose wilts on the opening of the blouse of one of the Siren bar maids.

Distractions

The sirens distract the mariners from the fundamental objective of getting home. The redeeming present requires concentration. Here distraction claims many bar occupants: the barmaids distracted by their

360

attention to the royal calvacade, don't hear boots; Simon by the news of his son, can't talk; Lenehan by his desire for drink, doesn't sense Simon's coolness; Bloom by the certain adultery of Molly, plans to send money to Martha; Lenehan by drink, almost forgets to give Blazes the message from Rochford; the barmaids by their interest in Blazes, don't get the drink order for Bloom and Richie right away; Simon by drink, can't play Martha in another key; Richie by his preoccupation, doesn't notice that Bloom is in mourning clothes; and the bar maids by Dollard's singing, don't see Bloom leaving.

The biggest distraction is loss of identity, inevitable on the sirens' island and epidemic in the bar. Simon goes blank in conversation after Lenehan gives him the unwelcome news that his son Stephen had been regaling important intellectual company earlier in the day. The blank Simon is referred to just as "he" from line 273, when he receives the news, until after he sings at line 440, when he is crying. Even when he first sings for a drink, no one in the bar (the barmaids, Lenehan and Boylan) listens. In free fall financially, Simon is addicted to pubs where in the past he received some respect because of his wit and singing ability; now, however, he is siren singing for his sauce.

Molly's singing costumes to create stage identity are mentioned in the Goodwin story. In the song "Love and War," the soul or identity is absorbed by both. Bloom in his fake identity writes to Martha and lies to Richie about the nature of the letter he writes right in front of him. In the song "The Croppy Boy," the British police captain is disguised in false identity as a priest to catch rebels seeking independence. After the aria from *Martha*, the narrator combines Simon and Leopold into "Siopold, Consumed," for consumption of identity in mournful music.

Music, Time and Death

The episode is constructed with many parallels to music, both in terms of typical lyrics and structure. An overture announces the themes in summary as the sirens' song of seduction is an overture to a big surprise. The themes are sequenced on the basis of rules for a certain kind of fugue, even though a fugue would not normally have an overture. In a fugue pattern, the melody is given in one voice and then slightly later is repeated in other voices, while the first voice continues. In other words, the fugue, like the memory, repeats the past voice.

Within this overall pattern, words in the text are arranged in groups that mimic chords and celebrated inversions of chords. The text even mentions five people together in the bar as a "fifth," which means both a certain chord made up of five notes as well as a common size whiskey bottle. The relationships of words in the text also mimic the time or horizontal relationships of one group of musical notes to the next—sliding into, bunched with, combined with etc. Some passages are sharp staccato like in attack and others are drawn out or slurred together. This construction combines the medium and the message, both on the surface and in the deep meaning.

Time is the leitmotif, a musical technique made famous by Wagner whereby one theme identified with one character or one force is used repeatedly. This emphasis on time is pressed home in the following instances: "time ever passing. Clockhands turning"; Blazes asks if the race wire is in yet and for the exact time; the clock whirrs and clacks; we hear the time; the time is sounded on Miss Douce's thigh; "time makes the tune"; and even a mention of metempsychosis. Time's hand maiden memory gets heavy billing with "God be with old times," the telling of old stories, Bloom's reference to Richie's poor memory and Bloom under the influence of music remembers his first meetings with Molly. The fundamental property of time is repetition without redemption.

Time's inevitable companions decay and death are featured in many refrains. The barmaid announces a member of the viceregal calvacade is "killed looking back." The piano is described as a "coffin." The tuning fork gives a "dying" call. Bloom thinks ". . . down among dead men. Appropriate." Bloom remembers Dignam and the rat at the cemetery. The confessing boy dies in "The Croppy Boy." Bloom mentions dying martyrs; Dollard has the "fat of death." Reincarnation and repeats in music (da capo) appear in the text as we observe these limited ego-bound bundles of the infinite consciousness struggle for even the illusion of happiness in the bar isolation of time and death.

The color green signals death to soul potential as the sirens were surrounded by green water, the sirens sat in a green meadow, one

362

barmaid wears Water of the Nile (a greenish perfume[18]), and the fake priest in The Croppy Boy is Father Green. And we have direct references to binding and lethal birdlime [from the Proteus (3rd) episode and *Hamlet*].

The World as Will

The foundation for this episode is the philosophy of Arthur Schopenhauer that music is a direct reflection of the World as Will. The narrator remarks: "Words? Music? No: it's what's behind." The following is a brief summary of Schopenhauer's concept, which is "behind" this episode as the sirens' lower halves are hidden behind the blinds.

The Will has produced the world, all physical forces, all matter and all living kind. The Will or will to life is a primal force existing outside of time that is characterized by blind, unconscious and repetitive striving. The Will is ethically evil because progress is impossible. Hence the pessimism displayed in this episode. The Will force remains eternal while mere phenomenal individuals are born and die. The Will manifests itself as perpetual struggle, as all entities fight for existence and suffer. Because the nature of the Will force itself is constant and repetitive striving, its human products are constantly striving for happiness or satisfaction but never achieve a permanent state of joy. Just as soon as one wish is satisfied or one problem solved, another one comes along. As a result, suffering is the natural condition of life.

All the arts can catch a glimpse of the pure Will but music most of all since it can be a direct copy of the Will. Music directly reflects the Will because it affects the human heart, just as the Will does. Like the Will, music operates in the dimension of tension and resolution.

In this philosophy, each part of the human body corresponds to a particular desire through which the Will manifests itself, for example the teeth for hunger and the genitalia for sexual desire. The Will is refracted through time, space and causality into the multiplicity of forces, individuals and forms (that "form endearing") experienced in the world. Like the opening summary of themes repeated in the body of the episode, the Will is repeated in the body of each human. Forms in the world are perceived through our built-in (*a priori*) notions of time, space and causality. This is the World as Idea, all perceived reality being conditioned by built-in human limitations.

The Will has different degrees of "objectification"; mere matter corresponds to the lowest grade of objectification while human consciousness corresponds to the highest. The lowest living creatures are marked by conformity to the species and the highest by discrimination or individuality. Despite being born of this flawed clay, the individual person can by restraint and control and, oddly, by voluntary suffering break away to achieve a calm Buddha-like state free of the Will force.

Right in line with the sexual undertone of this theory of Will, Bloom thinks: "Will? You? I. Want. You. To." The sirens' experience is representative of the suffering in life. You are rowing along and you come to an island you didn't even know was there. The girls sing and immediately the rowers have a new wish to satisfy. In today's world, the sirens would write advertising copy to stimulate the desire for expensive products. The point of Homer's story is that being subject to the sirens' song, that is vulnerable to the wish fulfillment process, means inevitable corruption and soul death. Restraint, fundamental restraint, is the antidote. Both our hero Odysseus and our hero Bloom overcome the process by self-control. Odysseus has himself strapped to the mast. Bloom ties his hands with the cats cradle. If Bloom were ever going to use booze, it would be on the day and at the moment he personally hears Blazes leave to go to Molly. But he doesn't.

The Will force is embodied in Bloom's thoughts about, and the narrator's description of, Simon's singing of "All is Lost Now":

Tenderness it welled: slow, swelling, full it throbbed.
That's the chat. Ha, give! Take! Throb, a throb, a
pulsing proud erect.
***

Bloom. Flood of warm jamjam lickitup secretness
flowed to flow in music out, in desire, dark to lick flow
invading. Tipping her tepping her tapping her topping
her. Tup. Pores to dilate dilating. Tup. The joy the feel
the warm the. Tup. To pour o'er sluices pouring
gushes. Flood, gush, flow, joygush, tupthrob. Now!

364

Language of love.

These most suggestive passages frame the narrator's statement about what's behind the music.

Miss Douce feels the Will force as she plays with the top of the white, smooth beer pull while listening to music:

> On the smooth jutting beerpull laid Lydia hand, lightly, plumply, leave it to my hands. All lost in pity for croppy. Fro, to: to, fro: over the polished knob (she knows his eyes, my eyes, her eyes) her thumb and finger passed in pity: passed, reposed and, gently touching, then slid so smoothly, slowly down, a cool firm white enamel baton protruding through their sliding ring.

Notice the use of the word pity from Joyce's aesthetic theory; Siren Lydia is lost in pity, but instead of sympathy she feels the personal pull of sex.

Simon is first presented paring the overgrown tops of his fingernails, signifying the manifestation of the Will in his claws and his desire to possess and hold down Stephen. Simon says he has only been "vamping," our paternal vampire. The vampire, like the pub patrons, must continue to drink. The barmaids are referred to as bronze and gold because earth elements are the lowest degree of objectification of the Will. Along these lines, Bloom thinks the following: "Chords dark. Lugugugubrious. Low. In a cave of the dark middle earth. Embedded ore. Lumpmusic." The sirens laugh at Bloom's individuating characteristics, which none the less give him a higher objectification status.

The point about Dollard starting too high on the scale in the song "Love and War" is that he is war and war is lower than love on the scale of objectification of the Will. The lower orders of the Will constantly struggle with the higher. The exact degrees of objectification of the Will are reflected in the efforts of the blind piano tuner; he sets the tones of the piano with the exact amount of separation. He is blind like the Will and is seen endlessly striving, first trying to get to the bar to tune the piano and then returning because he forgot his tuning fork. At the end of the episode, he reappears in the bar still striving to find his fork.

Bloom's self control is symbolized by the cats cradle he wraps around his hands. This would prevent him from drinking but also makes a small stringed instrument. Because of the short length of the string, this instrument would produce only high notes suitable for a melody. Schopenhauer makes several direct analogies to music: the slow moving low notes in the bass are akin to the lowest grades of objectification like the mass of the planet; the in-between accompaniment notes are like plant life; and the high running and connected notes of the melody are akin to the highest grades of objectification, the intentionally connected intellectual life of man. The change of key, or a new mode, is like death; Simon can't manage to confront it.

Bloom has already advanced in this system because of his empathy with the suffering of others—here even with the whore. In this episode, he voluntarily suffers the indignity of being present at the launch of the cuckolding visit; this voluntary suffering will, with the knowledge that life inevitably produces suffering for all, bring him to a state of restraint and detachment on the way to being free of wants and cares in this life prior to death. On his way out of the bar, Bloom thinks: "Get out before the end (read of life). Thanks that was heavenly. Where's my hat." His hat, his realization.

The Will to live is directly connected with the attachment of the personal ego to the cares of this world and its hospital wards time, sex and fear of death. And to anticipate somewhat, the approach of avoiding through restraint and detachment the ego and Will impulse leads to the void: "No will: no idea: no world." Watch for this concept to appear in Stephen's conversation with Bloom in a later episode.

Schopenhauer also provides a description of these Dubliners using clock and musical images:

> . . . like clockwork, which is wound up, and goes it knows not why; and every time a man is begotten and born, the clock of human life is wound up anew, to repeat the same old piece it has played innumerable times before, passage after passage, measure after measure, . . . with insignificant variations.

Farts and Songs

The episode ending fart is, I believe, presented as the analogue of the strictly personal musical experience and its cousin the pornographic arts. The description of Bloom's final fart, "Pprrpffrrppffff," contains in repetition the musical notations for soft (pp) and loud (ff).

First Letter and Traditional Schemata

The first letter **B** in the first word Bronze also opened the 5th and 7th episodes and again stands (compared to the figure for eternity) for limited realization.

The traditional schemata given by Joyce for this episode are organ—ear, art—music, color—none, symbol—barmaids, and technique—fugue per canone. Linati lists Coral as color and as Persons Ulysses, Menelaus, Leucothea (AKA Ino), Parthenope, Orpheus and the Argonauts. Coral is mentioned in connection with the bar as part of the island image. Parthenope was in some versions of the legend the name of a siren who threw herself into the sea after failing to attract Odysseus. Perhaps she reappears as the whore in the sailor's straw hat.

Song of Solomon

Simon Dedalus sings solos, the soloman. Soloman leads to Solomon (mentioned in the episode), supposedly the singer of the Song of Songs and a son of David. Snippets from the Solomon legends and the Song of Solomon[19] are woven into the music of the episode. But this is not Solomon the wise ruler, but Solomon the dispossessed. Fallen Solomon was restored to power only after he found the magic ring while eating a fish; the fallen Simon Dedalus looks longingly at a headless sardine. As Simon plays the dispossessed Solomon, Richie and Bloom, his rivals in a sense for Stephen's home, are eating food "fit for princes"—the rival princes that would be the other sons of David.

Parallel to the Mass and Purification

The use of words with double meanings related to the bar and Church, such as curate and libation, pull the Mass into the pub. Instead of the one offering in the Mass of wine as the blood of Christ, the pub features the antidote to the Mass, various polytheistic offerings for the imbiber and music to drive away guilt. The betrayal force of the Mass energizes the story of "The Croppy Boy"[20].

In Joyce's list of Jewish ritual (given in a later episode), the reference for this episode is "music, Shira Shirim," which means the Song of Songs. In art, restraint is called for in the dramatic method.

Structure, Art and Aesthetics

This episode carries plenty of unexpectedness and strangeness. Just let yourself go and read it aloud. Joyce said it took him five months to write this episode and that afterwards he couldn't stand to listen to music, because he knew its tricks too well.

The basic structure of an overture announcing in summary form the themes in the body of the work is similar to an opera. The narrator's voice, like the orchestra part, is coded with emotive information about the characters and the action. The use of a particular rhythm and flow in the voice helps convey the message. Here are some of the voice rhythms:

In the Overture, you hear the insistent "listen to us" message of the sirens, which is composed entirely in demanding long stresses:

Bronze by gold heard the hoofirons, steelringing.

Every syllable in that line is stressed, quite an unusual pattern. Notice the sequence made by the number of syllables in each word: one (bronze), one (by), one (gold), one (heard), one (the), two (hoofirons), three (steel ringing). Compare this sequence with Dollard's similar thoughts while playing the piano.

The forever young sirens' sexual energy is conveyed in pulsating lines like these:

When all agog miss Douce said eagerly:

—Look at the fellow in the tall silk.

—Who? Where? gold asked more eagerly.

******

She darted, bronze, to the backmost corner . . .

And the seductive alliterated S's from sirens' song:

Miss Kennedy sauntered sadly from bright light, twinning a loose hair behind an ear. Sauntering sadly, gold no more, she twisted twined a hair.—It's them has the fine times, sadly then she said.

368

The pedestrian, short steps of boots:

> The boots to them, them in the bar, them barmaids came. For them unheeding him he banged on the counter his tray of chattering china.

The connected smooth and resolved sounds for Bloom:

> Bloowhose dark eye read Aaron Fignater's name . . . huguenot name. By Bassi's virgins Bloom's dark eyes went by. Bluerobed, white under, come to me . . .

Bloom goes by the sirens and the language itself is a picture of passing:

> By went his eyes. The sweets of sin. Sweet and the sweets. Of sin.

The rhythm of Kennedy and Douce slowing down in laughter:

> Ah, panting, sighing, sighing, ah, fordone, their mirth died down.

The idle rhythm of the idle Simon Dedalus with nothing to do:

> Into their bar strolled Mr. Dedalus. Chips, picking chips off one of his rocky thumbnails. Chips. He strolled.

The cocky sound announcing Blazes Boylan:

> Jingle jaunty jingle.

This brilliant work goes on and on, in subject, in rhythm, in patterns of repetition, in return to tonic themes. Often the flow reinforces the lyrics just like a Bach Chorale: Listen to Bloom under the spell of music and sex:

> Bloom. Flood of warm jam jam lickitup secretness flowed to flow in music out, in desire, dark to lick flow invading. Tipping her tepping her tapping her topping her. Tup. Pores to dilate dilating. Tup. The joy the feel the warm the. Tup. To pour o'er sluices pouring gushes. Flood, gush, flow, joygush, tupthrob. Now! Language of love.

The episode is full of instances of writing imitating music—it rises and falls, it repeats, it reverses, a phrase is broken up and the parts are repeated and expanded or reduced, and on and on and on. The contrast between the personalities of Douce and Kennedy is emphasized, Douce being like a fast, high tripping melody and Kennedy being slower,

lower and less agitated. The text also repeatedly points to a gold by bronze contrast between them, perhaps major and minor.

Joyce gives as the technique a fugue per canone, a fugue according to a rule. Notice that musical architecture this blends nicely with the concept of Bloom's restraint and repetition of the past. For those of you who want to work on it, a fugue of this type consists of the following sections:

1. opening in which the subject, answer and countersubject are presented in the home key and another key;

2. exposition consisting of a complete statement of subject and answer by all voices;

3. free middle section;

4. climax in which the subject is presented in its most exciting aspect; and

5. coda with a desire for the home key.

My guess is that the subject is the sirens or attraction/distraction/limitation and the answer is Bloom or restraint/compassion. Perhaps Blazes is a countersubject. Just to give you an example, I would give the following thematic pattern for the first 192 lines (when Simon comes in): A-Sirens, B-Bloom, B-Bloom, A-Sirens, B-Bloom and A-Sirens or in musical terms ABBABA. Abba in Aramaic, Jesse's native language, means father and was used by Jesus to address his god. Ba was the soul in Egyptian mythology. The birth of the soul from the father. Blazes leaving the bar to go to Molly is probably the climax, and the blind piano tuner reappears in the coda with a desire for the home key. There's that word key again.

It is hard, at least in the United States, to feel the slow corruption and death in the pub since we don't have as many and fewer visit them. Joyce takes on the pub, a major Irish social institution, with a highly successful use of The Odyssey. As always, the emphasis is the effect on the soul viewed as the world of possibilities or self-realization. The action of the characters remains distinct in memory long after reading the episode. Simon is particularly well drawn, in the death meadow of his own making.

****

ENDNOTES

1. Bloom, H. *The Western Canon* (New York: Riverhead Books, 1995) p. 261.
2. Restuccia, p. 151.
3. Boyle, R. *James Joyce's Pauline Vision* (Carbondale: Feffer & Simon, 1978) p. 10.
4. Graves, Greek Myths, p. 730.
5. Ibid, p. 778.
6. Berard, V. *Les Pheniciens et L'Odyssee* (Paris: Librairie Armand Colin, 1902) vol. II., p. 334.
7. Bowen, Z. *Musical Analysis of the Sirens Episode in Joyce's Ulysses*, Literary Monographs, Vol. 1, edit. by E. Rothstein and T. Dunseath (Madison: University of Wisconsin Press, 1967) p. 254.
8. Bowen, p. 256.
9. Bowen, p. 258.
10. Joyce wrote a poem by this name.
11. Campbell, J. *Transformations of Myth Through Time* (New York: Harper and Row, 1990) p. 165.
12. *Sirens* Encyclopaedia Britannica, 1983 Edition, Micropaedia, Vol. IX, p. 236.
13. Powers, p. 32.
14. Graves, Greek Myths, p. 778.
15. Schwartz, p. 167.
16. Danielou, A. *The Myths and Gods of India* (Rochester: Inner Traditions International, 1991) pp. 188 et. seq. for all of the following material.
17. Campbell, Transformations, p. 112.
18. Gifford, p. 295.
19. Concerning the story of Solomon, all information is from Legends, vol. IV, pp. 160 et seq.
20. Lang, p. 163.

Episode 12 (Cyclops)

Basic Themes
Perspective. Distorted perspective.

With only one eye and no concern for his fellow creatures, Homer's Cyclops has distorted perspective, no depth perception physically and a limited "one I" emphasis spiritually.

Joyce's Cyclops is the anti-Semitic, misogynistic, chauvinistic Irish "Citizen," full of hatred and violence in his xenophobia. His distorted perspective produces blind love for Ireland and blind hatred for everything else. He sits in state in Barney Kiernan's pub in Little Britain Street waiting for the Irish faithful to pledge their allegiance by buying him another drink.

Homer contrasts the Cyclops with Odysseus, whose name derives from Outis (No man) and seus (Zeus or divine or farsighted). This derivation indicates that vision in depth results from dissolution of ego (no man), which in turn brings into focus the individual as part of the unity. In the unity, the separate "I" ego is put out. Joyce contrasts the violent Citizen with Bloom, who expounds the message of universal love and anti-violence.

Many distorted perspectives blur this episode. They include the fiercely held political opinions of the Citizen and the overly critical views of the meanspirited "I" narrator. A second narrator (using a different tone than the "I" narrator) renders the many and long asides, which are distorted by the use of various literary styles inappropriate to the context and content. Textual treatment of much subject matter features either gross reduction or gross exaggeration. The Citizen's connection with the legendary Irish warrior Cuchulain, who could at will expand or contract in size, generally sponsors the distortion.[1]

In this force field of distorted perspective, images from the Old Testament suffer gross reduction. Gentle Jacob's spirituality appears reduced and contained as Jacob's Biscuit tin, which holds free biscuits in the bar. Jacob's ladder, a two-way connection between heaven and earth, appears in anorexic form as a chimney sweep's ladder to remove soot. Ascending the ladder has been a traditional symbol of intensification of consciousness.[2] At the top of Plato's ladder of refining experience, unity is experienced as love and difference as beauty. For the Citizen, however, difference is them and unity is us, them versus us. In this force field of violence, images of Ireland and violence suffer gross inflation. At the grossly exaggerated climax (*klimax* in Greek means ladder) of this episode, the Citizen throws the empty Jacob's biscuit box at Bloom and Bloom ascends to heaven in the chariot of Elijah.

The image of the Cyclops, irrevocably bound by his Paleolithic bestiality to survival cave life, is contrasted with that of Prometheus, a noble creature representative of human development. As interpreted by Shelley, Prometheus not only brought fire to mankind but was the symbol for the renunciation of violence—he was bound to the rock his regenerating liver to be eaten each day only until he renounced his oath of violence against the gods. Here the efforts of Prometheus are signified by those of the chimney sweep; his job is to clean the chimney flue, allowing the open fire of love and preventing in the otherwise soot clogged flue the fires of hate.

As part of the exaggeration, Bloom is presented in the roles of Elijah and the Messiah. Bloom plays the Messiah of universal love to the xenophobic Citizen as Yahweh. In this case, the emphasis is on Yahweh as the xenophobic Jewish tribal god. As Joyce has a character remark, both the tribal Irish and the Old Testament Jews still wait for a redeemer.

Action in The Odyssey

Our lost Greek group, driven by the winds, arrives in the land of the Cyclops. The Cyclops are described, even before the action begins, by an omniscient narrator as follows: they are a "forward and lawless folk," who don't plant but nonetheless enjoy wheat, barley and grapes that grow wild on the land (pre-Neolithic); they herd sheep and goats; and they live in hollow caves, have no councils or oracles of law, care only for their families, if any, and beyond that don't care for each other. In general, the picture is of the psychology of a small survival group—concern is vested not in all humans or all Cyclops or all members of a Cyclops family but just in the one individual Cyclops. The Me Me Me generation of Cyclops. Oddly, there is no mention in his description of their single eye.

The Greeks land on a wooded island near the mainland. They marvel at the undeveloped state of the island, much as would a modern real estate developer. This island (read Ireland or Little Britain) is described as having wild goats, untilled land, an absence of ships (look for the Irish navy), soft meadows, good soil, good harbors, a well of bright water coming from a cave and many poplar trees. Notice this description is based on the Greek's own culture and their own limiting personal perspectives. The next day the Greeks feast on the local goats and imbibe wine they brought with them from a prior landing, where in their own bestiality they killed all the inhabitants. This wine is so strong it has to be mixed 20 water to 1 wine. From the island, the Greeks can see smoke on the mainland and hear human-like voices and sheep. Later we gather that even though the Greeks could see and hear the Cyclops on the mainland, the Cyclops could not see or hear the Greeks on the island. Greeks with vision, Cyclops without.

The next day, spurred on by curiosity, Odysseus and some of his men sail in just one ship to the mainland (read England). Their aim is to "make proof of these men, what manner of folk they are, whether forward, and wild, and unjust, or hospitable and of god-fearing men." This curiosity will kill a number of Greeks. This speech creates unusual perspective, given the fact the omniscient narrator has already told us what kind of men the Cyclops are.

On the sail over to the mainland, the Greeks see a cave roofed over with laurels, with a high outer court built of stones indicating masonry, and surrounded by tall pines and oaks. Even though they haven't arrived yet, the Greeks observe that this cave is occupied by a monster of a man tending sheep and that he is not social with others of his own kind "but dwelt apart in lawlessness of mind." Notice that even though the Greeks can see this detail on the sail over, the Cyclops still can't see the Greek ship.

With 12 men and some of the potent wine (farsighted he is always thinking ahead), Odysseus sets out to determine whether the giant was "like to any man that lives by bread" (that is, by settled agriculture or Neolithic). Arriving at the cave, they find the giant is out and marvel at the evidence of his industry—milk, cheese and young goats and sheep perfectly stored and organized in the cave's interior (order does not guarantee law and order). Note the giant apparently has no family and no significant other. Odysseus's men urge cautious departure with some food, but Odysseus foolishly wants to wait and meet the giant, optimistically counting on the protection afforded by Zeus to visiting strangers. While they wait, the Greeks free load on the giant's cheese.

The giant returns to his cave bearing a log for the fire, shepherds the female goats and sheep inside the cave, leaves the males outside and closes the door by rolling a giant rock into the entrance, apparently from the inside. Odysseus and crew are hidden in the cave and are not detected immediately; the Cyclops doesn't expect company. Finally the giant notices them and asks in the same beautiful language that Odysseus uses, rather than a simple, lusty language we would expect from a lawless giant, who they are and whether they are traders or sea-robbers. Notice that the Cyclops narrows the possibilities based on his own limited perspective.

Terrified by the size of the Cyclops and their trapped condition, Odysseus manages to answer that the sea drove them to this land by the will of Zeus. Feeling the need for help, Odysseus describes Zeus as "the avenger of suppliants and sojourners . . . and the god of strangers." Name dropping, Odysseus mentions Agamemnon. Notice that this response does not explain why they are hiding in the cave and eating the Cyclops's cheese. It also lacks perspective because it assumes that the Cyclops would know and honor Zeus and Agamemnon.

Cyclops responds menacingly that Zeus is paid no heed in the land of the Cyclops. Then the Cyclops gives away his intentions by asking about the location of their ship. Odysseus answers that his ship was wrecked by Poseidon, little knowing that the Cyclops is a son of Poseidon. Apparently in response to taking the name of Poseidon in vain, the Cyclops picks up two Greek crewmen, bashes their brains out and eats them, entrails bones and all. The rest of the Greeks cringe and wail to Zeus, but no avail. After the Greek repast, the gorged Cyclops falls asleep. The cunning Odysseus decides to wait. This delay costs four more Greeks.

In the morning, the giant goes outside to do his chores, a good little giant, leaving the cave mouth closed by the stone. Later he returns for a Greek lunch (two more). After lunch he leaves replacing the stone. Having found a huge club in the cave, Odysseus develops a plan to use the club to blind the one eye of the giant. The club is described as of fantastic size. They cut it down to a fathom's length (only six feet), sharpen the point and harden the point in the fire (you get it—the six foot pencil). They hide the finished weapon under dung in the cave. The Greeks draw four lots as to who with our hero will try the weapon on the giant; being picked apparently means that you are not in the immediate line of fire for the next meal.

The giant returns and this time brings the entire flock into the cave and closes the entrance. He does his chores and then snacks on two more Greeks. Odysseus offers wine in exchange for freedom. This is cunning because Odysseus is in no position to bargain. Without a word, the giant in a macho move gulps down two giant cups of the potent wine undiluted. In demanding the second, the giant extols the gift wine over his local brew with a reference to Zeus bringing rain for the vines; previously he had denied Zeus. He asks for Odysseus's name—alcohol producing the beginning of sociability. With the third undiluted drink, Odysseus gives his name as "Noman," outis of Odysseus means no man in the sense of anonymity. The giant tells Noman that in exchange for his gift of wine, Noman will be the last to be eaten. Happy with his own joke, the unsuspecting beast falls asleep under the influence (BUI) and in his own vomit. The remaining Greeks thrust the spear into the sleeping giant's eye and Odysseus spins it. The gory damage blinding the giant's eye and his blood curdling cries are described in detail.

Other Cyclops hear the cries and gather at the cave's mouth, which is still closed. They ask Polyphemus (we learn the giant's name) what is wrong, complaining that his cries are disturbing their sleep. Notice their limited concern for others. Polyphemus responds that "Noman" is destroying him "not at all by force." Interpreting this response literally that no one is present and from the perspective of a limited desire to help, the Cyclops crowd disperses believing that Polyphemus is ill. Polyphemus, now blind, rolls the stone away from the cave mouth and stretches his arms out across the entrance in an attempt to catch the Greeks as they try to escape. He doesn't ask for help from the other Cyclops, and none is offered. Odysseus and his men wait until the next morning when the flock goes outside according to their normal routine. Then they escape tied between the sheep.

The Greeks quickly drive the sheep to their ships and make a fast get away. On the sail back to the nearby island, Odysseus is unable to restrain his martial ego and yells out to Polyphemus that his own cruel deeds did him in by the law of Zeus. The giant, now acting more like a volcano, tears off the top of the mountain and throws it just in front of their ship, apparently relying just on sound for aiming. The impact of the rock landing in the water washes the Greek ship back to the mainland, but they get away again because the giant can not see to find them.

Back on the water, Odysseus yells out to Polyphemus a second time that he is Odysseus "the waster of cities, son of Laertes," Odysseus in his martial lineage. Polyphemus responds that an oracle had so warned him and invites Odysseus back to give him a proper stranger's greeting and the blessing of Poseidon. Odysseus declines this invitation suggesting that Poseidon heal his eye. Polyphemus prays to Poseidon that Odysseus never make it home or experience loss when he gets there. Polyphemus throws another gigantic rock at their ship that hits in the water just behind them, and this time the resulting wave helps them reach the island haven. Apparently the Cyclopean technology does not include boats. The Greeks pray, bemoan their losses, eat and drink and leave Cyclops Land by oars.

A different source, included in Joyce's permanent library, states that Jupiter cast all the Cyclops into hell because of their fierce and cruel nature. There they made thunderbolts for Jupiter.[3]

Thersites from *The Iliad*

Thersites, a character from *The Iliad*, appears in this episode as the mean-spirited "I" narrator. Famed as the ugliest Greek at Troy, Thersites always complained about everything, not just the military food. Thersites is described as cross-eyed (lack of perspective), lame, hunch backed, and narrow in chest with a long, pointed and mostly bald head. His famous brush with the eyes came after Achilles had wounded the valiant Penthesilea, the female Amazon warrior chief fighting for Troy. Without regard for honor or her valor and beauty, Thersites put out her eyes with his spear as she lay dying. He then laughed at Achilles, accusing him of lacking gall in his liver (remember Prometheus). Achilles killed Thersites with one blow.

The Name Odysseus

The name Odysseus breaks down into Outis or noman and seus. Joyce determined that seus was Zeus, which means divine or farsighted.[4] These characteristics return in Bloom, whose lack of ego fosters the divine or farsighted perspective. The divine in this case is not religious in the traditional sense but an appreciation of the unity of mankind. Acting out of that understanding and appreciation gives "life"—compassion, love and caring. The premium placed on unity invigorates the universal love speech of Bloom in the pub, the heavy references to the life of Jesus and the aside featuring the post-death soul journey as described in the Tibetan Book of the Dead.

Cyclops and Polyphemus

Graves reports Cyclops means ringeyed, as in the view of a volcano from above.[5] Berard is of the view that the word is a combination of eye and surround as with barbed wire.[6] The original pre-Hellenic Cyclops were masons, particularly builders of walls around cities.[7] An admirable symbol for a xenophobe. Polyphemus means famous, in contrast to the anonymity of Odysseus.

Prometheus Bound and Unbound

The original Greek legend of Prometheus as reworked by Aeschylus and Shelley provides important structural supplement for this episode. Prometheus, like Odysseus's name, means farsighted or prophetic.[8]

The basic legend goes as follows. Prometheus served as representative for mankind before the gods. In an offering of a sacrificed animal, he tried to trick Zeus in order to save the best parts for mankind. Punishing Prometheus for mocking the mighty one, Zeus denied fire to mankind, fire being key to their development. Prometheus, with assistance from Athena, stole fire from the sun carrying it to mankind in the pith of a giant fennel. For this insubordination, Prometheus was sentenced by Zeus to eternal punishment, chained to the mountain his regenerating liver eaten every day by a giant vulture.

As part of his spin control, Zeus published the falsehood that Athena had invited Prometheus to heaven for an illicit love affair. The Citizen blames Ireland's woes on an adulteress, Parnell's mistress Mrs. O'Shay. To offset the advantages of the stolen fire, Zeus sent to mankind the beautiful Pandora and her famous jar (not box). She visited Prometheus's brother Epimetheus, whose name means hindsight or afterthought. Forgetting his brother's warning against accepting gifts from the gods, he received her and opened her jar to the lasting distress of mankind. Only hope remained in the jar; it was at the bottom.

The legend as reworked by Aeschylus in *Prometheus Bound* involves further twists. First of all, Prometheus brought to "short lived" humans not only fire but also the power of intellect, which allowed them to cast off superstition and to develop skills. Even bound on the rock, Prometheus was proud of his independence and chided Hermes's acceptance of his role as a mere messenger. Jupiter was to fall, according to a prophecy, unless he could get the secret known only to Prometheus. Fearful of this prophecy, Jupiter traded, setting Prometheus free in exchange for the information that an offspring of the god Thetis was destined to be greater than Jupiter. To avoid the revealed prophecy and save his position, Jupiter arranged for a mere mortal woman to marry the god Thetis and their offspring was Achilles. Aeschylus's rework of the myth provides Joyce's parallel for the saving of the stern and xenophobic Jewish tribal god by Jesus, who was born of a mortal woman and god and preached the radical doctrine of universal love.

In Shelley's version *Prometheus Unbound* (PUB), Prometheus was freed from the rock chains just as soon as he renounced the curse against Jupiter with the line "I wish no living thing to suffer pain." As a model for the image of Bloom, Prometheus is described as "the highest perfection of moral and intellectual nature, impelled by the purest and the truest motives to the best and noblest ends." In his own Preface[9] dealing with influences for the poem, Shelley states the view that the forms in which art is expressed are due more to the minds of the times than the artist's genius, the forms being "the endowment of the age in which they live" and the individual artist's genius "the uncommunicated lightning of (his) own mind." The forms endowed with the times inspire the asides used in this episode. They paint a very sorry picture of this age in Ireland. This very sorry picture is of grossly distorted perspective.

Shelley's lyrical drama contains multiple cross references to the Cyclops chapter of The Odyssey. Volcanoes, earthquakes, tyrannical gods and those "eyeless in hate" make the connection. As Bloom would have it, eternal love triumphs in Shelley's version and tyrannical Jupiter is displaced in a Hollywood ending. According to Mrs. Shelley's notes, this ending reflected the personal philosophy of Shelley—that love should and would conquer and drive out the notion that mankind is partially evil. In one of Shelley's scenes, creatures helping Prometheus arrive in the "car of the hours" from the seat of power. This, I believe, is the ground for the otherwise puzzling references to the "castle car" and the "castle," the seat of political power in Dublin, in the scene in which Martin Cunningham saves Bloom from the Citizen.

These renditions of the Prometheus legend add further fuel to the distortion of perspective by giganticism that marks this episode. These artistic allegories presume to reach by ultimate extension to provide interpretation of the heart of the entire relationship between the gods and humankind. These efforts match the patriotic fervor of the Irish bar flies to conquer the English with an Irish navy.

Traditional Schemata

The traditional schemata given by Joyce for this episode are organ—muscle for violence, art—politics for struggle, color—none, symbol—Fenian ("ourselves alone" for limited survival group outlook), and technique—giganticism for distorted perspective. The correspondences are Noman—the "I" narrator, stake—cigar, and challenge—apotheosis or Bloom's Elijah chariot ride at the end. The Linati lists Galatea, a sea nymph that rejects Polyphemus, and Prometheus.

Time and Place

The time is 5:00 p.m. and the place is Barney Kiernan's pub, the Citizen's normal hangout. Bloom apparently arranged at the funeral to meet Martin Cunningham at this pub at this time in order to help with the life insurance policy for the Dignam family. The pub is near the court house. Like Odysseus's visits to Cyclops territory, Bloom enters the pub twice.

Action in Ulysses and Parallels to The Odyssey

The opening, in the complaining voice of the "I" narrator, is a masterful blend:

> I was just passing the time of day with old Troy of the
> D.M.P. at the corner of Arbor hill there and be damned
> but a bloody sweep came along and he near drove his
> gear into my **eye**. I turned around to let him have the
> weight of my tongue when who should **I see** dodging
> along Stony Barter only Joe Hynes.
>
> Lo, Joe, says **I**. How are you blowing? Did you **see** that
> bloody chimneysweep near shove my **eye** out with his
> brush? [emphasis added]

To whom is the narrator speaking in the first paragraph? Not to Joe. Not to the reader. This is the first distortion in perspective. The first paragraph speaks in the past tense as a narration of a historical event. The second moves into a conversation with Joe constructed in the present. The coupling of these two paragraphs gives a distortion in tense. This distorted opening recalls the odd opening of the related chapter of The Odyssey. The English of this narrator is brutal: "…says Joe…says I."

The "I" narrator has an egocentric orientation. Notice that the first sentence begins with "I" and ends with "eye." The second sentence begins with "I" and contains "I see." This proximity associates "I" and "eye" in the perspective realm, "I" for ego and "eye" for sight that is at best relativistic and confused and in this episode blinded by rage. This is our first "brush" with perspective in this episode.

The chimney sweep and his equipment (long-handled brushes and ladder) introduce the symbolic power of the fire of Prometheus and Jacob's ladder. The near miss of the narrator's eye by the sweep's gear gives us a start on the Cyclops story. The reference to Troy brings in the Trojan war from *The Iliad* and the reference to the D.M.P. (the Dublin Metropolitan police force) brings in force. Blowing (from "How are you blowing?") is for volcano, force and fire.

The complaining "I" narrator is not named, and he is one of our Nomen; there are at least four in the episode. The second narrator of the 33 asides is equally anonymous. The "I" narrator is a bad debt collector with curious notions as to his powers, indicating lack of legal perspective. Inspired by the character Thersites from *The Illiad*, he is meanspirited and complains about everyone and everything. He sponges off others in the bar, but complains that Bloom doesn't buy a round of drinks. He is in the company of the deniers.[10] Let's call him the collector.

The collector first talks about old Troy, identified as a former member of the police force, force being one of our main subjects in love and hate. Then the collector talks to Joe Hynes, who owes Bloom a debt and has just received his salary from the paper for covering the Dignam funeral.

The collector says he is inclined to have the chimney sweep arrested for "obstruction" (read of full vision by limited perspective). Note the suggestive language used: "I'm on two minds not to give that fellow in charge for obstructing the thoroughfare with his brooms and ladders." The phrase "give that fellow in charge" means in one sense arrange for his arrest, charging him. The same phrase also inevitably suggests the powers that be (fellow in charge), particularly Jahweh from the Old Testament who placed Jacob's ladder in the middle of the desert roadway. The thoroughfare or the way in the symbolic realm would be the beatific vision of the unity in the Kingdom. This vision is obstructed by the mean spirit of the collector and by a xenophobic tribal god.

The collector tells Joe he is trying to collect a debt owed by Geraghty the plumber to Moses Herzog the Jewish grocer for the purchase of tea and sugar. Circumcision is mentioned so the debt owed by the gentile to the Jew can be viewed in relation to the debt of the Christians to the Jews—Jesus was a Jew. The groceries not paid for are described as "any God's quantity of tea and sugar," bringing in the theft by Prometheus from the Gods of fire. In the distortion field of this episode, however, fire is in the mundane and reduced energy form of caffeine and calories.

The gentile debtor's defense is that the grocery store is not licensed (read Christians say Jews were delicensed by Christ). This defense may make sense to a plumber, who must be licensed and otherwise can not enforce contracts, and may even be correct in the legal perspective, but it does not make sense in the human one. Then the text proceeds, without warning, to a description by the second narrator in legalese of the court complaint that would be filed by the seller grocer in order to collect the debt. This is an accurate description of such a pleading in the legal realm but is the wrong focus for the action. This aside shares the same subject matter of this part of the episode but not the correct perspective. The legal language in any such lawsuit is not important; this emphasis involves a distortion. That's the whole point of this and, I think, all the asides. Like the Citizen, they miss the main point. Distortion by misemphasis.

The collector and Joe consider charitably paying their respects to an unnamed friend who is in an insane asylum off his head from drinking (mental distortion). Like the liver of Prometheus, the Dublin livers are being eaten every day by booze, which is designed to give a distorted perspective on life. The collector and Joe decide instead on a less charitable program affording more personal entertainment value, to go to Barney Kiernan's pub to tell the Citizen about the discussion on foot and mouth disease at the City Arms Hotel. They pass buildings that reflect British economic and legal control in Ireland. The collector thinks critically about Joe—he is a decent fellow when he has funds, which is rarely. The second aside describes Ireland and its commercial products in overblown terms similar to the description by Homer of the uninhabited island on which the Greek crew stopped. This aside is apparently a parody of the prose used in 19th century translations of Irish poetry and legends.[11] The reference to the land of holy Michan is to St. Michan's parish. In its church, corpses famous for their preservation were found.[12] There the human corpses sleep as they did in life, "warriors and princes of high renown." The Citizen's idol, Parnell, lay there before burial.[13]

The collector and Joe arrive at the Citizen's regular hangout, Barney Kiernan's pub. It features items from famous criminal trials (read Prometheus). They find in his "gloryhole" the Citizen famous for his fierce promotion of Irish causes and for his mangy dog Garryowen. The famous Citizen is the local Polyphemus (means famous) in his cave, his glory hole. As a chauvinistic xenophobe bound by his destructive oath of violence, he is also the spirit of the unredeemed Jewish tribal god. Like the two narrators, the Citizen is never named. He is one of our many nomen; in his case individuality has been engulfed by hatred. He has aggressive ego but not individuality. Like the Cyclops, the Citizen can speak well and learnedly, a distorting contrast between context and text. The Citizen has with him in the pub his papers relating to the Irish question, just as Polyphemus had a well organized cave.

The Citizen, the collector and Joe exchange greetings by using a series of lines, starting with "stand and deliver," which are the secret passwords of the Irish Ribbonmen, a group in opposition to the landlord class of Orangemen (Protestant) in Ireland.[14] To tie the Citizen to the Cyclops, Joyce has the narrator describe the Citizen as follows: "Then he rubs his hand in his eye and says he—What's your opinion of the times?" The phrase "in his eye" is inexact English usage; "one of his eyes" would be proper. The phrase "in his eye" is correct only if the Citizen has only one eye.

The collector is impatient for a beer. He speaks to Joe only a few lines before asking for a drink. Note that while the Citizen never buys, he criticizes Bloom for not buying a round, a projection of his own condition and another failure of perspective. Joe orders a round of three pints, the large size, for the collector, the Citizen and himself. For no apparent reason, the Citizen throttles his dog by the neck. The next aside, in the same 19th century language as the last one, describes an Irish hero with unrelieved exaggeration or giganticism and includes a list of famous Irish heroes. These Irish heroes, with some exaggeration, include Buddha and Napoleon. The Cyclops gulps down the gift beer, betraying his host's generosity.

Joe pays for the three pints with a sovereign. To the collector's question whether he robbed the poor box, Joe ascribes his funds to work and a wheeze (grace on a loan) from Bloom. This generosity the Citizen will choose to forget when he decides to assault Bloom with a deadly weapon. The collector says he saw Bloom looking at fish with his "cod's eye." Joyce signifies projection by this choice of words, that what one sees is often determined by what's inside. A short aside delivers Bloom "the prudent soul" in terms of Irish legend as Rory, Rory O'More having been a reasonable and humane Irish independence leader in the 17th century.[15] He apparently did not allow the ends distort his means.

The Citizen reads the obits and complains that the newspaper (*The Irish Independent*), originally started by Parnell to support Irish independence, now prints the names of British decedents. The Citizen doesn't recognize the human unity even in death. The name of one deceased is Cockburn, which Joe says he knows from bitter experience (venereal disease). A short aside describes in inappropriately radiant romance revival language[16] the arrival of Alf Bergan and the passing in front of the pub of Mrs. and Mr. Breen (the signal for Elijah). Apparently Alf has been eavesdropping on the Breens so he can enjoy the U.P. postcard joke even more. Alf tells the story again, first heard in the Lestrygonians (8th) episode, but is interrupted by the Citizen speaking Irish to the dog ("Bi i dho husht"). This apparently means shut up. They talk about the hanging at Mountjoy (read the crucifixion). Bob Doran, drunk and asleep in the bar on his annual bender, wakes up hearing Alf ordering a pony, a half pint. The beer pull is described in an aside in romance language mixing Irish and Greek legend.

The Citizen notices Bloom outside the pub. Bloom is loitering in front waiting for Martin Cunningham on the charitable mission of keeping the Dignam life insurance proceeds in the hands of the family and away from their creditors. The Citizen refers to Bloom as the "bloody freemason," as the Cyclops were masons and certainly not liberated.

Alf shows letters purportedly from a hangman advertising his services in the most sleazy way and using incorrect English. Bob Doran, waking up, asks who (sic) everyone is laughing at. Alf reports that he thought he just saw Willy Murray (Joyce's uncle's name) with Dignam on the streets and can't believe that Dignam was buried in the morning. This is a distorted reuse of the Jesus resurrection story.

An aside involves contact with Dignam in the land of the dead. It traces in a parodied form of Theosophical language the Bardo journey of his soul down through the chakras. Don't miss the Sanskrit spoofs—talafana for telephone, alavatar for elevator, etc. Dignam's soul,

385

which should be attached to higher matters of the higher chakras, is troubled by mundane matters, the cost of the funeral and the location of a lost boot his son was looking for (stepping into the boots of the father). This aside concludes with an irrelevant Irish epic voice: "fleet was his foot on the bracken."

Dignam's death is mourned and drunken Doran takes the blasphemous position that no good god would have taken Dignam. This comment registers the distorted perspective that god is all powerful and must be good in human terms. Dignam is described by the narrator as a "beam of heaven," echoing Jacob's ladder. Bloom and Christ are associated by placement in the text.

Then the Citizen invites Bloom into the pub, assuring Bloom the dog won't eat him. Bloom asks the bartender if Martin Cunningham has been in (he hasn't). Joe reads one of the letters from the hangman. Joe offers a drink to Bloom, who accepts a cigar instead (the hot spear of Odysseus). Now it is important to understand that Bloom will be accused of not buying a round after Joe has bought him a cigar. However, Joe owes Bloom money, and Bloom has been patient in waiting for payment and gives further extension in the bar. The cigar could reasonably be considered interest.

A mixed romance and biblical aside criticizes hangmen as the "knights of the razor." The pub group next discusses whether capital punishment works. Bloom defends the negative position from the "advanced" perspective that the punishment does not produce deterrence. This annoys the collector, whose perspective is retribution. Racism raises its ugly head as the collector thinks the dog smells Bloom's Jewish odor. The executed's erection (parody the resurrection) is discussed; Bloom explains the "phenomenon" scientifically, and the collector and the group become exasperated with Bloom's didactic inclinations. An aside in medical language gives a flavor of their reaction. Note that "phenomenon" breaks down into pheno (which suggests illuminated gas) and men on, or fire men on. Prometheus and Christ.

Doran tries to get the Citizen's dog to give a paw, the smallest of connections, but is attacked instead. Doran talks about training dogs by kindness and demonstrates this successfully by giving the dog some biscuit crumbs out of the Jacob's biscuit tin. Doran, still drunk, nearly falls on the dog in the process (parody the unity). Bloom and the Citizen argue Irish independence politics while the collector gives us some Bloom history: he lived in the City Arms Hotel; and from the collector's perspective tried to wheedle money out of an old widow, also an occupant of the hotel. The collector can't imagine Bloom helping someone just out of compassion.

Bloom says to the Citizen, "You don't grasp my point," one of many references to points and eyes and objects in eyes. The Citizen fulminates in Irish to the effect that you are either with us or against us, a limited survival group perspective. With this and reflecting loss of head in general, a long aside in a parodied version of the social pages newspaper style reports the execution, by hanging and beheading, of Robert Emmet, the Irish patriot. The social page flavor of the report and the immediate betrayal of Emmet by his sweetheart give this aside the Pangloss tone, or too forgiving or oily.[17] This tone is wrong for a report of an execution. In this aside, the elegantly attired and right proper provostmarshal Tomlinson speaks in the worst Cockney accent, again giving us the contrast between text and delivery vehicle. This aside carries the message that the Irish always betray the Irish. Later we learn that the hypocritical Citizen has himself betrayed the Irish by taking over the leasehold of an evicted Irish tenant.

After more fulminating by the Citizen about the Irish language and more discussion about dog training, the Citizen talks to his dog. An aside written in superficial social page newspaper style reports about a dog reciting his own verse. Joe buys another round, and there is no hint that the Citizen or the collector feels an obligation to reciprocate. Joe uses the phrase "Could you make a hole in another pint," another reference to the Cyclops story. Bloom refuses again and explains his mission concerning the life insurance policy for the Dignam family, mainly the widow. Bloom makes a slip in discussing a legal point in favor of the "wife's admirers," which he corrects to advisers, again reflecting the Irish betrayal theme. Bloom explains the legal point about the priority of the family over the lender-mortgagee of the policy, further increasing the enmity of the collector and others against the perspective of a learned lecturer. The collector remembers, in order to bring him down, that Bloom almost got into serious legal trouble because of selling tickets to the Hungarian privileged lottery.

Drunk Doran asks Bloom to extend his sympathies to the Dignam family, and an aside renders the sympathy conversation in overpolite social jargon. The collector remembers another one of Doran's annual benders when the whores, in referring to his limp penis, asked him if he had an old or a new testament. Bloom's new testament of love is full of blood and life giving energy; the old testament of Citizen Yahweh is wrung out and full of life denying wrath. The pub group continues to discuss local politics, and the Citizen refers to one politician as an "exploded volcano," another old testament to violence. They discuss hoof and mouth disease and again the collector is irritated by Bloom's knowledge and desire to educate. The collector recalls with relish that Bloom lost his job in the cattle trade because he "gave lip to a grazier."

After a bit the conversation turns to Irish sports and the Citizen is toasted as the champion shot putter (for Polyphemus the rock thrower). Against the grain of the conversation, Bloom mentions that violent exercise is not good for everyone, for example rowers. This example brings the subject back to context or perspective. Bloom promotes tennis as good for the eye, since depth perception is critical in tennis. An aside in parliamentaryese parodies the discussion. Then onto boxing organized by Blazes, who won a big bet after spreading false rumors (distortion by disinformation), and more on traitors. An aside in sports page style reports the boxing match (more violence). The boys turn the screw on Bloom by discussing the upcoming concert tour with Blazes as the organizer (organ high her). A short aside in some kind of romance language describes Molly. Calpe is Gibraltar, Molly's origin.

J.J. O'Molloy and Ned Lambert come in, and Ned buys half pints for O'Molloy and himself. The collector muses about O'Molloy's money problems; he recently had to pawn a watch and did so under the false name Dunne (the poet puts time away). They discuss and laugh at Breen, but Bloom, once more against the grain, expresses sympathy for his wife. The Citizen calls Breen and by extension Bloom a half and half, neither fish nor flesh or a "pishogue," not a real man whose proof is in violence. Bloom tries to explain and the bar conversation swirls around the legal aspects of the U. P. post card caper and a recent Canadian swindle case, a fraudulent sale of purported passage to Canada promising a new perspective on life. The forgiving perspective of one Dublin judge for debtors is discussed (read Jesus forgiving sins). An aside features a probate case in which the 12 tribes of Ireland sit Sanhedrin-like as judges, again a reference to a limited survival group perspective and the speedy night trial of Jesus.

The Citizen becomes more and more anti-Semitic in his references to strangers in the house of Ireland, and Bloom tries to avoid further trouble by pretending not to notice, turning the other cheek. He generously tells Joe not to worry about paying off his debt right away and asks for his help with Mr. Crawford on the Keyes ad. They discuss advertisement, and Bloom gives repetition as the secret of success. The Citizen ascribes to an adulteress and a dishonored wife (Parnell's mistress Mrs. O'Shay, an Englishwoman) all the problems of Ireland.[18] This is also a dig at Bloom, to remind him of his wife's reputation.

In an aside in the best romance revival tradition,[19] Knights John Wyse Nolan and Lenehan arrive. They report to the Citizen on the City Council meeting about the Irish language. We wonder why the Citizen didn't attend the meeting. The Citizen becomes more and more xenophobic in relation to England. Lenehan relates his sorrow in not betting on Throwaway, which came in at 20 to 1 (the water to wine mixing proportions in our Greek story). They discuss the other horses, the favorite Sceptre (suggesting royal control) and Zinfandel (suggesting spirit). Lenehan relates that he, Blazes and Blazes's lady friend (later identified as Molly) had bet on Sceptre: "Takes the biscuit, and talking about bunions. Frailty, thy name is Sceptre." These images suggest the Eucharist (biscuit) and the Church are the losers since they produce spiritual frailty. The winner Throwaway suggests loss of ego in compassion.

O'Molloy, the Citizen and Bloom argue law and history, and Bloom stands up to the Citizen with the remark that "Some people . . . can see the mote in others' eyes but they can't see the beam in their own." This combines the metaphor attributed to Jesus and our Greek story of the beam in the Cyclops eye. Note how subtle this remark is. It first of all accuses the Citizen of projection, his own faults onto others. It also says, through the radiant meaning of "beam," that those who criticize others can't find their own radiance, again our connection theme. The Citizen responds "Raimeis," Irish for nonsense, and says "There's no-one as blind as the fellow that won't see, if you know what that means." Won't see as opposed to can't see. He launches into a recitation of the former glories of Ireland, seemingly irrelevant in the context of the discussion, and the resulting pub group lament for the unjust fate of Ireland ends with the hope that at least the trees of Ireland will be saved. This reference leads to an aside on a wooded wedding done in the society page newspaper style with people named for trees. Then we learn from the collector's musings that the Citizen preaches one message but acts another. He is not welcome in Shanagolden where he grabbed the holding of an evicted Irish tenant.

Alf Bergan shows newspaper pictures of other bestial behavior: a head butting match and a negro lynching in "Omaha, Ga." (sic). After a discussion of the need for an Irish navy (now there's an idea) and the punishment of Irish sailors aboard English ships, the narrator issues a mongrelized Lord's Prayer pledging faith in violence and brutality. Bloom objectively suggests that discipline would be necessary in the Irish navy as well, a point the others miss as they are carried away by the patriotically energizing but economically impossible notion of an Irish naval force. After digressions on all the countries that have betrayed Ireland's bid for independence, Bloom weighs in against persecution as perpetuating hatred among nations. Bloom tries to define nation and, of course, errs on the over inclusive side. The boys enjoy a joke about his definition, since on a literal basis it sharply limits the care group to one. The Citizen asks Bloom to name his nation, and to his reply of Ireland the Citizen spits. Part of the spittle hits Joe Hynes, who takes out his handkerchief to dry off. This prompts an overblown aside on the handkerchief in the language of advertisement; this aside misses the point since the handkerchief is not important in the story.

Growing bolder, Bloom claims that his race is being persecuted right that very minute, nearly burning himself with the butt of his cigar. The Citizen tries to characterize this sentiment as Zionism with its negative connotations, that anything which benefits Israel is justified—this of course is the Citizen's position on Ireland. But Bloom lances back with a charge of injustice. John Nolan exhorts Bloom to respond to discrimination with force, to stand up to it like a man. Bloom replies that force never works a permanent solution and is the opposite of life, which is love. Bloom, our Prometheus Unbound, then exits the pub quickly.

The Citizen in his symbolic role as the Jewish tribal god mocks Bloom as the new apostle of universal love and claims that Bloom beggars his neighbor, more projection by the Citizen. An aside in the style of graffiti mocks the many meanings of love as distorted by sentimentality and sexuality.[20] (Joyce's definition of love is the desire of good for another.) In a discussion of the violence done by imperialists against blacks in the colonies, the name Casement is recalled by the Citizen, he the mason and user of stone doors.

With Bloom gone, Lenehan speculates that Bloom has left to collect on Throwaway at 20 to 1, on the logic that Bloom had given him a tip on the horse. Joe says Bloom is "a bloody dark horse himself," again a very true remark from an unlikely source. The pub group grows angry with Bloom since he didn't buy a round even though (they think) he had just won big on the horse race. Joe and the collector go to the bathroom for the famous critical musing by the collector while urinating. He apparently has venereal disease, which causes pain during urination because the exit tube is blocked (like the chimney that needs sweeping). It eventually causes blindness or very distorted perspective.

John Nolan defends Bloom before the inflamed pub group on the grounds that he has advanced ideas that could be used to gain peaceful independence for Ireland. The Citizen, however, wants no part of objective moderation. Martin Cunningham, Jack Power and Crofton arrive in the "castle car" (the name of a tram starting from the political center of Dublin), and their arrival is described in an aside in Shakespearean dialogue. In this aside, the "host" serves the arriving party only after learning they are the king's messengers (read the Jews waiting for their messiah). Cunningham is looking for Bloom, so the conversation about the absent Bloom continues with "wise" Nolan defending him and the Citizen and others attacking. Cunningham bends in the breeze of the conversation flowing against Bloom with this remark: "He's a perverted jew . . . from a place in Hungary and it was he drew up all the plans according to the Hungarian system. We know that in the castle." The Citizen jokingly calls him the new Messiah for Ireland, again the right message in the wrong mouth, and Martin notes that both the Jews and the Irish are still waiting for their redeemer. Now fully committed to hatred, the Citizen attacks Bloom's manhood and the paternity of his children. In spoof religious reporting, an aside describes the many ascetic priests and monks in Ireland (since Bloom the compassionate can't be a real man).

At this point Bloom comes back into the pub preparing to go with Martin and the others on their mercy mission for the Dignam family. The Citizen alerts his dog to attack Bloom, and Martin hurries Bloom out of the pub. A nautical aside reminds us of Odysseus's hurried departure from danger by ship. The Citizen yells at the departing Bloom, "Three cheers for Israel," again the right message but in the wrong mouth. Others try unsuccessfully to restrain the Citizen. Bloom, like Odysseus, yells back that Jesus was a Jew. This totally blinds the Citizen in rage. In the symbolic sub-text, this works either way—the Citizen as a Catholic claiming Jesus as his own or as the Jewish tribal god rejecting Jesus as the Messiah. The Citizen throws the empty Jacob's biscuit box (signifying lack of compassion since empty and parodying the thunderbolt) at the retreating Bloom but misses because the sun (where Prometheus got the fire) is in his eyes (bad vision). His departure and the landing of the tin are burlesqued in asides in state reporting and scientific perspective styles. Discovering his miss, the Citizen sends his dog after Bloom.

Now we know that Bloom will not be hit because he lives in the fourth chakra of the heart, which means "not hit." Stephen will, by contrast, be hit in a later episode before his Bloom-inspired conversion. The presence of Bloom in this chakra is indicated directly by his love speech and his charitable actions on behalf of the Dignam family. The Connector Fact for the fourth chakra is Israel, whose six-pointed Star of David, made by two interlocking triangles, is the same as the pictorial version of the fourth chakra. The upward pointed triangle stands for aspiration, for Bloom and the amplification of the spiritual life, and the downward pointed one is for inertia and the boys in the pub. They are arguing, as the triangles are interlocked. In addition, the smoke from Bloom's cigar produces the smoke color associated with this fourth chakra. The wish fulfilling aspect of the fourth chakra is parodied in the absurd desires for Ireland, such as an Irish Navy.

In the last aside parodying the perspective of the Bible, Bloom's departure is described in the vestments of the Elijah legend. Even this, though, must lose and confuse its perspective:

> And they beheld Him even Him, ben Bloom Elijah, amid clouds of angels ascend to the glory of the brightness at an angle of fortyfive degrees over Donohoe's in Little Green street like a shot off a shovel.

This is the climax of the episode as Elijah as the son of Bloom (ben Bloom Elijah) climbs to the heavens. Elijah is the son of Bloom since the spirit of Elijah proceeds from the compassion of Bloom.

Parallel to the Mass and Hairy Man

The Gold Cup race and Jacob's biscuit box further the tie of pub to church. The biscuitbox is a reflection of the container of the viaticum, the Eucharist administered to the ill.[21] This pub communion is for the spiritually ill.   One of the asides is a parodied form of the Commemoration of the Saints in the Mass, which comes just before the Consecration. In Joyce's parody of the Commemoration, scores of Saints and other Church dignitaries parade from nearby Nelson's pillar to Barney Kiernan's pub. In the spirit of giganticism, the description of the procession includes instances of all important Catholic religious modes: Saints, rituals, sacred objects, symbols and so on. Coded in the names of the parading saints are those of all the participants in the pub, even the dog Garryoven who appears as S. Owen Caniculus.

In Zoroastrianism, the forces of light (Ahura Mazda) contend with the forces of darkness (Ahriman or Angra Mainyu). The Citizen can be viewed as Ahriman, which in *Finnegan's Wake* becomes "hairy man." The Citizen in one of the asides is described as ". . . covered . . . with a strong growth of tawny prickly hair in hue and toughness similar to mountain gorse (Ulex Europeus)." As Angra Mainyu (angry man you), he creates evil and strife.

Purification

Bloom's experience with the Citizen is described in a later episode in terms of Jewish ritual as the holocaust, an exaggerated description of Bloom's anti-Semitic experience. The holocaust was a special kind of animal sacrifice to Jahweh. It involved burning the entire animal for sacrifice, as opposed to reserving part of the animal for personal consumption (the issue in the Prometheus myth). The holocaust describes Bloom's anti-Semitic experience with the Citizen whose rage is all consuming.

Proper focus is the lesson in aesthetics.

Art, Structure and Aesthetics

I might as well get it off my chest right away. I don't like the asides. They seem to be more writing showoff than integral members of this artistic group. As parts, they don't contribute enough to the whole to justify their magnitude and their distraction from the action. In my view, they more disrupt rather than contribute to integritas because there are too many. We could try to save them through the analysis that they are strangers like the Greeks in the land of the Cyclops or that they are designed to produce the very turbulent result of which I complain, as symbolic of the results of distorted perspective. But there are just too many of them and they are too long.

The conceptual connection is the striking feature of this episode. The trunk theme which holds the episode together and from which all branches hang is the notion of perspective, which is fashioned in the "eye – I" couplet.

The pub talk is wonderful and highly convincing as high Dublin slang. The portrait of the Citizen is priceless. The unusually detailed connection with the trials of Odysseus produces a rich result.

****

ENDNOTES

1. Schwartz, p. 37.
2. Frye II, p. 85.
3. Bacon, F. *The Wisdom of the Ancients* (Montana: Kessinger Publishing Co., no date) p. 207.
4. Ellmann, James Joyce, p. 61.
5. Graves, Greek Myths, p. 757.
6. Berard, p. 115.
7. Graves, Greek Myths, p.238.
8. Gifford, p. 314.
9. All Shelley cites are from *The Complete Poems of Percy Bysshe Shelley* (New York: The Modern Library, 1994) pp. 225 et. seq.
10. Ellmann, R. *Ulysses on the Liffey* (Oxford: Oxford University Press, 1972) p. 110.
11. Gifford, p. 316.
12. Gifford, p. 317.
13. Schwartz, p. 54.
14. *Joyce's Ulysses Notesheets in the British Museum*, edit. P. Herring (Charlottesville: University Press of Virginia, 1972) p. 19.
15. Gifford, p. 326.
16. Critical Essays, p. 274.
17. Ellmann, Ulysses on the Liffey, p. 111.
18. In the Notes to *Exiles*, Joyce says "The two greatest Irishmen of modern times—Swift and Parnell—broke their lives over women. And it was the adulterous wife of the King of Leinster who brought the first Saxon to the Irish coast.
19. Critical Essays, p. 275.
20. Critical Essays, p. 275.
21. Lang, p. 163.

Episode 13 (Nausicaa)

Basic Themes

The Prelude to Procreation casts its illusory spell.

Young and most eligible Gerty MacDowell yearns and burns in her consuming quest for romance and marriage.[1] Prone to hormone driven illusions, she all too quickly clothes Bloom, who is intently watching her on the beach, in the raiment of a uniquely gallant, intellectual and sensitive knight. Consumed by her Prelude, she lifts her skirt to reward his admiring gaze with a revelation of her grail.

Gerty folds the unlikely Bloom into the misty vapors of her marriage dream and knowingly excites him sexually. Watching her expose her bloomers, Bloom masturbates to ejaculation in synch with the rise and fall of a roman candle in a local fireworks show.

Consumed by this romantic illusion, Gerty fails to perceive the stark reality of marriage, even though it is right in front of her. In her immediate presence are three quarreling and demanding children, tended by her two friends Cissy and Edy. Gerty's illusory romantic yearns and burns are served in a parody of mediocre art,[2] the style of romance pulp fiction. Joyce said, *"Nausikaa* is written in a namby-pamby jammy marmalady drawersy . . . style with effects of incense, mariolatry, masturbation, stewed cockles, painter's palette, chitchat, circumlocutions, etc etc....."[3]

These romantic sentiments born of genetically hardwired passions blackmail Gerty's soul. To continue the species she must be blinded to her individual self potential, the "great sacrifice." Gerty is lame in the leg resulting from a chance "fall," which restricts her freedom compared to the fleet tomboy Cissy, who is less interested in males. Lameness from a fall suggests original sin from the First Fall in the Garden of Eden. Since the First Fall created time and death and the resulting necessity for sex, her lame but most shapely leg advertises the age old necessity for procreation.

In dealing with her personal version of the curse from the Fall, Gerty is comforted by Eve's romantic successor, the Virgin Mother, the symbol of motherhood everywhere. A nearby chapel dedicated to the

Virgin in her role as the Star of the Sea (protector of seamen) issues music that wraps serpentine-like around the experiences of Gerty and Bloom. The Virgin protects seamen while Bloom kills semen. The association of the Virgin Mother with Gerty places the Virgin Mother in the position of an illusory "come on" for the Church, a trap for the emotional and sentimental.[4] In Joyce's view, the comforting Virgin Mother is an illusion since Jesse's announced relation to God, and thus the Church's relation to God, is built on the much more difficult relationship of father and son.

Bloom writes in the sand "I AM A," a phrase which contains "ama" or love in Latin, "Ma" for mother and "Ma" the Sanskrit root meaning to construct or exhibit contained in maya for illusion. The projected illusion of young feminine charm yields to the reality of children as ma is contained in maya. The projected illusion of permanent sexual virginity in the Holy Mother yields to the reality of blood letting, her correspondingly necessary menstrual discharges and the passion of Jesus her son.

While Gerty loses soul to sentimentalism, Bloom loses soul to "realism." This long distance sexual experience constricts Bloom's normal compassion. In his post-emission mood, Bloom reduces Gerty to a depersonalized sex object. As Bloom achieves tumescence of his sexual organ, the blood is missing from his heart. He makes fun of her lameness and blames her for his now sticky shirt. While Gerty seems likely to return to the same spot the next day in hopes of furthering their relationship, he won't be there for her. As Bloom has ejaculated, he has once again failed in the will power and responsibility department to bring the male to Molly. He rationalizes his self-indulgent action as necessary to relieve seminal fluid build up, but each such limited personal satisfaction makes easier avoiding the issue of sex with Molly and having another son.

The Hindu gods of the world dream and the destroyer of illusions make veiled appearances in order to reinforce these basic themes strongly suggested by the Nausicaa chapter of The Odyssey. Bloom and Stephen begin to close as Bloom on Sandymount Beach picks up a piece of notepaper that could be the same one Stephen dropped in the Proteus (3rd) episode. Both mock the vital essence, Stephen by leaving a dried booger on the rocks and Bloom by leaving dying semen in his shirt.

Action in The Odyssey and Some Parallels

Odysseus is asleep on the beach after his harrowing escape from Calypso's island. He has come ashore in the land of the Phaeacians, the sea going folk. They are now defended by the isolation of their island and their superior sailing abilities. On their civilized island they have built walls and temples and measured out their lands. They are now led by the wise Alcinous, who has a beautiful daughter (sound like a fairy tale yet?).

While asleep in the castle under the watchful eyes of two handmaidens (Gerty is with two friends), the beautiful princess Nausicaa is visited in a dream by Athena in the guise of a young girl. Athena plants duty guilt in Nausicaa with respect to the family clothes she has neglected to care for ("shining raiment") and convinces Nausicaa this duty is important in terms of her reputation among her future in-laws. Gerty is also hard wired to get married and have children. Athena tells Nausicaa her maiden status will not last long. Athena even suggests that she go to the washing area by mule since that is more seemly. Notice the care for the opinions of others, which results in a significant loss of soul freedom.

Athena leaves for Olympus, which is described in terms of perfect weather (what an absurdly romantic notion!). Nausicaa "of the fair robes" (our Gerty is a smart dresser) awakens to review the dream with her parents. Wise Alcinous understands his daughter's matrimonial driven desire to wash the clothes of her five brothers and heartily agrees to furnish the wagon and mules for the project. Nausicaa with her "handmaidens" (Bloom has his own) and provisions by Mom start out with Nausicaa driving. Listen to the romantic presentation:

> . . . while the maiden brought forth from her
> bower the shining raiment. This she stored in the
> polished car, and her mother filled a basket with all
> manner of food to the heart's desire, dainties too she
> set therein . . . Then Nausicaa took the whip and the
> shining reins, and touched the mules to start them; then

398

there was a clatter of hoofs, and on they strained without flagging, with their load of the raiment and the maiden. Not alone did she go, for her attendants followed with her.

Now when they were come to the beautiful stream of the river, where truly were the unfailing cisterns, and bright water welled up free from beneath, and flowed past, enough to wash the foulest garments clean . . .

Everything is just dandy. Note in this romantic presentation that the inclusion of detail is relevant only from the point of view of how good little Nausicaa is feeling. The romantic is personal.

The girls, including the Princess, wash the clothes in the "black water" and "in busy rivalry" (our Dublin girls will joust). Environmentally sensitive, they clean the pebbles afterwards. After their own bath and lunch, they play with a ball that lands in the stream and is "swept away" (not a quote). Their resulting cries awaken our hero who, because he recently washed ashore, is naked and covered with white sea foam and salt, providing the connection for seamen and semen. Hearing female voices, Odysseus covers himself with a branch (Adam in the garden post-Fall) and "sallies forth like a lion . . . with blazing eyes." Bloom's eyes are hungry. Bold Nausicaa does not flee from Odysseus's savage appearance. Odysseus wisely decides to praise her rather than "grasping her knees" in supplication; notice violence is not an alternative considered, even though the clothes of her brothers are there for the taking. A good choice for a young girl thinking about marriage. Odysseus briefly explains his situation and extols her beauty, wishes her success in marriage and home, and asks for a garment. This approach works, and Nausicaa "of the white arms" advises him of her royal status (good for protection), calls from hiding her handmaidens and provides him bathing supplies and some of shining raiment to wear. These are royal robes, probably sea-purple.

The clean and clothed Odysseus sits down discretely apart. Nausicaa and her handmaidens are moved by his beauty and grace (he cleans up well!). Nausicaa says: "Would that such an one might be called my husband, dwelling here, and that it might please him here to abide! But come, my maidens, give the stranger meat and drink." Gerty is equally quick to embrace the idea of marrying Bloom based on physical appearance alone. Getting ready to go back, Nausicaa "has another thought" and asks Odysseus, in the interests of her reputation, to walk behind the wagon with the handmaidens and when they get close to town to stop and wait in a sacred grove. In this speech, we learn about the Phaeacian culture: a temple to Poseidon furnished with heavy stones is set in the earth near the harbor where each man has his mooring for his very own black ship, the symbol of the identity of the Phaeacians; and they "care not for bow nor quiver, but for masts, and oars of ships, and gallant barques . . . ." She further recommends that after waiting awhile, he enter the city by himself and seek out the Queen. Odysseus complies.

Athena shrouds Odysseus in a mist (Joyce's episode is filled with mirages and illusions). The mist allows him to make a stealthy entrance and avoid curious questions; he must look different from the locals. Athena, disguised as a young maid with a water pitcher, leads him to the palace and directs him to Queen Arete (remember aesthetic arrest), who married Alcinous her Uncle. She is famous for ending feuds (peace by Mary). The palace thresholds are of bronze, the walls brazen with a blue frieze and the doors gold and silver hued. Golden hounds astride the doors guard against death and age, the fall out from the Fall in the Garden. The Phaeacian women are masters at the loom; our Gerty embroiders her own panties. The local trees bear fruit all year long, as Gerty does each month. The mist falls off Odysseus just as he supplicant on his knees directs a prayer to Queen Arete for help in getting home. An advisor to the King suggests that Odysseus should not "sit upon the ground in the ashes by the hearth" but should be treated royally. The King raises him by the hand and puts him in a Prince's chair. Odysseus goes on to tell his story. The Phaeacians help Odysseus get home, and Poseidon punishes them.

Names

Samuel Butler published the view that Nausicaa is a self-portrait of the female author of The Odyssey. He based this view on the inclusion in the text of intimate knowledge of court life and the "preponderance of female interest." This same preponderance of interest informs the opinions of the narrator in this episode. Graves notes that by contrast to most of the other episodes, this one does not deal with an allegorical death.[5] Ulysses means thigh wound, and later we learn that Odysseus has survived such a wound, a common form of royal death.[6] Odysseus has a royal thigh wound, Gerty is lame in the leg from a "fall," and Bloom's sex life is limited to masturbation.

Gerty MacDowell has the first name Gertrude, the same as Hamlet's mother. She usurped honor for lust as Gerty usurps self for marriage. The episode contains several quotes from *Hamlet*. Gerty's full name is derived from a sentimental novel *The Lamplighter*.[7]

Wordsworth

As with Shelley in the last, the spirit of Wordsworth perfumes this episode. His sentimental poetry is one target of the mock sentimental presentation of Gerty and her thoughts.

Wordsworth's spirit makes a cameo appearance as an elderly man walking on the beach. He is described by one of the girls as "the man that was so like himself" (romantics write about themselves). Bloom describes him from a different perspective: the "nobleman . . . Blown in from the bay . . . Enjoying nature now . . . government sit (sinecure) . . ." Wordsworth the noble poet moved back and forth to and from France, extolled nature and his own personal reactions to it, and ended with a government job (sinecure) for the County of Westmorland distributing stamps.[8] Like Molly's father's corner in stamps, Wordsworth's monopoly position on stamps in his County suggests the limitations of the personal and romantic mode.

As you read this episode, remember that Wordsworth wrote *Ode to Immortality* (about children sporting on the shore), *An Evening Walk*, *The Cuckoo* and especially the *Lyric Poems* , which contained an experiment in the poetical use of the language of conversation of the middle and lower classes (our Gerty). Features from these poems are coded into the text.

Virgin Mary and Not So Maiden Leda

In Catholic theory, the Virgin Mary is conceptualized as the second Eva or Eve. In biblical typology, Mary came to Eve and Jesus came to Adam to purify the original couple. Eva reverses to Ave in Ave Marie for the Virgin Mother. Since Eve was the chosen instrument of the snake, this episode makes frequent references to devils, snakes and other reminders of the Garden. Bloom thinks of young Gerty as a green apple.

In the Catholic view, Mary conceived the child Jesus by the intervention through her ear by the Holy Ghost, "Big he and little she." Joyce castigates this view as sentimentally and romantically illusory. Compare the gentle story of the Virgin's ear tickle with the dramatic and violently realistic description in Yeats's poem (*Leda and the Swan*) of the conception by full carnal copulation between the human Leda and Zeus in the form of a swan:

A sudden blow: the great wings beating still

Above the staggering girl, her thighs caressed

By the dark webs, her nape caught in his bill,

He holds her helpless breast upon his breast.

The progeny from this violent carnal coupling included the battling twins Castor and Polydeuces, reflected in the contentious twins Tommy and Jacky. Poseidon made Castor and Polydeuces the saviors of shipwrecked sailors,[9] a subject encountered in the episode and a duty taken over by the Virgin as Star of the Sea. For her maternal service, Leda was deified as the goddess Nemesis, the meaning of whose name is reflected in every mother's soul sacrifice.

In this episode, the white dove of the Holy Ghost is replaced by the black bat, the symbol of murderous sentimentality. Joyce apparently suggested to Budgen a painting for this episode that showed the bat superimposed on a roman candle trail connecting Bloom and Gerty.[10]

First Word, First Letter and Traditional Schemata

The first letter is a capital **T** in the first word "The." The word "the" standing alone is a dead object in the English language. Like a woman intent on marriage, it can take life only from those words close to it. Joyce told Louis Gillet that he had decided to end *Finnegans Wake* with the word "the" because it was "the least accented, the weakest word in English, a word which is not even a word, which is scarcely sounded between the teeth, a breath, a nothing."

The traditional schemata given by Joyce for this episode are organ—eye and nose, art—painting, color—gray and blue (for chastity, the Virgin and hope), symbol—virgin, and technique—tumescence and detumescence. Correspondences: Phaeacia—Star of the Sea chapel; and Nausicaa—Gerty. The Linati scheme lists as additional persons handmaidens, Alcinoos, Arete, and Ulysses and the sense or meaning as "the projected mirage."

Action in Ulysses

The hour is about 8:00 p.m. Bloom is killing time on Sandymount Beach because he can't go home yet. Blazes could still be there. He is near the spot on the beach where Stephen composed poetry in the Proteus (3rd) episode. Bloom has just come from the Dignam residence in Sandymount and charitably helping the family with the insurance policy, which he did after leaving the Citizen. He drank cider at the Dignam home and urinated behind a wall on the way to the beach. He is tired.

Three young girls are near Bloom on the beach. Two of the young girls, Cissey Caffrey and Edy Boardman, are caring for Cissy's younger brothers, difficult 4 year old twins Tommy and Jacky, and one smiling and vomiting baby Boardman. The third young girl, Gerty, is slightly removed from them and not involved with the children. She is daydreaming in illusory sentimental terms about boys and getting married. She doesn't think about children, even though examples are right in front of her, or abusive husbands, even though her father was.

Also nearby is a chapel dedicated to the Virgin Mary as Star of the Sea, her role to save seamen. Her name in this capacity is *Maria Maris Stella*. This name originally started with the meaning of Mary "as a drop of water from the sea" (*Maria Stilla Maris*). Over time and through several translators, drop (*stilla*) became star (*stella*).[11] Notice that Bloom's drops of semen are associated with the star of the roman candle.

So right on the surface of the episode are the mirages and illusions that lead to marriage and the stark reality of family life, bawling and fighting children and abusing husbands, and the comforting religious illusion created by the most famous of all mothers.

The episode opens thus:

The summer evening had begun to fold the world in its mysterious embrace. Far away in the west the sun was setting and the last glow of all too fleeting day lingered lovingly on sea and strand, on the proud promontory of dear old Howth guarding as ever the waters of the bay, on the weedgrown rocks along Sandymount shore and, last but not least, on the quiet church whence there streamed forth at times upon the stillness the voice of prayer to her who is in her pure radiance a beacon ever to the stormtossed heart of man, Mary, star of the sea

This obviously sentimental presentation is typical of romantic pulp fiction. It features alliteration, which like romanticism and Gerty call attention to themselves. The letter alliterated is S, whose soft hiss sound suggest the hidden presence of the serpent. The mood of the quoted language is drugged languor. It promises embraces, glows, love, protection, purity and radiance. Its purring tone reflects Homer's Nausicaa chapter and is typical of Wordsworth. The sunset blushes and Gerty blushes, the ultimate sexual come on to be mimicked by her cosmetics. Compare this sunset blush mood with the following dead-pan opening line from Beckett : "The sun shown, having no alternative, on the nothing new."[12]

The evening folding the world in an embrace is basically meaningless, as is most sentimental literature. Only the mood counts, and mood counts only in the zone of the personal. The rest of the first paragraph alludes to the primary personal tools, the genitalia: the promontory the mons veneris, the lighthouse on it the penis, the weedgrown rocks the male pubic hair and testicles and the quiet church the vagina. They are close to Cock Lake. This initial emphasis on the personal reflects Nausicaa's interests and Gerty's daydreams. The initial emphasis on the sexual reflects the emphasis in the case of the Holy Mother on her virgin genitalia, her holy hole. And this is no minor matter; it is the human copying machine.

Compare the opening lines of this episode with the opening from George Eliot's *The Mill on the Floss*, a romantic novel about denial of opportunities to a girl:

> "A WIDE PLAIN, where the broadening Floss hurries on between its green banks to the sea, and the loving tide, rushing to meet it, checks its passage with an impetuous embrace."

Note the similar tone in the Catholic prayer to Mary as Star of the Sea:

> O thou who findest thyself tossed by the tempests in the midst of the shoals of this world, turn not away thine eyes from the Star of the Sea, if thou wouldst avoid shipwreck.

Compare also Wordsworth's *Tintern Abbey:*

> For I have learned
> To look on nature, not as in the hour
> Of thoughtless youth; but hearing oftentimes
> The still, sad music of humanity,
> Nor harsh nor grating, though of ample power
> To chasten and subdue. And I have felt
> A presence that disturbs me with the joy
> Of elevated thoughts: a sense sublime
> Of something far more deeply interfused,
> Whose dwelling is the light of setting suns,
> And the round ocean and the living air,
> Blue sky, and in the mind of man:
> A motion and a spirit, that impels
> All thinking things, all objects of all thought
> And rolls through all things.

For Joyce, the sad music of humanity is the inbred desire to continue the species. This music dominates the last episode of his novel, as Molly's thoughts speak the will to life.

The next material in the episode introduces Cissy Caffrey and Edy Boardman (read bored of man) and their normal children charges. The twins Tommy and Jacky are wearing sailors hats bearing the name H.M.S. Belleisle, or His Majesty's ship named Beautiful Island. This name echoes the paradisiacal conditions in Olympus as described by Homer and in the pre-Fall Garden of Eden. Sandcastles for the twins and pretend games to mollify the baby begin training in illusion at an early age.

The descriptions with respect to the children as "sufferers," "apple of discord," "headstrong" and "selfwilled" suggest the reality of family life as an echo of the exercise of free will by the original couple in the Garden. Since the discord in "apple of discord" is over a sand (pretend) castle, the creation of illusions is indicted as part of the original sin.

Gerty is initially presented in a conspicuously delayed entrance. The question "But who was Gerty?" announces her. This theatrical entrance focuses on the issue of her identity—mother or individual. Gerty is first seen "lost in thought." Gerty apparently doesn't want, as far as any male prospects are concerned, to be associated with the children. She is described in cloying terms by reference to the opinions of others. She has an unusually white complexion, a Connector Fact for Nausicaa of the white arms. Gerty is concerned with her menstrual discharges. She combines in unstable combination the boldness and disobedience of Eve and the reticence and obedience of Mary ("Inclination prompted her to speak out: dignity told her to be silent"). She can not stand anything unsavory, but at the same time her energy is devoted to improving her looks, clothes and "chances" according the dictates of fashion magazines. These minor inconsistencies are multiplied several fold in the book-ending image of Molly.

Beyond the boundaries of marriage prospects, her soul seems to be missing and her possibilities restricted. Later in this episode a bat flies around—the bat as the symbol of the spirit and linked to murderous sentimentality. Her grandfather Giltrap owned a dog named Garryowen (also the name of the dog with the Citizen in the last episode), associating Gerty's matrimonial desires with dependent dog-like limitations.

Gerty is tied to the Virgin Mary through their common choice of blue for personal accent and the waxen pallor of their faces. Since Mary is famous as a mother and Gerty yearns for marriage, their predetermined roles as mothers and the resulting constriction of their individual soul realization (the "great sacrifice" and "Two sweet to be wholesome") registers the gender based fall-out resulting from the Fall in the Garden. In this state, she trusts to "fate," the philosophical counterpart of dependence. Her current boyfriend Reggy Wylie (read why lie or accept illusions) had been riding up and down in front of her house on his freewheel bicycle. But his father now keeps boyfriend Reggy indoors studying to get into Trinity (!!!). Gerty thinks only of Reggy's good points, as the romantic mist narrows her field of vision and judgment. She remembers their first kiss but missed the reality inherent in Reggy's remark right afterward about getting "refreshments."

Gerty lavishes much attention at her female shrine, spending considerable time and trouble on her fancy panties. She dyes them blue. They are called "undies" for not dies, the human copying machine. Like a good little copying machine, she daydreams sentimentally of embraces (not pounding sex) and wedded bliss in her comfy and cozy little home without (despite their immediate presence) any provision for the sufferings and noise of children. She wears a hat of "nigger straw," for an association with the dead souls in the Wandering Rocks Episode and the prostitute in the Sirens episode. Gerty has sold her soul to marriage prospects, giving marriage an aspect of a commercial bargain. In these circumstances, the institutions of prostitution and marriage share fundamentals. Her black straw hat is trimmed with a "slightly shopsoiled" eggblue chenille, another reference to the dirt of original sin coming through Mary's pure blue.

In the middle of Gerty's thoughts, the benediction service sounds at the nearby chapel. A benediction service does not include the consummating mass. As Mary was impregnated by the Holy Ghost through the ear (the "Jew Bang"), so Bloom and Gerty experience the service in Mary's chapel through sound:

> And then there came out upon the air the sound of voices and the pealing anthem of the organ. It was the men's temperance retreat conducted by the missioner, the reverend John Hughes S.J., rosary, sermon and benediction of the Most Blessed Sacrament

407

. . . the old familiar words, holy Mary, holy virgin of virgins. How sad to poor Gerty's ears!

Hear staccato sounds of the organ in these words: "And then there came out upon the air . . . ." The organ of the ear, the Virgin Mary pun. Men's temperance in Dublin is tied to virginity. Gerty doesn't like the sound of permanent virginity. She is ready for the sacrament of sex. Gerty's drunken father beating her mother doesn't disturb her marriage vision.

Sure enough, one of the twins kicks a ball down to Bloom's location, as the ball swept away from Nausicaa toward Odysseus. Bloom tries to throw it back to Cissy, but it Falls short and " it rolled down the slope and stopped right under Gerty's skirt near the little pool by the rock." What a coincidence, a ball, a rock, and a pool under her skirt, given what is about to happen. Bloom is described by the Gerty influenced narrator as a gentlemen and gallant. Gerty tries to kick the ball to Cissy but she misses (her lame leg), and Cissy says "If you fail try again" (have sex until you conceive).

At this point Gerty takes her first direct look at Bloom, and notices his "saddest" expression. The song to the Virgin wafts in another mirage—that Mary never abandoned anyone who asked for her help. The baby tries to say pa pa, but instead says ha ja. This baby, like all others, is above average. After urinating, the baby says Ha ba (remember this when we get to the bat). The children are getting on Gerty's sensitive nerves.

Gerty is pleased to detect Bloom staring at her. She starts to think about him, and in the flush of his interest she emphasizes only his good points. Before long, she is already thinking, "It was he who mattered and there was joy on her face because she wanted him because she felt instinctively that he was like no-one else." This is the female human copying machine gearing up for action; it reduces individuation to sexual selection in preparation for copies to be collated. She immediately idealizes him, Gerty's form of tumescence, and thinks of their embrace. The maternal process having been stimulated, she wants to comfort him (like the Virgin).

The sounds coming from the chapel remind Gerty of her confession of sexual yearnings, which the priest blessed as natural. She has been trying to synchronize her yearnings with the teachings of Catholicism.[13] Now the twins are really bothering her. She refers to them as "Little monkeys common as ditchwater." The primate unity. Gerty thinks in critical terms about Cissy running to show off (she is not lame) and her limited appeal to males. Gerty's critical attitude in this regard shows that the female human copying machine is single-minded in its objectives. This critical attitude reaches full amplitude in Molly's reveries in the last episode. The chapel prayers to Queen Mary resume. The Host is being prepared with a chant in Latin of "Falling in adoration down," tying to lameness and original sin the need for the Host that continuously saves us.

Using classic body language, Gerty takes off her hat and lets down her wonderfully full and sensuous hair. Bloom responds with a "swift answering flash of admiration." Influenced by Gerty's thoughts, the narrator says Bloom is eyeing her "as a snake eyes its prey." This casts Bloom as the snake. Gerty blushes a glorious rose, the color of the summer sunset. The word "caricature" is used. Because of Gerty's suggestion that the others leave because of the late hour (so Gerty can be alone with Bloom), Cissy goes down and asks "Uncle Peter" (Bloom) for the time. Noticing that he takes his hand out of his pocket to reach for his watch, Gerty thinks that Bloom has enormous control over himself (since he didn't keep on rubbing). This is the first inkling that Gerty knows that Bloom is masturbating while watching her. Bloom stops watching Gerty in order to look at his watch. Bloom's watch has stopped at 4:30, the time when you know what happened to Molly. Cissy reports to Gerty that Uncle Peter's "waterworks" are out of order; while this is meant by Cissy to refer to his timepiece or his watch, the full meaning of this expression also feeds on the mutual exclusivity of urination and ejaculation.

Further idealizing Bloom and continuing the ear penetration theme, Gerty thinks his voice is cultured. In the chapel, one of the candles nearly burns the flowers, an image of the heat of sexual attraction that leads to fireworks, the famous roman candle. At the same time,

Bloom winds up his watch. Gerty watches Bloom put his hands back in his pockets and feels her menstruation coming on. Note the connection between masturbation and menstruation. As he masturbates, she swings her foot faster. Her blush increases, and Bloom is "literally worshipping at her shrine."

Departure preparations by the other two girls mingle with images from the benediction service. The presiding father has to read his lines from a card. The other girls tease Gerty about her lost boyfriend Reggy. Referring indirectly to her new candidate Bloom, Gerty answers loud enough for him to hear, "I can throw my cap at who (sic) I like because it's leap year." Again the hat serves as a spiritual manifestation. The bell rings for the Host in the chapel as the father wearing a veil (read illusion) gives the benediction with the Host in his hand. This service stops with the Host in the father's hand short of the consummating mass, just as Bloom's masturbation by hand equally lacks consummation and leaves the human Host in his shirt.[14] Likewise, Gerty's menstruation leaves her birth potential in her blue undies.

A bat flies from the resounding belfry into the night air and makes a "tiny lost cry." Gerty doesn't think about the bat. The bat is the dark side of the Holy Ghost, which pictured as a dove is released when the Son is present; in the middle ages, the black bat symbolized black magic and darkness; and in Egypt as ba (which our baby has already uttered and Bloom says later), it symbolized the separate soul. For me, the bat is the lost soul of Gerty and every other woman to whose maternal functions her soul possibilities have been sacrificed. Even to Jesus, Mary related primarily as a mother. To link the bat and its "tiny lost cry" with Gerty's lost soul, we read of "the cry of a young girl's love, a little strangled cry . . . that has rung through the ages."

Gerty is interested in romantic poetry and novels. She even would like to paint a picture, of the lighthouse because it would be easier than painting a man (read focus on the penis rather than the whole man). From a poem in the newspaper, she recalls the line "Art thou real, my ideal?" She is dying to know why Bloom is in mourning clothes and whether he is married:

Heart of mine! She would follow, her dream

of love, the dictates of her heart that told her he was her all in all, the only man in all the world for her for love was the master guide. Nothing else mattered. Come what might she would be wild, untrammeled, free.

Now keep in mind that this wild, untrammeled, free Gerty doesn't even know Bloom's name and has only been looking at him for a few minutes. This kind of freedom is tyranny.

At this point, the father in the chapel puts the Host back in the tabernacle and locks it. Both events, the father in the chapel and the show on the beach, are combined in the same line: ". . . Father Conroy handed him his hat to put on and crosscat Edy asked wasn't she coming but Jacky Caffrey called out . . . ."

The fireworks show starts, which can be seen from the beach back over the city. The others move to a different position further away for a better view, but Gerty stays and leans back on the rocks disclosing to Bloom her legs and panties. Just as a roman candle ignites, Bloom ejaculates inside his pants on his shirt. At the magic moment, he grunts "O" (signifying Onan and closed oval). Gerty knew what he was doing and enjoyed her part in the process. She remembers the lodger who masturbated in bed and who was with the Congested Districts Board (too much sperm). I think she starts her menstruation at the same moment as Bloom's ejaculation.

The point of view swings over to Bloom. He blushes under Gerty's glance of shy reproach and like her leans back on a rock. Still reflecting Gerty, the narrator shames Bloom. As Gerty leaves, she waives incense-like a perfumed cotton wad, perhaps to cover the odor of her menstruation.

Bloom's thoughts, now the sole focus of the text, reveal a different experience compared to Gerty's. This difference and the line "Art thou real, my ideal?" drop teasingly into the episode the metaphysical issue of inner experience and outer reality, idealism versus empiricism. The general mist/illusion image suggests that inner experience/idealism is unreliable as a guide to reality. Related is the view that subjective or romantic literature such as Wordsworth's would not plumb any depths other than Wordsworth's.

411

Watching Gerty leave, Bloom realizes she is lame and thinks of her as a hot little devil (the Garden again) who would be a curiosity to conquer, a cruel view even of depersonalized sex objects. He imagines correctly that she is menstruating, the scarlet letter for motherhood. He thinks about her for only a few seconds, a cruel contrast with poor Gerty's life dreams.

Bloom enjoys an absolutely absurd macho mood as a result of his "conquest." He congratulates himself on his restraint in not masturbating in the morning bath. He thinks critically about M'Coy and the limited musical talents of his wife. He denigrates the interest of women for sex: "I'm all clean come and dirty me." He condemns their lack of punctuality except for a date. He believes "They believe in chance because like themselves," the chance process of conception. He muses on their critical attitude towards each other, a concept that is borne out in Gerty's (and later Molly's) thoughts. These are small thoughts, unworthy of Bloom's normal spiritual condition.

He thinks about menstruation in terms of what it must feel like and what it does to women: "Devils they are when that's coming on them. Dark devilish appearance." The Fall in the Garden, orchestrated by the Devil, resulted in the need for constant birth and consequently menstruation. He remembers selling cuttings from Molly's hair when they were poor. In this mock macho mood, Bloom considers working Molly as a prostitute.

Composing his wet shirt, he blames Gerty, that "little limping devil," and rationalizes his masturbation as necessary to get rid of his sperm build up. He is glad he urinated behind the wall near Dignam's house because otherwise he could not have ejaculated. He thinks this cause, the release of semen, is sacred and that sperm gives strength. He images the awkwardness of a conversation with Gerty, because of what he perceives their intellectual differences to be. He thinks of the excitement they experienced together as a kind of language between them. He associates to prostitutes and the occasion he nearly approached the respectable Mrs. Clinch (!) thinking she were one. Bloom remembers having a prostitute in Meath street while she tickled his ear with dirty words. She referred to his "arks," connecting ejaculations with the arcs of the roman candles and the ark of the covenant.

Bloom thinks about the rise and fall of his own fireworks with "Up like a rocket, down like a stick." As he composes himself, we learn that he is not circumcised and therefor fails the acid test of Jewishness.

In contrast to Gerty's illusions, Bloom thinks about the realities of marriage: potwalloping, constant caring for children, boozing and abusing husbands, the wife's second class citizen status and the widow's home (generally wives die last). Monkeys and the courtship of other animals are referred to several times to emphasize the kinship in sexual reproduction of all of nature's creatures. He thinks about Molly masturbating, the smell of women and the smell of sperm. Seeing the old man on the beach, Bloom thinks about following him but decides not to because it could make the old man feel awkward, as the newsboys made Bloom feel outside the newspaper office (in the 7th episode). Bloom can't identify the mystery man on the beach (since the romantic Wordsworth is too wrapped up in himself).

Bloom sees the Bailey light house on Howth Point and thinks about the "wreckers," those who used fake lights to lure ships into the rocks for plunder (more illusions). Next in his thoughts is *Grace Darling*, a poem by Wordsworth about a heroine who saved shipwrecked passengers. Then the different wave length colors of light. These images are in the genre of mirage and illusion that, like Gerty's, lure and plunder the human soul. The reference to Rip van Winkle, "twenty years asleep in Sleepy Hollow," suggests the reality of long-term marriage and child raising. By the time the children leave home, the mother's soul is rusty and the wrinkles are permanent. He thinks about sex with Molly and the plunderer Blazes: "He gets the plums and I the plum-stones." Parable of the Plum pits.

Then Bloom sees the bat and thinks "ba," the ancient Egyptian term for the life-breath. The life-breath was represented in Egyptian iconography by a bird with a human head. It left the body at death but returned to resuscitate the body, if it had been properly preserved.[15] Another deferred return like Rip van Winkle. The life-breath image also suggests the Holy Ghost, whose influence on the human spirit has been

413

deferred and must take a back seat to procreation. Bloom thinks about the Holy Ghost's Egyptian counterpart Osiris: "They believed you could be changed into a tree from grief. Weeping willow."

The bat as the "little man in a cloak" prompts Bloom to think about Archimedes setting fires at a distance with a mirror, a crude analogue of the fertilization of the Virgin Mary by the Holy Ghost and Bloom's recent long distance sexual experience. Bloom's thoughts about sailors keep Mary as the Star of the Sea in our minds. Bloom remembers Milly on a cruise sporting a blue scarf, to bring her within the ambit of Mary, Gerty and pending motherhood. Bloom gets ready to leave and recognizes it is too late to go to the play *Leah*. He thinks about going to the hospital to visit Mrs. Purefoy and, true to charitable form, tries to view with compassion his recent experience with the Citizen.

Then Bloom, presumably as a message to Gerty, writes with a stick in the sand "I AM A" but does not complete the sentence. His thoughts touch on the transience of human existence and the difficulty of connecting (the parenthetical expressions are mine):

I.

Some flatfoot tramp on it in the morning [Odysseus]. Useless. Washed away. Tide comes here. Saw a pool near her foot [Nausicaa and Gerty]. Bend, see my face there [Narcissus], dark mirror, breathe on it, stirs. All these rocks with lines and scars and letters [Proteus signs]. O, those transparent! Besides they don't know. What is the meaning of the other world. I called you naughty boy because I do not like [subjective orientation from Martha's letter].

AM. A.

No room. Let it go.

Mr. Bloom effaced the letters with his slow boot. Hopeless thing sand. Nothing grows in it [the sterile soul]. All fakes. No fear of big vessels [big ferry boat of spirits] coming up here. Except Guinness's barges [human ecstasy]. Round the Kish in eighty days. Done half by design. [my additions]

The phrase "I AM. A." with no conclusion can have many meanings. The identification of Bloom is incomplete because in this macho mood Bloom has lost his compassionate identity.

After his sand writing, Bloom throws the stick he used to write ("his wooden pen"), and it lands stuck upright in the sand. Images of this stick, the stick remaining from the roman candle and the cross begin to combine as images of detumescence. With echoes of Christ's visitation on earth, Bloom thinks: "We'll never meet again. But it was lovely. Goodby, dear. Thanks. Made me feel so young." The gender gap: refreshment for Bloom, disappointment for Gerty.

Near the end, Bloom's sleepy stream of consciousness contains many references to other episodes: pike hoses, for Rauol (from the book Sweets of Sin), Mulvey (an earlier suitor of Molly mentioned in the 18th episode), Rip Van Winkle's rusty gun, his wife's perfume from Martha's letter, red slippers from his dream, the Agendath scheme in the promised land, and Bloom's fetish for ladies' drawers. Then he tries to convince himself that he will forge a paternal place with Molly in the next fertility cycle: "return next in her next her next." Bloom masochistically characterizes the action just concluded by reference to Molly in bed at 4:30 p.m.: "O sweety all your little girlwhite up I saw dirty bracegirdle made me do love sticky we two naughty Grace darling she him half past the bed . . . ."

In the ending, Bloom, the bat, the priest and Gerty are all organized around the sound from the canarybird cuckoo clock in the priest's house. On the hour (9 times for 9 o'clock), it chimes "cuckoo," and the sound affects all the characters. In the context of the major references in this episode, the captive canary bird coming out of the clock announcing the time suggests a mocking Holy Ghost coming from the eternal into space-time to announce the cuckold condition of all humans. Cuckold is the condition into which humans fell from the Garden of Eden; all humans are cuckolded by time and mortality. As part of this overall condition, Gerty is cuckolded by her belief that exclusive possession of a sex partner and birth of children is critically important. To this value she sacrifices her individual realization and retreats from her soul potential. Bloom is cuckolded by his male macho mood and retreats into its shadow, masochism. Presiding over this "temperance retreat" are Church officials issuing sentimental promises about the reliability of help from the Holy Mother. The self-restraint of temperance suggests Gerty's sacrifice of soul for motherhood. The allusion to Wordsworth's poem *The Cuckoo* taints as cuckold the personal in literature. The muse is conjugal only with authors in the classical mode.

Illusions in Maya

In the Hindu pantheon, the maintainers of the illusion of this world include Shiva's son known as Kumara (the "chaste one") or Skanda (the "Spurt of Semen"), our Gerty and Bloom. The destroyer of illusions is Shiva, who appeared in the Lotus-eaters (5th) episode as the composed woman near the hotel getting in the carriage. Bloom, the destroyer of Gerty's illusions in this episode, remembers the composed woman. Illusion can be dispelled by looking at reality the enlightened way, for an example used in the episode seeing combined white light (humanity) rather than the separate colors of the spectrum (egos).

Parallel to the Mass

The faithful in the temperance retreat pray in adoration of the Virgin, as Bloom adores Gerty's virginal lower half. Monthly menstruation among the women of Dublin is associated with the multi-location of Christ's blood in the sacrificial Mass simultaneously in the many Dublin churches. Gerty's use of perfume in hopes that Bloom will return the next day provides the incense, the "come" on for tomorrow.[16]

Onanism

Bloom's erotic experience is described in a later episode in terms of Jewish ritual as the "rite of Onan." In the Bible story of Onan (Genesis 38), Judah had, contrary to the Hebrew Code, married a Canaanite woman named Bath-shua. She gave him two sons Er and Onan. A patriotic Canaanite, Bath-shua wanted all her sons to marry Canaanite girls so their children would be Canaanite.

Judah, apparently regretting his initial marriage decision away from the Hebrew gene pool, married their first son Er (means the childless) to Tamar, who was Hebrew, so their children would be Hebrew (comes from the mother). Fighting for the Canaanite gene pool, Bath-shua used artifices against her Hebrew daughter-in-law Tamar. She convinced Er not to have intercourse with his wife Tamar. After three days, an angel killed Er (Yahweh is impatient for children). Then according to custom, father Judah gave Tamar as wife to the deceased Er's brother Onan. Under threat from Judah, Onan had intercourse with Tamar. But under subversive instructions from his mother Bath-shua, Onan depleted his sperm population by spilling his seed on the ground before intercourse with Tamar. But Yahweh wasn't fooled. Onan was also struck down by Yahweh for removing the paper from the human copying machine; Onan means mourning.[17] Finally star-crossed Tamar tricked her father-in-law Judah into intercourse with her, and their children were the forebearers of Judges and Kings, prominent lineage being a big deal in the Hebrew Scriptures.

Seen in full light, the story of Onan is not so much about masturbation as about avoiding your duty to procreate, the responsible use of your seed, a guilt which weighs heavily on Bloom's mind. But more fundamentally, the ultimate moral of this story is one of illusion, the illusion pursued by both Judah and Bath-Shua that the narrow divisions of humanity are important, Canaanites versus the Hebrews. Instead of all humanity, they narrowed their vision of concern to a Cyclops-like limited survival group, in essence a selfish orientation born of ignorance of the reality of the human condition. Onanism and Bloom's macho anti-feminist reaction to Gerty are among the ultimate expressions of that selfish, illusory orientation.

Masochism

The smell of masochism and its related father fixation already stick to Bloom. Masochism, a form of emotional distortion, provides motivation for his masturbation. The following contains a general explanation of this psychological phenomenon. As with any obsession, it restricts Bloom's possibilities, as the marriage dream does Gerty's.

Masochism was named after the author Leopold von Sacher-Masoch ("SM"), who was mentioned in an earlier episode. SM turned his own unusual sexual experiences into fodder for several novels, the most famous being *Venus in Furs*. Masochism was explicitly a subject in Joyce's play *Exiles* and, if you credit Joyce's letters, a force in his

417

relationship with Nora. Joyce even tried to get Nora to read Masoch's books (she didn't read any of Joyce's).

Masochism is a distortion in emotional reality arranged by the victim. The suffering male voluntarily organizes his own torture by a female he loves. This love must be a particular type, one based on fascination with beauty and charm. This type of love is traditionally associated with Venus.

In psyche speak, the suffering male's psychological condition relates to his childhood experience of a negative father image. The suffering male considers fatherhood in a negative light. The entire masochistic experience eventually results in a positive rebirth through the portal of the oral mother away from emotional distortion caused by the negative father image. Curing the problem results in a change in relation to the father and of the father image. At this point, the masochistic Bloom has a negative image of his own father and his role as a father.

The self-torture usually consists of arranging for the adored female to be unfaithful as well to whip the self-styled victim. For fetish reasons, the torturing female must be dressed in furs. The fur performs as a fetish that allows the tortured male to continue to believe that his mother has a phallus. A successful fetish is often the last object (pubic hair) one sees before the evidence that disturbs the distorted vision. The mother phallus is necessary because at this point, under the influence of masochism, the father must not be needed.

The female in *Venus in Furs* is named Wanda von Dunajew. I kid you not, done a Jew. Bloom is being tortured by Molly's infidelity that he has helped arrange by staying out of the house. Later Molly thinks he even arranged for Milly to leave home for the same reason. Frequent mention is made of Molly's fur boa, a snake-like fur piece, which combines the serpent, phallus and furs. This particular combination suggests masochism in the Garden of Eden, that Eve and Adam wanted to be punished. The torturing female is often described as a cat with its prey, a subject of Bloom's musings in the Calypso (4th) episode. A victim in search of torture, the masochist often sets love affairs in motion by ads in newspapers and uses false names.[18] Bloom has done just that and his letters from Martha carry the tone of the whip.

The suffering male in *Venus in Furs*, Severin, has been sponging off his father and following his Venus Wanda all around Europe. He is finally cured when Wanda becomes particularly cruel and joins forces with a Greek man to whip suffering Severin. Under this final pressure, Severin is somehow liberated from the control of his Venus. Analyzed psychologically, Severin asks to be beaten in order to drive out of himself the disturbing image of his father.[19] With his rebirth, Severin ceases to sponge off his father and returns home to a natural relationship with and to work for him in his last years.

Bloom has had several disturbing visions of his father. He is uncertain about his own role as a father of more children. In this episode, while Bloom still experiences the negative image of fatherhood, he subjects himself to Gerty's sexual torture in order to beat out his father sperms. He beats out the father image. Later Bloom, like Severin, achieves a rebirth through his relations with Molly after he meets Stephen with the Greek last name Dedalus and brings him home to Molly.

Adultery and *Onanism a' Deux*

In the view of the Catholic Church, Bloom' masturbation is as bad as Boylan's adultery with Molly. All recreational sexual activity is equally bad in the view of the Church. Only sperm in the bank is the right accounting for this energy. The outrageousness of that position even in 1904 Dublin is the point Joyce wants to make.

Gerty on the rock may be doing her own self-rubbing by means of her leg swing crescendo. If so, the beach scene is an *onanism a' deux*, which spreads the virus of human separateness in recreational sex. As we will learn later, Molly also carefully arranges for some sperm depletion *a la* Onan.

Art, Structure and Aesthetics

The style of this episode reminds me of pink cotton candy. The parody of the sentimental style is magnificent. The narrator has an attitude and assumes an author-like pose in commenting on the actions of the characters. This is improper in the dramatic mode, where the object is presented only in relation to the object (not the narrator). Here all objects are given in relation to first Gerty and then Bloom. The narrator is not distanced from the characters and the actions. The narrator is cuckolded by Gerty's desires.

This episode gave me an experience that Joyce describes as aesthetic arrest. It happened when the tie between lameness, original sin, Mary, illusion and procreation came together. It was onanistic. The Prelude to Procreation leads directly into the next episode.

****

ENDNOTES

1. Apparently the marriage rate in Ireland at this time was low. Gifford, p. 393.
2. Schwartz, p. 189.
3. Letter to Budgen dated 1/3/20.
4. Boyle, p. 22.
5. Graves, Greek Myths, p. 728.
6. Ibid, p. 731.
7. Gifford, p. 384.
8. *Wordsworth* Encyclopedia Britannica, 1983 ed., Macropaedia, vol. 19, p. 928.
9. Graves, Greek Myths, p. 248.
10. Budgen, pp. 208-209.
11. Pelikan, J. *Mary Through the Centuries* (New Haven: Yale University Press, 1996), pp. 93-99.
12. *Murphy*, first line.
13. Schwartz, p. 140.
14. Blamires, p. 138.
15. Gifford, p. 400.
16. See generally, Lang, pp. 172-174.
17. Legends, vol. II, pp. 32-33.
18. Deleuze, G. *Coldness and Cruelty* (New York: Zone Books, 1989) p. 18.
19. Deleuze, p. 60.

Episode 14 (Oxen of the Sun)

Basic Themes

Procreation: pro life and pro creation. Mother creates life and artist creates art. Condoms and artistic immaturity restrict possibilities.

These sacred efforts, birth of life and art, are powered by those fundamental forces of human nature, the sex instinct and the creative imagination.[1] These births share in the sacred by way of their link back through the "Land of the Dead," human ancestors for baby Purefoy and historical English prose for the novice author Stephen. These births link back to the gods, who originally created mankind and language. These sacred efforts are Joyce's double doors to the gods.

In the maternity hospital, Mother Purefoy's prolonged contractions finally deliver a son. For the woman, procreation is nature's most fundamental ordinance and life is sacred. In the common waiting room of the same maternity hospital, Stephen's contractions of his self-indulgence begin to deliver his own son, his second or spiritual birth that will inspire his creative imagination to significant art. For the artist, artistic creation is nature's fundamental ordinance and art is sacred. Joyce pairs mothers and artists because Joyce believes these processes share fundamental denominators. Creating artists often describe their condition as being pregnant.[2]

Both the mother's and the artist's contractions are purifying ordeals. The mother creates life through suffering and, in Bloom's phrase, "at the risk of her own." In the process, she converts personal sexual attraction to maternal compassion. Likewise, the artist creates more significant art through suffering and "at the risk of his own." The artist sheds his own personal subjectivity (his own) in molting toward classical detachment. Both are purified in the conversion from a profane to a sacred state. In both these efforts, love must be present in order to create a portal to the eternal.

Last seen at about 3:00 p.m., Stephen reappears at about 10:00 p.m. drinking beer with medical students in the common room of the maternity hospital. This is the same hospital where Mother Purefoy has been lying in for three painful days. The hospital's common room is where caring fathers await the sacred event. But Stephen's noisy drinking party profanes the common room and even disturbs the expecting mothers. How Stephen got there under these circumstances is not explained. I believe he is celebrating his date with Nora that afternoon and early evening. Given his incipient sexual and personal feelings for Nora, the profane use of the sacred is very much on his mind.

Stephen and Bloom are together for about an hour. Stephen is drunk on his pursuit of pleasure, Bloom sober on his errand of mercy. The profane and the sacred. They begin to connect ever so slightly. Stephen makes the statement about a pregnant mother that "once a woman has let the cat into the bag . . . she must let it out again or give it life . . . to save her own." Bloom responds, "At the risk of her own." This is the first meaningful dialogue between them; significantly, Bloom corrects Stephen's analysis concerning the mother's motivation from a selfish orientation to a compassionate one. This is the direction the Bloom experience moves Stephen. This is the beginning of the epiphany Stephen experiences with Bloom. Stephen prepares for art based on empathy in the halls of maternity that echo the fundamental human unity.

Stephen begins his release from self, his insulation having been burned off by the high voltage experience with Nora. Vulnerable, Stephen is destabilized by fear of thunder. The thunder and its association in the fourth episode (through the common Sanskrit root "Da") with self-control, charity and mercy signal the direction of Stephen's potential spiritual growth through the father principle. As indicated in the Nausicaa (13th) episode, Da is baby talk for Dad.

The slaughter by Odysseus's men of the sacred Oxen of the Sun for an eating orgy sponsors the general subject of profanity, which through impiety involves separation from the eternal powers and among human individuals. As the sacred Oxen bellowed while roasting on the spit, Joyce includes multiple references to vivesection, an operation on a living organism into order to separate and examine its individual parts in operation. The conversation in the common room includes several subjects that involve such separation: saving either the mother or the child in a troubled birth, and separating Siamese twins.

The subject of separation of the living reaches its climax as Stephen adjourns the group to Burke's pub. In leaving, the boys run by the nurse and Doctor and out of the hospital without any interest in the status of Mother Purefoy. They are hurriedly bent only on their own pleasure of one last brew before closing time at Burke's. Burke is the name of the famous Irish *deadbody* thief. He dug up bodies to sell for medical dissection. The boys leave the sacred maternity ward for the profane pub famous for dead bodies. From life to death. From the spiritual point of view, their behavior is an abortion, a hurried exit reflecting death. Stephen aborts what little compassion has been generated by his initial meeting with Bloom.

As ecstatic intoxication serves as the booster stage for both the human sexual instinct and creative imagination, Dionysius is the deity featured in this episode. As the icon for the forces of passionate ecstasy and the god of earliest Greek dramatic art,[3] Dionysius was "twice born" and the "child of the double door." He was so named because of his second birth from the thigh of Zeus after his mother was killed by lightning. This double set matches Joyce's double doors to the gods. Nietzsche, the philosopher of Dionysian vitalism, also gets good exposure in this episode. Careful guidance is necessary since the Dionysian booster stage is capable of damaging the launch pad. Bloom in the role of Hermes begins to guide Stephen.

Ecstasy helps in the spiritual launch because it helps defeat the gravity of ego. Here is Northrop Frye on this subject:

> [ecstatic is] a state in which the real self . . . enters a different order of things from that of the now dispossessed ego . . . . It seems clear from all accounts that the ecstatic state, no less than the erotic state, is one that one cannot remain in very long. Many writers who enter it in their great moments develop a ferocious ego for their rest periods.[4]

Personal spirituality can develop from personal ecstasy because ecstasy starts the move away from self and toward an appreciation of the unity.

In this episode, Stephen has experiences necessary as a preliminary matter to develop the ability to dispossess his ego, which is required in order to escape the romantic subjective approach to art and move on toward the sacred. Bloom leads the way with a moment of meditation focused on a beer bottle. While Stephen momentarily starts to move away from ego, he suffers a relapse at the end of the episode and returns to ferocious ego profanity, which leads him to more booze and the red-light district.

The sacred Oxen of the Sun were the icons of Helios, the god of generation. Circe explicitly warned Odysseus of the gravity of disturbing the herds. The sacred oxen did not reproduce but were maintained in herds of a constant number. Despite warnings from Circe, Odysseus's men slaughtered the sacred Oxen of the Sun for a feeding orgy. They treated the Oxen as mere meat. Their profane misuse continues in the values exhibited in this episode by Stephen and his young Irish drinking friends—drunken disregard of lying in mothers, sex pursued for sex's sake and a life pursued for ego's sake.

Joyce interpreted the killing of the sacred oxen, the icons of Helios the god of generation, as a "crime committed against fecundity by sterilizing the act of coition." This "over the top" interpretation has to be digested in order to experience the unifying concept of this episode. Fecundity is sacred, in life and art. Sterilization is profane, in life and art. This last point is hard to digest since safe sex (with a condom) seems only reasonable and since unprotected sex accords with the dictates of the Catholic Church, at this point one of the main bad guys. But there it is, straight from the horse's mouth.

Allusions to the Jewish festival of Pesah, which celebrates the Exodus from Egypt, and to the related Christian Last Supper announce that Stephen is pregnant with change from the profane to the sacred. Both Pesah and the Last Supper were on Thursday evening. After this Thursday evening (thunder day) discursive drinking session, Stephen's potential for spiritual growth is announced by the long awaited nourishing (sacred) but deluge-like (profane ending) rain that breaks the Dublin drought. The episode is full of allusions to spiritual development—from enchantment, to the Parable of the Prodigal Son, to the Eleusian mystery initiation ritual and to much much more.

Stephen's spiritual progress runs parallel with other embryological or epigenetic processes alluded to in this episode. The common trait these processes share is development in stages. The next stage arises out of and is dependent on the former stages. The process builds on what has gone before and does not start anew. It is a process that emphasizes continuity and innovation, but not each separate step. These other epigenetic processes include the fertilized human egg in the womb, evolution of living creatures on the earth, the progress historically of English prose styles and, most important, the collective unconscious of humanity. In the human spiritual realm, the human unity is the view of continuity that de-emphasizes the separate ego.

The emphasis on epigenetic processes arises out of *fin de siecle* intellectual currents about hereditary processes. One current involved a fascination with hereditary degeneration, toward the profane. Another involved evolutionary biology, toward the sacred survival of offspring. These currents fostered Jung's ideas about the evolution of the collective unconscious, the biological history that unites the human race. This collective includes, according to Jung, a layer related to Mithraism, a religion competitive with Christianity in the Roman Empire. Jung believed that Mithraism is the descendant most closely resembling the original mother of all religions for the Indo-Europeans. Jung believed that Mithraic images feed dreams in Western civilization. Accordingly, Joyce includes the icons of Mithraism in the dense layers and detail of this episode.

The most famous conjunction of the sacred and the profane occurred in the Catholic concept of the Incarnation of Jesus. The sacred god-head had space-time intercourse with the mortal Mary, known to Catholics as the Holy Mother of God. Given her maternal role in creating the sacred of all sacreds, the Holy Mother serves in this episode as a prototype for the artist in the delivery of the eternal. The profane Stephen wonders how close as an artist he can come to the sacred eternal. He hubristically believes that he can do better than the Holy Mother did.

The episode ends in Burke's pub with a deliberately confusing and incoherent spray of colloquialisms and dialectic bartalk current to the times. Issued in the den of the profane with the proxy for the Anti-Christ

(MacIntosh) present, this spray is a mocking allusion to the highly subjective literature of the 20th century. That literature speaks (in Joyce's view) in the many subjective tongues of Babel and lacks connection with the impersonal grave and constant. The confusion of Babel, you will remember, prevented the completion of construction of the tower that was to bridge from earth to heaven. Likewise, the highly subjective literature of the 20th century does not, in Joyce's view, reach to the eternal. Compared to Joyce's, such literature diddles its readers.

Action in The Odyssey

In Chapter xii, Circe treats Odysseus and his men, after their return from Hades, to some of the best life has to offer, the bare flesh of her hand maidens and bread and red wine. Then she tells him the bad news: that they must pass the Sirens and Scylla and Charybdis and then finally come to the Isle of Thrinacria (identified as Sicily, the land of three headlands or the trident). Remember Joyce has gone out of order compared to Homer. Speaking of three, Hermes, the reference for Bloom's guidance role, is best known as Hermes Trismegistus, Hermes the Thrice Great.

Circe informs Odysseus that the many herds of oxen and sheep on the island are very special since owned by Helios, the god of generation. You would think that since Helios is the god of generation, his herds would multiply. But these animals have "no part in birth or in corruption"; they do not reproduce and while they can be killed, they do not suffer a natural death. Accordingly, they are representative of eternal not immortal life. These sacred animals are guarded by goddesses and nymphs; two of the guardians are named—Phaethusa and Lampetie, children of Helios. Circe warns Odysseus that if they even hurt the sacred animals, they will not reach home, but if they leave the Oxen undisturbed they may yet reach home (no guarantees). Circe also says that if his men hurt the animals but Odysseus doesn't, he will escape but in "evil plight with the loss of all thy company."

Odysseus tells his men that Circe has bade them avoid the island. The crew, tired from the strenuous passage between Scylla and Charybdis and hungry, rally behind the plea of principal crewperson Eurylochus to land on the island. Odysseus consents but commands the crew to swear to him that they will not disturb the sacred herds and only eat the meat Circe gave them. They swear on command. After arriving on the island, they rest and dutifully feast only on Circe's meat. However, the next morning the weather is up preventing their departure. Odysseus repeats the warning, this time adding that the animals on the island belong to the god Helios and are sacred. The ill winds (from the south and east) blow for 30 days during which the crew's store of corn and wine runs out. They hunt and fish, using their own resources, but find little fare. They are very hungry but not starving.

Odysseus goes to shelter from the wind, prays and, you guessed it, falls asleep. Meanwhile, Eurylochus convinces the crew to kill some of the sacred cattle in order to avoid death by starvation. In an cautionary effort, they plan to appease the god Helios by sacrificing some of the meat now and, after they return home, by mounting a statue to Helios (the check is in the mail). Eurylochus further argues that if Helios is going to sink their ship in retribution, he would rather experience that death by drowning than one by starvation. Notice that this argument rests on the uncertain premise that since they are hungry, they will starve.

Odysseus returns but too late and finds the sacred cattle roasting. Apparently no sacrifice is being made. And ominous signs have begun—flayed skins are creeping and pieces of flesh on the spits are bellowing. The crew is, however, not disturbed by these supernatural omens and continues to feast on the sacred meat for six days (note they went overboard and ate more than was necessary for mere survival). The bad wind lets up and they leave. But Eurylochus and company, having diddled the god Helios, get their due. Zeus sets a violent west wind upon them that destroys their boat by snapping the forestays supporting the mast. The falling mast strikes the head of the pilot who drops the tiller. The ship rolls over and the entire crew falls overboard and is lost. Odysseus stays on board to the last second and saves himself by lashing together the keel and the mast to make a raft. The violent winds take him back to Scylla and Charybdis. This time he stays on the Charybdis side, and while his raft goes down into the whirlpool, he hangs on the branches of the figtree above "like a bat." When his raft comes back up again, he jumps back on and rows out to safety.

Parallels to the Odyssey

Like the cursed ship that lost its forestays and then its mast, narcissistic Stephen becomes unbalanced in despair, bitterness and fear. Stephen's ego and Odysseus's crew suffer contractions. Helios, Greek for sun, was thought to spend each evening sailing around the ocean in a huge cup.[5] Here the boys are under sail in their own cups.

The ego wraps of the boys drinking beer and disturbing the expecting mothers are the references for the destruction of the sacred herd. Joyce generalized these soul limiting activities as "crimes committed against fecundity (read possibilities)." The bellowing of the Oxen on the spits returns in the huckster preaching of Alexander Dowie.

Parallels to the Passion of Jesus

Jesus in the Garden of Gethsemane (means the olive "oil-press"), alone before Satan and desolate in his soul, experienced blood-sweat despair before his arrest. Prostrate and certain of His death, Jesus prayed using the personal pronoun "my" before Father, the only time recorded in the Gospels[6]: "Abba, Father (my Father) . . . take away this cup from me . . . ." (Luke 14:36). Facing the Secret Cause in his human aspect and Satan in His divine, Jesus managed to find stillness in Himself to face the arrest and crucifixion and the death of his human nature. Likewise, Stephen's soul contractions begin to press out his profane self-indulgence and to remove the debauched cup from him.

Where Has Stephen Been?

Stephen has been absent from the action for about seven hours. He reappears in this episode dressed in the ritual trappings of Pesah, the Paschal Lamb meal of the Passover.

The first question always asked at Passover is: Why is this night different from all other nights? The answer is, I believe, because Stephen has been on his first date with Nora. Further, I believe that on that date she "took him in hand." This would explain Stephen's anticipation in the Proteus (3rd) episode of the soft touch and his fixation in this episode on the effect of sterilizing the act of coition.

In his first speaking lines, Stephen abruptly changes subjects to speak of "impossiblilizing Godpossibled souls" (sterilizing coition) as a sin against the Holy Ghost. The reaction of Bloom, fresh from his own

428

sperm suicide, is not given. This new subject is so much out of left field that it must come from Stephen's preoccupation with the subject. If this is the case, then both Stephen and Bloom have quite recently "spilled their seed," perhaps even at the same time.

The Sacred and the Profane

The sacred creates a different sense of time, space and being.[7] The sacred attitude allows one to experience the foundation of relevant space and to live in a real sense. Time "stops" and attention is involuntarily riveted. Bloom provides an example as he meditates while staring at a beer bottle. For the profane view, there is only homogenous and relative space and existence. There is no true orientation, only unrelated fragments in life. A diluted sacred sense produces a low-grade memory glow for the firsts in life—birth, home, job, sex—a glow seen in this episode. What characterizes these first experiences and the full blown sacred is focused human energy, from the first pressings of Dionysius.

To live in the sacred is to attempt to reproduce the original experience in the Garden of Eden. Living in the sacred is living in an impersonal, objective reality, not in purely subjective experience. The concept of the sacred sponsors the many references in this episode to cosmic creation, Christ, the Garden of Eden, the initiation at Eleusius, the Prodigal Son's change in attitude, and the change from youth to maturity.

Bloom, Compassion and the Collective Unconscious

Bloom renders compassion to the child bearing mother, Mrs. Purefoy, whose name means pure faith. Bloom's compassion, we note, is not spread on every problem in the field of human concerns, but only on those inevitably shared by all humans, the grave and constant or the ground of human being in each of us. To this force field, Bloom has made a connection. Jung's collective unconscious is part of this force field. The collective transcends but does not eliminate individual differences and connects all humans based on common patterns of experience.[8]

Water

A heavy rain during this episode ends a long draught in Dublin. Dionysius was associated with all the wet elements: rain, blood, semen and sap. In Hindu symbolism, Vishnu sends at the end of each Brahma lifetime a sweet and pure rain to quench the thirst of the world.[9] Water, Joyce's symbol of unity, announces the start of the sacred. As a deluge, it announces the end of the profane. The ark, which saved a sacred remnant of humanity from the flood, connects to the big ferry boat in Bloom's compassion.

Hermes and the Caduceus

In Greek mythology, Hermes represents the power of human fertility and is the guide to spiritual knowledge, that is knowledge of the eternal. This Greek pairing supports Joyce's view of the sexual instinct as a portal to the eternal. The ancient call for rebirth of the spirit was "Come unto me, Lord Hermes, even as into women's wombs come babes!"[10]

Hermes's traditional icon is the caduceus, a staff in the form of a cross. It has wings above and two snakes wrapped around the lower part of the staff. It is now the symbol of the medical profession here in the sacred service of maternity.

The two snakes wrapped around the staff of the caduceus traditionally represent knowledge and wisdom, or in the language of Jung the personal and the impersonal collective. According to legend, Hermes originally found the two snakes fighting on the ground and placed his staff between them. The snakes were arrested and stuck to the staff. Likewise, Stephen needs to arrest and keep these twin creative forces in balance. When Stephen's art combines in balance both the personal and the collective, then it will be pregnant with epiphanies. Then his art will serve as a guide to the eternal, the grave and constant in the human condition.

The entwined snakes on the caduceus staff look like the figure 8, our symbol for eternity, and also look like a pregnant woman. In this way, the caduceus is a visual image of the cognate forces represented by Hermes. A figure 8 appears in Joyce's notes for this episode.[11]

In order to combine the symbolic influence of Hermes with Dionysius, the caduceus appears in this episode in the form of the vine of the hops—the vine for the caduceus and hops for the intoxication from the beer made with the hops. The leaves from this combined vine image eventually encircle Stephen's head, signifying the fermentation and intoxication of his imagination. This imaginative construction occurs in a conversation about his artistic future, when "something more . . . than a capful of light odes can call your genius father."

Stephen needs a boost from Dionysius and guidance from Hermes because at this point his imagination has been sterilized by his exclusive cultivation of the personal, his profane narcissistic ego. As the condom allows the pursuit of sex primarily as personal pleasure, self-indulgent art proceeds primarily for the personal pleasure of the artist. Stephen and the boys drunk with beer and ego joke about sex for sex's sake with condoms and diaphragms, even to the point of making enough noise to disturb the expecting mothers. The group adjourns by reference to their separate walking sticks, profane counterpoint to the caduceus. Their separate walking sticks are bare; they have no snakes, no wisdom and no balance.

Stephen at this point can't create except in the romantic subjective, which he knows is not of general interest. At this point his artistic effort is on a par with a used condom.

Development

This episode presents several strands of embryological development all wrapped around each other like the snakes on the caduceus. (For those who want to believe Joyce had the power to sense the future, consider the image of the caduceus as the double helix of DNA passed on to and engineering baby Purefoy.) These several wrapped strands include the development of English writing style, plot development in The Odyssey, physical development of the human fetus in the womb, evolution of living creatures on the earth, the layered development of the collective unconscious, and change in the soul of Stephen.

These personal and collective strands suggest for humankind the now familiar view that each of us as an individual experiences during his

431

or her personal development a process similar to that the species as a whole has experienced over time. Importantly, each of these processes moves forward by development from the prior state and thereby participates in continuity across time. For example, in Darwinian evolution all present creatures represent the prior survival experience of the species as a unity.

This is what Joyce said he was doing:

> Am working hard at Oxen of the Sun, the idea being the crime committed against fecundity by sterilizing the act of coition. Scene, lying-in hospital. Technique: a nineparted episode without divisions introduced by a Sallustian - Tacitan prelude (the unfertilized ovum), then by way of earliest English alliterative and monosyllabic and Anglo-Saxon ("Before born the babe had bliss. Within the womb he won worship. Bloom dull dreamy heard: in held hat stony staring") then by way of Mandeville ("there came forth a scholar of medicine that men clepen etc") then Malory's Morte d'Arthur ("but that franklin Lenehan was prompt eve to pour them so that at the least way mirth should not lack"), then the Elizabethan chronicle style ("about that present time young Stephen filled all cups"), then a passage solemn as of Milton, Taylor, Hooker, followed by a choppy Latin-gossipy bit, style of Burton-Browne, then a passage Bunyanesque ("the reason was that in the way he fell in with a certain whore whose name she said is Bird in the hand") after a diarystyle bit Pepys-Evelyn ("Bloom sitting snug with a party of wags, among them Dixon jun., Ja. Lynch, Doc. Madden and Stephen D. for a languor he had before and was now better, he having dreamed tonight a strange fancy and Mistress Purefoy there to be delivered, poor body, two days past her time and the midwives hard put to it, God send her quick issue") and so on through Defoe-Swift and Steele-

Addison-Sterne and Landor-Pater-Newman until it ends in a frightful jumble of Pidgin English, nigger English, Cockney, Irish, Bowery slang and broken doggerel. This progression is also linked back at each part subtly with some foregoing episode of the day and, besides this, with the natural stages of development in the embryo and the periods of faunal evolution in general. The double-thudding Anglo-Saxon motive recurs from time to time ("Loth to move from Horne's house") to give the sense of the hoofs of oxen. Bloom is the spermatozoon, the hospital the womb, the nurse the ovum, Stephen the embryo.[12]

Some Help in Reading

Since some of the paragraphs in this episode are very hard to read, a detailed interpretation is provided below. For the first paragraphs, the interpretation is line by line. The reference to Saintsbury is to a book about prose rhythm (patterns of stress) used by Joyce in reconstructing earlier prose styles. My explanation is rather tedious just to read through in its entirety, so you might just sample or graze now and come back when you are reading the novel.

1. Paragraph 1. The first phrase (*Deshil Holles Eamus*) is a chant much as our earliest ancestors must have communicated group enthusiasm. You might chant it aloud. It is given in three repetitions. Note that the chant mantra is made up of one Irish word *Deshil*, one English word *Holles* and one Latin word *Eamus*. In terms of stress patterns (long or emphasized_and short or not emphasized u), each of these words has two long feet, making a spondee, which has a mesmerizing quality like a Hari Krishna chant. Thus: _ _ _ _ _ _.

Deshil means may it be right or go well, *Holles* is the street location of the maternity hospital and *Eamus* means let us go home. Translated for Mrs. Purefoy, this means a safe birth followed by going home. Translated for Stephen, this means his spiritual birth, his true homecoming to the sacred. Near the end of episode, Stephen and his crew leave the hospital and turn right to go to Burke's pub, definitely not home.

The second phrase (*Send us bright one, light one, Horhorn, quickening and wombfruit*) is a chant worshipping bright radiance from the god Helios, the sun father of all creation on earth. This prayer is for the continuation of life of the survival group through birth, a major subject in the Book of Genesis. This phrase initiates the sun and oxen themes and the name of the doctor (Horne) in charge of the hospital. Horne also suggests the Archangel Gabriel the hornblower, who announced the divine incarnation to the Holy Mother.[13]

The third phrase (*Hoopsa bayaboy hoopsa*) is the traditional cry of the midwife celebrating the birth of a male child.[14] It is used in the Eleusian initiation.

Each phrase is repeated three times in the nature of a consecration. These ritual imprecations indicate the sacred nature of the subject matter. They are chanted over and over to indicate the attitude that the birth of life is sacred. This is pious ritual. It announces an episode in which Stephen begins the contractions of his self-indulgence.

2. Paragraph 2 ("Universally that person's" line 7) is in the style of Roman historians Sallust and Tacitus.[15] The disturbed syntax in English of these sentences is the result of a literal translation from Latin, in Roman times the language of Europe. The disturbed or partial English syntax suggests an unfertilized ovum and Stephen's sterilized artistic imagination. Both have potential but are scrambled because separate. The Roman reference is our initial portal to Mithraism.

The first sentence says: Those who are smart think that the prosperity of a nation is best encouraged by promoting procreation, as long as original evil is not present, and not by promoting "exterior splendor." Note that this sentence merely equates prosperity and procreation on a conditional basis. That condition is the absence of original sin, which if present would unfortunately be retransmitted by generation. If present, extinction would presumably be better since otherwise hereditary degeneration, a *fin de siecle* obsession, into the profane would result from retransmission. Since Catholicism embraced both procreation and original sin, Joyce is pointing out this inconsistency in his assault on the doctrine of original sin as part of his treatise on the sacred and profane.

The second sentence says: Those who know think that
(a)"exterior splendor," or material benefits in space/time reality, is not
important because it may be the turbid and corrupted downward tending
surface of a higher and purer reality (the Hindu notion of maya and
metaphysical reality[16]) or (b) on the contrary, that nature's boon (used
synonymously with exterior splendor) can not make up for a failure of
continuing procreation so every citizen should be in favor of procreation
to keep the tradition going, the tradition being the command and promise
from the gods of abundance. This difficult second sentence continues the
subject of fertility or life, now in the realm of metaphysics. From the
sacred to metaphysics, ultimate physical reality. It introduces the general
subject of the relationship of the sacred cosmic powers to this physical
world and the sacred invocation in Genesis to go forth and multiply
humankind. Note that the response to the sacred invocation in Genesis is
hard-wired in the human sex desire.

3. Paragraphs 3 ("It is not why therefore" line 33) and 4 are in
the style of medieval Latin prose chronicles. The subject matter suggests
organization and planning to foster life.

The three sentences of the third paragraph say: Therefor
historically among Celts the art of medicine was honored; this art has
been written down; and so a plan was adopted to reduce the chance of a
problem in child delivery for rich and poor alike.

The two sentences of the fourth paragraph say: So when women
are pregnant, nothing is allowed to bother them when the time comes
because this process is the link from mortals through the generations
back to the gods (God made Adam); and even housecalls are made to the
each of the pregnant mothers to see how she is doing. The sacred to the
practical. Human organization copies the logos in the original creation.

4. Paragraphs 5 ("Before born babe bliss had" line 60) through
10 feature Anglo-Saxon alliterative prose in the style of Aelfric (c. 955-
1022). The letters **B** and **W** are alliterated. **B** looks like a pregnant mother
and **W** her milk enlarged teats. Repetition suggests the numerous sperm
population. Later the letter **H** is alliterated, for horn or oxen hoof beat.

Subjects introduced include angels, the Annunciation of the
pending birth of the Christ Child to the Virgin Mary, the great deluge,

and the wandering of land and seafloor. In the 6th paragraph, Bloom arrives, Bloom the compassionate and wandering Jew sperm. The sperm only wants to contribute. In the 7th, Dr. Horne is in charge with his nurses.

The nurse Callahan is barren because her fiancée died. Likewise, Stephen's artistic promise has not been realized. She admits Bloom, and as old acquaintances they catch up. Bloom apologizes for failing earlier to return her greeting on the dock. She blushes. She wonders if his wife has died.

5. Paragraphs 11 ("Therefore, everyman" line 107) and 12 are in the style of Middle English, such as used in **Everyman** (circa 1485). Like the introduction to that hoary piece, the 11th paragraph deals with the effect of the certainty of death on one's philosophy of life. This style was used in its day mostly in material for preaching, and accordingly the 11th paragraph preaches.[17] The same style was used in the Vulgate version of the Bible with particular effect in the Book of Job and like verses, so allusions to Job are included in the 12th paragraph.[18] In this style, the alliteration is generally less frequent and more sophisticated,[19] but here we have the awful "with wonder women's woe" and the better "chiding her childless." The subject of menstruation is brought up as a sign of barrenness, as a symbolic web is being woven from the bleeding of menstruation to the suffering of Jesus. Later there is a reference to the "reek of moonflower," or the presence of a menstruating woman as a cure for barrenness of other women.[20] Likewise, Christ died in blood on the cross as a cure for the spiritual barrenness of others. Birth is near and suffering is the preparation. Suffering is necessary for the possibilities of this life.

6. In paragraphs 13 ("And whiles they spake" line 123), 14 and 15, the style is that of the author of **Travels of John Mandeville**, fantastic medieval travel stories (c. 1336-71). This travelogue was delivered in short sentences introduced often by "and" or "also" and in a simple conversational style grouped into verse size groups.[21] Joyce parodies this style with the use in almost every sentence of the opening word "and." And Joyce's paragraphs are also faithful to the conversational style, don't

you think? They center on travelers and knights and use exaggeration—for example, Bloom's bee sting is a bite from a dragon.

Dr. Dixon invites Bloom into the common room of the castle (hospital) where the knights of learning (the students) are at meat. Bloom is cautious, the nurse Callahan urges against joining this group (stay with her), but Bloom accepts because he is tired (like Odysseus's crew). As he enters, the table is littered with knives, glasses, beer bottles and cans of sardines. This table mess is an echo of the Greek orgy on the sacred Oxen. The hops, from which the beer is produced, are described as serpents on the vine. Bread from Chaldee is mentioned. Bloom receives a glass of beer but pours most of it back into Dixon's glass.

In terms of spiritual themes, swords, demons, fighting, and castles all make appearances; these are emblems of the first chakra. We also have magic, Mohammed, metallurgy, trade, the enthusiasm of Dionysius, and tamer spirits as this section progresses. Bloom's return of the beer gives us generosity. This sequence makes a ladder of improvement of the spirit.

7. Paragraphs 16 ("This meanwhile" line 167) through 19 are in the style of Sr. Thomas Mallory and the *Morte d' Arthur* (1485). This style features compilation, free flowing easy sentences, stock phrases, some use of the introductory "and," a skillful weaving of conversation and narrative, and the dominant use of the iambic (short long).[22] These I find except for the iambic. The weaving of conversation and narration comes off with a Joyce smirk.

The nurse tells the boys to be quiet as they are disturbing the birth process. They quiet down reluctantly. Lenehan and Bloom toast each other. The group introduced by the narrator one by one is waiting for Mulligan. Stephen is the least sober but the most somber. Bloom sits by him since he is a friend of his father. Bloom is calmed by compassion.

The boys are witty, skeptical and critical of each other—the discursive ego wrap. They discuss birth and the moral choice in a troubled birth of saving the mother or her new child. The boys favor the mother (the choice of the individual) against the dictates of the Church that command the choice of the child (the choice of the survival group). Stephen quotes official Catholic doctrine on Eve, Mary and Lilith, the first wife of Adam and the heretical patron of abortions, and the Church approved portions of Aristotle on the introduction of the soul in the second month of the fetus. Bloom dodges the issue of saving the mother or the child with an expression of gratefulness for Church pence for both. Stephen wildly quotes Nietzsche, the patron of individual power and Dionysian vitalism.

Bloom thinks about his son's death at 11 days and bemoans the fact that Stephen "murdered his goods with whores." This trenchant phrase is from the parable of the Prodigal Son.[23] It is spoken by the faithful son (who remained at home with his father to till the fields) in condemnation of the returning wastrel, his brother who with his liquidated share of the family inheritance had gone to the city to play. Forced home by a drought (remember our story), the Prodigal Son now out of funds appears to have a change of heart and his father is overjoyed, celebrating with a feast that had never been given for the faithful son. The point of the story is that current attitude, and not prior deeds, is all important and total change is possible in spiritual development. The use of this parable foretells the spiritual transformation of Stephen the Prodigal Son by Bloom, who like the father and the faithful son has been there plugging away at compassion all the time without any feast. Since Bloom can't know with certainty that Stephen has used prostitutes, "whores" must refer to his wastrel, egobound companions—in general all those who sacrifice the sacred for the personal.

This section clearly reflects the theme that ego disturbs the spiritual birth process. Bloom is directly extolled for being meek, kind and true. He is shown as disengaged but compassionate. Ethical questions are discussed and various legitimate sources of answers are explored—scripture and civil laws.

8. Paragraphs 20 ("About that present time" line 277) and 21 reflect a reaction to the style of the Elizabethan prose chronicles (Elizabeth died in 1603). The Elizabethan style would honor the effort of the Cambridge school to maintain the purity of the English tongue by refusing admission of foreign elements and "ink-horn terms," such as technicalities and archaisms. The style would use intense alliteration,

long and short sentences, and undulation in minor and contrasted curves.[24]

Given Stephen's condition of youthful independence, this section flouts the Cambridge school by using much in the way of foreign languages and archaisms. The alliteration is circus material: "body without blemish, a belly without bigness . . . . With will will we withstand, withsay."

In paragraph 20, Stephen becomes the host in an episode full of allusions to the Eucharist. As host, he pours the beer. He toasts in a parody of the Last Supper. Using allusions from Yeats, he preaches "time's ruins build eternity's mansions," a reference to Yeats's reaction to the death of his brother.[25] In general, this phrase refers to the development of the spirit (eternity's mansions) from suffering (time's ruins). In the line "Desire's wind blasts the thorntree but after it becomes from a bramblebush to be a rose upon the rood of time," the thorntree and the rose recall Yeats's and Dante's imagery about the rose being a wormhole for the eternal in time and space. The sacred transcends time.

Stephen gives a speech about the word becoming flesh, the metaphysical doctrine in the Book of John describing Christ in the world (In the beginning was the word, and the word was with God, and the word was God). Stephen's critical concern as an artist is about tapping the sacred, his relationship as a human artist to the eternal. Stephen speculates about the Holy Mother's relationship to God in the Incarnation, the impregnation of Mary with the Christ child through the intervention of the Holy Ghost. This subject is famously treated in Yeats's poem *Leda and the Swan*, which ends with the question "Did she put on his knowledge with his power/Before the indifferent beak could let her drop?" Since in Catholic doctrine no mortal can know or unite with God but only have a relationship,[26] Stephen wonders if the Holy Mother "knew" Him, with overtones from the Bible of knowing as sexual intercourse. Likewise, Stephen wonders how close as an artist he can come to god, to the eternal.

The same issue of the relationship of the eternal to the human is also raised in Stephen's credo of either transubstantiation or consubstantiation but not subsubstantiation. In transubstantiation, the bread and wine are changed entirely into the body and blood of Christ with accidentals left over—suggesting that mortals can be changed entirely into the divine. In consubstantiation, the bread and wine would be commingled with the body and blood of Christ—suggesting mortals can share human and divine substance. In subsubstantiation, the bread and wine would defile the body and blood of Christ—suggesting humans are always lower than and can have no contact with the gods. Stephen hubristically believes that as an artist, he can get to transubstantiation or consubstantiation, and thus closer to the eternal powers than Mary did in the official Catholic version of the Incarnation.

In the 21st paragraph, Costello sings about the third month. The nurse comes in to admonish them a second time for making too much noise. All criticize Costello in birth terms—he is an abortion and illegitimate. By contrast, Bloom remarks on the sacredness of the occasion.

In terms of spiritual development, the Eucharist and its main theme of spiritual change are treated in these paragraphs. "Bodiment" is mentioned to include the Buddha. The notion of changing lust to love (Eve the mother of death changes to Mary the mother of life) is also included. Development moves on to consciousness, art and spiritual fathers. Stephen is disturbed by a visit of the spirit.

9. Paragraphs 22 ("To be short" line 334) through 24 mimic the 16th-17th century Latinate prose and solemn style of Milton, Hooker, Browne and Taylor. This prose is Latinate because the author thinks first in Latin. All of these authors are known for ornate or "organ-tone" language that runs on in relative clauses.[27] These are to be found in all three paragraphs. The opening words "To be short" mock the ornateness. Milton and this material share a temperamental earnestness unchecked by humor.[28] The organ tone of the Book of Isaiah is copied in Stephen's stern lecture about Ireland as Israel. Typical Browne subject matter, such as weird anthropology, and a few of his unusual words ("assuefaction minorates atrocities") are used.[29] A few of the sentences, such as the one starting the 24th paragraph with the crack of thunder, exhibit an effort to style the rhythm of the sentence to the nature of the subject matter.[30]

Stephen jokingly compares himself to the eternal son (reborn he will be his own son—like the son of man) and parodies the Biblical sayings of Jesus. Curious foreign sex rites (the right of first refusal by the Madagascar priest to the bride's virginity) are discussed as we move to anthropology. Nietzsche is mentioned again, this time as the Professor of French letters at Oxtail University, suggesting by the condom reference (made from ox gut) that his views on the ego stop spiritual growth. Stephen uses the line "Bring a stranger within thy tower it will go hard but thou wilt have the secondbest bed." This suggests the Church as the stranger in your soul that gives one Shakespeare's second best bed in the form of a cold relationship, not union with the divine, perhaps in the nature of sodomy.

Feeling lost and in despair, Stephen makes an Old Testament type speech about Ireland's corruption in serving the wrong masters, but he is also talking about himself. He knows love and compassion but doesn't feel it. He is not in the promised land. He compares his spirit to that of Egypt visited by the plagues because the Pharaoh would not let the Hebrews go (Stephen has not freed his spirit). He goes on to questions about the meaning of life ("whatness of our whoness hath fetched his whenceness").

In the 23rd paragraph, Costello continues the song about the mansion of wisdom, and development proceeds in the lab of secular knowledge and science. In the 24th, lightning and thunder strike, Stephen fears a storm in his heart and is in "desperation." His narcissistic ego has lost its mast and helmsman. Bloom unsuccessfully tries to calm Stephen with Hindu inspired explanations of the thunder and lightning phenomenon as "the discharge of fluid from the thunderhead . . . ." Sound signals the development of hearing in the fourth month.

10. Paragraphs 25 ("But was Boasthard's" line 429) and 26 are in the style of John Bunyan from *Pilgrim's Progress* (1675). As would only be appropriate, this section very successfully rendered in the Bunyan allegorical style reviews the state of Stephen's soul, the spiritual Pilgrim. Bunyan's style used proper names (such as Boasthard for Stephen and Calmer for Bloom) and moved toward the plain and

downplay of rhythm, the "Augustan style, blending Bible music with the ordinary"[31].

Bloom can not calm Stephen because of a "spike named Bitterness" (remember the bitter herb in the Passover meal and the spikes in Jesus). Stephen claims his religion shall be based not on "Believe-on-me" heaven but on the here and now, the "Bird in Hand." The narrator states Stephen is neither calm like the Buddha or godly like Jesus, the first mention of the dream team.

11. Paragraph 27 ("So Thursday sixteenth" line 474) starts in the style of the diarists Evelyn and Pepys (d. 1706 and 1703) and ends in the style of Defoe (d. 1731), particularly *The Journal of the Plague Year* (Bloom's being with Crawford's *Journal* is mentioned). True to the diary form, this paragraph reviews events that have taken place previously—Dignam's funeral, the drought and the rain. With the rain, the style changes to long "run on" sentences that bring together unrelated ideas. This style mimics the effects of swirling water bringing together unrelated objects.

Buck, on his way to the hospital, meets Bannon, who refers to his new girlfriend Milly as a "skittish heifer, big of her age and beef to the heel [thick ankles]." Back in the common room, Bloom apparently recounts his dream of Molly in red slippers and Turkish trunks, and the drinking group analyzes this dream as predicting change. Notice that in the last episode Stephen talked about having a similar dream himself. This would connect Stephen and Bloom through the collective unconscious.

References to hair and nails signal the fifth month of the fetus. In the spiritual realm, Catholic, Protestant particularly Methodist and new paganism are uneasy bed fellows in these paragraphs.

12. The first part of paragraph 28 ("With this came up" line 529) is in the style of Defoe, that "ageless" unmannered English prose.[32] Since the name Defoe suggests the foe, the first part features the following foes of spiritual progress: Lenehan, a gossiper and lounger who avoids suffering; hoof and mouth disease (Deasy's letter has apparently appeared in the paper), signifying original sin; and Frank Costello, who wasted his life because he didn't follow his passion.

Stephen says not to worry about hoof and mouth because the Russian doctor Reinderpest is coming—the Eastern Orthodox Church did not believe in original sin *per se* but characterized the normal human condition as an unnatural one cut off from god. St. Paul by faith alone and St. Peter, who was crucified upside down, appear here together with a rerun of the Parable of the Prodigal Son. The naked pockets of the returning Costello suggest the fetus's empty scrotum in the 6th month.[33]

13. The second part of the 28th paragraph ("An Irish bull" line 581) is in the style of Swift (c. 1667-1745), the famous satirist but also a clergyman and political journalist. His style was quiet to allow the irony to stand out. His stress pattern undulated from mono to polysyllabic feet.[34] Here is just the satire, not Swift's supreme style, playing on puns Papal Bull and Oxen bull throughout the History of Ireland. The boys joke about Nicholas or Pope Breakspear, the only Pope who was English and who gave lordship of Ireland to Henry II, referred to as "lord Harry". The father of the faithful is Henry VIII, who was both Head of Church and State in England and Ireland. Behind the satire, Joyce connects the slaughter of the Oxen of the Sun to the mutilation of spiritual office by the historical figures.

14. Paragraphs 29 ("Our worthy acquaintance" line 651) and 30 are in the style of Addison (d. 1719), a writer Joyce dubbed the "world's greatest hypocrite"[35] and thus a suitable style for Mulligan. The out-of-proportion gentlemanly style parodies Mulligan in the dimension of his own self image—respectability.

Buck and Bannon appear at the hospital. Bannon is in town to buy a military commission. Buck's imaginary fertilizing farm, where women would come to be impregnated by Buck, is the *reductio ad absurdum* of the Church's view that sex is solely for procreation. His farm is to be on Lambay Island, whose bird sanctuary status suggests the Holy Ghost is surely an endangered species in this plan. In the 30th paragraph, Dixon asks Buck if his fat belly means he is pregnant. Buck answers in a prostitute's voice while hitting himself below the diaphragm (site of breath or spirit) that his belly never bore a bastard. Buck's birth activities are tested only in terms of social respectability. By contrast,

Jesus was a bastard since he had no natural father, and the reborn Stephen will be a bastard since his own father.

15. Paragraph 31 ("Here the listener" line 738) is in the style of L. Sterne, the English novelist and author of **Sentimental Journey Through France and Italy** (1768).[36] Saintsbury says that he used "deliberate and constant . . . mechanical means, to enforce such emphasis as he aims at . . . ." The style that Joyce copied shows intensely just one or two figures in isolation, reporting every little detail about them whether or not important to the action. Sentiment is much in place, and the episode ends with a favorite Sterne device—the unfinished indecency.[37]

Bannon has apparently been seeing a girl (Milly) but didn't have a condom at the right time; he wears a locket with her picture. Bloom hears this but doesn't know Bannon is talking about Milly. Puns run on rain cloaks as condoms and Mr. Poyntz (point tease) for French ticklers. Buck is the Le Fecondateur (in French because of the Journey through France). Lynch discusses the diaphragm (referred to as the umbrella) as superior to the condom, since he would have more pleasure. These connections tie rain with fecundity. We learn that the couple Father Conmee met coming out of the fields of privacy in the Wandering Rocks (10th) episode was Lynch and his girl Kitty.

16. Paragraph 32 ("Amid the general" line 799) is in the style of Oliver Goldsmith, an Irish man of letters (d. 1774). Nurse Callahan comes in to tell Dr. Dixon that Mrs. Purefoy has delivered a boy. Costello and Mulligan make fun of her ("a monstrous fine bit of cowflesh"). Dr. Dixon rebukes them for this profanity. Buck backs off saying hypocritically that he honors father and mother. This paragraph introduces the Commandments.

17. Paragraph 33 ("To revert to" line 845) is in the style of Edmund Burke (d. 1797). His style was oratorical, and virtually every important passage contained a thought image and sentiment.[38] This section proceeds, you will note, in a sentimental vein in terms of an exaggerated version of Bloom's likes and dislikes. It is what is now called overwritten, a fault believed to proceed from the lack of emotional distance between author and subject.

This section sets forth Bloom's reaction (apparently in his unspoken thoughts) to the young blades, whose lack of pity he charitably puts down to the energy of youth. Costello, however, comes in for serious criticism as Bloom compares him to Shakespeare's worst characters—the slave Caliban and the hunchback Glouchester. Reading the enthusiasm of youth in the archetypes in the Bible, Bloom believes that the enthusiasm of youth could account for the desire of Adam and Eve in the Garden of Eden for fruit from the tree of knowledge of good and evil, the source of original sin. But Bloom also believes that such enthusiasm should not necessarily lead to the intentional disregard of the importance of the maternal function or of women in general.

In terms of spiritual development, the narrator describes Bloom's calming practice of repressing the rising choler in his heart.

18. Paragraph 34 ("Accordingly he broke" line 880) is in the style of Sheridan (d. 1816), an Irish born dramatist and resourceful politician.[39] Sheridan didn't make it into Saintsbury. Gifford suggests the style follows his political writings.

Here Bloom "broke his mind to this neighbor," making an important connection from the Eucharist to human interaction by the sharing of information, the highest form of which is art. Bannon has the cold side of a conversation with Bloom, repeatedly suggesting infidelity by Mrs. Purefoy and mistaken identity in the father (thus projecting Bannon's own spiritual condition). Crotthers and the others praise the old father Purefoy for his sturdy bullets, but Bannon holds to his profane position. Bloom wonders at the ability of "metempsychosis" to change these frivolous youth into doctors (profane to sacred) with just a piece of paper, a decree. Consider for a moment whether this is an error by Bloom, who should think metamorphosis rather than metempsychosis (which he dealt with earlier in the day), or whether this is intentional. Is the change from youth to maturity in the same person equivalent to reincarnation of a soul in a new body and life?

19. Paragraph 35 ("But with what" line 905) is in the style of the 18th century savage satirist Junius,[40] an exaggerated oratorical style.[41] He apparently frustrated his own purposes by his exaggerated attack.[42]

In a similar style, the narrator accuses Bloom of disloyalty to his country when all Bloom has done is to criticize in his own mind the views of others. He has dared to judge. We learn that Bloom holds some bonds for investment and much earlier had tried to seduce a maid, who is compared to Hagar, the mother of Ishmael. The narrator criticizes his masturbation and suggests he should practice what he preaches. Bloom is compared to the pelican, a symbol of Christ since it nourishes its young with its own blood.[43]

20. Paragraph 36 ("The news was" line 942) is in the style of Edward Gibbon (d. 1794), the English historian and author of the famous *Decline and Fall of the Roman Empire*. His smooth perhaps monotonous, undulating prose[44] with a delicate use of marked off phrases is copied here for the birth announcement.

Upon receiving the news the boys break into a "strife of tongues," suggesting the biblical legend of the Tower of Babel. Calm Bloom attempts to restrain the boys, and the important explanation is given by the narrator that the only bond between the boys is discursiveness. Their spiritual limitations are associated with stylistic and physical imperfections as they discuss, in an atrociously long sentence, the oddities of birth in a kind of sequential historical style. Physical imperfections in newborns are attributed to earlier copulation of humans with beasts, with the Minotaur as an example. In the midst of this discussion about distortions, Buck demonstrates the essence of sex for sex's sake by postulating a "nice clean old man" as the "supremest object of desire."

To the issue of saving only one of the Siamese twins to be separated, Stephen replies let no man put asunder what God has joined together. This is a profane use of a sacred concept about marriage.

21. Paragraph 37 ("But Malachias' tale" line 1010) is in the style of Horace Walpole's Gothic novel *The Castle of Otranto* (1764). Haines plays the part of the bloodstained usurper from that novel.[45]

Buck conjures a Gothic inspired vision of Haines returning from hell through a secret panel in the wall by the chimney (a version of the double door). In the vision, Haines carries a book of Celtic literature and poison in his hands. In this Buck created vision, Haines confesses to the murder of Samuel Childs. Haines, as a symbol of the profane, declares drugs to be his only hope and suddenly vanishes sounding of the cry of the black panther.

The actual Haines enters immediately thereafter by the regular door (the second of the two doors) to instruct Buck to meet him at the Westland Row station at ten after eleven. Haines leaves immediately. Haines's appearance also supports the Dionysian allusion, since at the end of Dionysian festivals the evil powers of the underworld returned.[46]

After Haines leaves, the seer (Buck) and the sage (Stephen) trade witticisms that tie together Manaan and the definition of the sentimentalist and identify Haines as Haines Childs, the third brother murderer (the second was tried and acquitted thanks to Seymour Bush). Viewed in analogy to the biblical fratricide by Cain of Able, Haines would be connected with the third participant in that murder, the devil who was considered in some quarters to be the father of Cain.[47] The black panther in Haines's dream is identified as his own ghost and his own father (and perhaps also his Id). The rat from Hades is mentioned. The "murderer's ground" is the Child's home. Child from "childs" signifies, I believe, youth and innocence. Haines and Buck disappear shortly, leaving Stephen under the influence of Lynch and then Bloom.

22. Paragraph 38 ("What is the age of the soul of man" line 1038) is after the style of "gentle pathos and nostalgia" and archaic phraseology of Charles Lamb (d. 1834).[48] Here an all knowing narrator describes the "age of the soul of man" by reference to Bloom's ruminations about his past. Bloom thinks about younger iterations of himself from the vantage point of his current middle-age. This is, of course, the pattern for this novel, Joyce looking back on himself. The flash back technique of the narrator is weird, almost circus-like in calling attention to itself. Bloom remembers himself as a school boy, and later as a travelling salesman of trinkets for his father. Then he thinks son, "these about him might be his sons . . . the wise father knows his own child." Finally, he thinks about his first sex with the one shilling prostitute, Bridie Kelly, in "Hatch" street between the police watches and under two raincapped clouds (the cautious Bloom apparently used two condoms).

447

The host reappears as the bread his mother's love put in Bloom's school bag.

23. Paragraphs 39 ("The voices blend" line 1078) and 40 are after the style of the romantic De Quincey (d. 1859), whose smooth variety has been described as a dream fugue.[49] Some of his works involve fantastic animals.[50] These characteristics are faithfully followed in this dream-like sequence.

This section presents an image of generations stretching back in time. It includes a dream-like jumble of visions from the day. Animals appear as stars in the heavenly constellations obeying the law of parallax, the relativity of viewing from different positions. The reference to stars as the "murderers of the sun" is in the sense that when the stars come out, the sun sets. A blend of Milly, Martha, Molly and Gerty appears as Virgo wearing the golden sandals of Hermes. The constellation Pegasus, symbolic of poetic inspiration, rises and Virgo, the sign of the virgin, descends and ends on the red triangular sign of Taurus, the sign of artistic consciousness and the logo for Number One Bass ale.[51] This is the journey of Stephen's virgin soul, particularly after his date with Nora.

24. Paragraph 41 ("Francis was reminding" line 1110) is after the style of Landor (d. 1864), who featured imaginary conversations between figures from classical literature in order to comment on the problems of his own time.[52] According to Saintsbury, he brought to prose a polyphony combining magnificence, simplicity and a kind of frigidity. The specimens quoted in Saintsbury involve meetings of lovers among the trees and leaves.[53] His subject matter changed abruptly.

Joyce uses reflections of these techniques. Costello mentions to Stephen their schoolboy friends Glaucon, Alcibiades and Pisistratus, ancient Greek characters from Plato's Dialogues whom they studied in school and apparently imitated in their play conversations. Lynch recalls his visit to the fields and of meeting Father Conmee upon returning.[54] Some of the rhythm is wonderful.

In terms of our main themes, Stephen "encircled his gadding hair with a coronal of vineleaves." This image, which must refer to Stephen's intoxication and not actual leaves, places the symbol of Dionysius on the source of Stephen's imagination. Stephen boasts of his poetic prowess to bring back the past. Lynch tells Stephen that Lynch hopes "something more, and greatly more, than a capful of light odes can call your genius father." Note the use of language of paternal birth for art. Dionysius had his second birth from the thigh of Zeus, the ultimate male.

Lenehan mentions Stephen's mother, which throws Stephen into a funk. The narrator calls the gathering a "feast." Sceptre's fall in the horse race, or the fall of authority, is bemoaned. Throwaway with multiple winner W. Lane on board has won. The reference to Phyllis is to a conventional name for a maiden and profanely suggests "fill this." Buck notices that Bloom is in a trance looking at the red triangle on the Bass ale bottle.

25. Paragraphs 42 ("However, as a" line 1174) and 43 are in the style of Macaulay (d. 1859), an English historian who created unreliable historical accounts that came out more reasonably than the sordid facts themselves.[55] His weighty prose carried trivial information. His section gets the common errors in the use of English, "him being" and the incorrect "individual" instead of "person."

The narrator tells us that Bloom is staring at the beer bottle with beer left in it and is thinking about a few "private transactions." The group refrains from pouring more beer from this bottle because Bloom is staring at it. Bloom meets someone's eyes, comes out of his trance and pours beer for him. I think that this person is Stephen—others think Lenehan. The group is described person by person for the fourth time and with particular reference, as in the Last Supper, to who is sitting next to Stephen. Bloom's day is summarized.

26. Paragraph 44 ("It had better" line 1223) is after the style of Thomas Huxley (d. 1895), a naturalist most noted for his lucid exposition of the theory of evolution and other scientific matters.[56] Saintsbury called his "admirably sinewy prose"[57].

Thrinacria (Sicily) is mentioned and compassion of a sort describes the cooperation of sperm and egg. Lynch suggests an all encompassing determinism as a kind of degeneration pervades the discussion. In this atmosphere suggestive of the collapse of the traditional values at the end of the 19th century,[58] Stephen jibes the Almighty by saying that after eating all the old and corrupt (natural deaths), He would like some young and innocent bob (death of the young). God is being mocked.

27. Paragraph 45 ("Meanwhile the skill" line 1310) is after the style of Dickens. The paragraph uses some of Dickens's words, such as "Doady," his sentimentality and repetition, and parodies Dickens's typical combination of humor and social criticism.[59] The style chosen is apparently from that section of *David Copperfield* (1849-50) in which a death marks the end of David's adolescence and the beginning of his adulthood,[60] the coming pattern for Stephen.

Despite the parodied sentimentality, the tone of this paragraph compliments the courage of mother Purefoy and the sacredness of the birth. In this formula, sentimentality is sexual impulse without responsibility or love. The literary analogue of lust would be sentimental literature whose appeal does not last. The paragraph ends with an echo from the Parable of Talents, the harbinger of change of attitude.

28. Paragraph 46 ("There are sins" line 1344) is in the style of Cardinal Newman (d. 1900), the famous English Catholic writer. Saintsbury described his prose as "Quietly exquisite" and an "unbroken, unslurred current of harmony"[61]. The narrator discusses the longevity of sin or "evil memories," as would Newman in one of his sermons. The reemergence of sins after laying dormant in the soul seems to place them in the personal unconscious, or in Hindu terms in karma.

29. Paragraph 47 ("The stranger still" line 1356) is in the style of Walter Pater (d. 1894)—delicate and quiet with particular care of the paragraph.[62] His subject the Renaissance, the reuse of classical materials, sponsors Bloom's recollection of when he first saw Stephen, at a party 17 years ago. Note that Stephen's father Simon is not mentioned in the recollection. At this party Bloom bested John Henry Menton at bowls, which Menton remembered in the Hades (6th) episode. Characteristically, Bloom doesn't remember his victory. Stephen, then five, was standing on an urn looking at his mother with remoteness and reproach. The "linseywool" outfit Stephen wore then serves to connect Stephen to Rudy, who was buried in wool. Back in the present, Stephen's bitterness shows through his "false calm." The reference to the

game of croquet mimics the collisions of atoms in the nuclear level of reality.

30. Paragraph 48 ("Mark this farther" 1379) is in the style of Ruskin (d. 1900). His style was marked by attention to details and each word (parodied by Joyce as "Mark this farther and remember") and by the influence of verse and cumulative clauses.[63] The narrator compares the current scene to the crib birth in Bethlehem. Change resulting from fear of lightning and the "utterance of the word" is immanent.

31. Paragraphs 49 ("Burke's! Outflings" line 1391) and 50 in the style of Carlyle (d. 1900) capture Stephen's call to move the drinking group from the hospital to Burke's pub just before closing time. Outfling suggests abortion. In these Carlyle based paragraphs, Stephen suffers a relapse in his spiritual development.

Carlyle's style changed markedly over his lifetime from bareness to "varied and accidented and finished with colour"; his style was described during his time as "prose run mad"[64]. "Prose run mad" is a suitable prose style for Stephen's hurried charge to Burke's. This pub, named after the dead body parts specialists (Burke robbed graves to provide bodies for medical dissection), suggests abortion and the Mass, both of which must be taken before "closing time." Still chained to the profane, Burke's is the proper spot for the boys. They run right past the news of the birth of baby Purefoy, still bent on their own rounds. Leaving the hospital, the rushing boys turn right to go Burke's. Bloom, though, stops to offer through nurse Callahan his proper regards to mother and child. Uncharacteristically lacking in tact, he asks Nurse Callahan when she will be visited by the "storkbird." The specific news of the birth is in terms of the weight of the placenta, the gravity of the connection among humans. Note that physical construction of the placenta is similar to the combined strands of development nurtured by Joyce.

The rioters run down the street in the rain. Dixon catches up and Bloom follows. A bystander mistakes Stephen for a priest, so Stephen gives the last blessing from the Mass. With "Halt: Heave to" they enter Burke's. There two order whiskies, "mead of our fathers," five order Bass Number Ones and two order Guinesses, nicknamed "ardilauns." Bloom is ridiculed for ordering a ginger cordial (cordiality being his specialty). In the second round that comes quickly given the approach of closing time, all order absinthe (spirituality absent) except Bloom, who has red wine ["Rome boose for the Bloom toff (gentleman)"]. Bloom sets his watch. Stephen pays. Bannon privately identifies Bloom as Milly's father. Lenehan blames his betting loss on one Stephen Hand who steamed open a telegram from Bass, the owner of Sceptre. Steaming for the message describes Stephen's experience with Nora.

Stephen notices that Mulligan and Bannon have left to meet Haines to catch the last tram back to the tower in Sandymount. With a new party (Bannon) in residence, Stephen is foreclosed from the tower. The mysterious MacIntosh reappears as the rioters leave; he is described as formerly an important citizen now eating dry bread (Satan formerly an important angel now in his lair of the profane eating day old manna). Stephen invites Lynch to Nighttown. Feeling paternal, Bloom follows in order to protect Stephen.

The spray language used in this ending part suggests the babel of individual voices fueled by ego drive, characteristic of Joyce's view of literature in the 20th century.

Lynch sees a poster advertising Elijah and the gospel preacher Dowie (pronounced "Do we" for the unity). The episode ends in the huckster sermon style of the gospel preacher Alexander J. Christ Dowie speaking directly to the reader while apparently farting. His message is this: believe it or not at your peril; the Deity is in charge and not to be mocked; and living a profane life mocks the Lord. A combination of medicine (Hermes) and ecstasy (Dionysius) as the portal to the spiritual life ends the episode:

> You'll need to rise precious early, you sinner there, if
> you want to diddle the Almighty God. Pflaaap! Not
> half. He's got a coughmixture with a punch in it for
> you, my friend, in his back pocket. Just you try it on.

Traditional Schemata, First Letter and First Word

The traditional schemata given by Joyce for this episode are organ—womb, art—medicine, color—white, symbol—mothers, and technique—embryonic development. The correspondences are Thrinacria—hospital, daughters of Helios—the nurses, Helios—Dr.

Horne and Oxen—fertility. The initial letter **D** in the first word Deshil looks like a pregnant stomach.

The Virgin and Big Bird

Once again the profane Eve sacred Virgin Mary distinction is emphasized. In the Incarnation (the impregnation of Mary by the Holy Ghost and birth of Christ from Mary), the sacred Deity became manifest in time and space in the grand epiphany. The modem for this momentous event in the relationship of the eternal to the temporal was conception by god in a human mother. She conceived the incarnated Christ as a result of some kind of intercourse with the Holy Ghost. The nature of that intercourse is on Stephen's mind. Stephen has just felt Nora's hand.

This issue is key because Joyce believes that human sexual intercourse under the right conditions is one of the human channels to the eternal powers. In this way of looking at things, the choice by god of intercourse with the Holy Mother under the most proper circumstances is indicative of the power of this channel. Joyce appears to believe, for example, that if sex with shame was involved in the expulsion from the Garden of Eden, sex without shame is involved in the way back in. Moreover, the virgin birth serves as the critical juncture of fecundity and the sacred. Congress with the Holy Mother stands as the symbol of the two births celebrated in this episode, the sacred birth of the child to continue the human race and the virgin or second birth in the spirit. This subject was featured in the night discussion between Jesus and Nicodemus from the Sanhedrin (John 3:1). Jesus said man must be born again from above, reborn as a child, a new man; this new relationship with god as father results in a new relationship with other humans.

Stephen wonders in this tradition whether the Holy Mother, who of all humans certainly had the best chance, "knew" God at the moment of conception of Jesus. The more important branch of the pun on "knew" is of how much of God's transcendent energies Mary was aware. Catholic dogma allows even Mary only to approach God, but not know or unite with God. Stephen has found attractive the Oriental doctrines, echoed by Schopenhauer and Emerson, which teach that Stephen, like all things, has the divine spark within him (the narrator tells us Stephen is a "perverted transcendentalist"). Like Bloom mesmerized by looking at the

453

beer bottle, Stephen begins to stand outside himself and gets his first glimpse of the unity. This occurs, *a la* Vico, after he is frightened by thunder.

In Stephen's mind, the discussion about connections to the eternal relates to his art, which he wants to connect with the same source. Eve as the first mother is the home page for the collective unconscious, and Stephen wonders if Mary as the feminine side of the church is the browser to the eternal. He believes the server will always be busy to the church's browser, and that the artist can be superior to the church in downloading the word (the eternal), or making the word flesh.

His argument about Mary's role is a Hobson's choice: "Or she knew him, that second I say, and was but creature of her creature, *vergine madre, figlia di tuo figlio* (Virgin Mother, daughter of thy son, from Dante in *Paradiso*), or she knew him not and then stands she in the one denial or ignorancy with (Saint Peter and the Church) . . . " In other words, if Mary knew God then God became a creature of her creature, sex and human, and God would necessarily be downgraded by her sex and birth instincts. If she didn't know Him or what was happening, then she was ignorant of the eternal and can only be an unwitting vessel, like the Catholic Church and perhaps like a bottle of beer that allows Bloom to meditate on higher matters. As for the Church and Mary, Stephen says: "Let the lewd with faith and fervour worship."

Stephen takes the hubristic position that his art can browse the eternal better than the Holy Mother: "Mark me now. In woman's womb word is made flesh but in the spirit of the maker all flesh that passes becomes the word that shall not pass away. This is the postcreation." This "maker" is the artist. The artist's results are better since permanent, even better than the impermanent Christ who lived and died. Creating in classical restraint with respect to the grave and constant in human fortunes, the artist is acting "in the spirit of the maker" since the artist is detached and removed like god. The artist addresses in a permanent record (for example a book) the human impermanence, the fundamental condition of humans that god created ("all flesh that passes becomes the word that shall not pass away"). With this hubris, the youthful Stephen diddles the deity.

Jung and the *Fin de Siecle* Fascination with Degeneration

The particular combination of entwined embryological processes contained in this episode reflects intellectual developments current to the times, especially Jung (this episode was written in 1920).[65] As early as 1909, Jung had developed from theories in evolutionary biology his own psychological theory: that the unconscious mind retained a "vitalistic biological residue" from the earlier development of mankind and that each person traced this historical development of mankind in his or her own personal development. Ontogeny repeats phylogeny. This theory developed in an age that was fascinated with the concept of hereditary degeneration, that everything was getting worse.

The older layers of the collective unconscious (the "land of the dead") speak, according to Jung, in dreams images from pre-Christian pagan mythology, particularly for Aryans those of Mithraism. This religion is, in Jung's view, the clearest surviving example of the original sun based (thus Helios) Ur-religion of our very first Indo-European ancestors. This collective layer produces, per Jung, a cosmic life force linking all Aryan peoples.

Mithraism was favored by the early Roman rulers and competed with Christianity in the Roman Empire until 312 CE, when the Cross on Constantine's battle gear won the day on the field of battle and the Empire officially went Christian. Mithraism featured a rebirth, a last supper of Mithra on earth and rituals like the Catholic Mass involving consecrated water, bread and blood with priests and bells. The main event in Mithraic ritual was the revelation by the priest of the image of Mithra killing with a sword a wild bull (read youthful egoism). According to Jung, this original Aryan religion was also partly reflected in the ancient Teutonic religion involving Thor, the god of thunder whose claps on Thursday awaken Stephen from his egoism. Vico believed that thunder first awakened our primitive ancestors to a belief in other worldly powers.

By breaking through, by way of Jung's techniques, to these ancient archetypes and their associated energies, one could avoid the hereditary degeneration and decay (Nietzsche's "hereditary taint") with which the age was fascinated. This fascination produced in the literary realm Brian Stoker's ***Dracula***, whose vampire was the consummate image of the hereditary degenerate and the probable source for the vampire/bat symbol that continually appears in this novel. In this connection, it is important to note that once struck and sucked, Dracula's victims of the neck bite wanted more.

Jung's concept of the collective unconscious is that part of us which is outside of time; it represents the continuity and bond by which we feel that we are never extinguished.[66] Jung's personal guide in his active imagination, his Virgil to Dante, to the collective land of the dead was Philomen (name means love all men, perhaps Bloom as guide to Stephen). Jung was influenced by the Theosophical Society books on occultism by Mead and ideas of Max Muller about an early mythopoetic age prior to the diffusion of the original Indo-European people into Greece, India, Persia, etc.[67]

The parallels with this episode are striking. We have several embedded embryological processes going on. The opening three paragraphs are an invocation and petition to the ancient form of Aphrodite in the Ur-religion of man, since the birth process is the obvious source of mankind. Hereditary degeneration appears in this episode through the subjects of Eve and original sin, and vitalism appears as the forces for birth. Joyce's powerful prose gives us a vision of the Collective Land of the Dead.

The Mithraic god Kronos representing boundless time or destiny is pictured in a body wrapped by a serpent caduceus style, a thunderbolt engraved on his chest, and holding a long scepter and keys. The signs of the zodiac are engraved on his body. Hell in Mithraic religion was presided over by Ahriman and Hecate and the monsters that issued from their impure union. This religion featured a fierce determinism moderated by the influence of Mithra as "mediator." In the main image, Mithra conquers the wild bull and transforms the energy of its seed into the civilized benefits of useful plants and herbs. From the death of the wild bull was born a new life, better than the old one. Mithra symbolizes order in nature, the most important aspect of which is generation.[68]

The Mathraic concepts inform Joyce's choices for this episode. Stephen's change is very much like the conquering of the wild bull. The caduceus has been discussed already. The monsters are discussed by the boys. The thunderbolt appears as lightning. Stephen loses the keys. These details populate a haze permeating the layers in this episode, much as material resides in the collective unconscious.

The Eleusian Mysteries and More Hermes

Socrates, with whom Stephen has been linked, said his Eleusian experience was one of the greatest experiences of his life. Stephen's experience in this episode partakes of many of the reported attributes of an experience at the Eleusian mystery initiation.

Like the Eleusian initiates who probably consumed a psychedelic parasite (ergot), Stephen's intoxication serves as part of a purification ritual to dissolve his ego and achieve illumination. The Eleusian authorities in charge were the goddesses Demeter and Persephone and the serpents (the caduceus) as representatives of the Great Mother Goddess. At the critical moment in the initiation, a golden stave of wheat was raised by the presiding authorities, much as the host made from wheat is raised in the Mass and the malted beverage made from the hops is raised in this episode. In the Eleusian scenes left to us, the successfully converted candidate was pictured as an old man, notable for being more withdrawn from historical life and focused on the eternal. Profaning this image, Buck says the supreme object of desire is a nice clean old man. The successful Eleusian candidate realized in the first initiation that the eternal is present in the mortal life, realized in the second the combined male/female biological background (the collective unconscious) of us all and then in the third and final initiation came to Apollo, the god of spiritual consciousness and light who informs the muses. Here in Joyce's land of Helios, we are back to the Appollonian source of epiphanies for art and literature.

The spirit of Hermes protects the journey Stephen begins in this episode. Hermes generally protects those who are on the right personal voyage.[69] The windfall gain is a gift from Hermes; and fortuitously Bloom finds Stephen and Stephen finds Bloom. Stephen says his salary was received for a song—his natural gift of song that was the first stage in his artistic progress. The Hermes attitude is best reflected in the youthful, playful imagination of the artist.[70] As Hermes is responsible for the safety of divine property, he is in the right place at the right time—the maternity hospital helping the latest additions in the continuity of human kind, which reaches back to the gods.[71]

Hermes was the Greek interpretation of the Egyptian god Thoth or Ibis, which the Greeks translated as logos.[72] Stephen the hubristic artist diddles the deity's exclusive franchise on the logos. In the next episode, Hermes appears as a dog in the red light district.

Passover—Last Supper

Pesah or Passover begins on Thursday. This novel begins on a Thursday. The day before Passover is commemorated by the Fast of the First Born, which describes Bloom's paternal condition coming into this day. Trumpets blow three times at three special times during this holy Jewish day; and the introductory paragraphs of this episode repeat three times to mimic the trumpets. Passover celebrates release from Egypt, as Stephen is about to be released from narcissistic youth.

The Company for a Passover meal must be a minimum of ten or a minyan, which are present in the original group—Dixon, Lynch, Madden, Lenehan, Crotthers, Stephen, Bloom, Costello—plus the two nurses Callahan and Quigley. The Head is to take the first cup, as Stephen has surely done. The ritual is organized around the pouring of five cups of wine, the fifth being for Elijah and filled from the glasses of the participants. This episode is organized around successive pourings of beer, and at the end Bloom generously pours the beer in his glass into another's. The Passover participants eat bitter herbs, as Stephen is fixed with the spike of bitterness. Of the plagues visited by Jahweh on Egypt (referred to in the ceremony), all except the frogs appear in this episode in one way or another. The frogs represent fruitfulness and appeared, we remember, on Molly's dress. Her fruit is plagued by drought.

The Paschal Lamb is Rudy, whose sacrifice paved the way for the meeting of Bloom and Stephen. The avenging angel that killed the first born, unless the house was marked with blood of the lamb, is the thunder that kills Stephen's foolishness of youth unmarked by suffering. A place is always set at the Passover dinner for Elijah, and Bloom joins the group.

The Last Supper is the Christian counterpart to the Jewish Pesah. The Christian concept reflects a kind of embryological development from the Jewish concept. The Last Supper is the foundation for the Eucharist, the instrument of spiritual change. The haze of details in the drinking bout in the hospital also includes allusions to the Last Supper, the last supper at which Stephen is a narcissistic youth. His companions are the counterparts of the all too human disciples who fled when Jesus was arrested. We have the late arriving Mulligan and Bannon joining the original group, for a total of 12. They are listed several times, which for Joyce is a blunt clue. Haines makes a brief appearance for the 13th. Together they are one (Stephen or Bloom) plus twelve (as at the Last Supper). Peter and John, like the nurses, were not present at the Last Supper the entire time but went to get the lamb, as the nurses do the child. Like Luke, they include a doctor and medical students. Haines like Judas is never really there in the spirit. Haines gives Stephen the "heel" by leaving abruptly, as Judas was said to do when he left the Last Supper early after Jesse's prediction of betrayal.

At the Last Supper, the disciples were lead to the upper room by the man with the water pitcher (in order not to alert the Temple authorities where Jesus would be).[73] Here Stephen has supplied the beer, presumably from outside the hospital. Jesus knew at the Last Supper that his hour had come to "depart out of this world unto the Father." Stephen is about to become his own spiritual father. The room for the Last Supper was in the nature of a hostelry, the same type of room where Jesus was born. Jesse's first and last suppers were in the same type of room. And Stephen is about to change in a maternity hospital, where he probably arrived.

Purification

Stephen's condition parallels that point in the Mass when the Host or bread is being consecrated by lifting it to the cross and the bell rings three times for the entry of Jesus as Christ into the host in the transubstantiation.[74] Here Stephen is being prepared by reaching a state of desperation akin to Jesse's night in the Garden of Gesthemane and being with or held up to Bloom, that repository of reserved compassion. The bell rings three times in the hospital, signaling the beginning of his spiritual change. The Eucharist is communion, coming into union with, oneness.[75]

In the purification process, the prolonged delivery by Mrs. Purefoy is referred to in a later episode in terms of Jewish ritual as the "heave offering," that portion of a tithe gift retained by the priests. As "heave" denotes to select, the priests selected the portions to be retained by them. "Heave" means to separate or raise as in an offering. The heave offering was usually of agricultural products—bread and wine (Numbers 18:24). They were raised by the priest in offering to god. These meanings suggest the separating and raising of the just born baby Purefoy and the raising of the glasses of beer. Together with the heave action of the mother in the birth process, these meanings connect the spiritual allusions in this episode. In art, the heave must separate out the personal.

Structure, Art and Aesthetics

This is a very difficult episode to read and understand. It has depth in the subject of the sacred versus profane that I have not even tried to plumb. At times I felt like Dave in the *Space Odyssey* looking into the slab and being blown away by the depths of the stars inside the slab.

Don't take for granted writing in the styles of past masters of English while entwining multiple themes. That is a masterful achievement.

You have to answer for yourself whether the ground has been adequately prepared for a massive change in Stephen. That his change would be instantaneous rather than gradual is possible in youth. Also ask what dramatic point is made by giving the specific action of this episode such a distorted cubist-type exterior. Does this exterior mimic the flux in Stephen's soul?

The evolving language styles that wrap the episode suggest development toward more realism, and that direction relates generally to the change in Stephen toward more objectivity. It is entertaining to consider the changing styles in view of the linguistic theory that the structure of language from time to time reflects our evolving view of the structure of the physical world.[76] You might speculate at this stage on the structure of language that would be appropriate to describe those forces or energies in the eternal. Would it be calm and ordered or dreamy?

460

This episode is a separate object successfully marked off and is coherent from part to whole and whole to part. But does it radiate? Is it fortunately rendered? The picture of Stephen's condition and his meeting with Bloom is, in my opinion, so buried in the noise of the episode that their force is reduced. Joyce is too subtle. The radiance suffers as a result.

****

ENDNOTES

1. These, as we know, are Joyce's portals to the gods.
2. Frye II, p. 75.
3. CW, p. 39.
4. Frye II, p. 82.
5. *Helios* Encyclopedia Britannica, 1983 ed., Micropaedia, Vol. IV, p. 1001.
6. Edersheim, A. *The Life and Times of Jesus the Messiah* (New York: Longmans, Green, and Co., 1917) p. 539.
7. The following is a summary of Mircea Eliades's *The Sacred and the Profane* .
8. See generally Hillman, J. *Insearch Psychology and Religion* (Woodstock: Spring Publications, 1967).
9. Campbell, Mythic Image, p. 143 et. seq.
10. Mead, S. *Thrice Greatest Hermes* (London: John M. Watkins, 1906) vol. l, p. 86 quoting the Greek Hermes Prayers.
11. Joyce's Ulysses Notesheets, p. 261.
12. *The Letters of James Joyce*, edited by S. Gilbert (New York: Viking Press, 1957) vol. I, p. 139-140.
13. Blamires, p. 147.
14. Gifford, p. 408.
15. See Gilbert p. 298 for the concept that this was changed later. Unless otherwise indicated, my source for the style is Gifford.
16. For a modern version of this issue, see Murdoch, Iris *The Sacred and Profane Love Machine*.

17. Saintsbhury, G. *A History of English Prose Rhythm* (Bloomington: Indiana University Press, 1912) p. 44.

18. Ibid., pp. 53-54.

19. Ibid., p. 49.

20. Gifford, p. 413.

21. Saintsbury, p. 63-66.

22. Ibid., p. 82-90.

23. In the language as it appears from Wyclif in Saintsbury.

24. Saintsburty, pp. 115-122.

25. Gifford, p. 415.

26. See this issue in the AP.

27. Saintsbury, pp. 163 to 168.

28. Ibid., p. 169.

29. Gifford, p. 419.

30. sll sl ssll sl ll lss llss slsl ssls ll sl llsl. Try it.

31. Saintsbury, p. 239.

32. Critical Essays, p. 324.

33. Ibid., p. 325.

34. Saintsbury, p. 241-242.

35. Critical Essays, p. 326.

36. Gifford, p. 427.

37. Critical Essays, p. 327.

38. Saintsbury, p. 273.

39. Gifford, p. 429.

40. Ibid., p. 429.

41. Saintsbury, p. 257.

42. Critical Essays, p. 326.

43. Gifford, p. 429.

44. Saintsbury, p. 281.

45. Gifford, p. 431.

46. Boorstin, D. *The Creators* (New York: Random House, 1992) p. 203.

47. Kugel, J. *The Bible As It Was* (Cambridge: Harvard University Press, 1997) p. 86.

48. Saintsbury, p. 350.

49. Ibid., p. 311.

50. Critical Essays, p. 330.

51. Gifford, p. 434.

52. Ibid., p. 434.

53. Saintsbury, p. 328.

54. Critical Essays, p. 331.

55. Gifford, p. 436.

56. Ibid., p. 436.

57. Saintsbury, p. 441.

58. Blamires, p. 155.

59. Critical Essays, p. 332.

60. Janusko, R. *The Sources and Structure of the "Oxen of the Sun" Episode of James Joyce's Ulysses* diss., Kent State Univ. 1967, p. 157.

61. Saintsbury, p. 381.

62. Ibid., p. 420.

63. Ibid., p. 392 et. seq.

64. Saintsbury, p. 366.

65. Unless otherwise indicated, the source of all of the material under this heading is Noll, R. *The Jung Cult* (Princeton: Princeton University Press, 1994).

66. Jung experienced a self deification involving an internal merger of the Mithraic Aion and the Aryan Christ (look for a merger of Stephen and Bloom and Shakespeare in the next episode). After this, it was necessary for Jung to reenact the life of Christ and symbolically suffer the death on the Cross and the Descent into Hell—the Realm of the Mothers. Keep these basic ideas in mind as the rest of the novel unfolds.

67. And those of Bachofen about the passage of the human race through the three stages of (1) hetairism, polygamy and equality whose goddess was an ancient form of Aphrodite (2) matriarchy, the lunar and mother earth phase based on egalitarian values whose goddess was Demeter and (3) following a Dionysian transition, patriarchy with the sun, law and man whose god was Apollo. Jung found the

concept of deity to be an expression of the libido that from its brutal Roman days had been repressed by the joint forces of Mithraism and Christianity.

68. Cumont, F. *The Mysteries of Mithra* (New York: Dover Publications, 1902) p. 104 et. seq.

69. Unless otherwise indicated, all material on Hermes is from Kerenyi, K. *Hermes Guide of Souls* Trans. M. Stein (Dallas: Spring Publication, 1976).

70. In the *Iliad* where the heroic life is set off against certain fate and death, Hermes is kept at a distance. His skill is unheroic evasion as Bloom will duck the difficult moral issues discussed by the boys. As the mature balancer or unifier of opposites who sits at the junction of order and chaos, Hermes appears in Bloom who takes both sides in the discussion. Hermes likes to associate with persons and often makes them invisible, here reflected in Bloom's lack of ego. In The Odyssey, Hermes is the guide of souls when the world is defined by fluctuation rather than deep roots. Odysseus our mast journeyer and tied to Bloom is descended from Hermes through his mother's side. Hermes is named "painless," as Bloom in this episode rests from his journey and does not chide anyone.

71. Hermes is the ruler of dreams and so Bloom accounts from his recent dream. Hermes is the gatekeeper and Bloom is worrying about Molly and Milly's sacred gates and is the spiritual gate for Stephen. Hermes is the delight in meeting and finding, the messenger to and from the gods; he steals from the other gods and offers penetrating vision. As such, he must appeal as a symbol of the artistic imagination. Hermes was left an oracle of bees, and Bloom has been treated at this hospital for a bee sting. Hermes is connected to games of chance as part of the larger field of accidental happenings, and the results of the horse race and Bloom's alleged bet are still bothering some of the participants in this episode. As the god of doorways, Hermes is remembered in the line that Molly fills the door: "Full of a dure."

72. Budge, vol. 1, p. 400.

73. For all the statements concerning Passover, see Stallion, J. *Passover*

(San Jose: Resources Publications, 1988).

74. The rat returns in this episode from the Hades episode because the debate over the change in the Eucharist involved the question of whether after the consecration the rat would eat bread or Jesus.

75. The Mass begins with "sprinkle me with hyssop," a plant used in Hebrew purification rituals particularly for the ritual cleansing of lepers. Here the vine of the hop is cleaning Stephen's spirit. Bloom is the very model of meekness enjoined by the Epistle part of the Mass. The revivalist ending in the episode about diddling God sounds thus in the Mass: "Be not deceived; God is not mocked . . ." The Gospel portion of the Mass features the only son who is raised by the Lord, as Stephen will raise Rudy for Bloom. Stephen says he has received his drinking money for a song and the Offertory (when the plate is passed) says: ". . . and he put a new canticle into my mouth, a song to our God." As the altar is incensed, the Priest says "Set a watch, O Lord," and Bloom sets his watch. At the Consecration, the bell rings thrice as it does here.

76. Langer, S. *Philosophy in a New Key* (Cambridge: Harvard University Press, 1942) p. 88.

Circe (Episode 15)

Basic Themes

Invisible forces in the whorehouse purify Stephen and Bloom. Purified by maidenhead, they are prepared for an open life.

In the Odyssey, Circe's magic wand turns men into swine and then back again into better men. In the company of whores in Dublin's red light district, Stephen and Bloom descend deeper into swine states and then are initiated into greater self-respect and freedom through contact with the collective unconscious. Both these forces, Circe's magic wand and the collective unconscious, are energized by forces external to personal human consciousness and experience. Symbolized by Hermes in the form of a dog that changes breed often, invisible forces manipulate this episode.

Stephen and Lynch proceed from Burke's Pub to the Mabbot Street red light district. Protective and paternal Bloom follows. In Bella Cohen's brothel, Stephen and Bloom come together and paternal Bloom protects Stephen from the avaricious madam. In this odd context, both Stephen and Bloom are initiated into greater self-respect as a result of hallucinatory visions that tap the unconscious. As a result, we expect that Stephen's narcissism and Bloom's masochism will be exorcised.

Stephen and Bloom's hallucinatory visions are sourced from both personal experience and the impersonal collective experience (the archetypes or the collective unconscious). This construct follows the emphasis in Jung's theories, whose basic outline had already been published by the time this novel was written.[1] This Irish collective turns out to be comically efficient; it has already collected the events of the day. The collective is the source of many of the concerns in the grave and constant in Joyce's aesthetics. So here we are—right down at the "base" of it all in the whorehouse.

Dublin's red light district is known Nighttown. The name Nighttown suggests dreams, the theater of the unconscious. In dreams, the creative imagination and sexual instinct, Joyce's prime portals to the eternal, have lead roles. In dreams, reality blurs. Likewise, this episode's two planes of reality intersect, blend and blur in this dream-like presentation of Nighttown. The first is that limited by time, space and causality for the seven main characters of this episode. The second is that unlimited psychological realm in Stephen and Bloom's visions. Their visions distort reality. Bloom takes on the characteristics of Stephen, cause and effect melt, time runs both forward and backwards, and gender bends. These fluid visions, initially rigorously separated from, become more and more combined and interfused with concrete time and space events. As fluidity increases, so do the possibilities. Some of these dream-like episodes partake of the nature of nightmares, so appropriate for women of the night.

With Bella Cohen's whores in the "living room" and MacIntosh in the hallway, Stephen and Bloom experience their own personal version of the Apocalypse in the Book of Revelations, an apocalypse now. The hallucinatory presentation in Revelations is that author's vision of the eternal aspects of historical reality, the invisible influences in the world of Christ and his opponents, Satan and the Great Whore. The apocalypse connection sponsors the equal treatment in this episode in terms of "reality" of the hallucinatory visions and time and space events. The hallucinatory visions are presented as just as "real" as the time and space events. The message of the Book of Revelations is that the invisible forces are the most important factors in history. Likewise, the invisible forces in this episode liberate Bloom and Stephen to a more profound and open life.

The archetypes in the collective unconscious and the message of Revelations are based on the same underlying principle, that an important part of what you experience is an invisible force, an impersonal component based on a reality beyond your individual consciousness. This same principle infuses the fifth chakra, the "gateway of great liberation" through which release and purification are obtained in the chakra system. All these forces share fundamental principles with the power behind Circe's wand.

Odysseus acquired feminine side wisdom from his experiences with Circe, the sorceress who turns men into swine. If and only if Circe was approached properly, she would then turn the swine back again into men, this time better than before. In their initiation process, Stephen and Bloom descend deeper into and then are released from their own personal brand of swinishness, in both cases based on a lack of self-respect. In this most unlikely of venues, the whorehouse, both recover increased self-respect as they are initiated into maidenhead, feminine side wisdom, for males the most important part of the collective unconscious.[2]

After initially deciding to accept compromise and to return to his teaching job (his swine condition), Stephen finally decides once and for all to trust his destiny completely to his art. In the process, he is released from his mother's apron strings—the burn marks of mother guilt, lust, and narcissistic ego. After initially descending into deeper and compassion threatening masochism, Bloom decides to pursue his married life and paternity. In the process, he is released from masochism and lack of self-respect, the burn marks of the father's strap. With these purifying releases, Stephen respects his capacity to give birth to art, the son of

467

himself, and Bloom respects his capacity to give birth to a son, a new Rudy.

Inspired by Homer's contrast of swine and men, Joyce again draws the theme of sacred versus profane: spirit versus carnal, mass versus black mass, control versus instinct, Holy Ghost and pigeon versus egoism and vampire, marriage versus prostitution, love versus lust, families with children versus barren copulators, the genuine life versus the artificial life lived for respect (or money), holy water versus urine, true light versus artificial, and their literary relatives the dramatic versus the subjective. Joyce took this issue very very seriously.

The original meaning of profanity as writing about prostitutes supports Joyce's choice of venue for this episode. Profanity derives etymologically from disregard of the sacred in ritual, that is doing things wrong. Reflecting this background, profanity is represented in this episode in the physical dimension through distorted gesture or movement. Brothel sex often results in syphilis, which degrades muscle control. Like syphilis, guilt and lack of self-respect degrade spiritual control.

The red light district distortion display begins with the idiot's St. Vitus's dance, an irregular, involuntary and purposeless movement of muscle groups.[4] Momentarily sharing this local distortion in Nighttown, Bloom gets lost following Stephen. Movement is presented by explicit textual discussion as part of the larger issue of rhythm, the relationship in art of part to part and to whole. Rhythm in art is part of the larger philosophical issues of diversity in unity and the implication of the part for the whole.

Both Stephen (with Lynch) and Bloom (separately) arrive at Nighttown by train, the rails of common destiny. There they need the protection of Hermes, who appears in the form of a dog. This land of the unconscious is swarming with libido, incest, sadism, masochism and brutality all watched over by ineffective policemen. Joyce projects this invisible force field as the beast from the Book of Revelations.

Multiple references to the missing leg of the duck (the duck tucks one leg up during sleep) and the "eternal" tripod from Goethe's *Faust* indicate that the right relationship with sex is necessary for balance in art and in life. As Goethe believed, sexuality alone is not important but without effective sexuality nothing else can be done. For Stephen and Bloom, sexuality is the portal to the feminine side in the collective unconscious. It is an invisible influence in everything else.

Lurking in the shadows of this episode is the Buddhist deity known as Tara (her name is mentioned), a figure from the center of the world dream come to liberate us from illusory joys and fears.[5] In her benign aspect, she is a tear of divine compassion. In her wrathful aspect, she is known as Bella (the name of the whoremistress of the brothel), the source of constant hunger of life for life, a devouring combustion. The name Tara is composed of two Sanskrit roots, one of which means to liberate and the second means to scatter as in light. Bloom plays the liberating role, and Stephen the second when in a "miracle" he scatters street lamp light with his wand-like ashplant. Bloom comes by the same spot later and interprets the resulting scattered light as a fire (a devouring).

In terms of the symbolism of the Mass, Stephen in the climax scene uses his ashplant as a sword to knock out the artificial gas light in the brothel. This action seals his commitment to self-purification by rejecting compromise of his artistic goals. The counterpart in the Mass is the consecration of the Eucharist during which Christ is believed to come into the bread and wine, a process known as the transubstantiation. The sword is part of the symbolism of the Mass; the sword comes out of the mouth of the son of man in the Book of Revelations to strike the blow for freedom that kills the old and vivifies the new. At this dramatically critical moment, Stephen issues Siegfried's cry "Nothung" (not hung in English or not "I" in Sanskrit) and destroys the hold of his Mother memory and guilt. This one cry combines in Stephen's consecration a refusal to sacrifice his realization to loyalty or to a job. Thus consecrated in independence as Stephen Christ, Stephen is knocked down by a British soldier and rests in the fetal position on the ground among the woodshavings, the image of the body of the Eucharist (chip off the old block of Jesus rather than his father).

This climatic episode ends with Bloom standing guard over an unconscious Stephen; his unconscious condition reinforces the emphasis in this episode on the forces of the unconscious. Standing over his substitute for a son, Bloom has a vision of Rudy. In this final vision, Rudy is restrained and detached like the artist in the dramatic mode. Like the artist plugged into the archetypes, Rudy reads in the Hebrew book of his identity the Jewish legends that contain archetypes for modern European man.

Action in The Odyssey

In chapter x, Odysseus's ship comes to Circe's shores. Circe is sister to the wizard Aeetes and a daughter of Helios. She has magic powers that work invisibly either for harm or good.

Odysseus's ship arrives silently. On the third day after arrival (ample leisure time), Odysseus seizes his spear and sword (male effectiveness in this particular culture) and mounts the high ground. He sees smoke and flame from a structure located in the "thick coppice and the woodland," traditional symbols for the unconscious. He decides to go back to the ship for lunch (hunger and instincts). On the way back, he shoots a stag that was seeking water. Odysseus carries it back to the ship around his neck.

Odysseus divides his men into two groups, one headed by himself and the second headed by Eurylochus. The two groups draw lots for the venture to the mysterious structure in the thick coppice and woodland. Eurylochus's group loses and starts out. The unlucky group has no problem reaching Circe's Halls. Wolves and lions in the forest have been bewitched with drugs and are ineffective before men. At the gate, the group hears someone (Circe) singing; the narrator says she is working on an imperishable web of wool. The Greeks call, she opens the gates, and the group enters in "heedlessness." Fearing danger, Eurylochus remains outside. Circe serves a drugged cheese wine drink that makes the men forget their own country. Then she smotes them with her magic wand, turning them into swine with the mind of man. She pens the swine men and feeds them acorns. Note that the men must forget their own country before the magic wand will work on them.

Eurylochus returns to the ship and tells Odysseus what happened (somehow he knew even though it took place inside Circe's halls). He repeats in detail what has already been described. Despite

470

warnings from Eurylochus, Odysseus goes to the rescue. Odysseus explains that he must try to help "for a strong constraint is laid upon me." On the way to help, Odysseus meets a young version of Hermes. The young god predicts the same swine fate for Odysseus unless Odysseus takes moly, the "herb of virtue." With Moly, Hermes promises "I will redeem thee from thy distress, and bring deliverance." Hermes counsels Odysseus that the moly will protect him against Circe's drink and that after drinking, he should draw his sword from his thigh and spring upon Circe as if to slay her. Hermes indicates that as a result of this protocol, Circe will shrink back and want to have peaceful sex. Odysseus is counseled to accept her sex and make her swear an oath to release his men. Odysseus agrees. Hermes plucks a nearby plant from the ground. The plant is black at the root but milk white in the flower. The gods call it moly, and mortals are not able to dig it out of the earth. Note moly is nearby. Odysseus eats it. Moly, like Circe's wand, is energized by a higher power outside of it.

Odysseus goes to Circe's "Halls" with a heavy heart. He calls, and Circe answers, invites him in and gives him the drugged cup. Protected by the moly, he is not affected. She is stunned by the impotence of her drink. Following Hermes's suggestion, Odysseus draws his sword "from his thigh." Overcome, she suggests that he put his sword back in his sheath and that they make love so they can trust each other. Odysseus calls for her oath to release his men before he takes it all off. She complies.

Bathed and oiled by Circe's handmaidens, Odysseus refuses food (still no trust?). Circe asks him why he is devouring his own soul (through sorrow) rather than the meat and drink. Odysseus says he misses his companions who are yet to be redeemed, delaying sex to get his buddies back first. She brings them in and waves her wand, which changes the swine back into men, younger than before (time distortion) and more attractive and taller. They rejoice; Circe is moved to compassion. Circe says trust me, return to your ship, store your weapons and come back. They do and all are bathed, oiled and fed. The crew weeps and mourns for their permanently lost ones. Circe urges them to cheer up (seize the present), and they feast for a year. Eventually the crew feels it is time to go home. Circe agrees to let them go if they agree to go to Hades and seek out Tiresias for prophecy. Odysseus asks who their guide will be for this trip. She replies that they don't need one (self sufficiency—the father principle). The crew laments. Circe ties a ram and black ewe to their departing ship.

In the Hades chapter, Odysseus finally receives his prophecy from Tiresias. It includes a post-homecoming experience during which he is to go inland to people who do not understand the sea. He is to carry an oar that the inland farming people will mistake for a winnowing fan, a fan used to separate the desired from the waste parts of the grain. Then he will die by the sea.

Parallels to The Odyssey

Circe as the daughter of the god of generation has a natural association with the power of sex. And that power can turn men into profane swine or, if approached properly, open the sacred gates. Odysseus sleeps with Circe, a mortal with a goddess, only after he achieves the right relationship with her. He first disarms an aspect of her powers, reducing her from profane temptress to trustful and benign partner.

The swine condition prevalent in Nighttown is a heedless lust driven rush to sex. As Circe could turn men into swine only after they lost their desire for home, Bloom and Stephen are susceptible to the swine condition by reason of their guilt and lack of self-respect. In Stephen's case, his swine condition results from mother guilt, which leads to threatened compromise of his art and independence in the interest of preserving his job with Mr. Deasy. In Bloom's case, his swine condition results from father guilt, which leads to masochism and his lack of integrity to his heritage and to his role as husband and father.

The time distortion produced by Circe's wand sponsors the reality distortions in the visions. Her magic, her tricks, are reproduced in low-voltage form in the "tricks" in the brothel, a form of distorted love. The enchanted woodland around Circe's Halls appears in the surreal descriptions of the street entrance to Nighttown. Circe's singing is the music that brings customers into the brothel. The shot stag appears in the hat-rack antlers in the hallway of the brothel. The image of Odysseus carrying the stag on his shoulders returns in an image in the whorehouse mirror. Circe's imperishable web of wool suggests the human continuity in the collective archetypes.

The repeated descriptions in The Odyssey of the same events show up here in dream memories. Hermes promises redemption from distress, and Bloom and Stephen finally realize this relief. Odysseus is protected by the moly of virtue, as Stephen and Bloom are protected against profanity in the brothel by their initiations. Molly is Bloom's moly, his sacred even if cuckolded married love. Artistic connection with humanity and the collective unconscious is to be Stephen's moly. The plant moly, like human consciousness, is black at the root and white at the top.

The recommended firm approach to Circe is in relation to her role as temptress whose commercial representatives staff the whorehouse. Bloom and Stephen eventually manage the firm approach against the demons in their visions and, you will notice, do not use the whores even though they pay. This experience signals the end of Stephen's and Bloom's degenerate period. The trust love that Odysseus and Circe generate after he firmly denies her temptress aspect depicts modern married love, most poignantly represented here in the case of Stephen's favorite whore Georgina Johnson. Stephen is shocked to discover she is no longer in the profane pleasure business because she has married the commercial traveler Mr. Lamb. She has moved from self-abasement to self-respect.

The Fetish—the Wand and the Hat Trick

The double meaning of fetish provides foundation for this episode. The first meaning of fetish is a magic charm or object, like Circe's wand, which has supernatural powers that can come only from the external and impersonal gods. The second and related meaning of fetish is a psychological condition that provides to a non-genital object (such as a foot or item of underclothing) the power to generate some kind of sexual gratification. Bloom, who ejaculates on Molly's panties, has this psychological condition. This second meaning can be generalized as a wrong approach in terms of realizing the maximum goal.

473

These two meanings of fetish infuse the hat trick with the basic meaning of this episode. The hat trick, mentioned several times in the episode, is a ruse used to disguise the fact that you have defecated in a public place. If someone comes along at a point when your guilt would be obvious, you use the hat trick. This involves covering the evidence with your hat. You tell the by-stander that a wounded bird is under the hat and ask the by-stander to hold the hat until you can summon help. The by-stander is left holding the hat until he or she discovers the turd while expecting the bird. You, however, have lost your hat in order to cover up your guilt.

Since hat trick also means three goals in one game, you can see this one coming in the context of the Trinity. The Holy Ghost, which is represented by a bird and for Joyce means the spirit in each person, completes the Trinity that according to St. Augustine is present in each person. The point Joyce wants to make is the cost of guilt, religious and psychological. You lose your realization, symbolized throughout the novel by your hat, if you feel guilty about your humanity. If you feel guilty because a turd is under your hat (repressed emotion), you are going to lose realization potential. The Catholic Church tells you through the doctrine of original sin that you do have a turd in your hat and that you should feel guilty about it. If you feel guilty about your natural human condition, you will lose self-respect. Guilt is the wrong approach, like the fetish substitute. You won't get the real thing.

In this episode, Joyce shows us what is really under the hat in human consciousness. True to then modern psychological theory, the turd in the hat is the negative residue of parental relations, for Stephen the mother and Bloom the father, resulting from the inevitable dependence of the child. The human invisible influence.

The fetish provides the energy curve for the visions. Like Circe's wand and the misdirected sexual reaction, the visions raise the energy level and flout normal reality. The visions explode away from normal reality into a fragmented, cubist-type emotional reality characteristic of dreams. Joyce's must have been interesting.

Hermes

Often Hermes is depicted with three women who stand for the three potential fates—Aphrodite for the life of lust, Hera for the life of the loyal marriage and Athena for the life of a hero. Accordingly, Hermes is featured in this episode dealing with the proper relation to the female. As the guide to the knowledge of the eternal, Hermes is symbolized by a dog. This is appropriate since the dog with a strong sense of smell can find the invisible trail, the trail of the invisible forces. Bloom follows Stephen's invisible trail in Nighttown. Since invisible influences take many forms, the dog in this episode changes breed often. Hermes is also the patron of fatherhood or self-respect, which Bloom seeks through the flesh and Stephen through his art.

These connections weren't enough for Joyce. He treats Moly as a state of mind that is the gift of Hermes:

> My latest is this. Moly is the gift of Hermes, god of public ways, and is the invisible influence (prayer, chance, agility, presence of mind, power of recuperation which saves in case of accident. This would cover immunity from syphilis) . . . . In this special case his plant may be said to have many leaves, indifference due to masturbation, pessimism congenital, a sense of the ridiculous, sudden fastidiousness in some detail, experience.[6] [emphasis added]

Joyce has generalized the meaning of moly as the many invisible influences in the spirit.

Like moly, fatherhood or self-respect results from a consciousness (white flower) integrated with its unconsciousness (dark root). It is the gift of Hermes that is achieved by the right relation with the female.

Revelations and the Shrink

This episode stages an apocalypse in a whorehouse. The Greek word *apocalypsis* carries the metaphorical sense of uncovering or removing the lid, as in losing your hat.[7] Likewise, the visions in this episode reflect the removal of the lid from the repressed unconscious.

Why the resistance of Stephen and Bloom to revealing repressed memories is lowered is not explained. Perhaps it results from gaining an effective relationship with the female power.

The apocalyptic visions in the Book of Revelations present a written account of one view of the divine reality of the world. It contains a studious collection of allusions to many events in the Old Testament and contains the author's vision of the true meaning of the scriptures. The Book of Revelations contains a prophecy of terrible future events to be followed by a new Heaven on earth. Before the final restoration, the chief architects of distress are to be the Antichrist Satan and the "Great Whore," the invisible influences for evil in the Christian religion (MacIntosh is always invisible in this episode). At the final restoration, the final judgment is to be in the form of a court trial, and the original tree and waters of life from the Garden of Eden are to be restored.

In the whorehouse, the Great Bella rules as whoremistress and the corrupt waters containing the residue of commercial consummation are carried out by a representative of the Antichrist. Commercialization, even of the sacred gate, is the Great Whore. Bloom is subjected in his own visions to numerous court trials. As a result of their initiations in this episode, Stephen and Bloom find the tree and waters of life in Part III of this novel.

The Book of Revelations is first and foremost a different view of reality promoted by a divine vision. The purpose of Revelations is to change the reader's attitude about the world. The target attitude is registered in Revelations itself, a book which identifies itself with the divine presence. In Revelations the normal space time world is destroyed so that the reader's normal attitude about the world will be destroyed (atomic zen). Northrop Frye characterized the modern version of this target attitude as dissolution of ego and termination of psychological repression.

Both Stephen's narcissism and Bloom's masochism share a misdirection. Stephen's condition will, if his narcissism is not checked and runs on the Freud course, result in a fetish, the direction of sexual energy upon oneself. The victim of this condition, because of a lack of love on the part of the parents, can never discharge sexual energy with satisfaction on another person. In this analysis, the inordinate kind of self-love of the narcissist results at bottom ironically from a lack of self-respect. The masochist like Bloom also produces a fetish, a misdirection of sexual energy, since the masochist needs to be subjected to pain and humiliation in order to achieve satisfaction. Curing each of these conditions requires a changed relation, in heterosexual love, to the female.

Stephen and Bloom have their own revelation, a changed view of the emotional world, as a result of their visit in the realm of the female to the unconscious.

Traditional Schemata

The traditional schemata given by Joyce for this episode are organ—locomotor apparatus (feet and such), art—magic, symbol—whore, and technique—hallucination. The Linati meaning of the episode is "man-eating," or loss of male self-respect. Magic succeeds by illusion and prostitution by profanity. Both feature tricks. The correspondence is Bella—Circe.

Action in Ulysses

In reading this long episode drawn in the form of a play, the most dramatic of forms, note that the italics passages in parentheses are designed to be stage directions. The time is midnight in Dublin's well known red light district. The day is Friday, the date June 17. Friday is the day Christ died a profane death only to arise in a sacred defeat of his human condition.

The surreal opening stage directions introduce Mabbot Street as a mysterious and dangerous portal to Nighttown. It has uncobbled tram tracks (read loss of control), red and green will of the wisps and danger signals. This portal is drawn in terms that suggest the female sex organ. The houses in Nighttown, like the commercialized genitalia, are dirty and the doors are left open. This is the gateway to a commercial sperm release, a profane version of the gateway of great liberation.

The poor light given by Nighttown street lamps is a rainbow fan penumbra of separate colors rather than unified white light, a symbol of wholeness. In this poor light, what are later identified as children are first described as stunted men and women (the destiny of these children), a distortion of time sequence. The children squabble in front of the ice cream vendor who sells snowcakes.

The first appearances in Nighttown, like the archetypes of the collective unconscious, are totally impersonal: "The Call," "The Answer," "The Children," "The Idiot." Whistles call and answer as in the first episode where they introduced Biblical typology and Buck's mock mass. Typology apparently reigns in the profane as well as the divine dimension.

The Call is "Wait, my love, and I'll be with you." The Answer is a direction to meet "Round behind the stable." Neither speaker is visible. This exchange by invisible parties, apropos of the unconscious, distorts cause and effect. What is described as The Answer should be the Call and vice versa. The Answer (let's meet behind the stable) contains the lustful impatience and should come first. The Call should be the answer, "Wait, my love, and I'll be with you." Patience, love and unity are coded into this answer.

Also apropos of the unconscious is the ambiguity of the meaning of this exchange. It is probably a customer calling for a prostitute, introducing the subject of an improper relationship with the female. The stable suggests both profane swine and the birth of the sacred Christ child in the manger. "Round," instead of around, suggests the ego lock from the symbolism of prior episodes.

An idiot surrounded by a chain of children jerks by. This grouping symbolizes the negative effects on adulthood (the idiot) resulting from experiences in childhood (the circle of children). The idiot suffers from locomotor ataxia, a foot and eyesight impairment resulting from syphilis, the swinelove disease of the brothel and the profane life. The children call him Kithogue or left-handed—unlucky (Hermes)—which suggests his problems are not his fault (more invisible influence). His mother may have given him the disease, as Stephen's mother gave him his guilt.

The children command the idiot to salute, and he does so repeating "Ghahute" for salute. The next and curious question from the children is: "Where's the great light?" Apparently the idiot usually talks about the great light. He responds "Ghaghahest," which translates in the

Ghahute-salute lexicon to Sasalest or celestial. The children release him since apparently he gave the right answer. The celestial light is symbolic of impersonal awareness and the object of many spiritual systems, including the Hindu search for the invisible influences. The celestial light is distinguished from the light of personal consciousness, here depicted by the inferior street lamp light.

Then a pigmy on a rope, "pig me" being an allusion to masochism, swine and Circe. The rope reference, for prehuman (ape) behavior, extends Circe's wand produced swine condition back along the genetic trail to the ancestors of mankind. Their invisible influence is still contained in the collective unconscious. A stunted man picks through trash. Dirty syphilitic children grab at their mother's skirt, suggesting the mother of all fixations. A drunken navy lurches through, signifying loss of control. Two policemen with hands on their staffholsters are only vaguely present, and the holstered staff is identified with uncertain control. Cissy Caffrey, from the Nausicaa episode and now ambiguously in the red light district, sings a song about giving jolly Molly the leg of a duck. Two off-duty and drunk British soldiers are in the area and fart through their mouths. A Virgo, a domineering woman, mocks them and petitions for more power to the Cavan (wild) girl. Cissy joins this petition for women's rights.

Stephen and Lynch arrive at Nighttown by tram. On the way, Stephen hurt his hand in some kind of fight at Westland station, probably over the key to the tower. Like the visions (and the collective unconscious and original sin), Stephen never manages to remember personally what happened at the station. Bloom is following Stephen, but he is behind because he didn't get off the tram when he should have and moreover he stopped to buy some food (read lack of control). Bloom follows the same invisible trail and finds Stephen really by luck.

Stephen enters on a high note into this nighttown swamp of the lowest condition of humanity, where the only hope is the twelve year old daughter will get enough tricks. Stephen walks into the red light district chanting in Latin from the Mass for Paschal time, about holy water flowing from the restored temple. Profane water in the whorehouse and holy water from the temple register the issue of purification from within.

479

Meanwhile, pimps solicit Stephen's interest in maidenhead. Ironically, Stephen gains the spiritual version of maidenhead, feminine side wisdom, as a result of this visit. Stephen and Lynch pass by the British soldiers who, assuming from Stephen's black clothes that he is a parson, jeer him since he should not be in the red light district. Cissey sings two more suggestive songs about giving the leg of a duck. When the duck is asleep, one leg is up, signifying an erect penis. Stephen and Lynch are joined by a dog, the symbol of Hermes, which starts out as a liver and white spaniel and changes breed often.

In a curious passage abusive of space-time reality, Stephen scatters the inferior light from the street lamp with his ashplant. His ashplant signifies his art, and this event serves as a symbol of the limitations of his current art, his art with artificial not celestial light at the end of it. In Tantric iconography, the image of the effect of the Kundalini snake arising through the chakras in the body is a glow in the head of the snake. Here in Nighttown of the unconscious, the Kundalini snake has been converted to a street pole producing artificial light, much as the magician traditionally changes a snake into a solid vertical object such as a pole. Later a drunken navvy removes the pole after clearing snot from his nose, the symbol of the divine essence.

A bawd mistakes Stephen and Lynch for medical students from Trinity. Edy Boardman (from the Nausicaa episode), also ambiguously in Nighttown, bickers relative red light district ethics with Vertha Supple (can she bend!). Edy refers to the bed as the "mantrap." Stephen's last Latin line is "They are made whole," as Odysseus's men were restored. Right after this, Stephen looks back, apparently at the light he scattered with his ashplant. This phrase, "They are made whole," echoes the subject of artificial versus celestial light.

Stephen and Lynch are mid-way in a metaphysical discussion of importance to the meaning of the episode. Drunken Stephen suggests that gesture or movement in general could be the universal language to unite all peoples; it could serve as a substitute for the gift of tongues, the presence of the Holy Ghost among the followers of Jesus that allowed them to speak to all nations. Stephen is referring not to common speech but rather to language expressing the first form (in the Platonic sense), which Stephen says is structural rhythm (remember *consonantia* from the Introduction). So Stephen proposes structural rhythm as the universal language of eternal forms since rhythm serves as a basic foundation in art. The concept of rhythm promises unity in variety, and a meaningful unity for humankind. All these concepts fuse under the rubric of relationships: artistic rhythm being about part to part and to whole, and human rhythm being about relationships, to each other and the eternal powers. This theoretical rhythm gives broader meaning to the locomotor ataxy of the idiot.

As part of their conversation about rhythm or relationship, Stephen has discussed the effect on males of distorted love. Stephen supports his position by the introduction of examples of the effect of bad relationships with women on Shakespeare, Socrates and Aristotle. Note that these two young men on the verge of commercial sex in the whorehouse are talking about distorted love as part of the general subject of rhythm in the aesthetic sense. Stephen experiments with gesture language, a form of rhythm, by trying to communicate to Lynch, just by making shapes with his hands, the phrase from Omar: Loaf, jug of wine and thou (with obvious Mass overtones). In doing this, Stephen holds his hands in the shape of an X, the Maltese cross that suggests togetherness in suffering.

Stephen tells Lynch they are going to visit his favorite whore Georgina Johnson. In describing her, Stephen parodies the Mass—she robbed his youth and vitality and gladdened the days of his youth. The twin boys from the Nausicaa episode climb gaslamps to tickle their loins, probably the only light they will ever experience. In response to Lynch's miracle suggestive statement to "take your crutch and walk," a drunken navvy clears snot from his nose and picks up a street lamp (remember this is a hallucination). He weaves through the fog and crowd. A glow of fire appears in the south.

Bloom comes walking into the same general area of Nighttown under the railroad bridge. He has dropped behind in his effort to follow and protect Stephen because he stayed on the tram too long and had to back-track. He got on the first class car and did not in time see Stephen and Lynch exit the third class car near Mabbot Street. Even though

481

lagging, he has already stopped to buy bread and chocolate and stops again to buy pig and sheep feet at the porkbutchers Olhausen's; he can't resist—the life of the pig.

Bloom has been running and has a stitch in his side, which suggests the legacy of Eve the seductress is preventing him from catching up with the spiritual. He sees the street lamp light scattered by Stephen (this could happen only in a hallucination) and first wonders what it is: "A flasher? Searchlight?" Remember that this scattered light signifies Stephen's current artistic output. A flasher would be the sexual counterpart of the exhibitionist author, the author that shows through. The searchlight is the counterpart of the pornographic—showing something in a positive or negative light. Next Bloom thinks the scattered light might be the Aurora Borealis or a steel foundry or a fire on the south side, even Blazes's home on fire. Note these possibilities descend from the celestial, to Hades (steel foundry) and finally to a kinetic projection of Bloom's hate for Blazes.

Bloom then uses "cross" twice hurrying to find "him," perhaps the spiritual him. Two cyclists "swim" by grazing Bloom; they are carrying paper lanterns (safety lights) and ringing bells. They suggest the influence of the Buddha, who was born with webbing between his feet and toes (good for swimming) and with a pattern of a wheel on his foot. He urged his followers to make lights unto themselves. His influence is missing at this point.

Immobilized in the street by the stitch in his side, Bloom is almost run over by a sandstrewer operating on the tram tracks. In Nighttown, the sandstrewer looks like a dragon. The sand dispensed by the sandstrewer serves to keep the tram cars on the tram tracks, the common destiny of the profane. In the street, Bloom raises a policeman's white gloved hand in an attempt to stop the sandstrewer. In the red light district, the sandstrewer has trouble stopping (heedless). Bloom's last second, stifflegged escape from the path of the sandstrewer causes the driver, the "motorman," to ask if Bloom is doing the hat trick, defecating on the tram line. The sand strewing machine slides over the chains and keys, the switches, where it might have changed destinies—which is what this episode is all about.

Safe from danger, Bloom thinks about insurance from The Providential (Hermes) and locates his potato talisman. He finds excuses for the sandstrewer driver in typical Bloom forgiving fashion. He associates to the "Mark of the beast" in connection with cattle and food poison. Feeling light in the head (announcing a non-ego controlled vision), Bloom sees a sinister Spanish figure whose dark facial appearance suggests treatment for syphilis with mercury (this would be Mercury, the dark side of Hermes). The gender of the dark face is uncertain, as male and female begin to bend and merge in the visions. Bloom calls him/her senorita Blanca (Miss White), by sharp contrast to his/her blackened face, and Bloom asks where he is. Miss White responds in a way that suggests Bloom has correctly used a password and, accordingly, tells him the street location. Because of the reference to password, Bloom thinks Blanca is a spy for the Citizen. Bloom pushes on making several allusions to Hermes (signposts, public boon, lost his way) and keeping to the right (which sounds like ethics).

Jacky Caffrey, one of the twin boys from the Calypso (4th) episode, accidentally runs into Bloom. He thinks the collision might have been part of a pickpocket attempt, as would the wrong relation with the female. The dog, now a retriever, approaches sniffing the ground, like Hermes finding the invisible trail.

Bloom experiences a vision of his father Rudolph as an elder of Zion with talon-like hands. Father Rudolph berates son Bloom for wasting his money, lacking in soul and associating with gentiles—a foot race with "Harriers" (means both cross country runners and a kind of hawk) many years ago in which Bloom cut his hand. Bloom becomes child-like and shamefully hides his non-kosher purchases from his father. His mother in normal dress, together with Molly in Turkish outfit (complete with camel), also appear in the vision to make Bloom feel more guilty and further reduce his self-respect. Note that Bloom's self-respect problems started with his father and have continued in relation to his wife Molly.

Bloom is enchanted by Molly, but she lords over him. Stressing her independence, she demands to be addressed as Mrs. Marion rather than Mrs. Leopold, per Blaze's letter. She taunts him by asking about his

483

cold feet, which now refer to the pig feet he is carrying and his long idle penis. Molly's camel bows to her as she shouts "Nebrakada Femininum!" (blessed feminine). Notice the connection to Stephen's chant in the Sirens (12th) episode in which he also uses "Nebrakada Femininum." Bloom mentions he is buying her lotionwax as a present, trying to substitute generosity for masculinity. He lies in saying he doesn't have the lotion because the store closed early. The soap he does have appears in the vision as the sun rising on the morrow to render a poem. The purchase of the "special recipe" on the following day is recorded in the face of the soap, as time loses its hold in this hallucination. Then Molly disappears.

In time and space, Bloom hears a proposition from a bawd about the availability of fifteen year old maidenhead in a house providing total privacy, except only for a drunk and sleeping father (Stephen's and Bloom's condition). In response, Bloom has a vision of Bridie, his first sex partner, who flaps her bat shawl and runs away down the street, then of Gerty blaming him for her "bloodied clout" (bloody undies) and then of his old flame Mrs. Breen wearing a man's overcoat. Mrs. Breen demands a respectable explanation why he is in Nighttown, but she doesn't explain her own presence (this is ok in visions). He acts guilty and lies about Molly always wanting to visit Nighttown to see negroes. This vision continues stereotypically with a song and dance routine by Tom and Sam about someone in the house with Dina "playing on the old banjo." The language is sexually suggestive and indicative of Bloom's knowledge of who is in the kitchen with Molly.

Bloom seizes Mrs. Breen's wrist and suggests they embrace for old time's sake. This firm approach works, and they reenact old palour games and recall a joint outing to the races. But her husband appears with Alf Bergan to break up the fun. Mrs. Breen is still hot for Bloom, but Bloom now plays the faithful husband. She asks if he has a present for her, and with this question the vision shifts to Richie Golding, Bloom's dinner partner. Richie appears with three ladies' hats on his head (remember Hermes with three women as the potential fates of man). Bloom and Mrs. Breen continue the recall to a day at the races at Leopardstown. On the way back from the races, Dancer Moses held a poodle in her lap which "bridles up." Mrs. Breen asked if Bloom had ever heard of or knew or read about . . . . but doesn't finish the thought. This excites Mrs. Breen, but the subject is never given and she fades away. The dog is now a terrier, the tenacious type of dog trained to find and kill rats.

The vision of Mrs. Breen fades away as Bloom in time and space approaches Hellsgate, the opening to Nighttown. There a woman is shamelessly urinating in the street. Near there gaffers (who carry construction materials up ladders) are listening to a story while two armless gaffers are wrestling (imagine that!). The story is about gaffer Cairns coming off the construction scaffolding and pissing in a pail. Unknown to him, the pail contained porter, a type of beer and a double pun for the transport of spirits. This image, like the hat trick, further depicts the negative residue in the human unconscious. Note that in this episode, the productions of the elimination functions, triggered in the unconscious, end up in a hat or a pail of spirits. Since Bloom thinks this porter pail story is a coincidence, his unfinished story with Mrs. Breen must involve some similar indiscretion. The loiterers are "spattered with size and lime of their lodges." Size in lime is symbolic of Freemasonry of the cement of brotherhood.[8]

Whores call to Bloom by reference to his middle leg. The navvy and Privates Carr and Compton pass by looking for the "bloody house." Bloom thinks about fate (Hermes) bringing him together with Stephen and his presence of mind (more Hermes) saving him from the sandstrewer. He sees chalk graffiti for "Wet Dream," which reminds him of something Molly drew on the frosted glass in a coach (perhaps on the way back from the Glencree dinner). Whores in the doorways smoking cigarettes blow rings that (as "The Wreaths") speak to Bloom in images of the book he is bringing to Molly: "Sweet are the sweets. Sweets of sin."

Feeling insecure and uncertain about his food purchases, Bloom feeds them to the dog, which is now a mastiff (Hermes includes a stiff mast, or fatherhood). This action sets off in Bloom a masochistic vision of being questioned by the police (the watch) and tried for committing a nuisance, cruelty to animals. In this jurisdiction, generosity is cruelty. In this vision, the gulls testify to his earlier gifts of "kankury kake" (gull talk). Bloom testifies to his effort to prevent cruelty to horses and circus animals, but Seignior Maffei, the sadist from the book *Pride of the Ring*, appears to extol the use of force for control. Bloom tries to evade trouble by identifying himself as the other Leopold Bloom, the dentist and the cousin of a rich Egyptian pasha. But this ploy doesn't work because his Henry Flower identity card falls out of his hat. This is all about lack of genuine identity. He even tries to bribe the policemen by offering sex with his mistress Martha.

Still in the trial vision, Bloom feels guilty about the flower Martha sent him, so he lies about that. The dark Spanish figure returns leading a veiled figure who turns out to be Martha Clifford with a crimson halter around her neck. She accuses him of breach of promise and gives her real name as Peggy Griffin. Bloom gives the Masonic distress sign for help. He lamely defends himself by reference to his wife's father's military position (about as far from the genuine Bloom as you can get) and claims to be an author-journalist, a possible compromise Stephen is facing. Bloom's author claim is denied by the editor Crawford and Beaufoy, the newspaper prize winning author from the Calypso (4th) episode. Beaufoy criticizes Bloom for fouling his article (Bloom used it to wipe) and chides him for lack of a university education. Bloom defends with "university of life. Bad art." His former house maid, Mary Driscoll, appears to accuse him of a vile suggestion.

Still in the trial vision, Bloom is tried for offenses that expand to include an emergency bowel movement in a plasterer's bucket, a heedlessly quick rather than a delayed release. This may be what Mrs. Breen was referring to. O'Molloy, Bloom's defense counsel, argues that his ancestors (the collective archetypes) are to blame, and since he is oriental he is not responsible for his actions. Bloom assumes the oriental part by speaking pidgin Chinese. O'Molloy shifts his defense, which is illogical because part of a hallucination in the unconscious, to Bloom's natural modesty and shows slides of his heavily mortgaged property at Agendath Netaim (the promised land flyer). Bloom lists some society character references, but his accusers expand to include phallic society ladies in furs who charge him for lewd letters he has sent them. Since actual letters seem unlikely, Bloom is now being tried for his guilty thoughts. The phallic ladies are sadistic in their pursuit of justice (justice is just before generous). One mentions Venus in furs. The charges against Bloom echo the activities in Masoch's novel by that title.

Still in the long trial vision, the ladies begin to flog Bloom's now bare bottom, a treatment which he masochistically enjoys. The women and jury accuse him of being a cuckold. A bed, presumably Molly's, jingles. The charges expand to insurrection and slave traffic. Bloom's alibi is that he was at the funeral. The dog, now a beagle, changes into Paddy Dignam, who speaking with the voice of Esau courtesy of metempsychosis confirms Bloom's alibi. U.P. is identified with a burial docket number. Paddy and Tom Rochford ("My turn on now") disappear underground through a coalhole. This long trial vision ends as "kisses" like dancing angels settle on Bloom.

Back in time and space, Bloom finds himself in front of a brothel. From the window he hears open fifths being played on a piano within. An open fifth is a two note chord separated by five steps (do and so of do re mi fa so). It has a distant but harmonious sound. Traditionally a chord would have three notes (do mi so) rather than just two, the second (mi) being a third from the bottom note (do) and a third from the top note (so). The interval of a third is particularly sweet and harmonious, and two thirds sounded together form the major harmonic element of Western music. The missing third in the chord, leaving it "open," refers in the Circe context to the relationship with the female (with whom the third leg is important). In the Trinity, the missing sweet third would be the missing Holy Ghost, who proceeds from the Father and the Son closing the Trinity only when their relationship of love is appropriate.

Note that luck (Hermes) plays a major role in Bloom's finding Stephen. In front of the brothel, Bloom meets Zoe ("life" in Greek), a whore from Bella's house. Zoe is wearing a zany outfit, a sapphire slip closed with three bronze buckles. Somehow she knows that Bloom is looking for someone inside (perhaps because both Bloom and Stephen are wearing black). Seemingly knowledgeable about Nighttown, Bloom asks if this house is Mrs. Mack's. Zoe identifies the house as Mrs.

Cohen's (Jewish) and #81 (the eternal plus one). She also informs Bloom, without his asking (more luck), that the madam herself is working at that very moment with the horse vet who in barter gives her racing tips. Winning bets on the tips help her pay for her son's tuition at Oxford, the ladder to respectability. This knowledge, acquired by chance (more Hermes), proves valuable to Bloom later on.

Taking the initiative, Zoe feels Bloom's magic area (he hangs right) and thinks he has syphilis ("hard chancre"). But the lump in his pocket turns out to be his talisman potato (Hermes's protection), which she takes. Stimulated, Bloom has an inflated vision with Zoe as womanicity herself in an oriental Jewish setting. It starts with Bloom's hyper-extended vision of Jerusalem as the bride of Christ from Revelations, but Zoe's garlic breath quickly ends that promising celestial vision.

Back in time and space, Bloom caresses Zoe's breast and refuses her request for a cigarette. With this marginal input of sex and dominance, Bloom's starved self-respect hyperinflates a wildly extravagant vision of himself. He is a public agitator against tobacco and then the famous reform Lord Mayor of Dublin, Leopold the First, who introduces Bloomusalem where all is free, including love. This vision reveals in Bloom a thirst for recognition and respect from others. He becomes Bloom the triumphant, the omnipotent, the generous, the law giver and the entertainer.[9] But even his own hyperinflated vision of himself carries the virus of lack of self-respect as its representative the mob eventually turns against him. MacIntosh, the first to speak against him, testifies that his name is really Higgins, Bloom's mother's maiden name. Dr. Mulligan reports Bloom's sexual problems, and Dr. Dixon diagnoses him as the "new womanly man." [The god resident in the fifth chakra is Shiva in hermaphroditic form ("Half-woman Lord")]. Bloom announces he wants to be a mother. He instantly bears eight male children with various metallic faces (for James Bond fans, one is named Goldfinger) and becomes the Messiah. He is attacked again by the Artane orphans and the Prison Gate girls, whose acrostics spell the most vulgar of four letter words ("If you see Kay" and "See you in tea"). Appearing in Christ's image, Bloom is stoned and burned inquisition style with the black robed in attendance (black mass). This long vision takes place during the few seconds Bloom is on the landing of Mrs. Cohen's.

Back in time and space, Zoe says that Bloom can talk until he is black in the face (Mercury); Bloom must have been talking during the vision. Bloom rubs her breast mechanically, and she talks him into the brothel. As he crosses the threshold, Bloom has another vision of himself as captive infant and Zoe as a hawk seizing his hands with her talons. Ineffective as always, Bloom trips at the door, and she steadies him with a "Hoopsa," the birth cry from the Oxen (14th) episode now heralding the imminence of initiation into stability. Inside, the hallway contains a macintosh coat (guess who), stuffed animals (the dead life and pigs *a la* Circe) and an antlered mirror (cuckold). An ape-like whorehouse gaffer with a "goatee beard upheld" (downward pointing triangle?) and carrying a "waterjugjar" passes by going outside; you can imagine what profanity is in the water. In the Apocalypse, the "mother of fornications, [is] the great harlot, [who] sitteth upon many waters."

In the "living room" of the brothel, a moth circles around the gas fed chandelier light that is covered by mauve colored tissue paper. The constantly unsatisfied desire of the moth results from its inability to see any other light in the presence of this gas fed lamp. Likewise, the limited vision whores circle moth-like around and relight the gas lamp during the episode. Lynch and Stephen are in the "living room," where the customer selects his girl, with whores Kitty Ricketts and Florry Talbot (some commentators say Zoe - animal, Kitty - mineral and Florry - vegetable). Kitty wears the emblems of torture, a boa and chains. Zoe's last name is Higgins, the same as Bloom's mother's maiden name. Her full name, Fanny Higgins, is the same as Bloom's grandmother. This coincidence indicates that Bloom is sullying his feminine side inheritance.[10] The pattern on the floor is rhomboid, a distorted parallelogram for more distortion.

Stephen and Lynch have shown patience in the process of seeking sex. Lynch is seated on the floor and Stephen is playing on the piano. They haven't rushed to the bedrooms. Stephen plays a series of empty or open fifths, two notes also called the tonic and the dominant, all of which are suggestive in this situation. Stephen discusses a composer who set verses from the Psalms to music for two voices introduced by empty fifths. He discusses this subject with Lynch's cap. The description of this music is a micro-presentation of the pending Stephen/Bloom relationship. Bloom is the home based tonic and Stephen the higher dominant tone which tends to resolve to the tonic (so to do). Stephen describes the empty fifth as the largest interval that is harmonious and as the ". . . greatest possible ellipse. Consistent with. The ultimate return. To the octave [and the tonic note]." These astrological and musical terms suggest that Stephen recognizes that he has done all that is possible in terms of his own separate ego and is as far from home as he can get consistent with a successful return to the tonic or ground. Think of the crucifixion.

Bloom comes into the common room in the brothel just as a gramophone outside plays "The Holy City." At the exact moment of Bloom's arrival, Stephen launches into a discussion of the reciprocating interaction between self and experience [first announced in the Scylla and Charybdis (9th) episode]. Stephen gives an Aristotelian version of psychic reality, that what you seek in new experience is inevitably a function of your own past experience, which has been registered in your soul. As a result, what you find in new experiences is your potential self as it was destined to become, the invisible influence of the soul. Remember from the Proteus (3rd) episode the theory of Parmenides about pre-existing change. In this limited sense, Stephen seeing Bloom recognizes Bloom in himself. Put another way, Stephen was inevitably destined because of his past experience to meet Bloom in the whorehouse and have the experience recorded in his soul.

Stephen doesn't know why Bloom is in the whorehouse, so he makes the natural assumption. Fat Florry, stimulated out of her sleep by Stephen's intellectual conversation, mentions a newspaper article she read recently about the end of the world and the arrival of the Antichrist (a vision reports the safe arrival of the Antichrist in the Thames). Just as Stephen first sees Bloom, Stephen quotes "A time, times and half a time" from the Book of Revelations (12: 13-14), the description of the amount of time (2 1/2 units) the Mother of God was safe from the serpent. A Milton inspired vision of Rueben J. Dodd as the Antichrist carrying his dead son on a pole visits apparently just Stephen. The vision continues with "The End of the World," a two-headed octopus in kilts appearing as the "Three Legs of Man" walking the tightrope and being brokered by the revivalist preacher Dowie (Stephen and Bloom are about to be revived). The revivalist preacher appears as Elijah and sounds the personal Christ theme as an amalgamation of the eastern and western religious traditions. Confronted in the vision with Elijah who is to precede Christ at the end, the whores confess their first time fall. Zoe says she did it for fun. Stephen blesses the beatitudes that parade by, but instead of Blessed are the meek we have instead Blessed are the following: "beer beef battledog buybull businum . . . ." Notice that right after the eight carnal beatitudes beginning with the first letter "b" and the discussion about the end of the world, the subject of beauty (first letter b) is discussed in the bosom of the light image. We as readers are invited to conclude blessed is beauty.

This Revelations inspired end of the world discussion reflects the personal experience of Stephen and Bloom, who are ending one kind of spiritual life and beginning another. In this context, the end of the world from Revelations is interpreted not as a historical event for all mankind but as an individual gnostic event. The Catholic Church's historical interpretation of the end of the world is mocked by putting it in the newspaper (safe arrival of Antichrist). Sharing the gnostic view of Revelations, Stephen comes back to himself "in the end the world without end."

Still in Stephen's Revelations vision, Lyster, Best and Eglinton, from the library discussion in the 9th episode, appear to discuss aesthetics and truth. Keats is mentioned so the reader will remember beauty and truth and truth and beauty. The vision expands to include Mananaan MacLir, the Irish counterpart of Poseidon and Shiva. He intones the rootwords of the gods ("Aum! Hek! Wal!) and announces Hermes Trismegistos (Thrice Great Hermes), the cult of the Shakti (female regenerative power), and the zodiac. Also mention is the crab from the sign of Cancer (from the zodiac), which is identified with the sexually suggestive number 69. Mananaan thinks "Punarjanam," Sanskrit for born again, and "patsypernjaub," Sanskrit forgoing into the fire unto death. The "dreamy creamy butter" with which Stephen identifies is the Hindu counterpart of the wafer in the Mass.

In time and space, the gas jet makes noise and Zoe adjusts the mantle. She lights a cigarette by the flame. Lynch lifts her slip with the poker, and she refers to the "beauty spot of my behind."

In the next vision that visits Bloom, his grandfather Virag arrives from the chimney flue on pink stilts and "sausaged" into several coats, including a macintosh. He gives an amusing, objective description of the whores in relation only to their physical nature. Virag reviews what he tried to teach Bloom and explores various sexual subjects, including the automatic nature of the sexual instinct and viragitis, masculine psychology in a woman. Criticizing Bloom for his masochism, Virag asks Bloom whether he likes or dislikes women "in male habiliments." Virag instructs that insects like the moth seek only the near light because of their "complex unadjustable eye"; they cannot adjust to see other lights. Remember the Hindu image of not being able to see the celestial light because of the light of ego consciousness.

Bloom treats the Garden of Eden legend as an "analogy to his idea" why women fear serpents (which is not explained—serpents eat children?). Bloom rues rule by instinct or pig status: "Instinct rules the world. In life. In death." Instinct is one of the invisible forces. The moth Gerald, known by name to Virag, returns to give us a poem and fly into the gas light shade again. The last line after the moth Gerald experiences the ultimate light intoxication is "Pretty, pretty . . . . petticoats" (Bloom's fetish). Henry Flower appears draped in the mixed images of the Spanish, the Hebrews and the savior.

Back in time and space, Stephen is still on the subject of return (from the dominant to the tonic) and regards himself with the phrase "Filling my belly with husks of swine," a metaphor mixing the prodigal son and Circe stories. He concludes that he must compromise his independence and by telegram apologize and defer to Deasy in order to get his teaching job back. In this mode, he describes himself as a minor chord, a "finished artist" and "out of Maymooth (the priesthood)." This is Stephen's nadir, his swine condition. He reaches this commercial compromise in the common room of the brothel where lack of self-respect reigns supreme and MacIntosh is nearby. He feels "I will arise and go to my," a thought that is not completed but spiritual death is indicated. Philip Sober and Philip Drunk quarrel in his head. Philip Drunk, representative of the compromise, connects the octave to reduplication of personality or reincarnation and wonders if he was someone before—perhaps Mac something (MacIntosh) or Swinburne (burn the swine).

In a Bloom vision, Virag describes essential male-female relations using the Hindu terms lingam (male sexual principle) and yoni (female sexual principle) and continues on to describe Jesus as the pope's bastard (had no natural father) and son of a whore with two left feet (so shown in a famous painting). Zoe tells of a priest who came for a visit but experienced only a "dry rush"; this is a comment on the Catholic Church's lack of connection to the eternal. Kitty extends the visionary image with the story of Mary Shortall (read the Virgin Mary) and Jimmy Pidgeon (read the Holy Ghost). Their child who couldn't swallow would be Christ refusing drink on the cross. Their child who was smothered in convulsions in the mattress would be the sex instinct that defeats the sacred child. They "all subscribed for the funeral" through guilt in the Mass. The exchange in French between Mary and Joseph is about how she got in her pregnant condition—it was the sacred pigeon.

After a brief return to conversation among Lynch and the whores, Virag continues in Bloom's vision the subject of the Virgin Mother and the Roman Centurion Panther paternity theme. At this point, Virag turns into a baboon. The emphasis on the Virgin reflects, I believe, the notion that Stephen's soul is a virgin (the concept elucidated in Joyce's notes to his play *Exiles*). Stephen tells Zoe that she would prefer Luther but to beware of agony. Luther characterized reason as a whore. Florry thinks Stephen is a "spoiled priest . . . or monk." Lynch affirms that Stephen is a cardinal's son. Given Stephen's apparent decision to make the necessary compromises to keep his teaching job, the combination of Stephen and his father (who would have advised him to be practical and keep his job) makes an inflated appearance as a Cardinal ("Simon Stephen cardinal Dedalus") and issues a ditty about "Conservio

493

is prison" (the conservative route binds the soul). The Cardinal disregards the swarm of midges, symbols of the damned.

In time and space, Zoe hears the squeaking door ("theeee" for thee or you) and says the devil is in the door. At the same time, an unidentified male form takes the macintosh waterproof and hat from the hall rack and leaves (my guess is MacIntosh). He talks to the other whores outside on the doorstep. The whorehouse is MacIntosh's Ithaca. Bloom, in the image of Napoleon, exercises his Masonic magic against the Antichrist form leaving in the mist. Bloom wonders if this devil creature is Blazes: "If it were he? After? Or because not? Or the double event?" That is, Blazes could be there in the whorehouse after he did Molly, or because he didn't do Molly.

Just as Bloom is thinking about the influence of light and color on personality, Bella Cohen, the whoremistress and our Circe, makes a dramatic entrance. She has just finished "doing" her tipster the vet (Circe with many animals). She is as masculine (moustache) as Bloom is feminine. Impacted just by her physical presence, Bloom has a long vision from his deepest repressed zones fueled by lack of self-respect. This is the key vision and swine nadir for Bloom. In this guilt vision, initially Bella's fan instructs him. He cowers before the fan, expressing a masochistic desire to be dominated, and he becomes psychologically impotent before "petticoat government." The fan serves in this fetish role because the fan was an interpretation by the inland farmers of Odysseus's oar, an interpretation based on their own limited experience. Their fan was used to separate the valuable seed from the chaff. At this point, the fan is floating the chaff in Bloom's psyche.

In the guilt vision, the fan possesses Bloom, right out of classical masochism. Bloom expresses a desire to be dominated based on the rationalization that it is too late for him to change. He thinks he will end up like his widower father sleeping with his dog. The fan instructs him to tie Bella's bootlace. In his prostration, he kneels and ties Bella's bootlace, Bella who has a hoof for a foot. In this kneeling and supplicant posture, Bloom speaks of limited life goals and remembers his humiliating mistakes. At Bella's command, he humbly lowers to the floor. At that moment, Bloom becomes a female pig and Bella becomes the male Bello (Italian for beautiful in the masculine). Bello has now assumed the combined female/male role as the final torturer in Masoch's *Venus in Furs*. As we shall see, it has to get worse before it gets better on Circe's island, in masochism and in the visions.

Still in the guilt vision, Bello abuses Bloom pig and eventually sits on its face. Disclosure of Bloom's cross dressing career leads Bello to dress Bloom pig in women's clothes. Bloom pig remembers being a female impersonator named Gerald (same name as the moth) in a play named "Vice Versa" (pun on versatile vice or versus vice) in high school and suffering from incontinence (more parallels to the classic masochistic character). In this state, the sins of his past ("evil memories") visit Bloom pig. He is assigned latrine duty. Bello shoves his arm in Bloom's pig vulva to measure its depth. (By the way, the pear shaped uterus with the fallopian tubes attached looks like a deer head with antlers.) Bloom's confused sex merits "shis" and "hrim" as personal pronouns. Bello puts hrim up for auction sale as a sex tool. The Caliph appears in the auction crowd in ordinary disguise and buys Bloom for his harem.

Still in the guilt vision, Bello examines Bloom's penis and asks him if he can do a man's job. Bello chides Bloom pig as impotent and reminds hrim of what is going on at shis house, where the red beast of Blazes is feeding on Molly. Bello knows that Blazes has knots and warts on his penis and a bush of red hair coming out his behind (he must have visited the whorehouse). Bello taunts hrim with the possibility of a Blazes sired child. Bello tells Bloom he is a "lame duck." Bello gives hrim a look in a magic glass at Milly in sexual intercourse with a Mullingar student. Bello predicts the wooers at home will damage shis statue (of Narcissus) and look in shis hiding places (secrets of his bottom drawer—the id).

Still in this same masochistic guilt vision, Bloom tries to gather strength to use against Bello from shis willpower, memory and suffering (of shis race)—Bloom's   heritage and identity. This doesn't work as Jews appear to reject him by casting dead sea fruit on hrim and pronouncing the ritual for a dying Jew. The nymph in the picture above Molly's bed comes to hrim with comfort, and Bloom is now in the picture among the yew (you) trees. The nymph thanks Bloom for

495

rescuing her from the profane magazine (Bloom cut her picture out the magazine *Photo Bits*). Together they remember what has happened in the Bloom bedroom, including urination in the orange one-handled pot. In the vision, the sound of urination is inflated to the sound of a waterfall. Bloom appears in juvenile clothing in response to a memory about a school outing to the trees. He is accused of masturbating in the trees. He reenacts his first time with Molly on Ben Howth, but this time he manages to get burrs all over his clothes and to fall over the cliff. This portion of the vision reflects the legend of the magician Simon Magus, who died while trying to fly off the roof of the Roman Forum in a contest with St. Peter.

Still in the same masochistic guilt vision, the nymph chides Bloom for looking at her backside (in the museum in the 8th episode) since she has no profane eliminations, normally eating electricity. Kitty, Florry, Lynch , Zoe and Virag enter the woods. Bloom extols the warmth of women. The nymph describes herself as "stonecold and pure," the vision of Venus or Aphrodite from Masoch. Bloom's masochistic vision reaches its climax as the nymph suggests eliminating shis desire: "No more desire . . . Only the ethereal. Where dreamy creamy gull waves o'er the waters dull." Notice the connection with sentimental literature.

In response to this suggestion to abandon his bedrock compassion in favor of total resignation, Bloom in the guilt vision pops a trouser button (our Bloom goes hard) and two sluts going by sing a song about Bloom not knowing what to do to keep it up (it's up now). This breaks the spell. Bloom seizes the hand of the nymph, and in the ensuing struggle the nymph tries unsuccessfully to castrate him. He accuses her of illegitimate sexual experiences. She turns out to be only a plaster cast that breaks from his firm grip. The break releases a cloud of stench from hell. This climax in Bloom's vision transforms male Bello back into female Bella and Bloom from a female pig back into a man. Back in time and space, Bella tells him "You'll know me the next time," since Bloom has just unblocked his repressed emotions. Taking the offensive, Bloom criticizes Bello's looks and the expected size of her genitalia. She accommodates by farting through her genitalia. Bloom recovers his potato talisman by a direct and effective request to Zoe. From here on, he takes charge. With self-respect, the father is back.

In time and space, Stephen pays for two, himself and Lynch. Stephen pays first with a pound note (20 shillings) and then again, because he is drunk, with a gold coin (which must be a half sovereign or 10 shillings). The price is 10 shillings (one-half sovereign) per whore. Stephen has paid 30 shillings, overpayment for two (20) and correct payment for three. Bella asks if Stephen is paying for three, and Stephen thinks this question means he has underpaid. With apologies, Stephen gives her two crowns or 10 shillings more. Stephen is willing to pay for Bloom, a further connection between their characters. Now Stephen has paid a total of 40 shillings, overpayment even for three. The avaricious Bella is satisfied not to mention the excess. But Bloom notices. He pays for himself by putting in a half sovereign (10 shillings) and taking out the pound note (20 shillings), which he returns to Stephen. Bella admires this move since it recognized that Stephen had overpaid.

Now Stephen has paid 40 less 20 or a net of 20 shillings and Bloom 10. The pot is right. The total paid (30) relates to the phrase used earlier by Stephen: "a time, times and half a time" (21/2). Note that this fee is never recovered. Stephen has paid his way. Note the repeated use of sovereign and half sovereign. Consider the connection of a half sovereign with a whore. Half sovereign reflects loss of spiritual control and the presence of an invisible influence.

The girls immediately claim their cut, no employee trust in the brothel. The cut transaction assumes that there is no change in the whorehouse (monetary or spiritual). As the girls get up, Florry's foot is asleep per the basic distorted movement image. Stephen tells the fox riddle with a changed last line: "To get out of heaven." He knows that with compromise in life and commerce in sex, he is in foul waters and out of heaven. At Bloom's suggestion, Stephen gives the rest of his money to Bloom for safekeeping. Stephen returns to the fox riddle and speculates that the fox killed his own grandmother (as Stephen is about to do).

Stephen meditates on the fact that his favorite whore Georgina Johnson is not available for his temporary pleasure because she has married a commercial traveler named Mr. Lamb. This event, which unsettles Stephen, represents a change from the profane whore to the self-respecting wife Mrs. Lamb, lamb signifying humility and purity. Stephen is much impacted by this development. Stephen lights a cigarette (with a reference to Lucifer matches) and drops it on the floor. Bloom prevents a fire by picking it up and throwing it in the fireplace grate (control). Since Stephen is very drunk, Bloom suggests that he eat something, but Stephen responds by quoting from Wagner[11] to the effect that intense desire destroys us all. Zoe responds with "Hamlet, I am thy father's gimlet!" A cocktail replaces spirit in the brothel.

In time and space, Zoe suggests she read Stephen's palm; he resists. With a cursory glance at Stephen's palm, she finds Mars for courage, but Stephen is planning on selling out at this point. Lynch kids him about his fear of learning the future. Lynch mentions the pandybat, and Stephen remembers the time (memorialized in AP) when Father Dolan unjustly spanked him with such a bat for not having his glasses (they were broken) and allegedly being lazy. Punishment of Stephen by the Fathers parallels Bloom's troubled paternal image and his visions of punishment by phallic women. As Zoe reads his hand, Stephen says he could never read the handwriting of God except in the criminal thumbprint of the church. We learn that Stephen was born on Thursday, the same day of the week on which the novel opens. Reading his palm, Zoe says she detects imagination and a strong sense of morality and predicts "You'll meet with a . . ." but refuses to finish. (My guess is that Zoe sees Stephen meeting with Nora and interprets that in her own experience as a sexual encounter, which would be bad for her business.)

Fearing psychic harm to Stephen, Bloom intervenes forcefully, substituting his own palm for Stephen's. Bella and Zoe have trouble reading Bloom's. Zoe predicts travels beyond the sea, for a connection with the prophecy for Odysseus, and guesses correctly that he is henpecked (most married men of his age in the brothel would be). The image of a black rooster (in the bird family with the Holy Ghost) appears as a symbol of the spiritual condition in the brothel. Bloom attributes a scar on his hand to an accident 22 years ago when he was 16. Stephen, showing he is sensitive to any connection, notes that he is now 22 and 16 years ago "twentytwo tumbled." To complete the connection, Stephen notices he hurt his hand somewhere. The reader knows this happened at a fight at Westland row station. Stephen doesn't remember, more invisible influence. Through their common hand injuries signifying suffering, Bloom is shown as an older Stephen.

In time and space, Zoe and Florry try to figure out what Bloom is thinking. Meanwhile, he has a masochistic vision of Blazes and Lenehan going by in a hackneycar #324. Blazes announces his four scores with Molly and revels in her female smell on his hands. Bloom imagines that in the next visit to Molly, Blazes will hang his hat on Bloom's antlered head and Bloom will assist as a servant while Blazes rides Molly horse style. Molly is in her "pelt," to continue the Masoch connection.

At this all important moment, Stephen and Bloom in time and space are near the "gilt edged" (read guilt edged) mirror over the mantelpiece. Lynch notices this alignment and points to the reflection saying "The mirror up to nature." The reflection in the mirror somehow combines the faces of Stephen and Bloom together with the hat-rack antlers. Stephen and Bloom both gaze in the mirror only to see the face of Shakespeare, which curiously is beardless and rigid. This facial image is crowned by the reflection of the antlered hat rack in the hall. This combination, Stephen-Bloom-hat rack or Shakespeare-hat rack, depicts the face of the cuckold. Stephen and Bloom have been cuckolded by their lack of self-respect and Shakespeare by his vengeance.

This ultimate combination is the mirror image of Joyce while his creative imagination is hamstrung by guilt or repressed emotions (perhaps about the possibility of carrying venereal disease). In the Bloom version of this vision, Shakespeare reminds Bloom that he has an ego (is not invisible), but as the sermon continues Shakespeare loses control over pronunciation in trying to say that he lost his father on Thursday. At this lowest of points, with Stephen still ready to compromise his art, Shakespeare is speechless and rigid, without imagination. Bad life and bad art.

Back in time and space, Bloom notices the girls whispering and asks to be let in on their joke (he is the joke). They predict the death of his wife and a second marriage (the second will be a new relationship with Molly in the same sense that Stephen will be born again). Given the widow reference, images of widow Dignam and her children in tow appear in a vision. Shakespeare, still rigid in the face, gurgles that he who weds second kills first, reflecting the Hamlet plot but also the death of the old spirit to the birth of the new. Shakespeare's face changes to the face of Martin Cunningham (from the 6th and 12th episodes). Beginning to wrestle again with the decision whether to compromise to keep his job and reacting to the vision of the horns in the mirror, Stephen quotes biblically that the horns of the wicked will be cut off and those of the righteous exalted. Compromise also triggers his recollection from Greek legend of the half beast Minotaur conceived by Queen Pasiphae with the sacred bull. Considering compromise with whores, he is drawn to the biblical image of the curse on Noah's daughters since they saw his penis when he was drunk: "his ark was open." An open ark wouldn't float.

In time and space, the whores call for Stephen to speak French (parlez vous), but he gives them a disjointed speech in English punctuated by marionette-type jerks (as if controlled by others). The speech features exotic entertainments available in Paris, including a heaven and hell show and the rape of a nun by a vampire man (there it is again—the ultimate subjectivist). Lynch cheers him on. Providing material for the black mass, Stephen describes angels as prostitutes, apostles as ruffians and sex acts as side shows. Bella particularly enjoys this speech since it brings the sacred down to her level. Stephen relates a dream of a watermelon, which the whores interpret as a masturbation device. Stephen remembers a widow shown to him by Beelzebub, Satan's lieutenant. Bloom tries to intervene to stop this blasphemy, but Stephen rejects his interference with the following declaration using the Icarus-Daedalus image: "No, I flew. My foes beneath me. And ever shall be. World without end. . . Pater! Free!"

Stephen experiences a vision of his compromised self and his father flying as Icarus and Daedalus bearing the family flag. His father appears as a buzzard (since he feeds on the death of others). The fox

500

appears in Stephen's vision with huntsmen and the rabble in pursuit, echoes of Stephen's exile from respectability. The scene changes to the race track where the crowd acting as oddsmaker gives 10 to 1 on any horse in the field except the favorite, which suggests the difficulty of rejecting job compromise and going one's own way against the grain of respectability. Horse images go past; the first must be Throwaway but sounds like Swift (this would be Joyce). Following Throwaway are the horses from Deasy's pictures. Deasy brings up the rear.

Back in time and space, off-duty British soldiers Privates Carr and Compton, with Cissey Caffrey in tow, walk by outside Bella Cohen's whorehouse singing the Yorkshire Girl song. The lyrics involve two men away from home unknowingly idolizing to each other the same girl back home, eventually realizing her identity and returning to find her married to yet a third man. This song is about woman as temptress, not woman as loyal mate. An energized Zoe plays a waltz on the nickelodeon. About to compromise his art to a job, Stephen dances with the whore in the structured rhythm of the profane. Stephen's profane dance is counterpoint to Dante's choirs of angels in Paradise revolving in a celestial dance.

In a vision of uncertain source, dancing instructor Prof. Maginni appears to advertise his lessons in "the poetry of motion." Stephen and Zoe dance in time and space. In a merger of time and space and vision, dancers of the hours appear to join them. The dance of Stephen and Zoe increases in intensity while Maginni in the vision asks for balance and restraint. The dancers representing the later afternoon hours appear with false bloom and "dark bat sleeves" (falsity and trouble). The night hours are even more dangerous with "daggered hair and dull bells." The bells in the vision produce the same sound heard at the end of the Calypso episode: "Heigho!" Maginni directs a mixing of the dancers, Stephen and Zoe mixing with the hours weaving patterns. The dance involves changing partners frequently—where else but in a whore house! Stephen changes Zoe for Kitty. A merry-go-round turns the room in the vision. Stephen spins off Kitty to Lynch and shouts he will do a solo dance (*pas seul*, which sounds like no soul). As everyone spins around him, Stephen does leg kicks. Stephen's father interrupts the vision to warn Stephen

"Think of your mother's people!" Stephen responds with "Dance of death." An image of total chaos filled with Satan appears in the vision.

At this critical point, Stephen's mother appears in his vision. She rises through the floor, just as the King Hamlet's ghost did in Hamlet's mother's closet. Stephen says "Ho" from "Heigho," signifying by voice pitch rise the third overtone, the note representing the female principle. As in the dreams reviewed in the 1st episode, she is from the grave and would pull Stephen to a spiritual grave. The choir obligingly sings the layman's hymn commending a dying person to God and to the choir of virgins. Buck as jester accompanies the mother image in the vision. She is referred to as "The Mother," not just Stephen's mother. Stephen is "horrorstruck," since his mother wants loyalty and compromise. In time and space, Stephen initially thinks the vision is a fury or erinyes resulting from a magic trick. But The Mother and Buck press on, and Stephen accepts the vision as such. Like Bloom, he argues his innocence, pleading cancer as the real mother killer. This is the wrong attitude since it assumes the possibility of guilt. He asks her about love, but she is only interested in duty; she wants him to repent, to bow. In time and space, Stephen becomes pale from his emotional reaction to this mother vision; Bloom takes effective action by opening the window.

Stephen's vision continues to a climax as a green crab (of cancer) representing The Mother's god sticks its claws in Stephen's heart. Stephen violently rejects her and her god with the manifesto that he will serve only his own intellectual imagination. In this moment, he finally and once and for all rejects any compromise. His Mother identifies her grief with Christ on the cross and the Sacred Heart cult, as her sacrifices for Stephen have not been appreciated. With Siegfried's cry of "Nothung" (which makes his sword magical provided Siegfried is not afraid), Stephen in time and space lifts his ashplant (read his art) and smashes the gas fed ceiling lamp, the artificial light source. This eliminates the Mother image. Stephen's old world ends: "Time's livid final flame leaps and, in the following darkness, ruin of all space, shattered glass and toppling masonry." No longer will the ashplant of his art end in artificial light.

In time and space, Stephen runs out into the street without his ashplant (his art). He is totally reborn anew. He tears his coat in the process, to further the connection to Christ on the cross. In the ensuing excitement, Bella attempts to gouge Bloom for the damage to the lamp, but he very effectively resists her claim noting that only the shade (read dead souls in Hades) has been damaged (his blow allows more light through). Bloom successfully compromises her damage claim using his knowledge about her son at Oxford and her aversion to scandal! Bloom picks up Stephen's ashplant, signifying that the Bloom force field can now influence Stephen's art. Bella thinks he is going to hit her with it (Odysseus with the knife over Circe). But he is only showing what damage has been done. Bloom goes outside into the street carrying the ashplant and saying he needs mountain air (a Connector Fact to Goethe's *Faust*). In a narrator's vision, almost everyone in the book and then some follow Bloom. He is now going beyond society's norms.

Outside Bloom catches up with Stephen, who in time and space is talking to Privates Carr and Compton and Cissey Caffrey. The privates, English soldiers off their Irish colonial duty, think Stephen has insulted Cissey, apparently a whore; we don't hear the allegedly insulting remark. Voices defend him in a mixture of time and space and vision. Cissey says Stephen ran up behind her even though she was already with the soldiers (they were actually off urinating), and this offended her dignity. Notice that Stephen couldn't tell she was with anyone (more invisible influences), and again the issue is the right relationship with the female. The soldiers threaten violence. Bloom tries to protect Stephen. In a conversation with the soldiers, Stephen refers to killing the invisible influences of priest and the king in his own head (this is the result of his rebirth). Various characters signifying the King and the conflict of Ireland versus England appear to Stephen in a vision. Talking to Old Gummy Granny, Stephen associates the Blessed Trinity with the hat trick (3 goals in one game of hockey or covering excrement otherwise in public nuisance).

In time and space, Bloom asks Cissey as representative of womankind who connect nations and generations to save Stephen with the truth, but she refuses, romantically thinking the men are fighting over

503

her. In Stephen's continuing vision, Hell and Armageddon arrive in Dublin with brimstone fires and war. This chaos is celebrated in a black mass with kidnapped Mrs. Purefoy as the host on the altarstone: "goddess of unreason, lies, naked, fettered, a chalice resting on her swollen belly," birth and life kidnapped for the profane. The Revs. Malachi O'Flynn and Haines Love preside in ritual in the black mass. Love's head is on backwards. The Antichrist and Adonai duel with words over god and dog. A black mass is celebrated to the devil.

Cissey finally forgives Stephen, but Private Carr, all worked up now, wants to hit him anyway (no control). He thinks Stephen has slandered the British King and Jesus. While hypocritically using profanity about his own King and Jesus, he strikes Stephen with the coward's blow, a running stiff arm blow on a defenseless Stephen, in the interests of protecting Cissey's honor and collective loyalty and obedience. Stephen falls, and Bloom retrieves Stephen's hat (as he did Parnell's) while the retriever dog barks. Then Bloom tries to take command of the situation.

The local police arrive. They tend to believe the soldiers' version of the event and threaten to write up Stephen. Kelleher, who at this moment was bringing two customers to Mrs. Cohen's house, saves the day by hinting to the policemen that Bloom is loaded from the race win and Stephen is the son of an important man. Kelleher, a police spy and an undertaker, saves the day with the corrupt police by the suggestion of a bribe and influence (invisible). The violence and aftermath are in perfect "reality." Bloom and Kelleher lie to each other about why they are in Nighttown.

Stephen is on the ground in the fetal position. Bloom wakes him, and Stephen mumbles "Black Panther. Vampire." This is a description of the forces that have just left his soul. Stephen then cites fragments of the Fergus rules poem (who rules now?). The governance issue is relevant since priest and king have just been killed in Stephen's head. In a similar if more portentous moment, Jesus cried out "My God, why hast thou forsaken me?" As Christ conquered death, Stephen conquers priest and king, centurions of death to the imagination. Bloom thinks Stephen is talking about a girl. While Joyce is talking about Nora, on the surface this is a mistake by Bloom. Notice in a later episode a similar mistake is made by Molly as Bloom falls asleep.

Bloom cites the Masonic oath of secrecy, which suggests that he has been initiated into something. Standing guard over Stephen as a secret master because of his initiation, Bloom sees an image of Rudy in an Eton suit reading a book in Hebrew and kissing the page. Rudy bears the objects traditionally attributed to Hermes. His vision suggests the sacrificial lamb. The episode ends with this image.[12] This image is the invisible influence on Bloom.

Light

Light is a strong symbol in this episode, from the early reference to the "great light," to the red light district, to red warning lights, to dim lanterns, artificial light from pole lamps, the artificial light Stephen scatters with his ashplant, and finally the chimney lamp that Stephen breaks in the whorehouse. These images create various forms of false light compared to the great celestial light of the spirit. The swirling world of forms and visions are combined in this episode with the image of the great light because, as Joyce put it in a letter to Lady Gregory: "All things are inconstant except the faith of the soul, which changes all things and fills their inconstancy with light"[13].

The "miracle" is in light. As Stephen goes by the lamppglow of "Rare lamps with faint rainbow fans" (separate parts of the spectrum not the whole white light), "He flourishes his ashplant, shivering the lamp image, shattering light over the world." This "miracle" of scattered light corresponds to Stephen's limited literary output so far, a personal and relativistic replay of artificial light. The next subjects in the text after the "miracle" are the growling spaniel and then the discussion about structural rhythm (relationship of whole to part and part to whole) being the fundamental aspect of art. Light is related to structure in the visible world because light carries information of that structure. In the same general sense, art and the sacred in life carry information of the eternal.

Stephen is in the whorehouse at night. The room is dimly lit by only one mauve tissue covered gas fired lamp. At the moment of expiration of his old life, Stephen breaks the glass lamp cover and the tissue paper, which broken would give more light. At Christ's human death, the veil covering the entrance to the most sacred room in the Temple, the holy of holies, was rent, and the middle and chief candle in the golden candlestick went out.

Modern Twilight

The mysterious and dimly lit aspects of this episode help make Joyce's basic point about the twilight regions of the psyche being explored through the visions. As reflected in Joyce's comments recollected by Arthur Powers, these explorations are the main point of modern literature:

> . . . (the classical or traditional form of writing) is a form of writing which contains little or no mystery . . . and since we are surrounded by mystery it has always seemed to me inadequate. It can deal with facts very well, but when it has to deal with motives, the secret currents of life which govern everything, it has not the orchestra . . . the modern mind, which is interested above all in subtleties, equivocations and the subterranean complexities which dominate the average man and compose his life . . . classical literature represents the daylight of human personality while modern literature is concerned with the twilight, the passive rather than the active mind . . . we are now anxious to explore the hidden world, those undercurrents which flow beneath the apparently firm surface . . . We believe that it is in the abnormal that we approach closer to reality . . . When we are living a normal life we are living a conventional one, following pattern which has been laid out by other people in another generation, an objective pattern imposed on us by the church and state. But a writer must maintain a continual struggle against the objective . . . The eternal qualities are the imagination and the sexual instinct, and the formal life tries to suppress both. Out of his present conflict arise the phenomena of modern life . . . In my Mabbot Street scene I approached reality closer

in my opinion than anywhere else in the book except perhaps for moments in the last chapter.[14]

Notice that in Mabbot Street Nighttown where church and state, the formal and conventional qualities, are at their weakest, the sexual instinct has the lead role in the hallucinations, visions from the creative imagination from behind the valence of the conscious active mind. The breakdown of formal and conventional qualities in life is mirrored by a similar breakdown of the formal qualities of literature in this episode, constructed as a play within a novel.

Initiation

Stephen and Bloom both undergo significant initiations in this episode. Their initiations allow Stephen to avoid compromise and to connect and Bloom to be effective, both aspects of stability and psychic adulthood.

At Eleusis, the mother of all initiations, only the priestess (Pythia) could mount the sacred tripod. The same tripod image occurs in Goethe's **Faust** part 2 when Faust matures to the ethic of the immanence of the divine—the counterpart of Stephen Christ. This tripod stability is what both Stephen and Bloom achieve. The third leg of the male is the penis, or more generally manhood in a mature sense. In Stephen's case, the tripod's third leg is his ashplant, his art cleansed of self-indulgence. Without his ashplant, Stephen is knocked down, the ultimate in the lack of balance. He is to start anew as an artist.

In the case of woman in her role as seductress, the correct approach is a violent rejection. Lust and narcissism have been Stephen's seductress, masochism Bloom's. Here both Stephen and Bloom reject the seductress. Stephen frees himself from his mother guilt and redeems these forces, byproducts of incestuous libido, in order to redeem and fulfill himself.[15] Bloom frees himself from father guilt in order to free himself to father a child.

Orestes and Mothers and Fathers

Several allusions generalize the mother figure Stephen confronts. She is referred to as "The Mother," rather than individually by her name or as Stephen's mother. In this process, she is generalized into the mother archetype.

507

Because of his disloyalty at her death bed, Stephen is accused of matricide. The most famous mother murderer was Orestes. He murdered his mother because she murdered his father (and thus the natural path to manhood). He is cleared of guilt by the heroic Athena in Aeschylus's play *Eumenides*, which promotes the patriarchal over the matriarchal order. Likewise, Stephen's mother's claim on his loyalty would murder Stephen's spiritual father. Stephen claims his innocence before his mother's death, and his patriarchal self sufficiency overcomes matriarchal dependency and loyalty.[16] In terms of the oedipal complex suggested by Stephen becoming his own father, Stephen will once and forever "rest the tease" (Orestes).

Note that in combination Stephen and Bloom achieve freedom in the soul from the psychological problems typically faced by humans, youthful preoccupation with the mother image and older preoccupation with the father image. Stephen and Bloom freed from guilt give us the Joyce who wrote this novel.

The Fifth Chakra

The fifth chakra, the next one after the heart chakra, is known as the "gateway of great liberation." This concept is similar to that represented by the image of Tara. The bicycles with wheels remind us of the chakras. Shiva appears in the fifth chakra in androgynous form to unite male and female power. This combined outlook is the feminine side wisdom that Stephen experiences and Bloom already has in combination. In the mental outlook of the fifth chakra, psychic reality is trusted as the only reality, an understanding that franchises the standing of the visions in this episode.

Faust, Siegfried and Narcissus

Stephen's initiation has many parallels with Faust in Goethe's play. After the wild Walpurgis Night and dancing with witches, Faust escapes the net of sexual passion with which Mephistopheles hoped to catch his soul. Faust escapes by virtue of his pure, selfless earthly love for Gretchen, whom he had earlier doomed by his lust. In Part Two, Faust is initiated from a subjective, self-centered world into a larger more objective world where he learns beauty and power by visiting "The

Mothers." This is a realm inhabited by what Goethe called "archetypes"; the following is Mephistopheles's instruction to Faust about going there:

> When you at last a glowing tripod see,
> Then in the deepest of all realms you'll be.
> You'll see the Mothers in the tripod's glow,
> Some of them sitting, others stand and go,
> As it may chance. Formation, transformation,
> Eternal Mind's eternal re-creation.
> Images of all creatures hover free,
> They will not see you, only wraiths they see.
> So, then, take courage, for the danger's great.
> Go to that tripod, do not hesitate,
> And touch it with the key![17]

Here well before Jung, Goethe's archetypes speak Mother. Goethe phrased this visit not in psychological terms but rather in the deeper metaphysical realm of being and becoming, our initiation chamber for this episode and the realm of the fifth chakra. The realm of "formation, transformation . . . recreation . . ." provides the stream of endless possibilities at the base of Joyce's Big Vision.

Finally Faust, like Prospero in **The Tempest**, banishes all magic from his power and stands only as a man. He leaves behind his reckless egoism and longing for all-embracing experience and self-expansion. His goals assume a human aspect. He finds a version of the unity, a cooperative world in which he does not lose himself. Goethe's final chorus sings to "The Eternal-Womanly" which "Draws us above." Goethe ends with the conclusions that all which is earthly is but a symbol of the eternal and that Grace is an understanding love that in its purest, most selfless form comes only in an earthly mother's love for her children or from the Virgin. Joyce delivers the same message in his own way in the last episode.

The legend of Siegfried is tied into the episode because unafraid (without guilt) he vanquished the gods of the old order (Wotan) with his sword. Fearless Stephen freed from guilt puts out the false light of the brothel with his ashplant and banishes compromise from his life and art.

Narcissus disappeared in the pool after he saw his own reflection. Here Stephen sees in the mirror the combined image of himself and Bloom as a rigid and cuckolded Shakespeare who can't even talk straight. The risk of narcissism, according to Francis Bacon in *The Wisdom of the Ancients*, a book in Joyce's permanent library, is that a person of great beauty or talent will do nothing and prove to be the cause of his or her own destruction.[18] In the context of Stephen's life, this possibility is reflected in the image of Shakespeare who can't even talk. Stephen in his narcissism has to this point produced very little art.

Black Mass

A black mass celebrating Satan is coded into this episode.[19] Black masses were apparently popular with the daring in Dublin at this time. For starters, consider the black mass is to the mass as the vampire is to the dove. The black mass is centered in the magical power of woman sourced originally from the primal earth mother goddess, whose invisible influence is now temporarily repressed by patriarchal religions. The mythical power of woman is projected by patriarchal forces as devil-worship seeking vengeance (if you are against a female deity, you say she uses devil worship). In a black mass, the sorceress leads a defiance of Jesus. The black mass in this episode celebrates the arrival of the Antichrist, with overtones of the Easter 1916 Uprising in Dublin that resulted in a massacre of Irish civilians by the British.

The black mass is typically a four act drama that perverts and turns the Catholic Mass inside out. After the introit, Jesus is denied by Satan, and with drug encouragement a whirling dance the Witches' Round is performed. Stephen does this dance with the whores just before his initiation. The black mass drug of choice is belladonna; here Bella turns Bloom into woman, a donna. In the second act, woman herself is the altar. Mrs. Purefoy is kidnapped for this purpose and presented as the goddess of unreason; fecundity is perverted for these purposes. The Eucharist is a cake baked on her body. Toads are torn up (see passing references to toad). The third act of the black mass gives license to illicit intercourse, which of course is our whorehouse. This extends to incest, particularly mother-son after which the son remains faithful; here incest and oedipal libido fuel Stephen's mother nightmare. At dawn,

Satan is burned; this shows up in one of Bloom's explanations of the light scattered by Stephen as a fire on the south side.

The black mass wafer was an aphrodisiac; in the introduction to Nighttown, desire for ice or snowcake turns children into stunted men and women. This is cold lust contrasted with warm love. Note the names of the presiding minister for the black mass—Rev. Hugh C. Haines Love. He shares names with Blazes Boylan (Hugh) and Haines. Co-presider Father Malachi O'Flynn has the first name as Buck. As you already know, they are the bad guys.

In Stephen's sacred mass, the counterpoint to the black mass, Stephen is consecrated by rejecting compromise and dependence totally and forever. Unconscious on the ground covered with woodchips, he becomes the sacred body, the substitute son as Christ is in the Eucharist. At the beginning of the next episode, Bloom helps him up as the counterpart to the Greater Elevation in the Mass. As midnight has passed into Friday, we are ready for Friday Mass, the Mass of the Pre-Sanctified. Bloom plays the role of the presanctified host.

Stephen and Bloom

Translating their initiations into theological terms, Stephen and Bloom begin to merge in terms of the first and second persons of the Trinity. The son must be a likeness of the Father in order for the Holy Spirit to issue. Molly will serve as the Holy Spirit. Jesus considered himself the son of God in the sense that his power on earth had come from God. In the same sense, Stephen becomes the son of Bloom as he receives Bloom's power and proceeds in Bloom's likeness as he registers the human unity.

Stephen and Bloom merge in the sense that Joyce felt that his personality and power as an author reflected the combination of elements from these two characters. What Bloom brings to the merger is the dispassionate compassion that allows him to plug into the common human experiences without going ballistically subjective. What Stephen brings to the merger is raw talent and pure dedication to his intellectual imagination and his art.

Biblical Analogies

Several images from the Book of Revelations, abook of recorded visions, stir this episode. Stephen's sense of Christ is what is revealed to him in his vision. His sense of Christ is to lead the genuine life—totally true to yourself, your higher self as you perceive it. The vision in Revelations of Christ in gold among the seven golden candles surfaces as Bloom and his eight metallic children (the extra one is Stephen). The vision in Revelations of the son of man with white hair and a white head reappears in demonic parody as Miss White with the mercury stained face. The four animals before the throne in Revelations appear in this episode: a lion, a bull, a hybrid part animal part human and an eagle. Stephen's favorite whore becomes Mrs. Lamb, while in Revelations the lamb breaks the seven seals. The throne of heaven contains an unopened book that the lamb opens and reads; after Bloom gains his manhood, Rudy appears to him in the form of a lamb reading and kissing a book written in Hebrew.

According to Revelations, those loyal to the beast of Satan have a mark put upon their right hand; Bloom has an old scar on his right hand that he incurred in a foot (lowest member) race with some Gentiles, leading an inauthentic life of competition, and Stephen recently hurt his right hand (my guess is fighting Mulligan for the key). The general purpose of the Antichrist of Revelations is to deny the father and the son, but he who like Bloom acknowledges the son also acknowledges the father and denies the Antichrist.

Purification

The chaos in the whorehouse is described in a later episode in terms of Jewish ritual as Armageddon, the last battle between good and evil described in the Book of Revelations.

The counterpart in the Mass is the Mass itself, as opposed to the Black Mass. The Mass is designed to achieve liberation from sin.

The counterpart in artistic development is contact with the collective unconscious, library for the grave and constant in human affairs.

First Letter and First Word

The first letter is **T** in the first word "The," signifying the cross. The T also looks like the lotus plant, a symbol of human consciousness, whose crossbar is the pad that rests on the surface and whose stem descends to the earth below the water. Like the initiate in the fifth chakra, the lotus lives in but does not partake of its immediate environment.

Structure, Art and Aesthetics

This wonderfully funny episode gets my vote. The hallucinations worked for me as a mode for presenting the archetypes in the personal and collective unconscious. However, some work on the reader's part is necessary to make the episode credible.

As to Bloom's lack of self-respect, it is necessary for the reader to project the current situation back in time in order to justify his masochistic condition. Lack of self-respect is not a necessary correlate to the charity and generosity that Bloom has shown in the novel. Stephen's dramatic and instantaneous change is credible because of his youth. The notion that a visit to female power in the collective unconscious immediately cures serious guilt by opening up new possibilities is troublesome.

Despite the problems, I evaluate this episode in the most forgiving of moods. The most dramatic form the play, the cultural descendant of Dionysian festivals featured in the last episode, is used to memorialize the moment Stephen and Bloom connect in the land of the archetypes, the source of the grave and constant. Art and life merge.

****

ENDNOTES

1. Joyce had a copy of Jung's *Die Bedeutung des Vaters dur das Schicksal des Einselnen* (1909) [The Significance of the Father in the Destiny of the Individual] in his permanent library collection. Ellmann, The Consciousness of Joyce, p. 115.

2. I don't know whether Joyce took this concept, something like the *anima,* from Jung or anticipated it.

3. Brown, p. 132.
4. *Chorea* Encyclopedia Britannica,1983 ed., Micropaedia, vol. II, p. 888.
5. Danielou, Myths, p. 274 and Campbell, Mythic Image, p. 52.
6. Budgen, p. 230.
7. See Frye I, p. 135 and following for most of the material on Revelations in this section.
8. Gifford, p. 460.
9. Blamires, p. 173.
10. Blamires, p. 177.
11. Gifford, p. 511.
12. Concerning the final scene, please be advised that Blake during his youth was arrested after a row with a drunken soldier who accused Blake of speaking seditiously against the King. Ackroyd, P. *Blake* (New York: Knopf, 1996).
13. Letters, p. 53.
14. Power, A., *conversations with James Joyce* ed. C. Hart (Chicago: University of Chicago Press, 1974) p. 73-74.
15. Jung, C. *Psychology of the Unconscious* Trans. B. Hinkle (New York: Moffat, Yard and Company, 1916) p. 254. Listen to this: "Thus the libido which lies inactive in the incestuous bond (with the mother) repressed and in fear of the law and the avenging Father God can be led over into sublimation through the symbol of baptism . . . and of generation (spiritual birth) through the symbol of the descent of the Holy Ghost. Thus man becomes a child again . . . ."
16. Stephen and Orestes are connected by several details. Attacked by the Furies, Orestes falls prostrate on a couch for 6 days. See Stephen on the couch in the brothel. Orestes bites off his own finger; Stephen hurts his hand fighting with Buck presumably over the key. Orestes is continuously washed with pigs' blood as Stephen's lust turns him into a pig. Orestes pursued and driven crazy by the furies traveled in Apollo's colors for protection; Stephen is in the sacred garb of the parson and loses touch with reality. The furies represent mother night the ancient goddess of the earth. Orestes means mountaineer, which connects to Faust Part 1, also set on a mountain top.

17. Goethe, J. *Faust* Trans. G. Priest (New York: Alfred A. Knopf, 1957), 182 (lines 6283 et. seq.).
18. (Montana: Kessinger Publishing Company) p. 230.
19. This material is from Siverstein, N. *Joyce's Circe Episode: Approaches to Ulysses Through a Textual and Interpretative Study of Joyce's Fifteenth Chapter.* diss. Col. Univ., 1960, who uses Michelet's because Stephen mentions that author.

Part III—Summary

In the Nostoi or homecoming section of The Odyssey, Odysseus finally arrives in Ithaca. United with Telemachus, they slay the suitors. In Part III of this novel, Bloom is with Stephen on the way to or at Bloom's home and Bloom is with Molly in their bedroom. Armed with a new confidence, Bloom slays Molly's suitors in characteristic Bloom fashion.

Compared to prior episodes, more generalized kinds of images drive the details as Part III serves Joyce's program to "eternalize" the characters. With this program, the meaning moves from the personal to the impersonal.

In the progression of its three episodes, Part III outlines Joyce's view of the interrelationship of art and human existence. This is Joyce's redo of the Vico chart. In tabular form, the progression through the last three episodes is refracted through factors that include the following:

Episode	Trinity	Vico Stage	Artist
Eumaeus	Conjunction improper	Subject/object merged	subjective
Ithaca	Conjunction proper	Subject controls object	control
Penelope	Holy Spirit issues	Subject/object independent	detachment

515

Joyce fashions the final three episodes as a progression toward Joyce's view of the more real, more true and more absolute and fundamental. Joy's art follows Hindu metaphysics. The final "Amen" vision is of the impersonal ground of being and how the part implies the whole. It shows Molly's personal instincts fueling the species. She is representative of ultimate reality, an open rather than self-contained system built on possibilities. She affirms. I am that I am. I will be that I will be. I will be natural.

In the Trinity, the progression in the relationship of Father and Son is from improper to proper conjunction. In Eumaeus, the conjunction is improper because Bloom is didactic and possessive and Stephen is aloof. In Ithaca, the conjunction is proper because a mutual respect develops between Stephen and Bloom that allows each to enjoy their similarities while respecting their differences. A likeness of Bloom begins to develop in Stephen. With the proper conjunction of Father and Son, Joyce's version of the Holy Spirit issues forth in Molly in the last episode.

Molly is more fundamental because of her natural fertility, the fundamental of the human condition. Her natural fertility sponsors the human sex instinct and is the creative source with which the artist must be in touch to fulfill the highest art. The sexual instinct and creative imagination, two of the most natural human impulses, serve as Joyce's portals to the gods.

In these last three episodes, Joyce's artistic approach as to both style and subject matter progresses through the literary analogue of the three stages in the recurring cycle of human civilization as set forth by Vico. Each stage has a central core that informs the nature of authority and the resulting relationship of subject to object. Joyce uses this subject/object relationship in terms of the connection between the narrator and the material of the episode.

Through the progression of styles used in the three episodes and Molly's book-ending monologue, Joyce presents his view of the maturation of art. The progress of artistic maturity follows the pattern from subjective dislocation to control to detachment. It flows from the personal to the impersonal. In human perception, the analysis of reality moves from a youthful self-indulgent orientation to the restrictive Law of the Fathers and then to the open-ended Flow of the Mothers.

All of these factor progress toward the more fundamental. In this progression, new possibilities increase in art and life. Molly in the last episode reigns in the holy of holies, the infinite possiblities of life.

Eumaeus (Episode 16)

Basic Themes

Delayed recognition of the Ambush at Home. Ambush of subject by object.

In the Odyssey, Odysseus finally arrives home at Ithaca. The usurpers with superior numbers are still in charge at the mansion, the potential ambush at home. Odysseus meets Telemachus at the hut of the swineherder named Eumaeus, the name selected by Joyce for his episode. But initially Odysseus remains in disguise. Odysseus recognizes Telemachus, but Telemachus doesn't recognize the disguised Odysseus. Eventually the disguise disappears, Odysseus is revealed and together they slay the wooers. They retake their home and Telemachus becomes a man.

Stephen's early and dazed moments of consciousness in this episode are coded with references to Christ's resurrection and reappearance to the disciples at Emmaus after His crucifixion. At first He recognizes them but they don't recognize Him. Finally, as they break bread together, the disciples recognize Him. Upon recognition, He disappears.

As this episode proceeds in a cabmen's shelter, a didactic and possessive Bloom senses only the commercial value of Stephen, and aloof Stephen doesn't recognize the value of Bloom, whose charity is in disguise. As a result, they don't connect immediately. Eventually, in the next episode, they break bread together, Stephen recognizes the value of Bloom and then young Stephen disappears into the dawn.

517

Odysseus's Eumaeus is Christ's Emmaus is Bloom's cabmen's shelter. The impostor is revealed by his departure. Likewise, the narrator of this and the next episode is an impostor for Joyce who, in the final episode, is revealed by his departure—the artist in the dramatic mode. The narrator, like the impostor sailor Murphy, is revealed by his lack of departure.

The sense of this episode indicated by Joyce is the "Ambush at Home." Odysseus and Telemachus have returned to Ithaca to a dangerous situation. Christ was ambushed in Jerusalem. Likewise, an ambush awaits Stephen as an artist in Dublin and at Bloom's home.

In the Vico cycle, the analogy is to first stage, the theocratic or mythical age of the gods. The first Vico stage features a powerful deceit of the imagination, weak reasoning, inability to generalize and tendency to assign natural powers to the gods. Most importantly, subject and object are merged in this mentality. Subject Zeus and object lightning are the same thing. First stage mentality possesses the narrator of this episode. Subject and object are merged as the narrator (subject) is servant to his material (object).

For most of this episode, Bloom and Stephen sit side by side in a cabman's shelter, the counterpart of the swineherd's hut. A cabman's shelter is a place where cabs wait for their next job and members of the public can, regardless of the hour, find refuge and a bite to eat. The crowd in this nighttime shelter is representative of common humanity, the source of the grave and constant.

Didactic Bloom suggests that Stephen should work, in singing tours to be organized by Bloom. Fresh from his Circe initiation, Stephen recognizes Bloom's suggestion would ambush his artistic goals and refuses to work. In Joyce's aesthetics, the analogy is to the first principle *integritas*, or marking off from the rest. As Stephen said in SH, "isolation is the first principle of artistic economy." Stephen marks himself off from common society, by refusing ordinary work, in order to accomplish in his personal life what he must accomplish in his art—independence. But at this point Stephen still goes too far. He fails to recognize that he must be sufficiently connected with humanity in order to appreciate the grave and constant in the human condition.

From the artist's perspective, the risk of ambush at home is a merger of subject and object, author and material. The author not sufficiently removed from his or her material ambushes his or her own work. Joyce gives us in the narrator for this episode a deliberate example of such an ambush. The narrator is an impostor for Joyce. The narrator, apparently a tired old man, is easily influenced by the crowd.[1] The narrator consistently uses cliched words and phrases. These flaws reflect a lack of independence that is fatal to production of high art.

In the shelter, Bloom and Stephen talk to a drifter (D.B. Murphy) who claims he is a home bound sailor just off the ship *Rosevean* (she floated up the river "at one" at the end of the 3rd episode). But the reader knows better because Murphy has the time of arrival wrong (11:00 versus 1:00). Murphy tells several tall tales of sea voyages in an effort to impress the group. Even though home bound and despite a claimed absence of several years, Murphy is apparently in no hurry reach his purported home and wife in Queenstown Harbor. The crowd fails to recognize his true status, but Bloom intuits that Murphy is just out of prison, is an impostor as a sailor and guesses that a nasty surprise (ambush) awaits Murphy at any home he may have. Both Murphy and the narrator of this episode tell stories and are impostors.

Water and the sea are used by Joyce to signify the common ground of being. They are symbolic in Shivaism of common inertia since water always tends to become level and remain still. This episode features images of the sea and the idle members of society that hour by hour merely sit and stare at it. The many references to victims of drowning stem from the following note in Joyce's Notesheets: "sea drowns body crowd ditto soul." Other details used by Joyce emerge from the myth of the wandering Murkandeya, who fell out of the mouth of Vishnu into the milky waters of the cosmic ocean. Murkandeya failed to recognize the true nature of reality until he had this experience. Then his perception of impostor reality departed. In Sanskrit, the word "Upanishad" (the title of various treatises mentioned in the 1st episode dealing with the subject of reaching knowledge of the ultimate reality) means sitting close in to a teacher or near approach, as Stephen sits with Bloom.

In terms of Hindu symbology, Bloom plays Vishnu the remover (Bloom removes woodchips from Stephen). The Vishnu/Bloom tendency is cohesive (compassion) and centripetal, "toward a center, toward more concentration, more cohesion, more existence, more reality, all that tends toward light, toward truth. . . . ."[2] The drifter plays Rudra, the centrifugal force toward dispersion and the lord of tears. The presence of Rudra's proxy and the bricks on the ship he claims he arrived on suggest that suffering is the common ground of being.

The counterpart to this episode in the Mass is the Greater Elevation. Bloom helps Stephen up. In this portion of the Mass, the consecrated wafer and wine are raised by the Priest and shown to the congregation. The Greater Elevation prepares for Communion (etymology—common union). The Friday Mass is the Mass of the Presanctified.

Bloom plans to bring Stephen home "to lay down his wife for him" in the interest of eliminating Blazes. In the language of the Trinity, the Son can come to the Holy Spirit only through the Father. In the language of art, the author can achieve the highest powers only through the father principle of self-sufficiency and in contact with "feminine" creative inspiration. Stephen with Bloom, future plans for Stephen with Molly exchanging Italian for singing lessons, and Bloom with Molly. A common union through Bloom the father. A communion.

Action in Ulysses

This episode is continuous with the last episode, when Stephen was knocked down and Bloom was standing guard over him. Bloom helps him up and brushes him off. Stephen's early moments of consciousness are coded with references to Christ's resurrection.

Bloom and Stephen walk to a cabman's shelter after Bloom unsuccessfully looks for a cab. Near the shelter a group of Italians argue in their native language. In the shelter, Bloom buys a roll and coffee for the dazed Stephen, who rejects both. The shelter operator is rumored to be one of the Invincibles.

Several other people are in the shelter; they appear to be common folk. One, D.B. Murphy, claims to be a sailor just off the *Rosevean*. Murphy tells exotic tales of his sea travels and documents them with a post card showing natives in South America. Bloom notices the card is addressed to a Mr. Boudin in Chile and contains no message. The crowd accepts the story, but Bloom is skeptical. Dazed Stephen doesn't care.

Bloom suggests everyone would work in his ideal state, but Stephen declines. A working whore comes by looking for a trick. As they leave, Stephen and Bloom pass through a street sweeper. Stephen is panhandled by Lord John Corley. Watching, Bloom feels possessive. At the end of the episode, they walk off arm in arm and Stephen sings a song.

The opening line is "Preparatory to anything else [Bloom brushes the woodchips off Stephen] . . . ." The first word "Preparatory" prepares us for Vico's first stage and the first aspect of Joyce's aesthetic theory.

Narrator

Notice that the flow of Joyce's presentation shifts from the narrator's description of the conversation to the actual conversation itself. This technique tells the reader the narrator is not omniscient. Note how the narrator changes tone depending on the mental state of the subject being discussed. The narrator's tone is suggestive generally of the mental state of common humanity, susceptible to influence by others. Generally the style is what Joyce called "relaxed." The whole effect is banal. The narrator viewed as an author does not arise above his material.

Work

Notice all the people working. Lord John panhandles and talks about work; the corporation night watchman watches the stones; the cabshelter operator serves coffee; Murphy has purportedly just returned from sea duty; the cabman waits for a hire; the whore trolls for a trick; and the street sweeper driver makes his rounds. Notice also the degrading nature of this work. It would not produce a greater elevation of humanity.

Bloom suggests that in his ideal state everyone would work, but Stephen demands an exemption from the draft. Bloom assures him that he could work writing for the newspapers (a compromise Stephen rejected in the 9th episode). Bloom grandly plans commercial musical tours featuring Stephen and Molly but leaving time for Stephen to "practise literature," as if art were a sideline like woodworking. Stephen can not work and fully serve his art (as Joyce found out in spades as he worked in a bank by day writing business correspondence and worked on this novel at night).

Stools

Stephen asks why the stools are put up on the cabshelter's tables at closing time, and Bloom gives the common sense answer—in order to clean up in the morning. By contrast to the tripod as the symbol of balanced consciousness, the upended stool can be read as sleep or a visit to the unconscious, which cleans the soul. Stephen has just had his cleansing in the last episode.

While sharing their common interest in music on the walk back to Bloom's home, Bloom and Stephen come upon a horse-drawn street sweeper. With the image still in mind of the up-ended stools for cleaning, the reader is treated to a another powerful stool and cleaning symbol. The horse drawing the sweeper defecates three "globes of turds," that is stools, which the brush in the sweeper immediately behind the horse will clean up. The subject creates the very object the subject is designed to clean up. Likewise, the Church creates a sense of sin that the Church cleans up in confession and with the Eucharist. Stephen and Bloom pass between the turds and the sweeper wagon. They pass through the gap in the chains (connecting the horse and the sweeper wagon) made by an upright in the form of a cross. In traditional iconography, the horse represents the human emotions and the driver the control function. The gap in the chains under the cross-shaped upright represents the freedom provided by Stephen's non-guilt oriented view of Christ.

On the Way Home

The episode ends with Bloom and Stephen walking arm and arm towards Bloom's home, Bloom taking pains to take Stephen's right arm (Bloom's left in Stephen's right). In this joinder, Bloom gives Stephen the right-handed way of society and Stephen gives Bloom the left-handed way of individualism. Stephen feels strange in contact with another human and begins to recover consciousness.

Stephen then sings "All ships are bridged." The word "bridge" suggests a connection between separate and drifting ships. Stephen's singing this song indicates he is beginning to feel a bridge to Bloom, previously considered by Stephen to be a totally separate being. The driver of the sweeper car, as representative of the commonality ("might as well be the sleeper car"), watches them walk away, and his mundane observations about the retreating Stephen and Bloom are woven together with lines Stephen sings from a song. Stephen sings about Peggy and her boyfriend going in a "low-backed car" to be married by Father Maher. Perhaps Father Maher is "may her," or Stephen's experience with Nora, which permitted him to gain artistic effectiveness.

Since the date with Nora is not explicitly disclosed in the action, the Nora subject has impostor status in the novel. Murphy's imposture is as a seaman discharged from service on the *Rosevean*. Nora discharged the semen off Stephen's loaded ship of suffering; she ambushed them at home. Nora is preparatory to anything else.

Action in The Odyssey

In the related chapters xvi through xviii, Odysseus finally reaches the beaches of his homeland Ithaca. The Phaeacian escort sails away immediately. Once again the big O is asleep at an important moment, and Athena has to wake him. Odysseus doesn't recognize his homeland right away because Athena has covered it with a mist. He has the treasures from his martial activity but doesn't know what to do with them. Included in his treasures are a number of tripods, the symbol of balance from the last episode.

Athena is initially disguised as a herdsman. Odysseus asks where he is. Athena won't tell but gives him the following hints: the land is not fit for the driving of horses (too many rocks for the wild passions) and is narrow (discipline required) but produces in abundance (the life of true satisfaction). With these hints, Odysseus figures out he is home. Revealing her identity, Athena compliments his guile. Athena says she has a plan for him, but warns it will involve much suffering. Odysseus needs assurance that he is home; she provides it and compliments his

523

patience in finding out about his family. She scatters the mist, and Odysseus on his knees kisses the now recognizable home soil. She advises him to hide his treasures in local caves[3] and disguises him as a beggar with withered skin, wasted hair and dimmed eyes. She advises him to stay with the swineherd Eumaeus until she has gathered Telemachus. The swineherd lives on the estate in a humble hut apart from the mansion.

The swineherd Eumaeus doesn't recognize the disguised Odysseus but treats him well as a stranger. The herder tells Odysseus what has transpired at the mansion. Odysseus spins his impostor tale: that he is the bastard son of Castor from Crete, fought at Troy, had trouble returning (using part of the true story), and was to be sold as a slave but managed to escape. He also relates, as part of his tall tale, that he has heard tidings of Odysseus and that he will be coming home soon. The herder doesn't believe the part about Odysseus, thinking that the stranger is just inventing good news to make his own way easier. The herder provides food and shelter to the disguised Odysseus.

Athena catches up with Telemachus at Menelaus's mansion in Sparta. At her urging, Telemachus gets ready to leave. Several bird omens appear. A soothsayer named Theoclymenus visits as Telemachus is about to depart. For some unknown reason, Theo's lineage is given. Theoclymenus asks for passage and confesses that he is wandering because he killed one of his own kin. Telemachus grants his request for passage. With Athena's help, Telemachus avoids the naval trap laid by the wooers by using a circuitous route on the return home.

Right in the middle of the description of Telemachus's voyage, the text cuts back to Odysseus in disguise and the swineherd in the hut. Odysseus asks for advice about begging in the main mansion and about the master's father and mother, and the herder complies. Odysseus provides more detail in his cover story: that he was kidnapped by some traders (ambush by the commercial life); and the traders enlisted the aid of a serving women of the same nationality who worked in the family house (an "ambush at home" and an "inside job"). Then the action shifts mid-paragraph back to Telemachus arriving home at Ithaca.

Telemachus, directed by Athena, arrives at the hut where Odysseus is hiding. He doesn't recognize his father because of the disguise. Odysseus defers and offers him a seat, but Telemachus instinctively declines. While the swineherd is out, Athena changes Odysseus back to normal, and father and son reunite in tears and proceed to plan their attack on the suitors. When the swineherd returns, Athena changes Odysseus back to the beggar disguise. Odysseus and Telemachus smile knowingly at each other in response to the herder's remarks.

Odysseus, still in disguise, and Telemachus go separately to the mansion per their plan. At the mansion, each wooer has a stool and brazier for his every pleasure. Odysseus in disguise as a beggar is beaten by the wooers with stools.

Parallels to The Odyssey

The associations with this episode are ripe. The cabman's shelter is the swineherd's shelter. The swine are the common folk represented by their proxies in the cabman's shelter. Telemachus and Odysseus are finally together, as are Bloom and Stephen.

Recognition is deferred with Odysseus of Ithaca, Telemachus of Odysseus and Stephen of Bloom. As with Odysseus and his tripods, Bloom has his treasure but doesn't know what to do with him. Stephen is still in the mist of his stupor, the mist on the beach at Ithaca. The concept of preparations against the suitors is suggested in the episode's first word Preparatory. The danger at home is being killed by the suitors and Stephen's being dragged down through work to the low common denominator of humanity.

The sailor's tall adventure tales suggest the cover story of Odysseus. The "double" character of Odysseus is double cast in the episode: Bloom gets the real identity and the sailor the impostor. The all too coincidental bird omen at Sparta appears as the all too coincidental tall tale by the sailor of a sharp shooter named Simon Dedalus. Over his shoulder, he shoots eggs that are behind him. Like Stephen's father by the same name, he kills the young coming behind him. The curious lineage of the soothsayer Theoclymenus is found in that of Lord John Corley, whose ancestors are traced to a washerwoman in the mansion of

525

the Malahides. The soothsayer who killed his own kin shows up as the rumored identity of the shelter keeper as one of the Invincibles who turned on his own. Stephen still kills his artistic kin by the romantic subjective mode. The swindle in Odysseus's story is reflected in the arguments of the Italians.

The impostor virus from Odysseus's disguise infects the shelter occupants. Most pretend to be something they are not: the operator of the shelter one of the Invincibles; the drifter just out of prison an international sailor; and even Bloom who tries to establish his own identity through a photo of Molly. The shelters of life are an impostor for real living, which inevitably involves suffering.

Merger of Subject and Object

The merger, or more generally the relationship, of subject and object is the general theme of this episode. As we have seen, the issue of the relationship of the subject artist to his object materials is one of the founding fathers of this novel.

The narrator of this episode, the impostor for Joyce, is soft and relaxed and is carried away by his reactions. The narrator's words and phrases are cliched, reflecting low ambition and a lack of artistic freedom. Merger of artistic subject and object is the artistic ambush at home. So far Stephen has been ambushed in his parental home and ambushed his own art.

In Vico's theocratic or mythical age, myths and metaphors reign in art, words are concrete not abstract and the prose is discontinuous. Reflecting that orientation, this episode features cliched descriptions, wandering prose, and an alert, concrete oriented Bloom conversing with a normally conceptual but now dazed Stephen. The dazed Stephen signals the nature of the literary style.

The relationship of subject and object also sponsors a host of more mundane subjects in this episode. They include the following: maneaters (subject eats the object); disguises and impostors (subject is not truly the indicated object); Bloom's musing on whether traffic creates boat routes or vice versa (subject and object mutually interact); the gospels, superstitions about Parnell and other tall tales (object distorted by desires of subject); relationship of subject words to signified objects; and the relationship of subject Christ to everyman object.

A very special version of the relationship of subject and object is the theory of the Incarnation, the immanence of the divine Christ in Jesus. This topic and its special relationship to the artist and his materials are explored in depth below.

Resurrection, Emmaus and Incarnation

"Preparatory to anything else," Bloom brushes most but not all the shavings off Stephen and hands him his hat and ashplant, signifying Stephen's pending maturation to result from the Bloom force field. The subsequent images in the opening scene present humorous references to the resurrection. The old Stephen being dead, the new one arises from the shavings, from the tomb of his youthful ego. As our human proxy for the risen Christ, Stephen is naturally thirsty, hungry and dazed (he yawns). In his first words, he naturally enough voices anger at Lynch, his Judas.

It is no coincidence that this episode is named Eumaeus. After the resurrection, the first reappearance of Christ recorded in the Bible (Luke 24) was to two disciples on the road to Emmaus (means thermal springs). Christ was not immediately recognized, the eyes of the disciples being "holden." As an impostor, Christ explained all the prophecies in the Old Testament as about the Christ whose suffering was necessary for God to come in glory. The disciples asked the imposter to stay with them for a meal and the night. As Christ broke the bread, they finally recognized Him. Immediately He disappeared. Shortly thereafter, He reappeared to Peter and his group in Jerusalem, showed the doubting disciples His pierced hands and feet, and asked for food—fish he ate. They walked to Bethany together, and then He disappeared into heaven. Twice the risen Christ was initially not recognized and disappeared upon ultimate recognition.

The artist comes after Christ, remains removed from common society and attempts to resurrect eternal concepts about humans. Like Christ at Emmaus and Bethany, the artist disappears by detachment when he is in the highest mode. This is the homecoming in art. Stephen's artistic life is compared to Christ's divine nature, and the possibility of working and participating in normal society is compared to the flesh of

527

Jesse's corporeal nature. The job as the flesh takes its purest form in the streetwalker who visits the shelter in her "rounds." She is apparently the same one who appeared in the Sirens (11th) episode. In this context, the risk of ambush at home is ambush by the flesh.

Christ is viewed as the role model "to show the understudy in his title role how to." The artist is the understudy. Coming later, the understudy artist is Christ's successor, in this sense his resurrection, for the presentation through art of the eternal in this world. The Word in Catholic doctrine refers to the expression by God of His understanding of His own Being, which understanding acts as His creative agent.[4] Like God, Joyce the artist presents through the word an understanding of his own being as representative of humanity as a whole.

Joyce views Christ as the merger of the eternal and temporal, god and man. In Joyce's experience, the coincidence was often the meeting ground for the eternal and temporal, so the coincidence is used frequently in this novel. This artistic effort to show the eternal through the temporal by coincidence or otherwise is not easy because of the proverbial "difficulty of making both ends (god and man) meet."

The subject of the incarnation function of the artist is coded into the long first paragraph. It informs the references to Bloom's attempt to find a mode of transport (for the eternal), Beaver Lane for feminine side creativity, stables for birth, Amiens (French for friend) Street and Amiens railway station terminus for connections, the North Star for guidance and, if you needed anything more, a direct reference to Ibsen, one of Joyce's literary gods.

The general concept of the incarnation of spirit in the flesh, or the eternal in the temporal, takes a multitude of forms in this episode. The forms include Lord John Corley, who is out of a job (because the Incarnation is over), the rumored return of Parnell, Christ who came to the Jews according to the flesh, the soul in the body, the verities in classical music, classical form in Greek sculpture and heaven in this life. In Stephen's case, it appears in his God-given tenor voice. The reverse of the incarnation, the temporal in the divine, visits in multiple references to feet of clay in the idol, Achilles's heal and Stephen receiving a "dose."

The word "Incarnation" denotes the state of being in the flesh and unravels to the state of being in the car (In car nation). This word play inspires Stephen's episode ending song about the car (vehicle) which is "lowbacked," the flesh.

Homecoming is featured, particularly the delayed homecoming of Murphy. He claims to live in Queenstown Harbor, symbolic of creative inspiration (read in the spirit). Like Stephen, he has not been able to visit home because having been incarcerated (Stephen by his narcissistic ego). Incarceration and incarnation.

Common Ground of Being

The common ground of being is suggested in the opening section by the obvious overuse of the word "it," pointed confusion in the intended reference of the personal pronouns "he" and "his," and throughout the episode by the following suggestive words and phrases: "terminus," "gone the way of all buttons (flesh)," "kindred," "if I were in your shoes," "genus homo," "hoi polloi," the "averageman," "simple soul," "lower orders," "dictates of humanity" and "feet of clay." The tram tracks of the Dublin United Tramways Company suggest common destiny. All traffic has been suspended on the railways. Bloom and Stephen pass the most common stops of humanity—the morgue and the bakery of daily bread.

The common ground of being is presented as tired, low in aspiration and accomplishment, selfish and subject to inertia. This presentation is made by the limited actions and interests of those in the shelter (Joyce's Notesheets say "cabm. shelter image of society") and more powerfully by the use of cliched language by the narrator throughout the episode. The shelter occupants' conversation is limited to patriotism, hero worship and argument. They even read to each other from a day-old newspaper. The narrator's voice speaks the language of this tired and limited tribe. The entire atmosphere is banal. Bloom thinks in stereotypes about classes of people and nationalities (even the Jews). He rationalizes Molly's infidelity from the category of a decision carrying personal responsibility to the category of a predetermined event in which individual spiritual decisions play little part.[5]

529

In the shelter, Bloom shares the common with Stephen; he buys the common fare of coffee and a hard roll for Stephen. But Stephen declines both offerings as symbols of the mindset he rejects; the liquid is an impostor for invigorating coffee and the hard role of common work is not for him. Much of what goes on in Bloom's mind and in the conversation of the others in the shelter is common and boring. I am reminded powerfully of television and its appeal to the lowest common commercializable denominator. Bloom's recollection of the Parnell case is very much like a soap opera.

In this milieu of the constant but not the grave in human fortunes, Stephen yawns repeatedly. Bloom continues to be compassionate, but in this episode he exhibits bourgeois values—didacticism and a jealous desire for possession of Stephen's attention and respect, and a yearning for economic status. Bloom plans a singing tour for Stephen and Molly; he will organize this one.

Several instances of error, the common condition of the common man, are included. Lord John thinks he saw Bloom with Boylan; Bloom thinks Stephen is orthodox Catholic; the newspaper account of the funeral is wrong; Bloom's name is spelled wrong in the article (Boom signifying thunder and Jew Bang); and Bloom confuses Indian yogis with Aztecs (who performed religious rites similar to the Mass[6]).

Bloom and Stephen briefly talk about the soul and God, generally talking past each other. Stephen is in the conceptual and Bloom in the concrete. In speaking of the human soul, Stephen uses "simple" in the sense of complete without addition or modification or parts while Bloom uses the same word in the sense of ordinary. These different senses are characteristic of the conceptual Stephen and the concrete Bloom.

Vishnu and Rudra

Bloom is once again identified with Vishnu, the cohesive principle in the Shivait cosmology. Vishnu is the "remover," and in the first sentence Bloom helps Stephen to his feet (remember the rising of the entelechy, the form of being) and removes wood chips from his clothes.

Vishnu is the source, the plan of life, so Bloom continues to dream many plans for himself, Molly and now adding in Stephen.

This episode plays host to the myth of Vishnu and Murkandeya. This myth presents the world as a dream of the gods, the ultimate merger of object world with subject god. After the world had become totally corrupted as part of its normal cycle, Vishnu burned all life and returned the remaining universe to his body. Using his internal body heat, Vishnu generated the dream of a new universe complete with individual humans, animals and plants. This impostor dream world was inside his body. In this dream world Murkandeya was a wandering saint who has lived for hundreds of years. But Murkandeya didn't know he was just a dream character and accepted Vishnu's impostor dream world and his own personality as real. In his happy wanderings through this dream world, the saint happened one day to fall out of Vishnu's mouth into the cosmic milk-white ocean. From the ocean surface, the saint could see the partially submerged and self-luminous sleeping Vishnu supported in this ocean by the giant snake Ananta (denotes the Endless or the Remainder or Residue). This was the ultimate reality.

Swimming in the ocean, the saint became frightened and bewildered. Finally, the saint gathered strength and swam over to Vishnu to ask questions (what an opportunity to solve the mysteries!). But Vishnu would have no questions and picked the saint up and put him back into his cosmic mouth. Inside Vishnu's body once again, the saint experienced the same impostor world as before, still thinking he was real. Soon, however, he fell out into the cosmic ocean a second time. This time he saw a luminous young boy who addressed the saint as one would a child. The saint, whose dignity was offended by the boy, demanded respect. The boy explained himself as a manifestation of Vishnu, and the saint was transformed. Back in the mouth and the Vishnu dream world a third time, the now transformed saint, finally understanding ultimate reality as a dream of Vishnu, sat alone in the forest listening to the sounds of the gander (ham-sa). No more ego.

This myth is the type that Vico posited as typical of the mythical stage. It is designed to communicate to the intuition and imagination the concept of maya as impostor reality and the underlying unity of opposites. The opposites in the myth are the two visions of reality: one is the saint's initial view of himself as real, the view inside the Vishnu; and the second is the view from outside of Vishnu of the ultimate reality of the world as a dream by Vishnu. The transformed saint unified both views in reaching wisdom.

Connector Facts bring the Murkandeya myth into the episode. Bloom and Murphy share characteristics of the wandering saint; Bloom is "all at sea for a moment" and "can't make head or tail." Murphy is the wandering sailor seeking respect. Since the universe is suspended, the trains have stopped. Falmouth (fall from the mouth) and Bournemouth (born from the mouth) are mentioned in connection with a "new lease of life" by travel for the common man. Two sides of reality are shown with the sailor's postcard. Vishnu is played by Skin-the-Goat, the purported Invincible, who operates the lighted cabshelter and draws for coffee "spurts of liquid from his boiler affair," a reference to Vishnu's internal heat. Bloom sees the horse drawn sweeper in a new focus, as the saint did the dream world upon returning the second time. The sweeper driver is described as the "lord of his creation, on the perch, busy with his thoughts."

The drifter is identified with Rudra. This identification is made by his gray hair (ash), red color (Rudra means the red one) and blue tattoo (Rudra's blue neck from swallowing Vishnu's sperm), and his tattoo of the number 16, which is associated with both Rudra and homosexuality. As Rudra the centrifugal force, the drifter has allegedly sailed all around the globe. As Rudra the Lord of Tears, the drifter claims he is just off the ship carrying bricks, the symbol of suffering by the Jews in Egypt. But he has the time wrong; the drifter says he was off at eleven and we know she came up the Liffey at one o'clock.

Shivaism, the pre-Aryan religious heritage in India, is a collective heritage of religious and human experience that emphasizes the connection of all living beings. The Shivait doctrines are associated with Tantra, the left-handed way. Lefthandness is mentioned frequently in this episode. In Tantra doctrine, return to basic sexual activity, even anal penetration, is used to jump start the kundalini process,[7] so this episode contains references to homosexuality (perhaps the low-backed car fits in here). Ganesha, the son of Shiva, guards the anus;[8] Stephen refers to his own elephant ears.

Homosexual Theme

At this time (1904), homosexuals were the ultimate impostors, forced to live in the closet as to their essence. Think of Oscar Wilde, mentioned in this episode, as the divorce of subject and object. The sailor's 16 tattoo was a code number for what was then illegal and persecuted. When the sailor is asked what the tattoo number is for, he evades that question by answering another question put at the same time about a sailor being eaten by the sharks: "Ate. A Greek he was." Ate suggests oral, and 8 as one half of 16 completes the cliched allusion to the Greek. The episode ends with the driver of the sweeper wagon watching them walk arm in arm in the middle of the night with the lines of the song pasted in: "and looked after their lowbacked car." The low back is the buttocks, the vehicle for the left-handed way of Tantra.

Lord John Corley

Stephen meets Lord John Corley in the common ground of being and humanity. The Lord's lineage is traced to an ancestor who was a washerwoman in the mansion of the Lord Talbot de Malahide. Delayed mention is made of common lines through a mother. Lord John says he is out of a job, needs help in finding one and needs a loan.

Seeing Lord John successfully panhandle Stephen, Bloom calls Lord John a "hangerson." Now this word can be read either as a hanger son or as a hangers on. The hanger son must refer to Christ on the cross, and the rest of the material can be interpreted in this light—Christ coming allegedly from the line of the House of David, out of a job and seeking funds. The hanger son could also be the Father who allowed his Son to be crucified. Since the main incarnation in Jesus is over, Lord John is out of a job and just making ends meet. He is hanging on after the son was hanged. He says he would even work as a sandwichman (carrying the wisdom of Hell sign) or a crossing sweeper (the symbol for a priest or the Church). The Church is to continue the role of Christ. Lord John also shares traits with the soothsayer Theoclymenus from The Odyssey; his lineage was also given, and he was wandering because he killed one of his own kin. Perhaps this is an allusion to Jahweh, or the

Father who killed his own Son, and never wants to be seen (Joyce's joke—because he has Malahid, bad skin, and craves respect).

Reaching for coins to help Lord John, Stephen first finds the remains of biscuits and finally two half crowns. The biscuit crumbs would be the Eucharist in which the Lord makes limited appearances. Half a crown would be the kingdom of the spirit but not Caesar's kingdom, as Stephen renders a half crown to the Lord. So Stephen meets the Lord John in the poor and down and out; as Christ said, as you treat the poor, so you treat me.

Plato's Dialogues

With Stephen's presence, the pattern of references to Plato's dialogues in Part I returns in Part III. The reference for this episode is Plato's *Republic*, in which the ideal state is described. Work is emphasized, artists serve the state and controls are severe. These aspects return in Bloom's ideal state involving work for everyone and Stephen's dazed condition as an artist. Plato's recommendations for the ideal state are based an assumption of severe limitations in human possibilities. His state was essentially a controlled shelter to protect against human weaknesses.

Traditional Schemata and First Letter

The traditional schemata given by Joyce for this episode are organ—nerves, art—navigation, color—none, symbol—sailors, and technique—narrative (old). The Linati adds the sense or meaning as "The Ambush at Home." The Correspondences are given as Eumaeus—Skin-the-Goat the shelter operator, Odysseus as Pseudangelos (impostor)—the sailor, and Melanthious (Odysseus's goatherd who turns against Odysseus)—Lord John Corley.

The nerves are featured in Stephen's dazed condition. They communicate to the subject brain news of effects on the object body; they connect object and subject. Navigation by sailors is discussed in terms of shipwrecks, the destiny of most soul voyages. The symbol is sailors because they adventure out and then come home to tell tall tales, like the artist. The technique is narrative old because the domain is the substratum of being among humans. Note the parallels and contrasts with the 3rd episode Proteus for which the technique was narrative young and in which Stephen searched for the underlying reality of nature.

The cabman's shelter, I am told, is an eight-sided small enclosed building; all occupants are inside together.[9] Eight will press hard in the meaning of the last episode as the symbol for eternity. Any sharply enclosed building divides the inside from the outside, as does the disguise.

The first letter P in Preparatory looks like the elevation of the host in the Mass. In Egyptian hieroglyphics, which will become paramount in the next episode, a reversed P stands for preparatory to holiness.[10]

Parallel in the Mass and Jewish Ritual

In the Mass of the Presanctified on Good Friday, the scene begins with the priest "lying prostrate on the altar steps"[11]. This parallel with the prostration of Stephen at the beginning of the episode is unusually direct. It points to Stephen as the priest of the imagination. Bloom elevates Stephen as the priest does the Host. The Mass commences with a reading by a person otherwise unconnected with the ceremony. In SH, Joyce referred to this person as a "strange unconnected reader." This allusion complements the isolation of the artist.

Bloom takes Stephen to the shelter where the night congregation has gathered. The congregation is the common body for worship. Early on Friday morning Bloom plays host to Stephen for coffee and a hard roll. Bloom is presanctified as the host because of his earlier loss of ego, which produces the compassion for Stephen. After his symbolic death, elevation and purification by Bloom, Stephen is to be translated into the host for the reader communion at large, the author of this novel.

Since the Host has already been presanctified on Holy Thursday, the service on Friday does not include a transubstantiation ("trans," the coming across of the divine from the void). The most that Stephen can achieve on Friday is consubstantiation, a condition in which the substance is only partly divine and partly the accidents of mortality.[12] This is the incarnation of the eternal in the flesh. As "con" connotes bound up with, consubstantiation echoes the beginnings of Stephen's connection with Bloom. Again the merger of subject and object.

The reference to this episode in terms of Jewish ritual in the next episode is "atonement," the reconciliation of Jahweh and his people. On the Day of Atonement, Yom Kippur, the high priest for the only time during the year burned incense in the Holy of Holies in the Temple. This Bloom will do in the next episode.

In art, the artist must atone his experience by detachment.

The Trinity

At this point, the Father Bloom and the Son Stephen are not in the proper relationship in order for the Holy Spirit to issue. Bloom is didactic and possessive and Stephen is aloof. Accordingly, Joyce deliberately flaws the art of the episode in order to reflect the absence of the Holy Spirit.

Art, Aesthetics and Structure

The control of the means, the writing, in this episode is in a new league. The boring banality comes only through the literary style, not directly in the text. The method of narration, rather than what is narrated, carries the main theme. This is heady stuff. When you are at the same time experiencing both the banal mode of the prose and the boring material being presented, think about falling out of the mouth of Vishnu into the cosmic ocean.

The theory of literary style, Joyce's favorite topic, appears on the surface in this episode. Ibsen and Dante, two of Joyce's literary gurus, are mentioned. Several references to coincidences reflect Joyce's belief that coincidences are wormholes to meaning. And there is this very direct reference:

> Added to which was the coincidence of meeting, discussion, dance, row, old salt of the here today and gone tomorrow type, night loafers, the whole galaxy of events, all went to make up a miniature cameo of the world we live in especially as the lives of the submerged tenth, viz. coalminers, divers, scavengers etc., were very much under the microscope lately.
> [emphasis added]

For Joyce, the master of indirection, this directness is like hitting a mule with a board—just getting his attention (an old joke

536

referred to in this episode). While this material includes a direct reference to those in the shelter (under the microscope) as a symbol for society in general, it also introduces the issue of how close to real life can literature come and remain art. To what extent must subject art "rise" above its object basic material? Elsewhere the narrator says no photo (total merger of subject and object) can be art. Again a question is asked but not answered.

Art as the confidence trick is suggested by the following:

. . . .[the conversation between the shelter operator and the sailor, both impostures] reminded him forcibly as being on all fours with the confidence trick, supposing, that is, it was prearranged as the lookeron, a student of the human soul if anything, the others seeing least of the game.

Here is the artist as the "looker on" and "student of the human soul" with the reader seeing the "least of the game."

Literature like all art is a confidence trick, a double or impostor for reality and a subject only partially related to its object. But like Odysseus in his disguise who could provide information about Odysseus, it can relate eternal truths; and like Odysseus in disguise getting the lay of the land as part of a successful homecoming, it can help you come home to yourself, your real self not your bourgeois self built on the opinions of others.

****

ENDNOTES

1. Schwartz, p. 232.
2. Danielou, Myths, p. 149.
3. Twelve tripods were found recently in a cave at Polis on the island of Ithaca according to **The Oxford History of Greece and the Hellenistic World** (Oxford: Oxford University Press, 1986) p. 61.
4. **Incarnation**, Encyclopedia Britannica, 1983 Ed., Micropaedia, Vol.

V, p. 321.

5. Critical Essays, p.377.
6. Jung, Psyche and Symbol, p. 178.
7. Danielou, Myths, p. 148.
8. Danielou, Shiva, p. 90.
9. Gifford, p. 534.
6. Adams, W. *The House of Hidden Places* (African Heritage Classical Research Studies Series, publication date missing) p.101. This book was in the permanent library of Joyce (Ellmann, The Consciousness of Joyce).
11. SH, p. 116 and Lang, p. 36.
12. Lang, p. 264.

Ithaca (Episode 17)

Basic Themes

Control.

Control produces bad relationships. Control produces bad art. Proceeding from ego, control produces illusion. Institutional control restricts individuality and human possibilities.

This episode, Joyce's favorite, is constructed entirely of questions and answers. Like those used in science to explain relationships in the natural world, the method of questions and answers implies an authority. The authority is in the position of control—to choose the questions and give the answers.

The issue of control in human relationships plays out in two pairs, Stephen with Bloom and Bloom with Molly. These relationships are the exclusive subject in the surface presentation of the last 100 pages of the novel. Only the two pairs of humans are presented. Having escaped the control of religious and cultural institutions, Stephen now faces a human relationship with Bloom. In the most intimate of human relationships, Bloom now faces dealing with Molly's infidelity. She has made no effort to disguise her activities of the day.

Stephen experiences the Bloom force field in the secular communion of friendship. Initially, Bloom is neither didactic nor possessive with Stephen. Stephen takes off his shell and is no longer aloof from Bloom. They connect in a noble form of eros, mutual respect for their differences and celebration of their similarities. Stephen and Bloom build their communal celebration of their shared interests in "heterodox resistance," rejection of the conventional life ruled by the Law of the Fathers. However, when Bloom asks Stephen to live with them and exchange singing for Italian lessons, the threatened control drives Stephen into the night even though he has no where to go.

After Stephen leaves, Bloom resolves Molly's infidelity with compassion born of equanimity. Even though Molly is apparently asleep, Bloom lifts her nightgown and kisses her bottom, despite the probability of waking her. This seems an unlikely move the day before. Even without ego, Bloom manages an erection; signs of things to "come." Bloom does not attempt to control Molly or her infidelities. He accepts the situation as it is. He is more masculine and assertive with Molly even though not controlling. She continues her control efforts through an interrogation of Bloom. The ending images suggest renewal in the Bloom marriage.

Self-realization proceeds within this eros according to the analysis in Plato's dialogue *Phaedrus*: the characters imaginatively project their personal god onto the image of the other and in eros move their soul toward the reflection of that god. Stephen projects onto Bloom an intellectual Jesus and Bloom onto Stephen the "ecstasy of catastrophe." Bloom projects the image of the Promised Land on Molly. Molly's images of Bloom are reserved for the last episode.

In this form of eros, the characters serve as mirrors for each other, much as the still pond did for Narcissus. Through this process, humans become more like their gods. You will note that this form of eros is fed by noble versions of the sexual instinct and the creative imagination. The mirror metaphor indicates that self-realization or self-knowledge can be obtained only in connection with other humans. Each must relate to others and understand humanity in order to know himself. The part must imply the whole. Stephen must met Bloom and through him humanity into order to progress individually and as an artist. Plato's metaphor sponsors the many mirror images in this episode.

In this episode, the authority is the narrator as author. The narrator/author of the last episode was slavishly subject to the attitude of the tribe. Here Joyce has created the other extreme—a most authoritative narrator/author who commands the material both asking and answering the questions in a sternly objective style. This narrator/author, like the teacher in the Nestor (2nd) episode, is in control. With the author focused exclusively on control, proper perspective is lost. Bad art is the result. Again the author/narrator is an impostor for Joyce.

Reflecting loss of perspective, this episode zooms wildly in and out to close or long range perspective. From microscope to macroscope. The artist's exclusive interest in control and loss of perspective also dehydrates the emotions. In this episode described by Joyce as "dry rocks," all emotion is arrested. As a result, life drains right out of the picture. What is left is the impersonal in control. Joyce described it as a "mathematico—astronomico—physico—mechanico— geometrico—chemico sublimation of Bloom and Stephen" where "all events are resolved into their cosmic, physical, psychical, etc. equivalents." As in human relationships, the control artist dries up the art.

The voice of authority speaking in dry mathematical and scientific terms is the modern mask of the Law of the Fathers. The purpose of the Law of the Fathers is control. Control in turn limits self-realization of the individual. In this Law, the primary assumption is made that opposites cannot be reconciled. In Aristotelian terms, non-A can never equal A. This assumption controls possibilities and permissible relationships.

Joyce condemns these assumptions by presenting the Law of the Fathers within a stylistic framework that is lacking in fundamental perspective. Joyce presents art nurtured by the Flow of the Mothers as reaching a higher truth, a greater reality. Art so nurtured shows the way beyond science to reconciliation of opposites. Representing respectively the scientific and artistic outlooks, Bloom and Stephen come into proper conjunction. By merger in Joyce, they atone the two outlooks on life.

Changes in Stephen and Bloom away from control in the human realm represent the direction Stephen and any other author needs to go to produce proper art. The artist must free the material from his personal control and connect with the grave and constant. This is how Robertson Davies put the problem of control by the author; he is speaking about an author being creative:

> So, if the creative process cannot be forced, can it be encouraged or assisted? . . . but in the end it comes down pretty much to the artist's ability to get out of his own way. He must not force; he must not strain. In his encounters with the creative process within him he must not dictate, or bully, or make conditions. He must, in fact, give up control and abandon himself to what happens.[1]

These requirements for the highest art parallel the fundamentals in human love. Proper love, the desire of good for another, can only flower in a relationship based on respect and lack of possession. Within such a relationship, the lovers sense the unity. That same unity is at the base of Joyce's aesthetics, the grave and constant in the human condition and empathy in terror, pity and joy. It is in the spirit of this kind of love that Bloom treats Molly's infidelity with equanimity, and their bed behavior holds promise for the future and a new Rudy.

As the Son proceeding from the Father, Stephen declines Bloom's offer to stay at their home and leaves into the early morning hours with no fixed destination in mind or purpose to guide him. Having experienced Bloom, Stephen will become more like him, more open and accepting of relationships. The Son proceeds in the likeness of the Father. Like the artist in the dramatic mode, Stephen disappears. Molly and Bloom share the bed but keep their secrets. Their relationship is to proceed based on understandings and misunderstandings. Their souls will not merge.

The analogy in Joyce's aesthetics is *consonantia* or rhythm, the relationship of part to part and to whole. The analogy in the Vico cycle is to the second stage, the aristocratic or heroic age of paternal authority. In this stage, control is predominant in governance and subject and object

541

are more separated in thought. This stage sponsors the Law of the Fathers and its artistic proxy the control oriented author.

The condition of human existence under the Law of the Fathers, separated and interested in control, is associated with the Fall in the Garden of Eden. Joyce implies that God's interest in control (don't eat this don't eat that) was the major cause of the Fall. And the Fall produced separation. In the institutional religious realm, the Law of the Fathers requires the absolute separation of God and humankind. In the realm of material reality, opposites must remain just that. Joyce indirectly tells us that with these assumptions, the tree of life for the individual spirit receives the wrong kind of light. This is a very big point—that the emphasis on control and separation of opposites encoded into our major systems of knowledge, views of material reality and major spiritual assumptions produce or at least encourage separation and control among humans.

The end of the episode demonstrates the potential for movement toward greater togetherness in ordinary human relationships. This movement is associated in human relations with love rather than possession and in knowledge systems with the assumption of the possible unification of opposites in the infinity of being. These systems include the philosophy of Giodarno Bruno and the Hindu/Buddhist view that all humans share the divine component. The goal of these systems is unification with god. (Ironically, the latest discoveries in quantum physics suggest a similar kind of connection in the universe through quantum fields.) The personal tool of these systems of unification is meditation designed to seek the impersonal unity beyond the personal. Tools for meditation and images of unified opposites end the episode as Bloom is arrested by sleep.

Suggestive of Stephen's artistic future, he vaguely agrees to Bloom's plan to barter Italian for singing lessons with Molly, which lessons would place him in contact with the symbol of the creative inspiration. But he declines to stay the night, appropriate to maintaining his distance from what is about to become the material for this novel. Stephen walks out through the north gate of the Blooms' garden into the resonant Eccles Lane in the early hours of near dawn. Bloom, the master of community, feels cold isolation as Stephen leaves. What Stephen feels and where he goes are left to our imagination.

As Stephen leaves, Bloom returns to what in Joyce's view is the best you can get on this earth, the prospect of heterosexual union and family with his wife. Molly's bed, as the Ark of the Covenant, now contains from Blaze's profane visit the remains of manna (crumbs) and the imprint of Aaron's rod (some flakes of Plumtree's potted meat). Molly misinterprets murmurs made by Bloom as he falls asleep as a request for breakfast eggs in bed. The significance of their physical togetherness in bed is intensified by the image thrown upward on the ceiling by the bed lamp of inconstant but full concentric circles, a reference to Dante's vision of the Godhead. The contrast with the half circle fan shape (arc subtended by a chord) signifying separateness gives the main theme of relationships in a visual presentation.

Action in The Odyssey and Parallels

Telemachus and Odysseus, pursuant to their plan, proceed separately to the mansion where the wooers are still in command (as a usurping narrator is in this episode). Odysseus is in disguise as a beggar and before the usurpers checks his emotions in order not to give away his true identity (emotions are arrested in this episode in the presence of usurping narrator). Odysseus in disguise says Odysseus would have come home earlier except that he has been gathering treasures; and Bloom continues his bourgeois day dreams of riches. Father and son are finally together in the proper relationship of mutual respect and assistance, Odysseus with Telemachus and Bloom with Stephen.

The suitors don't recognize Odysseus in disguise. Penelope, not consciously knowing that Odysseus is home but feeling something finally sets up a contest for her "hand." The winner must string Odysseus's bow (this involves bending the bow) and shoot one arrow through 12 targets, which requires great strength. The targets are gray iron loops attached with a stem to the handle (the symbol for sperm). None of the suitors can even string the bow; the main suitor waits until last and, sensing his own defeat as well, suggests the contest be postponed until due sacrifices can be made to Apollo (the Big Archer).

This dodge is, of course, the wrong attitude as to the gods, who must always be consulted first.

But Odysseus, still in disguise, forces the issue, arms the bow and shoots one arrow through all 12 loops. Drugged by their many months of being in control at the mansion, the suitors still don't recognize Odysseus or sense danger. This is also the artistic fate of authors interested in control. Reprogrammed by Athena from beggar disguise into his manly heroic condition, Odysseus turns the mighty bow on the suitors. He and Telemachus proceed to kill them one by one and retake their home. Athena helps by providing a light in the action area, as Molly turns on a light in the bedroom. Odysseus starts with the leader Antinous and then Eurymachus. Likewise, Bloom and Stephen throw off their oppressors, signified by Blazes and Buck. After the killing, the mansion is fumigated of death stench with sulfur, and 12 unfaithful servants are dispatched as well. In this episode, Bloom dispatches the smell of Blazes with incense and dispatches Molly's suitors not with violence but with equanimity (arrested emotion).

At first Penelope doesn't believe the good news, thinking that the stranger may be a god. But she is convinced after the stranger recounts how their marriage bed was carved whole from an olive tree (apparently gods can't see in the bedroom or are not interested in these domestic details). Our Bloom losses track of the furniture because Molly has moved it, but he does make it back to her bed.

Garden of Eden and Possibilities

Joyce finds the issue of the nature of relationships in human experience in the patriarchal legend of the Garden of Eden. Adam and Eve ate of the tree of knowledge of good and evil but not of the tree of life. Joyce interprets the knowledge of good and evil as a metaphor for systems in the Law of the Fathers that assume the absolute separation of opposites in the finite (e.g. good and evil are irreconcilable opposites). Joyce interprets the tree of life as a metaphor for the unity and possible infinity of being. The result of eating the fruit of the tree of the knowledge of good and evil but not of the tree of life was equivalent to expulsion from the Garden. Joyce indirectly indicts God's interest in control as the cause of the resulting hardships on and separation among humans.

Expulsion had disastrous consequences. Before the expulsion, Adam and Eve were with God and lived an idyllic life apparently in immortality. The consequences of the expulsion were registered in the negative effect on relationships and the mortality of humans. Without the recognition of unity, God was separated from human kind, and the forces in the universe became the impersonal and cold interstellar void. Without the recognition of unity, Adam was emotionally separated from Eve. They "covered" themselves from each other in their guilty shame. This emotional separation, operating through the human archetypes, keeps humans apart and incomplete.

The expulsion created the seemingly unbridgeable pair of opposites: separation versus the unity. On the one side is separation of opposites with restriction, consistency, control, possession and limitation. In short, the Law of the Fathers. On the other side is unification of opposites in the unity with liberation, inconsistency, equanimity, freedom, love and infinite possibilities. In short, the Flow of the Mothers.

This theme is initiated in the sublime first question and answer that indirectly traces individual human isolation to the Fall in the Garden. It is nurtured in occult shadows through veiled references to Yeats's figure of interlocked gyres (spinning triangles) and then finally is exposed in direct textual references.

Action in Ulysses

Bloom and Stephen leave the cabman's shelter and walk arm in arm to Bloom's home. They walk together on "parallel courses . . . returning." Returning to home applies naturally to Bloom and symbolically to Stephen. In the description of this walk and by reference to street names, the Fall of the human race in the Garden of Eden is retraced. Their parallel courses would, in a system of opposites like standard geometry, remain separated. Later Joyce specifies that apparently parallel lines actually meet in the center of the earth.

In the first Q&A, "United" at a "normal" pace (read unity was the normal condition in the Garden) Stephen and Bloom walk from Beresford Street (read bare ford or bare crossing as Adam and Eve were naked after the Fall in the Garden) to Lower and Middle Gardiner Streets (moving through the Garden) and then to Mountjoy Square (for sex to which they are condemned by death by expulsion from the Garden). At that point, Bloom and Stephen slow down and "each" (separately) moves into a street named Gardiner's Place (for the world created by the Big Gardener), and then by "inadvertence" walk on Temple Street (read institutional religious instruction). Still separate, they haltingly move through Temple Street to Hardwicke Place (read suffering). Then "disparate" (even more separate), they pass at a "relaxed pace" through the circus (for a curved street) in front of St. George's Church. In the circus, they walk on a "chord" diametrically across the circle made by the curved street, a chord being a straight line across the circle. The shape produced by the chord and the curved portion of the street is a half circle or fan shape, suggesting individual separation and restriction in comparison to a full circle. The liberating opposite of this image is the imperfect but full concentric circles that appear on the ceiling in Molly's bedroom.

At the end of the first answer, the control-oriented narrator adds in a didactic tone, "the chord in any circle being less than the arc which it subtends." Opposites, such as a curved arc and straight line chord, can never be equal. In standard geometry, the finite chord is always less than the arc. Note Joyce's choice of the word "subtends", which leaves an odor of a lower tendency. The chord separates the circle. Through this association, the first Q&A associates human separation with the Law of the Fathers. On the other hand, Bruno famously cited as an example of opposites uniting in infinity the lack of any difference between the smallest possible chord and the smallest possible arc.

In the second Q&A, Stephen and Bloom are described as a "duumvirate," meaning a partnership or a unification. The second question concerns their conversational subjects. The answer is a list of various subjects of knowledge. The item in the middle of the list is a paraheliotropic tree, a tree that seeks light and signifying the tree of life. The list of subjects includes the presabbath (Friday), the day when Adam and Eve (then known as Ish and Ishah) were expelled from the Garden because of eating from the prohibited tree of knowledge of good and evil.

In the Jewish vision of Paradise, the tree of knowledge surrounds the gigantic tree of life, and it is necessary to clear a path through the tree of knowledge in order to reach the tree of life.[2] The answer in the second Q&A is a picture of that arrangement, a light seeking tree of life in the middle of various subjects of knowledge. But because of the Fall in the Garden and systems of knowledge that assume the separation of opposites, this tree is receiving only artificial light (gaslight and arc and glowlamps). The tree of life would die in this artificial environment. This second Q&A, by the way, is in my view the most satisfying art in the entire novel.

Note the subjects on the way in toward the tree of life: "Music, literature, Ireland, Dublin, Paris, friendship, woman, prostitution and diet." These have been liberating influences for Stephen. Note that these subjects become less effective in liberation the closer they are placed to the dying tree of light. Note the control related subjects on the way out away from the tree of life: "exposed corporation emergency dustbuckets, the Roman catholic church, ecclesiastical celibacy, the Irish nation, jesuit education, careers, the study of medicine, the past day, the maleficent influence of the presabbath, Stephen's collapse." These have been authorities in Stephen's life that would control him (Joyce tried to study medicine in Paris) and restrict his possibilities. Note that these influences are generally chronological and the stronger influences are closer to the dying tree of life.

The next several Q&As explore the general subject of separation and unity in the relationship of Stephen to Bloom in terms of their differences and affinities. These include their mutual tenacious resistance to orthodox beliefs, their reactions to experience, likes and dislikes, reactions to the community and prior connections.

In the fourth Q&A, Stephen expounds the view that literature reflects "the eternal affirmation of the spirit of man." Bloom dissents, given that he has been carrying the book *The Sweets of Sin*. In this same answer, Bloom agrees "covertly" to Stephen's correction of the date of conversion of Ireland to Christianity by St. Patrick from 432 to 260. The year 260 is in the reign of Cormac MacArt, the last pagan King who suffocated on his own vomit (the Academy award in subjectivism).

Note the association of conversion with MacArt, whose name means the person (Mac) and Art—that would be person art or the romantic subjective, literary vomit. Bloom attempts to explain the suffocation scientifically by reference to body chemicals, but Stephen attributes the cause of conversion "to the reapparition of a matutinal cloud (perceived by both from two different points of observation, Sandycove and Dublin) at first no bigger than a woman's hand." This is a reference to the rain cloud from the Elijah story, rain that brought renewal as Nora did to Joyce leading with her hand. Nora moved Stephen from the blind alley of masturbation to sexual relationship with the potential for love. The parallax reference (two different points of view) suggests Stephen's date with Nora was in the direction of Sandycove; in fact, Joyce's date with Nora included the summer fields near the Dodder River, which viewed from Bloom's home is in the direction of Sandycove.[3] By now you realize the Nora connection to Bloom, since he also literally and figuratively took Stephen in hand in his distress. Both Stephen and Bloom will father their own son as a result of proper relationship with the female.

In the fifth Q&A, Stephen and Bloom agree that artificial light, such as that from streetlights, has a negative influence on paraheliotropic trees. Note that Joyce has returned to the tree in order to emphasize the image of the tree of life. A heliotropic tree or plant bends toward the sunlight. In the context of the image of the trees of knowledge and life, the street light (produced by the City) would be the artificial light disseminated by authorities that does not feed the tree of life. The authorities signify the Law of the Fathers.

In the sixth Q&A, Bloom reflects that he hasn't had an intellectual conversation like this one for a long time; the last one was more than 10 years ago, reflecting the same hiatus as in sexual relations with Molly. In a question about this sequence,[4] Bloom reflects that individual development is necessarily accompanied by a restriction on community, "the converse domain of interindividual relations." On this subject of the individual and the unity, Bloom thinks about birth when he came to many and was received as an individual ("From inexistence to existence he came to many and was as one received"), his adult life during which he has been isolated in the same way as anyone ("existence with existence he was with any as any with any") and his death when he would be perceived by the remaining community as nothing ("he would be by all as none perceived"). These three highly concentrated phrases reduce this complex subject to the linguistic counterpart of a mathematical formula. Human relationships are described in terms of a mathematical formula whose foundation assumptions have grave implications for the human results. The method implies the result.

When they reach Bloom's house, Bloom discovers he has forgotten his key for the front door, the regular way in. Bloom, now effective, improvises. In terms suggesting monkey (key again and continuing the human story), he hangs from a pipe and drops down to the cellar entrance (read the collective unconscious). The word "fall" is used twice, and Bloom survives his fall uninjured, having "regained new stable equilibrium." The new equilibrium, gained by initiation in the Circe episode, is spiritual balance free of guilt. The description of Bloom's drop (read into the human condition) also includes references to the Ascension and methods for dating Easter, the Christian ordained methods for bridging the Fall. Bloom has bridged the separation resulting from the Fall with compassion.

Once inside, Bloom lights a light, removes his shoes and is gone for four minutes for a purpose not explained, perhaps into the hallway to make sure Blazes has left. Then he lets Stephen in the front door. Over the door, glass in the shape of a fan makes a half circle, signifying separation by an arc subtended by a chord.

Their entrance is described in ritualistic terms. In going to the kitchen, they go past a "lighted crevice of doorway on the left" (the bed room?) and then down steps curiously described as "more than five." Bloom kneels to light a fire, and Stephen remembers others kneeling in school and at home, but always in submission (controlled relationships built on restriction and limits). He also sees on a drying line strung up in the kitchen four handkerchiefs and one pair of gray hose attached to the line by wooden pegs. One of the control pegs is right you know where. I think these relate to the archery targets in The Odyssey and four scores with Molly by Blazes.

Bloom makes hot water for cocoa, which means god food[5] and is derived from the tree known as Theobroma cacao. The water Q&A unexpectedly zooms out to long range in perspective; the fire Q&A radically zooms in on details. Bloom's hand is connected to Nora's with this description of Bloom's hand: "his firm full masculine feminine passive active hand." Bloom does, but Stephen the hydrophobe declines to, wash his hands.

Unlike at the cab shelter, Bloom now uses discretion in choosing his subjects of conversation, not giving unsolicited advice to Stephen. This is described as avoiding "didactic counsels," another reference to concepts involved in proper art. The same point is made by reference to Bloom's unsuccessful practice of attempting to gain instruction in solving personal problems by randomly opening pages of Shakespeare; no didactic instruction there either.

Bloom gives Stephen and himself the same type of cup and the cream (read spirit) usually reserved for Molly's breakfast (where we started in the 4th episode). Ever sensitive, Bloom decides not to use his special mustache cup of imitation "Crown Derby," since there is only one and it would serve as an icon of authority. By the way, the special mustache cup has a bar across the top, in order to protect the user's mustache from foam. Looking at the top of the cup, the bar creates a chord across the circle made by the rim, our symbol of separation.

The cocoa is described with reference to the Mass —"Epps's mass product, the creature cocoa." They drink in "jocoserious silence," a good description of Joyce's overall method. Bloom notices a small tear in the right side of Stephen's jacket.

The torn race tickets discarded on the dresser apron and Bloom's previous intimations of the result of the Gold Cup horse race (Throwaway) prompt a review of the subject of premonition. In this review, the description of Bloom blends into the prophet filled Hebrew tradition: "with the light of inspiration shining in his countenance and bearing in his arms the secret of the race, graven in the language of prediction." This is Dublin's secular counterpart of Moses coming down

550

from the mountain and breaking the tablets (torn race tickets) containing among other matters the prediction of Hebrew destiny. Even though he didn't bet, Bloom is satisfied because he had brought "Light to the Gentiles," the candle and the truth to Stephen. The torn race tickets, which are losing tickets, are numbered 8 87 and 88 6, both reflecting separation and a fall from 8 for infinity or eternity. The winning tickets, in the language of the Trinity, would have to be 888.

Bloom remembers a poem he composed at age 11. It contains a reference to his name and a desire to be in print. An innocent version of the romantic subjective. The very next question relates to the major factors separating Bloom and Stephen: name, age, race and creed. Then to sandwich this grave list of separating factors, the next questions are about anagrams the youthful Bloom made on his own name and a poem to Molly. His youthful verse is self-conscious and, appropriate to the author in control mode, even contains the author's name. In this mode, the author claims possession: "You are mine. The world is mine." These are all separating factors. Even subjective art causes separation. Bloom's failure to complete a song for a pantomime on *Sinbad the Sailor* is mentioned. The next question dwells on their respective ages.

Anagrams made by the youthful Bloom on his own name are also given: ". . . Ellpodbomool . . . Molldopeloob (Bloom is a dope with Molly)." Have some fun. Try the same anagram with Stephen Dedalus's name. One is Deadsetlusphen (dead set loose pen). Their names, their identity, control the arrangement of the letters. Making anagrams brings new possibilities into play.

The narrator reviews their prior connections: a meeting when Stephen was five, was with his mother and refused to shake hands with Bloom (they shake hands tonight); a meeting when Stephen was ten, was with his father and invited Bloom to dinner (gracefully refused); and finally Dante, who used to live with Stephen's family and later lived in the same hotel as the Blooms (read the art of Dante, which Stephen crossed with Bloom will produce).

Neither mentions the age gap. Concerning his race, "Bloom's thoughts about Stephen's thoughts about Bloom and about Stephen's thoughts about Bloom's thoughts about Stephen" were that "He thought

551

that he thought that he was a jew whereas he knew that he knew that knew that he was not." This is a burlesque on the reflective mirror theory of Plato. Their parentage, baptisms, and educations are given. The narrator states that they represent the scientific and the artistic temperaments.

Bloom considers the perfect ad—a cross of "triliteral monoideal symbols, vertically of maximum visibility (divined), horizontally of maximum legibility (deciphered) and . . . to arrest involuntary attention, to interest, to convince, to decide." This concept combines the cross, Bloom's ideal ad and Joyce's theory of literature. The cross represents the combination in Christ of the divine or eternal (vertical) and human (horizontal) natures. See "divined" and "deciphered." The eternal in the temporal. Also consider in this context that the letters "ad" are also used to refer to AD, after the death of Christ on the cross. Bloom's ad would, in Joyce's aesthetics, be pornographic art since it intends to interest in order to convince and decide, in other words to control purchasing decisions. Likewise, the Church's use of Christ to create guilt would be in the interest of control of souls. By contrast, Stephen's view of Christ is to produce love and freedom and his view of art is to find the eternal in the temporal to produce aesthetic arrest.

Consider in this connection the following ad:

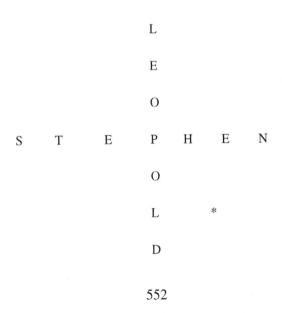

Notice that after the axis at P, the influence of Bloom on Stephen is represented in math graphs as the 4th quadrant, marked * in the above diagram. In that quadrant, Stephen as he becomes older will become more like a hen, that is gain feminine side wisdom or value the more inclusive, the greater in possibilities. The juncture is at P, and they urinate together in a separate parting of the waters.

Bloom gives as examples of good ads "K.11. Kino's 11/- Trousers," which suggests Rudy's death, and "House of Keys. Alexander J. Keyes," the meaning of which is disclosed in the final episode. His example of the worst is "What is home without Plumtree's Potted Meat? Incomplete. With it an abode of bliss." Bloom recounts for Stephen his previous original suggestion to the owner of Wisdom Hely's for an ad for writing supplies. It consisted of girls writing on paper while riding on a cart. Note this ad like all ads is pornographic by its very nature; it is designed to create desires. Stephen counters with two suggestions that combine aspects of ads and aspects of literature. Here is literary theory on the surface.

Stephen's first suggestion is for a hotel ad (Nora was working at a hotel when Joyce first met her). A young woman in a hotel room impatiently paces back and forth waiting for a coach that finally arrives. She leaves, apparently in response to the arrival of the coach. An anonymous man in the dark corner of the room, who apparently was with her in the room, reads what she has repeatedly written (left-handed) while waiting for the coach—"the Queen's Hotel the Queens's Hotel. . . ." This anonymous author is certainly not in control. The name Queen's Hotel suggests the articulated female sex organ with many visitors, Bloom's house this day. This ad also describes the place of work of Nora, Finn's Hotel, and Stephen's/Joyce's arrival there to take her away, a subject very much on his mind.

This hypothetical ad created by Stephen does not work as an ad for the hotel because it does not create desire for the hotel; the hotel is incidental. It moves away from the pornographic. The story in the ad, based on Stephen's own personal experience, turns out to contain a meaningful coincidence since Bloom's father committed suicide in a hotel of the same name. So viewed as "proto" literature, Stephen's creation is subjective—driven by his then hot experience with Nora—and as a result connects with Bloom only because of luck and in a different dimension (the creator's experience is love of a woman and the audience's related experience is Bloom's loss of a father). It is grave but not constant and does not result in any unification of Bloom with any of the characters. Not so incidentally, it also keeps two major subjects in the novel in front of the reader.

Stephen's second suggestion is an ad based on the parable of plums, with its heavy voyeur overtones. Bloom thinks this is another meaningful coincidence because of the connection of plum with Plumtree's potted meat, a gift that Blazes brought with him and "no home should be without." But the Bloom marriage has been without. This time Bloom's reaction to the parable ad shares the sense intended by the creator; Bloom's voyeur sexual activities and resulting impotence unite him in empathy with the two maids in the parable, also voyeur sufferers. This "proto" literature is in the dramatic mode and speaks to both the grave and constant in the human condition. Impotence caused by guilt is a human problem many including Bloom share. Generalized fully, impotence raises the issue of the divinity potential of artist.

The narrator states that the problem most often on Bloom's mind was "What to do with our wives." Generalized, this subject is the proper relation with the female. His various solutions include liberal instruction, which he thinks is appropriate given that she had "in disoccupied moments" given automatic writing in various languages. The narrator states that her intellectual deficiencies were made up for by the fact she is earth mother (the arms of balances point toward the center of the earth) and best understands Bloom.

Stephen and Bloom discuss famous Jews who lived after the forced Babylonian exile of the Jews (597—539 BCE). This subject is appropriate since Bloom and Stephen are returning from guilt based exile from the female. They compare letters from the ancient Hebrew and ancient Irish alphabets, in order to connect the word and spirit in this association of Jew to Irish. These letters are written on the flyleaf of the book Bloom borrowed, *The Sweets of Sin*. Bloom gives the esoteric numeric values assigned to the Hebrew letters in the Kabbalah tradition (Jewish mysticism). In that system, the Hebrew letters selected by Bloom have the following meaning:

> ghimel – opposites such as wealth and poverty and spatial directions
>
> aleph – mediator between opposites
>
> daaleth – knowledge and ignorance
>
> goph – inner sight.[6]

These esoteric readings of Hebrew reinforce the main themes of this episode.

They sing and discuss other relationships between Irish and Hebrew, the relevant community groups in which their respective senses of isolation and community have developed. Note that they are stressing their unity rather than their separation. Their mutual reflections "merge."

Taking a cue from the description in the Book of Isaiah (64:4) of straining to reach God by eyes and ears, the text gives a rendition of concealed identities by reference to the visual and auditory realms. Bloom registers in the visual, the eye of science and reason, while Stephen registers in the auditory, the ear of faith and the artist.[7]

The discussion about concealed identities is the core passage for the application of the mirror metaphor from Plato. In that metaphor, eros leads one to project his own god unto the personality of a beloved and then soul-wise move toward that imaginative image mirrored in the beloved. That movement soul-wise increases self-knowledge. The 106th and 107th Q&As are as follows:

> What was Stephen's auditive sensation? (in other words, what did Stephen hear?)
>
> He heard in a profound ancient male unfamiliar melody the accumulation of the past. (In other words, the wisdom of the Hebrew Scriptures. Note that borrowing from Schopenhaeur's Will, melody is used as a metaphor).
>
> What was Bloom's visual sensation? (what did Bloom see?)
>
> He saw in a quick young male familiar form the predestination of a future.

555

Keep in mind in reviewing these answers that time-wise Bloom represents the mature future of Joyce after the youth of Stephen. Then to the concealed identities:

> What were Stephen's and Bloom's quasisimultaneous volititonal quasisensations of concealed identities? (In other words, what image did they see in the other at the same time?)
>
> Visually, Stephen's: The traditional figure of hypostasis, depicted by Johannes Damascenus . . . as leucodermic, sesquipedalian with winedark hair. (Stephen now in visual.)
>
> Auditively, Bloom's: The traditional accent of the ecstasy of catastrophe. (Bloom now in auditive.)

Stephen sees in Bloom the image of Christ, leucodermic (pale as in without skin pigment), sesquipedalian (user of long words) and winedark hair (red hair described with Homer's favorite trope for the color of the sea, signifying the unity). This is an intellectual Jesus, Stephen's own god, which he has projected onto Bloom. Hypostasis means the substance or essence or underlying reality and secondarily refers to the combined god-man nature of Jesus as Christ (unification of opposites). Johannes Damascenus held the view that Christ's human and divine characteristics were united and inseparable.

Bloom hears in Stephen the joy of suffering, Bloom's own god of compassion. It also refers to group masochism,[8] the traditional Jewish condition. This is Bloom's god projected onto Stephen.

These projections, characteristics born in reactions to religious traditions and brought about by their relation to each other, are the subject of the merger of their mutual reflections. The concealed identities subject leads to the next Q&A about what other careers had been possible for Bloom and the role models for each. The other possible careers or identities were the church, the bar and the stage. They are also concealed identities.

The next subject is the "allied theme" of the legend of Little Harry Hughes, which Stephen is prompted to sing. This theme must be allied to the theme of potential identities, like Bloom's possible careers. In the song, little Harry Hughes loses his "head" to a Jewish girl's penknife after hitting his ball twice into the Jewish house. After that,

556

Harry lies among the dead. Reduced to its basics, this verse gives the legend of the fall of the head.

Stephen condensed interpretation of the "legend" is in the context of soul potential: destiny of Harry which "comes when he is abandoned [by his friends] and challenges him reluctant and, as an apparition of hope and youth, holds him unresisting. It leads him to a strange habitation [remote room in the Jew's house] . . . and there, implacable, immolates him, consenting." This sounds like both the passion of Jesus and Stephen's own destiny projected into a future with a Bloom residence.

Bloom's reactions are strange: to the line that the second ball "broke the jew's windows all," Bloom "With unmixed feeling. Smiling, a jew, he heard with pleasure and saw the unbroken kitchen window." The unbroken window he sees is his own. To the verse about the loss of head, Bloom has mixed feelings, reacts to the jew's daughter as if his own and considers ritual murder (read crucifixion).

The text then describes three reactions of the "host," which eventually plays out to be Bloom. The host is identified by the narrator as the "victim predestined" and "reluctant, unresisting." This gives to Bloom the characteristics of the victim Harry Hughes and bolsters the mirror image of eros from Plato. Bloom goes on to several memories of Milly.

Bloom invites Stephen to stay the night, which he promptly declines. They do vaguely agree on a program of exchanging singing and Italian lessons (Molly with Stephen in art and language). The narrator discusses Bloom's desires to make the world a better place. Bloom is dejected. Stephen empathizes by "affirming [Bloom's] significance as a conscious rational animal proceeding syllogistically from the known to the unknown and a conscious rational reagent between a micro and a macrocosm ineluctably constructed upon the incertitude of the void." This is a philosophical statement of the process of deduction and the Law of the Fathers. Bloom disagrees and believes instead that "he had proceeded energetically from the unknown to the known through the incertitude of the void," a statement of induction and the Flow of the Mothers. Deduction has limits since the syllogism can not proceed to conclusions that are inconsistent with the known. Induction knows no such limits.

As Stephen leaves the house, the lines in the text are shaped like downward oriented triangles (apex at the bottom), or the cross section of cones, and the departing procession drips in images of Jewish and Christian ceremonies of Exodus and renewal. Bloom bears a "Lighted Candle in Stick" and Stephen a "Diaconal Hat on Ashplant." The 113th Psalm is mentioned, which in the King James is the 114th. The quote is "When Israel came out of Egypt, The House of Jacob from a foreign nation." The last line of Psalm 113 in the King James is "He enthrones the barren woman in her house by making her the happy mother of sons." Stephen goes out into freedom, and Bloom prepares to sire a son.

Outside, the view of the stars leads to Stephen's famous artistic line, "The heaven tree of stars hung with humid nightblue fruit," and a scientific lecture by Bloom, including a reference to the infinity of the cosmic and microorganism universes, bodies within bodies. The cat, the female principle, moves in and out with them. The light is on in the second story bedroom. From below, Bloom and Stephen see this bedroom light reflected through the roller blinds (the lines of literature showing the eternal light between the lines). Note that the light comes from the bedroom. Bloom refers to "the mystery of an invisible attractive person." Joyce's Holy Spirit likes the bedroom. Then the mirror image again: "each contemplating the other in both mirrors of the reciprocal flesh of theirhisnothis fellowfaces."

Bloom and Stephen urinate together, signifying togetherness in the basics, the natural artistic process of changing experience into art, and of the parting of the waters in Exodus. During this process, they look up at the light from the bedroom. They see a "falling star" from Vega in the Lyre towards Leo. The "centripetal" Bloom lets the "centrifugal" Stephen out by key. Like Stephen in the 1st episode, Bloom turns the key on the inside, signifying the human spirit. They shake hands across the threshold. Since this time neither has washed his hands, this act commingles any traces of urine on their hands, their union through art as the shared Exodus and as processed experience. Together they hear the 2:30 a.m. bell from St. George's and its third overtone echo.

Stephen interprets these sounds as the Latin prayer by the layman for the dying, this time not for his mother but for the death of his old self. Bloom once again hears "Heigho," signifying relationship.

Both hear the bell sounds in four sections each of two parts, a total of eight (for infinity or the eternal). The two-part section is symbolic of the heartbeat, and the four sections are symbolic of the fourth chakra of the heart. Bloom's Heigho suggests, by the way that word is pronounced with a rising voice, the rising interval of a third, the sweet interval signifying the feminine.

Then Stephen leaves through the garden, not the front door (the way he came in), but a voluntary departure through and from the human garden to independence and artistic detachment. He exits through the North gate into Eccles Lane. Visual moves to auditory as Bloom hears in Stephen's departure "The double reverberation of retreating feet on the heavenborn earth, the double vibration of a jew's harp in the resonant lane." The Notes say ".twanged a fourfold chord, scale of a jew's mouth harp." The double reverberations suggest their combined heart beats while together and predict Stephen's art will be echoes from their experiences together. Heart will become he art. Stephen having left, Bloom feels very alone in the cold of vast and empty interstellar space. Stephen's departure reminds him of the death of many friends. He sees the "disparition of three final stars" at daybreak, the "death" of stars at dawn.

Bloom goes back inside the house and into the parlor. There his head runs into the sideboard, which had been moved into a new position in the door opening. My guess is that for Blaze's visit, Molly moved it there to act as an early warning system in case of Bloom's early return, and then afterward in her laziness moved it back only partially or not at all. She has also moved other furniture, woman as energy and movement.

Notice that the chairs are given personality by the narrator; the easy chair sounds like Molly and the cane (Cain for possession) chair Blazes—the "large dull passive and a slender bright active." The big chair, the scene of vigorous activity that afternoon, is discolored in a way that suggests fluids. The seat of the cane chair is of "white plaited rush."

559

Guess what that is. The room is disturbed. The blatant narrator indicates the two chairs are significant for "symbolism."

Still in the parlor, Bloom lights an incense cone using the Promised Land flyer he had picked up in the butcher shop. The room apparently contains odors he wants to expunge. For this purpose, he furls the flyer into the shape of a cone, which he lights at the point end, and then uses the furled burning flyer to light the point of the incense cone (cone point to cone point). Note that the cross section of a cone has the same general outline as a pyramid.

He notices on the mantle under the mirror wedding gifts that he and Molly received; the gifts now speak of a dead marriage—a stopped clock, a dwarf tree (of the spirit), and an embalmed owl (embalmed wisdom). He looks at the back of these items through the "giltbordered pierglass" (read the mirror image for Bloom has been guilt before peers). He views himself in the mirror as a solitary ("ipsorelative") but interacting ("aliorelative") man. The narrator provides a central clue in the answer to why Bloom was aliorelative: "From infancy to maturity he had resembled his maternal procreatrix. From maturity to senility he would increasingly resemble his paternal procreator." This is the clue to why Stephen has a mother image problem and Bloom a father image problem.

Bloom sees in the mirror an image of books across the room, a perspective doubly removed from life (once in the book and twice in the mirror), and goes over to straighten them. Joyce lists the titles of the books, as he loves to do. The titles include *The Hidden Life of Christ*. Bloom contemplates the statue of Narcissus on the table. It has a broken hand glued back on, as Stephen has hurt his hand at Westland Row Station. He removes his clothes and organizes Molly's, which were discarded in the parlor. Plenty of circumstantial evidence is staring him in the face; Molly didn't even clean up.

He scratches his bee sting on his belly. His chest hair makes a triangle. He does the budget for the day, apparently a daily ritual. The accounting is detailed and treats with ultra-care and precision the transaction by which Stephen left his money in safekeeping with Bloom and received it back. It is treated as a receipt by Bloom, creating in double entry accounting a cash asset and an offsetting debt (to return the money), and the return is separately treated as a disbursement of cash and reduction of debt. Think of this accounting treatment as the picture of compassion. The credits include a commission from the *Freeman's Journal* in the amount of 1 pound 7 shillings and 6 pence. The payment of this amount to Bloom was not included in the narrative and, curiously, the amount is the same one mentioned by Blazes over the phone in the 10th episode.

Bloom takes off his shoes, because of an ache in his footsoles, and tears off part of his toe nail because it is too long. This is an echo of the artist in detachment pairing his fingernails, except with Bloom it is the nails on the feet of the wandering Jew. He thinks about his typically bourgeois dream house in the country, which he would buy not inherit (I paid my way), and about his pipe dream schemes for making vast wealth. In a review of Bloom's love of rectitude in his youth, the evolutionary theories of Darwin are mentioned. They fuel aspects of the last episode. We are told that Bloom's regular practice upon retiring is a "tranquil recollection of the past," again an image of the required resolution of experience in order to produce art.

The eclectic contents of Bloom's "drawers" provide additional information about his background. He inherited some money from his father that he has invested judiciously. His father's suicide note is there. Bloom wrote a prophecy about the Home Rule bill, which has not yet come to pass since he has not been in charge at home. The anal dildo-like device to be used as an aid in releasing gas during sleep is a joke about the unconscious in dreams, where individuality and unity merge through the collective unconscious. Notice that Bloom has condoms, so their lack of sexuality activity is motivated by more than a fear of children.

Bloom regrets the loss of his Jewish heritage. He reviews the events of his day which the narrator translates in terms of Jewish ritual: breakfast in the 4th episode as the burnt offering; delayed defecation in the 4th as the holy of holies; the bath in 5th as the rite of John (the Baptist); the funeral in the 6th as the rite of Samuel; the Keyes ad in the 7th as Urim and Thummin; the light lunch in the 8th as the rite of Melchisedek; the museum and library in the 9th as the holy place; the bookhunt in the 10th as Simchath Torah; the music in the 11th as Shira Shirim; the argument with the Citizen in the 12th as the holocaust; the visit to the Dignam residence between the 12th and 13th as the wilderness; the masturbation in the 13th as the rite of Onan; the hospital delivery in the 14th as the heave offering; the chaos in the 15th as Armageddon; and the walk home in the 16th as atonement. Each of these references to ritual was discussed in connection with the applicable episode. Blessing the day with ritual gives it sacred character. Please notice how instrumental the Jewish ritual concepts have been in the structure of each episode.

Bloom considers leaving Molly and imagines her efforts to find him, which include advertisements that read like looking for the lost Christ. Bloom moves from the parlor to the bedroom, a door to the bedroom apparently being through the parlor. This move is lightly documented at line 2063: "Bloom risen, going . . ."

Molly is in bed, apparently asleep. Her bed lamp is on. He initially considers not getting into the bed but eventually decides, adopting a practical outlook, that the advantages outweigh the disadvantages. As he turns out the light on his side, Bloom suddenly comprehends the joke about where Moses was when the candle went out. In the dark. The narrator states that Bloom still doesn't know who M'Intosh is. The bed is described as a nest of snakes. He gets into bed head to foot with Molly and notices in the bed crumbs and particles of potted meat as well as the imprint of a man. She and Blazes did it on Bloom's side, and she didn't even clean up the bed. In reaction, Bloom reviews the series of Molly's suitors.

Bloom feels competing emotions, envy and jealousy but also abnegation and equanimity. The forces of abnegation and equanimity eventually reconcile his spirit. This may seem like pure rationalization born of weakness, but I read it in context as the human being at his best using reason and compassion under extreme moral stress.

Joyce's Notes stress that in lying down, Bloom is facing east and his left side is toward the earth. He is lying on his left side with his left hand under his head and right leg on top of left. This is the exact opposite of the Buddha lion posture. Bloom, who slays the suitors with equanimity not with violence, is in the lamb posture. His right-hand thumb is on his nose, a technique used in Kundalini Yoga breathing exercises. Bloom is, in his final appearance, bathed in the image of unaffected sanctity of the Buddha. As Joyce put the point in SH, his Buddha sanctity is gained by equanimity rather than by the blood of revenge.

Bloom contemplates the wonder of universal human sexual attraction to the female spheres (an essence of the human unity) and, raising her nightgown, kisses Molly's bottom to the accompaniment of his own erection. He projects Molly's bottom as his promised land: ". . . the islands of the blessed, the isles of Greece, the land of promise . . . redolent of milk and honey . . ." This sexual overture and attraction, despite Bloom's masturbation that very afternoon, promises well for the future. Molly (who I think has been awake for some time) asks Bloom questions about what he has been doing all day and all night ("catechetical interrogation"). Bloom reports truthfully but leaves out some critical material, concentrating on Stephen whom Bloom inflates to a professor and author. Bloom doesn't ask Molly any questions about her day.

Molly inwardly dwells on the "limitation of fertility" in this marriage during the last 10 years, 5 months and 18 days. Bloom inwardly dwells on the "limitation of activity, mental and corporal" in this marriage since Milly reached puberty, 9 months and 1 day before, and left home. The narrator states that since then, Molly with no child to care for has customarily pestered Bloom with questions about what he has been doing while away from home. These instruments of control have circumscribed their relationship. The control function normally exercised by the mother with respect to the child in protective compassion has been turned on the husband in the interests of jealous control.

Bloom gets sleepy and "inconstant" concentric circles made by the reflection from the lamp on Molly's side play on the ceiling. Both Bloom and Molly are lying on their left side, head to foot, facing away from each other. Molly has her head propped up resting on her left hand. Bloom has the thumb and index finger of his right hand on his nose.

Molly is described explicitly as "Gea-Tellus," the earth mother and goddess of life and death, and big with seed. Bloom is described as "the childman weary, the manchild in the womb" by reference to a famous photograph by Apjohn, a friend of Bloom's. These allusions are right on the surface. They manifest unification of opposites, for example life and death, child and man, and mandchild in the womb.

The art photographer's name Apjohn indicates *a la* Darwin the source of the human race in apes and signifies the combination of opposites in the human. The word human derives from humble and points through humane toward refinement. The narrator questions whether Bloom is returning to the womb:

Womb?weary?

He rests. He has traveled.

The episode ends as Bloom falls asleep uttering lines born of **Sinbad the Sailor**:

Going to dark bed there was a square round Sinbad the
Sailor roc's auk's egg in the night of the bed of all the
auks of the rocs of Darkinbad the Brightdayler.

These lines also feature the unification of opposites, square and round and bright and dark. Note the association of guilt (Sinbad) with possession (roc's auk's) of the egg otherwise lying in the bed of manifold possibilities (night of the bed of all the auks of the rocs). The egg is for the unlimited possibilities of the future. The bed of all the auks of the rocs would be the collective unconscious and Darkinbad the Brightdayler would be the effect of the collective unconscious on the daytime ego. And all of this is the hand of the past and the unity on the present and future individual.

The night of the bed is dream consciousness where the dreamer is both subject and object and where, since anything is possible, the circle can be squared (which is impossible in waking consciousness because pi can not be fixed at a finite number). Dante also used this squaring the circle metaphor in his concluding images in **The Divine Comedy**. The Roc is the giant bird from the tales of Sinbad; the Auk is a similar sound association that we have already heard from Manaanan Maclir. It is a primitive sound containing A for the self in man and the deity in the cosmos, U from AUM for dream consciousness and K for hardness of any kind (reality). Bloom goes to sleep. He is at rest, arrested.

The last question is "Where?" It is not answered. It evokes the joke about where Moses was when the candle went out. In this last series of questions, the narrator asks the kind of questions Molly would normally use in a control oriented inquiry about what Bloom has been doing: With? When? Where?

In the original edition, a large dot ended the episode, as in Q.E.D. Joyce's syllogism from the opening letters of Parts I, II and III is S.M.P. That apparent syllogism, Stephen Molly therefor Poldy, is no syllogism at all. It is not from the Law of the Fathers. It stands for a proposition born of an entirely different system—Stephen experiences the female in the right relationship and becomes his own father. The episode ending period represents the point or circle where the eternal enters. The circle introduces infinity because pi is a number which is not finite. It just keeps going on and on beyond the decimal point. Joyce's Notes say O produces infinity.

Phaedrus

Plato's dialogue **Phaedrus** is the father of this episode. The paternal influence is greater than for any of the other episodes with a dialogue connection (1st—3rd and 16th—18th). Concepts from the same dialogue also mother the last episode.[9]

This dialogue features a conversation between Socrates and Phaedrus, an ill matched pair. Young Phaedrus is a trendy and bohemian intellectual while old Socrates is an old-fashioned seeker of personal wisdom. This comparison resonates with Stephen and Bloom. The meaning of the dialogue is imparted partially by the text and partially by the form, just as with Joyce.

The subject of discussion is love (between an older man and young boy), and Socrates uses eros as a subject to examine his favorite subject self-knowledge. Socrates makes the point that self-knowledge can be usefully increased only in connection with a relationship with other humans and in the context of an understanding of the human soul and man's place in the cosmos. Understanding the part requires understanding the whole. Socrates describes the soul as immortal self-motion, which returns in Stephen's definition of literature as the "eternal affirmation of the spirit of man." Man must be understood in terms of ends, not historically or as a process of development (move over Pierre Teilhard De Chardin).

Socrates describes eros that stops at sexual love as the reflection of a limited self-knowledge and noble love as the reflection of a greater grasp of reality. At a noble level, the lover projects onto the beloved the image the lover aspires to (Plato calls this the lover's god). Then the lover sees in the beloved the projected image of the lover's god. This moves the lover's soul toward the image. In this process, the lover gains an external image of himself through the mirror of the beloved and gains more self-knowledge. In the highest version of self-knowledge, the person will gain knowledge of the eternal Forms, or Beings. Joyce uses this mirror concept in the concealed identity projections by Stephen and Bloom and the several other allusions to mirrors. Think of Joyce's literary productions as similar mirrors.

This projection and reflection process is referred to as "erotic art," since the projection involves eros and the creative imagination. The lover is moved toward the image he has created. You will recognize these components as ancestors of Joyce's portals to the eternal, the sexual instinct and the creative imagination.

This process is possible only if the lover is not under the control of some outside force, signified among others by the myth of Typhon. Typhon was the giant monster child of Mother Earth. Typhon took Zeus prisoner, but Zeus was saved by the heroic Athena, who castrated Typhon.[10] For Plato, the earth bound monster signifies the inability to gain vision of the eternal Beings, perhaps primarily by reason of its sex instinct. For Joyce, Typhon is any system that artificially limits possibilities.

In the dialogue. Socrates and Phaedrus playfully exchange the speaking roles of the lover and beloved. Stephen and Bloom do the same. Stephen gets older and Bloom goes to sleep as a manchild.

On the level of generalization, Plato treats eros as a god and the erotic impulse as one of the divine disturbances of the conventional life: prophetic from Apollo; mystic from Dionysius; poetic from the Muses;

566

and the erotic from Eros and Aphrodite. Joyce follows suit by including in this episode rather mundane versions of these divine disturbances, for example sleep walking. He does dress with dignity and respect the nobly erotic secular communion of Bloom and Stephen.

Why Questions and Answers?

Questions and answers necessarily focus the level of reality, an issue in this episode. The way a question is asked effectively determines the way it can be answered. For example, to the question "who made the world," the proper response may be to reject the question. The assumptions made by the question may be illusory. In this sense, questions and answers are perfect specimens of control and the Law of the Fathers. Molly uses questions to control Bloom.

The unanswered last question "Where?" echoes the famous question—where was Moses when the candle went out? The answer is in the dark. Note that the question asks for location and the answer gives condition. The answer has slipped into a different dimension beyond the control of the question. Away from the Law of the Fathers.

Questions and Answers and Art

The relationship between Molly and Leopold has been veiled because of her sorrow at the loss of Rudy and her apparent decision to avoid any more children by avoiding sexual intercourse altogether. Her sorrow at the loss of the first son has prevented the creation of the second son, much as guilt for the death of Jesus prevents self-realization. In this episode, the Blooms are together in bed but their relationship is restricted to possessive questions by Molly (what have you been doing?) and evasive answers by Bloom. Of all the many happy possibilities for a married couple in bed, this is among one of the most limited methods of interaction possible.

Note that questions and answers are used to construct the entire episode; they are the art of the episode. Questions and answers about the Blooms' questions and answers in bed; the control author's method and their "dry rocks" marriage. As the Blooms' questions and answers produce among the possibilities a limited human emotional interaction, the use of questions and answers as a extremely static literary method produces among the many happy art possibilities an episode limited in emotion—no pity no terror no joy. This guy is good.

The Garden Legend Redux

Bloom and Stephen experience the Dublin after-shock of the Fall in the Garden of Eden. The after-shock is, however, given a new interpretation—the inevitable separation of one person from all others resulting from self-realization, particularly during youth. In this interpretation, the erect and talking serpent symbolizes the human sense of development, of self-realization. Bloom, the detached elder, has learned the wisdom of empathy that can bridge the Fall. Stephen is about to.

This interpretation of the Fall is much in the same vein as Stephen's view of Satan as the youth of Christ. Bloom used the same method of analysis in the Oxen episode, accounting for the desire for the god-like fruit from the tree of the knowledge of good and evil as a product of youth.

In the kernel of the myth stripped of its didacticism, Adam and Eve, after all, only do what is natural to humans, particularly as their sense of self-consciousness initially deepens. According to Jewish legend, the flesh of the apple from the tree of knowledge actually did what the serpent promised: it brought on increased self-realization—their eyes were opened and their "teeth set on edge."[11] This development was characterized by Yahweh as bringing Adam and Eve closer to god status, the desire for which tempted Eve in the first place. This is scriptural authority for Joyce's belief that self-realization is part of the path to God. Interested in control, God expels them from Eden.

The Fall Legend seasons this Q&A concerning Bloom's relations with Milly:

Did that first division, portending a second division, afflict him?
Less than he had imagined, more than he had hoped.

The second division is the departure of Milly from home. The first division is the Fall. Bloom is afflicted but less than he would have imagined, because he has the secret that cures the wounds from the Fall. That secret is detached compassion that bridges the separation.

After Bloom encounters the rearranged parlor (an echo of removal from the Garden), you can feel the lingering presence of the serpent in the description of the furniture:

> One: a squat stuffedeasychair, with stout arms extended and back slanted to the rere, which, repelled in recoil [viper strike], had then upturned an irregular fringe of a rectangular rug [disorder] and now displayed on its amply upholstered seat a centralised diffusing and diminishing discolouration [juice from the apple]. The other: a slender splayfoot chair of glossly cane [Cain] curves...its seat being a bright circle of white plaited [means interwoven with a hint of devious] rush.

[parenthetical added]

The natural human development in self-realization, the reason for the Fall, often proceeds in the teeth of the rules, but disobedience is not at its essence. At the core is personal isolation, which in turn results in the necessity for sex to regenerate eros and the sense of connection, without which is death of the spirit. As Joyce reportedly said to Arthur Power, "[copulation is not the death of the soul because] there you are dealing with a mystery which can become anything and transform everything. Love-making can end in love, it often does, and so its possibilities can be limitless"[12]. This philosophy brightens Joyce's view that the sexual instinct is one of the two eternal human qualities.

With a "naked" approach to the myth of Adam and Eve, that is stripped of its didacticism, the relationship between the powers that be and humans changes. Without disobedience, the moral of the story is no longer a guilty sense of sin and the need for obedience directed by the control oriented church. Instead, the naked approach promotes human self-realization of individual essence as the initial path to the eternal. The Fall does occur but its essence is not disobedience but the separation among humans, even between man and wife. What is wrong with Adam and Eve is their separated condition, which makes them ashamed of their nakedness in the presence of each other. This Fall is to be bridged in maturity, according to Joyce's own experience, by heterosexual union with a mate producing children and empathy with mankind in general, the Full Monty in communion and unity.

Life and Art

Stephen and Bloom as characters move in the direction of emotional disengagement, that is toward the characteristics of proper literary art. Bloom is no longer didactic or possessive. Stephen leaves, as promised by the Buddha milk bowl symbolism in the Proteus episode, no longer the worn out ascetic but now the veteran of intense empathy with Nora and restrained empathy with Bloom. He is more like Bloom. The empathy experiences of Stephen are reflected in the compassionate character of Bloom, as the extension in time of Stephen. The start of Stephen's new approach is symbolized by the handshake on the threshold, "the exodus from the house of bondage." As a result, Stephen's soul now has the potential for empathy with the grave and constant in the human condition, the source of meaningful art. Stephen remains self-sufficient, as proper art must be appreciated in and for itself, not as promotion for another aim, and love must not reach for possession. His pattern is that of Jesus and the Buddha—Stephen becomes individual in a way that allows both uncompromised loyalty to his individuality and empathy with mankind free of desire and aggression, the engines of authority and the Law of the Fathers.

The words "arrest," "kinetic" and "didactic" right out of Joyce's aesthetic theories appear frequently. For example, kinetic appears in a description of Bloom's earlier attempts at poetry (after their merger the earlier Bloom is Stephen) and arrest appears in his nighttime practice of a tranquil recollection of the past and "the automatic relation to himself of a narrative concerning himself . . . . " The distance Stephen gains from his material is symbolized by leaving Bloom. Stephen goes off without an indicated current destination or purpose in order to emphasize that eventually he will write about Bloom and Molly.

Stephen and Bloom urinate side by side and turn the events of the day into processed water as the artist processes experience into art. With proper art, the water can be turned into wine again. In order to be effective, art must appeal to those common human denominators present in the archetypes produced through history, such as the historical Hebrew and Irish experience, which the artist radiates through ordinary life. Mincuration is the way of all flesh.

The episode ends with Bloom falling asleep and murmuring Sinbad the Sailor inspired dream images. In dreams, the sleeper is both subject and object, the perspective of the artist in the dramatic mode, and the possibilities are limitless. In dream land, Bloom the individual is combined with the unity through the collective unconscious.

Since our Two Partners have merged in a sense (technically the type of merger is *cummunicatio idiomatum* — the exchange of attributes used to describe the mixture of human and divine in Christ), descriptions of Bloom can apply to Stephen and vice-versa. Their names are combined as Stoom and Blephen.

Parallels to the Mass

The secular communion of Stephen and Bloom is bathed in images from the Mass. Ascension is mentioned, candles are used and reference is made to railings, which surround the altar and separate it from the congregation. Consistent with the reinterpretation of the Garden legend as the necessary product of youth, the altar railings separate the priest from the congregation during the early part of the Mass but communion during the later part unites them. In this pattern, the early part of the Mass equates with youth and the later communion with maturity.

The procession into the Bloom kitchen follows the procession in the Good Friday Mass of the Presanctified. The Host, saved from Thursday Mass, is returned to the main altar and the light is turned on to indicate the presence of the sanctified Host. Consider Molly's hose, an object of intense interest on the preceding Thursday, as an indication of the presence of Joyce's presanctified host. The lighted charcoal of the incense appears in Bloom's coal fire. The priest performs a Lavabo; Bloom washes his hands. The priest mixes water and wine and Bloom cocoa and water. The catechism for the Good Friday Mass refers to the lancing of Jesse's side on the cross, and Bloom notices the fissure in the side of Stephen's jacket, his outer protective shell. Molly's light is on.

The Mass breaks a fast for the faithful because at this time (1904), abstaining from even water was necessary in order to prepare properly for communion. Hot water and a spoon are used in the Greek Orthodox Mass (Joyce's favorite Mass) and by Bloom in the kitchen. The mixing of the water, wine and host in the Mass symbolizes the mixture of the divine with human, the reconciliation of opposites. Humanized, this Dublin communion is made with cocoa, water and cream, and these ingredients, particularly the cream linked with Molly's mother's milk, humanize the mass. This Dublin Mass is back to the basics in communion, a community meal as a symbol of charity. Bloom is "host" and Molly "hostess."

So early on a Friday morning, Bloom breaks Stephen's fast by ushering him into communion with others. The post-communion procession of the newly baptized faithful informs the departure of Stephen from Bloom's home. Bloom's new attitude will also break the fast with his wife. He like Stephen will father a new son.

As there is no transubstantiation in the Good Friday Mass, the best that can be achieved on earth is consubstantiation, part divine and part human. Stephen as artist will continue in that type of role, to find the eternal in the flesh of the here and now. In this process, the artist must from his own experiences achieve the detached distance of the intellectual imagination. Consecration is a metaphor for the continuous operation of that facility.[13] As the process of sanctification in the Mass is invisible, so is the change in Stephen.

Holy Trinity and Pyramid of Light

The Holy Spirit in the Roman Catholic view is the invisible power of love in the world that operates in part through the sacraments. It became manifest to the apostles in tongues of fire. It is the creative spirit in the Holy Trinity, and its essence is free spontaneity.

In the Dublin trinity, Molly stands for the creative free spirit without guilt with which Stephen must connect. Bloom refers to Molly in the "mystery of an invisible attractive person" and has already felt her tongue of fire. Singing and Italian lessons will provide the venue for the connection of the son to the spirit, as these two experiences in Joyce's life (music and the Italian language of Dante) opened his soul to creativity. Molly's role as the creative free spirit sponsors the image of literature as the light in her bedroom coming through the roller blinds—light between the lines.

Bloom invites Stephen to Molly in the interests of replacing Blazes as Satan. In Catholic theory, the Son can come to the Holy Spirit only through the Father, another version of the Law of the Fathers. Joyce describes Stephen as coming to Milly through Molly and to Molly through Milly, in either event in connection with the feminine principle. Stephen and Bloom see Molly's light just as they are urinating, urine being the symbol of art as a natural process involving processed experience. As Stephen experiences relationships, he begins to move into an emotional reality described by the orthodox version of the Trinity based on separate Persons in relationships. The Sabellian "I am everything" self-sufficiency view of the Trinity is replaced by one based on relationships, with emphasis on the feminine Holy Ghost.

Similar trinities were spawned in the ancient Egyptian religions, whose influence remains in Bloom's Freemasonary. For the Egyptians, the trinity of Father-Son-Holy Ghost was Osiris or Ra (father), Thoth or Athor (son) and Maat (female counterpart to son).

The symbology of the Pyramid of Light as revealed by Adams in the *House of Hidden Places,* a book in Joyce's permanent library, is the template for a great deal of the detail in this episode. The pyramid at Ghizeh is, according this view, the House of Osiris (the father principle) in whose detailed inner architecture the initiation ritual of the ancient *Book of the Dead* finds visual meaning. The Book of the Dead is also known as the *Book of the Master of the Hidden Places*, a title which must have appealed to Joyce's view of the import of his new approach to literature.

The goal of this initiation ritual was for the dead to achieve union with Osiris as a result of purification in the Eternal Light and thus achieve infinite serenity and victory over death. With this goal, the connection to art and arrest or stasis is immediate. Just to cement the connection, the son of god is Athor (sounds just like author). This god (also known as Hathor or Thoth[14]) is the opener of leads to the secret places of heaven, counterparts to Joyce's epiphanies.

The soul of the candidate was weighed for purification in the balance scales against a feather. If too heavy, the candidate was consumed by a giant dog. If found light enough, the candidate was entitled to the ultimate secret revealed in the initiation process in the Osiris House of Hidden Places—the interdependence of life, love and joy. This is the secret of the House of Keyes, which is decoded in the last episode. Compare this trinity of the spirit (father-life, son-love and spirit-joy) with Dante's concept of the Godhead as three interlocking and mutually reflecting circles.

According to Adams, the relationship of the base of the pyramid in the form of a circle (going through the points of the base) to the length of the side (which in turn depends on the angle of steepness) corresponds closely with the number for pi (3.1416 ad infinitum). The four sides of the pyramid are pointed exactly to the four poles. These engineering marvels bear fruit in this episode in terms of the many and prolonged references to magnetic direction and the seemingly odd topic of squaring the circle. Squaring the circle means finding by geometry the exact area of a circle. This would be done, if possible, by converting the circle through geometry to a square, whose area is neatly contained and can be easily computed. The area of a circle is, however, not a finite number since pi, a number which never stops after the decimal point, is involved. The approximate area of a circle can be squared, but never the exact area.

The circle represents the infinite. The unsuccessful attempt to square the circle suggests the unsuccessful attempt of authority to limit the immeasurable potential of man. The circle extended in time and space makes a sphere, which is the spatial manifestation of Molly and life in the final episode. The prescribed path of the Initiate through the inner rooms to the Hidden Places in the sacred Pyramid of Light is reflected in the main movements in this episode. The pyramid's long opening tunnel is the counterpart of the parallel courses that Bloom and Stephen arm in arm trace on their way home, union being the tunnel to the opening in art. After going down the stairs, the first stop of the Initiate is at the Well of Life with its square perpendicular shaft. Bloom conducts Stephen down "more than 5 steps" into the kitchen and lights a fire in the fireplace (the chimney is the shaft), food and heat for life. The fireplace kindles the memory of Stephen, the well of life for literature. The Chamber of the Moon, where monthly Osiris renews his birth, is Molly's monthly in the chamberpot (next episode). The flow of sparkling waters beneath the Royal Arch of the Planetary Systems appears as Bloom and Stephen's urination in the garden outside under the planets.

Stephen departs just before dawn through the north gate of Bloom's garden and down the alley stones of Eccles Lane; the initiated leaves the Pyramid of Light through the "double gate of the horizon" or the "gate of ascent" through the north side of the pyramid. This northern portal in the pyramid features two downward pointing chevron shaped lintels above the gate. They are reflected in the chevron shaped lines in the texts and the echoes in Eccles Lane.

Bloom's bumping his head in the parlor on the sideboard suggests the low Hidden Lintel, which allows access to the Queen's chamber and the King's chamber, the innermost chambers of the sacred pyramid. The two chairs in the parlor indicate the Hall of Double Truth. The dead wedding presents reflect the internal pyramid structures that give a picture of petrified flame, and the dead marriage of the Blooms reflects the Place of Central Fire for Ordeal. Bloom seeing the books doubly removed in the mirror is a metaphor for the sacred mirror of Ank, which records that time and space are doubly mirrored in the mind of Ra and in "reality."

Bloom plays the role of Osiris symbolized by the star Sothis (Sirius). At a certain time of year, this star rises on the horizon just before dawn at the same spot the sun will rise in about 40 minutes. When the sun does rise, Sothis appears to set or vanish. This coincidence of location on the horizon was meaningful because it heralded the start of the annual rise in the Nile, the symbol of all things good. Sothis is also known as the dog star and the guardian and watchman, as Bloom is the guardian for Stephen who is the rising sun/son in literature. After Stephen leaves, the dawn receives considerable attention with direct textual reference to "The disparition of three final stars" at day break. Stephen's guardian and Sothis, Bloom goes below the consciousness horizon to sleep as manchild. The hieroglyph for Sirius was the triangle, which means Eternal Light.

Molly in this pattern is Maat, the female counterpart to Athor, or the pattern of order. Maat shares the ostrich feather with Amen, the hidden one. Molly remains in the bedroom out of sight while Bloom and Stephen are together. Her double relation through motherhood to the human and to the divine gives her the throne. She is featured in the last episode as a great Amen final cadence with four repeating words. These four repeating words suggest the earth spinning. The sacred pyramid was oriented so that as the earth spun, the same side of Isis's chamber would directly face the sun every four years.

The Shooting Star and the Zodiac Tell All

At an important moment, Bloom and Stephen see a shooting star move from Vega in the constellation Lyra (also known as Alpha Lyrae) to Leo (the fifth sign in the Zodiac). By now the reader senses the lyrical romantic subjective literary method in Alpha Lyrae, the starting point. Leo, the end point and 5th sign of the Zodiac, signifies masculine fixed, or solar power of the self-sufficiency father principle. Leo is the astrological counterpart of self-sufficiency and the dramatic method. So the path of the shooting star announces in the macrocosm Stephen's change as an artist in the microcosm.

The name Zodiac combines zoe (life) with chakos (wheel) and pictures the process in Hindu metaphysics "by which primordial energy, once fecundated, passes from the potential to the virtual, from unity to multiplicity, from spirit to matter, from the non-formal world to the world of forms and then returns."[15] With our memory of the debauched Stephen dancing in the round with Zoe, it is an appropriate template to present the last image of Stephen's change.

Seventh Chakra

The seventh chakra, the abode of absolute bliss where the initiate becomes at one with god, is symbolized as a downward oriented, thousand petalled lotus containing the Great Void inside the yoni triangle. This symbol is contained in Stephen's line "the heaventree of stars heavy with humid nightblue fruit." The stars would be the thousand lotus petals. The seventh chakra's theme of liberation is shown as a stream of nectar, which the humid nightblue fruit would release. The Great Void is the cold interstellar space Bloom feels. In this highest

576

chakra, the mind dances at the feet of Ista-devata, the female power. Here Bloom's mind dances in dream language as he goes to sleep head to toe with Molly, whose melon rump is his promised land.

Dante Again

At the end of *The Divine Comedy* after hell and purgatory, the narrator Dante sees in Paradise the ideal young woman Beatrice (pronounced Bee ah **treach** a), whose mere image brought him spiritual renewal during life. She is referred to in the last episode as Portinari, her family name that Dante tried to keep secret. St. Bernard of Cairvaux asks the Virgin Mary to let Dante see the Divine Majesty, which she grants. Dante sees a glimpse of the Trinity and the union of Man with God. He describes it as "Three orbs of triple hue, clipt in one bound" each reflecting the others. Note the parallel with the secret of the Hidden Places in the pyramid—the interdependence of life, love and joy.

As they urinate, Bloom and Stephen see the reflection in the roller blinds (lines in literature) of Molly's lamp. When Bloom is in bed with Molly, the concentric rings of reflected light from the same lamp dance above the bed, just as Dante saw them. The same source of light shows through the lines of literature and announces the trinity above the Blooms' marriage bed. The inspiration for art and the completed trinity come from the same source—the proper relation between the father and son that allows the spirit to issue forth.

Dante is featured in the closing images of this penultimate episode because Dante is one of Joyce's literary gods and because Dante's experiences in life have important parallels with those of Joyce and those in this novel. Like Joyce and like Stephen as I have interpreted this novel, Dante was transformed by a female, Beatrice for whom he wrote *Vita Nouva*. Like Joyce and Stephen, Dante was exiled from his native and spiritual home Florence. The name Dante means "the giver," signifying the charitable spirit which informs Bloom's soul and Joyce's literary works.

The union of God with man is presented in the three joined images each reflecting and relating to the others, the collective of the human condition. In Joyce's world, the union of human with human in love and joy is the union of human with god. If this equation doesn't hold, Joyce would not be interested in god.

Stephen and Bloom as Leonardo da Vinci?

The narrator describes Stephen as the artistic temperament and Bloom as the scientific, and Joyce described the successful artist in himself as a combination of the two. Bloom makes a daily list of his receipts and disbursements that is included in this episode in all its seemingly unimportant detail. Molly's bed is curiously described as a nest of vipers. Joyce's permanent library contained a copy of Sigmund Freud's *Leonardo da Vinci and a Memory of His Childhood* (originally published in 1910), which may provide clues to these and other odd aspects of this episode.

Freud describes the fuel for Leonardo's enormous artistic endeavors and scientific investigations as sublimated erotic energy originally directed at his mother. During one period of Leonardo's life, his artistic and scientific efforts were in competition. Not only did they compete for his time, but the scientific tendency to see more and more problems requiring more and more artistic solutions prevented Leonardo during this period from completing his paintings. Here is Freud's discussion of Leonardo's problem during this period:

What interested him in a picture was above all a problem; and behind the first one he saw countless other problems arising, just as he used to in his endless and inexhaustible investigation of nature. He was no longer able to limit his demands, to see the work of art in isolation and to tear it from the wide context to which he knew it belonged.

In other words, failure of *integritas*, the mark-off function.

The famous Mona Lisa smile is, according to Freud, probably a memory of his early years, a highly charged time with his natural mother. Leonardo was illegitimate and lived alone with his mother for several years before being taken into the house of his father. According to Freud, Leonardo regained his artistic power to complete works upon finding his mother's smile adorning one of his models. He went on to paint his late masterpieces, all with the same famous bewitching and sinister smile, described as a vampire smile by W. Pater. The model's smile, according to Freud, liberated Leonardo's sublimated erotic energy.

As support for this interpretation, Freud fastened on Leonardo's own report (in his diary) of the memory of a recurring childhood vision or dream of a vulture[16] pounding its tail ("coda" in Italian) in his lips. In view of Leonardo's purported "homosexual-typical" personal traits and the odd detailed accounting in Leonardo's diary of sums spent on his beautiful boy students (in the absence of accounting for larger sums for other items), Freud interpreted the vulture memory as a trace of his largely sublimated erotic impulse for his mother, an erotic impulse that resulted from too much too early from his single parent mother. Too much community too early. Freud describes this experience as one path to narcissism and homosexual urges.

As part of this explanation, Freud describes the famous Mona Lisa smile as a warning of the unification of opposites in woman, a combination of positives and negatives in the relation of the male to the female. To the male adult, the combination is of seductive and tyrannical, compassionate and cruel, kind and deceitful, graceful and feline; and to the male child, the combination is tender but potentially menacing if the child is loved for the wrong reasons. He notes the Egyptian mother god Mut, which appeared as a vulture with a penis. Joyce's Notes indicate that he ruminated on this aspect of the female—in its most pronounced form, the murder by the female spider of the procreating male.

Like Leonardo, Bloom and Stephen are initiated into effectiveness as they achieve stability in relation to the female. Leonardo's incomplete paintings are Stephen's earlier attempts at art. So Bloom gets into bed with his Mona Lisa. Apropos of the warning in Mona Lisa's ambiguous smile, Molly's bed is described as the nest of vipers. Consider the tail in the mouth from Leonardo's recurring vision in the context of Bloom and Molly sleeping head to foot and Bloom kissing Molly's tail.

Like Leonardo as an artist, Bloom has overcome his lack of self-respect and ineffectiveness as a male. The statue of Narcissus desiring desire is arrested and mute testimony to forces overcome by Stephen. Happily, Mona Lisa in Italian is not only part of the name of the subject of the painting also denotes thread bare ascetic, the life Stephen has overcome.

Narcissus and the Last Echo

In the terms of this episode, Narcissus would stand for the pole of individual isolation without connection to the unity. His hand is broken since he can't connect. Molly has put him back together. The counterpart limitations of romantic subjective art are featured in the following wonderfully succinct description: "the statue of Narcissus, sound without echo, desired desire." The sound of subjective art is sound without echo because it does not echo in the reader. It does not connect with the reader because it is not of general interest—it does not relate to grave and constant in the human condition.

Mathematics and Godel

Joyce borrowed the concepts of one/many, ipsorelative, and sequence from Bertrand Russell's *Introduction to Mathematical Philosophy*, a treatise about the foundations of mathematics, the king of the sciences that assume the absolute separation of opposites.

Joyce presents the view that truth from the knowledge of unity is broader than the truth that can be obtained from systems that assume the separation of opposites. This view anticipates the theorem of Kurt Godel published in 1931 to the effect that any internally consistent theorem must necessarily be incomplete (can not reach all true statements). In other words, provability is weaker than truth.

Molly's Suitors

When Bloom lists the series of Molly's suitors (including Blazes) and dispatches them with equanimity (ARREST), the list is necessarily of men that Bloom thinks have lusted after Molly, not necessarily those who have been successful. The fact that Blazes has been successful and is included in the list does not mean they all have. But the truth is left uncertain, as it must be in Bloom's mind.

Yeats (and a Little More Dante)

Yeats is suggested by the very odd bit of information about Molly that "In disoccupied moments she had more than once covered a sheet of paper with signs and hieroglyphics which she stated were Greek and Irish and Hebrew characters." This is a forceful clue to link some aspect of this episode to Yeats, who reported that at least two of his female acquaintances engaged in "automatic writing." This writing, which involved suspension of the will and production of occult knowledge, was according to Yeats the result of their psychic gift of being in touch with spiritual communicators. Something like the Apostles speaking in many tongues. The first Yeats medium, although she knew consciously only English and a little French, allegedly produced automatic writing which "contained words and phrases and answers to questions in Greek, Latin, Hebrew, German, Welsh, Provencal, Irish, Chinese, Coptic, Egyptian Hieroglyphs, and several other languages"[17].

Joyce's reference to this automatic writing channel suggests that creative inspiration proceeds from the collective through the more inclusive feminine side wisdom or, stated differently, a satisfactory relation with the female. Molly's preoccupation with the letter Q in Quebec (which follows immediately after the automatic writing statement) appears to be related to the cat (the Q looks like a seated cat), our symbol of the female principle, and to the birth of life (the Q also looks like a sperm entering an egg).

When Bloom furls the promised land flyer (into the shape of a cone) in order to ignite the incense cone on the mantle, the image combines (1) Dante's symbol of Hell as a burning cone in the earth carved out by Lucifer's landing and (2) Yeats's symbol of interlocking and spinning cones or triangles.[18] Adding to the mix is Joyce's view that the domain of art is cone shaped, that is proceeding from the narrow to the broader or the part to the whole.

In the interpretation inspired by Dante, the burning Promised Land flyer represents suffering or Hell on this earth. Bloom uses the burning flyer to light the incense cone. The incense cone, signifying the incense that Odysseus used to fumigate the death of the usurpers, represents for Joyce the calming equanimity Bloom brings to the sufferings of this world. Bloom brings the two cones together in ignition, the fast burning flyer igniting the slow burning incense cone. The flyer is consumed. The fast burning flyer for Zion signifies the subjective ego that Bloom has overcome. The slow burning incense cone is his compassion and charity.

In the interpretation inspired by Yeats, spinning two triangle shapes make interpenetrating cones. Yeats referred to these as interpenetrating "gyres," an odd word used in this episode. This figure was for Yeats a meaningful symbol of relationship in the world of opposites, which he referred to as antinomies, the most basic being subjective (ego based personality or the burning cone) and objective (community or the incense cone) forces in human experience. Bloom highlights this issue by ruminating on the human condition of being both solitary and interacting. A reconciliation of opposites.

Yeats developed in *A Vision* a schematic formula based on lunar phases indicating different mixtures of the subjective and objective. Since the date of this episode is June 17, it is of interest to note that phase 17, shortly after the full moon that gets a big play in this episode, is the phase when "Unity of Being" is most possible. The world soul, on the other hand, is in phase 22 of its historical cycle, and Stephen is 22, a fact that is drilled into the reader through mathematical calculations.[19]

Joyce developed a view of art that involves interpenetrating cones. One cone represents the selective faculty and the other the reproductive. The broad end of the selective cone is the artist's experience, which the artist distills into its essence, the narrow end of this cone. Then the interpenetrating reproductive cone takes the essence at its narrow end and renews it in new circumstances, the broad end of the reproductive cone.

This Yeatsian system seems to carry through the entire episode. Bloom goes to sleep and revisits the womb as "manchild," having unwound his memories. This is the very process that happens in Yeats's view of the afterlife. His consciousness returns to the narrow end of the cone where there is a point, like the one at the end of this episode.

Traditional Schemata

The traditional schemata given by Joyce for this episode are organ—skeleton for the fleshless and lifeless artistic approach of control author, art—science for the Law of the Fathers, color—none since emotion is lacking, symbol—comets for lights that come, leave and return as do souls, and technique—catechism (impersonal) for detachment. The suitors are Buck and Blazes and the bow reason. The sense of the episode is the "armed hope," as Odysseus and Telemachus are armed for the suitors and Stephen and Bloom walk home arm in arm in frail community.

Aesthetics and the Trinity

Above Molly and Poldy in the bedroom are the reflections from the lamp and shade in "an inconstant series of concentric circles." This image also suggests the three concentric concepts in Joyce's aesthetics: *integritas* (separation from the background), *consonantia* (relationship of part to part and to whole) and *quidditas* (the radiance or soul of the art object). These aesthetic concepts control the surface in this episode. Bloom and Stephen as one pair and then Bloom and Molly as a second pair are separated from the background. Their relationships to each other and to humanity in general are presented as part of the human rhythm, part to part and part to whole, which is in various degrees harmonious. The radiance of these relationships is projected for us on the ceiling in the light from the lamp that symbolized the art of literature, eternal light between the lines.

The rhythm of *integritas*, *consonantia* and *quidditas* blends into the related rhythm of the Trinity: the Father creates the world of separate and self-bounded objects that we live in; the Son, distanced from the Father by his condition as part divine and part human, comes to time and space to instruct as to relationships; and with Father and Son in the correct relationship, the Holy Spirit generates love, the radiance. The Son proceeds from the Father and the Holy Ghost proceeds from both. Likewise, the relationships of *consonantia* proceed from what is separated out in the function of *integritas*, and *quidditas* proceeds from both what is separated and their relationships.

St. Acquinas applied *consonantia* to the dynamic, "immanent procession of Son from Father within the unity of the Divine Trinity (Substance), as well as the immanent, dynamic presence of God in all creatures, and to the union of all creatures among themselves, which has the Divine Trinity as its ideal analogate."[20] This is Joyce's ultimate presentation as well.

The novel indicates that the bottom line on the relationship of one human to another is at best married sexual love that produces children together with detached empathy for mankind as a whole. Likewise, the bottom line on the relationship of each individual to the eternal powers that be is at best one of distanced engagement like that made by the artist. The rest of us non-artists, like Bloom who sees his books in the mirror, have to participate even more indirectly with the eternal powers, by experiencing the art made by the artist who at best achieves a distanced engagement with the eternal. This degree of detachment is fundamental to the proper function in art of the grave and constant; it allows the limited degree of unification in pity, uniting in sorrow but not merging with the human sufferer. The secret cause, the inevitability of death and its relationship to life, becomes an issue only because of the limited degree of knowledge of the eternal powers, those forces contained in the tree fruit in the Big Garden. There must have been trees of knowledge in the Garden other than of good and evil. If only Eve could have shoplifted a bite from the fruit of the tree of life.

At the end of this episode, the universals are stripped of their individuating conditions as Molly dissolves into mother earth, the source of life and inspiration, and Bloom dissolves into the manchild in the womb, the possibilities of the future. Now the future is pregnant with hopeful change, armed hope. We learn in the next and last episode that Molly interprets Leopold's going to sleep remarks about the roc's auk's egg as a request for an egg breakfast in bed. This is the request that will break their fast in bed. Though ever thoughtful, Bloom will take charge in bed in the morning; in parallel, Stephen will master the temper and art necessary to produce this novel. The Blooms' love that flowers the future is this novel, the book dedicated to Nora.

Structure, Art and Aesthetics

The reconciliation of message and medium in this episode is almost beyond belief. Joyce tackles epistemology with aesthetics in a morality play about metaphysics.

Note the ebb and flow of the beautiful answer about the water source. Some of the questions involve rhetorical pomposity. The pomposity is sponsored by the aristocratic Vico stage that features in jurisprudence and authority modalities the application of the right words and solemn formalities.

Often the text involves a series of beautiful images rolling to a climax cut short by a ridiculous falling off or short ending. Perhaps this stylistic device reflects the troubled combination of the eternal and the carnal in human heterosexual attraction, both of which deflate in sexual climax. But to Joyce, it provides the only peep show to what we are missing and the way back into the Garden through connections.

The primary sense of the words in the first part of the episode (Stephen with Bloom) is a masculine, fixed meaning. At the end, however, the sense of the words becomes more ambiguous. Compared to prior episodes, the characters are more shallow, in order to allow the eternal meaning more prominence.[21] The meaning shifts from surface meaning to obvious allegory suddenly and even rudely. Our Two Partners become comets swinging from the solar light out to the outer orbit of isolation and back again. Events in the Eccles Street microcosm are tied to events in the macrocosm of the stars. The Trinity turns on when Bloom and Stephen urinate, imitating the natural process of artistic creation. Subtle references to ancient Egyptian symbolism add venerated depth to the images.

I feel too humbled by the majesty of this episode to give any more definitive reading of its merits. This is to my view one of the greatest art objects in the history of Western civilization.

****

ENDNOTES

1. Davies, R. *The Merry Heart* (New York: Viking, 1996) p. 312.
2. Legends, vol. 1, p. 70.
3. Costello, p. 226.
4. Summarized as n, n+1, n+2, n+4, n+8, n+9 and n+20.
5. Tindall, p. 222.
6. Drucker, J. *The Alphabetic Labyrinth* (London: Thames and Hudson, 1999) p. 146 et seq.
7. Boyle, p. 10.
8. In the Notes, this idea is "Judaism misfortune not religion (Hcinc)."

9. The following description is taken from Griswold, C. *Self-Knowledge in Plato's Phaedrus* (New Haven: Yale University Press, 1986)
10. Graves, Greek Myths, p. 134.
11. Legends, vol. I, p. 74.
12. Power, p. 108.
13. Most of the material in this section is from Lang, pp. 183, 259-264.
14. In this analysis of equivalencies, I am speaking on that gross level of connection that is good enough for artistic symbols, not a more sophisticated knowledge resulting from deeper study and more refined nuances.
15. Cirlot.
16. Later shown to be properly translated as a kite, a different kind of bird, not as a vulture. Remember the kite in the Aeolus (7th) episode.
17. Ellmann, R. Yeats *The Man and the Masks* (New York: W.W. Norton, 1979) p. 198.
18, Ellmann, Yeats, p. 231.
19. Ellmann, Yeats, pp. 241 et seq.
20. Noon, p. 48.
21. Gross, J. *Joyce* (London: Fontana, 1971) p. 84.

Penelope (18th Episode)

General Themes

Yes—being—possibilities. House of Keyes, the key is yes.

The last episode is constructed exclusively of Molly's thoughts while she is in bed with Bloom who is asleep. She begins with "**Yes because he never did a thing like that before as ask to get his breakfast in bed . . .**"

Molly's natural slogan includes "**Yes**" because her instinct is birth and affirmation. Keyes, from the House of Keyes whose ad Bloom tried to place, breaks down into two words: key and yes.[1] The key is yes. Molly, like Yahweh, affirms: I am what I am. She champions the natural.

And the letter "Y" is the joinder for **key** and **yes**, a letter that looks like the female birth plumbing.

Her natural slogan includes "Yes **because**," since she is, with respect to the condition of "being" or to "**be**," the "**cause**." As a fertile woman, she is the cause of being when she has children. But in addition, she like every woman in this role is a repository of being itself. She is a fundamental part of life itself. This repository of the fundamental, Joyce believed, is the source the artist must tap and is the source of *quidditas* or the epiphany.

Her natural slogan includes, "Yes because **he never did a thing like that before** . . ." because the life affirmative cause of being is more new possibilities. Possibilities feed such diverse engines of being as personal self-realization and the impersonal process of Darwinian natural selection. Human babies are new possibilities personified.

Molly's "Yes because . . . " is responsive. It makes sense, we learn from Derrida, only as a response to a question. With Vico-like circularity, Molly provides at the end of her episode the question that her opening "Yes because . . ." answers.[1] At the end, she recalls the question she enticed Bloom to re-ask on that outing on Howth Head:

> . . . and I thought well as well him as another
> and then I asked him with my eyes to ask again yes and
> then he asked me would I yes my mountain flower and
> first I put my arms around him yes and drew him down
> to me so he could feel my breasts all perfume yes and
> his heart was going like mad and yes I said yes I will
> Yes.

The question Molly answered then and answers now is the same question: will you? Her answer is yes because. The references to nature through the flowers and to the Will force of Schopenhauer transpose the question and answer into the nature of all being. At the bottom line, it becomes impersonal: ". . . I thought well as well him as another . . ."

The part implies the whole because Molly, while pursuing the interests of the species, thinks she is pursuing her own personal interests. Again Joyce follows Schopenhauer (***The Metaphysics of the Love of the Sexes***).

Three important things happen in this episode as far as plot is concerned: Molly registers a request from Bloom for breakfast (eggs) in bed; Molly menstruates into the orange, one-handled pot; and Molly decides to have another child by Bloom.

The beginning announces Molly as Everywoman and the Earthmother, the foaming source menstruating for eucharistic renewal. Her sexual and maternal instincts serve as the earthly representative of the Holy Spirit, Joyce's view of God's presence in the world. Not the priests, not the ritual, not the Mass but Molly's instincts to create new life are the breath of God over his creation. As Molly's menses ends this novel with prospects of renewal of life, the Flow of the Mothers liberates the lock-up of the Law of the Fathers. Fixed forms that limit nature are not in her make-up.

The analogy in Joyce's aesthetics is *quidditas*, the whatness or essence of the art object. This episode gives the *quidditas* of the entire novel. The essence, presented through Molly, is the nature of the human condition and by extension the nature of being. The essence flows in art and life when maximum possibilities are nurtured by acceptance of the natural human condition rather than restricted by control in the interest of non-human objectives. Molly represents human possibilities. She brings forth. She is the repository of the open-ended process of becoming.

The analogy in the Vico cycle is the last stage, the human or secular stage in which subject and object are totally separated. Laws based on human reason and human experience replace aristocratic control. The artistic counterpart of Vico's human stage is the dramatic method. Using the same full separation of author and material, Joyce gives us the power and majesty of art created in the dramatic style fully empowered. That art gives birth to the *quidditas*, the possibilities of the human condition.

Molly and the Artist

Like the artist, Molly must receive before she can give. Molly's thoughts circle around the selection of a mate and reproduction. Molly receives flattering attentions as part of egotistical love, selects her mate, receives sperm and then gives back children and compassion for them. Likewise, the artist in the selective facility receives and selects experiences and in the productive facility gives back art. Here is Joyce, in SH, on the role of the artist:

> The artist, he imagined, standing in the position of mediator between the world of his experience and the world of his dreams—a mediator, consequently gifted with twin faculties, a selective faculty and a reproductive faculty . . . the artist who could disentangle the subtle soul of the image from its mesh of defining circumstances most exactly and re-embody it in artistic circumstances chosen as the most exact for it in its new office, he was the supreme artist.

Like Elijah, Molly as mother must "come before." Like Penelope, Molly unweaves her menses and then weaves her egg. The artist unweaves the "subtle soul" from his experience and then weaves it in new material.[2] Marion Tweedy, her maiden name, for the web of tweed.

This episode, created solely in the thought patterns of Molly, is created with only two capital letters (one on Yes as the first word and a second on Yes as the last word) and one period at the end. Otherwise, 37 remarkable pages proceed without punctuation, capital letters or apostrophes. In this respect, this episode is the modern secular counterpart of the Hebrew Scriptures, which were originally written in the same format and without vowels.[3] This mode of presentation allowed full flexibility in interpreting the scriptures because different vowels could be used resulting in different meanings. As a result, the Torah was believed to have the potential to give all possible meanings, to cover all possibilities.[4] Molly, the patron of possibilities, is presented in Joyce's analogue of the Torah's possibilities.

Joyce's secular scripture presents simultaneously an indelible portrait of Molly as one human being and as representative of the forces of procreation. Molly menstruates in the chamber pot her own blood and water, her own Eucharist. With this connection, the novel has moved in the search for the eternal powers from the Mass to Menstruation, a development from control to the natural. Symbolic of the redemptive power of menstruation in relation to the Host that stirs the faithful, menstruate unfolds to men stir eight (for infinity or eternity).

Unlike Stephen and Bloom, Molly feels no guilt and is not self-conscious; she is all natural. She feels no guilt over and does not try to hide her activities with Blazes. Her thoughts and desires are routinely inconsistent. Her inconsistencies present the fertility of the possible as the manifold source of the creative imagination. This source of possibilities is not limited by logical consistency. Her inconsistencies mirror the merger of opposites in the infinite. The sexual instinct and the creative imagination, portals of expanded possibilities to the eternal.

With pregnancy on her mind, Molly remembers that an excited Bloom was at her pregnant breasts for himself and even for cream for the tea. As Everywoman, she reviews her considerable history as a sexual competitor for males. As Earthmother, she muses about a man who could have "planted" her. Like the earth, Molly's thoughts appear to spin and return through words repeating at intervals. Her thoughts in only eight loomed sentences are connected in a huge web spun by the Spider Woman that eats her mate. Like the creative imagination, the web pulsates insistently as her thoughts born of body wisdom and energy hasten to their Hidden Places.

Molly and Sex

Molly's monologue is a paean to the sexual energy in her body, her own chamber music filling the chamber pot in the Queen's chamber. Her memories expose her youthful nature as a totally self serving, catty, mean-spirited competitor for all attractive men, a competition destructive of female friendships that elevates concern for personal appearance over the soul. These predator tracks are traced in her memories of youthful relationships on Gibraltar and in Dublin. Even now she tries to find out whom Bloom has been with and even regards Milly as a rival. This stage of female ego exiled upon itself is bolstered by the equation of sex appeal and self worth. I attract males therefor I am or ". . . I feel I want to I feel . . ." As a youthful sexual competitor, she stands beside our other products of youth: the narcissism and romantic subjective artist mode in youthful Stephen, the youthful drive in the Garden for realization and Satan as the youth of Christ.

Molly's attitude toward sex is, like Gerty's, bathed in the

perfume of the romantic impulse for flowers. In Gerty's episode, the counterpart of the subjective romantic literary approach was signaled by our frequent flyer the vampire. Sure enough, Molly's mouth and teeth are emphasized, she thinks of the song "Winds from the South" (Stephen's vampire poem), and she is of the opinion that she is menstruating because she has too much blood. The onset of her bleeding sounds like the arrival of the vampire to draw blood: "that thing come on me." She even thinks about giving fellatio to the statue of Narcissus, self 8 self. The nature of the episode as a coda in musical terms recalls Leonardo and the tail (coda) in his lips.

In the language of the Eucharist, the transubstantiation for Molly is to become pregnant, to become the host for life. This condition changes her self-serving romantic orientation into the selfless mother's love for the life of her child. In birth and renewal of human life, the mother's profane body and blood otherwise discharged in menstruation is changed into the sacred substance and accidents of the child. Likewise, the artist must change from the emotional subjective to the dramatic literary approach to give birth, love and independent life to his or her created characters.

Atonement and the Scapegoat

The plot of this novel reaches a state of atonement for Stephen on the one hand and Bloom and Molly on the other. Stephen has begun the process of at one ment, the discovery of the unity, and Bloom and Molly will proceed in their own matrimonial version of unity conditioned by their own personalities.

On the day of Atonement in Hebrew ritual, the high priest atones for the entire Hebrew community by putting blood from the sacrificial bull and goat on the horns around the altar in the holy of holies. A second goat, selected by lot and with a piece of crimson wool tied between its horns, is sent out into the wilderness where Azazel, a demon, resided. The second goat was deemed to escape, thus the scapegoat, was deemed to carry away the sins of Israel (Lev.16:8). When the scapegoat reached the wilderness, a second strip of crimson wool tied to the door of the sanctuary turned white (Yoma:6 Mishnah 8).

Bloom was clearly marked as the scapegoat to Azazel in the

Circe (15th) episode (15: lines 776 and 1889). Bloom has reached the wilderness and in compassion and equanimity has accepted Molly's sin. He carries her sin. Molly is the sanctuary. Her altar has been marked with blood. Her crimson menstruation, if it continues, will mean that the scapegaost has not carried off her sins. If her crimson menstruation ceases, because she is pregnant, then atonement will have been realized.

The Trinity

The Father and Son through Bloom and Stephen have come into the proper conjunction. Accordingly, the Holy Spirit, the unseen life giving force, should issue love in the world. And here she is, the holy mother spirit, with the emphasis on her holy holes. Bathed in images of the Holy Spirit, the Earthmother and Egyptian female deities, she dares the atheists to "go and create something . . ." The Holy Spirit is the spontaneous creative force of God in the world. She is known metaphorically as the force that broods over His creation. Molly broods over her menses, her birth potential. Known in the Kaballah as the Shekinah, the feminine principle, and in New Testament as the Paraclete or advocate, Molly becomes the solicitor of sex. According to Molly, the power of sex, particularly for a woman the first time, "makes you feel like nothing on earth."

Joyce's ultimate creation is Molly as a human personality who reflects female psychology, the unconscious and the ultimate source of being. This episode consists only of her interior monologue, Molly to Molly. She is presented in a style isolated by a uniqueness among the many styles used in this novel.[5] Since this episode ends the novel, this selection indicates that this frame of reference is the ultimate reality—Molly with Molly, not Molly with Bloom. Her ego is presented as "exiled upon itself." Her child is her Exodus. For her, Bloom is first and foremost not a unique human opportunity for maximum self-realization. She rates him as a provider for the nest, and a poor one at that. He has lost four jobs already, and she is afraid he will lose the *Freeman* job over something as unimportant as politics or Freemasonry. She even muses about never again getting in the "same boat" (the symbol of unity) with Bloom. She remembers the last time his ineptness brought water in the boat and ruin to her clothes, her all important courting feathers. While she has urges for children by him and compassion for their care, her openings to Bloom are not in a dimension that will allow merger of their humanity. He will connect on her web site for children and family support.

Like Stephen and Bloom, Molly and Bloom must come together as soul strangers. This separateness is presented as originating in the Fall in the Garden, which has been recreated in her bedroom with Blazes as the serpent. Her Yes to Bloom is still the Mona Lisa's sinister smile, not that of the Holy Mother.

The Medium is the Message

More than any other, this episode communicates by the medium. Molly uses merged subject and verbs but without the apostrophe, for suggestive examples Id for I'd and wed for we'd. Contractions (with the apostrophe) are what an about to deliver pregnant mother has, so the menstruating Molly doesn't use them.

Her thoughts are presented without proper punctuation because in her force field everything is connected by feeling, not by thinking. "Yes because" does not produce an explanation other than by way of motivation. The language of her presentation expresses liberation into greater possibilities human and otherwise through the use of the following: words with shifting meaning; a narrative procedure based on periodic flow; syntax without punctuation and thus without containment; a view that looks both forward and backward in time; and a catalog of inconsistencies that maps almost every statement she makes. Her desires loosen the boundaries.

Bodies and Spheres

Molly's thoughts are body thoughts, born of the wisdom and energy of her body. As potential mother, Molly is the medium of vital connections because the maternal birth is the life line back to God in the Garden and forward to the future. Her body mixes the temporal and eternal dimensions of life. Her menstrual discharge is the black mass to the renewal of birth. The eight giant webbed sentences of this episode reflect the prone 8 for infinity, as well as a picture of Molly's holy holes.

593

On its side, the 8 can also look like a mobius strip, a shape in which the inside of the structure becomes the outside and vice-versa.[6] In her thoughts, Molly's insides become her outside.

Joyce wrote to Budgen:

> Her monologue turns slowly, evenly, though with variations, capriciously, but surely like the huge earthball itself round and round spinning. Its four cardinal points are the female breasts, arse, womb and sex expressed by the words because, bottom (in all senses bottom button, bottom of the glass, bottom of the sea, bottom of his heart) woman, yes.

The repetition of these four words is meant to give the impression of a spinning earth. If this is the case, the spin is highly irregular and capricious because the pattern does not repeat on a regular basis.[7]

Joyce's design, according to his letters, was to create an image of the earth as "pre-human." Earth in a sense is the mother of all life. Molly's thoughts have a Darwinian amoral cast. Joyce's view of life in the long run presents individuality as only skin deep and the deep reality of life as continuity.

The spherical shape of the earth also serves Joyce's symbolic purposes. The rotating sphere provides continuous returns, a physical presentation of Joyce's view of cyclical history and the continuity of basic human patterns. Since every part of the surface of the sphere has the same shape and is equidistant from the center, the sphere is a physical presentation of Joyce's megacept that the part implies the whole. Feeling the same parallels as Joyce, the pre-Socratic Greek philosopher Parmenides described all "reality" as the shape of a sphere and Gaston Bachelard in *The Poetics of Space* postulated the sphere as representation of the nature of being. In *Phaedrus*, Plato described the eternal Forms or Beings as divine intelligence situated on the surface of the heavenly sphere.

Molly's mother's name, Lunita Laredo, translates as little moon, the little moon to the big mother earth. She had little influence on Molly's early life; she either left or died when Molly was a child. Molly was raised by her father with the help of Hester Stanhope, who later called Molly by the nick-name Doggerina. This nickname suggests a female dog, which recalls our learning in dog and god.

Molly's mother was apparently a Spanish Jewess, a very unusual bride and thus a new possibility for a member of the British occupying forces at Gibraltar. Molly is a mixture from a Spanish Jewish mother and an Irish Protestant father. Leopold Bloom is a mixture from an Irish Catholic mother and a Hungarian Jewish father. Molly starts in Gibraltar, the control rock, as a sexual competitor and ends up in Dublin as a compassionate mother, another picture of the maturation of artistic approach.

In terms of how Bloom fares in Molly's thoughts, he starts well, then wanes increasingly through the middles sentences and then returns to favor in the end. Joyce referred to this variation as an "amplitudinously curvilinear episode." This shape gives the moon in relation to Molly's natural cycle and her melodious spheres. The impersonal from ultimate reality sponsors the dilution of Molly's motivation in choosing Bloom – might as well be him as another. The process is what has the power; it proceeds even with a less than ideal choice. The only objective of the process is continued life.

Action in Ulysses

This episode carries on directly from the ending of the last episode. Bloom and Molly are in bed head to toe. He is asleep, she awake in some sense. She interprets what Bloom has said on falling asleep as an egg breakfast in bed request and as a suggestion of conjugal reunion. She gets up to use the chamber pot for her monthly. She passes both blood and urine. The discharge purifies her of the possibility of being pregnant by Blazes and soils her plans for the next sexual rendezvous with him on the following Monday. In this most natural way, her rebirth possibilities prevent the next sexual meeting with the profane Blazes.

She goes back to bed. During her monologue, she remembers her loves. Her list is short, compared to Bloom's. Her first was Lt. Mulvey in Gibraltar. When he was shipped out from Gibraltar, she promised him sexual favors on his return, even if she were then married. Her second, Lt. Gardener, died in the Boer war. When Gardener left, she gave him Mulvey's ring. He is missing from Bloom's list of suitors.

595

Next are d'Arcy, who kissed her in the corridor in the concerthall, Blazes and his great big red one (the only certain full consummation other than Bloom), Stephen as a potential and Bloom.

In the end, she yearns for a child and affirms her desire for a full relationship with Bloom. She plans to leave early in the morning for the market and then return to an anxiously uncertain husband with the special fixings for his surprise breakfast, my guess is an egg omelet with vegetal fillings from the earth. They will start to have sex not in spite of but because of the menstruation.

Action in The Odyssey and Parallels

Odysseus convinces Penelope of his true identity by his intimate knowledge of their immovable marriage bed that he carved whole out of a living olive tree. Molly makes reference to the all too loose and noisy nature of their bed, which prompted her to use the floor with Blazes.

In a crafty effort to delay and diffuse the expected outrage of the community to the killing of so many of her eligible bachelors, Odysseus fakes a wedding feast that would commemorate Penelope's wedding to one of the suitors. This surely is Molly's sex with Blazes.

Molly is from Gibraltar because in one epilogue to The Odyssey, Odysseus goes out beyond the Gates of Hercules, the north end of which is Gibraltar. Here Molly remembers Ulysses S. Grant coming to Gibraltar.

According to Tiresias's prophecy, Odysseus is to die by the sea. Meanwhile our Bloom the manchild is in the ocean of unconsciousness.

Kundalini, The Buddha and Utimate Reality

My emphasis throughout this guide on the Kundalini is justified by Molly's recollection, in reaction to Bloom's sleeping with his hand touching his nose, of a Hindu God. In Kundalini exercises, the novitiate is instructed to breathe in through one nostril and then out through the other, a difficult process made easier by closing one nostril by finger pressure. Bloom is touching his nose.

Molly represents the female power at whose feet the initiate dances in the seventh, the highest chakra. Bloom is head to her feet asleep on his left side dreaming in the land of the archetypes, the seven veils of the divine inspiration. Molly remembers Bloom identifying this

Hindu god as the Buddha recumbent on its side, reminiscent of our Bloom.

The Kundalini symbolizes the development of the impersonal life, as Molly moves from sexual competitor to mother and points beyond in the impersonal ultimate realities. Yoga means "to grasp the real essence, the inner structure, in its living reality as a dynamic substance and the laws of that matter"[8]. So this episode is Joyce's yoga, which features in Molly's dialogue the sexual instinct and creative imagination ("go and create something"). Bloom now shares the sexual instinct and Stephen the creative imagination. They share modalities with god the creator.

The nature of the ultimate reality presented by Joyce through Molly is a custom blend of Schopenhaeur's Will Force and Darwin's selection and continuity process. It is impersonal and cyclical. In its natural form not restricted by the Law of the Fathers, it promotes human possibilities within the constraint of the continuity of life. The part implies the whole because Molly's birth impulse is not a personal decision for her but is an instinctive product of the evolution of the species. Her birth instinct implies the species and the species implies her birth instinct.

The Passover

The images of the Passover, so important in previous episodes, continue here in Molly's menses. The kill by the avenging angels passing over is delivered in the chamber pot as Molly menstruates her dead egg and lining. She remains vulnerable to the avenging angels because she is still in the house of bondage of herself, Molly as a woman whose sexual desires must be satisfied, and not Molly the compassionate mother. Molly, who lost her own mother early in her life, is missing the mother element here. Like a flower and like a neglected rose, her menses has wilted.

Molly and the Giants

The thunder, which scared Stephen in the Oxen episode, apparently awakened Molly from sleep following her repeated self-indulgence in stimulation with Blazes. In Vico's analysis, thunder is the aspect of nature that brought the giants to reverence. Likewise, it has partially tamed Molly, because her religion is fear of hell. But her reverence has a limit. Her consistent test is whether something is natural. In her view, what the Church designates as sin is bad (Sinbad) unless its natural. If it is natural, it can't be a sin. And naturally enough, she doesn't understand why she has to confess to a priest (representative of the Law of the Fathers) if she has confessed to God, who already knows anyway.

As Earthmother, Cybele was the mother of giants. Molly feels her giants in Blazes's large penis. The Earthmother was invoked by the Romans by sinking their arms down towards the earth.[9] Recall the image of the arms of the balance pointing to the center of her earth. Cybele was attended by lions, accounting for the references to Blazes as an old Lion.

Molly is drawn to Stephen as the Great Mother was to her son Tammuz or Adonis, her son and lover and representative of nature's rebirth in the spring (flowers and vegetables). Every menstruation is a death of her son and lover. Perhaps in deference to the homage at the ending of Goethe's **Faust** to the eternal feminine, Joyce described Molly as "sane full amoral fertilizable untrustworthy engaging limited prudent indifferent Weib" and as ". . . the indispensable countersign to Bloom's passport to eternity"[10].

The Fall in the Garden and Plato's Original Couple

The images from the primordial legend of the Fall in the Garden continue in this episode. The Fall was initiated by a breach in human relationships, Eve's treachery toward Adam. As the snake tricked her, she tricked Adam into eating of the apple. This treachery violated the relation of human to human, and thus to God. As a result, they were separated from God as they were separated from each other.

Molly wishes she could go back to the "original couple of uniting parties." Her memory traces of making love for the first time with Bloom at Howth Head in the rhododendrons are presented in ideal overtones. This is "firtree cove" where she broke the bag (hymen or high men or hi men). Firetree cove is all that is left of the tree of life.

Adam's first mate, Lilith, who was independent minded and refused sex on Adam's missionary position terms, is suggested by the Blooms' servant girl. Bloom apparently made a pass at her and invited her to share their Christmas table on equal terms. Molly fired her because she was a thief and too uppity (Lilith now allegedly steals children). After that, Eve with the right attitude was made from Adam's rib. Molly's skirt "opening up the side" suggests Eve's birth from Adam's rib.

The serpent in the Garden earns multiple allusions: Lt. Gardener's penis that looked like it had an eye (the Big Gardener produced the serpent); the solicitor who was flirting with the young girl at Pooles Myriorama; and the dean or bishop who sat next to Molly in the "jews temples garden." Blazes's name suggests the Great Fiend and his big red penis a combination of the initially upright serpent and the poisonous apple. Blazes, accompanied by his barren sisters, first set his eyes on Molly in DBC and there first noticed her foot. This reflects the serpent's punishment; he had his feet chopped off. Now feet are his fetish. The serpent was initially upright in the garden, and was banished to the ground for his role. Given the momentous apple, Molly remembers wives who poisoned their husbands in favor of a lover.

After the Fall, Adam and Eve lost their original covering of a "horny skin . . . enveloped with the cloud of glory"[11]. This lost horny skin covering is reflected in several Connector Facts: Molly's loss of her suede gloves in the DBC rest room on the occasion when Blazes first eyed her; Molly's recollection of feeling Bloom to determine if he had been circumcised; Bloom's devotion to her coverings, her gloves and drawers; and Bloom's being worried about blood poisoning after he cut off a corn on his toe.

The serpent tricked Eve into eating the apple by showing her that Adam's rule not to even touch the tree of knowledge under the pain of death was not true. Eve interpreted the death threat as mortal death, as opposed to spiritual death. The serpent pushed Eve against the tree and nothing happened. Likewise, Blazes spanks Molly on the backside. When convinced by the touch test and by the example of the serpent to eat the apple, Eve first just ate the skin and finally the flesh. Likewise, Molly requires Blazes to finish outside of her the first three times and in the fourth allows onanized Blazes the ultimate in flesh. Adam before the Fall was gigantically tall but afterwards was short. Guess what that means.

The corrupting nature of the relationship with Blazes is indicated by Molly's thoughts that he should buy her expensive presents.

After they were first married, Adam called himself Ish and Eve Ishah, names which carried syllables from the name of God. But after they went astray, God's syllables were withdrawn and instead of "Ish there would remain Esh, meaning fire, a fire issuing from each and consuming the other." Molly's sex drive has consumed her and her human relationships. Her sex with Blazes produced no satisfaction, only more itch.

Plato's original couple was one person combining both sexes, so Molly indicates that sometimes she wishes she were a male so, sure enough, she could have sex with someone as desirable as she. Bloom, you remember, mused about being a woman so, sure enough, he could be a mother.

Atlas Shrugged

Molly was born on Gibraltar and her memories refer to the two mountains that frame the Strait of Gibraltar. The one on the North in Gibraltar was known to the Greeks as Kalpe, which means water pitcher or jug. The one on the south in Africa was Abilla or high mountain and is now called monkey mountain.[12] Atlas was said to hold up both mountains, Atlas who carries the burden for others. The Strait suggests the female sex opening; beyond the Straits was the end of the world.

The water jug appears as the chamber pot that receives Molly's monthlies. Monkey mountain is referred to in Molly's thought that monkeys used the caves in Gibraltar to return to Africa. Molly as Everywoman serves as Atlas because she bears the pains of childbirth that holds up the human race. This month she shrugged.

Archetypes

With the provocative comment by Molly about monkeys using caves in Gibraltar to go back to Africa, we know that Gibraltar somehow stands for consciousness against the collective unconscious of Africa. For related holes, Joyce's working notes for this episode include: "her cunt, darkest Africa." Africa, the origins and the symbol of the unconscious.

Amen

Molly's monologue is the amen of this novel. Amen in Hebrew

derives from *aman*, which means to support, to sustain and to be firm. These notions complete the allusions to continuity and Aristotle's concept of being—rising and holding firm within a limit. The limit is the human.

Molly's kind of love is the amen to life on earth as we know it. The unity of life is, at the bottom, impersonal. Detached compassion matches it best.

First Letter and Traditional Schemata

The first letter is Y in "yes." You can do that one now, given the emphasis in this episode. The top two branches of the Y represent the fallopian tubes. The E represents identity from Plutarch's Delphi and S the river Nile, whose cyclical inundation replenished the holy soil.

The traditional schemata given by Joyce for this episode are organ—flesh, art—none, color—none, symbol—earth, and technique—monologue female. Linati lists for Time the prone 8 for infinity as well as the female genitalia.

Yes

The book ends with Molly's yes. Joyce reportedly told Louis Gillet:

> In order to convey the mumbling of a woman falling asleep, I wanted to finish with the faintest word that I could possibly discover. I found the word yes, which barely pronounced, which implies consent, abandonment, relaxation, the end of all resistance.

Structure, Art and Aesthetics

Here we have the pure dramatic style in an interior monologue. This is the ultimate achievement in the dramatic—the purely personal rendered in the dramatic objective incarnating the eternal. Subject and object are totally separated, the dramatic mode. Subject and object shimmer and dance, shifting roles.

With its style in language vulgar and authority modality in human experience, this episode derives from Vico's last stage based on human nature. In the Vico system, the cycle will, absent a break-out such as that resulting from the Jewish Covenant of God, inevitably cycle back to the mythical age of the gods. The Joyce break-out is here, beginning and ending with Yes, an Ode to Joy. **Joy in Joyce**.

****

ENDNOTES

1, Rabate, J. *Joyce Upon the Void* (New York: St. Martins Press, 1991) p. 63.
2. Rabate, p. 43.
3. Kugel, p. 5.
4. Nadel, p. 4 et. seq.
5. Brown, p. 34.
6. Rabate, p. 46.
7. 'Yes' is used 84 times, 'because' 46 times, 'bottom' 19 times and 'woman' and 'women' 66 times. Starting each phrase with yes, the pattern appears to be random with respect to the use of the other three words.
8. Hauer quoted in Jones, C. *The Psychology of Kundalini Yoga* (Princeton: Bollingen Series XCIX Princeton University Press) p. xxxviii.
9. Gilbert, p. 399.
10. All from Gilbert.
11. All of this obscure material about the Garden is from Legends, vol. 1, pp. 70 et. seq.
12. Berard, pp. 245 et. seq.

Epilogue

The best novel of the 20th century. A novel that starts with "Stately" and ends with "Yes." It moves from patriarchal restriction of possibilities in the interests of control to the maternal expansion of possibilities in the interests of potent art and life. Increased possibilities are the junction for Joyce's views of the eternal, metaphysics and the human condition.

Joyce expresses in his literary architecture the eternal patterns of repetition through cycles and the harmony of part and whole, Joyce's architecture of metaphysics. The sexual instinct and creative imagination, in Joyce's view human burn marks from the divine, create these same patterns. Joyce's artistic patterns share fundamentals with the recurring patterns found in nature—spirals, waves and other tapestries that have developed through reproduction of survival patterns in life forms. One pattern in nature, the fractal, is particularly Joycean. In this pattern, each subsection of the entire design is an image of the whole. Each subsection is different in size but not in shape. Each part resembles another and the whole. Joyce's architecture of part implying whole is fractal.

As Leonardo reproduced the patterns of moving water in the hair curls of his subjects, Joyce has reproduced what he saw as the fundamental patterns of human nature and ultimate reality in this novel. Joyce merges art and metaphysics. Joyce's musical pulse within these patterns reminds me of the following recent description (by Brian Greene in *The Elegant Universe*) of the superstring theory of ultimate reality: "[in this realm] musical metaphors take on a startling reality, for the [superstring] theory suggests that the microscopic universe is suffused with tiny strings whose vibrational patterns orchestrate the evolution of the cosmos."

Music, the art in which form and substance are one, provides the best analogy for Joyce's literary art. I hope his artistic vibration patterns brought you Joy in Joyce.

Bibliography

Ackroyd, P. *Blake* (New York: Knopf, 1996)

Adams, W. *The House of Hidden Places* (African Heritage Classical Research Studies Series, no date)

APA DSM –III-R *Diagnostic Manual of Mental Disorders*, 3rd Edition,revised

Auerbach, E. *Mimesis The Representation of Reality in Western Literature* (Princeton: Princeton University Press, 1953)

Avalon, A. *The Serpent Power* (New York: Dover Publications, 1953)

Bacon, F. *the wisdom of the ancients* (Montana: Kessinger Publishing Co., no date)

Baron, N. and Bhattacharya, N. *Vico and Joyce: The Limits of Language in Vico and Joyce*, edit. by D. Verene (New York: State University of New York Press, 1987)

Beets, M.G.J. *The Coherence of Reality* (Holland: Eburon, 1986)

Berard, V. *Les Pheniciens et L'Odyssee* (Paris: Librairie Armand Colin, 1902)

Blamirez, H. *The New Bloomsday Book: A Guide Through Ulysses* (N.Y.: Routledge, 1996)

Blavatsky, H.P. *Isis Unveiled* (Pasadena: Theosophical University Press, 1976)

Bloom, H. *Shakespeare: The Invention of the Human* (New York:

Riverhead Books, 1998)

Bloom, H. *The Western Canon* (New York: Riverhead Books, 1995)

Bohm, D. *Wholeness and the Implicate Order* (New York: Ark Publications, 1980)

Bonwick, J. *Irish Druids and Old Irish Religions* (London: Griffith, Farran & Co.,1984)

Borstein,D. *The Creators* (New York: Random House, 1992)

Bowen, Z. *Musical Analysis of the Sirens Episode in Joyce's Ulysses*, Literary Monographs, Vol. 1, Edit. by E. Rothstein and T. Dunseath (Madison: University of Wisconsin Press, 1967)

Boyle, R. *James Joyce's Pauline Vision* (Carbondale: Feffer & Simon, 1978)

Brown, R. *James Joyce and sexuality* (Cambridge: Cambridge University Press, 1985)

Brivic, S. *The Veil of Signs* (Evanston: University of Illinois Press, 1991

Bruno, Giodarno *Cause Principle and Unity* trans. J. Lindsay (New York: International Publishers, 1962)

Budge, E. *The Gods of the Egyptians* (New York: Dover Publications, 1969)

Budgen, F. *James Joyce and the Making of Ulysses* (Bloomington: Indiana University Press, 1960) p. 107

Burgess, A. *Re Joyce* (New York: WW Norton, 1965)

Cahill, T. *The Gifts of the Jews* (New York: Doubleday, 1998)

Campbell, J. *Early Hindu and Buddhist Myths* audiotape, Big Sur Tapes (1993)

Campbell, J. *Masks of the Gods Creative Mythology* (New York: Arkana, 1968)

Campbell, J. *Masks of the Gods Occidental Mythology* (New York: Arkana, 1991) pp. 301-302

Campbell, J. *Masks of the Gods Oriental Mythology* (N.Y.: Penguin, 1962)

Campbell, J. *Mythic Worlds, Modern Words* (New York: Harper Collins, 1933)

Campbell, J. *Myths to Live By* (New York: Penguin Books, 1972)

Campbell, J. *Primitive Mythology* (New York: Arkana, 1991)

Campbell, J. *The Campbell Companion* (New York: Harper Collins, 1991)

Campbell, J. *The Mythic Image* (Princeton: Princeton University Press, 1974)

Campbell, J. *The Novels of James Joyce* audiotape, Big Sur Tapes (Tiburon, Ca)

Campbell, J. *Transformations of Myth Through Time* (New York: Harper and Row, 1990)

Cixuos, H. *The Exile of James Joyce*, trans. by S. Purcell (New York: David Lewis, 1972)

Colum, M. and P. *Our Friend James Joyce* (Garden City: Doubleday & Company, 1958)

Coomaraswamy, A. *Buddha and the Gospel of Buddhism* (New York, G.P. Putnam's Sons, 1916)

Coomaraswamy, A. *Dance of Shiva* (New York: Noonday Press, 1957)

Cooraraswamy, A. *Selected Papers* Vol. 2 (Princeton: Princeton University Press: Bollingen Series LXXXIX, 1977)

Costello, P. *James Joyce Years of Growth* (N.Y.: Panteheon, 1992)

Cumont, F. *The Mysteries of Mithra* (New York: Dover Publications, 1902)

Dannielou, A. *Shiva and Dionysus*, trans. K. Hurry (London: East - West Publications, 1982)

Dannielou, A. *The Myths and Gods of India* (Rochester: Inner Traditions International, 1991)

Davies, R. *A Voice From the Attic*

Davies, R. *The Merry Heart* (New York: Viking, 1996)

Deleuze, G. *Coldness and Cruelty* (New York: Zone Books, 1989)

Drucker, J. *The Alphabetic Labyrinth* (London: Thames and Hudson, 1999)

Edersheim, A. *The Life and Times of Jesus the Messiah* (New York: Longmans, Green, and Co., 1917)

Eliade, M. *The Sacred and the Profane*

Ellmann, R. *James Joyce* (Oxford: Oxford University Press, 1982)

Ellmann, R. *The Consciousness of Joyce* (Toronto: Oxford University Press, 1977)

Ellmann, R. *Ulysses on the Liffey* (Oxford: Oxford University Press, 1972)

Ellmann, R. *Yeats The Man the Masks* (New York: W.W. Norton, 1979)

Erickson, E. *Childhood and Society* (New York: W.W. Norton , 1950)

Ferris, K. *James Joyce and the Burden of Disease* (Lexington: The University Press of Kentucky, 1995).

Frazer, J. *The Golden Bough* (N.Y.: MacMillan, 1963)

Freeman, K. *Ancilla to the Pre-Socratic Philosophers* (Oxford: Basil Blackwell, 1948)

Freud, S. *Dictionary of Psychoanalysis*

Frye, N. *Words with Power Being a Second Study of The Bible and Literature* (San Diego: Harcourt Brace Jovanovich, 1990)

Frye, N. *The Great Code The Bible and Literature* (San Diego: Harcourt Brace Jovanovich, 1990)

Gifford, D. *Ulysses Annotated* (Berkeley: University of California Press, 1988)

Gilbert, S. *James Joyce's Ulysses* (New York: Vintage Books, 1970) p. 51.

Goethe, J. *Faust*, trans. G. Priest (New York: Alfred A. Knopf, 1957)

Goldberg, S. L. *The Classical Temper* (New York: Barnes & Noble, 1961)

Gorman, H. *James Joyce* (New York: Rinehart & Company, Inc. 1939)

Graves, R. *The Greek Myths* (London: Penguin, 1955)

Graves, R. *The White Goddess* (New York: Farrar, Strauss and Giroux, 1948)

Greene, M. *A Portrait of Aristotle* (Chicago: University of Chicago Press, 1963)

Griswold, C. *Self-Knowledge in Plato's Phaedrus* (New Haven: Yale University Press, 1986)

Gross, J. *Joyce* (London: Fontana, 1971)

Guthrie, W.K.C. *A History of Greek Philosophy* (Cambridge: Cambridge University Press, 1965)

Harrison, J. *Prolegomena To the Study of Greek Religion* (Cambridge: Cambridge University Press, 1922) (first edition 1903)

Heidegger, M. *An Introduction to Metaphysics* (New Haven: Yale University Press, 1959)

Herring, P. *Joyce's Uncertainty Principle* (Princeton: Princeton University Press, 1987)

Hillman, J. *Insearch Psychology and Religion* (Woodstock: Spring Publications, 1967)

Hinnells, A. *Esoteric Buddhism* (Boston: Houghton, Mifflin & Co.,

1883)

Huxley, A. *The Perennial Philosophy* (New York: Harper & Row, 1944)

James Joyce's Ulysses Critical Essays edit. C. Hart and D. Hayman (Berkeley: University of California Press, 1974)

Januska, R. *The Sources and Structure of the "Oxen of the Sun" Episode of James Joyce's Ulysses* diss. Kent State University

Jones, C. *The Psychology of Kundalini Yoga* (Princeton: Bollingen Series XCIX Princeton University Press)

Joyce, J. *A Portrait of the Artist as a Young Man* (New York: Viking Press, 1956)

Joyce, J. *Stephen Hero* (New York: New Directions, 1944)

Joyce, J. *The Critical Writings* Edit. by E. Mason and R. Ellmann (Ithaca: Cornell University Press, 1959)

Joyce, S. *My Brother's Keeper* (New York: The Viking Press, 1969)

Joyce's Ulysses Notesheets in the British Museum, edit. P. Herring (Charlottesville: University Press of Virginia, 1972)

Jung, C. *Man and His Symbols* (New York: Doubleday & Company, Inc., 1964)

Jung, C. *Psyche and Symbol* (Princeton: Princeton University Press, 1991)

Jung C. *Psychology of the Unconscious* (New York: Moffat, Yard and Company, 1916)

Kenner, H. *Dublin's Joyce* (Bloomington: Indiana University Press, 1956)

Kerenyi, K. *Hermes Guide of Souls* (Dallas: Spring Publication, 1976)

Kimball, J. *Odyssey of the Psyche* (Carbondale: Southern Illinois University Press, 1997)

Klein , M. *A Shout in the Street* (New Directions)

Kugel, J. *The Bible As It Was* (Cambridge: Harvard University Press, 1997)

Lang, F. K. *Ulysses and the Irish God* (Lewisburg: Bucknell University Press, 1993)

Langer, S. *Philosophy in a New Key* (Cambridge: Harvard University Press, 1942)

Letters of James Joyce, edit. S. Gilbert (New York: Viking Press, 1957)

Mead *Thrice Greatest Hermes* (London: John M. Watkins, 1906)

Murray, G. *Five Stages of Greek Religion* (New York: Columbia University Press, 1925)

Nadel, I. *Joyce and the Jews* (Iowa City: University of Iowa Press, 1989)

Noll, R. *The Jung Cult* (Princeton: Princeton University Press, 1994)

Noon, W. *Joyce and Acquinas* (New Haven: Yale Univ. Press, 1957)

Odyssey of Homer trans. by Butcher and Lang (New York: P. F. Collier & Sons, 1909)

611

O'Faolain, E. *Irish Sagas and Folk Tales* (Oxford: Oxford University Press, 1954)

Ovid, *Metamorphoses* (London: Penguin, 1955)

The Oxford Dictionary of World Religions edit. J. Bowker (Oxford: Oxford University Press, 1997)

The Oxford History of Greece and the Hellenistic World (Oxford: Oxford University Press, 1986)

Pater, W. *The Renaissance* (London: MacMillan, 1873)

Pelikan, J. *Mary Through the Centuries* (New Haven: Yale University Press, 1996)

Plato Dialogues of Plato, trans. by R. E. Allen. (New Haven: Yale University Press, 1984)

Plutarch *Moralia* (Cambridge: Harvard University Press, 1936)

Power, A., *Conversations with James Joyce* edit. Hart (Chicago: University of Chicago Press, 1974)

Rabate, J. *Joyce upon the Void* (New York: St. Martins Press, 1991)

Radin, *The Trickster* (New York: Philosophical Library, 1956)

Restuccia, F. *Joyce and the Law of the Father* (New Haven: Yale University Press, 1989)

Reynolds, M. *Joyce and Dante* (Princeton: Princeton University Press, 1981)

Russell, B. *A History of Western Philosophy* (New York: Simon and Schuster, 1972)

Saintsbury, G. *A History of English Prose Rhythm* (Bloomington: Indiana University Press, 1912)

Shelley, P. *The Complete Poems of Percy Bysshe Shelley* (New York: The Modern Library, 1994)

Silverstein, N. *Joyce's Circe Episode* diss. Columbia University, 1960

Stallion, J. *Passover* (San Jose: Resources Publications, 1988)

Syme, D. *The Jewish Home* (New York: UAHC Press, 1974)

Tindall, W. *A Reader's Guide to James Joyce* (Syracuse: Syracuse University Press, 1995)

Tymoczka, M. *The Irish Ulysses* (Berkeley: The University of California Press, 1994)

Vreeswijk, H. *Notes on Joyce's Ulysses Part I* (Amsterdam: Van Gennep, 1970)

Yeats, W.B. *Rosa Alchemical in Mythologies* (New York: P. F. Collier & Sons, 1959)

Zimmer, H. *Myths and Symbols in Indian Art and Civilization* (Princeton: Bollingen, 1946)

Figure 1

Figure 2

Lightning Source UK Ltd.
Milton Keynes UK
UKOW04f0827220118
316602UK00001B/85/P

9 781581 127621